AF600140

Evolution and Revolution in Linguistic Theory

Evolution and Revolution in Linguistic Theory

EDITED BY
Héctor Campos and Paula Kempchinsky

Georgetown University Press / Washington, D.C.

Georgetown University Press, Washington, D.C. 20007

Printed in the United States of America.
10 9 8 7 6 5 4 3 2 1 1995
THIS VOLUME IS PRINTED ON ACID-FREE OFFSET BOOKPAPER

Library of Congress Cataloging-in-Publication Data

Evolution and revolution in linguistic theory / Héctor Campos, ed.
p. cm.—(Georgetown studies in Romance linguistics)
Includes bibliographical references.
1. Linguistic analysis (Linguistics) I. Campos, Héctor.
II. Series.
P126.E94 1995
415'.01—dc20
ISBN 0-87840-248-9 95-1843

Contents

Preface

One of Carlos Otero's early articles in linguistics was titled "Mínima introducción a la lingüística." Some thirty years later he is a leading proponent in the Minimalist Program in Linguistic Theory. Thus his own trajectory in the field of linguistic theory exemplifies "the growth of a linguist's mind" (the title of a chapter in his 1970 book, *Introducción a la lingüística transformacional*). In a recent article he admits to a certain degree of optimism about the current state of research into cognitive systems, of which language is a fundamental component. It is only fitting then that the contributions to this volume, presented in his honor, should represent some of the latest work in linguistic theory.

Carlos Peregrín Otero did his graduate work at the University of California in Berkeley and subsequently joined the faculty of the Department of Spanish and Portuguese at the University of California, Los Angeles, in 1959. At UCLA he has taught courses in literature (in fact, his dissertation was on the Spanish poet Luis Cernuda), literary theory, history of the Romance languages, and Spanish phonology, morphology, and, of course, syntax. In recent years he has also taught undergraduate honor seminars on linguistics and the cognitive sciences.

At UCLA he founded and directed for many years the Program in Romance Linguistics and Literature. This program, which gives graduate students the necessary academic space in which to pursue course work in both the Department of Linguistics and the associated language departments (French, Italian, and Spanish and Portuguese), is emblematic of Carlos's success at bridging the gap that all too often exists between linguistics and language departments.

The versatility that Carlos has shown in his teaching is mirrored in the breadth of his published work. Within the field of linguistics alone his published work ranges from syntax to phonology to his revolutionary work on the development of Spanish, aptly titled *Evolución y revolución en romance*, which inspired the title of this book. Alongside his work in linguistics are his writings on political and social theory, both concerned with the wider question of "the nature of human nature." As if this were not enough, he has also made significant contributions to scholarship in Spanish literature. There is certainly an element of personal experience in Carlos's observations in a recent paper about the different natures of scientific inquiry (as in linguistics, the field of rational inquiry par excellence) and humanistic scholarship.

Some of the contributors to this volume were students of Carlos; others have been colleagues and "fellow travelers" for many years. The personal debts owed to him are noted by some in the acknowledgements that accompany their individual articles. Carlos has been an important source of moral support for younger faculty in linguistics at UCLA. Colleagues in the discipline, both at UCLA and elsewhere, have benefited from his insights. As a mentor and teacher he is honest and encouraging, freely sharing his intuitions about the matter at hand. Nine years after finishing our graduate studies at UCLA, we continue to turn to Carlos for advice and guidance. We are honored to consider him both our teacher and our friend.

In a poem by Cernuda, written at the time of the Spanish Civil War, we find the following lines:

Escribir en España no es llorar, es morir
Porque muere la inspiración envuelta en humo,
Cuando no va su llama libre en pos del aire.

[To write in Spain is not to cry but to die // because inspiration dies sheathed in smoke // when its flame cannot freely go in pursuit of air]. When asked how it was that he came to remain in the United States, Carlos has sometimes been heard to reply, "Because Franco took so long to die." Fortunately for Spain, Franco did finally die, and fortunately for us, Carlos has continued to make his home here in spite of that fact. Muchas gracias, Carlos.

We would like to thank first all of the contributors to this volume, who responded warmly to our request to participate in this book. It was indeed a pleasure to work with such a group of distinguished and busy researchers who even managed to meet the deadlines we stipulated.

There are two people who deserve special recognition. We very much doubt that this volume could have been brought to fruition without the collaboration of Judith Strozer. When we first talked to Judy about our idea for this book, she felt honor-bound to inform us that Carlos had once told her that if she ever heard of any such plans, she was to quash the idea immediately. This is our opportunity to state publicly that she complied with his request. That said, her suggestions and moral support at the various stages of this project have been crucial and greatly appreciated.

We also want to give special thanks to Eric Holt, graduate fellow in the Department of Spanish at Georgetown University, who did the necessary and very time-consuming task of formatting the articles and checking bibliographic references, as well as making useful editorial suggestions. The final editing process would have been impossible to complete on time without his assistance. Finally, it is to Eric that we owe the inspired suggestion that the title of this volume pay homage to one of Carlos's own works.

We are also thankful to the secretarial staff of the Department of Spanish and Portuguese, as well as to Dean Judith Aikin from the College of Liberal Arts at the University of Iowa and to Dean Emeritus James E. Alatis of the School of Languages and Linguistics at Georgetown University, for their help and encouragement. Our special gratitude goes to Patrick Shoemaker for his constant moral support, to Patricia Rayner from Georgetown University Press for her useful editorial suggestions, and to Dr. John Samples, director of the Press, for his support in making this book come to light.

Héctor Campos
Paula Kempchinsky

On the Metrical Unity of Latinate Affixes*

LUIGI BURZIO
The Johns Hopkins University

1 Introduction. The Latinate subset of English suffixes breaks down into two subclasses, which I will refer to as Class I and Class II, following established terminology. The suffixes of Class I cause changes in the stress pattern, as illustrated in (1). Here and elsewhere italicized characters identify the stress of the unsuffixed stem.

(1) CLASS I AFFIXES: Restressing
a. *al:* *a*ccidéntal, m*e*dícinal, *o*ríginal, p*a*réntal, pr*e*fíxal, p*y*rámidal, tr*i*úmphal, *u*nivérsal
b. *ic:* l*i*nguístic, r*e*alístic, *a*llérgic, *o*ceánic, astr*o*nómic, g*y*mnástic, h*o*méric, *i*diótic, pr*o*phétic
c. *ion/ation:* c*o*ngregátion, c*o*nsecrátion, d*e*marcátion, *i*nsulátion, *i*ntegrátion, int*i*midátion, aff*i*rmátion, all*e*gátion, central*i*zátion, comb*i*nátion, comp*i*látion
d. *ous:* adv*a*ntágeous, c*o*urágeous, *o*utrágeous, *i*ncéstuous, m*o*méntous, v*o*lúminous, r*i*dículous, t*e*mpéstuous

In contrast, the suffixes of Class II generally preserve the stem stress, as in all the cases in (2):

(2) CLASS II AFFIXES: Stress neutral
a. *able:* acc*é*ptable, ad*á*ptable, aff*ó*rdable, exp*á*ndable, opp*ó*sable, ref*ú*ndable, resp*é*ctable, surp*á*ssable, sust*á*inable, ab*ó*lishable, *á*lterable, *á*nswerable, ch*é*rishable, c*ó*lorable, del*í*verable, inh*á*bitable, inh*é*ritable, int*é*rpretable, p*é*rishable
b. *ist:* pharmac*ó*logist, perf*é*ctionist, emp*í*ricist, gen*é*ticist, rom*á*nticist, extr*é*mist, h*ú*morist, propag*á*ndist, t*é*rrorist, am*é*ricanist, c*á*pitalist, g*é*neralist, indiv*í*dualist, m*ó*dernist, m*ó*narchist

c. *ism:* absent*é*eism, al*á*rmism, def*é*atism, esc*á*pism, extr*é*mism, m*ó*dernism, m*ó*narchism, c*á*pitalism, f*é*deralism, l*í*beralism, l*í*teralism, n*á*turalism, r*á*dicalism, am*é*ricanism, f*á*voritism
d. *ant/ent/ance/ence:* cons*ú*ltant, cont*é*stant, def*é*ndant, dep*é*ndant, det*é*rminant, exp*é*ctant, inh*á*bitant, r*é*gistrant, rel*á*xant, res*í*stant, res*ú*ltant, v*í*sitant, compl*í*ance, del*í*verance, inh*é*ritance, res*é*mblance, res*í*stance, s*é*verance, s*ú*fferance, abs*ó*rbent, antec*é*dent, coex*í*stent, cons*í*stent, conv*é*rgent, dep*é*ndent, remin*í*scent, subs*í*stent, transc*é*ndent
e. *ment:* ab*á*ndonment, acc*ó*mplishment, ach*í*evement, adv*á*ncement, am*é*ndment, ber*é*avement, bomb*á*rdment, dev*é*lopment, emb*ó*diment, env*é*lopment, acc*ó*mpaniment, g*ó*vernment, impóverishment
f. *ize:* propag*á*ndize, anthropom*ó*rphize, europ*é*anize, it*á*licize, rom*á*nticize, comp*ú*terize, g*é*latinize, mon*ó*polize, revol*ú*tionize, c*á*pitalize, mun*í*cipalize, fam*í*liarize, p*ó*pularize, am*é*ricanize
g. *y:* félony, m*á*triarchy, m*ó*narchy, b*ú*tchery, *ó*rthodoxy, *á*ccuracy, conf*é*deracy

In the past, from Chomsky and Halle's (1968) SPE to Halle and Kenstowicz (1991), stress neutrality has consistently been analyzed as a form of evasion of stress by the suffix, or immunity of the suffix to the stress principles. This idea has been implemented in various ways. In SPE the distinction between the two classes of suffixes was taken to be a difference in the type of boundary involved. Class II affixes were thought to be associated with a word boundary '#,' and Class I affixes with a morpheme boundary '+.' The restressing character of Class I affixes then followed from the fact that the stress rules reapplied at each successive cycle and were given the power to alter previously assigned stresses. In contrast stress neutrality followed from the assumption that rules of word stress, while applying across morpheme boundaries, did not apply across word boundaries, hence leaving the stem unaffected on later cycles, as succinctly stated in (3a,b), respectively.

(3) Chomsky and Halle (1968) SPE:

a.	párent + al	Stress rules reapply
b.	américan # ist	Stress rules fail to reapply

In Kiparsky's (1982) influential 'Lexical Phonology' model, the distinction was made not by different types of boundaries, but rather by different stages at which different affixes were attached, in a sequentially organized morpho-phonological derivation. Class I affixes were taken to be attached at 'Level 1,' which would also contain the rules of word stress, while Class II affixes would be attached at 'Level 2,' presumed not to contain rules of word stress, as in (4):

(4) Kiparsky (1982) 'Lexical Phonology':

a. Level 1 | Morphology: Class I affixation
Phonology: Stress rules, . . .

b. Level 2 | Morphology: Class II affixation
Phonology: . . .

The alternative model developed by Halle and his associates, which we will refer to as 'Cyclic Phonology,' later abandoned the hypothesis of (4) that the distinction between the two classes of affixes concerned both morphology and phonology in parallel and postulated a purely phonological distinction in terms of a lexical diacritic specifying which phonological rules they triggered. Specifically, Class I affixes were supposed to trigger those phonological rules that are 'cyclic,' and were for that reason referred to as 'cyclic' affixes in that theory, while Class II affixes were correspondingly presumed to trigger only the noncyclic rules, and were thus referred to as 'noncyclic' affixes. This schema is illustrated in (5):

(5) Halle and Vergnaud (1987a,b), Halle and Kenstowicz (1991) 'Cyclic Phonology':
a. Cyclic Phonology (main stress rules), triggered by cyclic affixes (= Class I)
b. Noncyclic Phonology (other stress rules), triggered by noncyclic affixes (= Class II)

The organization in (5) does not immediately account for stress neutrality, however, unless the set of noncyclic stress rules is taken to be null. In Halle and Vergnaud (1987a,b) this is in fact not the case, and no specific account of stress neutrality is given. This unresolved issue is addressed in Halle and Kenstowicz (1991), who give an explicit account of neutrality by modifying the Halle and Vergnaud framework. Their analysis is described and illustrated in (6):

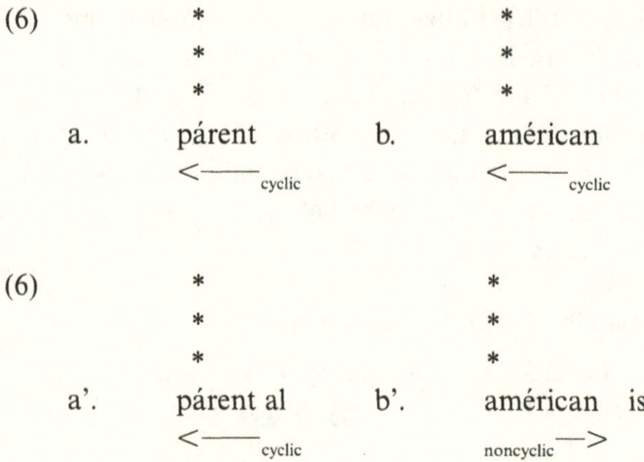

(i) Cyclic rules: right-left parse; 'Stress Erasure Convention'
(ii) Noncyclic rules: left-right parse; 'Crossover Constraint'

In (6a) a first application of the cyclic stress rules, which parse syllables into feet from right to left, results in the metrical grid given. In (6a′) a second application of the cyclic rules correspondingly results in the new grid. There is no preservation of earlier metrical structure here, because cyclic rules are in that theory associated with the 'Stress Erasure Convention,' which eliminates earlier metrical structure at each new cycle. In (6b) the cycle is just as in (6a), but in (6b′) the suffix is noncyclic, triggering only noncyclic rules. The latter are presumed to be rather similar to their cyclic counterparts, except for three crucial differences: (i) non cyclic rules parse the structure from left to right (Halle and Kenstowicz's innovation to the Halle and Vergnaud framework); (ii) they are not associated with the Stress Erasure Convention; and (iii) they are subject to the 'Crossover Constraint,' which states that a parsing procedure cannot jump over preexisting metrical structure. As a result of the conjunction of (i) and (iii) Class II suffixes like *ist* in (6b′) remain unparsed, hence evading stress much as in earlier models. As a result of (ii) the stem stress will then surface unchanged.[1]

In this paper I will present an alternative account of stress neutrality, based on the hypothesis that neutral suffixes are subject to normal parsing into feet, like non-neutral ones, though two different modes of metrification distinguish the two classes, as will be illustrated in (7) below. One important aspect of my proposal is the assumption that metrical structure is part of the underlying representation of words, subject to well-formedness conditions, that is, the assumption that there is no stress 'assignment,' but rather stress 'checking.' I argue further that there is a requirement that morphemes be metrically 'consistent,' that is, to the extent possible, they surface with the same metrical structure in all their occurrences, just as they in fact tend to consistency of segmental and semantic structures in all their occurrences. Metrical consistency of both stem and suffix, however, will only be achievable in specific cases. More generally, the two will be incompatible, hence requiring that either the stem or the suffix metrify in a new way, which is inconsistent with other occurrences of the same morpheme. Our proposed distinction between Class I and Class II is now that with Class I suffixes the suffix prevails, imposing its own metrification on the stem, graphically as in (7a), whereas with Class II suffixes the stem prevails, imposing its own metrification on the suffix, as in (7b):

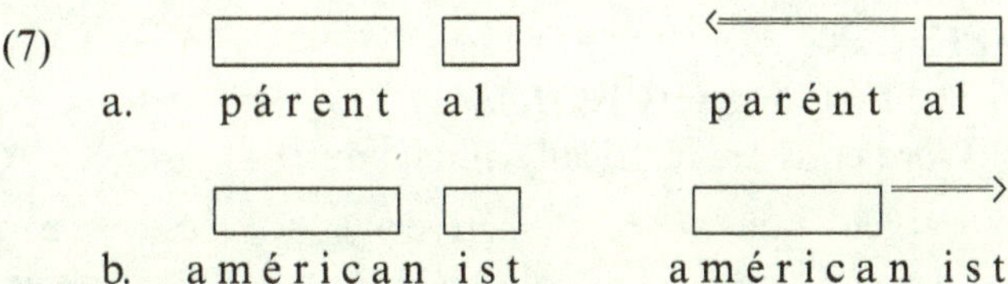

We will see later that from this general perspective it is in fact possible to predict which suffixes will behave in which way. The main part of the paper will be a collection of arguments for this approach and against any form of 'stress evasion,' hence excluding all past approaches, and thus suggesting that any model of the lexicon or of the phonological component that has stress evasion as an available option is seriously inadequate.

2 Basic framework. To make the proposal in (7) concrete, it will be necessary to introduce some basic machinery, which we draw from Burzio (1987) and later related work. We begin by considering the two well-known generalizations of English stress given in (8) and (9):

(8) a. Stress heavy penultimate: *agénda, appéndix, horí:zon*
    b. Otherwise, stress antepenultimate: *américa, ásterisk*

(9) a. Stress superheavy final: *pervért, decí:de*
    b. Otherwise, stress penultimate: *inhábit, imágine*

The pattern in (8) is the one characteristic of nouns and suffixed adjectives, while that in (9) is characteristic of verbs and unsuffixed adjectives. The 'superheavy' syllables of (9a) are syllables whose structure exceeds that of normal heavy syllables by one consonant, a heavy syllable being standardly defined as one with either one postvocalic consonant or a long vowel.

In Hayes (1982, 1985) and much subsequent work, the two patterns in (8) and (9) were analyzed in terms of a single parsing algorithm by supposing that English word ends are metrically ambiguous, in the sense that the parsing, proceeding from right to left, can start at two different points in the structure. Specifically, Hayes proposed that, at the right edge of an English word, either a full syllable or a single consonant may be 'extrametrical,' namely, ignored in the parsing. The parsing then constructs either a monosyllabic foot *(H)* or a bisyllabic one *(σL)*, where 'H' and 'L' stand for heavy and light syllables, respectively. This approach, which has been influential, is synoptically illustrated in (10):

(10) After Hayes (1982), (1985):
  (i) The foot inventory is: *(H)/ (σL)*
  (ii) Word ends are metrically ambiguous: . . . *)σ#/ . . .)C#*

a.	a(gén)	da	b.	per(vér)	t	c.	(pér)	vert
	a(mé ri)	ca		in(há bi)	t		(ás te)	risk
	←			←			←	

Starting with Burzio (1987) I have presented a different approach, which maintains Hayes's intuition that there is a single parsing mechanism at work in both (8) and (9) and that the difference reduces to properties of word ends. My implementation of this intuition is rather different, however. A central assumption I have introduced is that syllabification is in general free to parse phonetically empty structure beyond the audible edges of words. Given then the well-known principle that requires consonants to syllabify as onsets whenever possible, this will entail that final consonants will always be onsets, since they can always be followed by a null vowel in the manner of (11):

(11) per.vér.tø, in.há.bi.tø

In this hypothesis there will thus never be truly 'final' consonants: all English words end in a vowel, overt or null. It is easy to see that this idea now reduces the stress of the items in (11) to the penultimate/antepenultimate pattern of *a.gén.da/a.mé.ri.ca* in (8). More generally, it will reduce the pattern of (9) above to that of (8), as we see below. In addition the 'null vowel' hypothesis, which extends to other languages, accounts for the phenomenon of 'superheavy' syllables and the fact noted by Hayes (1982:229) and otherwise unaccounted for that in English and other languages ". . . superheavy syllables may occur only in . . . final position." In our proposal all syllables become normal; the term "superheavy syllable" is now only a description of a sequence of two syllables, the second of which has a null vowel, its occurrence only peripherally reflecting the distribution of empty structure.

General motivation for Hayes's extrametricality disappears as well on this approach, since feet can now be taken to be uniformly binary *(Hs)* or ternary *(sLs),* as in (12). (See Burzio (1994) for more extensive discussion and further arguments.)

(12) After Burzio (1987):
(i) The foot inventory is: *(Hσ)/ (σLσ)*

a. a(gén da) | b. pér(ver tø) |
a(mé ri ca) | in(há bi tø) |
<——┘ <——┘

Despite the demise of Hayes's extrametricality, a partially similar device is necessary in this approach as well, however, in order to handle nouns ending in a consonant (that is, a null vowel), as in (13):

(13) (pér ver) | tø
(ás te ris) | kø
<——┘

Specifically, we suppose that final syllables with null vowels are optionally extrametrical, much as final syllables in general were in Hayes's framework. Note, however, that the type of extrametricality invoked by (13) is in fact attested independently of null vowels, with a class of special syllables that we refer to here as "weak" (W). The class of weak syllables is illustrated in (14a–e), and—internally to our 'null-vowel' hypothesis—(14f).

(14) Word ends are metrically ambiguous: . . . *W)#/ . . .) W#*
W class: *y, ive, ure,* [*son*], ø
a. an(típathy) / (éffica)cy
b. ob(jéctive) / (ádjec)tive
c. ad(vénture) / (áper)ture, (témpera)ture

d. a(póstle) / (végeta)ble
e. de(cémber) / (chárac)ter
f. per(vértø) / (pérver)tø

The extrametricality of the right-hand examples in (14a–e) is essentially factual, since it must be postulated in any theory that recognizes (8) above as a basic generalization of English. The reason is that the stress pattern of the latter examples exceeds that generalization by exactly one syllable. In particular the extrametricality of (14a–e) must be postulated in Hayes's theory as well, crucially in addition to Hayes's normal extrametricality, as, for example, in *(éffi)<ca>[cy],* where '< >' marks the normal extrametricality of Hayes's system, and '[ ]' the extrametricality of the special syllables in question. Our system in (12)–(13) thus accounts for the two patterns in (8) and (9) by simply extending the extrametricality needed for (14a–e) to the case in (14f), whereas the system in (10) does so by introducing unrelated machinery.

As shown by (14), weak syllables are apparently syllables with the high vowel corresponding to orthographic *y,* syllables *ive* and *ure,* and syllables with sonorant nuclei like those of *particip*[L], *charact*[R]. As noted in Burzio (1993, 1994), there are reasons for supposing that the distinguishing characteristic of weak syllables is in fact acoustic weakness, their metrical behavior reflecting the rather general alignment of metrical structure and acoustic prominence observable crosslinguistically. If this is correct, then the inclusion of syllables with null nuclei in this class will obviously be appropriate.

Weak syllables have another property besides their ability to be extrametrical. When they are metrified as part of a binary foot *(Hs),* that foot fails to attract primary stress, as illustrated in (15), which covers the same spectrum of weak syllables as (14). We refer to this class of feet as "weak" also.

(15) Weak Foot: *(σ W)*

a. cóntro(vèrsy)	b. ínno(vàtive)	c. árchi(tècture)
d. táber(nàcle)	e. álli(gàtor)	f. bérnar(dìnø)

It seems natural to take the phenomenon in (15) to further reflect the acoustic weakness of weak syllables. Like weak syllables, weak feet can also be taken to be acoustically weak relative to other feet, because they are structurally minimal, namely binary, and they incorporate a weak syllable. Given the above definition of "weak foot," the position of primary stress in English is now fully predictable as being on the rightmost *non-*

weak foot, the italicized restriction presumably reflecting the general alignment of stress and acoustic prominence as noted.

3 Stress neutrality and weak syllables. We are now ready to make the proposal in (7) above more concrete. Specifically, we propose, as in (16) below, that stress neutrality is a by-product of the rather general ambiguity of word ends in English, namely the double option of either metrifying a final weak syllable or not.

(16) Stress neutrality results from the ambiguity of word ends, namely: . . . *) W* versus . . . *W).*

Assuming then, as in (7b) above, that with neutral suffixes the stem 'prevails,' we consider the cases in (17) to see how suffixes can be integrated into the metrical structure of the stem under the hypothesis in (16).

(17)	a.	ac(cép tø)	b.	propa(gán da)	c.	a(mé ri ca)nø
		ac(cép ta)ble		propa(gán dis)tø		a(mé ri ca)(nìs tø)

The case in (17a) is rather straightforward. Here, the first syllable of the suffix *able* supplants the final syllable of the stem *accept* (i.e. the null vowel), while its second syllable *ble*—a weak syllable (compare (14d)), remains extrametrical. As a result, the rightmost foot of *acceptable* is identical to the one of *accept,* whence the identical stress. The case in (17b) is rather similar, as the first syllable of the suffix also supplants the final one of the stem, while the second syllable of the suffix, again being weak, remains extrametrical. In the case in (17c) on the other hand, none of the suffixes can be incorporated into the final foot of the stem, but here the other option available to weak syllables can be resorted to. By metrifying that syllable, the suffix can now form a separate foot of its own, hence leaving the preceding one undisturbed. Furthermore, since the new final foot is weak, it will only bear secondary stress, leaving the primary stress on its original stem position. Note that perceptual evidence does not independently confirm the presence of a secondary stress on *ist* in (17c), but that is because the perceptual prominence of syllables with secondary stresses is generally nondistinct from that of unstressed heavy syllables with unreduced vowels (see Burzio, 1994).[2]

We will see below that the type of account of stress neutrality illustrated in (17) and based on the ambiguity of weak syllables can be extended to all cases.[3] One might ask at this point why the same ambiguity should not suffice more generally, yielding neutrality with all suffixes that end in a weak syllable (like *al, ic*) incorrectly. We will see that there is a principled answer to this question, but in the meantime we consider the following as a preliminary account. We suppose that Class I suffixes are lexically marked as having metrically unambiguous ends, specifically by means of a foot boundary that either includes or excludes the final weak syllable, depending on the suffix, as in (18):

(18) Nonneutral suffixes are marked with unambiguous ends: *a)lø, icø), ou)sø, . . .*

a.	(páren)tø	b.	(línguis)tø	c.	(mómen)tø
	pa(rénta*)*lø		lin(guísticø*)*		mo(méntou*)*sø
a′	(py′rami)dø	b′.	(hóme)rø	c′.	(rídicu)le
	py(rámida*)*lø		ho(méricø*)*		ri(dículou*)*sø

Note that some equivalent markings seem required in any theory so as to distinguish, for instance, *al* or *ous,* which place stress according to the pattern in (8) above, from *ic,* which follows the pattern in (9), placing stress always on the immediately preceding syllable as (18) shows.[4] In our analysis, the same independently needed diacritic will also serve to distinguish nonneutral suffixes from neutral ones. The latter suffixes will simply lack the diacritic.

4 Arguments against stress evasion. We now turn to the actual arguments for our account of neutrality in (16) above and against approaches based on stress evasion. The evidence considered will concern 'Latinate' suffixes only, and those in (2a–g) in particular. Accordingly, the thesis in (16) will be defended only relative to Latinate suffixes, leaving open the question of the neutrality of Germanic suffixes like *less, ness, ful, ly.* See Burzio (1994), however, for arguments that the latter is also not reducible to stress evasion.

4.1 Bound stems. Our first argument is based on the observation that the two metrifications needed to account for stress neutrality under (16), namely one including and the other excluding a final weak syllable (or the equivalent options handling (8) versus (9) in other theories), are independently needed to account for cases where the same suffixes occur with bound stems, where there is obviously no issue of neutrality. This is shown by (19), where each column instantiates the type of foot and metrification given at the top. The diacritic '♠' used here and later indicates the existence of other variants of the same item. (Unmetrified, nonorthographic null vowels are omitted here.)

(19)

(σ L σ) W	(H σ) W	(. . . W)
a.		
inde(fátiga)ble,	ine(lúcta)ble,	♠hos(pítable)
in(dómita)ble,	de(lécta)ble	
in(dúbita)ble,		
i(néquita)ble,		
i(névita)ble,		
i(néxora)ble,		
in(súpera)ble,		
(mísera)ble,		
(vérita)ble,		
(vúlnera)ble,		
b.		
an(tágonis)t,	perio(dóntis)t,	(sólip)(sìstø),
mi(sógynis)t,	obscu(rántis)t,	ob(scúran)(tìstø),
pro(tágonis)t,	ana(báptis)t	♠(sy'stema)(tìstø)
re(cídivis)t		
c.		
a(náchronis)m,		(sólip)(sìsmø),
an(tágonis)m,		(écume)(nìsmø),
me(tábolis)m,		(málapro)(pìsmø),
ven(tríloquis)m,		(sy'ner)(gìsmø)
as(tígmatis)m		
d.		
con(cómitan)t,	be(nígnan)t,	
ex(trávagan)t,	re(dúndan)t,	
e(xúberan)t,	re(púgnan)t,	
pro(túberan)t,	re(lúctan)t,	
	in(dígnan)t	
e.		
ex(périmen)t,	com(pártmen)t,	(témpera)(mèntø)
me(dícamen)t,	com(pórtmen)t,	
pre(dícamen)t,	de(pártmen)t,	
	em(bánkmen)t,	
	in(stálmen)t	
f.		
	an(tágo)(nìze),	
	me(tábo)(lìze)	

g.[5]

	(áppeten)cy,	(áller)gy,
(éffica)cy,	(cásual)ty,	(líber)ty,
(éner)gy,		
(lítur)gy,	(ámnes)ty,	e(cónomy),
(léthar)gy,	(dýnas)ty,	a(nátomy),
(cálum)ny,	(ínfan)try,	a(nómaly),
(májes)ty,	(índus)try,	pe(ríphery),
(próper)ty,		(táxi)(dèrmy),
(póver)ty,		(métal)(lùrgy),
(cával)ry		(cére)(mòny)
		(ácri)(mòny),
		(áli)(mòny),
		(cóntro)(vèrsy),
		(cáta)(lèpsy),
		as(sémbly)
		an(típathy),
		al(lótropy)

We note that the left and middle columns in (19b–e) instantiate normal metrification for items of these classes—that is, nouns and suffixed adjectives—while the right-hand column corresponds to a metrification still attested but rarer with these classes and more typical of verbs. As could be shown by considering a larger sample of cases, the instances on the right are in fact less numerous than the others, essentially as with underived items or items with Class I suffixes. While the behavior of overt weak syllables *ble* and C*y* of (19a,g) is slightly more complex (see Burzio (1994) and below), the stress of the items in (19) is on the whole rather unremarkable, the cases in (19f) also showing the parse typical of their class, namely verbs.[6] We thus take the suffixes in (19) to be parsed like ordinary syllables, which leads to the conclusion that stress evasion is superfluous as an account of the neutrality of these suffixes, since the parses independently attested in (19) suffice.

4.2 Exceptions to neutrality. The second of our arguments is that only the thesis in (16) correctly predicts certain cases of nonneutrality, such as those in (20):

(20) a. (dócu)(mèntø) => (dòcu)(ménta)ble
b. c*i*rcumvéntable, *i*mpleméntable, r*e*compénsable, *i*nterchángeable, m*a*niféstable, *a*scertáinable,

r*e*concílable, *e*xtradítable, r*e*alízable, cr*i*ticízable, r*e*cognízable, *u*tilízable, *o*xydízable, g*e*neralízable, d*i*agnósable, pr*o*secútable, *e*xecútable, s*u*bstitútable, c*u*ltivátable, r*e*gulátable, man*i*pulátable

The verb *document* in (20a) exhibits the normal metrification of verbs, incorporating the null vowel. However, because the final foot is weak (and there is another foot preceding it), that final foot bears only secondary stress. When *able* is attached, the structure of the final foot will be preserved as usual, just as it was in (17a) above, except that the final foot of the adjective is now no longer a weak one, since the *a* of *able* does not yield a weak syllable. Because of this, primary stress will then shift forward to the final foot, resulting in nonneutrality.[7] The cases in (20b) are all analogous to (20a), as are the ones in (21):

(21)	a.	(ánec)(dòte)	=>	(ànec)(dótistø)
				[like: *o*pportúnist, m*e*tallúrgist]
	b.	(máni)(fèstø)	=>	(màni)(féstan)t
	c.	(ádver)(tìse)	=>	♠(àdver)(tísemen)t

The cases in (22) are also rather similar:

(22)	a.	(prótes)t	=>	pro(tésta)ble
	b.	(rémedy)	=>	re(média)ble
	c.	♠(súrvey)	=>	sur(véya)ble
	d.	(módify)	=>	(mòdi)(fía)ble
	e.	(tránsla)te	=>	trans(láta)ble
	f.	(tríum)ph	=>	tri(úmphan)t
	g.	(lúxury)	=>	lu(xúrian)ce
	h.	♠(ímpreg)(nàte)	=>	im(prégna)ble

The left-hand forms in (22a–g) all have the stress pattern of nouns ((8) above) for various reasons, some idiosyncratic. When a suffix like *able* is attached to such a metrical structure, neutrality simply cannot be achieved for reasons that will be made clear in 4.6 below, whence the stress shifts in (a–e). The shifts of (22f,g) follow in analogous fashion from the fact that *ant*/*ance* exist in only one metrical variant, as in (19d) and as noted in note 6 (hence like *al* and *ous* of (18)). This enables these suffixes to be neutral in the same manner as *able* when attached to verbs in general, but not in these particular cases. Finally, in the case in (22h), which involves attachment of *able* to a truncated verb in *ate,* neutrality cannot be achieved because the resulting structure **(impregna)ble* would instantiate an ill-formed foot *$(\sigma H \sigma)$. In sum the stress shifts of (20)–(22) are entirely predictable from the assumption that the suffixes are metrified. In contrast within a stress-evasion account of neutrality there would be no reason at all for this curious set of exceptions.

4.3 Vowel shortening. Our third argument is based on cases in which a Class II suffix occurs with a stem that has been affected by vowel shortening, such as those on the left in (23), contrasting with those on the right, in which stem vowels remain long (relevant vowels underscored).

(23) Vowel Shortening with Class II Suffixes

a. *able*

(ádm*i*ra)ble, (cómp*a*ra)ble, ♠(cógn*i*za)ble, ♠(rép*a*ra)ble, ir(rép*a*ra)ble, ♠(réf*u*ta)ble, ir(rév*o*ca)ble	opp*ó*sable, ref*ú*table, rest*ó*rable, . . . *í*zable

b. *ant/ent/ance/ence*

(ásp*i*ran)t, (ígn*o*ran)t, ♠(éxc*i*tan)t, (cógn*i*zan)t, cla(ríf*i*can)t, sig(níf*i*can)t, (ábst*i*nen)t, (cónf*i*den)t, co(ínc*i*den)t, (prés*i*den)t, (rés*i*den)t, (préc*e*den)t	adh*é*rent, persev*é*rance, endúrance, disp*ú*tant, disapp*é*arance, poll*ú*tant, ♠exc*í*tant

c. *ment*

(chást*i*semen)t, ♠ad(vért*i*semen)t (íncr*e*men)t, (éxcr*e*men)t	acqu*í*rement, ♠advert*í*sement, caj*ó*lement, repl*á*cement, eng*á*gement, conf*í*nement, app*é*asement, agr*é*ement, adv*í*sement

d. *y/ist*

te(léph*o*ny)/ist, me(trósc*o*py)/ist,	(hy'pn*o*tis)t, ♠(árch*i*vis)t, ♠(álleg*o*ris)t, (mílit*a*)(rìstø), (sát*i*ris)t, exp*í*ry, ♠alleg*ó*rist, ♠arch*í*vist, ♠pr*í*vacy, encyclop*é*dist, esc*á*pist, extr*é*mist, manic*ú*rist

e. *ism*

(sém*i*)(tìsm), (rább*i*)(nìsm) — extr*é*mism

(mílit*a*)(rìsmø), (prósel*y*)(tìsmø),
in(fánt*i*lis)m, (álb*i*nis)m,
(phílist*i*)(nìsmø)

f. *ize*

(álleg*o*)(rìze), (mílit*a*)(rìze), — ♠concr*é*tize

(sát*i*)(rìze), (ímm*u*)(nìze),
(prósel*y*)(tìze), ♠(cóncr*e*)(tìze),
(óx*y*)(dìze)

The argument stems from the fact that, when stem vowels shorten, the position of stress is no longer characterizable in terms of 'stress neutrality,' but is correctly predicted only by the view that there is metrification of the suffix in the manner indicated by the analyses. The examples in (24) below, exhibiting the same variation between left-hand and right-hand cases as those in (23), show that such shortening of stem vowels is a general property of Latinate affixation common to Class I suffixes, as in (24a–d), as well as to prefixes, as in (24e).

(24) Vowel Shortening with Class I Suffixes/Prefixes

a. *al*

vág*i*nal, antíp*o*dal, — homic*í*dal, anecd*ó*tal,
centríf*u*gal, hor*i*zóntal, — caricat*ú*ral

b. *ous/y*

ínf*a*mous/y, carnív*o*rous, — des*í*rous, ♠dec*ó*rous
blásph*e*mous/y, ♠déc*o*rous,
gángr*e*nous, monót*o*nous/y

c. *age*

concúb*i*nage

d. *ation*

♠ . . . *iz*átion (with short *i*) — ♠ . . . *iz*átion (with long *i*)

e. *prefixes*

ímp*i*ous, ínf*a*mous/y, ínf*in*ite, — bip*ó*lar, subl*ú*nar, prem*ó*lar
irrép*a*rable, omníp*o*tent, unív*a*lent,
bíc*y*cle, unív*o*cal, súbs*e*quent,
ímm*i*grant

In Burzio (1993, 1994) I propose a unified analysis of the shortening of (23)–(24), sometimes referred to as 'morphological' shortening, and several other descriptive types of shortening, in particular the 'trisyllabic' shortening of *divi:ne/divinity*, etc. I have argued that the rather unsystematic character of the morphological shortening in (23)–(24) compared with the more systematic character of trisyllabic shortening follows from independent principles of metrical theory, specifically the principle of metrical consistency alluded to in section 1 above. In the cases in (23)–(24) metrical consistency of the stem, namely, preservation of stem stress, can be achieved only if shortening does not occur, since penultimate stress requires a heavy syllable. The observed variation can then be interpreted as satisfaction of either contending requirement: shortening as in the left column, or stress preservation as in the right column. In contrast trisyllabic cases like *di(vínity)* can satisfy both shortening and stress preservation at the same time unproblematically, since antepenultimate stress on a light syllable is well formed, as in *a(mérica)*, etc. In this view the only difference between 'morphological' and 'trisyllabic' shortening is the position in which the candidate vowel happens to be: either in the penultimate or the antepenultimate syllable. It is thus a completely general fact that Latinate affixes induce shortening of stem vowels. Regardless of the exact account of morphological shortening, however, the question at hand is why it should be incompatible with stress neutrality, as in (23). The thesis in (16) provides an immediate answer: neither metrification nor nonmetrification of the final weak syllable can guarantee stress preservation once shortening applies, as shown in (25):

(25)	a.	*as(p*í*ran)t	/	*as(p*í*rantø),
	b.	*tele(ph*ó*nis)t	/	*tele(ph*ó*nistø)
	c.	*hyp(n*ó*tis)t	/	*hyp(n*ó*tistø)
	d.	*mili(t*á*rI)ze	/	*mili(t*á*rIze)
	e.	*ad(m*í*ra)ble	/	*ad(m*í*rable)
	e′.	*blas(ph*é*mou)s	/	*blas(ph*é*mousø)

The reason is that in (25) all left-hand cases instantiate ill-formed feet **(Lσ)*, while the right-hand ones in (a–d) instantiate equally ill-formed feet *(σHσ)*. The case in (25e) **ad(mírable)* might, however, be expected, since the first syllable of the suffix is light, yielding *(σLσ)*. Some cases with that structure are in fact attested, such as *di(vísible), des(pícable)*. In general, however, it appears that *ble* remains extrametrical. We attribute this to metrical consistency. As we see in more detail in section 4.6, neutrality of *able*, unlike that of *ist* (but like that of *ant*), rather consistently requires nonmetrification of the final weak syllable. In turn this is due to the fact that (like *ant*) *able* is attached primarily to verbs. The metrification *a)ble* is thus the one that satisfies consistency, whence exclusion of **ad(mírable)* of (25e), and cases like *di(vísible)* being the exception. Analogous consistency with the prevalent metrification *ou)s* will correspondingly exclude *blas(phémousø)* in (25e′), otherwise well formed.

In contrast to the above account there will be no particular reason why, if the suffixes in (23) can evade stress, they could not continue to do so when they trigger morphological shortening. Earlier analyses based on stress evasion might have attempted to capture these facts as in (26):

(26)
- 'Morphological' shortening is a 'level 1/cyclic' rule.
- When triggering it, a suffix must be 'level 1/cyclic,' whence its nonneutrality in the presence of shortening.
- Class II suffixes are therefore systematically ambiguous: either 'level 1/cyclic,' thus triggering shortening, or 'level 2/noncyclic,' thus being neutral.

The account in (26) is not tenable, however. The reason is that Class II suffixes are never nonneutral when there is no vowel shortening (except in the cases in section 4.2, already accounted for). In past analyses Level 1/cyclic classification implied metrification of the suffix, which in turn implied nonneutrality. Since morphological shortening is unsystematic with Level 1/cyclic suffixes (witness (24)), the account in (26) predicts that there should be instances in which suffixes like *ist* are nonneutral and yet there is no shortening. But this is not the case.

In sum the facts in (23) above are only consistent with the hypothesis that all Latinate affixes are metrified, the failure of stress preservation in the left-hand cases following in the manner of (25).

4.4 Suffix size. A fourth argument against stress evasion is that no stress-neutral suffix is larger that a weak foot. This fact follows immediately from (16). The reason is that any structure larger than a weak foot will necessarily be or contain a strong foot, which will thus bear primary stress, hence excluding neutrality. In contrast there is no reason why stress evasion should be applicable only to suffixes of a particular size. While relevant suffixes here are not very numerous, they all behave as we predict. Thus, *átion, ólogy, ómeter* are all nonneutral, bearing primary stress.

4.5 Parametric variation. A fifth argument for (16) above is that it correctly predicts that languages such as Italian, whose word ends are not ambiguous in the way postulated for English, should not have stress-neutral suffixes. In fact the hypothesis that existence of weak syllables is a language-specific fact can account for the whole cluster of differences summarized in (27):

(27)	Phenomenon	English	Italian
a.	Apparent maximal structure of final syllables:		
	ro.bust	CVCC	
	robust.to		CV
b.	"Shorter" stress pattern:		
	convért, depósit	yes	
	convérto, depósito		no
c.	"Extra long" stress pattern:		
	génerative, índustry	yes	
	generatívo, indústria		no
d.	Weak feet:		
	bérnadìne, désignàte	yes	
	bernardína, designáto		no
e.	Stress-neutral suffixes:		
	am*é*ricanìst, propag*á*ndist	yes	
	americ*a*nísta, propag*a*ndísta		no

Non-existence of weak syllables in Italian will exclude final null vowels and hence the apparent superheavy syllables of (27a). The same condition that excludes final codas in English will then force all final syllables to end in an overt vowel in Italian. If parsing of a null vowel is what lies behind the apparently shorter stress pattern in (27b), that pattern will be correctly precluded in Italian. Then, if extrametricality of weak syllables is what lies behind the extra-long pattern of (27c) ((14) above), Italian will also lack that and, lacking weak syllables, it will also lack the weak feet of (27d). Finally, the stress neutral suffixes of (27e) will be correspondingly lacking in Italian if weak syllables are crucial to them, as in (16) above.

In contrast to this, in the traditional view that a subset of the Latinate affixes can evade stress in English, it will be purely accidental that a language such as Italian should never avail itself of that option.

4.6 Predictability of stress neutrality. Our sixth and final argument is that only the thesis in (16) can in fact predict which English suffixes will be neutral and which will not. Let us suppose that the general principle of metrical consistency discussed above imposes consistency of the stem, that is, 'neutrality,' over consistency of the suffix, putting aside for the moment why this should be the case. In (28), (a) is thus ranked over (b):

(28) a. Stem Consistency
     b. Suffix Consistency

This ranking imposes that any suffix that can be neutral will, satisfying (28a), and leaving only those suffixes that cannot be neutral to satisfy (28b) instead, presumably by fixing the position of the rightmost foot boundary in lexical representation in the manner of (18) above. What we need to do then is consider each possible structural combination of stem and suffix and determine whether it can yield neutrality under the hypothesis in (16), that is, by an appropriate parse of the weak syllable. As it turns out, this is a simple exercise.

We begin by noting, as in (29) below, that most English suffixes end in a weak syllable (either with a null vowel or not) and furthermore that most are either monosyllabic or bisyllabic.

(29) a. Most English suffixes end in a weak syllable (italicized):
     ic*ø*, al*ø*, i*ty*, ist*ø*, a*ble*
     b. Most English suffixes are monosyllabic or bisyllabic.

We put aside the few cases that do not conform with (29a), such as *-fy*, discussed in note 3, which would not affect our point. We also put aside the few suffixes such as *ation, ology, ometer*, which do not conform with (29b) and whose behavior has already been accounted for. Under the conjunction of (29a,b) all relevant suffixes will then reduce to the three structures in (30):

(30) a. W   b. L W   c. H W

Considering now how suffixes combine with stems, we make the further observation that suffixes are generally either concatenated with the stem externally to its final foot, as in (31a), or overlapped with that foot by one syllable, as in (31b):

(31) a. *concatenation*: a(mérica)nø → americanist
└‹─┐
istø

b. *σ-overlap*: propa(gánda) → propagandist
└‹──┐
istø

The combination of (30) and (31) will now give us six logical possibilities to examine. It is clear that 'stress neutrality' will result when the rightmost foot boundary of the stem is preserved, hence allowing all preceding metrical structure to remain intact as well (recall discussion of (17) above). We then essentially need to look only at the effects of suffixation on that boundary for each of the six possibilities. This is done in (32):

(32)

	concatenat.	s -overlap	neutrality	suffix sample
a. W	. . .) W	. . . W)	always neutral	*ive, ure, y, er, or*
b. L W	*. . .) L W	. . . L) W	only under overlap	*able, al, ic, ity, ous*
c. H W	. . .)(H W)	. . . H) W	always neutral	*ate, ist, ize, ent ment*

In (32a) the suffix consists of a single weak syllable. When that syllable is attached by concatenation, the resulting structure is well formed, because a weak syllable can be extrametrical. When that same syllable is attached by overlap, the structure is still well formed, since weak syllables can also be metrified. The prediction is therefore that all suffixes that are of this form should be neutral. This seems correct: suffixes *ive, ure* are neutral (e.g., *prevéntive, depárture*), as is nominal/adjectival/diminutive *y* (e.g., *presidéncy, súgary, Bílly*), as are agentive/comparative *er* and agentive *or,* which have syllables with sonorant nuclei.[8]

Turning to (32b), the sequence *LW* cannot be neutral when attached by concatenation, because it can be neither extrametrical nor metrified as a separate foot (given (12) above), hence requiring that the rightmost foot boundary of the stem be reset. In contrast when that sequence is attached by overlap, neutrality will result, because the weak syllable can remain extrametrical. The ensuing prediction seems again correct: suffixes *able, al, ic, ity, ous,* all have the structure in question, but only *able* is neutral. The reason is that only *able* is attached by overlap. In turn this is due to the fact that only *able* attaches to verbs, that metrify a final null vowel, replaced by the *a* of *able.* Note too that the sequence *al,* nonneutral as an adjectival suffix attached to nouns, is in fact neutral just like *able* when attached to verbs, as in *perúse* → *perúsal,* etc., just as expected.[9] Note further that *able* itself is not neutral when attached to items that have the metrical structure of nouns (hence by concatenation), as in (22a–e) above.[10]

Finally, suffixes with the structure *HW* are predicted to be always neutral, as in (32c). When they are concatenated, they can stand as an independent foot in the manner of (17c) above. When they are attached by overlap, they can leave the weak syllable extrametrical. Again, this seems correct as *ate, ist, ize, ant, ment* are all neutral (but see note 10).

We can now return to (28a,b) and consider why stem consistency namely, stress neutrality, should be preferred to suffix consistency. If we suppose that lexical organization incorporates a principle of 'economy,' requiring maximal reuse of existing structures including metrical structure, then it will be a simple numerical fact that stress neutrality satisfies that principle to a greater degree than suffix consistency. The reason is that for each individual suffix there are at most two possible metrical structures: one including and one excluding the final weak syllable, while there are many more stems. So, inconsistency of an individual suffix, as in *is)tø/ istø),* versus consistent *a)lø* will entail an increase in the number of metrical structures by exactly one. In contrast inconsistency of the corresponding stems will entail a much larger increase, like the one found with *al* in *áccident/accidéntal, médicine/medícinal, órigin/oríginal,* and so forth. That is, the increase here will be by a number commensurate with the number of stems the suffix takes, though likely smaller than that number as not all stems necessarily remetrify (e.g., *cláuse/cláusal*). Hence, 'economy' or maximal preservation in fact predicts that in general (28a) should have priority over (28b), as we supposed, and in turn that all suffixes that can be neutral will be, as we have seen is the case (with the qualification of note 10).

5 Conclusion. In this article I have presented an analysis of the stress neutrality of Latinate suffixes like *able, ist,* and others that departs significantly from past analyses, all of which in various different forms relied on the notion that these suffixes evade the stress principles. Specifically, I have argued that stress neutrality of Latinate suffixes results from integration of the suffix into the metrical structure of the stem and that the latter is made syntactically possible under further conditions by the general metrical ambiguity of word ends—a language-specific property of English. I have given six arguments to support the latter analysis and to refute stress evasion, summarized in (33).

(33) (i) Stress evasion is superfluous, since the modalities of metrification of the same suffixes with bound stems suffice to account for neutrality.
(ii) Only metrification and not stress evasion correctly predicts the classes of exceptions to neutrality in (20)–(22).
(iii) Only metrification correctly predicts that when stem vowels shorten, stress neutrality will no longer obtain.
(iv) Only metrification correctly predicts that no neutral suffix will have a syllabic structure larger than a weak foot.
(v) Only reliance on the ambiguity of weak syllables correctly predicts that a language that does not have weak syllables will not have stress-neutral suffixes.
(vi) Only by assuming metrification of all suffixes can one predict which suffixes will be stress neutral and which will not.

NOTES

* The present work is a revised version of Burzio (1991), which was reprinted in Rivista di Grammatica Generativa 16: 1–27. Portions of the work presented here were made possible by NEH Fellowship for University Teachers FA-27660-88 for the academic year 1988–89.

1. The motivation for the left-to-right parse of Halle and Kenstowicz (1991) is in part to more naturally account for the initial stress and apparent ternary foot of cases like *(wìnnepes)sáukee.* We argue in Burzio (1994), however, that the need to postulate special devices for this class of cases, including the left-to-right parse, is a contingency of an incorrect foot typology that excludes ternary feet. Note that in the system we propose below in the text and in Burzio (1994), directionality of parsing plays no role, since stress is not assigned by rule. The differences across languages commonly attributed to directionality of parsing must therefore be expressed differently, and in fact can be, without difficulty.

2. For instance, the final syllables of *syllabify* and *organize* compare in perceptual prominence, despite the fact that final stress is present only in the latter item, as we see in the next note.

3. This account predicts that vowel-ending suffixes should not be stress neutral since they have no weak syllable. That prediction is correct, as shown by the behavior of *fy*, nonneutral in *ácid/ a(cidify), húmid/ hu(midify), pérson/ per(sónify), sólid/ so(lidify)*, etc. The correct stress pattern of items in *fy* thus follows from supposing (contrary to past analyses) that there is no secondary stress on *fy*, which in turn is consistent with the fact that syllabification will not induce a null vowel here. In contrast, a secondary stress would predict **(ácidi)(fy) / . . . *(sólidi)(fy)* on a par with, e.g., *a(mérica)(nìze), (óxyge)(nàte)*, in which both *ize* and *ate* are neutral as predicted.

The null-vowel hypothesis thus predicts that in general vowel-ending verbs should exhibit the stress patterns of nouns ((8) above), which is largely correct (note also *rémedy*), though cases like *agrée* require further comment, as do nouns like *kangaróo* also.

4. But see Burzio (1994) for an attempt to predict that difference and, more generally, the one between (8) and (9), formerly stipulated.

5. Note that the items *(àller)gy* through *(càval)ry* in (19g), unlike the rest of the left-hand column, actually instantiate binary rather than ternary feet. As I argue in Burzio (1994), rightmost feet can be binary and headed by a light syllable, provided that the other syllable is heavy and that the foot is word initial—namely, that lack of syllables makes it impossible to construct a ternary foot, as in these cases. This point will not affect the rest of the discussion.

6. We may also note that *ant* in (19d) appears only as *an)tø,* while in (19f) *ize* appears only as *ize).* For the former case it is easy to show, however, that its stress-neutral behavior requires only that single metrification (as in *con(súltan)t,* etc. See also discussion of (25) below). For the case of *ize,* however, a handful of neutral cases will in fact require the alternative *i)ze* (like *propa(gándi)ze*). Hence, the claim that the metrification needed for bound stems suffices to account for neutrality under (16) is not completely true if made relative to each individual suffix, in particular for *ize.* But it is nonetheless true for all other individual suffixes, as well as for the suffixes taken as a group.

7. There is, however, dialectal variation. For some speakers there is no stress shift in these cases. The exact account of this variation is not immediately obvious.

8. Some of the suffixes just cited belong to the 'Germanic' rather than the 'Latinate' class (they do not induce vowel shortening, for instance), but this does not affect the text point, to the extent that Germanic suffixes are also parsed into feet, as argued in Burzio (1994).

9. There are, however, further restrictions not accounted for by the text. In particular the stem is generally required to be *oxytonic* with a few exceptions, such as *bury/ burial.*

10. It is important to note that in the text account stress neutrality could still be achieved even with suffixes of the type *LW* attached by concatenation, whenever the final foot of the stem has the structure *(HL)* in the manner illustrated in (i).

(i) (H L) L W=>(H L L) W

That is, a binary foot *(HL)* can expand to ternary in this fashion, since a ternary with a light median is well formed. This would predict a specific class of cases in which neutrality obtains even with *LW* suffixes attached by concatenation, such as *al* or *ic.* That prediction is incorrect, however, as shown by *(tita)n* → **(titani)cø* and many other examples. This fact requires that we interpret (28) above in a more specific manner. In particular we must take it to mean that stem consistency prevails over suffix consistency only if it has a sufficiently significant effect on the bulk of the stems that the suffix takes. In other words the creation of an additional metrical allomorph for the suffix (suffix *in*consistency) must be sufficiently well justified in terms of stem consistency measured in numbers of metrical allomorphs saved for stems (see text discussion below). With suffixes such as *ic,* stem-consistency can only be achieved for the class of cases in (i) and other isolated instances (*aórta/aórtic*), and for this reason suffix consistency prevails instead. This is analogous to the fact that *ant* and *able,* which could be neutral in (22f) and (23a) above, respectively, as in **(tríum)(phàntø), *ad(mírable),* are not, the reason being the small number of stems that would motivate the new parse of the suffix.

REFERENCES

Burzio, L. 1987. English Stress. In *Certamen Phonologicum Papers from the 1987 Cortona Phonology Meeting.* P. M. Bertinetto and M. Loporcaro, eds. Torino: Rosenberg and Sellier.

Burzio, L. 1991. On the Metrical Unity of Latinate Affixes. In *Proceedings of the Eighth Eastern States Conference on Linguistics.* G. Westphal, B. Ao, and H.-R. Chae, eds. Columbus Ohio State University. Reprinted in *Rivista di Gramatica Generativa* 16:1–27.

Burzio, L. 1993. English Stress, Vowel Length, and Modularity. *Journal of Linguistics* 29:359–418.

Burzio, L. 1994. *Principles of English Stress.* Cambridge: Cambridge University Press.

Burzio, L. To appear. Metrical Consistency. In *Proceedings of the DIMACS Workshop on Human Language.* E. Ristad, ed. Providence, R.I.: American Mathematical Society.

Chomsky, N., and M. Halle. 1968. *The Sound Pattern of English.* New York: Harper and Row.

Halle, M., and M. Kenstowicz. 1991. The Free Element Condition and Cyclic versus Noncyclic Stress. *Linguistic Inquiry* 22:457–501.

Halle, M., and J. R. Vergnaud. 1987a. Stress and the Cycle. *Linguistic Inquiry* 18:145–84.

Halle, M., and J. R. Vergnaud. 1987b. *An Essay on Stress.* Cambridge: MIT Press.

Hayes, B. 1982. Extrametricality and English Stress. *Linguistic Inquiry* 13:227–76.

Hayes, B. 1985. *A Metrical Theory of Stress Rules.* New York: Garland Publishing.

Kiparsky, P. 1982. Lexical Phonology and Morphology. In *Linguistics in the Morning Calm.* I. S. Yange, ed. Seoul.

Reconstruction and Picture Nouns in Spanish*

HÉCTOR CAMPOS
Georgetown University

1 Four problems for reconstruction in Spanish. The anaphor "himself" in (1) may be bound either by the subject of the main clause or by that of the embedded clause:

(1) [Which picture of himself$_{i,j}$] did John$_i$ say that Peter$_j$ saw?

To account for the ambiguity of (1), it has been proposed that the moved argument may be reconstructed to its base position or to any position it has moved through.[1] Thus (2a) may be reconstructed either as (2b) or (2c):

(2) a. [$_{CP}$ [Which picture of himself]$_i$ did [$_{IP}$ John say [$_{CP}$ t_i that [$_{IP}$ Peter saw t_i]]]]?
b. John$_i$ said [which picture of himself$_i$] Peter saw?
c. John said Peter$_j$ saw [which picture of himself$_j$]?

In (2b), "John" binds "himself" while in (2c), "Peter" binds it, thus obtaining the desired readings for the anaphor.[2] The equivalent of (1) in Spanish is also ambiguous, as shown in (3):

(3) ¿[Cuál foto de sí mismo$_{i,j}$] dijo Juan$_i$ [$_{CP}$ que [$_{IP}$ Pedro$_j$ había visto t]]?[3]
'[Which picture of himself$_{i,j}$] did Juan$_i$ say [$_{CP}$ that [$_{IP}$ Pedro$_j$ had seen t]]?'

Since subjacency does not force the *wh*-phrase to move through the intermediate CP in (3) because CP rather than IP is a bounding node in Spanish, it is possible for the *wh*-element to skip the lower CP.[4] If the *wh*-element has not moved through CP, there is no motivation to reconstruct into the intermediate CP in (3). Thus the fact that "himself" may refer to *Juan* in (3) if the *wh*-element has not moved through the intermediate Comp is in need of a new explanation.

While the example in (3) does not conclusively show that the *wh*-element did not move through Comp, there are other constructions where the anaphor inside the *wh*-phrase may be interpreted as coreferential with the matrix subject and where it can in fact be shown that the *wh*-phrase has not gone through the intermediate CP.

Torrego (1983) has noticed that a certain class of verbs in Spanish may appear without a complementizer in front of a tensed sentence. This is shown in (4a). Notice, however, that while the complementizer is optional in (4a,b), it is obligatory in (4c):

(4) a. Supongo (que) verán fotografías de sí mismos.
'I suppose (that) they will see pictures of themselves.'
b. ¿Qué fotografías de sí mismos$_{i,j}$ suponen ellos$_i$ [$_{CP}$ (que) [$_{IP}$vieron *t* [Marta y Miguel]$_j$]]?
'Which pictures of themselves$_{i,j}$ do they$_i$ suppose$_i$ [$_{CP}$ (that) [$_{IP}$ [Marta and Miguel]$_j$ saw *t*]]?'
c. ¿Qué fotografías de sí mismos$_{i,j}$ suponen ellos$_i$ [$_{CP1}$ *t* *(que) [$_{IP}$ propondrá su padre [$_{CP2}$ que [$_{IP}$ vean *t* [Marta y Miguel]$_j$]]]]?
'Which pictures of themselves$_{i,j}$ do they$_i$ suppose [$_{CP1}$ *t* *(that) [$_{IP}$ their father will propose [$_{CP2}$ that [$_{IP}$ [Marta and Miguel]$_j$ see *t*]]]]?'

Torrego (1983) has argued that the obligatory presence of the complementizer with this class of verbs is indicative of a trace in CP. Since the complementizer is not obligatory in (4b), we may conclude that the *wh*-phrase did not move through this intermediate CP and thus that there is no trace in that intermediate CP.[5] This follows from Subjacency, since CP, rather than IP, is a bounding node in Spanish. In (4c), on the other hand, the presence of the complementizer is obligatory. This also follows from subjacency. In (4c) the *wh*-phrase must stop in CP1 if subjacency is not to be violated. What is interesting to observe, though, is that whether or not the *wh*-phrase moves through the intermediate CP1, the anaphor inside the *wh*-phrase can be interpreted as coreferential with the subject of the main clause.[6] (4b) is unexpected, then, if reconstruction is possible only to positions the *wh*-phrase has moved through.

Coreference is also possible across a *wh*-island, as shown in (5):

(5) ¿[Cuáles fotos de sí mismo$_{i,j}$] no sabe Pedro$_i$ [$_{CP1}$ por qué [$_{IP}$ Juan$_j$ vio *t*]]?

'[Which pictures of himself$_{i,j}$] doesn't Pedro$_i$ know [$_{CP1}$ why [$_{IP}$ Juan$_j$ saw *t*]]?'

It is clear that in the examples in (5) there is no intermediate trace in CP1 as [Spec,CP] is occupied by *por qué* 'why.' Again, the reading where *sí mismo* refers to *Pedro* is unexpected if reconstruction is possible only to intermediate positions through which the *wh*-phrase has moved.[8]

Finally, *wh*-words need not move to CP by S-Structure in Spanish. In this case, the anaphor may also refer to the subject of the main clause:

(6) ¿Juan$_i$ dijo que Pedro$_j$ había visto cuál foto de sí mismo$_{i,j}$?
'Juan$_i$ said that Pedro$_j$ had seen which picture of himself$_{i,j}$?'

If the *wh*-word moves to CP in LF it is not clear how the sentence can be reconstructed with the *wh*-word in the intermediate CP.[9] [10]

So the question that must be addressed is how (3), (4b), (5) and (6) can be reconstructed to the intermediate CP if they have not gone through the intermediate CP. Before we present our solution, it will be necessary to look at the behavior of anaphors inside picture nouns in Spanish in more detail.

2 On the structure of picture nouns.

2.1 Picture nouns in Spanish and English. Chomsky (1986) posits a PRO inside the picture NP in (7) to account for the contrast between (7a) and (7b):

(7) a. They$_i$ told [PROi stories about them$_{*i,j}$].
b. They$_i$ heard [PROj stories about them$_{i,*j}$].

The claim that picture nouns may contain a PRO subject is further motivated by Stowell (1989:239) who, following Clark (1986), Roeper (1986), and Abney (1987), also proposes a PRO in NP to account for the following constructions:

(8) a. John disapproves of [the PRO$_i$ hatred of oneself$_i$].
b. John$_i$ needs [a PRO$_i$ talking to t_i].
c. Bill resented [the PRO$_i$ destruction of the city [PRO$_i$ to prove a point.][11]

Let us consider picture nouns in Spanish. As in English, an anaphor inside a picture noun phrase may be bound by an antecedent external to the noun phrase. This is shown in (9):

(9) a. Juan$_i$ mostró una foto/fotos/la(s) foto(s) de sí mismo$_i$.
 b. Juan$_i$ showed a picture/pictures/the picture(s) of himself$_i$.

In (9), *Juan* and *sí mismo* 'himself' are interpreted as coreferential in both English and Spanish. In both English and Spanish the examples in (9) are ambiguous. In the first reading *Juan* is interpreted as the agent of his own picture; in the second reading *Juan* is only the 'patient' of the picture that someone else took. These two readings will become relevant when we look at long-distance dependencies in Spanish.

We may explore the structure proposed in Chomsky (1986) and suggest that the ambiguity of the Spanish example in (9a) is best captured by the following structures:

(10) a. Juan$_i$ mostró [una PRO$_i$ foto de sí mismo$_i$].
 Juan$_i$ showed [a PRO$_i$ picture of himself$_i$].
 b. Juan$_i$ mostró [una foto de sí mismo$_i$].
 Juan$_i$ showed [a picture of himself$_i$].

PRO would appear in the picture noun phrase only when it is controlled, as shown in (10a). When there is no antecedent for the agent of the picture noun, PRO is not projected syntactically, as shown in (10b).

However, there is one crucial difference between English and Spanish. In Spanish, but not in English, the anaphor may be bound by a long-distance antecedent.[12] This is shown in (11):

(11) a. Pedro$_i$ dijo que María vio la/una foto de sí mismo$_i$ en la mesa.
 b. *Pedro$_i$ said that María saw the/a picture of himself$_i$ on the table.

It is also interesting to observe that, in spite of the ambiguity found in (9a), where *Pedro* may or may not be the agent of the picture, in (11a) *Pedro* must be interpreted exclusively as the agent of the picture.

If the picture noun phrase contained a control *PRO* in subject position, as in (10a), this long-distance control would be hard to motivate since control is supposed to be a local phenomenon, and the difference between English and Spanish would not follow from any principle and would need to be stipulated.

To account for the difference between English and Spanish, we could entertain the hypothesis that *pro,* rather than a control *PRO,* appears in these constructions.[13] We would thus be able to explain why these constructions are possible in Spanish but not in English. Thus, (11a) would have the structure shown in (12):

(12) Pedro$_i$ dijo que María encontró [la *pro*$_i$ foto de sí mismo$_i$] en la mesa.
Pedro$_i$ said that María found [the *pro*$_i$ picture of himself$_i$] on the table.

How would *pro* be licensed in (12)? Rizzi (1986) has proposed that *pro* is subject to a licensing and an identification condition:

(i) licensing condition: *pro* is governed and Case-marked by X^0_y;
(ii) identification condition: *pro* is recovered through rich agreement and specification.

The licensing condition in (i) claims that *pro* is licensed by a governing head X^0 of type *y,* which assigns Case to *pro,* where the class of licensing heads would vary from language to language. AgrS would then be an appropriate governing head in Spanish and Italian, but not in English or French, thus allowing for silent subjects in the former but not in the latter languages. Rich agreement is what seems to make X^0 an appropriate licensing head. Notice that the noun *foto* 'picture' is clearly marked as FEMENINE and SINGULAR in Spanish.[14] Because there is no nominal agreement in English, *pro* would fail to meet the government condition (i) in English, while this condition would be met in Spanish.[15] In the case of a *pro*-subject AgrS, apart from being an appropriate governing head of type X_y, also assigns Nominative Case to *pro,* thus licensing *pro* in subject position in Spanish. I would like to suggest that the N^0 (plus its agreement and number) assigns Genitive case to *pro.* We thus obtain constructions such as *la sua fotografia* 'the [his/her] picture' in Italian or *la seva fotografia* 'the [his/her] picture' in Catalan, where *pro* is phonetically realized.[16] Thus *pro* would be licensed in Spanish but not in English because it is governed and receives Case by an appropriate head X^0.

Regarding the identification condition, in the case of *pro* in subject position AgrS identifies it. However, when *pro* is inside a noun phrase, there is no rich agreement to identify it. Nevertheless, this identification can be done via binding: *pro* will acquire the features of its antecedent.[17] Thus *pro* is also identified in (12).

With respect to Binding Theory I will assume that *pro* has the features [−ana, +pron] and, following Campos (1991), I will assume that *pro* in Spanish has the feature [+B],[18] which requires it to be bound sentence-internally. Thus, in (12) *pro* is free in its governing category (the embedded IP) but bound sentence-internally as required by its [+B] feature. Thus *pro* is licensed in NP in Spanish.

Notice that if *Pedro* fails to c-command *pro* or if *Pedro* is a discourse topic, the sentence becomes ungrammatical:

(13) a. *El hermano de Pedro$_i$ dijo que María vio la foto de sí mismo$_i$.
'The brother of Pedro$_i$ said that María saw the picture of himself$_i$.
b. —¿Conoces a Pedro$_i$?
—*Sí, y María dijo que había visto la foto de sí mismo$_i$ en el periódico.
—Do you know Pedro$_i$?
—*Yes, and María said that (she) had seen the picture of himself$_i$ in the paper.'

In (13a) *sí mismo* may refer to *Pedro's brother,* but not to *Pedro.* This suggests that *pro* in picture noun phrases must have a c-commanding antecedent sentence-internally.[19] [20]

I conclude, therefore, that *pro,* which will be interpreted as the agent of the picture, will appear as the subject of the picture noun when there is a sentence-internal antecedent. If there is no explicit agent for the picture, *pro* does not appear. Thus the ambiguity of (9), repeated here as (14a), is to be represented as in (14b,c), rather than as in (10a,b):

(14) a. Juan mostró una foto de sí mismo.
Juan showed a picture of himself.
b. Juan$_i$ mostró [una *pro*$_i$ foto de sí mismo$_i$].
Juan$_i$ showed [a *pro*$_i$ picture of himself$_i$].
c. Juan$_i$ mostró [una foto de sí mismo$_i$].
Juan$_i$ showed [a picture of himself$_i$].

In (14b) *Juan* is interpreted as the agent of the picture; in (14c) somebody else took the picture and *Juan* appears in it.

The structures proposed in (14b,c) directly explain the long-distance anaphoric binding noted in (11), repeated here as (15a):

(15) a. Pedro$_i$ dijo que María vio la/una foto de sí mismo$_i$.
Pedro$_i$ said that María saw the/a picture of himself$_i$.
b. Pedro$_i$ dijo que María vio [la/una *pro*$_i$ foto de sí mismo$_i$].
Pedro$_i$ said that María saw [the/a *pro*$_i$ picture of himself$_i$].
c. *Pedro$_i$ dijo que María vio [la/una foto de sí mismo$_i$].
Pedro$_i$ said that María saw [the/a picture of himself$_i$].

The anaphor in (15c) is not bound in its governing category (the embedded IP), hence the ungrammaticality of (15c). In (15b), on the other hand, the anaphor is bound by *pro,* which is itself bound sentence-internally by *Pedro,* thus satisfying its [+B] feature. This explains why (15a) can only be interpreted as *Pedro* having taken the picture himself, rather than as someone else having taken it.

Consider now the English examples. Since there is no nominal inflection (gender) in nouns in English, *pro* would not be licensed. *PRO,* on the other hand, could be a possible subject of NP in English. Thus while *pro* could be found in NP in Spanish, *PRO* may be found in English. This parallels the behavior of *PRO/pro* inside IP, where *PRO* is possible only when there is no (verbal) agreement. And the fact that *PRO* appears in noun phrases when there is no inflection, while *pro* appears when there is nominal inflection, parallels the proposal of Huang (1984, 1987) whereby the weak verbal inflection of Chinese allows *PRO* to appear as a subject of a tensed clause, whereas the strong inflection of Spanish, on the other hand, would license *pro* in the same position. Thus we see that our proposal that *PRO/pro* may appear in the same position is motivated elsewhere in the grammar.

The corresponding English structures are shown in (16):

(16) a. Peter$_i$ showed a picture of himself$_i$.
b. Peter$_i$ showed [a PRO$_i$ picture of himself$_i$].
c. Peter$_i$ showed [a picture of himself$_i$].

The English example in (16a) is ambiguous as its Spanish counterpart in (14). However, the ambiguity of the English examples is represented as (16b,c), where *PRO* appears in (16b) when *Peter* is interpreted as the agent of the picture noun. In contrast to Spanish, though, the long-distance binding of the anaphor is not possible:

(17) a. *Peter$_i$ said that Mary showed a picture of himself$_i$.
b. *Peter$_i$ said that Mary showed [a PRO picture of himself$_i$].
c. *Peter$_i$ said that Mary showed [a picture of himself$_i$].

Example (17c), similar to (15c), is ungrammatical because the anaphor is not bound in its governing category (the lower IP). (17b) is also ungrammatical, however (cf. 15b), because there is no long-distance control of *PRO.* So in (17b) *PRO* fails to be controlled by *Pedro,* in which case *himself* is not bound in its governing category, either.

We thus see that the ambiguity exhibited by (14a) and (16a), as well as the difference between Spanish and English regarding long-distance anaphoric binding, can be explained if we assume the structures in (14b,c) and in (16b,c), respectively.

2.2 Picture nouns and *wh*-questions. Consider now *wh*-questions in picture nouns. *Wh*-questions may either move to CP or be left *in-situ* in Spanish.

(18) a. ¿Juan$_i$ mostró cuáles fotos de sí mismo$_i$?
b. ¿Cuáles fotos de sí mismo$_i$ mostró Juan$_i$?
'Which pictures of himself$_i$ did Juan$_i$ show?'

In both examples in (18) *Juan* may or may not have taken the picture. The ambiguity of (18a) can be represented at LF as in (19):

(19) a. ¿[Cuáles x] Juan$_i$ mostró [x *pro*$_i$ fotos de sí mismo$_i$]?
[Which x] Juan$_i$ showed [x *pro*$_i$ pictures of himself$_i$]?
b. ¿[Cuáles x] Juan$_i$ mostró [x fotos de sí mismo$_i$]?
[Which x] Juan$_i$ showed [x pictures of himself$_i$]?

Sí mismo 'himself' satisfies Condition A at LF by being bound by *pro* in (19a) and by the main subject in (19b).[21]

The ambiguity of (18b) can be represented as in (20):

(20) a. ¿[Cuáles *pro*$_i$ fotos de sí mismo$_i$] mostró Juan$_i$?
'[Which *pro*$_i$ pictures of himself$_i$] did Juan$_i$ show?
b. ¿[Cuáles fotos de sí mismo$_i$] mostró Juan$_i$?
'[Which pictures of himself$_i$] did Juan$_i$ show?'

Following Chomsky (1993), I will assume that the trace of the moved *wh*-element is a copy of the original *wh*-element. Then the examples in (20) reduce to those of (19) at LF. The ambiguity that results in these constructions is explained because the two representations in (19), the one with *pro* and the one without it, yield licit outputs.

Wh-questions may also appear in intermediate Comp positions in indirect and semiquestions.[22] Let us consider first an indirect question where the anaphor is interpreted as being coreferential with the embedded subject.

(21) a. Pedro dijo que cuáles fotos de sí misma$_i$ mostró María$_i$.
Pedro said that which pictures of herself showed Maria.
'Pedro asked which pictures of herself$_i$ María$_i$ showed.'
b. Pedro dijo que [cuál x] María$_i$ mostró [x *pro*$_i$ fotos de sí misma$_i$].
Pedro said that [which x] María$_i$ showed [x *pro*$_i$ pictures of herself$_i$].
c. Pedro dijo que [cuál x] María$_i$ mostró [x fotos de sí misma$_i$].
Pedro said that [which x] María$_i$ showed [x pictures of herself$_i$].

In this case *María* may or may not be interpreted as the agent of the pictures. This case is parallel to the one shown in (19). The fact that the construction is ambiguous follows from the fact that the two representations in (21b,c) yield a legal output.

From the intermediate Comp position in (21a) the anaphor may also be able to corefer with the main subject. This is shown in (22):

(22) Pedro$_i$ dijo que cuáles fotos de sí mismo$_i$ mostró María.
Pedro$_i$ said that which pictures of himself$_i$ showed María
'Pedro$_i$ asked which pictures of himself$_i$ María showed.'

Notice, however, that sentence (22) is not ambiguous. In this case, and different from the examples discussed above, *Pedro* must be interpreted as being the agent of the pictures; somebody else could not have taken them.

The two potential LF representations for (22) are shown in (23). Only (23a) is well formed:

(23) a. Pedro$_i$ dijo que [cuáles x] María mostró [x *pro*$_i$ fotos de sí mismo$_i$].
Pedro$_i$ said that [which x] María showed [x *pro*$_i$ pictures of himself$_i$].

b. *Pedro$_i$ dijo que [cuáles x] María mostró [x fotos de sí mismo$_i$].
Pedro$_i$ said that [which x] María showed [x pictures of himself$_i$].

These facts follow directly from our claim. In (23a) the anaphor *sí mismo* 'himself' is bound by *pro,* while in (23b) it is not bound at all, hence the ungrammaticality of (23b).[23] We thus explain why the only possible reading is that in which *Pedro* must be interpreted as the agent of the picture.[24]

The behavior of anaphors inside picture noun phrases is replicated in semiquestions. In (24) the anaphor may refer either to the embedded or to the main subject:

(24) a. Pedro no sabe cuáles fotos de sí misma$_i$ mostró María$_i$.
'Pedro doesn't know which pictures of herself$_i$ María$_i$ showed.'
b. Pedro$_i$ no sabe cuáles fotos de sí mismo$_i$ mostró María.
'Pedro$_i$ doesn't know which pictures of himself$_i$ María showed.'

In (24a) *María* may or may not have taken the pictures. In (24b), on the other hand, only *Pedro* could have taken the pictures. These facts reduce to those of (22). Assuming a unique representation for picture nouns, the behavior of the anaphors in (22) and (24b) could not be accounted for.

Consider now the case of long extraction. Since the reading where the anaphor is coreferential with the embedded subject can always be explained by reconstruction into the argument position at LF, we will concentrate on the case in which the anaphor is referential with the main subject. Consider (25):

(25) ¿Cuál foto de sí mismo$_i$ dijo Pedro$_i$ que el periódico había publicado?
'Which picture of himself$_i$ did Pedro$_i$ say that the newspaper had published?'

In (25) *Pedro* must be interpreted as having taken the picture.

Contrast the example in (25) with that of (26):

(26) ¿Cuál foto de sí mismo$_i$ dijo Pedro$_i$ que no sabía si el periódico había publicado?

'Which picture of himself$_i$ did Pedro$_i$ say that he didn't know whether the newspaper had published?'

The example in (26), different from that of (25), is ambiguous between *Pedro* being or not being the agent of the picture. The corresponding derivations for (25) and (26) are shown in (27a,b), respectively:

(27) a. [$_{CP1}$ Cuál foto de sí mismo$_i$ [$_{IP}$ dijo Pedro$_i$ [$_{CP2}$ que [$_{IP}$ había publicado el periódico *t*]]]]?
[$_{CP1}$ Which picture of himself$_i$ [$_{IP}$ said Pedro$_i$ [$_{CP2}$ that [$_{IP}$ had published the newspaper *t*]]]]?
b. [$_{CP1}$ Cuál foto de sí mismo$_i$ [$_{IP}$ dijo Pedro$_i$ [$_{CP2}$ *t* que [$_{IP}$ no sabía [$_{CP3}$ si [$_{IP}$ el periódico había publicado *t*]]]]]]?
[$_{CP1}$ Which picture of himself$_i$ [$_{IP}$ said Pedro$_i$ [$_{CP2}$ *t* that [$_{IP}$ not knew [$_{CP3}$whether [$_{IP}$ the newspaper had published *t*]]]]]]?

Since CP is a bounding node in Spanish, Subjacency forces the *wh*-element to move through CP2 in (27b = 26) but not in (27a = 25).

Consider first (27a). Since the *wh*-element has not moved through the intermediate Comp, the only possible reconstruction structure is the one for which a copy of the original *wh*-element appears in object position as shown in (28), where there are two potential structures:

(28) a. ¿[cuáles x] Pedro$_i$ dijo que el periódico había publicado [x *pro*$_i$ fotos de sí mismo$_i$]?
[which x] Pedro$_i$ said that the newspaper had published [x *pro*$_i$ pictures of himself$_i$]?
b. *[which x] Pedro$_i$ dijo que el periódico había publicado [x fotos de sí mismo$_i$]?
[which x] Pedro$_i$ said that the newspaper had published [x pictures of himself$_i$]?

In (28b) the anaphor fails to be bound in its governing category, while in (28a) it is bound by *pro.* Thus (27a) can only be interpreted with *Pedro* being the agent of the pictures. This follows from our claim that in (28a) there is a *pro* subject in the picture noun phrase. If there were only one structure for picture nouns, the lack of ambiguity of (27a) could not be accounted for.[25]

Since the *wh*-element has proceeded through the intermediate CP2 in (27b), we may reconstruct the *wh*-phrase in this intermediate CP2 as shown in (29):

(29) ¿[Cuál x] Pedro$_i$ dijo [$_{CP2}$ [x fotografía de sí mismo$_i$] que [$_{IP}$ no sabía [$_{CP3}$ si [$_{IP}$ el periódico había publicado *t*]]]]?
[Which x] Pedro$_i$ said [$_{CP2}$ [x picture of himself$_i$] that [$_{IP}$ not knew [$_{CP3}$ whether [$_{IP}$ the newspaper had published *t*]]]]?

Notice that in (29) *Pedro* may serve as an antecedent to the anaphor *sí mismo* 'himself' and *Pedro* may be interpreted as the nonagent of the picture. The fact that the *wh*-element moved through CP2 in (27b) explains why *Pedro* may be coreferential with the anaphor and also why *Pedro* may be interpreted as the nonagent of the picture.

In (27b) *Pedro* may also be interpreted as being the agent of the picture. This follows from the fact that the *wh*-element may be reconstructed in the original argument position, thus obtaining the same representations as in (28).

The facts discussed in this section argue in favor of the structures proposed in (14), where a *pro* subject appears only when the *pro* subject has a sentence-internal antecedent.

Summarizing, then, we have shown that picture noun phrases may appear with or without a *pro* subject, as shown in (14). In the former case the antecedent of *pro* is interpreted as being the agent of the picture noun phrase; in the latter case, although there is an implicit agent outside the sentence, it is not syntactically represented. Let us now return to the four problems noted in section 1.

3 Solving the paradox. The following examples required an explanation in section 1:

(30) a. ¿[Cuál foto de sí mismo$_{i,j}$] dijo Juan$_i$ [$_{CP1}$ que [$_{IP}$ Pedro$_j$ había visto]]? (=3)
'[Which picture of himself$_{i,j}$] did Juan$_i$ say [$_{CP1}$ that [$_{IP}$ Pedro$_j$ had seen]]?'

b. ¿Qué fotografías de sí mismos$_{i,j}$ suponen ellos$_i$ [$_{CP1}$ (que) [$_{IP}$ vieron [Marta y Miguel]$_j$]]? (=4b)
'Which pictures of themselves$_{i,j}$ do they$_i$ suppose$_i$ [$_{CP1}$ (that) [$_{IP}$ [Marta and Miguel]$_j$ saw]]?'

c. ¿[Cuáles fotos de sí mismo$_{i,j}$] no sabe Pedro$_i$ [$_{CP}$ por qué [$_{IP}$ Juan$_j$ vio]]? (=5)
'[Which pictures of himself$_{i,j}$] doesn't Pedro$_i$ know [$_{CP}$ why [$_{IP}$ Juan$_j$ saw]]?'

d. ¿Juan$_i$ dijo que Pedro$_j$ había visto cuál foto de sí mismo$_{i,j}$? (=6)
'Juan$_i$ said that Pedro$_j$ had seen which picture of himself$_{i,j}$?'

In the examples above reconstruction to the intermediate CP is not possible since there is no trace of the *wh*-element in the intermediate CP, either because the *wh*-element has not gone through the intermediate CP (30a,b,d) or because the intermediate CP is occupied by some other element (30c). Thus we need to explain how the anaphor inside the picture noun phrase is able to corefer with the main subject if it cannot be reconstructed into the intermediate CP. Another fact to explain is why the subject of the embedded clause may be interpreted as either the agent or the nonagent of the picture noun while the subject of the main clause must be interpreted exclusively as the agent of the picture noun.

These facts follow directly from our analysis. For the constructions above there are two potential structures. In the first construction there is a *pro* inside the picture noun phrase as shown in (31):

(31) a. ¿[Cuál x] Juan$_i$ dijo [$_{CP}$ que [$_{IP}$ Pedro$_j$ había visto [x *pro*$_{i,j}$ foto de sí mismo$_{i,j}$]]]?
[Which x] Juan$_i$ said [$_{CP}$ that [$_{IP}$ Pedro$_j$ had seen [x *pro*$_{i,j}$ picture of himself$_{i,j}$]]]?

b. ¿[Cuáles x] ellos$_i$ suponen [$_{CP}$ (que) [$_{IP}$ [Marta y Miguel]$_j$ vieron [x *pro*$_{i,j}$ fotos de sí mismos$_{i,j}$]]]?
[Which x] they$_i$ suppose [$_{CP}$ (that) [$_{IP}$ [Marta and Miguel]$_j$ saw [x *pro*$_{i,j}$ pictures of themselves$_{i,j}$]]]?

c. ¿[Cuáles x] Pedro$_i$ no sabe [$_{CP}$ por qué [$_{IP}$ Juan$_j$ vio [x *pro*$_{i,j}$ fotos de sí mismo$_{i,j}$]]]?
[Which x] Pedro$_i$ does not know [$_{CP}$ why [$_{IP}$ Juan$_j$ saw [x *pro*$_{i,j}$ pictures of himself$_{i,j}$]]]?

d. ¿[Cuál x] Juan$_i$ dijo que Pedro$_j$ había visto [x *pro*$_{i,j}$ foto de sí mismo$_{i,j}$]?
[Which x] Juan$_i$ said that Pedro$_j$ had seen [x *pro*$_{i,j}$ picture of himself$_{i,j}$]?

In (31) the *pro* in the picture noun phrase may be coreferential either with the subject of the embedded clause or with that of the main clause. Thus, at reconstruction *pro* is able to bind the anaphor inside the picture noun phrase. In this way we obtain the reading that either the subject of the main clause or that of the embedded clause is the agent of the picture noun.

The second potential construction is the one without *pro* in the picture noun phrase:

(32) a. ¿[Cuál x] Juan$_i$ dijo [$_{CP}$ que [$_{IP}$ Pedro$_j$ había visto [x foto de sí mismo$_{*i,j}$]]]?
[Which x] Juan$_i$ said [$_{CP}$ that [$_{IP}$ Pedro$_j$ had seen [x picture of himself$_{*i,j}$]]]?
b. ¿[Cuáles x] ellos$_i$ suponen [$_{CP}$ (que) [$_{IP}$ [Marta y Miguel]$_j$ vieron [x fotos de sí mismos$_{*i,j}$]]]?
[Which x] they$_i$ suppose [$_{CP}$ (that) [$_{IP}$ [Marta and Miguel]$_j$ saw [x pictures of themselves$_{*i,j}$]]]?
c. ¿[Cuáles x] Pedro$_i$ no sabe [$_{CP}$ por qué [$_{IP}$ Juan$_j$ vio [x fotos de sí mismo$_{*i,j}$]]]?
[Which x] Pedro$_i$ does not know [$_{CP}$ why [$_{IP}$ Juan$_j$ saw [x pictures of himself$_{*i,j}$]]]?
d. ¿[Cuál x] Juan$_i$ dijo que Pedro$_j$ había visto [x foto de sí mismo$_{*i,j}$]?
[Which x] Juan$_i$ said that Pedro$_j$ had seen [x picture of himself$_{*i,j}$]?

In the construction without *pro* the anaphor may be bound only by the embedded subject. This also explains why only the embedded subject may be interpreted as the nonagent of the pictures. The subject of the main clause fails to bind the anaphor in (32).

We thus see that the paradoxical examples from section 1 receive a direct explanation from our claim that there are two underlying structures for picture nouns.

4 Some potential counterexamples and speculations. In the previous section we motivated two underlying representations for picture nouns. The representations of (14b,c) are repeated here as (33) for convenience:

(33) a. Juan$_i$ mostró [una *pro*$_i$ foto de sí mismo$_i$].
Juan$_i$ showed [a *pro*$_i$ picture of himself$_i$].
b. Juan$_i$ mostró [una foto de sí mismo$_i$].
Juan$_i$ showed [a picture of himself$_i$].

Binding Theory predicts that anaphors and pronominals should be in complementary distribution. A pronominal, however, may appear inside a picture noun phrase, as shown in (34):

(34) Juan$_i$ mostró una foto de él$_i$.
Juan$_i$ showed a picture of him$_i$.

The genitive pronoun may be interpreted as a possessor (*Juan's picture*), as well as the agent or the patient of the picture. However, when *Juan* is interpreted as the patient of the picture, he cannot be interpreted as the agent of the picture at the same time. Since *pro* appears when there is a sentence-internal antecedent in the analysis we sketched in section 2, we predict for (34) a picture noun structure without *pro,* as in (35):

(35) Juan$_i$ mostró [una foto de él$_i$].
Juan$_i$ showed [a picture of him$_i$].

If *él* 'him' is a pronominal, (35) would constitute a violation of Condition B of the Binding Theory as *él* 'him' would be bound in its Complete Functional Category (CFC). What we would like to suggest here is that genitive pronominals behave like possessives. Compare the behavior of *de él* 'of him' with that of *su/suya* '(of) his' in (36):

(36) a. Juan$_i$ dice que yo mostré su$_{i,j}$ foto/una foto suya$_{i,j}$.
'Juan$_i$ says that I showed his$_{i,j}$ picture/a picture of his$_{i,j}$.'
b. Juan$_i$ mostró su$_i$ foto.
'Juan$_i$ showed his$_i$ picture.'
c. Juan$_i$ dice que yo mostré una foto de él$_{i,j}$.
'Juan$_i$ says that I showed a picture of him$_{i,j}$.'
d. Juan$_i$ mostró una foto de él$_i$.
'Juan$_i$ showed a picture of him$_i$.'

In spite of its behaving like a pronominal in (36a), the possessive *su/suya* 'his' behaves like an anaphor in (36b). Notice the parallel behavior of the genitive pronoun.

These facts suggest that possessives are pronominal anaphors but, different from PRO, possessives may have a governing category and they may be lexical. We could pursue the possibility that GENITIVE Case (parallel to Tns/Agr, which assigns NOMINATIVE) counts as an accessible SUBJECT to determine the CFC, and then the pronominal status of these elements may be maintained, as they would be free in NP.[26] But we still need to explain why the GENITIVE would not make the NP a CFC in (33).

I have no specific claim to make about possessives here. But if genitive pronouns are treated like possessives, in that they may be bound (although not obligatorily) in their CFC, then the structure in (33) does not present a counterexample to our claim.

A second issue to address is the difference between English and Spanish regarding the agent of the picture noun. Consider (37):

(37) a. Which picture of $himself_i$ did $Peter_i$ see?
b. Which picture of $himself_i$ did $Peter_i$ say that Mary had seen?

In both examples of (37) Peter may be interpreted as the agent or the nonagent of the pictures. Spanish is different, though:

(38) a. ¿Cuáles fotos de sí $mismo_i$ vio $Pedro_i$?
b. ¿Cuáles fotos de sí $mismo_i$ dijo $Pedro_i$ que María había visto?

Only in (38a) can *Pedro* be interpreted both as the agent and the nonagent of the pictures. In (38b) *Pedro* is necessarily the agent of the pictures. In section 2 the facts of Spanish were shown to follow from the structures in (33). The facts of English also follow from our analysis. (39) shows the two possible reconstructions for (37a):

(39) a. [Which x] $Peter_i$ saw [x PRO_i picture of $himself_i$].
b. [Which x] $Peter_i$ saw [x picture of $himself_i$].

In (39a) *Peter* is interpreted as the agent of the pictures; in (39b) *Peter* is not the agent. Hence the ambiguity of (37a).

There are four possible reconstructions for (37b). Notice that only the first two are licit:

(40) a. [Which x] $Peter_i$ said [x PRO_i picture of $himself_i$] that Mary saw?
b. [Which x] $Peter_i$ said [x picture of $himself_i$] that Mary saw?
c. *[Which x] $Peter_i$ said that Mary saw [x PRO picture of $himself_i$]?
d. *[Which x] $Peter_i$ said that Mary saw [x picture of $himself_i$]?

Example (40a) provides the reading in which *Peter* is both the agent and patient of the picture, while (40b) provides the reading in which *Peter* is just the patient and there is an understood agent. In (40c) and (40d) the anaphor fails to be licensed. In (40c), because of the long distance from its antecedent, PRO fails to be controlled and thus the anaphor is not bound in its governing category. In (40d) the anaphor also fails to be bound in its governing category, thus violating Condition A.

A third issue concerns anaphors over a *wh*-island in English. Frank (1992) has noted the following example for English:

(41) Which picture of himself$_i$ does Carl$_i$ wonder whether Mary prefers?

Notice that, parallel to the facts of Spanish discussed in section 1, the anaphor may refer to the main subject in spite of its not having gone through the intermediate CP. *Carl* in (41) may be interpreted both as the agent and the nonagent of the picture. However, consider the examples in (42):

(42) a. ?Which picture of Spain doesn't Carl know whether Mary prefers?
b. *Which picture of himself$_i$ doesn't Carl$_i$ know whether Mary prefers?

Example (42a) is a subjacency violation, hence its marginality. In spite of the parallel structure of (42b) it is worse than (42a). The anaphor seems to fail to be connected to its antecedent in (42b), contrary to what happens in (41).

Suñer (1991, 1993)[27] has argued that verbs such as 'wonder' in (41), which take an indirect question complement, may have a double CP, as in (43), while verbs like 'know,' which take a semiquestion complement, have only one CP, as in (44):[28]

(43) [Which picture of himself$_i$] does Carl$_i$ wonder [$_{CP}$ [$_{CP}$ whether [Mary prefers *t*]]]?
(44) *[Which picture of himself$_i$] doesn't Carl$_i$ know [$_{CP}$ whether [Mary prefers *t*]]]?

The facts above suggest that the higher CP in (43) may be available for landing and hence for reconstruction, as shown in (45):[29]

(45) [Which x] Carl$_i$ wonders [$_{CP}$ [x picture of himself$_i$] [$_{CP}$ whether [Mary prefers *t*]]]?

Since *Carl* may also be interpreted as the agent of the pictures, *PRO* may be licensed in this intermediate CP position:

(46) [Which x] $Carl_i$ wonders $[_{CP}$ [x PRO_i picture of $himself_i$] $[_{CP}$ whether [Mary prefers *t*]]]?

Since *PRO* does not seem to be licensed long-distance, as shown in (40c), *PRO* must be licensed at LF in the intermediate CP position in (46).

We thus explain the grammaticality of (43), where *Carl* may be interpreted both as the agent (46) and the nonagent (45) of the pictures. The impossibility of (44) in either reading follows from the fact that the *wh*-phrase fails to reconstruct in the intermediate CP, and hence the anaphor incurs a violation of Condition A.

If this proposal is on the right track, we expect Spanish to behave like English in these constructions if the higher CP in (43) is a possible landing site. This is borne out:

(47) ¿[[Cuál foto de sí $mismo_i$] se pregunta $Juan_i$ $[_{CP1}$ *t* $[_{CP2}$ si María ha visto *t*]]]?
[[Which picture of $himself_i$] wonders $Juan_i$ $[_{CP1}$ *t* $[_{CP2}$ whether María has seen *t*]]]?

If the *wh*-element were to skip CP1, we would obtain a subjacency violation in (47). If the *wh*-element moves through CP1, then the *wh*-element may be reconstructed there, as in the English example (45). We thus explain why *Juan* may be interpreted as the nonagent of the picture. The interpretation in which *Juan* is interpreted as the agent of the picture follows from the *pro* subject in the picture noun, as suggested above.

A last problematic issue has to do with the level at which Condition A applies. As noted in the discussion of indirect questions and semiquestions,[30] we noted that Condition A must necessarily apply after reconstruction in Spanish. Consider example (24b), repeated here as (48a), and compare it with the English equivalent in (48b):

(48) a. $Pedro_i$ no sabe cuáles fotos de sí $mismo_i$ mostró María.
b. $Pedro_i$ doesn't know which pictures of $himself_i$ María showed.

In (48a) *Pedro* can only be interpreted as the agent of the picture. To account for this fact, we have assumed that Condition A applies after reconstruction at LF, thus obtaining the following contrast:

(49) a. Pedro$_i$ no sabe [cuál x] María mostró [x *pro*$_i$ fotos de sí mismo$_i$].
Pedro$_i$ doesn't know [which x] María showed [x *pro*$_i$ pictures of himself$_i$].
b. *Pedro$_i$ no sabe [which x] María mostró [x fotos de sí mismo$_i$].
Pedro$_i$ doesn't know [which x] María showed [x pictures of himself$_i$].

Example (49b) violates Condition A and hence only (49a) is a possible structure, where *Pedro* is interpreted as the agent of the pictures. If Binding Theory were to apply at S-structure (before reconstruction), we would expect *Pedro* to be either the agent or patient of the pictures. Thus these facts suggest that Binding Theory cannot apply at S-structure.

Example (48b), on the other hand, is ambiguous in English:

(50) a. Peter$_i$ doesn't know [which PRO$_i$ pictures of himself$_i$] María showed.
b. Peter$_i$ doesn't know [which pictures of himself$_i$] María showed.

These facts seem to suggest that Condition A must apply 'before' reconstruction in English but 'after' it in Spanish. Since control *PRO* must be interpreted locally, we may be able to motivate why the *wh*-element may have to stay *in-situ* in (50a), rather than be reconstructed, as in (49a).[31] However, there is no motivation for the *wh*-element in (50b) to stay *in-situ* in English but to be reconstructed as in (49b) in Spanish.[32] This difference does not follow from any of the principles of the framework we are assuming here, and it must be stipulated at this point. I leave this issue open for further research.

Summarizing, then, we have claimed that picture nouns in Spanish have the two underlying representations shown in (51), depending on whether XP is interpreted as the agent (51a) or the nonagent (51b) of the picture noun:

(51) a. XP$_i$ . . . [la [*pro*$_i$ foto de sí mismo$_i$]]
XP$_i$ . . . [the [*pro*$_i$ picture of himself$_i$]]
b. XP$_i$ . . . [la [foto de sí mismo$_i$]]
XP$_i$ . . . [the [picture of himself$_i$]]

We have shown how these representations can explain a number of long-distance anaphor dependencies without the need of reconstruction. These structures were also shown to explain certain differences regarding the interpretation of XP in English and Spanish. Finally, we have suggested that English has the same structures as (51), but *PRO* instead of *pro* is the subject of the picture noun phrase. This explains why the anaphor must be local in English and why, where reconstruction is blocked, the result is an unbound anaphor. This work has concentrated exclusively on the syntax of the noun 'picture' in both English and Spanish. It remains to be studied whether other picture nouns behave similarly.

NOTES

* I would like to thank Juan Uriagereka, Norbert Hornstein, David Lightfoot, and those who attended the lecture when this paper was presented at the University of Maryland at College Park for their valuable insights and comments on a first version of this paper. I am grateful to Carlos Otero, Raffaella Zanuttini, and Robert Frank for detailed comments and suggestions. Part of this research was made possible by a sabbatical leave granted by Georgetown University. The usual disclaimers apply.

1. See Huang (1993:109) and references there cited. For reconstruction see Chomsky (1976, 1993); for an alternative analysis see Barrs (1986). See also Lasnik and Uriagereka (1988:137, 157) and Freidin (1992:section 8.2), among others.

2. In the minimalist program of Chomsky (1993) the trace of a moved element is a copy of the original element, as in (i):

(i) [Which picture of himself] did John say [which picture of himself] that Peter saw [which picture of himself]?

At PF only the first *wh*-element is pronounced. At LF, the anaphor raises to the verb by an operation similar to cliticization (CL_{LF}, see Chomsky 1993), and the *wh*-elements are translated into operator-variable configurations, as in (ii):

(ii) a. [Which x] John self-said [x picture of t_{self}] that Peter saw [ ]?
b. [Which x] John said that Peter self-saw [x picture of t_{self}]?

In (i.a) *John* and *himself* are interpreted as coreferential; in (ii.a) *Peter* and *himself* are.

Since long dependencies were not discussed in Chomsky (1993), there is no discussion as to the nature of the category [ ] following *saw* in (ii.a), if any. It could be a category bound by the whole *wh*-phrase [*x picture of* t_{self}], but this would mean that [*x picture of* t_{self}] is both a variable and an operator at the same time.

What is crucial for our purpose, though, is that whether we adopt Chomsky's or the traditional reconstruction analysis, *self* will be able to refer to the matrix subject only if the *wh*-phrase has gone through the intermediate CP during the derivation. For ease of exposition we have adopted the traditional LF representation of reconstruction constructions.

3. Where *sí mismo* 'himself' and *Juan* are coreferential, *Juan* must be interpreted as being the one who took the picture. See section 2.

4. See Torrego (1983, 1984).

5. If an adjunct is moved, the presence of the complementizer is also obligatory, as predicted by Torrego (1984):

(i) ¿Cuándo$_i$ supones [$_{CP}$ t_i *(que) [$_{IP}$ vimos a Marta t_i]]?
'When$_i$ do you suppose [$_{CP}$ t_i *(that) [$_{IP}$ we saw Marta t_i]]?'

The obligatory presence of the intermediate trace in CP, and hence of the complementizer, follows from ECP.

6. As in (3), when the anaphor is coreferential with the main subject, the subject is interpreted as the agent of the picture noun.

7. A similar observation is made for English in Frank (1992:178). See section 4.

8. Where *sí mismo* 'himself' refers to *Pedro, Pedro* is interpreted as being the one who took the picture.

9. If *sí mismo* refers to *Juan, Juan* is necessarily the agent of the picture noun.

10. If the sentential complements of perception and causative verbs are to be analyzed as IP complements, there would be no intermediate CP position available. Notice that in these constructions coreference with the main subject is also possible:

(i) a. ¿[Cuál foto de sí mismo$_{i,j}$] vio Luis$_i$ [$_{IP}$ mostrar a José$_j$]?
'[Which picture of himself$_{i,j}$] did Luis$_i$ see [$_{IP}$ José show]?'
b. ¿[Cuál foto de sí mismo$_{i,j}$] hizo Luis$_i$ [$_{IP}$ mostrar a José$_j$]?
'[Which picture of himself$_{i,j}$] did Luis$_i$ make [$_{IP}$ José$_j$ show]?'

11. However, as Abney (1987:100) has noted, picture nouns may not always have a PRO subject, otherwise the grammaticality of (i) could not be explained:

(i) They$_i$ heard [stories about each other$_i$].

12. Notice that long-distance anaphoric relations are not otherwise possible in Spanish:

(i) *Pedro$_i$ dice que María siempre habla de sí mismo$_i$.
'Pedro$_i$ says that María always speaks about himself$_i$.'

13. Suñer (1978, 1982, 1984) has argued for the existence of a control *pro* in Spanish. We are proposing a regular (noncontrol) *pro* for these constructions.

14. For the existence of a NUMBER and a GENDER phrase node within the noun phrase see Picallo (1991).

15. Since there is singular/plural agreement in English, GENDER agreement seems to be the licensing feature for *pro* in NP. Notice that in IP, GENDER is not the crucial licenser (there is no gender agreement in verbal agreement in Spanish), but rather, PERSON (I, II, III) and NUMBER (SINGULAR, PLU-

RAL) are. We may thus be dealing with two different kinds of *pro*. I leave this issue open for further research.

16. These constructions also existed in Old Spanish (see Penny 1991:126):

(i) a. la mi muger
the my wife
'my wife'
b. el mio fiel vassallo
the my loyal subject
'my loyal subject'

These constructions disappeared by the early sixteenth century. But the genitive can still be seen when the possessive is used postnominally:

(ii) la mujer mía
the wife mine
'my wife'

17. Notice that the same is observed in the case of control *PRO*:

(i) Las chicas prefieren [PRO vivir contentas].
The girls prefer [PRO to-live happy-FEM-PL].
'The girls prefer to be happy.'

PRO acquires its *phi*-features via Control and thus the adjective is able to agree with *las chicas* 'the girls'.

18. See Iatridou (1986) and Enç (1989), among others.

19. Pollard and Sag (1992:264) mention some examples with picture nouns in English where the anaphor is possible in contexts where there is no possible c-command. Notice that the equivalent examples in Spanish are ungrammatical:

(i) a. The picture of herself$_i$ on the front page of the *Times* made Mary$_i$'s claims seem somewhat ridiculous.
*La foto de sí misma$_i$ en la portada de ABC hizo parecer ridículos los alegatos de María$_i$.'
b. The picture of herself$_i$ on the front page of the *Times* confirmed the allegation Mary$_i$ had been making over the years.
*La foto de sí misma$_i$ en la portada de ABC confirmó el argumento que María$_i$ venía repitiendo desde hacía tiempo.'
c. John$_i$'s intentionally misleading testimony was sufficient to ensure that there would be pictures of himself$_i$ all over the morning papers.
El testimonio despistante de Juan$_i$ fue suficiente para que aparecieran fotos de sí mismo$_i$ en todos los matutinos.'

20. In Campos (1991) it is suggested that *pro* [+B], parallel to the Greek pronominal *idhios* 'him(self)', need not have a c-commanding antecedent, as shown in (i):

(i) [El hermano de Pedro$_i$]$_j$ dijo que María lo conocía *pro*$_{i,j}$.
[The brother of Pedro$_i$]$_j$ said that María him knew *pro*$_{i,j}$.
'Pedro's brother said that María knew him.'

This suggests that *pro* in NP does not behave exactly like *pro* in IP. See also note 15.

21. If we assume that Condition A requires the anaphor to cliticize, we may assume the following representations:

(i) a. ¿[Cuáles x] Juan$_i$ mostró [x *pro*$_i$ sí$_i$-fotos t_{si}]?
[Which x] Juan$_i$ showed [x *pro*$_i$ self$_i$-pictures t_{self}]?
b. ¿[Cuáles x] Juan$_i$ sí-mostró [x fotos de t_{si}]?
[Which x] Juan$_i$ self-showed [x pictures of t_{self}]?

In the representations that follow cliticization structures will not be shown, for ease of exposition.

22. See Suñer (1991, 1993).

23. Chomsky (1993) argues that the two possible referents for the anaphor are best captured by the following LF representations:

(i) a. John$_i$ wondered which picture of himself$_{i,j}$ Bill$_j$ saw.
b. John wondered [which x, x a picture of himself] Bill saw.
c. John wondered [which x] Bill saw [x picture of himself].

Notice that these representations do not allow us to capture the ambiguity noted for Spanish.

24. At S-Structure we would have the two following representations:

(i) a. Pedro$_i$ dijo que [cuáles *pro*$_i$ fotos de sí mismo$_i$] [María mostró].
Pedro$_i$ said that [which *pro*$_i$ pictures of himself$_i$] [María showed *t*].
b. Pedro$_i$ dijo que [cuáles fotos de sí mismo$_i$] [María mostró].
Pedro$_i$ said that [which pictures of himself$_i$] [María showed].

Notice that if Binding Theory applied to the S-Structure representations in (i), we would expect both representations to be well formed, since in (i.a) *pro* would serve as an antecedent to the anaphor, while in (i.b) *Pedro* would be its antecedent. This is not borne out, however. As mentioned above, the only reading we obtain here is the one in which *Pedro* is interpreted as the agent, and not as a non-agent. These facts show, then, that Condition A cannot apply at S-Structure; it must apply at LF, thus supporting Chomsky's (1993) claim that the level of S-Structure can be dispensed with. For discussion of the problem raised by the English facts see section 4.

25. Notice that the English equivalent of (27a) is ambiguous. This follows because CP2 is an available landing site for the *wh*-element. So the English sentence would be reconstructed as in (i):

(i) a. Which picture of himself did Pedro say that the newspaper had published?

b. [which x] Pedro$_i$ said [x PRO$_i$ picture of himself$_i$] that the newspaper had published *t*?
c. [which x] Pedro$_i$ said [x picture of himself$_i$] that the newspaper had published *t*?

I will assume that in this intermediate CP both the anaphor and *PRO* are able to corefer with *Pedro.* This alternative is not available in Spanish as the *wh*-element does not proceed through CP2. When CP2 is available (as in 27b), the two readings are available, as expected.

26. Also, as noted in Lasnik and Uriagereka (1988:37–38), (i) is possible in English:

(i) They read [each other's book].

If GENITIVE were to make NP a CFC, then "each other" could not be bound by "they".

27. See also Plann (1982), where this construction is treated within the framework of the time.

28. The claim for a double CP structure is strongly supported by the facts of Spanish, where a complementizer may precede the *wh*-element in verbs that take indirect questions but is impossible with verbs that take semiquestions:

(i) a. Luis se pregunta (que) cuándo llegará María.
Luis wonders (that) when will-arrive María.
'Luis wonders when María will arrive.'
b. Luis no sabe (*que) cuándo llegará María.
Luis not knows (*that) when will-arrive María.
'Luis doesn't know when María will arrive.'

29. However, this is incompatible with Suñer's (1991) claim that the higher CP contains an interrogative operator. If so, (42) would be expected to be a strong subjacency violation.

30. See examples (21) and (24), respectively.

31. If PRO is a [+ana] element, it may need to cliticize by CL_{LF}. Thus reconstruction would be blocked.

32. We may want to pursue the claim that the rich morphology of the noun somehow blocks the cliticization of the anaphor in (48a), but notice that such cliticization is possible in other cases (see example (47), for instance).

REFERENCES

Abney, S. 1987. *The English Noun Phrase in its Sentential Aspect.* Ph.D. Dissertation. MIT.

Barrs, A. 1986. *Chains and Anaphoric Dependence.* Ph.D. Dissertation. MIT.

Campos, H. 1991. Silent Subjects and Objects. In *Current Studies in Spanish Linguistics.* H. Campos and F. Martínez-Gil, eds. Washington, D.C.: Georgetown University Press.

Chomsky, N. 1976. Conditions on Rules of Grammar. *Linguistic Analysis* 2:303–51.

Chomsky, N. 1986. *Knowledge of Language: Its Nature, Origin, and Use.* New York: Praeger.

Chomsky, N. 1993. A Minimalist Program for Linguistic Theory. In *The View from Building 20: Essays in Linguistics in Honor of Sylvain Bromberger.* K. Hale and S. J. Keyser, eds. Cambridge: MIT Press.

Clark, R. 1986. *Boundaries and the Treatment of Control.* Ph.D. Dissertation. University of California, Los Angeles.

Enç, M. 1989. Pronouns, Licensing, and Binding. *Natural Language and Linguistic Theory* 7:51–92.

Freidin, R. 1992. *Foundations of Generative Syntax.* Cambridge: MIT Press.

Frank, R. 1992. *Syntactic Locality and Tree Adjoining Grammar: Grammatical Acquisition and Processing Perspectives.* Ph.D. Dissertation. University of Pennsylvania.

Huang, C. T. J. 1983. A Note on the Binding Theory. *Linguistic Inquiry* 14:554–561.

Huang, C. T. J. 1984. On the Distribution and Reference of Empty Pronouns. *Linguistic Inquiry* 15:531–74.

Huang, C. T. J. 1987. Remarks on Empty Categories in Chinese. *Linguistic Inquiry* 18:321–37.

Huang, C. T. J. 1993. Reconstruction and the Structure of VP: Some Theoretical Consequences. *Linguistic Inquiry* 24:103–38.

Iatridou, S. 1986. An Anaphor not Bound in its Governing Category. *Linguistic Inquiry* 17:766–72.

Lasnik, H., and J. Uriagereka. 1988. *A Course in GB Syntax.* Cambridge: MIT Press.

Penny, R. 1991. *A History of the Spanish Language.* Cambridge: Cambridge University Press.

Picallo, M. C. 1991. Nominals and Nominalizations in Catalan. *Probus* 3:279–316.

Plann, S. 1982. Indirect Questions in Spanish. *Linguistic Inquiry* 13:297–312.

Pollard, C. and I. Sag. 1992. Anaphors in English and the Scope of Binding Theory. *Linguistic Inquiry* 23:261–303.

Rizzi, L. 1986. Null Objects in Italian and the Theory of *pro. Linguistic Inquiry* 17:501–557.

Roeper, T. 1986. Implicit Arguments, Implicit Roles, and Subject/Object Asymmetry in Morphological Rules. Manuscript. University of Massachusetts, Amherst.

Stowell, T. 1989. Subjects, Specifiers, and X-Bar Theory. In *Alternative Conceptions of Phrase Structure.* M. Baltin and A. Kroch, eds. Chicago: University of Chicago Press.

Suñer, M. 1978. Perception Verb Complements in Spanish Same or Different? *Canadian Journal of Linguistics* 23:107–27.

Suñer, M. 1982. Big *PRO* and little *pro.* Manuscript. Cornell University.

Suñer, M. 1984. Controlled *pro.* In *Current Issues in Linguistic Theory.* Vol. 26: *Papers from the XIIth Linguistic Symposium on Romance Languages.* P. Baldi, ed. Amsterdam: John Benjamins Publishing Company.

Suñer, M. 1991. Indirect Questions and the Structure of CP: Some Consequences. In *Current Studies in Spanish Linguistics.* H. Campos and F. Martínez-Gil, eds. Washington, D.C.: Georgetown University Press.

Suñer, M. 1993. About Indirect Questions and Semi-Questions. *Linguistics and Philosophy* 16:45–77.

Torrego, E. 1983. More Effects of Successive Cyclic Movement. *Linguistic Inquiry* 14:561–65.

Torrego, E. 1984. On Inversion in Spanish and Some of its Effects. *Linguistic Inquiry* 15:103–29.

Bare Phrase Structure

Noam Chomsky
Massachusetts Institute of Technology

1 Some leading ideas in the study of language. This paper[1] is an extension of earlier ones (Chomsky 1991, 1993) that were concerned with two related questions: (1) What conditions on the human language faculty are imposed by considerations of virtual conceptual necessity? (2) To what extent is the language faculty determined by these conditions, that is, how much special structure does it have beyond them? The first question in turn has two aspects: what conditions are imposed on the language faculty by virtue of (A) its place within the array of cognitive systems of the mind/brain, and (B) general considerations of simplicity, elegance, and economy that have some independent plausibility?

Question (B) is not precise, but not without content, as in the natural sciences generally. Question (A) has an exact answer, but only parts of it can be surmised, given what is known about related cognitive systems. To the extent that the answer to question (2) is positive, language is something like a 'perfect system,' meeting external constraints as well as can be done. The 'minimalist' program for linguistic theory seeks to explore these possibilities.

Any progress toward this goal will deepen a problem for the biologial sciences that is already far from trivial: how can a system such as human language arise in the mind/brain, or for that matter, in the organic world, in which one seems not to find systems with anything like the basic properties of human language? That problem has sometimes been posed as a crisis for the cognitive sciences. The concerns are appropriate, but their locus is misplaced; they are a problem for biology and the brain sciences, which, as currently understood, do not provide any basis for what appear to be fairly well-established conclusions about language.[2] Much of the broader interest of the detailed study of language lies right here, in my opinion.

The leading questions that guide the minimalist program came into view as the principles-and-parameters (P&P) model took shape. A look at recent history may be helpful in placing these questions in context; needless to say, these remarks are schematic and selective, and benefit from hindsight.

Early generative grammar faced two immediate problems: to find a way to account for the phenomena of particular languages ('descriptive adequacy'), and to explain how knowledge of these facts arises in the mind of the speaker-hearer ('explanatory adequacy'). Though it was scarcely recognized at the time, this research program revived the concerns of a rich tradition, of which perhaps the last major exponent was Otto Jespersen.[3] Jespersen recognized that the structures of language "come into existence in the mind of a speaker" by abstraction from presented experience, yielding a "notion of structure" that is "definite enough to guide him in framing sentences of his own," crucially, "free expressions" that are typically new to speaker and hearer. These properties of language determine the primary goals of linguistic theory: to spell out clearly this "notion of structure" and the procedure by which it yields "free expressions,'" and to explain how it arises in the mind of the speaker—the problems of descriptive and explanatory adequacy, respectively. To attain descriptive adequacy for a particular language L, the theory of L (its grammar) must characterize the state attained by the language faculty. To attain explanatory adequacy, a theory of language must characterize the initial state of the language faculty and show how it maps experience to the state attained. Jespersen held further that it is only "with regard to syntax" that we expect "that there must be something in common to all human speech"; there can be a "universal (or general) grammar," though "no one ever dreamed of a universal morphology."

In the modern period these traditional concerns were displaced in part by behaviorist currents and in part by various structuralist approaches, which radically narrowed the domain of inquiry while much expanding the data base for some future inquiry that might return to the traditional—and surely valid—concerns. To address them required a better understanding of the fact that language involves infinite use of finite means, in one classic formulation. Advances in the formal sciences provided that understanding, making it feasible to deal with the problems constructively. Generative grammar can be regarded as a kind of confluence of long-forgotten concerns of the study of language and mind and new understanding provided by the formal sciences.

The first efforts to address these problems quickly revealed that traditional grammatical and lexical studies do not begin to describe, let alone explain, the most elementary facts about even the best-studied languages. Rather, they provide hints that can be used by the reader who already has tacit knowledge of language and of particular languages. This is hardly a discovery unique to linguistics. Typically, when questions are more sharply formulated, it is learned that even elementary phenomena had escaped notice and that intuitive accounts that seemed simple and persuasive are entirely inadequate. If we are satisfied that an apple falls to the ground because that is its natural place, there will be no serious science of mechanics. The same is true if one is satisfied with traditional rules for forming questions or with the lexical entries in the most elaborate dictionaries, none of which come close to describing simple properties of these linguistic objects.

Recognition of the unsuspected richness and complexity of the phenomena of language created a tension between the goals of descriptive and explanatory adequacy. It was clear that to achieve explanatory adequacy a theory of the initial state must hold that particular languages are largely known in advance of experience. The options permitted in universal grammar (UG) must be highly restricted; limited experience must suffice to fix them one way or another, yielding a state of the language faculty that determines the varied and complex array of expressions, their sound and meaning, in a uniform and language-independent way. But this goal receded still further into the distance as generative systems were enriched in pursuit of descriptive adequacy in radically different ways for different languages. The problem was exacerbated by the huge range of phenomena discovered when attempts were made to formulate actual rule systems.

This tension defined the research program of early generative grammar—at least, the tendency within it that concerns me here. From the early 1960s its central objective was to abstract general principles from the complex rule systems devised for particular languages, leaving rules that are simple, constrained in their operation by these UG principles. Steps in this direction reduce the range of language-specific constraints, thus contributing to explanatory adequacy. They also tend to yield simpler and more natural theories, laying the groundwork for an eventual minimalist approach. These two aspects of inquiry are logically independent: it could turn out that an 'uglier' and richer version of UG reduces permissible variety, thus contributing to the primary empirical goal of explanatory adequacy. In practice, however, the two enterprises have proven to be mutually reinforcing and have progressed side by side.

These efforts culminated in the P&P model, which constituted a radical break from the rich tradition of thousands of years of linguistic inquiry, far more so than early generative grammar, which could be seen as a revival of traditional concerns and ways of addressing them (which is why it was more congenial to traditional grammarians than to modern structural linguists). The basic assumption of the P&P model is that languages have no rules at all in anything like the traditional sense and no grammatical constructions (relative clauses, passives, etc.) except as taxonomic artifacts. There are universal principles and a finite array of options as to how they apply (parameters). Furthermore, it may be that Jespersen's intuition about syntax-morphology can be captured, with parameters limited to the lexicon, indeed to a narrow part of it: functional categories. So I will henceforth assume.

The P&P model is in part a bold speculation rather than a specific hypothesis. Nevertheless, its basic assumptions seem reasonable in the light of what is currently at all well understood and do offer a natural way to resolve the tension between descriptive and explanatory adequacy.

If these ideas prove to be on the right track, there is a single computational system C_{HL} for human language and only limited lexical variety. Variation of language is essentially morphological in character, including the critical question of which parts of a computation enter the phonological component, a question brought to the fore by Jean-Roger Vergnaud's theory of abstract Case and James Huang's work on *wh*-constructions.

This account of the P&P approach overstates the case. Languages may vary in parts of the phonology that can be determined by readily available data, as well as in "Saussurean arbitrariness"; that is, the sound-meaning pairing for the substantive part of the lexicon. We put these matters aside, along with many others that appear to be computationally irrelevant; that is, not entering into C_{HL}: among them, variability of semantic fields, selection from the lexical repertoire made available in UG, and nontrivial questions about the relation of lexical items to other cognitive systems.

Like the earliest proposals in generative grammar, formulation of the P&P model led to a huge expansion in empirical materials, by now from a wide variety of typologically different languages. The questions that could be clearly posed and the empirical facts with which they deal are novel in depth and variety, a promising and encouraging development in itself.

Insofar as the tension between descriptive and explanatory adequacy is reduced in this way, the problem of explanation becomes far harder and more interesting. The task is to show that the apparent richness and diversity of linguistic phenomena is illusory and epiphenomenal, the result of interaction of fixed principles under slightly varying conditions. And still further questions arise, namely, those of the minimalist program. How 'perfect' is language? One expects 'imperfections' in the formal part of the lexicon. The question is whether, or to what extent, this component of the language faculty is the repository of departures from virtual conceptual necessity, so that the computational system C_{HL} is not only unique but optimal. Progress toward this further goal places a huge descriptive burden on the answers to the questions (A) and (B): the interface conditions and the specific formulation of general considerations of simplicity. The empirical burden, already severe in any P&P theory, now becomes extraordinary. The problems that arise are therefore extremely interesting. It is, I think, of considerable interest that we can at least formulate such questions today and even approach them in some areas with a degree of success. If the thinking along these lines is anywhere near accurate, a rich and exciting future lies ahead for the study of language and related disciplines.

2 The minimalist program. All these investigations have been based on several underlying factual assumptions. One is that there is a component of the human mind/brain dedicated to language—the language faculty—interacting with other systems. A more specific assumption is that there are just two such interacting systems: an articulatory-perceptual system A-P and a conceptual-intentional system C-I.[4] The particular language L is an instantiation of the language faculty with options specified. L must therefore provide 'instructions' to be interpreted at these two interface levels. L is then to be understood as a generative system that constructs pairs (π, λ) that are interpreted at the A-P and C-I interfaces, respectively. π is a PF representation and λ an LF representation, each consisting of 'legitimate entities' that can receive some interpretation at the relevant level (perhaps interpretation as gibberish). A linguistic expression of L is at least a pair (π, λ) of this sort—and under minimalist assumptions, at most such a pair, meaning that there are no 'levels of linguistic structure' apart from the two interface levels PF and LF; specifically, no levels of D-structure or S-structure.

We say that a computation (derivation) converges at one of the interface levels if it forms an interpretable representation in this sense, and converges if it converges at both interface levels, PF and LF; otherwise it crashes. We thus adopt the (nonobvious) hypothesis that there are no PF-LF interactions;[5] similarly, that there are no conditions relating lexical properties and interface levels, such as the Projection Principle. The notion "interpretable" raises nontrivial questions, to some of which we return.

It seems that a linguistic expression of L cannot be defined just as a pair (π, λ) formed by a convergent derivation. Rather, its derivation must also be optimal, satisfying certain natural economy conditions, for example, conditions of locality of movement, no 'superfluous steps' in derivations, and so on. Less economical computations are 'blocked' even if they converge.

Current formulation of such ideas still leaves substantial gaps. It is, furthermore, far from obvious that language should have anything like the character postulated in the minimalist program, which is just that: a research program concerned with filling the gaps and asking how positive an answer we can give to question (2) of the first paragraph: how 'perfect' is language?

Suppose that this approach proves to be more or less correct. What could we then conclude about the specificity of the language faculty (modularity)? Not much. It could be that the language faculty is unique among cognitive systems, or even in the organic world, in that its principles satisfy minimalist assumptions. Furthermore, the morphological parameters could be unique in character. Another source of possible specificity of language is the conditions imposed at the interface, what we may call "bare output conditions." These will naturally reflect properties of the interface systems A-P and C-I (or whatever they turn out to be), but we have no idea in advance how specific to language these properties might be; quite specific, so current understanding suggests.

In brief the question of the specificity of language is not directly addressed in the minimalist program, except to indicate where it should arise: in the nature of the computational procedure C_{HL}, in the properties of the bare output conditions and the functional component of the lexicon, and in the more obscure but quite interesting matter of conceptual elegance of principles and concepts.

It is important to distinguish the topic of inquiry here from a different one: to what (if any) extent are the properties of C_{HL} expressed in terms of output conditions, say filters of the kind discussed in Chomsky and Lasnik (1977) or chain-formation algorithms in the sense of Rizzi (1986) in syntax or conditions of the kind recently investigated for phonology in terms of optimality theory (Prince and Smolensky 1993, McCarthy and Prince 1993)? A related question is whether C_{HL} is derivational or representational in character: does C_{HL} involve successive operations leading to (π, λ) (if it converges), or does C_{HL} select two such representations and then compute to determine whether they are properly paired (or select one and derive the other)? The questions are rather subtle; typically, it is possible to recode one approach in terms of the other. But the questions are nevertheless empirical, turning basically on explanatory adequacy. Thus, filters were justified by the fact that simple output conditions sufficed to limit the variety and complexity of transformational rules, advancing the effort to reduce these to just Move-α (or Affect-α, in the sense of Lasnik and Saito 1984) and thus to move toward explanatory adequacy. Similarly, Rizzi's proposals about chain formation were justified in terms of the possibility of explaining empirical facts about Romance reflexives and other matters.

My own judgment is that a derivational approach is nonetheless correct, and the particular version of a minimalist program I am considering assigns it even greater prominence. There are certain properties of language, which appear to be fundamental, that suggest this conclusion. Under a derivational approach computation typically involves simple steps expressible in terms of natural relations and properties, with the context that makes them natural 'wiped out' by later operations and not visible in the representations to which the derivation converges. Thus, in syntax, head-movement is narrowly 'local,' but several such operations may leave a head separated from its trace by an intervening head, as when N incorporates to V leaving the trace t_N, and the $[_V$ V-N] complex then raises to I leaving the trace t_V, so that the chain (N, t_N) at the output level violates the locality property satisfied by each individual step. In segmental phonology, such phenomena are pervasive. Thus the rules deriving the alternants *decide-decisive-decision* from an invariant underlying lexical form are straightforward and natural at each step, but the relevant contexts do not appear at all in the output; given only output conditions, it is hard to see why *decision,* for example, should not rhyme with *Poseidon* on the simplest assumptions about lexical representations and optimal output conditions. Similarly, intervocalic spirantization and vowel reduction are natural and simple processes that derive, say, Hebrew *ganvu* 'they stole' from underlying *g-n-B,* but the context for spirantization is gone after reduction applies; the underlying form might even all but disappear in the output, as in *hitu* 'they extended', in which only the /t/ remains from the underlying root /ntC/ (C a 'weak' consonant).[6]

In all such cases it is possible to formulate the desired result in terms of outputs. For example, in the head-movement case, one can appeal to the (plausible) assumption that the trace is a copy, so the intermediate V trace includes within it a record of the local N → V raising. But surely this is the wrong move. The relevant chains at LF are (N, t_N) and (V, t_V), and in these the locality relation observed by successive raising has been lost. Similar artifice could be used in the phonological examples, again improperly, it appears. These seem to be fundamental properties of language, which should be captured, not obscured. A fully derivational approach captures them and indeed suggests that they should be pervasive, as seems to be the case.

I will continue to assume that the computational system C_{HL} is strictly derivational and that the only output conditions are the bare output conditions determined externally at the interface.[7]

We hope to be able to show that for a particular language L, determined by fixing options in the functional part of the lexicon, the phenomena of sound and meaning for L are determined by pairs (π, λ) formed by maximally economical convergent derivations that satisfy output conditions. The computation C_{HL} that derives (π, λ) must, furthermore, keep to natural computational principles (e.g., locality of movement) and others that are also minimalist in spirit. A natural version of this requirement is that the principles of UG should involve only elements that function at the interface levels; specifically, lexical elements and their features, and local relations among them. Let's adopt this proposal, sharpening it as we proceed.

In pursuing a minimalist program we want to make sure that we are not inadvertently 'sneaking in' improper concepts, entities, relations, and conventions. I assume that an item in the lexicon is nothing other than a set of lexical features, or perhaps a further set-theoretic construction from them (e.g., a set of sets of features), and that output conditions allow nothing beyond such elements. The point of the occasional forays into formalism below is to ensure that C_{HL} keeps to these conditions, introducing no further elements, expressing only local relations, and deriving stipulated conventions where valid. Naturally the more spare the assumptions, the more intricate will be the argument.

3 The computational system. A linguistic expression (π, λ) of L satisfies output conditions at the PF and LF interfaces. Beyond that, π and λ must be compatible: it is not the case that any sound can mean anything. In particular they must be based on the same lexical choices. We can then think of C_{HL} as mapping some array of lexical choices A to the pair (π, λ). What is A? It must at least indicate what the lexical choices are and how many times each is selected by C_{HL} in forming (π, λ). Let us take a numeration to be a set of pairs (*l*, *n*), where *l* is an item of the lexicon and *n* is its index, understood to be the number of times that *l* is selected. Take A to be (at least) a numeration N; C_{HL} maps N to (π, λ). The procedure C_{HL} selects an item from N and reduces its index by 1, then performing permissible computations. C_{HL} does not converge unless all indices are zero.

If an item is selected from the lexicon several times by C_{HL}, the choices must be distinguished; for example, two occurrences of the pronoun *he* may have entirely different properties at LF. *l* and *l′* are thus marked as distinct for C_{HL} if these are two selections by C_{HL} of a single lexical item.

We want the initial array A not only to express the compatibility relation between π and λ, but also to fix the reference set for determining whether a derivation from A to (π, λ) is optimal, that is, not 'blocked' by a more economical derivation. Selection of the reference set is a delicate problem, as are considerations of economy of derivation generally. For the moment let us take N to determine the reference set, meaning that in evaluating derivations for economy we consider only alternatives with the same numeration. At least this much structure seems to be required; whether more is needed is a hard question. We return to the matter in section 7.

Given N, C_{HL} computes until it converges (if it does) at PF and LF with the pair (π, λ). In a perfect language, any structure Σ formed by the computation—hence π and λ—is constituted of elements already present in the lexical elements selected for N; no new objects are added in the course of computation (in particular, no indices, bar-levels in the sense of X′ theory, etc.). Let us assume that this is true at least of the computation to LF; standard theories take it to be radically false for the computation to PF.[8]

Output conditions show that π and λ are differently constituted. Elements interpretable at the A-P interface are not interpretable at C-I, or conversely. At some point, then, the computation splits into two parts, one forming π and the other forming λ. The simplest assumptions are (i) that there is no further interaction between these computations and (ii) that computational procedures are uniform throughout. We adopt (i) and assume (ii) for the computation from N to λ, though not for the computation from N to π; the latter modifies structures (including the internal structure of lexical entries) by processes sharply different from those that take place before entry into the phonological component. Investigation of output conditions should suffice to establish these asymmetries, which I will simply take for granted here.

We assume, then, that at some point in the (uniform) computation to LF there is an operation Spell-Out that applies to the structure Σ already formed. Spell-Out strips away from Σ those elements relevant only to π, forming Σ_P and leaving Σ_L, which is mapped to λ by operations of the kind used to form Σ. Σ_P is then mapped to π by operations unlike those of the $N \rightarrow \lambda$ mapping.

We then assume that each lexical entry is of the form {P, S, F}, where components of P serve only to yield π (phonological features), components of S serve only to yield λ (semantic features), and components of F (formal features, e.g., the categorial features [$\pm$N, $\pm$V]) may enter into computations but must be eliminated (at least by PF) for convergence. Since we take computation to LF to be uniform, there is no way to stipulate that elements of F are eliminable only after Spell-Out. But the mapping to PF has different properties and may contain rules that eliminate F-features in ways not permitted in the N $\rightarrow \lambda$ computation.

The lexical entry for "book," for example, might contain the phonological feature [begins with stop] stripped away by Spell-Out and mapped to PF, the semantic feature [artifact] that is left behind by Spell-Out, and the formal feature [nominal] that is both carried over by Spell-Out and left behind, interpreted at LF, and eliminated in the course of computation to PF, though relevant to its operation.

Let us assume further that Spell-Out delivers Σ to the module Morphology, which constructs wordlike units that are then subjected to further processes that map it finally to π. To fix terminology, let us continue to call the subsystem that maps the output of Morphology to PF the phonological component and the subsystem that continues the computation to LF after Spell-Out the covert component. Other terms are familiar but have had misleading connotations. I will have little to say about the phonological component here, except with regard to the matter of ordering of elements in the output (see section 6).

The simplest assumption is that Spell-Out can apply anywhere, the derivation crashing if a 'wrong choice' is made. After Spell-Out neither the phonological nor covert component can have any further access to the lexicon, a requirement for any theory, on the weakest empirical assumptions (otherwise sound-meaning relations would collapse). It is unnecessary to add stipulations to this effect. Because of the way C_{HL} is constructed, to which we return, an element selected from the lexicon cannot be embedded; hence the issue is narrow, arising only at the root of a phrase marker. If the phonological component adds a lexical item at the root, it will introduce semantic features, and the derivation will crash at PF. If the covert component does the same, it will introduce phonological features, and the derivation will therefore crash at LF.

Questions remain about lexical items lacking semantic or phonological features: can these be added at the root by the phonological or covert components, respectively? Empirical consequences seem to arise only in connection with functional elements that have 'strong features' in the sense of Chomsky (1993), that is, those that must be 'satisfied' before

Spell-Out. Suppose that root C (complementizer) has a strong feature that requires overt *wh*-movement. We now want to say that unless this feature is checked before Spell-Out it will cause the derivation to crash at LF to avoid the possibility of accessing C after Spell-Out in the covert component. Slightly adjusting the account in Chomsky (1993), we now say that a checked strong feature will be stripped away by Spell-Out, but is otherwise ineliminable.

4 Phrase markers in a minimalist framework. The development of X′ theory in the late 1960s was an early stage in the effort to resolve the tension between explanatory and descriptive adequacy. A first step was to separate the lexicon from the computations, thus eliminating a serious redundancy between lexical properties and phrase structure rules and allowing the latter to be reduced to the simplest (context-free) form. X′ theory sought to eliminate such rules altogether, leaving only the general X′-theoretic format of UG. The problem addressed in subsequent work was to determine that format, but it was assumed that phrase structure rules themselves should be eliminable.

In the papers on economy and minimalism cited earlier, I took X′ theory to be given, with specific stipulated properties. Let's now subject these assumptions to critical analysis, asking what the theory of phrase structure should look like on minimalist assumptions and what the consequences are for the theory of movement.

At the LF interface lexical items and their constituent features must be accessed.[9] Accordingly, such items and their (semantic and formal) features should be available for C_{HL}. It is also apparent that some larger units constructed of these items are accessible, along with their types; for example, noun phrases are interpreted differently from verb phrases. Of the larger units only maximal projections seem to be relevant to LF-interpretation. If so, output conditions make the concepts minimal and maximal projection available to C_{HL}, and on minimalist assumptions, nothing else apart from lexical features. Minimal and maximal projections must be determined from the structure in which they appear without any specific marking; as proposed by Muysken (1982) they are relational properties of categories, not inherent to them. There are no such entities as XP (X^{max}) or X^0 (X^{min}, terminal element) in the structures formed by C_{HL}, though we may use these as informal notations, along with X′ (X-bar) for any other category. Given a phrase marker, a category that does not project any further is a maximal projection XP and one that is not a projection at all is a minimal projection X^0; any other is an X′, invisible at the interface and for computation.[10]

We also hope to show that computation keeps to local relations of XP to terminal head. All principles of UG should be formulated in these terms, and only such relations should be relevant at the interface for the modules that operate there.[11]

Given the numeration N, C_{HL} may select an item from N (reducing its index) or perform some permitted operation on the structures it has already formed. One such operation is necessary on conceptual grounds alone: an operation that forms larger units out of those already constructed; call it Merge. Applied to two objects α and β, Merge forms the new object γ. What is γ? γ must be constituted somehow from the two items α and β; the only alternatives are that γ is fixed for all α, β, or that it is randomly selected; neither is worth considering. The simplest object constructed from α and β is the set {α, β}, so we take γ to be at least this set, where α and β are the constituents of γ. Does that suffice? Output conditions dictate otherwise; thus verbal and nominal elements are interpreted differently at LF and behave differently in the phonological component (see note 9). γ must therefore at least (and, we assume, at most) be of the form {δ, {α, β}}, where δ identifies the relevant properties of γ; call δ the label of γ.

The label must be constructed from the two constituents α and β. Suppose these are lexical items, each a set of features. Then the simplest assumption would be that the label is either (a), (b), or (c):

(1) a. the intersection of α and β
    b. the union of α and β
    c. one or the other of α, β

The options (a) and (b) are immediately excluded: the intersection of α, β will generally be irrelevant to output conditions, often null, and the union will be not only irrelevant but contradictory if α, β differ in value for some feature, the normal case. We are left with (c): the label δ is either α or β; one or the other projects and is the head of γ. If α projects, then γ = {α, {α, β}}.

For expository convenience we can map γ to a more complex object constructed from additional elements such as nodes, bars (primes, XP, etc.), subscripts, and other indices. Thus we might represent γ informally as (2) (assuming no order), where the diagram is constructed from nodes paired with labels and pairs of such labeled nodes, and labels are distinguished by subscripts:

(2) 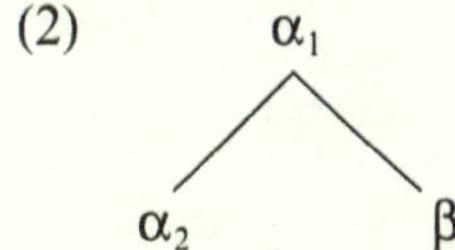

This, however, is informal notation only: empirical evidence would be required for postulation of the additional elements that enter into (2) beyond lexical features, and the extra sets.

The terms "complement" and "specifier" can be defined in the usual way, in terms of γ. The head-complement relation is the 'most local' relation of an XP to a terminal head Y, all others within YP being head-specifier (apart from adjunction, to which we return); in principle there might be a series of specifiers, a possibility that seems to be realized (see section 7). The principles of UG, we assume, crucially involve these local relations.

Further projections satisfy (1c) for the same reasons. We call these projections of the head from which they ultimately project, restricting the term "head" to terminal elements and taking complememt and specifier to be relations to a head.

If constituents α, β of γ have been formed in the course of computation, one of the two must project, say α. At the LF interface γ (if maximal) is interpreted as a phrase of the type α (e.g., as a nominal phrase if its head *k* is nominal), and it behaves in the same manner in the course of computation. It is natural, then, to take the label of γ to be not α itself but rather *k*, the head of the constituent that projects, a decision that also leads to technical simplification. Assuming so, we take $\gamma = \{k, \{\alpha, \beta\}\}$, where *k* is the head of α, and its label as well, in the cases so far discussed. We keep to the assumption that the head determines the label, though not always through strict identity.

The operation Merge, then, is asymmetric, projecting one of the objects to which it applies, its head becoming the label of the complex formed. There can be no nonbranching projection. In particular there is no way to project from a lexical item α a subelement H(α) consisting of the category of α and whatever else enters into further computation, H(α) being the actual 'head' and α the lexical element itself; nor can there be such 'partial projections' from larger elements. We thus dispense with such structures as (3a) with the usual interpretation: *the, book* taken to be terminal lexical items and D+, N+ standing for whatever properties of these items are relevant to further computation (perhaps the categorial information D, N; Case; etc.). In place of (3a) we have only (3b):

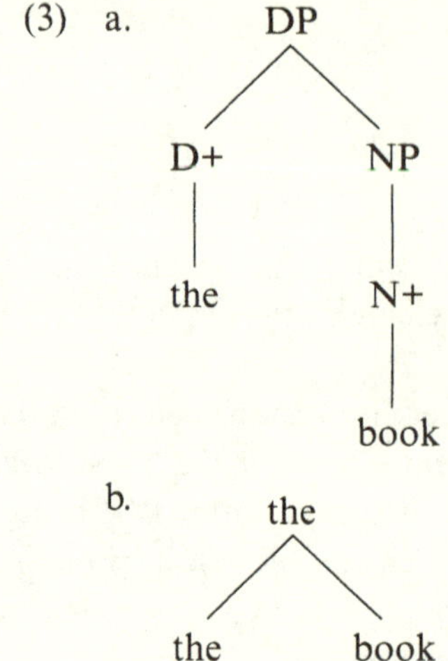

Standard X′ theory is thus largely eliminated in favor of bare essentials.

Suppose that the label for {α, β} happens to be determined uniquely for α, β in language L; we would then want to deduce that fact from properties of α, β, L; or, if it is true for α, β in language generally, from properties of the language faculty, and similarly if the label is uniquely determined for arbitrary α, β, L, as may be the case.

Suppose that we have the structure that we represent informally as (4), with *x, y, z, w* terminals:

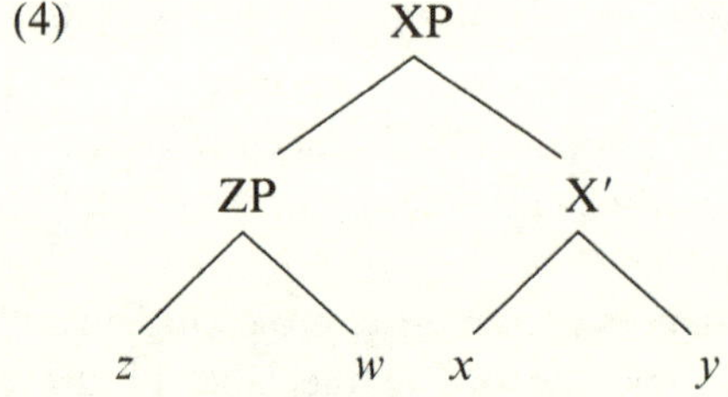

Here ZP = {*z*, {*z*, *w*}}, X′ = {*x*, {*x*, *y*}}, XP = {*x*, {ZP, X′}}. Note that *w* and *y* are both minimal and maximal; *z* and *x* are minimal only.

The functioning elements in (4) are at most the nodes of the informal representation: that is, the lexical terminals *z, w, x, y;* the intermediate element X′ and its sister ZP; and the 'root element' XP standing for the full structure formed. In the formal representation the corresponding elements are *z, w, x, y;* {*x*, {*x*, *y*}} = P and its sister {*z*, {*z*, *w*}} = Q; and the root element {*x*, {P, Q}}. These alone can be functioning elements; call them the terms of XP. More explicitly, for any structure K,

(5) a. K is a term of K
b. if L is a term of K, then the members of the members of L are terms of K

Terms correspond to nodes of the informal representations, where each node is understood to stand for the subtree of which it is the root.

In (4), *x* is the head of the construction, *y* its complement, and ZP its specifier. Thus (4) could be, say, the structure VP with the head *saw,* the complement *it,* and the specifier *the man* with the label *the,* as in (6):

(6)

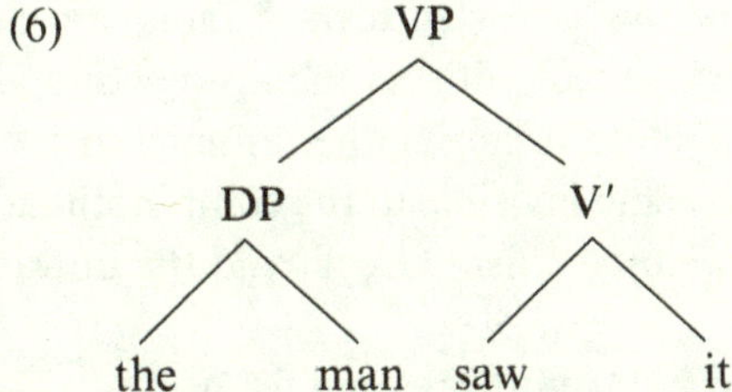

Here V′ = VP = *saw* and DP = *the.*

Note that this very spare system fails to distinguish unaccusatives from unergatives, a distinction that seems necessary in the light of differences of behavior that have been discovered. The simplest solution to the problem would be to adopt the proposal of Hale and Keyser (1993) that unergatives are transitives; I will assume so.

The structure (6) will yield the sentence "the man saw it" when further inflectional elements are added by Merge and the specifier of the VP is raised (assuming this particular form of the predicate-internal subject hypothesis, as I will throughout). This example involves the second operation that forms phrase markers, the operation Move (Move-α). Given the phrase marker Σ with terms K and α, Move targets K, raises α, and merges α with K to form the new category with the constituents α, K. This is the operation of substitution, a term borrowed from earlier theory that is now somewhat misleading, though we continue to use it. As matters now stand, either K or α could project. The operation forms the chain (α, *t*); α c-commands *t,* which is a copy of α.[13] We return to adjunction. The only other operation is Delete (Delete-α), which leaves the structure unaffected apart from some indication that α is not 'visible' at the interface.

In the case of (6) *the man* raises overtly (pre-Spell-Out), targeting the highest Agr phrase, while *it* raises covertly, targeting the lowest Agr phrase, each of the raised elements becoming the specifier of the targeted category. As noted, there is another option: the raised phrase itself might have projected, so that the targeted Agr phrase would become the specifier of the raised nominal phrase, which would now be a D′, not a DP, since it projects to a higher phrase. In preminimalist work this obviously unwanted option was excluded by conditions on transformations and stipulated properties of X′ theory. But we no longer can—or wish to—make recourse to these, so we hope to show that the conventional assumption is in fact derivable on principled grounds—that it is impossible for Move to target K raising α, then projecting α rather than K. For the case of substitution the result is immediate within the minimalist framework under the strong formulation of the principle Greed of Chomsky (1993), which licenses movement of α only as a step toward satisfying one of its own properties. If α raises and merges with K, then projecting, α is now an X′ category, not X^{max}. Therefore it can neither enter into a checking relation nor be moved further, being invisible to the computational system C_{HL}. Accordingly, the raising cannot satisfy Greed, and the unwanted option is excluded.

I will assume that Greed holds in this strong form:

(7) Move raises α to a position β only if morphological properties of α itself would not otherwise be satisfied in the derivation.[14]

Thus Greed cannot be overridden for convergence. We cannot, for example, derive (8a) by raising, violating Greed to satisfy EPP (the strong DP-feature of Infl), and (8b) cannot be interpreted as something like (c), with covert raising:

(8) a. *It is believed [a man to seem to *t* that . . .]
b. *There seem to a lot of us that . . .
c. It seems to a lot of us that . . .

Similarly, DP cannot raise to [Spec,VP] to assume an otherwise unassigned Θ-role. There can be no words "hit" or "believe" with the Θ-structure of *hit, believe* but no Case features, with *John* raising as in (9) to pick up the Θ-role, then moving on to [Spec,Infl] to check Case and agreement features:

(9) a. John [$_{VP}$ *t′* [HIT *t*]]
b. John [$_{VP}$ *t′* [BELIEVE [*t* to be intelligent]]]

The only possibility is direct raising to [Spec,Infl] so that the resulting sentences "John HIT" and "John BELIEVES to be intelligent" are deviant, lacking the external argument required by the verb.[15] We thus have a partial analogue to the P&P principle that there is no raising to a Θ-position. And we can assume that, for substitution at least, it is the target that projects. We will see that there are independent reasons for the same conclusion.

Raising of α targeting K is barred by (7) unless some property of α is satisfied by its moving to, or through, this position, and that property would not have been satisfied had this operation not applied; there is no movement to or through a position unless that operation is necessary in this sense. Consistent with Greed, such movement would be permitted if there were no other way for α to reach a position where its features would eventually be satisfied. Suppose (as we assume) that movement is constrained by a 'minimal link condition' (MLC), meaning that α must make the 'shortest move' in a sense that must be defined. That could in principle require movement through a position that satisfies no properties of α. The situation should not arise in the kind of case just discussed: a substitution operation that 'creates' a new position, [Spec,K], by raising of α. It might well occur, however, in the case of adjunction satisfying the MLC.

Suppose that the structure K targeted by Move is a proper substructure of Σ. Thus suppose the operation is covert raising of the object to [Spec,AgrO] for Case and object agreement. Prior to this operation we have (in informal notation) the structure (10a) embedded in the larger structure (10b):

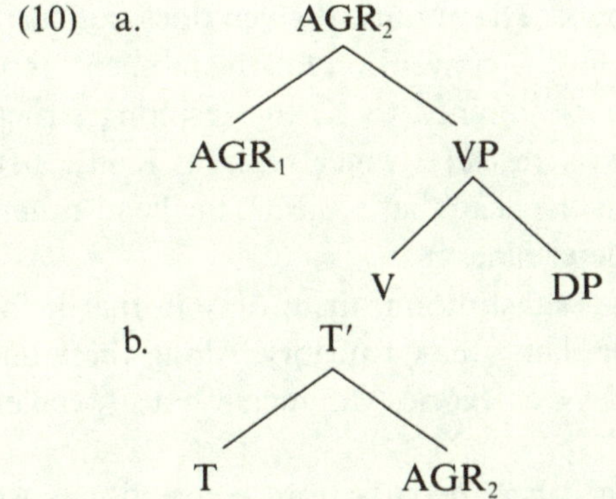

Here T′ is {T, {T, K}}, where K (namely (a)) is {Agr, {Agr, VP}}, VP = {V, {V, DP}}. If we target K, merging DP and K and projecting Agr as intended, we form (11) with the raised DP the specifier of AgrP (Agr^{max}):

(11)

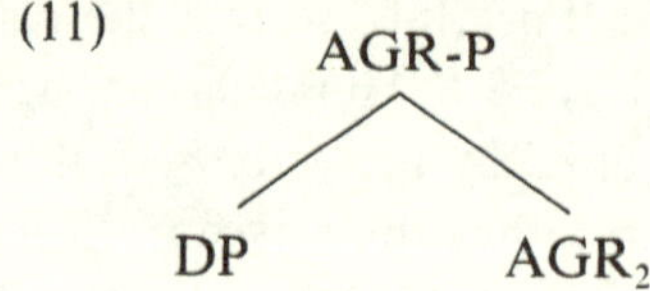

Here AgrP is {Agr, {DP, K}} = L, and the term T′ immediately dominating it is {T, {T, L}}, not {T, {T, K}} as it was before Move raised DP. Note that labels do not change, only constituents, if it is the target that projects, not the raised category.[16]

It remains to extend the discussion to adjunction, forming a two-segment category.[17] That adjunction and substitution both exist is not uncontroversial; thus, Lasnik and Saito (1992) adopt only the latter option while Kayne (1994) adopts (virtually) only the former. Nevertheless, I will assume here that the distinction is necessary; that is, that specifiers are distinct in properties from adjuncts and, generally, A- from A′-positions.[18]

We have so far considered operations that form Q = {*k*, {α, K}}, where *k* is the head (= the label) of the projected element K. But we now have a second option, in which Q is a two-segment category, not a new category. Plainly we need a new object constructed from K but not identical with its head *k*. The minimal choice is the ordered pair <*k*, *k*>. We thus take Q = {<*k*, *k*>, {α, K}}. Note that <*k*, *k*>, the label of Q, is not a term of the structure formed. It is not identical to the head of K, as before, though it is constructed from it in a trivial way.

Suppose that we adjoin α to K where K is embedded.[19] For substitution we were able to derive the conventional assumption that the target projects, not the raised element. The argument given does not carry over to adjunction, but let us adopt the convention for the moment, returning to the matter. Thus when α is adjoined to K, the resulting structure is necessarily [K, K] = {<*k*, *k*>, {α, K}}, which replaces K in a structure containing K. Recall that it is the head that projects; the head either is the label or, under adjunction, determines it.

Adjunction differs from substitution, then, only in that it forms a two-segment category rather than a new category. Along these lines the usual properties of segments vs. categories, adjuncts versus specifiers, are readily formulated.

The bare theory outlined here departs from conventional assumptions in several respects. One is that an item can be both an X^0 and an XP. Does this cause problems? Are there examples that illustrate this possibility? I see no particular problems, and one case comes to mind as a possible illustration: clitics. Under the DP hypothesis clitics are Ds. Assume further that a clitic raises from its theta-position and attaches to an inflectional head. In its theta-position, the clitic is an XP; attachment to a head requires that it be an X^0 (on fairly standard assumptions). Furthermore, the movement violates the head-movement constraint (HMC, a tentative posit that we hope to derive), indicating again that it is an XP, raising by XP-adjunction until the final step of X^0-adjunction. Clitics appear to share XP and X^0 properties, as we would expect on minimalist assumptions.

If the reasoning sketched so far is correct, phrase structure theory is essentially a given on grounds of virtual conceptual necessity in the sense indicated earlier. The structures stipulated in earlier versions are either missing or reformulated in elementary terms satisfying minimalist conditions, with no objects beyond lexical features. Stipulated conventions are derived (with a gap yet to be filled, for adjunction). Substitution and adjunction are straightforward. We return to further consequences.

5 Properties of the transformational component. We have so far considered two operations, Merge and Move, the latter with two cases, substitution and adjunction. The operation Merge is inescapable on the weakest interface conditions, but why should the computational system C_{HL} in human language not be restricted to it? Plainly, it is not. The most casual inspection of output conditions reveals that items commonly appear overtly 'displaced' from the position in which they are interpreted at the LF interface.[20] This is an irreducible fact of human language, expressed somehow in every theory of language, however the displacement may be concealed in notation; it is also a central part of traditional grammar, descriptive and theoretical, at least back to the Port Royal Logic and Grammar. The only question is: what is the nature of these transformational devices (whether one chooses to call them that or not)? On minimalist assumptions we want nothing more than an indication at LF of the position in which the displaced item is interpreted; that is, chains are legitimate objects at LF. Since chains are not introduced by selection from the lexicon or by Merge, there must be another operation to form them: the operation Move.

In the early days of generative grammar speculation about this matter invoked parsing and semantic considerations—improved parsability on certain assumptions, the separation of theme-rheme structures from base-determined semantic (theta) relations, etc. (see Miller and Chomsky 1963, Chomsky 1965 for review). The minimalist framework, with the disparity it imposes between Θ-role assignment and feature-checking, requires such an operation, as Kenneth Wexler has observed. Our concern here is to ask how spare an account of Move the facts of language allow.

This question was a second focus of the effort to resolve the tension between descriptive and explanatory adequacy alongside the steps that led to X′ theory. A central concern was to show that the operation Move-α is independent of α; another was to restrict the variety of structural conditions for transformational rules. These efforts were motivated by the dual concerns discussed earlier: the empirical demands posed by the problems of descriptive and explanatory adequacy, and the conceptual demands of simplicity and naturalness. Proposals motivated by these concerns inevitably raise the new leading problem that replaces the old: to show that restriction of the resources of linguistic theory preserves (and we hope, even enhances) descriptive adequacy while explanation deepens. The efforts have met with a good deal of success,[20] though minimalist assumptions would lead us to expect more.

Consider first the independence of Move-α from choice of α. While this currently seems a reasonable supposition, it has so far been necessary to distinguish various kinds of movement: XP-movement from X^0-movement; and among XPs, A-movement from A′-movement. Various kinds of 'improper movement' are ruled out, essentially by stipulation; for example, head-raising to an A′-position followed by raising to Spec. A further goal would be to eliminate any such distinctions, demonstrating on general grounds, without any special assumptions, that the 'wrong kinds' of movement crash; not an easy problem.

Some of the general constraints introduced to reduce the richness of descriptive apparatus (hence the variety of transformations) also have problematic aspects. Consider Emonds's structure-preserving hypothesis (SPH) for substitution operations (Emonds 1969). As has been stressed particularly by Jan Koster, it introduces an unwanted redundancy in that the target of movement is somehow 'there' before the operation takes place; that observation provides one motive for nonderivational theories that construct chains by computation on LF (or S-structure) representations. The minimalist approach overcomes the redundancy by eliminating the SPH: with D-structure gone, it is unformulable, its consequences derived—we hope to show—by the general properties of Merge and Move.

It has also been proposed that something like the SPH holds of adjunction: thus, heads adjoin to heads and XPs to XPs. This extended SPH introduces no redundancy and is not affected by the minimalist program, though we would like to deduce it from more elementary considerations.

The descriptive facts are not entirely clear, but they might be something like this. Suppose that only YP can adjoin to XP, and that pre-Spell-Out only Y^0 can adjoin to X^0, though covert operations may adjoin YP to

X^0; for example, VP-adjunction to causative V. We then have two problems: (i) to explain why the SPH holds at all, and (ii), if it does, why it differs before and after Spell-Out, apparently violating the (optimal) uniformity assumption on C_{HL}.

The answer to the second problem may lie in the nature of the Morphological component. Recall that at Spell-Out, the structure Σ already formed enters Morphology, a system that presumably deals only with wordlike elements, which we may take to be X^0s—that is, either an item α selected from the lexicon (hence with no constituents) or such an item with an element adjoined to it (hence $\{<\alpha,\alpha>, \{\alpha, \beta\}\}$):

(12) Morphology gives no output (so the derivation crashes) if presented with an element that is not an X^0.

On this natural assumption the largest phrases entering Morphology are X^0s; if some larger unit appears within an X^0, the derivation crashes. The pre- versus post-Spell-Out asymmetry follows.

It remains to explain why Y^0 adjoins only to X^0; for example, why can a verb not raise from VP and adjoin to an XP, escaping HMC (a tentative posit, which we hope to derive), and then move on to adjoin to an Infl element? Recall that we assume that one case of Y^0-adjunction to XP is legitimate, namely, when Y^0 is also a YP, as in the case of clitics. The question arises for nonmaximal Y^0.

Consider more closely the case we want to exclude, say, extraction of V from VP, adjoining to the higher AgrP:

(13)

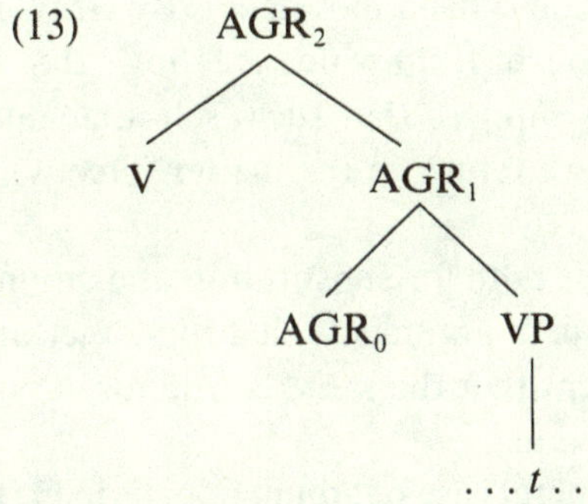

Here Agr_2 and Agr_1 are segments of a category formed by adjunction of V to Agr.

In (13) the V head of the chain (V, *t*) is V^{max} (VP), by definition. But its trace is not. A natural requirement is that chains meet the uniformity condition (14), where the 'phrase structure status' of an element is its (relational) property of maximal, minimal, or neither:

(14) A chain is uniform with regard to phrase structure status.

Adjunction of nonmaximal α to XP is therefore blocked, including (13). The argument carries over to substitution: quite generally, we cannot raise nonmaximal α targeting K, where K then projects. For example, D cannot raise from (nontrivial) DP to [Spec,Infl] (subject) position, leaving the residue of the DP. These consequences of the SPH for substitution and adjunction have commonly been stipulated; they follow from (14), within the bare theory.

We have seen that when Move raises α targeting K to form a new category L (substitution), then the target K must project, not α. The uniformity condition provides an independent reason for this conclusion when α is maximal. If α raises and projects, it will be an X′, not an X^{max}, so the chain will violate (14). There is also an independent reason for this conclusion when α is nonmaximal. Suppose that (15) is formed by Move, raising α to attach to target K, forming L, a projection of α:

(15)

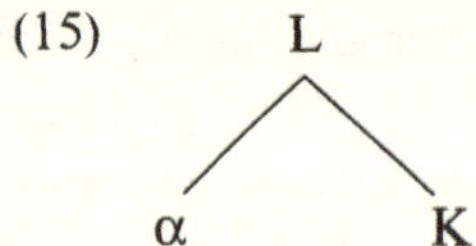

Since α is nonmaximal, the operation is head movement. By HMC it cannot have crossed any intervening head, from which it follows that K can only be the projection of α itself. Suppose that such 'self-attachment' is ruled out on principled grounds (we return to the matter directly). If so, it must be the target that projects.

Note that this argument holds both for substitution and adjunction. We therefore have several independent arguments that the target projects under substitution and an argument that the same is true for adjunction when the raised element is nonmaximal.

Consider more closely the general case of adjunction, as in (15), with L a segment. Suppose that L is projected from α, the case we wish to exclude. We have to determine what the head of the chain formed by the adjunction operation is: is it α, or the two-segment category [α, α]? The latter choice is ruled out by (14). But the former leaves us with a category [α, α] that has no interpretation at LF, violating Full Interpretation (FI) (the same problem would have arisen, this time for α, had we taken the head of the chain to be [α, α]).[22] Again, we conclude that the target must have projected.

The asymmetry of projection after movement thus seems to have solid grounds: it is only the target that can project, whether movement is substitution or adjunction.

One strand of the argument was based on the assumption that self-attachment is impermissible, as in (16):

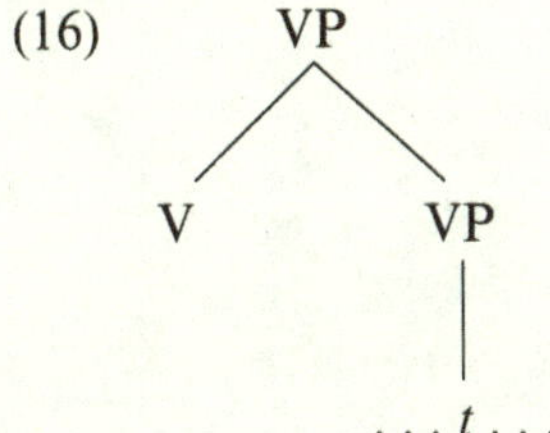

Thus suppose we have the VP "read the book" and we adjoin to it the head "read," forming the two-segment category [*read* [*t the book*]]. Under the intended interpretation of (16), with the target projected, we have formed the object (17), where γ is the target VP = {*read, read, the book*}} (omitting further analysis):

(17) {<read,read>, {read, g}}

Suppose, however, that we had projected the adjunct V ("read") in (16), yielding (18):

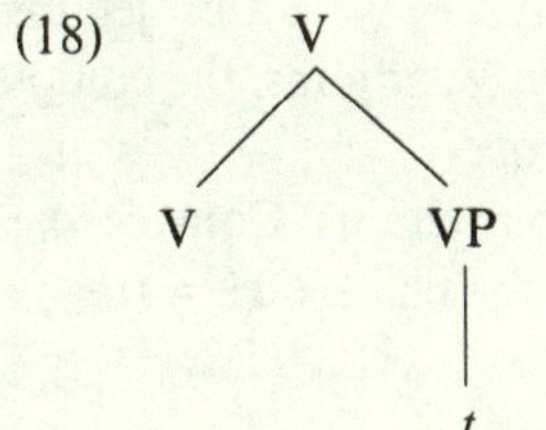

But this too is an informal representation of (17), just as (16) is, though the intended interpretations differ: in (16) we have projected the target, in (18) the adjunct. Furthermore, the latter interpretation should be barred.

Note that the problem is not limited to adjunction. Suppose that we raise the head N of NP to [Spec,NP]. Then in exactly the same way we will construct the same formal object whether we think of NP or Spec as projecting.

We might conclude that this is exactly the right result, with such ambiguity interpreted as a crashed derivation. Then such operations of 'self-attachment' (whether adjunction or substitution) are barred outright, as appears to be the case, incidentally filling the gap in the argument that the target projects under head raising.

Let's turn now to the case of raising of V (= V_2) in a Larsonian shell, as in (19):

(19)

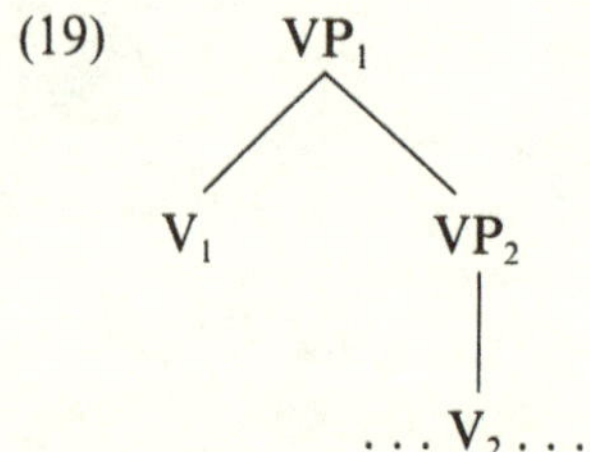

Since self-attachment is ruled out, the operation cannot have targeted VP_2 either as adjunction or substitution. It must be, then, that VP_1 is not a projection of the raised verb V_2 but rather a VP distinct from VP_2, as stipulated in earlier accounts. Thus, V_2 raises to an already filled position occupied by a 'light verb' *v* that has been selected from the lexicon and heads its own projection, VP_1. V_2 adjoins to *v* forming $[_v\ V_2\ v]$; the V_1 position is not 'created' by the raising operation. That conclusion, in fact, is independently imposed by economy conditions, which permit the raising of V_2 only to satisfy its morphological properties (Greed). Raising of V is legitimate only if the operation is necessary for satisfaction of some property of V. That would not be the case if VP_1 were a projection of V_2, but can be if it is a projection of V_1, to which V_2 adjoins, the complex then raising to satisfy morphological properties of V_2.

We now have several conclusions about chains. Consider again the basic structure (20), where α is the head of the chain CH = (α, *t*):

(20)

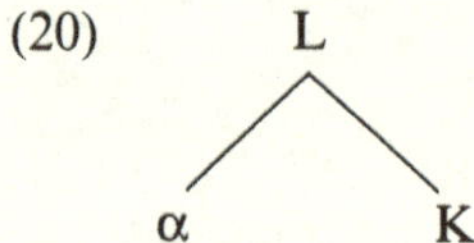

Whether the operation OP forming CH is substitution or adjunction, L is a projection of K, not α. If OP is substitution, then *t* is an $X^{max.}$ Suppose

OP is adjunction. If K is maximal, then α is maximal; pure heads can only adjoin to pure heads. If K is nonmaximal, then α too must be nonmaximal if OP is overt (pre-Spell-Out), though it can be maximal if OP takes place in the covert component, not entering Morphology. We eliminate the SPH for adjunction as well as for substitution. Furthermore, a number of the cases of 'improper movement' are eliminated, carrying us a step forward toward a bare principle Move with no breakdown into various kinds of movement.

We have so far sidestepped a problem that arises in the case of normal head adjunction. Take K to be a nonmaximal head in (20) and α to be a head. Since K projects to L, α is maximal. Thus α is both maximal and minimal. If that is true of *t* as well (e.g., the case of clitic-raising), then CH satisfies the uniformity condition (14). But suppose *t* is nonmaximal, as in the case of V-raising to Infl or to V. Then under a natural (though not necessary) interpretation (14) is violated; CH is not a legitimate object at LF, and the derivation will crash. That is obviously the wrong result. We might therefore assume that at LF, wordlike elements are 'immune' to the algorithm that determines phrase structure status:

(21) At LF, X^0 is submitted to independent word-interpretation processes WI,

where WI ignores principles of C_{HL}, within X^0.[23] WI is something like a covert analogue of Morphology, except that we expect it to be compositional, unlike Morphology, on the assumption that the N → LF mapping is uniform throughout.

Suppose that K in (20) is a maximal head and α a pure (nonmaximal) head; thus this is a case of head adjunction in which the target happens to be a maximal projection. The status of this case depends on the precise interpretation of (21). But the question need not concern us, since the case cannot arise: for reasons of c-command, a pure head α must raise from within the target K.

Suppose that (20) is formed by adjunction, so that L and K are segments, with L = K. So far, there are two ways in which (20) could have been formed: by strict merger of α, K (without movement), or by raising of α, forming the chain CH, α then merging with K. In either case, we form the structure γ = {<*k, k*>, {α, K}} with the three terms α, K, γ; *k* the head of K. Each of these is a category that is 'visible' at the interface, where it must receive some interpretation, satisfying FI. The adjunct α poses no problem. If it heads CH, it receives the interpretation associated with the trace position; if it is added by strict merger, it would presumably be a predicate of K (e.g., an adverbial adjunct to a verb). But there is only one role left at LF for K and γ. Note that the label <*k, k*> is not a term, hence receives no interpretation.

If γ is nonmaximal, the problem is obviated by (21) under a natural interpretation of WI. This should suffice to account for, say, noun incorporation to verbs or verb incorporation to causatives; the same would extend to VP incorporation to V if the LF interface permits such word structures (unlike Morphology). Furthermore, the target K in such cases often lacks any independent function, for example, an affix lacking a Θ-role. In these cases only α or the chain it heads is interpreted, and FI is satisfied.[24]

Suppose γ is nonminimal. We now have two terms, γ and K, but only one LF role. The structure is still permissible if K lacks a Θ-role, as in the case of covert adjunction to an expletive (independently of (21)). The only other possibility is that the adjunct α is deleted at LF, leaving just K. When would this take place?

One case is when α is the trace of successive-cyclic movement of the type that permits intermediate trace deletion, say, along the lines sketched by Chomsky and Lasnik (1993) in terms of a principle of economy of deletion for non-uniform chains; for example, *wh*-movement to [Spec,CP] with intermediate adjunction, as in (22):[25]

(22) Which pictures of John's brother did he expect that [*t′* [you would buy *t*]]

Another case is full reconstruction at LF, eliminating the adjunct entirely, thus a structure of the type (23) interpreted only at the trace:

(23) $[_{YP}$ XP $[_{YP} \ldots t \ldots]]$

It follows that 'scrambling' is permissible only if it is interpreted by reconstruction, as is argued to be the case by Saito (1989 and subsequent work). Similarly, it would follow that such constructions as (24) must be Condition C violations (under the relevant interpretation), and we predict a difference in status between (25) and (22), the latter escaping the violation because the head of the chain is not an adjunct:

(24) a. Meet John in England, he doesn't expect that I will
b. Pictures of John, he doesn't expect that I will buy

(25) Pictures of John's brother, he never expected that you would buy

The conclusions are plausible as a first approximation, though we enter here into a morass of difficult and partially unsolved questions of a kind discussed by Barss (1986), Freidin (1986), Lebeaux (1988), and earlier work; see Chomsky (1993) for some discussion.

On strictly minimalist assumptions these should be the only possibilities for adjunction; namely, (26):

(26) a. word formation
b. semantically vacuous target (e.g., expletive-adjunction)
c. deletion of adjunct (trace deletion, full reconstruction)

In particular, apart from (c) there will be no adjunction to a phrase that assigns or receives a semantic role (e.g, a Θ-role assigner or an argument, a predicate or the XP of which it is predicated). Since (c) is irrelevant to strict merger, the options for the current counterpart to 'base adjunction' are even narrower. We consider adjoined adverbials further in section 7.[26]

Adjunction is therefore an option, but a limited one with rather special properties, under natural minimalist assumptions.

In these terms we might return to the problem of improper movement. We want to show that the wide variety of such cases is excluded on principled grounds. Some fall into place. Thus, standard cases such as (27) cause no problem in the minimalist framework:

(27) *John is illegal [$_{IP}$ t_2 [$_{IP}$ t_1 to leave]]

The complement of *illegal* permits PRO (*it is illegal to leave*) so that (null) Case is assigned to the subject of the infinitive and further raising is barred by Greed, under the strong interpretation (7) (see Martin 1992).

Consider cases of the type (28), with t_2 adjoined to IP in (a) and in [Spec,AgrP] in (b):

(28) a. *John seems [that [t_2 [it was told t_1 [that . . .]]]]
b. *Why do you wonder whether John said that Bill [t_2 [left t_1]]

Here we do not want to permit the intermediate (offending) trace t_2 to delete, unlike (22). The distinction suggests a different approach to intermediate trace deletion: perhaps it is a reflex of the process of reconstruction, understood in minimalist terms as in Chomsky (1993). The basic assumption here is that there is no process of reconstruction; rather, the phenomenon is a consequence of the formation of operator-variable constructions driven by FI, a process that may (or sometimes must) leave part of the trace—a copy of the moved element—intact at LF, deleting only its operator part. The reconstruction process would then be restricted to the special case of A′-movement that involves operators.[27] Some other cases of improper movement also can be eliminated along lines considered here, for example, XP-movement passing through or adjoining to a pure Y^0 position, the trace then deleting. The general topic merits a comprehensive review.

So far, we have kept to the minimalist assumption that the computational procedure C_{HL} is uniform from N to LF; any distinction pre- and post-Spell-Out is a reflex of Morphology within the phonological component. I have said nothing so far about the 'extension condition' of Chomsky (1993), which guarantees cyclicity. The condition is motivated for substitution pre-Spell-Out by relativized minimality effects (in the sense of Rizzi 1990) and others, and does not hold post-Spell-Out if the Case-agreement theory of the minimalist approach is correct. It also cannot hold for adjunction, which commonly (as in head-adjunction) targets an element within a larger projection. We would like to show that these consequences are deducible, not stipulated.[28]

With regard to Merge there is nothing to say; it satisfies the extension condition by definition.[29] Questions arise only in connection with Move. Move targets K, raising α to adjoin to K or to be the specifier of K, K projecting in either case. K may be a substructure of some structure L already formed. That is a necessary option in the covert component but not allowed freely pre-Spell-Out as a result of other conditions, we hope to show.

There are several cases of pre-Spell-Out cyclicity to consider. One is of the type illustrated by such standard examples as (29):

(29) *Who was [$_{\alpha}$ a picture of t_{wh}] taken t_{α} by Bill

This is a CED violation if passive precedes *wh*-movement, but it is derivable with no violation (incorrectly) if the operations apply in countercyclic order, with passive following *wh*-movement. In this case natural economy conditions might make the relevant distinction between the competing derivations. Passive is the same in both; *wh*-movement is 'longer' in the wrong one in an obvious sense, object being more 'remote' from [Spec,CP] than subject in terms of number of XPs crossed. The distinction should be captured by a proper theory of economy of derivation—though the general problem is nontrivial.[30]

The relativized minimality cases fall into three categories: (a) head movement (the HMC), (b) A-movement, (c) A′-movement. In each case we have two situations to rule out: (I) skipping an already filled position; (II) countercyclic operations, that is, movement that skips a 'potential' position that is later filled. Situation (I) may fall under the Minimal Link Condition (MLC) (no innocuous assumption). As for (II), category (a) is not a problem; as we have seen, head-insertion is necessarily by pure merger, which satisfies the extension condition. The remaining cases to be excluded are countercyclic derivations in which an XP is raised to some Spec crossing the position of a lower Spec that is introduced later by movement. It is not easy to construct examples that are not ruled out in one or another independent way, but a closer look is plainly necessary.

It may be then that there is no need to impose the extension condition of Chomsky (1993) on overt operations. Furthermore, neither the phonological nor covert component can access the lexicon for reasons already discussed. The Morphology module indirectly allows variation before and after Spell-Out, as does strength of features. It seems possible to maintain the preferred conclusion that the computational system C_{HL} is uniform from N to LF, in that no pre- versus post-Spell-Out distinction is stipulated.

6 Order. Nothing has yet been said about ordering of elements. There is no clear evidence that order plays a role at LF or the computation from N to LF. Let us assume not. It must be then that ordering is part of the phonological component, a proposal that has been put forth over the years in various forms. It seems natural to suppose that ordering applies to the output of Morphology, assigning a linear (temporal, left-to-right) order to the elements it forms, all of them X^0s, though not necessarily lexical elements.

The standard assumption has been that order is determined by the head parameter: languages are head initial (English) or head final (Japanese), with further refinements possible. Fukui (1993) has proposed that the head parameter provides an account of optional movement, which otherwise is excluded under economy conditions, except in special cases when alternative derivations are equally economical. He argues that movement that maintains the ordering of the head parameter is 'free'; other movement must be motivated by Greed ('last resort'). Thus, in head-final Japanese, leftward movement (scrambling, passive) is optional, while in English such operations must be motivated by feature checking; and in head-initial English rightward extraposition is free, though barred in Japanese.[31]

Kayne (1994) has advanced a radical alternative to the standard assumption, proposing that order reflects structural hierarchy universally. Specifically, he proposes the Linear Correspondence Axiom (LCA), which states that asymmetric c-command imposes a linear ordering of terminal elements; any phrase marker that violates this condition is barred. From his specific formulation of LCA he draws the further conclusions that there is a universal Spec-head-complement (SVO) ordering, and that specifiers are in fact adjuncts. A head-complement structure then is necessarily an XP, which can be extended—exactly once, on Kayne's assumptions—to a two-segment XP. The proposal is very much in the spirit of the minimalist program. Let's consider how it might be incorporated into the bare phrase structure theory just outlined. That is not an entirely straightforward matter, because the bare theory lacks much of the structure of the standard X′ theory that Kayne adopts and partially reduces to LCA.[32]

Kayne offers two kinds of arguments for LCA: conceptual and empirical, the latter extended in subsequent work (see particularly Zwart 1993). The conceptual arguments show how certain stipulated properties of X′ theory can be derived from LCA. The empirical arguments can largely be carried over to a reformulation of LCA within the bare theory, but the conceptual ones are problematic. First, the derivation of these properties relies crucially not just on LCA, but on features of the standard X′ theory that are abandoned in the bare theory. Second, the conclusions are for the most part already derivable in the bare theory without LCA, though in somewhat different form.

Kayne adopts the standard X′-theoretic assumptions (30), illustrated for example in (3), above:

(30) Certain features (categorial features) project from a terminal element to form a head, then on to form higher categories with different bar levels.

The conceptual arguments and the conclusions about ordering crucially rely on these assumptions, which are abandoned in the bare theory.

To illustrate, consider two elementary structures central to Kayne's account (his (4), (13), notations modified):

(31) 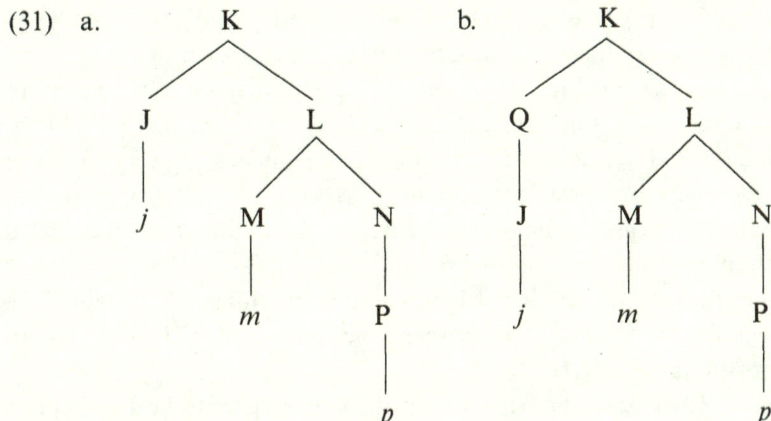

Putting aside the status of K for the moment, consider first (31a). Here *j, m, p* are terminals, selected from the lexicon. They project to J, M, P, respectively, the X^0 categories that are the actual heads. P then projects to the X^{max} category N, which combines with M to form the higher projection L. The categories are J, M, P (heads) and L, N (maximal projections); a tacit assumption is that projection to higher categories in (30) is optional. The c-command relation is stipulated to hold only of categories (not terminals). Asymmetric c-command (ACC) holds between J and M (irrelevantly, also J and N, P) and between M and P. Accordingly, the terminals dominated by these categories are assigned the linear ordering *j-m-p,* and the structure is admissible under LCA.

In (31b) there is a new category Q, an X^{max} projected from the head J. J does not c-command at all; Q c-commands M (and N, P) and L c-commands J, asymmetrically in both cases. The ACC relations do not yield a linear ordering: ACC(Q, M) entails that *j* precedes *m,* which precedes *p* as before; ACC(L, J) entails that *m* precedes *j.*

Therefore (31a) is admissible under LCA and (31b) is not. Turning to K, in (31a) the structure remains admissible under LCA whether K is a new category or a segment of the two-segment category [K, L]; ACC holds the same way in either case. The case of (31b) is different, however. Its inadmissibility follows from the fact that L asymmetrically c-commands J. But if c-command is restricted to categories as Kayne proposes, excluding segments of categories along with terminals, then L will no longer c-command J if [K,L] is a two-segment category. Hence, (31b) is inadmissible only if K is a new category; if Q is adjoined to L, (31b) is admissible. The segment-category (adjunct, specifier; A- vs. A′-position) distinction can be maintained in the case of (31a), where *j* projects only to a head, but not in the case of (31b), where *j* projects to an X^{max}; in the latter case we have only adjunction, and the distinctions disappear.

This seems an odd result, for several reasons. On conventional assumptions the admissible structure (31a) should be inadmissible however interpreted; we do not expect nonmaximal heads to be specifiers or to be adjoined to maximal projections. Furthermore, it is strange that the only admissible case of the segment-category distinction (and the related ones) should be for a dubious structure such as (31a). Finally, there are real questions as to whether it is possible to eliminate what seem to be fairly significant distinctions between specifiers and adjuncts, A- and A′-positions.

Turning to the bare theory, the counterpart to both (31a) and (31b) is (32):

(32)

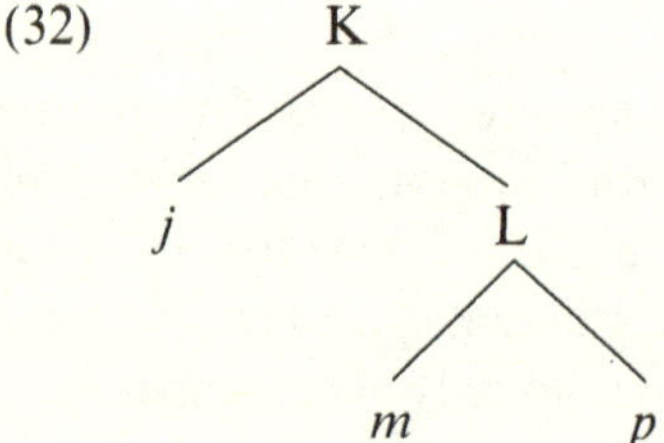

Here L is either *m* or *p*, K is either *j* or L, and K may be either a segment of [K, L] (*j* an adjunct in an A′-position) or a separate category (*j* a specifier in an A-position). The heads are the terminal elements *j, m, p* themselves; there are no head projections. There are no bar levels, only lexical elements and sets constructed from them. Assuming that L is not formed by adjunction, whichever of *m, p* is not projected to L is an X^{max} as well as a head. (32) cannot be interpreted as intended for (31a), with $[_J\ j]$ a head adjoined to the maximal projection $[_L$ M N]. Rather, if L projects to K, then *j* is a single-terminal maximal projection, either specifier or adjunct of the head-complement construction L. And if *j* projects to K, it is either a head with complement L, or L is adjoined to *j* (which is a bare head or both maximal and minimal, depending on higher structure).

The disparity between the systems mounts when we consider richer structures. Thus, Kayne (still adopting standard X′ conventions) compares (31) with an alternative in which the head $[_M\ m]$ is replaced by the X^{max} $[_{MP}\ [_M\ m]]$, inadmissible under LCA. But in the bare theory it again reduces to (32).

Despite the disparity let us ask how a modified LCA might be added to the bare theory. There is no category-terminal distinction, so either may c-command. Turning to (32), suppose that K is a separate category and L projects, so that *j* is a specifier in an A-position. ACC holds of (*j, m*), (*j, p*), so that *j* must precede *m* and *p*. But it would hold of (*m, p*) only if the single-terminal *p* (the complement of the head *m*) were replaced by a complex category. Hence, we have the order Spec-head-complement, though only for nontrivial complement.

Suppose that instead of terminal *j* we had branching J, with constituents α, β. L is an X′, neither maximal nor minimal, so it does not c-command.[33] Therefore the ACC relations are unchanged.

Suppose that K is a separate category and *j* projects. ACC holds as before; *j* is now the head of K with complement L.

Suppose that K is a segment, either *j* or L. There is no particular problem, but adjunct-target order (to which we return) will depend on the precise definition of c-command.

In brief LCA can be adopted in the bare theory but with somewhat different consequences. The segment-category distinction (and the related ones) can be maintained throughout. The intended interpretation of (31) is unformulable, correctly it seems. We draw Kayne's basic conclusion about SVO order directly, though only if the complement is more complex than a single terminal.

The conceptual arguments for LCA do not carry over to the bare theory. Thus Kayne shows how it is possible to derive such X′-theoretic stipulations as (33):

(33) a. The complement of a head cannot be a head.
b. A category cannot have two heads.
c. Every phrase must be headed.

He notes further that (33c) entails that coordination cannot be of the form [XP YP] but must have a coordinate element as head ($[_{\alpha}$XP $[_{and}$ YP]], etc.), again correctly. But, as noted, derivation of these and other consequences crucially requires not only LCA but also (30), assumptions abandoned in the bare theory, and in the latter the conclusions of (33) follow trivially without LCA, though with a slightly different formulation for (33a) and (33b) ((33c) is unchanged): (a) the complement of a head can be a head, which will be an X^{max}; (b) a category can have two heads, one a bare head that projects, the other an X^{max}.

Let us return now to (32), taking L = *m* with the single terminal complement *p*, both minimal and maximal. Since neither *m* nor *p* asymetrically c-commands the other, no ordering is assigned to *m, p;* the assigned ordering is not total, and the structure fails LCA. That leaves two possibilities. Either we weaken LCA so that non total orderings (but not 'contradictory' orderings) are admissible under certain conditions, or we conclude that the derivation crashes unless the structure $\alpha = [_{L}\ m\ p]$ has changed by the time LCA applies so that its internal structure is irrelevant; perhaps α is converted by Morphology to a 'phonological word' not subject internally to LCA, assuming that LCA is an operation that applies after Morphology.

Consider the first possibility: is there a natural way to weaken LCA? One obvious choice comes to mind: there is no reason for LCA to order an element that will disappear at PF, for example, a trace. Suppose then that we exempt traces from LCA, so that (32) is legitimate if *p* has overtly raised, leaving a trace that can be ignored by LCA. The second possibility can be realized in essentially the same manner, by assuming that LCA may (but need not) delete traces. Under this interpretation LCA may eliminate the offending trace in (32), if *p* has raised.[34]

In short, if the complement is a single terminal XP, then it must raise overtly. If XP = DP, then its head D is a clitic, either demonstrative or pronominal, which attaches at a higher point (determined either generally or by specific morphological properties, depending on how cliticization works).[35] If XP = NP, then N must incorporate to V (and we must show that other options are blocked). Clitics then are bare Ds without complements, and noun incorporation must be restricted to 'nonreferential NPs' (as noted by Hagit Borer), assuming the referential, indexical character of a noun phrase to be a property of the D head of DP, NP being a kind of predicate. Within DP the N head of NP must raise to D (as argued for different reasons by Longobardi (1990).[36]

We therefore expect to find two kinds of pronominal (similarly, demonstrative) elements: weak ones that are morphologically marked as affixes and must cliticize, and strong ones with internal structure, which do not cliticize, for example, in French, the determiner D (*le, la,* etc.), and the complex element *lui-meme.* In Irish the weak element is again D, and the strong one may even be discontinuous, as in *an teach sin* ('that bòok,' with determiner *an-sin* (Andrew Carnie, pc)). A phenomenon that may be related is noted by Esther Torrego. In Spanish, in (34a) the Case-marker *de* can be omitted, but not in (34b):

(34) a. cerca de la plaza ('near the plaza')
b. cerca de ella ('near it')

Deleting *de* in (34a), D = *la* can incorporate into *cerca* satisfying the Case Filter, but that is impossible in (34b) if the strong pronominal *ella* is not

D but a more complex word from which the residue of D cannot be extracted.

Since the affixal property is lexical, weak pronominals cliticize even if they are not in final position; for example, a pronominal object that is a specifier in a Larsonian shell. If focus adds more complex structure, then focused (stressed) weak pronominals could behave like complex pronominals. If English-type pronouns are weak, they too must cliticize, though locally, not raising to Infl as in Romance (perhaps as a reflex of the lack of overt verb raising). The barrier to such structures as "I picked up it" might follow. English determiners such as "this," "that" are presumably strong with the initial consonant representing D (as in "the," "there," etc.) and the residue a kind of adjective perhaps. Various consequences are worth exploring.

While apparently not unreasonable, the conclusions are very strong; thus, every right-branching structure must end in a trace on these assumptions.

What about ordering of adjuncts and targets? In Kayne's theory adjuncts necessarily precede their targets. Within the bare theory ordering depends on exactly how the core relations of phrase structure theory, *dominate* and *c-command,* are generalized to two-segment categories.

Consider the simplest case, with α attached to K, which projects:

(35)

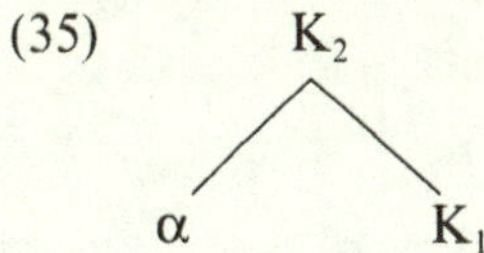

Suppose that K_2 is a new category, α the specifier. Take *dominate* to be an irreflexive relation with the usual interpretation. Then (35) (= {*k,* {α, K}}, *k* the head of K) dominates α and K; informally, K_2 dominates α and K_1.

Suppose, however, that the operation was adjunction forming the two-segment category [K_2, K_1] = {<*k, k*>, {α, K}}. Are α and K_1 dominated by the category [K_2, K_1]? As for c-command, let us assume that α c-commands outside of this category; thus, if it heads a chain, it c-commands its trace, which need not be in K_1 (as in head raising).[37] But what about further c-command relations, including those within (35) itself?

The core intuition underlying c-command is that

(36) X c-commands Y if (i) every Z that dominates X dominates Y and (ii) X and Y are disconnected

For categories we take X and Y to be disconnected if $X \neq Y$ and neither dominates the other. The notions "dominate" and "disconnected" (hence "c-command") could be generalized in various ways for segments.

Let us restrict these relations to terms, in the sense defined earlier: in the case of (35), to α, K (= K_1) and the two-segment category [K_2, K_1]. K_2 has no independent status. These decisions comport reasonably well with the general condition that elements enter into the computational system C_{HL} if they are 'visible' at the interface. Thus K_1 may assign or receive a semantic role, as may α (perhaps heading a chain), but there is no 'third' role left over for K_2; the two-segment category will be interpreted as a word by Morphology and WI (see (21)) if K is an X^{min}, and otherwise it falls under the narrow options discussed earlier.[38]

If that much is correct, we conclude that in (35) [K_2, K_1] dominates its lower segment K_1, so that the latter does not c-command anything (including α, not dominated by [K_2, K_1] but only contained in it).

Turning next to c-command, how should we extend the notion "disconnected" of (36ii) to adjuncts? Take adjunction to a nonmaximal head (Kayne's (16) reduced to its bare counterpart):

(37)

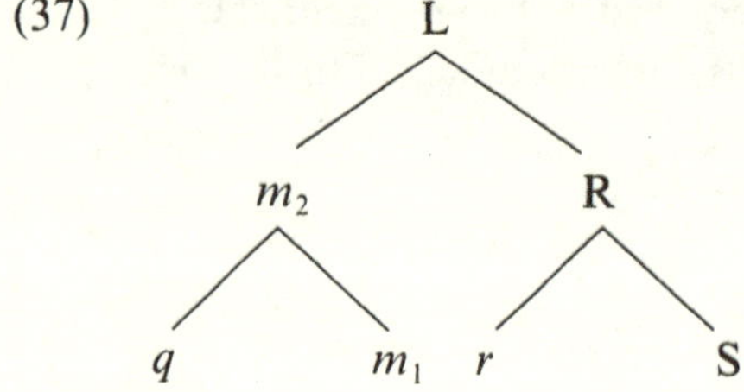

Here q is adjoined to the head m to form the two-segment category [m_2, m_1], a nonmaximal X^0 projecting to and heading the category L, which has label m. R is the complement of m and r its head, and S (which may be complex) is the complement of r. What are the c-command relations for the adjunct structure?

The lowest Z that dominates q and [m_2, m_1] is L; therefore, q and [m_2, m_1] asymmetrically c-command r and S, however we interpret "disconnected." What are the c-command relations within [m_2, m_1]? As noted, m_1 does not c-command anything. The other relations depend on the interpretation of "disconnected" in (36b). Kayne interprets it as "X excludes Y." Then q (asymmetrically) c-commands [m_2,m_1] so that q precedes m_1; and in general an adjunct precedes the head to which it is adjoined. If X, Y are taken to be 'disconnected' if no segment of one contains the other, then q c-commands m_1 but not [m_2,m_1], and again q precedes m_1.[39] If 'disconnected' requires still further dissociation of X, Y—say, that neither is a segment of a category that contains the other—then no ordering is determined for q, m_1 by LCA.

If m_1 is not a head but the complex category $[_m\ m\ P]$, so that q is an X^{max} for reasons already discussed, then q c-commands the constituents of m_1 under all interpretations of 'disconnect,' and the adjunct precedes the target (whether q is internally complex or not).

Left open then is the case of adjunction of a head to another head, that is, ordering within words. Whether order should be fixed here depends on questions about inflectional morphology and word formation.

Summarizing, it seems that Kayne's basic intuition can be accommodated in a straightforward way in the bare theory, including the major empirical conclusions, specifically, the universal order SVO and adjunct target (at least for XP-adjuncts). In the bare theory LCA gains no support from conceptual arguments and therefore rests on the empirical consequences. We take LCA to be a principle of the phonological component that applies to the output of Morphology, optionally ignoring or deleting traces. The specifier-adjunct (A-A′) distinction can be maintained, and there may be multiple specifiers or adjuncts, though the options for adjunction are very limited for other reasons. There are further consequences with regard to cliticization and other matters, whether correct or not, I do not know.

7 Some residual problems. In discussing the options for adjunction we had put aside such structures as (38), with an adverbial adjoined to the two-segment category [XP, XP], projected from α:

(38)

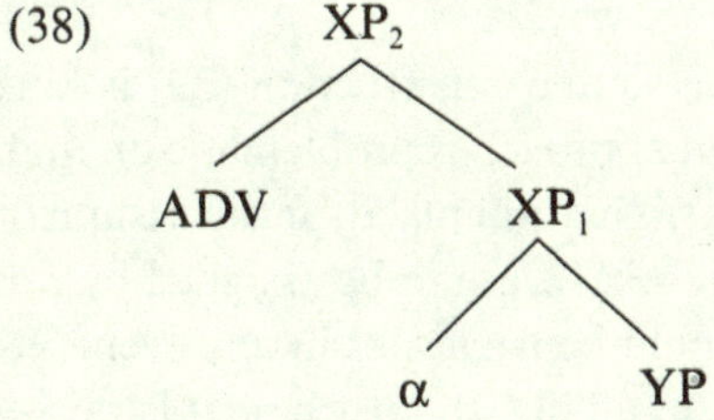

The construction is barred if XP has a semantic role at LF; say, if XP is a predicate (AP or VP), as in (39):

(39) John $[_{VP}$ often $[_{VP}$ reads $\left\{\begin{array}{l}\text{books}\\ \text{to his children}\end{array}\right\}$]]

Such structures as (38) could have been derived either by Merge or Move. The latter possibility can perhaps be ruled out in principle, under Greed: adverbs seem to have no morphological properties that require movement. The empirical evidence also seems to indicate that they do not form chains. Thus, an adverb in pre-IP position cannot be interpreted as if it had raised from some lower position.[40]

The only option then is Merge. The question is whether we have 'base adjunction' in the EST sense, at least above the level of word formation. So far, it is barred if XP is semantically active as in (39). The sentences themselves are fine, but the structures assigned to them by (39) are not.

Adverbials can, however, be adjoined to such phrases as AgrP or IP or to any X′. Adjunction to X′ by merger does not conflict with the conclusion that X′ is invisible to C_{HL}; at the point of adjunction the target is an XP, not X′.

Such constructions as (39) have played a considerable role in linguistic theory since Emonds's (1978) study of differences between verb-raising and nonraising languages (French and English). The basic phenomena, alongside (39), are illustrated by (40) (both well-formed in French):

(40) a. John reads often to his children.
b. *John reads often books.

A proposal sometimes entertained is that V raises from the underlying structure (39) to form (40a), but such raising is barred in (40b) for Case reasons; accusative Case is assigned to *books* by *read* under an adjacency condition of the kind proposed by Stowell (1981). French differs in the adjacency property or in some other way.

Apart from the fact that the source construction (39) is barred for the reasons discussed,[41] the general approach is problematic on minimalist assumptions. This framework has no natural place for the assumed condition of adjacency. Furthermore, it takes Case to be assigned by raising to [Spec,AgrS] so that adjacency should be irrelevant in any event. It is also unclear why the verb should raise at all in (40), or where it is raising to. It seems that either the standard analysis is wrong or there is a problem for the minimalist framework.

In fact the empirical grounds for the analysis are dubious. Consider such adverbial phrases as *every day* or *last night,* which cannot appear in the position of *often* in (39):

(41) *John every day reads to his children.

Nevertheless, we still find the paradigm of (40):

(42) a. John reads every day to his children.
b. *John reads every day books.

It seems then that the paradigm does not involve verb raising.

Furthermore, similar phenomena appear when raising is not an option at all, as in (43):

(43) a. John made a decision (last night, suddenly) to leave town.
b. John felt an obligation (last night, suddenly) to leave town.

Here the adverbial may have matrix scope, so that it is not within the infinitival clause. It can appear between the N head and its complement, though the N cannot have raised in the manner under discussion. In general, therefore, it is doubtful that raising has anything to do with the relevant paradigms.

The phenomena suggest a Larsonian solution. Suppose that we exclude (39) from the paradigm entirely, assuming that *often* appears in some higher position and thus does not exemplify (38) with XP = VP. The structure underlying (40) and (41) is (44):

(44)

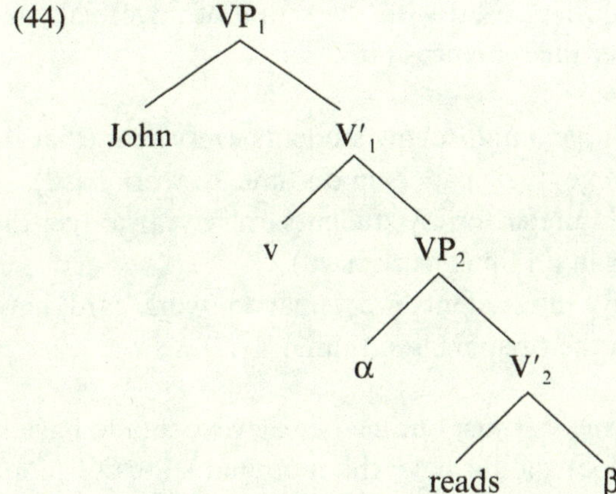

Here VP_1, V'_1 are projections of the 'light verb' *v;* and VP_2, V'_2 are projections of *read.* Whether the latter raises or not depends on whether *v* is selected in the initial numeration. Unless *read* raises, the derivation crashes because its features (specifically, its tense and agreement features) are not satisfied; by HMC it must raise to *v*. The phenomenon is structurally similar to ECM, with a phrase moving so that further movement can satisfy Greed; see below.[42]

Suppose that α in (44) is the adverbial *often*. Then if β = *to the children*, there is no problem. But if β = *books*, the derivation will crash; *books* cannot raise to [Spec,Agr] to have its Case checked because of the intervening α. The relativized minimality violation cannot be overcome by V-raising, which will not create a large enough minimal domain. Note the crucial assumption that the subject *John* is in [Spec,VP], the strong version of the VP-internal subject hypothesis that we have been assuming throughout; otherwise that position would be an 'escape hatch' for raising of *books*.[43]

Under this analysis the basic facts follow with no special assumptions. There is a Case solution, but it does not involve adjacency. The problem of optional raising is eliminated, along with those raised by (42) and (43).

Questions remain about other matters, among them: What is the basis for the French-English distinction? Why do the *wh*-variants of the adverbials in question behave like adjuncts, not arguments? What about CED effects in the case of adjuncts such as Adj in (45), which is in a complement position if 'base-generated' adjuncts are barred?

(45) They [read the book [$_{\text{Adj}}$ after we left]]

Another question has to do with the scope of adverbials in ECM constructions. Consider the sentences (46):

(46) a. I tell (urge, implore) my students every year (that they should get their papers in on time, to work hard).
b. I would prefer for my students every year to (get their papers in on time, work hard).
c. I believe my students every year to (work hard, have gotten their papers in on time).

Under the Larsonian analysis just outlined *every year* should have matrix scope in (46a), and (46c) should have the marginal status of (46b) with embedded scope if interpretable at all. The differences seem to be in the expected direction, though they are perhaps not as sharp as they might be. We would incidentally expect the distinction to be obviated in a verb-raising language such as Icelandic, as appears to be the case (Diane Jonas, pc).

Questions also arise about the relevance of the specifier-adjunct distinction to Case and agreement. In Chomsky (1993) I took the checking domain to include adjuncts as well as specifiers in the light of Kayne's (1989) theory of participial agreement. The assumption was that in passive and unaccusative the object passes through the [Spec,AgrO] position (A-movement), checking agreement with the participle, and then raises to subject, driven by Case; and in operator movement, the object adjoins to the Agr phrase (A′-movement), again checking agreement in the checking domain of Agr, then raising ultimately to [Spec,CP], driven by the operator feature. In particular Kayne found dialect differences associated with the two kinds of participial agreement.

Dominique Sportiche and Philip Branigan have observed that the operator-movement case is problematic because of such long-distance movement constructions as (47):[44]

(47) la lettre [qu'il a $[_{\text{AgrP}}$ *t′* $[_{\text{AgrP}}$ dit [que Pierre lui a [envoyé *t*]]]]]

Raising of the operator from *t* to *t′* (perhaps with intermediate steps) and then to [Spec,CP] is legitimate successive-cyclic A′-movement and should yield participial agreement with *dit* in the higher clause, incorrectly. That suggests that agreement (hence, presumably, Case as well) should be restricted to the specifier position, so that (47) would be ruled out as a case of improper movement if MLC requires lower adjunction on the way to *t′*. Assuming that the conclusion generalizes properly, we have another reason for the segment-category (specifier-adjunct, A-A′) distinction, as well as for a requirement of successive cyclic movement. The dialect differences noted by Kayne remain unexplained, however.

Under either analysis the example illustrates that agreement can be assigned without Case. The same is true of such simple adjectival constructions as (48):

(48) John is $[_{\text{AgrP}}$ *t′* Agr $[_{\text{AP}}$ *t* intelligent]]

Here *John* raises from the predicate-internal subject position *t* to [Spec, Agr] (*t′*) for agreement with the adjective (raised to Agr), then raises on to the subject position ([Spec,AgrS]) for Case checking, with agreement checked independently by AgrS so that there is double agreement.[45]

The counterpart would be a structure in which Case is assigned without agreement, that is, a structure of the form (49) in which α checks the Case of DP, which then raises to [Spec,Agr] for agreement:

(49) [DP Agr [. . . . [*t* α . . .]]]

This possibility is illustrated by transitive expletives (TEs) as analyzed by Jonas and Bobaljik (1993) and Jonas (to appear). Icelandic has structures of the following type (English words):

(50) $[_{\text{AgrS-P}}$ there $[_{\text{AgrS}}$ painted $[_{\text{TP}}$ a student $[_{\text{AgrO-P}}$ the house VP]]]]

The meaning is something like "a student painted the house," or the intelligible but unacceptable English counterpart (51):

(51) There painted the house a student (who traveled all the way from India to do it).

In (50) the expletive is in [Spec,AgrS] (subject) position; *painted* is the verbal head of VP adjoined to intermediate inflectional nodes and finally to AgrS; *a student* is raised to [Spec,Tense] with its Case checked by the trace of the raised Tense that heads TP; *the house* is raised (object raising) to [Spec,AgrO], where its Case and agreement are checked, and the VP contains only traces. Positions are motivated by placement of adverbs and negation in the overt forms. In the covert component, *a student* adjoins to the expletive for checking of its subject-agreement features, as in expletive constructions generally (we are assuming). The usual definiteness effect holds. Possibly, this reflects the fact that Agr, an inherently 'weak' element, requires a 'strong' element as its specifier—hence a definite (or specific) DP, either a full DP or the expletive; others remain in [Spec,TP] by Procrastinate. A similar argument might bear on the tendency for object raising to prefer definites; Agr, being weak, attracts the definite to its Spec, leaving indefinites behind by Procrastinate.[46]

We thus have the full range of expected cases: agreement and Case are fully dissociated,[47] and there is good reason to suppose that Agr (i.e., a set of *phi*-features) appears twice and Tense once in a proliferated Infl system of the type proposed by Pollock (1989), a conclusion strengthened by examples such as (51) that couple object raising with expletives and thus require three pre-VP positions for arguments.

These TE constructions at once raise two questions:

(52) a. Why do languages differ with regard to TEs, some (Icelandic) allowing them, others (English) not?
b. Are such structures permitted by economy principles?

Question (52a) presupposes some analysis of simple expletive constructions such as (53):

(53) a. There arrived a man.
b. There is a book missing from the shelf.

Since subject-verb agreement holds between the verb and the postverbal DP (*a man, the book*), the latter must have raised covertly to [Spec,AgrS] on our assumptions, much as it does overtly in "a man arrived." The fact that the overt raising option exists alongside (53a) raises no problem; they arise from different numerations, so that if reference sets for economy comparisons are determined by the initial numeration, as proposed earlier, the options are not comparable in terms of economy of derivation. Covert adjunction to the expletive must be driven by some unsatisfied feature, either Case or agreement or both. Suppose that partitive Case can be assigned by unaccusatives along lines discussed by Belletti (1988). Then covert raising in (53) would be motivated by agreement, as we have assumed for TEs.[48]

Assuming that much, why does English lack TEs? Example (51) suggests that the lack of TEs may be a rather superficial phenomenon. As noted, the sentence is unacceptable (as is (53a), to some degree), though intelligible, and with other lexical choices the construction ranges in acceptability, as Kayne has observed, improving as the subject becomes 'heavier':

(54) a. There entered the room a man from England.
b. There hit the stands a new journal.
c. There visited us last night a large group of people who traveled all the way from India.

Such constructions have been thought to result from an extraposition operation, but that is unformulable in our terms, which allow only one possibility: that they are TEs with the subject in [Spec,T] at LF but on the right overtly. The overt position could be the result of a process in the phonological component, perhaps motivated by properties of theme-rheme structures, which, as often noted, involve 'surface' forms in some manner.[49] Prominence of the theme might require that it be at an 'extreme' position: to the right, since the leftmost position is occupied by the expletive subject. Icelandic might escape this condition as a reflex of its internal V-second property, which requires a method for interpreting internal themes. The lexical restrictions in English presumably reflect the locative character of the expletive. If speculations along these lines prove tenable, question (a) of (52) may not arise: the TE option may be general.

Question (b) of (52) is harder, leading into a thicket of complex and only partly explored issues. Note first that no problem is raised by the fact that TEs alternate with nonexpletive constructions; they arise from different numerations. But it is not obvious that constructions of the form (55), with subject SU in [Spec,T] at Spell-Out, should be allowed at all:

(55) Expletive Agr [SU [T XP]]

If TEs of the form (55) are legitimate, we should expect to find such structures as (56) in Icelandic, with *seem* raising to AgrS and SU raising from *t* to [Spec,TP] (as demonstrated by placement of adverbials and negation).

(56) There seems $[_{TP}$ $[_{SU}$ a man] $[_{IP}$ *t* to be in the room]]

Assuming these to be legitimate,[50] we then have to explain why (57) is barred in English:

(57) *There seems (to me, often) $[_{IP}$ a man to be in the room]

Note that we do not have a direct contradiction. Thus, for UG reasons every language might bar (57) while permitting (56), with the associate having raised to [Spec,TP] of the matrix at Spell-Out. Both English and Icelandic would then have only (56), the surface form appearing in English as (58), given the speculative answer to (52a):

(58) There seems to be in the room [a man (who traveled all the way from India)]

Assuming this to be the correct resolution of the problem, we then ask why the structure illustrated in (56) is permitted but that of (57) barred. We cannot appeal to numeration in this case, because it is the same in the two examples.

We also have to explain why the form (59) is permitted, with *there* raising from the position of *t,* where it satisfies the Extended Projection Principle EPP in the lower (infinitival) clause:[51]

(59) There seems [*t* to be [a man in the room]]

The problem becomes harder still when we add ECM constructions. In these the embedded subject does raise overtly to a position analogous to *t* in (59), where it is barred (see (57); and it cannot remain *in-situ* as it does in (59):

(60) a. I believe [John to be [*t* in the room]] (. . . to have been killed *t*)
b. *I believe [α to be [John in the room]] (. . .to have been killed John)

Within the minimalist framework we expect the answers to these problems to come from invariant UG principles of economy.

The questions have to do with overt movement; hence, the relevant principle should be Procrastinate, which favors covert movement. Recall that Procrastinate selects among convergent derivations. Overt movement is permitted (and forced) to guarantee convergence.

To begin with, let's compare the effects in the contrasting cases (57) and (60). In each case the reference set determined by the initial numeration includes a second derivation; in the case of (57), the one that yields (59); in the case of (60a), the analogous one that yields (60b) with α the trace of raised I. Our goal is to show that in the case of (57) and (59) economy considerations compel raising of *there* from the embedded clause, while in the case of (60), on the contrary, the same considerations block raising of I from the embedded clause, requiring raising of *John* to satisfy EPP (that is, the strong DP-feature on the embedded Infl).[52] The options available suggest that the difference lies in theta theory.

Consider first (57) and (59).[53] Consider the structure that is common to the two derivations. In each at some stage we construct γ = (61), with the small clause β:

(61) $[_\gamma$ to be $[_\beta$ a man in the room]]

The next step must fill the specifier position of γ to satisfy EPP. Given the initial numeration, there are two relevant possibilities:[54] we can raise *a man* to [Spec,γ] or we can insert *there* in this position. The former choice violates Procrastinate; the second does not. We therefore choose the second option, forming (62):

(62) $[_\gamma$ there to be β]

At a later stage in the derivation we reach the structure (63):

(63) $[_\delta$ seems $[_\gamma$ there to be β]]

Convergence requires that [Spec,δ] be filled. Only one legitimate option exists: to raise *there*, forming (59). We therefore select this option, not violating Procrastinate, which does not arise.

Why then does the same argument not favor (60b) over (60a)? The common part of the derivations is (64):

(64) [$_\gamma$ to be [$_\beta$ John in the room]]

Again, we have two ways to fill [Spec,γ], insertion of I being preferred if it yields a convergent derivation. Suppose we insert *I*, then raising it to form (60b). Recall that we cannot raise I to the VP-internal subject position [Spec,*believe*]; as already discussed, that violates Greed (see (9)). Therefore the LF output violates the Θ-criterion; the argument chain (I, *t*) lacks a Θ-role. Note that we must assume now that the derivation crashes; if not, it will converge as gibberish, blocking the desired derivation of (60a).

We therefore conclude that violation of the Θ-criterion prevents convergence (see note 22), although the need for a Θ-role is not a formal property, like Case, that permits 'last-resort' movement. The conclusions are delicate. It remains for cases and consequences to be investigated further.

Much the same reasoning applies to such structures as (65):

(65) β is believed [α to be [DP XP]]

Before Spell-Out both positions α and β must be occupied. Hence, DP must have raised successive-cyclically, yielding (66) (DP = *John*, XP = *in the room*):

(66) John is believed [*t′* to be [*t* in the room]]

Suppose that the numeration included the expletive *there*. Then (65) would yield the possible outcome (67a) but not (67b) (DP = *a man*, XP = *in the room;* (67a) analogous to (59), (67b) to (57)):

(67) a. There is believed [*t* to be [a man in the room]]
b. *There is believed [a man to be in the room]]

Note that (67b) contrasts with (60a), in which overt raising of DP is required.

Suppose that the numeration included expletive *it* instead of *there*. The analogue of (67a) is now impossible because *it*, unlike *there*, is not an LF-affix, so that the features of DP of (65) cannot be checked. Suppose, however, that instead of such DP we had a phrase that required no such feature checking, say, a CP instead of [DP XP] in (65), as in (68):

(68) β is believed [α to have been proven [$_{CP}$ that . . .]]

Then we have the possible outcome (69a) but not (69b):

(69) a. It is believed [*t* to have been proven [that . . .]]
b. *It is believed [[that S] to have been proven *t*]

With a different numeration, lacking *it,* the embedded CP could have raised to matrix subject position, giving (70):

(70) [that . . .] is believed [*t′* to have been proven *t*]

Hence, it is not raising of the CP that is blocked in (68).[55]

Suppose that we have the numeration N that yields (71) with successive-cyclic raising, *t* and *t′* being traces of *John:*

(71) It seems that [John was believed [*t′* to be [*t* in the room]]]

An alternative derivation with the same numeration yields (72), *t* and *t′* traces of *John:*

(72) *John seems that [it was believed [*t′* to be [*t* in the room]]]

The two derivations have the common part (73):

(73) [$_{\alpha}$ to be [$_{\beta}$ John in the room]]

The next step is to fill [Spec,α] either by raising of *John* (violating Procrastinate unless this is necessary for convergence) or by insertion of *it.* By the earlier reasoning insertion of *it* is required, yielding only the incorrect output (72) and blocking the correct alternative (71). It must be then that derivation of (72) does not converge, even though all formal properties are satisfied. (72) is an example of superraising, violating relativized minimality; in the current framework the Minimal Link Condition (MLC). The conclusion seems to be, then, that violation of this condition—and, presumably, of the conglomerate of properties that fall under ECP generally—causes the derivation to crash. The natural conclusion is that a chain that violates ECP is not a legitimate object at LF; in the framework of Chomsky and Lasnik (1993) a chain with a trace marked * is not a legitimate object. If so, then there is no convergent derivation of (72), and (71) is left as the only convergent derivation, as required.[56]

One aspect of question (52b) still remains unanswered: why is the permitted TE structure (55), repeated here as (74a), not blocked by the alternative (74b) in accord with the reasoning just reviewed?

(74) a. Expletive Agr [SU [T XP]]
b. Expletive Agr [*t* [T [. . . SU . . .]]]

In other words, why is (50), repeated here as (75a), not blocked by (75b) with *there* inserted in the [Spec,TP] position instead of *the student* raising to this position in violation of Procrastinate?

(75) a. [$_{\text{AgrS-P}}$ there [$_{\text{AgrS}}$ painted [$_{\text{TP}}$ a student [$_{\text{AgrO-P}}$ the house VP]]]]
b. [$_{\text{AgrS-P}}$ there [$_{\text{AgrS}}$ painted [$_{\text{TP}}$ *t* [$_{\text{AgrO-P}}$ the house [$_{\text{VP}}$ a student . . .]]]]]

A possible argument is that the [Spec,TP] position must remain open for the subject *a student* after object raising. But that is not compelling. First, the trace of *there,* serving no function at LF, might well be deleted or replaced, so that [Spec,TP] would remain open; see note 53. Second, the same question arises if there is no object raising.

Consider the structure (76) that is common to the two competing derivations:

(76) [$_{\text{TP}}$ T AgrP]

The object may or may not have raised to Spec of the AgrP complement of T. The next step is to fill [Spec,TP]. Given the numeration, the choice, as before, is between raising of the subject *the student* or insertion of the expletive *there* by Merge. The former violates Procrastinate. Therefore, insertion of *there* is preferred—if it will lead to a convergent derivation. In the cases discussed earlier that was indeed the case: *there* was able to raise to Spec of the matrix clause, satisfying EPP. But in this case the matter is different because of intrinsic properties of *there.* Note that *there* bears Case but lacks intrinsic agreement, the latter determined not by *there* but by its associate, which raises to adjoin to it. Raising of the associate is driven by agreement, not Case, under the assumptions of the previous discussion (following Belletti 1988). Accordingly, if *there* is already in a Case position, it is prevented from raising by Greed; all its features are already satisfied. Hence, if *there* is in [Spec,TP], it cannot raise, and the derivation will crash.[57] Therefore, given (76), the only convergent derivation results from raising of the subject *the students,* overriding Procrastinate, and yielding (75b). Insertion of *there* yielding the alternative (75b) is not an option.

The assumptions here are those of Chomsky (1993), repeated earlier. The principle of Greed (last resort) overrides convergence; Procrastinate selects among convergent derivations. In addition we have several conclusions about expletive constructions, theta theory, economy, and convergence. These are strong assumptions with varied empirical consequences. So far, they seem both conceptually plausible and supported by sometimes rather intricate argument.

The basic assumption about reference sets that underlies the preceding discussion is that they are determined by the initial numeration, but determined stepwise; at a particular point in the derivation we consider the continuations that are permitted, given the initial numeration; the most economical derivation blocks the others. On that assumption we explain the full set of cases—although, it must be stressed, it is no trivial matter to generalize the reasoning to more complex cases, and the assumptions to which we have been led are far from solid.

Recall that the bare phrase structure theory allows multiple Specs in principle. Is this option realized? If so, we will have the structure (77):

(77)

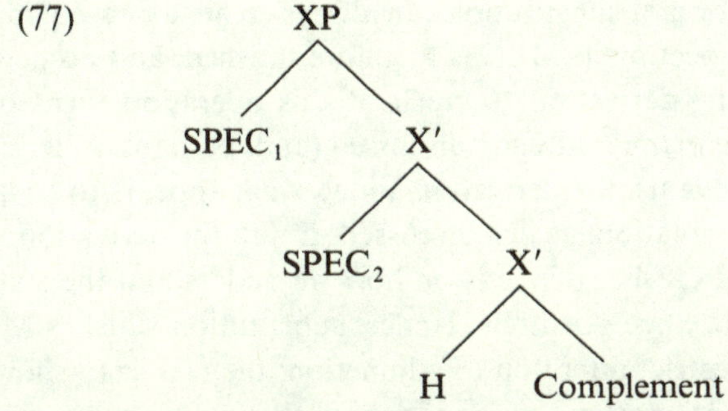

Here we may assume $Spec_1$ and $Spec_2$ to be equidistant targets for movement, being within the same minimal domain.

Such ideas and phenomena related to them have been investigated in recent work (Miyagawa 1993a,b; Koizumi 1993; Ura 1993). If a language permits (77), then it should allow multiple assignment of Case and agreement from the same head, since Spec is available for checking these features.[58] Suppose that the head H has a strong DP-feature. Then Case must be checked pre-Spell-Out at least at $Spec_2$, satisfying the strong feature of H. But $Spec_1$ is still an available position and could be filled by covert movement, so that the same Case is checked again by H. Furthermore, $Spec_1$ allows an escape hatch for superraising. Finally, it permits scrambling with A-position properties (binding, obviating weak crossover effects, etc.), unlike scrambling to an A′-position, which under earlier assumptions involves full reconstruction.

Ura (1993) has found that these properties correlate in a wide range of languages, lending strong empirical support to the conclusion that (77) is indeed an option that a language may have. A language might allow this option for some heads but not others (perhaps C but not Agr), in which case other properties follow, all matters now under investigation.

A major question left unresolved is the exact nature of the Minimal Link Condition (MLC). Specifically, we want MLC to deal with relativized minimality cases without any reference, direct or oblique, to the three categories: (i) HMC, (ii) A-movement, and (iii) A′-movement. Let's review the kinds of problems that arise.

MLC imposes a shortest-move requirement. Exactly how should we interpret that? We might understand MLC to mean that Move-α must attach α to the nearest target in the already formed structure in a way that does not cause the derivation to crash.[59] One natural strategy for implementing this idea would be to rely on the fact that multiple Spec positions are allowed in principle. Whether the 'nearest target' is a head H or an X^{max} HP, the operation of substitution can always create a new equidistant Spec, moving α to occupy it. MLC is therefore satisfied, and no new reason is added for the derivation to crash. If this operation turns out to satisfy Greed in the manner already discussed (and, perhaps, other conditions, if any are relevant), the derivation allows what appears to be a relativized minimality violation, as just discussed. If not, the derivation is illegitimate; whether it crashes depends on how we understand the status of illegitimate multiple Spec positions. Hence, substitution satisfies MLC.[60] We can therefore restrict attention to adjunction; the task is to show that 'improper movement' crashes, bearing in mind that a wide range of cases are admitted in principle when we keep to bare minimalist assumptions.

What is the 'nearest target'? Recall that self-attachment is ruled out for α, a head. The nearest target for α is therefore the head H that immediately c-commands α, or its (equidistant) specifier (or HP itself, if that too is equidistant). These are the nearest targets for nonminimal α as well if adjunction is barred within a minimal domain, as might be the case.[61]

Consider nonmaximal α (a pure head). Recall that substitution (i.e., raising to Spec or to a new head position) is ruled out; only adjunction is an option. Adjunction of α to X^{max} (either [Spec,H] or HP) causes the derivation to violate (14) (uniformity), therefore to crash. That leaves only the possibility that α adjoins to H, yielding HMC in this case. Adjunction of α to H does not cause the derivation to crash on the assumption that α can still raise for feature checking, either by excorporation or pied-piping of H.[62]

For maximal α MLC requires that α adjoin to H, to HP, or to [Spec,H]. It remains to be shown that all of these are cases of 'improper movement' that crash if α ends up in an A-position.

These remarks are intended only to sketch out the issues that remain when the operation Move is freed from any specific conditions. Whether the facts of the matter are consistent with that goal is at the moment unclear, though parts of the problem seem to be within reach.

To summarize, it seems that we can hope to eliminate the theory of phrase structure almost entirely, deriving its properties on highly principled grounds. Many consequences follow for the theories of movement and economy when these conclusions are combined with other minimalist assumptions. We are left with hard and challenging questions of a new order of depth and prospects for a theory of language with properties that are quite surprising.

NOTES

1. Most of what follows is based on lecture-seminars at MIT in the fall of 1993. Thanks to the participants for their many suggestions and criticisms in what was (as usual) a cooperative effort, insufficiently acknowledged. Thanks particularly to Samuel Epstein, John Frampton, Sam Guttmann, and Howard Lasnik for comments on an earlier draft.

2. For some discussion of this issue see Chomsky (1994), referring to (though not mentioning) Edelman (1992) and commentary on it. The terms "mind" and "mental" are used here innocuously, as when we informally class certain phenomena, and whatever is involved in accounting for them, as "optical" or "chemical."

3. For some discussion see Chomsky (1977:ch. 1).

4. The assumption that articulation and perception involve the same interface (phonetic representation) is controversial, and the obscure problems relating to the C-I interface even more so. The term "articulatory" is too narrow in that it suggests that the language faculty is modality-specific, with a special relation to vocal organs. Work of the past years in sign language shows that this traditional assumption is too narrow. I will continue to use the term, but without any implications about specificity of output system, while keeping to the case of spoken language.

5. Which is not, of course, to deny that a full theory of performance might involve operations that apply to the (π, λ) pair.

6. The work in optimality theory mentioned above does not consider such problems. In Prince and Smolensky (1993) there seems no barrier to the conclusion that all lexical inputs yield a single phonetic output namely, whatever the optimal syllable might be (perhaps /ba/). That would be ruled out by Prince and McCarthy's (1993) "containment condition" (suggested in passing in Prince and Smolensky (*op. cit.*:80) as a "non-obvious assumption" that they have "found essential"). But it is hard to see how this can be sustained in segmental phonology (as in the cases mentioned) without implausible and widely varying assumptions about parsability. It seems likely that these approaches will have to postulate intervening levels within the phonological component, raising the question of how they differ from rule-based approaches. They may well differ, at least in the domain of prosodic processes (which are hard to separate from segmental ones). At present it seems to me likely that Bromberger and Halle (1991) are correct in holding that phonology, unlike the rest of C_{HL}, is rule based, perhaps apart from some specific subdomain.

7. Recall that the ordering of operations is abstract, expressing postulated properties of the language faculty of the brain with no temporal interpretation implied.

8. Indications of syllabic and intonational structure are not contained in lexical items, nor is, apparently, much of the output phonetic matrix.

9. The PF level is too primitive and unstructured to give meaningful output conditions itself, but the phonological component does select items of particular kinds to be mapped to the PF output, thus indirectly posing what amount to output conditions for the computation to LF. In speaking of PF output conditions we really mean those determined by the operations of the phonological component, which indirectly reflect the actual A-P interface conditions.

10. See also Fukui (1986), Speas (1986), Oishi (1990), and Freidin (1992), among others. From a representational point of view there is something odd about a category that is present but invisible; but from a derivational perspective, as Epstein observes, the result is quite natural, these objects being 'fossils' that were maximal (hence visible) at an earlier stage of derivation.

11. In our terms head-head selection is a head-complement relation, and chain links are reflexes of movement. Further questions arise about Binding Theory and other systems.

12. Nothing essential changes if a lexical entry is a more complex construction from features.

13. I put aside here the question of whether chains are formed by successive applications of Move or by a single Form-Chain operation that could be 'successive cyclic,' as suggested in Chomsky (1993). I also dispense with a more precise account of Move along the following lines: given the phrase marker Σ, select K, α such that the root of K dominates or c-commands α; form γ by merging α, K (what we call "targeting K and raising α"); define the chain CH = $(\alpha_{1,} \alpha_2)$ relationally as the pair $<\alpha, \alpha>$, with the usual properties relative to γ. Note that there is no ambiguity in defining a chain this way, given that there are no 'copies' other than those formed by movement and given that independent selections of a lexical item are distinguished, as noted.

14. See Lasnik (1993) for argument for a weaker version.

15. On the nature of this deviance see section 7. For different approaches to the question see Brody (1993) and Bošcović (1993). Note that the same economy considerations bar raising-to-object, even if the object is a specifier in a Larsonian shell.

16. Problems could arise if X′ were targeted and the raised category were to project, but neither contingency is possible.

17. I put aside here the question of multiple-segment categories beyond two. Nothing essential changes if these exist.

18. Take A-positions to be those narrowly L-related in the sense of Chomsky (1993), A′-positions those non L-related, and the status of broadly L-related yet to be determined. Note that the specifier-adjunct distinction does not quite correlate with the A-A′ distinction.

19. The normal case and in fact the only case when heads are adjoined, since the target head H is always within the higher projection H′.

20. Technically, this is not quite correct; see note 9.

21. Not entirely, however. A look at the earliest work from the mid-1950s will show that many phenomena that fell within the rich descriptive apparatus then postulated, often with accounts of no little interest and insight, lack any serious analysis within the much narrower theories motivated by the search for explanatory adequacy and remain among the huge mass of constructions for which no principled explanation exists—again, not an unusual concomitant of progress.

22. A nontrivial question is whether violation of this principle (say, violation of the Θ-criterion) causes the derivation to crash or yields a convergent derivation interpreted as gibberish. We have no performance tests to differentiate the cases. There are other empirical differences, in principle. Thus if the derivation converges, it could block others under economy conditions. Such arguments are hard to construct; we return to one in section 7. The discussion of reconstruction as a process driven by FI in Chomsky (1993) suggests another line of argument, which would support the conclusion that a derivation crashes if it violates FI.

23. We evade here a certain ambiguity about adjunction to α that is simultaneously X^{max} and X^{min}. Is it X^0-adjunction? X^{max}-adjunction? Either, freely? The unanswered questions carry over to subsequent discussion. Specific answers are readily formulated; the question is which ones are factually correct. Note also that there may be a crucial difference between V-raising to Infl and V-raising to V. In the former case the Infl element may be 'invisible' at LF (see next note), so chain uniformity will not be violated, on an appropriate interpretation.

24. K presumably does not function at LF, having mediated the relation between Spec and raised head (see Chomsky 1993). A question arises about implementation; deletion raises technical issues in our terms (including a question of self-adjunction). Suppose for concreteness that checked functional features are simply understood to be 'invisible' to operations of the interface.

25. See note 13. Note that the concept of uniformity here is different from uniformity of phrase structure status discussed earlier.

26. Condition (b) partially generalizes a conclusion in Chomsky (1986), based on a suggestion by Kyle Johnson: that there can be no adjunction to arguments (partially, because of (c)). The motives required that the conclusion be generalized in very much this way, as has been pointed out a number of times.

27. That reconstruction should be barred in A-chains is thus plausible on conceptual grounds. It has some empirical support as well. Thus, under the relevant interpretation (i) can only be understood as a Condition B violation, though under reconstruction the violation should be obviated, with *him* appearing in the position of *t*, c-commanded by *me;* that the latter c-commands α is shown by such Condition C violations as (ii):

(i) John expected [him to seem to me [$_{\alpha}$*t* to be intelligent]]
(ii) Mary seems to him [*t* to like John]

That the raised subject does not fully reconstruct is shown by standard binding-theoretic facts as well as by the quasiagentive status commonly conferred in 'surface subject' position; e.g., in (iii):

(iii) PRO to appear [*t* to be intelligent] is harder than one might think

We assume here that the quasiagentive role is a by-product of the raising, motivated on other grounds. Note further that on these assumptions, *there*-adjunction does not reconstruct.

28. See Kitahara (1994, 1995) for an economy-based account that yields these consequences within standard X′ theory, involving structures that are not permitted in the bare theory outlined here.

29. One could define Merge differently, of course, allowing 'internal merger.' But there is no conceptual advantage in that; in fact, the definition is more complex.

30. See Collins (1994). For a different approach to (29) in terms of economy see Kitahara (1995).

31. See also Ueda (1990). Note that this proposal requires that ordering be imposed within the N → λ computation.

32. I depart from Kayne in understanding linear ordering to be literal precedence, not simply a transitive, asymmetric, total relation among terminals. That is clearly the intended interpretation, but Kayne's more abstract formulation allows very free temporal ordering even if LCA is satisfied. Thus, if a class of phrase markers satisfies LCA, so will any interchange of sisters (as Samuel Epstein notes), meaning that consistent with LCA a language could, for example, have any arrangement of head-complement relations (e.g., *read-books* or *books-read* freely). Kayne considers one case of the problem (fully left-to-right or fully right-to-left), but it is more general.

33. Note that L is part of the structure, however; otherwise we would have a new kind of structure, inadmissible in our terms. Thus the branching structure remains, and *m, p* do not c-command out of L.

34. On the latter interpretation we must assume that Morphology precedes LCA, so as to prevent the use of XP-adjunction to X^0 as an 'escape hatch' in the syntax, its effects disappearing by LCA before they cause Morphology to crash.

35. Note that V-raising (as in French) does not affect the conclusion that the clitic must raise overtly. If D remains *in-situ,* then whether the trace of V is ignored or deleted by LCA, it will still be a terminal complement, either to V itself or to some intervening element, and the derivation will crash.

36. Presumably the affixal character of N is a general morphological property, not distinguishing nouns with complements from those without (which must raise).

37. The assumption is not entirely obvious; see Epstein (1989) for a contrary view. Much depends on resolution of questions involving reconstruction after adjunction and word-internal processes at LF.

38. Suppose that, as has been proposed, the upper segment enters into calculating subjacency, scope, or other properties. Then we would hope to show that these effects receive a natural expression in terms of containment and domination, notions still available even if the upper segment is 'invisible' for C_{HL} and at the interface.

39. That q c-commands $[m_2,m_1]$ is required in Kayne's theory for reasons that do hold in the bare theory, where the assumption plays no role.

39. Operator phrases formed from adverbials can, of course, be moved, e.g., "how often." Here it is the *wh*-phrase that moves to satisfy a formal feature.

41. Note that although (39) is barred, *often* could be adjoined to V′ under present assumptions.

42. A number of questions arise here that we have left unsettled. Thus, HMC has only been stipulated, and we have to determine just how it and other MLC cases interact with Greed.

43. Recall that if the VP-internal subject is missing, the position cannot be filled by raising of DP to pick up the unassigned Θ-role. See (9).

44. Branigan (1992). See Friedemann and Siloni (1993) for a reanalysis of the phenomenon with a broader data base within a minimalist framework that distinguishes a participial phrase from AgrO.

45. See Cardinaletti and Guasti (1991) for further evidence for a structure like (48). Raising to Spec of the lower Agr is necessary for convergence if agreement features of the adjective must be checked and is permitted, because the features of the subject can be checked there as well without causing the derivation to crash, as it would with a transitive verb.

46. The observations, if valid, might be assimilated to the apparent tendency for rich overt inflectional morphology (Case and agreement) to appear either in Spec or related head (noun or verb) but not both. Such properties are natural if Case and agreement are manifestations of basically the same relation. See Chomsky (1991, 1993).

47. That is, different manifestations of the same relation with different features, *phi*-features vs. Case features; see last note.

48. See Lasnik (1993) for a somewhat different analysis and discussion of internal problems in the account in Chomsky (1993). Also Groat (1993). Note that we must assume that inherent Case assignment satisfies agreement, perhaps by raising to Spec of a functional category that assigns it (or that is associated with the Case assigner).

49. On movement operations within prosodic phrases see Truckenbrodt (1993) and Zubizarreta (1993).

50. Apparently, that is the case (Jonas pc).

51. Note that we want to distinguish "there be NP" constructions with strong existential import from the expletive constructions with small clause, which are much weaker in this respect, differing in other properties as well. For example, the sentence (53b) may be true even if there is no book, just a space on the shelf where a book should be. Similarly, "John has a tooth missing" does not entail the existence of a tooth. A fuller analysis of expletive constructions and the like will also bring in focal stress and other relevant questions that to my knowledge have yet to be examined properly.

52. Procrastinate then blocks further overt movement of *John* (for Case and agreement) to [Spec,AgrO], though overt movement would be required to satisfy EPP in "John is believed to be intelligent."

53. Covert raising of *a man* to matrix subject is required in (59) for convergence. This operation could involve replacement of the trace of *there,* which plays no LF role, or might simply skip this position if that trace is deleted, EPP having been satisfied.

54. Technically, there are others, but they will crash or violate Greed—or so it must be demonstrated, not a trivial problem in general.

55. The assumption here is that "I believe [[that he was here] to have been proven]," while not felicitous, is better than (69b). That is not obvious. See Koster (1978).

56. Discussion of the *it*-expletives thanks to John Frampton.

57. We assume then that the associate has its agreement checked directly from the head. Raising of *there* with adjoined associate is barred by Greed even if the features of the associate would be checked thereby, since *there* itself lacks agreement features.

58. The Cases assigned are always the same, but agreement may vary. This may reflect the fact that Case is an inherent feature of the Case checker (thus, transitive verbs check accusative, finite tense checks nominative), but there is no reason to view the *phi*-features of Agr the same way: perhaps Agr in these cases simply checks such features, whatever they are, lacking *phi*-features of its own. Note that we have tentatively reached a similar conclusion for expletive *there;* it does not have arbitrary *phi*-features, but lacks them. There are various technical problems overlooked here.

59. Another possibility, discussed in lectures some years ago, is that raising α over X to position Y could be blocked because raising X would be a shorter move, an approach that requires suspending Greed in evaluating the raising of X. Such an account might be framed in terms of the notion of 'shallowness' introduced in Oka (1993). There are other possibilities that merit consideration.

60. We need not be concerned with substitution that literally replaces the target K. That is excluded by recoverability of deletion; furthermore, substitution for K is meaningless if α is within K, as in all cases other than pure head adjunction, where substitution is also barred by the uniformity condition (14) and other requirements.

61. Also to be considered is targeting an adjunct. Considerations are similar.

62. Suppose H is not morphologically marked as accepting head adjunction. We would then have to assume that adjunction of α to H creates a violation within Morphology that is distinct from a crashed derivation, again distinguishing a word-internal process. Note that adjunction of α to H is not motivated by Greed, but that is irrelevant for adjunction, as discussed.

REFERENCES

Barss, A. 1986. *Chains and Anaphoric Dependence.* Ph.D. Dissertation. MIT.

Belletti, A. 1988. The Case of Unaccusatives. *Linguistic Inquiry* 19: 1–34.

Bošković, Ž. 1993. D-Structure, Theta Criterion, and Movement into Theta-Positions. Manuscript. University of Connecticut and Haskins Laboratories.

Branigan, P. 1992. *Subjects and Complementizers.* Ph.D. Dissertation. MIT.

Brody, M. 1993. Θ-Theory and Arguments. *Linguistic Inquiry* 24:1–24.

Bromberger, S., and M. Halle. 1991. Why Phonology is Different. In *The Chomskyan Turn.* A. Kasher, ed. Cambridge/Oxford: Blackwell.

Cardinaletti, A., and M. T. Guasti. 1991. Epistemic Small Clauses and Null Subjects. Manuscript. University of Venice and University of Geneva.

Chomsky, N. 1965. *Aspects of the Theory of Syntax.* Cambridge: MIT Press.

Chomsky, N. 1977. *Essays on Form and Interpretation.* Amsterdam: Elsevier North-Holland.

Chomsky, N. 1986. *Barriers.* Cambridge: MIT Press.

Chomsky, N. 1991. Some Notes on Economy of Derivation and Representation. In *Principles and Parameters in Comparative Grammar.* R. Freidin, ed. Cambridge: MIT Press.

Chomsky, N. 1993. A Minimalist Program for Linguistic Theory. In *The View from Building 20: Essays in Linguistics in Honor of Sylvain Bromberger.* K. Hale and S. J. Keyser, eds. Cambridge: MIT Press.

Chomsky, N. 1994. *Language and Thought.* Wakefield (R.I.) and London: Moyer Bell.

Chomsky, N. and H. Lasnik. 1977. Filters and Control. *Linguistic Inquiry* 1:11–46.

Chomsky, N., and H. Lasnik. 1993. Principles and Parameters Theory. In *Syntax: An International Handbook of Contemporary Research.* J. Jacobs, A. von Stechow, W. Sternefeld, and T. Vennemann, eds. Berlin: Walter de Gruyter.

Collins, C. 1994. Economy of Derivation and the Generalized Proper Binding Condition. *Linguistic Inquiry* 25:45–61.

Edelman, G. 1992. *Bright Air, Brilliant Fire.* New York: Basic Books.

Emonds, J. 1969. *Root and Structure-Preserving Transformations.* Ph.D. Dissertation. MIT.

Emonds, J. 1978. The Verbal Complex V′-V in French. *Linguistic Inquiry* 91:51–75.

Epstein, S. 1989. Adjunction and Pronominal Variable Binding. *Linguistic Inquiry* 20:307–19.

Freidin, R. 1986. Fundamental Issues in the Theory of Binding. In *Studies in the Acquisition of Anaphora.* B. Lust, ed. Dordrecht: Reidel.

Freidin, R. 1992. *Foundations of Generative Syntax.* Cambridge: MIT Press.

Friedemann, M. and T. Siloni. 1993. Agr_{OBJECT} is not $Agr_{PARTICIPLE}$. Manuscript. University of Geneva.

Fukui, N. 1986. *A Theory of Category Projection and its Applications.* Ph.D. Dissertation. MIT.

Fukui, N. 1993. Parameters and Optionality. *Linguistic Inquiry* 24:399–420.

Groat, E. 1993. English Expletives A Minimalist Approach. In *Harvard Working Papers in Linguistics* 3. H. Thráinsson, S. Epstein and S. Kuno, eds.

Hale, K., and S. J. Keyser. 1993. On Argument Structure and the Lexical Expression of Syntactic Relations. In *The View from Building 20: Essays in Linguistics in Honor of Sylvain Bromberger.* K. Hale and S. J. Keyser, eds. Cambridge: MIT Press.

Jonas, D. and J. Bobaljik. 1993. Specs for Subjects: The Role of TP in Icelandic. In *Papers on Case and Agreement* I. J. Bobaljik and C. Phillips, eds. *MIT Working Papers in Linguistics* 19.

Jonas, D. To appear. The TP Parameter in Scandinavian Syntax. In *Göteborg Working Papers in Linguistics.* C. Hedlund and A. Holmberg, eds.

Kayne, R. 1989. Facets of Past Participle Agreement. In *Dialect Variation and the Theory of Grammar.* P. Benincà, ed. Dordrecht: Foris.

Kayne, R. 1994. *The Antisymmetry of Syntax.* Cambridge: MIT Press.

Kitahara, H. 1994. Relativized Minimality, Superiority, and the Proper Binding Condition. *Harvard Working Papers in Linguistics.*

Kitahara, H. 1995. Target α: Deducing Strict Cyclicity from Principles of Derivational Economy. *Linguistic Inquiry* 26:47–77.

Koizumi, M. 1993. Topicalization in English as Adjunction to PolP. *Northeast Linguistics Society* 24.

Koster, J. 1978. Why Subject Sentences Don't Exist. In *Recent Transformational Studies in European Linguistics.* S. J. Keyser, ed. Cambridge: MIT Press.

Lasnik, H. 1993. Case and Expletives Revisited. Manuscript. University of Connecticut.

Lasnik, H., and M. Saito. 1984. The Theory of Proper Government. *Linguistic Inquiry* 15:235–89.

Lasnik, H., and M. Saito. 1992. *Move-α.* Cambridge: MIT Press.

Lebeaux, D. 1988. *Language Acquisition and the Form of the Grammar.* Ph.D. Dissertation. University of Massachusetts.

Longobardi, G. 1990. N-Movement in the Syntax and in LF. Manuscript. Università di Venezia.

Martin, R. 1992. On the Distribution and Case Features of PRO. Manuscript. University of Connecticut.

McCarthy, J., and A. Prince. 1993. *Prosodic Morphology I.* Manuscript. University of Massachusetts and Rutgers University.

Miller, G., and N. Chomsky. 1963. Finitary Models of Language Users. In *Handbook of Mathematical Psychology* II. R. D. Luce, R. Bush, and E. Galanter, eds. New York: Wiley.

Miyagawa, S. 1993a. Case, Agreement, and *ga/no* Conversion in Japanese. *Proceedings of Third Southern California Japanese/Korean Linguistics Conference.* Stanford: CSLI.

Miyagawa, S. 1993b. LF Case-Checking and Minimal Link Condition. In *Papers on Case and Agreement II.* C. Phillips, ed. *MIT Working Papers in Linguistics* 19.

Muysken, P. 1982. Parametrizing the Notion 'Head.' *Journal of Linguistic Research* 2:57–75.

Oishi, M. 1990. Conceptual Problems of Upward X′ Theory. Manuscript. Tohoku Gakuin University.

Oka, T. 1993. *Minimalism in Syntactic Derivation.* Ph.D. Dissertation. MIT.

Pollock, J.-Y. 1989. Verb Movement, Universal Grammar, and the Structure of IP. *Linguistic Inquiry.* 20:365–424.

Prince, A. and P. Smolensky. 1993. *Optimality Theory.* Manuscript. Rutgers University and University of Colorado.

Rizzi, L. 1986. On Chain Formation. In *The Syntax of Pronominal Clitics.* H. Borer, ed. *Syntax and Semantics* 19. New York: Academic Press.

Rizzi, L. 1990. *Relativized Minimality.* Cambridge: MIT Press.

Saito, M. 1989. Scrambling as Semantically Vacuous A′-Movement. In *Alternatives Conceptions of Phrase Structure.* M. Baltin and A. Kroch, eds. Chicago: University of Chicago Press.

Speas, M. 1986. *Adjunction and Projection in Syntax.* Ph.D. Dissertation. MIT.

Stowell, T. 1981. *Origins of Phrase Structure.* Ph.D. Dissertation. MIT.

Takahashi, D. 1993. Minimize Chain Links. Manuscript. University of Connecticut.

Truckenbrodt, H. 1993. Towards a Prosodic Theory of Relative Clause Extraposition. Manuscript. MIT.

Ueda, M. 1990. *Japanese Phrase Structure and Parameter Setting.* Ph.D. Dissertation. University of Massachusetts.

Ura, H. 1993. Super-Raising and the Feature-Based X′ Theory. Manuscript. MIT.

Zubizarreta, M. L. 1993. Some Prosodically Motivated Syntactic Operations. Manuscript. University of Southern California.

Zwart, J. W. 1993. *Dutch Syntax: A Minimalist Approach.* Ph.D. Dissertation. Groningen.

Deep, Free, and Surface Bound Pronouns*

Joseph E. Emonds
University of Durham, England

1 Two levels of lexical insertion. Investigations in formal syntax consistently discover dual usages for grammatical morphemes (='function words'). Often, such dual usages result from complementary distribution at a nonsuperficial level of structural analysis or from dual category membership.

The following examples typify complementary distribution. The same P (English *if,* Romance *si*) can introduce indirect questions in complement positions and conditionals in adjunct (adverbial) positions (cf. Emonds 1985:ch. 7, especially to show that both uses involve the feature WH). Similarly, the same P (English *for,* French *pour*) can introduce goals in complement PPs but benefactives in adjuncts. The same grammatical verb (English *do,* Japanese *suru*) inserted in the finiteness position I lacks the 'activity' feature, in contrast to the presence of this feature on this verb when it heads a VP (for the analysis of *suru* see Kubo 1992:ch. 4).

Dual usage resulting from complementary distribution is widespread cross-linguistically, since it reflects lexical items with more general (less stipulative) insertion conditions; nonetheless, the differing meanings and feature compositions associated with different syntactic positions imply some sort of brace or parentheses notation in the lexical entries for these morphemes.

Dual usages based on dual category membership are more language particular. In English the morpheme *too* doubles as an A(djectival) modifier and as an affirmative particle in clauses; *that* serves as both a complementizer and a determiner (which led to confusion in some traditional analyses of English relative pronouns); and nonverbal negative polarity modals such as *dare* and *need* also appear as regular verbs. Again, the lexical use of braces or parentheses seems indicated.

One may ask, why is there not more dual usage (e.g., why are triple usages of closed class items relatively rare), and, equally well, why is there not less? For the first question I will be content with the trivial observation that some presently uninvestigated level of 'intolerable ambiguity' must prevent too much of what might be called 'lexical economy' among the closed class grammatical morphemes. For the second question it must be that natural language lexicons prefer one entry containing the brace and/or parenthesis notations to proliferating separate entries.[1] Thus, items such as (1)–(4) must contribute significantly to lexical economy (as well as to ambiguity). Syntactic features playing a role in interpretation are in capitals, and interpretive properties themselves are in quotes.

(1) if, P, WH, +__S,
{ "question" if P heads a sister to an X^0
"condition" if P heads a sister to a V-headed phrase }

(2) do, V, { $[_{I, -MODAL}$ ___]
ACTIVITY, +___DP }

(3) that, { P, +___S
D, DEMON }

(4) need, { V, +___{ DP, to ^VP }
M, "negative polarity" } , "necessity"

The pervasive presence of dual usage in all languages, together with the fact that it is the locus of much language variation, suggests (5) as a maxim for the expected behavior of grammatical elements in particular grammars.

(5) Lexical entries of closed class items maximize use of the brace and parenthesis notation.

Further, under Borer's (1984:29) proposal that particular grammars consist solely of lexical entries for closed class items, (5) embodies a principal strategy for first language acquisition.

In other work I have argued that the dual usages induced by brace and parenthesis notation in closed class lexical entries correlate, in a certain range of cases, with whether an item is inserted in a given context prior or subsequent to the operation on that domain of transformational and other syntactic principles (e.g., abstract Case marking and selection of the modifying elements often termed Specifiers). A prime example of such a dual usage is furnished by the way in which the English verbal suffix *ing* satisfies its definitional contextual feature +V___, [+N] (Emonds 1991).[2] When *ing* is subject to (partially understood) semantic lexical restrictions, it is inserted prior to transformational computation and Case-marking within an XP domain and gives rise to restricted classes of derived nominals and adjectives (*thorough* {*learning* /**knowing*} *of the model, a subtlety very* {*pleasing* /**escaping*} *to children*); on the other hand, when these restrictions are ignored, *ing* is inserted productively in the same post-verbal context subsequent to 's-structure,' and then yields gerunds and participles (*thoroughly* {*learning* /*knowing*} *the model, a subtlety* {*pleasing* / *escaping*} *the children*). The dual usage of *ing* is lexically expressed by the following entry:

(6) ing, [+N], +V____, $\left(\left\{\begin{array}{l}\text{if N, then V must be ACTIVITY, and} \ldots\\ \text{if A, then V is PSYCHOLOGICAL, or} \ldots\end{array}\right\}\right)$

In order for the nominal and adjectival syntax of the restricted derived nominals and adjectives to follow without stipulation, it suffices that semantically conditioned insertion of *ing* occur prior to transformations (at a 'deep' level); *mutatis mutandis,* for the verbal syntax of gerunds and participles to follow without stipulation, it suffices that the free insertion of *ing,* which ignores the parenthesized material in (6), follows any syntactic operations (i.e., insertion occurs in phonological form).

My general proposal for lexical insertion developed from this study of *ing*—and in the light of other recent and ongoing work, especially Borer (to appear)—is that the following two principles account for all insertion of grammatical morphemes into 'post transformational' contexts or at two levels of a derivation:

(7) Deep Lexicalization (DL): Items associated with nonsyntactic, purely semantic features or principles of interpretation must satisfy lexical insertion conditions before transformations apply to domains containing them.[3]

(8) Phonological Lexicalization (PL): Items specified solely in terms of contextual and other noninterpretable features are inserted subsequent to any operation contributing to Logical Form.

To render DL and PL fully explicit, one must define the terms "purely semantic feature" and "interpretable feature" in (7) and (8). As in Chomsky (1965), "(purely) semantic feature" means not "contributes to meaning," but rather "plays no role in the syntactic component"; most syntactic features do indeed centrally contribute to meaning, as follows:[4]

In general I claim that universal grammar determines for all syntactic features what can be called host categories, which are for the most part unique: the host of PAST is I but not P or [Spec,A]; PLURAL occurs with the host D but not with P or V; ACTIVITY occurs with its host V but not with [Spec,P or D], and so on. Unmarked syntactic features always occur on their host; occurrence elsewhere under agreement, movement, and so forth, is permitted only by a principle of tree architecture I call "alternative realization" (Emonds 1987 and in preparation); in such positions syntactic features do not contribute to Logical Form. Thus, the 'interpretable syntactic features' in (8) are precisely those located on their UG-determined host categories.

With these definitions (7) and (8) taken together imply that an entry such as (6), whose only interpretable features consist of parenthesized (optional) semantic information, leads to a dual usage correlated with insertion either prior to transformational and other LF-visible syntactic operations (DL) or subsequent to them (PL).[5]

In this paper I will argue that a widely observed dual usage in the syntax of personal pronouns can also be correlated with whether the features of the pronouns are fixed prior to or subsequent to transformational/syntactic operations and suggest that this dual determination of syntactic features (i.e., of agreement with the antecedent) is in turn to be identified with deep versus phonological lexical insertion.

2 General properties of pronouns. Personal pronouns are forms whose entire content seems to be feature complexes of number, gender, person, case, and definiteness (e.g., *she, us,* etc.), the features that Chomsky (1981) terms '*phi*-features.' In line with Postal's (1968) classic treatise these feature complexes are Determiners or 'D' of the same class as demonstratives such as *this* and *that.* I also follow the proposal of Abney (1987) and take all noun phrases and pronouns as DP projections of D; a DP that contains more than a pronominal head D also contains an NP sister to D.[6]

These *phi*-features of D are archetypically both syntactic and central to interpretation (i.e., they determine the choice of antecedent). An unstipulated consequence of DL (7) and PL (8) in section 1 is that grammatical items such as pronouns, whose features are both syntactic and interpretable, are constrained by neither principle. Rather, such items remain available for any level that permits lexical insertion, which I take to be two: the pretransformational/syntactic level (conveniently termed "deep structure") and the post-transformational/syntactic level (termed "phonological form"). Thus, the theory of lexical insertion comprised of (7) and (8) predicts that pronouns should exhibit some kind of dual usage, correlated with whether they can be inserted at deep structure (and hence called deep pronouns) or in the phonological component (and hence called surface pronouns).

Studies on the relations between pronouns and their antecedents have indeed revealed two types of syntactic usage, which Reinhart (1983), probably the most astute research on the issue, calls free and bound forms. In what follows I will argue that these two usages are precisely those predicted by, respectively, deep and phonological feature determination and lexicalization. First, however, let us review a property shared by all pronouns and also some properties that differentiate bound and free pronouns without yet relating them to any theory of lexical insertion.

2.1 Extending Principle B. For purposes of discussing pronouns we may say that @ c-commands @′ if and only if the maximal XP headed by @ is a sister to a node dominating @′.[7]

Generative studies have long considered one established property of pronouns to be that DPs (more generally XPs) headed by proforms may not c-command their antecedent (Wasow 1979), as exemplified in (9).[8]

(9) a. *We told her_i that the teachers liked Mary_i.
b. *We told Mary_i that the teachers liked Mary_i.

Chomsky (1981:ch. 3) attributes this restriction on binding to the antecedent, not to the pronoun. From this point of view (9a, b) are analogous, since the co-indexed nouns in both violate his Principle C: a referring DP such as *Mary* cannot be c-commanded by a coreferential DP.

However, slightly varying (9b) renders it acceptable, while the same changes do not improve (9a):

(10) a. *We reminded her_i that the judges had chosen Mary's_i work.
b. We reminded Mary_i that the judges had chosen Mary's_i work.

Similar examples with inanimate antecedents can be constructed in which a lexical DP can be c-commanded by a coreferential noun-containing DP but not by a coreferential pronominal DP:

(11) a. A city_i is often thought to generate jobs around the city_i.
b. *It_i is often thought to generate jobs around the city_i.

(12) a. The guestrooms$_i$ should have the bathrooms for the guestrooms$_i$ nearby.
b. *They$_i$ should have the bathrooms for the guestrooms$_i$ nearby.

Some final examples where binding of a referring DP by a coreferential noun phrase and a coreferential pronoun produces different acceptabilities are given in (13)–(14):

(13) a. In our field, (the) syntacticians$_i$ cite (the) syntacticians$_i$.
b. *In our field, they$_i$ cite (the) syntacticians$_i$.

(14) a. The customer$_i$ seemed intimidated by the clerk, even before the customer$_i$ approached the counter.
b. *He$_i$ seemed intimidated by the clerk, even before the customer$_i$ approached the counter.

What seems to be transpiring is the following. There may well be some condition restricting binding of noun-containing lexical DPs as in (9b), but the blanket formulation provided by Principle C, which should exclude the (a) examples of (10)–(14), is too strong.[9] In addition to a revised Condition C (not a focus of concern here), a pronominal DP requires an antecedent, and this antecedent cannot be c-commanded by the pronoun. This latter restriction can easily be generalized to subsume Chomsky's Principle B as well. By Principle B a pronoun cannot have a c-commanding antecedent inside its 'Minimal Governing Category' (MGC), which is roughly the smallest constituent containing both the pronoun and a DP that stands in the grammatical relation of subject; for details see the discussion in Chomsky (1981: ch. 3). Putting these two conditions together yields the following:

(15) Antecedent Condition: A proform may not be in a c-commanding relation with its antecedent inside the proform's Minimal Governing Category.[10]

I have formulated (15) to cover not only pronominal DPs but also clausal proforms, whose adherence to (15) is exemplified in (16) and (17); in all these examples a c-command relation holds between the proforms and the antecedents.

(16) They encourage all [$_{MGC}$ who can afford [$_{IP}$ to]] [$_{IP}$ to visit Italy].

*[$_{MGC}$ They encourage all who can afford [$_{IP}$ to visit Italy] [$_{IP}$ to]].

(17) She said [$_{Si}$ the party was chic] only to guests [$_{MGC}$ who thought so$_i$ anyway].

*[$_{MGC}$ She said so$_i$ only to guests who thought [$_{Si}$ the party was chic] anyway].

Summarizing, the Antecedent Condition (15) replaces and generalizes Principle B of Chomsky (1981), subsuming the nonproblematic subcase of Principle C and an important condition on non-DP proforms as well. In section 3 below the Antecedent Condition will be generalized even farther.

2.2 Two types of pronouns. An interesting development in recent work on pronouns (Evans 1980, Reinhart 1983) has been the emergence of arguments for two fundamentally different types of DP antecedents for pronouns. These are exemplified in (18a) versus (18b–c):

(18) a. The ads [$_{VP}$ convinced (the) teenagers$_i$ that [$_S$ they$_i$ would stay in school]].

b. The ads [$_{VP}$ targeted (the) teenagers$_i$], so that [$_S$ they$_i$ would stay in school].

c. The ads [$_{VP}$ targeted (the) teenagers$_i$], but [$_S$ they$_i$ wouldn't stay in school].

Since the pronoun in (18a) is in a c-command relation with the antecedent DP, reversing the lexical content of the two DPs in (18a) violates (15); in (18b–c) there is no such c-command relation, and so the same procedure preserves acceptability (though it introduces the stilted style often associated with 'backwards pronominalization'):

(19) a. *The ads [$_{VP}$ convinced them$_i$ that [$_S$ (the) teenagers$_i$ would stay in school]].

b. ?The ads [$_{VP}$ targeted them$_i$], so that [$_S$ (the) teenagers$_i$ would stay in school].

c. ?The ads [$_{VP}$ targeted them$_i$], but [$_S$ (the) teenagers$_i$ wouldn't stay in school].

So far, the facts are as predicted by the Antecedent Condition (15); any antecedent relation it does not expressly forbid is permitted.

However, when the antecedents and pronominals in examples like (18) are varied in certain ways, it turns out that the c-command relation in (a) and the lack of it in (b–c) correlate with other differences, four of which will be introduced here and a fifth in later sections. Terminologically, we say that a pronominal DP is 'bound' when c-commanded by its antecedent as in (18a) and 'free' when not so c-commanded as in (18b–c).

(i) As brought out by Evans and Reinhart, when antecedents are quantified by *each* and *every,* a free pronoun must be plural while a bound pronoun is singular (and in some prescriptive usage must be; ! = excluded in such prescriptive usage).

(20) a. The ads [$_{VP}$ convinced every teenager$_i$ that [$_S$ {she$_i$/!they$_i$} (alone) would stay in school]].
b. The ads [$_{VP}$ targeted every teenager$_i$], so that [$_S$ {they$_i$ (all)/ *she$_i$} would stay in school].

And more clearly:

(20) c. *The ads targeted every teenager, but she didn't stay in school.[11]

(21) a. Did you satisfy each contestant that {he/!they} could win many prizes?
b. Did you satisfy each contestant, since {they/*he} could win many prizes?
c. Did you satisfy each contestant, and could {they/*he} win many prizes?

Tentatively, we say that a bound pronoun agrees syntactically with its antecedent (*each* and *every* being grammatically singular), whereas a free pronoun exhibits pragmatic agreement that reflects the fact that *each* and *every* imply plural cardinality (*John has {that /*each} weak heart*).

(ii) As also brought out by these authors, a DP quantified by *no* sometimes cannot serve as a pragmatic antecedent of a free pronoun, though it can uniformly serve as a syntactic antecedent of a bound pronoun. This test is easier to display with subject antecedents.

(22) a. No drivers were tested {while/on whether} they had been drinking.
b. *No drivers were tested, but they had been drinking.

(iii) Free pronouns alternate with 'epithets,' but bound pronouns do not.

(23) a. *Many drivers$_i$ were tested {while/on whether} the fools$_i$ had been drinking.[12]
b. Many drivers$_i$ were tested, but the fools$_i$ had been drinking.

(24) a. *We satisfied each contestant$_i$ that the sucker$_i$ could win many prizes.
b. We satisfied each contestant$_i$, since the suckers$_i$ could win many prizes.

(25) a. *The ads convinced the teenagers$_i$ that the layabouts$_i$ would stay in school.
b. The ads targeted the teenagers$_i$ so that the layabouts$_i$ would stay in school.

The pronominal properties of epithets have been examined in detail in a number of studies on the essentially equivalent construction in French (Milner 1978; Ruwet 1982,1990; Lamiroy 1992). Lamiroy (1992) concludes that the *Noms de Qualité* (epithets) are subject to Principle C—that is, they cannot be c-commanded by an antecedent, which is exactly the definitional characteristic of a free pronoun.[13] Thus, epithets share distribution with free pronouns, but not with bound ones.

(iv) French has two preverbal clitics *en* 'of/from+pronoun' and *y* 'to/at+pronoun' which license empty pronominal arguments and adjuncts of the form $[_{PP} [_P \emptyset] [_{DP} \emptyset]]$ or (for *en*) $[_{NP} \emptyset]$. These clitics exhibit no gender, number, and person features, presumably because the empty categories they license are not projections of D (the locus of *phi*-features), but rather are PPs and NPs. Usually, the antecedents of these clitics are inanimate DPs or NPs. Nonetheless, if specific conditions are fulfilled, these pronouns can refer back to animate antecedents; (26) gives some contrasting examples from Lamiroy (1985):

(26) a. Le frère$_k$ de Paul$_i$ pense que Marie en$_{i,*k}$ est amoureuse.
'The brother of Paul thinks that Mary thereof-is in love'
b. Le mari$_k$ d'Anne$_i$ est convaincu que Paul y$_{i,*k}$ pense toujours.
'The husband of Ann is convinced that Paul thereon-thinks still'

For purposes of exposition, we will speak of *y/en* as 'having antecedents' and 'being free' or 'being bound,' when rather the empty DP or NP arguments or adjuncts licensed by these clitics have antecedents and are free or bound.

The binding theory properties of these clitics have been discussed in perspicuous detail in a series of papers by Lamiroy (1985, 1991) and Ruwet (1990). These works focus on *en,* but Lamiroy (1985) mentions *y* in passing as having similar properties. Basically, an interesting dichotomy emerges if we separate the empty phrases licensed by *en,* like other pronouns, into those that are bound and those that are free, depending on whether their antecedents c-command them. As exemplified in (26), when *en* and *y* are free (not bound), they can refer back to human and other antecedents under loosely pragmatic conditions. Lamiroy (1985:note 6) points out that another type of free *en* permitting a human antecedent is the so-called partitive *en,* whose antecedent is an NP (under the DP hypothesis) and hence involves identity of sense rather than reference. In (27) the NP antecedent of *en* is italicized:

(27) $[_{DP}$ Un $[_{NP}$ *homme*]] en vaut un autre.
One man thereof-is-worth an other
'One man is as good as another'

Since under the DP hypothesis an NP does not c-command any material outside DP, binding theory principles, such as the Antecedent Condition (15), do not restrict an NP's ability to serve as an antecedent. (In passing, Lamiroy's appeal to identity of sense to exempt partitive *en* from the binding theory is thus unnecessary.)

The cases focused on by Lamiroy and Ruwet are those in which *en* is bound—in accord with (15), by a DP outside its Minimal Governing Category. It is Ruwet (1990) who establishes this class of cases, in contradiction to Lamiroy's earlier views; here, I will follow Lamiroy's (1992:56) subsequent reanalysis of Ruwet's paradigms. There are two subcases of bound *en* and *y* to be considered:

(a) "One can therefore retain that coreference is possible when [bound] *en* refers back to an inanimate DP, which one can represent by *en = de cela* 'of that/it'." [my translation, JE]. Two of Ruwet's crucial contrasts illustrate this restriction on bound *en:*

(28) a. *Joe$_i$ prévoit que les journaux {en$_i$ parleront/parleront de cela$_i$}.

'Joe predicts that the papers {thereof-speak/speak of that}.'

b. La constitution$_i$ prévoit qu'on pourra {en$_i$ modifier des parties /modifier des parties de cela$_i$}.
'The constitution foresees that one can {thereof-modify parts /modify parts of it}.'

(29) a. *Max$_i$ a suggéré à son médecin {d'en$_i$ parler/de parler de cela$_i$} à un spécialiste.
'Max suggested to his doctor {to thereof-speak/to speak of that} to a specialist.' (i.e., thereof = that = Max)

b. Ce beau paysage$_i$ suggère à Corot {d'en$_i$ faire/de faire de cela$_i$} plusieurs tableaux.
'That nice landscape suggests to Corot to {thereof-make/ make of that} several paintings.' (i.e., thereof = that = landscape)

As a first approximation, we can say that *en* and *y* license empty phrases that contain no marked (e.g., animate) *phi*-features and that antecedents of bound *en* and *y* must agree with this specification; in contrast, those of free *en* and y, as seen above, need not.

(b) There is nonetheless a circumscribed class of examples where animate antecedents bind *en* and *y*. However, the distribution of these antecedents is predicted by a general stylistic convention in French, which is especially characteristic of informal language: marked *phi*-features on an antecedent that are not contextually selected do not prevent agreement with pronominal DPs, which themselves exhibit no *phi*-feature contrasts, such as demonstrative *cela/ça* 'that.'

Lamiroy points out that exactly when *en* and *y* can be bound by animate DP, as in Ruwet's example (30a), these DP can also be pronominalized by *cela/ça,* 'that,' as in (30b). In these cases verbs such as *mériter,* 'deserve,' do not select animate subjects, so the animate subject can be pronominalized by *ça, en,* and so on. (In contrast, the animacy of the DP antecedents in (28) and (29) is selected by the agentive senses of *prévoir,* 'predict,' and *suggérer,* 'suggest,' and so prevents these pronominalizations.)

(30) a. Les intellectuels$_i$ ne méritent pas qu'on en$_i$ parle tant à la télé.
'Intellectuals don't deserve that one thereof-speaks so much on TV.'

b. Les intellectuels$_{i,}$ ça$_i$ ne mérite pas qu'on en$_i$ parle tant à la télé.
'The intellectuals, that doesn't deserve that one thereof-speaks so much on TV.'

Space prevents full discussion of the diverse examples that Ruwet and Lamiroy have constructed to demonstrate that *en* and *y* can be bound. Citing Blanche-Benveniste et al. (1984), Lamiroy illustrates that animate DP antecedents binding *en* are not selected as animates and can also be pronominalized (in French but not English) by a neuter demonstrative. For our purposes below, the stylistic convention on French pronominalization can be restated as follows:

(31) French Stylistics: A nonselected animacy feature on an antecedent may be ignored in determining agreement with pronouns lacking *phi*-feature contrasts (e.g., *ça, en, y,* etc.).

In light of (31) we can require that the empty phrases licensed by bound *en* or *y* have no marked *phi*-feature values and yet still agree with an antecedent that binds them. The only marked *phi*-features tolerated on that antecedent are then the unselected animacy features allowed by (31), features that are ignored. Consequently, animacy features (which are redundantly specified for non-third person pronouns) may bind *en* only with certain predicates. If a predicate selects an animate argument, this argument must agree with any pronoun it binds and hence cannot bind *en* or *y*. As seen earlier, an antecedent of a free *en* or *y* need not agree in this way.

We have now reviewed four ways in which the antecedents of free and bound pronouns differ. In the next section we see how these properties, and, in addition, one other of free pronouns, can be accounted for by the theory of Deep and Phonological Lexicalization presented in section 1; the guiding idea is that free pronouns are inserted prior to transformations and bound pronouns remain empty categories at this level.[14] In developing these ideas we will also generalize the Antecedent Condition (15).

3 Free pronouns as deep pronouns. This section argues that the properties of free pronouns (and epithets) result from their *phi*-features[15] and crucially from their antecedents being specified before transformations apply on the syntactic domains in which the pronouns occur; in classic generative terms, it argues that the *phi*-features and antecedents of free pronouns are present in deep structure.

If we combine the general Antecedent Condition (15) on pronouns (my extension of Chomsky's Principle B) with the defining characteristic of free (= nonbound) pronouns, we arrive at (32):

(15) Antecedent Condition: A proform may not be in a c-commanding relation with its antecedent inside the proform's MGC.

(32) A free pronoun and its antecedent may not be in a c-command relation.

I now make a crucial assumption for this section, whose justification is the material of section 4: that bound pronouns and their *phi*-features are not present pretransformationally; rather, at the pretransformational or deep level, a bound pronoun is simply an empty D with no features.[16] Under this assumption, and reinterpreting (32) as a condition on determining antecedents, we arrive at (33):

(33) A pronoun whose antecedent and *phi*-features are determined pretransformationally (that is, present at deep structure) cannot be in a c-command relation with this antecedent.[17]

The common behavior of epithets and free pronouns is combined by restating (33) as (34):

(34) Nonempty DPs lacking independent reference (= deep pronouns and epithets) with pretransformationally specified antecedents cannot be in a c-command relation with these antecedents.

One way to appreciate (34) more fully is to reflect on the usually vague notions of 'linguistic' versus 'pragmatic' antecedent. In general there are no syntactic relations between elements that do not stand in a c-command relation, certainly not if such elements are nonadjacent. Thus, it is plausible to restrict the relation of 'linguistic antecedence' to being by definition 'syntactic' or equivalently a subcase of c-command, since antecedence is par excellence a relation at a distance. 'Pragmatic antecedence' of a pronoun is then extended to coreference with any actually referring DP (whether linguistically present or not; e.g., ostention, split antecedents, etc.), provided that (i) the pronoun and the DP stand in no c-command relation and (ii) that the pronoun's *phi*-features do not conflict with the DPs actual reference. In this light (34) can be reformulated as follows:

(35) A nonempty DP in a pretransformational (deep) structure that lacks independent reference must have a pragmatic antecedent.

Further reflection suggests that (35) reduces to a requirement that a nonempty DP either has independent reference or does not (a purely logical dichotomy) and that if it does not, then it has a 'dependent' reference, namely, a pragmatically determined (nonsyntactic) antecedent. Conceptualized in this way, (35) is simply a subcase of what Chomsky (1986) terms 'Full Interpretation'; in particular, a DP specified for features must have some kind of reference.[18]

We are now in a position to understand the four paradigms characteristic of free pronouns discussed in section 2.2. First, the behavior of epithets has already been accounted for in (34) by the term 'lacking independent reference.' Second, when a DP quantified by *no* as in (22) fails to establish a reference in a universe of discourse, then it *a fortiori* cannot serve as a pragmatic antecedent. Third, DPs quantified by *each* and *every* can refer only to sets of plural cardinality in a universe of discourse and so can be pragmatic antecedents only of plural pronouns. Fourth, the French preverbal clitics *en* and *y*, which lack *phi*-features and are generally compatible with third person singular inanimates, nonetheless also tolerate animate antecedents, provided these clitics are free (not c-commanded by these antecedents). This is explained as follows: a pragmatic antecedent of a free pronoun must be compatible with the pronoun's *phi*-features, but, since *en* and *y* have no such features, this restriction does not limit the range of their antecedents. Thus, the reference of the free clitics is demonstrably looser than the inanimacy requirement imposed on bound *en* and *y*, which will be discussed in section 4.

A fifth contrast between free and bound pronouns amply illustrated in Reinhart (1983:section 7.2) clearly confirms the hypothesis that (only) free pronouns are specified for their *phi*-features and antecedents in deep structure. Two pairs of her examples follow:[19]

(36) a. People from LA adore it, and so do people from New York.

b. LA is adored by its residents, and so is New York.

(37) a. Zelda thought about Siegfried on his wedding day, and about Felix too.
b. Zelda bought Siegfried a present on his wedding day, and Felix too.

As observed by Reinhart, in these and variations on these structures the pronouns (*it* in (36) and *his* in (37)) in the understood ellipted clauses of the (a) examples unambiguously refer to an antecedent in the left-hand clause (respectively *LA* and *Siegfried*). In contrast, in the ambiguous (b) examples the antecedents may equally well be the overt DPs in the right-hand clause (respectively *New York* and *Felix*).

We are concerned in this section with free pronouns, which means the (a) examples of (36) and (37); the (b) examples of bound pronouns are discussed in the next section. According to the analysis here, (only) free pronouns as in the (a) examples have pretransformationally determined antecedents and *phi*-features. Thus, when at some post-transformational level Chomsky's (1981) Logical Form is computed, the contents of the left-hand clauses that are transferred to the ellipted ones necessarily include the already fixed references of the deep free pronouns of the (a) examples. Consequently, under the natural assumption that the reference of pronouns may not change during a derivation, the proposed model of deep pronouns correctly predicts that examples like (36a) and (37a) are unambiguous.

I conclude that free personal pronouns are precisely those whose antecedents and *phi*-features are present in deep structure, prior to any transformational or other syntactic computation. In addition both free pronouns and epithets must have pragmatic (i.e., nonsyntactic) antecedents, which is equivalent under Full Interpretation to compensating for their lack of independent reference. Then, as Deep Lexicalization (7) specifies, their required association with a nonsyntactic interpretation guarantees that lexicalization of a free pronoun precedes transformations. As further explained in note 3, such a non-syntactic interpretation can be due either to a parenthesized specification in the entries of the pronouns or to some general interpretive calculation. Thus, 'free pronouns' are accurately termed 'deep pronouns.'[20]

In order to obtain the results of this section it has been consistently assumed that bound pronouns are Ds that not only are lexically empty but whose *phi*-features and antecedents are also absent prior to transformations applying to the domains that contain them. The statements of this section would otherwise fail to hold in unqualified fashion. The final section will provide evidence for this crucial assumption in three ways: (i) by showing how surface insertion of bound pronouns is a natural prediction of the dual lexicalization theory of section 1, (ii) by explanations for the five properties of bound pronouns brought out in this and previous sections, and (iii) by a natural account of distributional properties of resumptive and other pronouns with obligatory antecedents.

4 Bound pronouns as surface pronouns. By definition bound pronominal DPs are c-commanded by their antecedents; by the Antecedent Condition (15) such an antecedent is outside the pronoun's Minimal Governing Category. By the crucial assumption of section 3, bound pronouns are empty Ds, unspecified for *phi*-features and antecedents prior to the operation of the syntactic component. It therefore remains (i) to state how the syntactic component specifies bound pronouns for features, antecedents, and phonological realization, and (ii) to independently justify both the crucial assumption of section 3 and any formulation of (i).

To this end let us return to Reinhart's examples (36b) and (37b), which contain bound pronouns:

(36) b. LA is adored by its residents, and so is New York.

(37) b. Zelda bought Siegfried a present on his wedding day, and Felix too.

According to the crucial assumption, the bound pronouns *its* in (36b) and *his* in (37b) are unspecified Ds prior to transformations and hence prior to computing Logical Form. Since bound pronouns are by definition c-commanded by their antecedents and are also subject to the Antecedent Condition (15), they must obtain syntactic features and antecedents by a principle such as (38):

(38) Pronoun Binding (PB): An empty D may receive *phi*-features and referential index only from those DPs c-commanding it and exterior to its MGC.[21]

In the examples of (36) and (37) other LF-interpretive processes, which we can lump together as 'VP-Interpretation' (VPI), transfer the contents of the left-hand clauses onto the right-hand ellipted structures. Now, suppose that PB and VPI freely apply in either order. If PB precedes VPI, then the interpretations of the ellipted clauses in (36b) and (37b) will contain references back to *LA* and *Siegfried* respectively (so-called 'strict identity'); if VPI precedes PB, then the interpretations will instead contain references back to *NY* and *Felix* (so-called 'sloppy identity'). In this way the crucial assumption about the empty status of bound pronouns in section 3 is independently justified, since assigning antecedents not at deep structure but in the course of a derivation correctly accounts for the ambiguities in (36b), (37b), and Reinhart's many similar examples. These ambiguous examples contrast with the unambiguous (36a) and (37a), in which the pragmatic antecedents are assigned at deep structure before VPI may apply.

The final step in specifying bound pronouns consists in the lexical insertion of their phonological forms. Deep lexicalization is ruled out, not because bound pronouns fall under PL (8) (on the contrary their *phi*-features are eminently interpretable, as we have just seen), but rather because of (35); that is, lexicalized pronouns are required to have pragmatic (non-c-commanding) antecedents. Nor should Pronoun Binding (38) itself subsume lexicalization, because PB applies in either order with interpretive principles of VPI and does not always entail a phonetically overt output.[22] Moreover, in the model of lexicalization assumed here, the only two levels for insertion are the deep (pretransformational) level and within the phonological component. Thus, on both counts, bound personal pronouns must be lexicalized in the phonological component (the level of PL), and are aptly termed "surface pronouns."

Pronoun Binding (38) and Phonological Lexicalization (8) are further supported by the fact that they correctly account for the four properties of bound pronouns discussed in section 2.2. A DP quantified by *each* or *every* is grammatically singular and so by the identity of *phi*-features required in (38) can only bind a singular pronoun. For the same reason any DP of the form *no* + NP, whether or not it has pragmatic reference, can serve as a bound pronoun's antecedent, since any filled DP has *phi*-features. Epithets do not alternate with bound pronouns because PB, being a purely syntactic principle, cannot introduce the lexical contents of such items. Finally, since the empty pronominal DPs and NPs licensed by French *en* and *y* are incompatible with PB imposing a +ANIMATE specification (thus also excluding first and second person features), the only antecedents that can bind them are either inanimates or those whose animate features may be ignored because of Convention (31).[23]

This analysis of bound pronouns is additionally confirmed by the simplicity with which it accommodates paradigms discussed in Dougherty (1969:note 13). He observes that in several contexts personal pronouns have an obligatory antecedent in a fixed structural position. The italicized antecedent-pronoun pairs in (39) through (41) exemplify such constructions:[24]

(39) Verb Phrase idioms:
hold one's breath, drop one's guard, make one's way, lose one's marbles, lose one's temper, etc.
Mary convinced *Bill* not to drop {*his*/**her*} guard.

(40) English tag questions:
a. *Mary* should vaccinate Sam, shouldn't {*she*/**he*}?
b. *Each change* will bother them, won't {*it*/**they*}?

(41) Dislocation constructions:
a. *Kids like that,* someone ought to control *them.*
b. I told *her* about the movie, *that friend of yours.*

Resumptive pronoun constructions, more numerous in languages other than English, also fall under this rubric. To my knowledge the antecedent in all such constructions c-commands the pronoun. That is:

(42) A pronoun with an obligatory antecedent in a fixed structural position must be bound.

This descriptive generalization fits with the dichotomy proposed in this study; namely, any pronoun with an obligatory antecedent in a fixed structural position is a 'surface pronoun' whose source is an empty deep structure D. The present framework thus has an exceptionless property: deep free pronouns never have obligatory antecedents in stipulated fixed postions. Further, by deriving constructions as in (39) through (41) from structures containing not pronouns but empty and featureless D, they are assimilated to all others with bound pronouns; these idiomatic and resumptive Ds all receive their features and antecedents automatically through the standard application of Pronoun Binding (38) and are regularly spelled out in the phonological component like other bound pronouns.

The common treatment of idiomatic and other bound pronouns by PB solves a problem of how to lexically represent idioms as in (39). The idioms can be listed as deep structure (pretransformational) fully specified VPs of the form *hold* $[_{DP}$ *Ø] breath, lose* $[_{DP}$ *Ø] marbles,* etc.; no special device for idioms such as a "lexical variable" is needed. Rather, these idioms need only contain stipulated empty determiner constants akin to constants that appear in other idiomatic expressions such as *bury*$[_{D}$ *the] hatchet, take* $[_{D}$ *a] powder, keep* $[_{D}$ *Ø] house, drop* $[_{D}$ *Ø] anchor, hold* $[_{D}$ *Ø] court,* etc.[25]

Finally, the present analysis of bound pronouns suggests a tantalizing analysis of English tag questions. It is a curious fact that this construction, for all the attention it receives as an exemplum of syntactic regularity and argumentation in elementary classes on generative grammar, has never been elegantly characterized in terms of Universal Grammar. However, if as argued here a bound pronoun is an empty D early in a derivation, and under the plausible assumption that English tags contain an empty VP that is interpreted like other ellipted VPs, we may characterize the genesis of an English tag question by (43):

(43) Right-adjoin WH+I+(Neg) to a projection of I.

An immediate advantage is that this hypothesis resembles tag question formations of other languages, which often simply right-adjoin a Neg or assertive morpheme or a combination of both in addition to the same rising intonation on the adjoined material as in English. WH in (43) represents rising intonation and also triggers I inversion in the English tag. The Universal Grammar prototype for tag questions is plausibly right-adjunction to I^{i} of [WH,(@),(Neg)], where @ is some assertive element. The English version (43) chooses to represent the assertive pole by copying the finiteness category I, which then gives rise to the following complex of syntactic consequences.

Even weaker versions of structure-preservation assume that the only bar notation categories that may be adjoined to a phrase (a projection of I) are necessarily maximal phrases, so that the directive (43) to adjoin WH+I+(Neg) can be satisfied only by adjoining a full XP *containing WH+I+(Neg)* to I′ or IP. Since such an adjunction is not structure preserving in the stronger sense (Emonds 1985:ch.3), it must be a root operation, and indeed tag questions are a quintessential root phenomenon. By a plausible reading of Economy of Representation any such adjoined XP should be minimal, that is, a CP=WH+IP projected from the copied I itself. Since the obligatory DP and VP constituents of such a transformationally generated IP are inaccessible to deep structure lexicalization, they must be empty. Moreover, this DP and VP will remain unlicensed and uninterpretable—unless rules of LF-interpretation and/or late lexicalization can rescue them. But, indeed, if the projected IP is adjoined low enough, to I′ rather than to the original root IP, the main clause subject DP will c-command the empty DP, so that Pronoun Binding (38) can provide the latter with both features and antecedent. Similarly, the interpretive principle VPI can license the covert VP in the tag, so that finally the entire transformationally projected IP is well formed. (44) exemplifies the structure for (40a) prior to I-to-C movement in the tag.

(44)

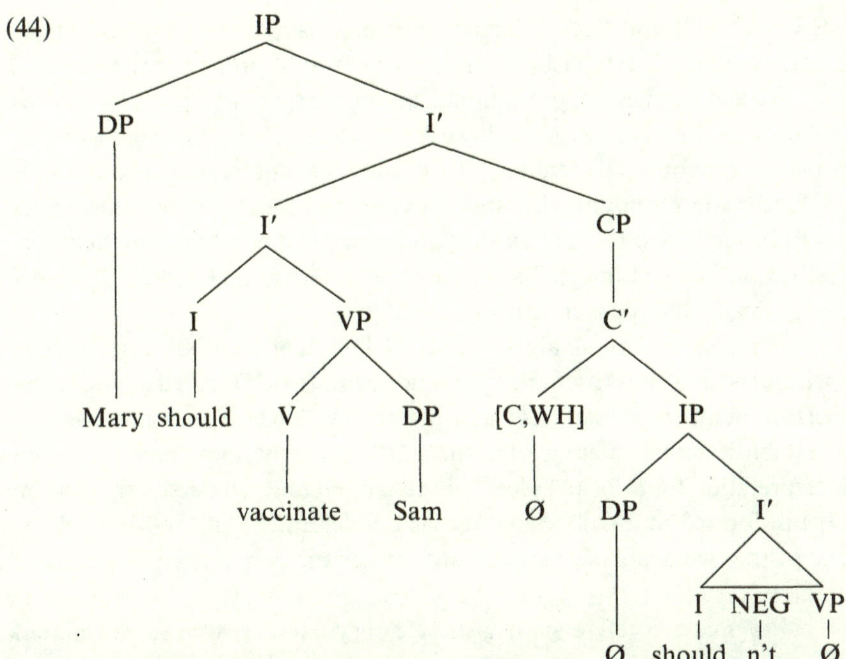

The empty DP in (44) is specified for its *phi*-features and antecedent in the root clause subject by the regular application of Pronoun Binding (38) and, like other bound pronouns, is later spelled out by lexical insertion in PF. So a second advantage of analyzing bound pronouns as underlying empty D is that Pronoun Binding accounts for the subject pronouns in English tag questions without stipulation. Consequently, for the first time in the history of generative grammar, the English tag rule can be formulated as a plausible subcase of a Universal Grammar option and one that fully conforms to the general principles regulating the transformational component.

5 Overview of mechanisms in the personal pronoun system. The results of this study can be summarized as follows. Studies of bound morphemes (derivational and inflectional morphology and clitics) and of other grammatical elements, reviewed in section 1, strongly suggest two quite distinct levels for lexical insertion (= satisfaction of contextual restrictions), one pretransformational (at 'deep structure') and the other post-transformational (in the phonological component). While many grammatical elements including personal pronouns can in principle be inserted at either level, two restrictive principles regulating insertion can be formulated as DL (7) and PL (8). These principles have been justified by their predictive abilities established outside the realm of pronominalization.

Recent studies of pronominalization, particularly those of Evans (1980) and Reinhart (1983), have revealed two distinct behaviors of personal pronouns, depending on whether an antecedent c-commands (= binds) the pronoun. This study argues that these different behaviors are to be explained by the fact that pronouns, like other grammatical formatives, are indeed inserted at two different derivational levels, pretransformationally and post-transformationally.

Personal pronouns are D-heads of DPs that lack NP sisters. They spell out sets of interpretable syntactic features of D called *phi*-features (person, number, gender, case, and definiteness), which in themselves fail to establish actual reference for their DP. Since the requirement of Full Interpretation for DPs includes their actual reference, a personal pronoun D is ill-formed unless D is marked as coreferential with another DP by one of the two available mechanisms, pragmatic coreference or syntactic binding.

Pragmatic coreference triggers a nonsyntactic search for a referent among possible referents of DPs, as restricted by the pronoun's *phi*-features. Hence, by DL (7) any pronominal D with a pragmatic antecedent must be inserted pretransformationally. Until now pragmatic coreference has been a loose term thought to cover different notions such as ostention, shared universes of discourse, and perhaps intersentential relations. But here pragmatic coreference or antecedent of a pronoun is widened and unrestricted: it can include the possible reference of any DP in the language, except those in a c-command relation with the pronoun or those whose reference conflicts with a pronoun's *phi*-features; cf. (34) and note 18. DP epithets, which also lack actual reference, search for their antecedents in exactly the same way. Thus, any pronoun that respects the non-c-command condition has in this sense a pragmatic antecedent and is a deep free pronoun.[26]

The other way for a pronoun to satisfy Full Interpretation (i.e., to acquire actual reference) is through the syntactic principle of Pronoun Binding (38). Reinhart's (1983:ch. 7) bound pronouns, as well as in those constructions exemplified in (39) through (42), are generated in this way. A central claim of this study is that these bound pronouns are entirely empty D categories in pretransformational (deep) structure, devoid of *phi*-features and coreferential indices at this level. This is expressed directly in the formulation of PB, which applies only to empty Ds. Consequently, a bound pronoun can only be lexicalized post-transformationally and is therefore called a surface bound pronoun.

In the light of this system the Antecedent Condition (15) can be seen as a theorem. Since the only sources for pronominal antecedents are Pronoun Binding and pragmatic coreference (the latter incompatible with c-command relations), the only sanctioned c-command relation between a pronoun and its antecedent is that of PB; the Antecedent Condition simply reproduces the c-command relations excluded by PB. Pronoun Binding, which subsumes Chomsky's Principle B, is the only pronoun-particular syntactic principle of Universal Grammar. Moreover, it is freely ordered with respect to VP Interpretation, a result that sheds some light on the relation between syntactic and LF-interpretive processes.

A central tenet of this system's descriptive adequacy is the condition on pragmatic antecedence (34), which prohibits a c-command relation between a pronoun and a pragmatic antecedent. Taking c-command as the broadest form of 'syntactic relation,' one can ask why pragmatic antecedence must exclude overlap with syntactic relatedness. Reinhart (1983: section 7.2) discusses this issue in terms of Gricean principles, although in my view unsatisfactorily. The exclusion of pragmatic antecedents in just those structures where binding is possible seems to me more likely because of the way Economy of Representation holds at a deep level—an empty, featureless D should be structurally more economical than a specified and spelled-out one, if both contribute the same way to propositional content. I leave for further investigation this conjecture that the bifurcation between pragmatic and syntactic antecedents results from considerations of economy.

All the empirical differences between bound and free pronouns discussed in sections 2.2, 3, and 4 follow without stipulation from the differing conditions and levels of derivation that define pragmatic versus syntactic (c-commanding) antecedents. In the interests of concreteness I terminate by recalling how two of these differences are predicted.

(i) The actual reference of an English DP quantified by *each* or *every* is plural, but its *phi*-feature (as shown by agreement patterns) is singular. Thus, a free pronoun with such a pragmatic DP antecedent must be plural, while a pronoun bound by this kind of DP may be (and in prescriptive usage must be) singular.

(ii) The different behaviors of bound and free French *en* and *y* follow entirely from their lack of *phi*-features and the differing mechanisms governing pragmatic and syntactic antecedents. In pragmatic antecedence the *phi*-features of the pronoun restrict choice of antecedent, so the complete lack of *phi*-features on these clitics imposes no restriction. In syntactic antecedence the *phi*-features of the antecedent are imposed on the pronoun, so the incompatibility of these pronouns with *phi*-features limits their distribution. Thus are explained the differing properties of bound and free *en* discovered in Ruwet (1990) and Lamiroy (1985, 1991).

NOTES

* I first started to think seriously about appropriate levels for types of lexical insertion when reading Carlos Otero's proposal for a post-transformational dictionary (Otero 1976). While I did not agree that all morphemes should be associated with syntactic categories only at surface structure (as then conceived), his work did convince me that many if not all of the grammatical bound morphemes necessarily must be (e.g., Romance clitics and verbal inflections). It is a pleasure to be able to set down here the ideas that have developed from this source in a volume dedicated to Otero's contributions. Carlos was a constant source of creative and challenging ideas during our decade spent as colleagues in Los Angeles in both areas where we shared so much, generative grammar and radical politics.

I wish to thank Miori Kubo for carefully reading a draft of this work and suggesting several improvements.

1. The importance of these notations in language-particular statements is explained in Chomsky and Halle (1968).

2. +N stands for N or A. That is, using the notion of Lieber, Selkirk, and Williams that an English suffix is the head of a word, then *ing* is a noun or an adjective bound to a preceding verb, which together with that verb forms respectively a noun or an adjective.

3. In Emonds (1985:ch. 4) I argue that activation of purely semantic interpretive processes—for example, the principle that optionally assigns the theta role of agent to an animate subject of an activity verb—require that any lexical item in that category be present at deep structure. Thus, Deep Lexicalization (7) is required not only for items lexically specified for particular purely semantic features, but equally well for syntactic items whose category contributes to triggering a nonsyntactic principle of interpretation. As discussed in section 4, the determination of a pronoun's or epithet's pragmatic antecedent is such a principle.

4. DL (7) thus reflects a kind of modular clustering of nonsyntactic information and processing at deep structure, in line with characterizing it as an 'interface' with conceptual structure in Chomsky (1993).

5. The notion that certain uses of grammatical formatives (= 'closed class items') are to be inserted subsequent to transformational and other syntactic operations on a domain has been present throughout the history of generative grammar. The earliest and perhaps most widely accepted proposal of this type is Chomsky's (1957) classic *do*-insertion into clauses whose finiteness (tense) features are morphologically unsupported by a modal; cf. example (2) in the text. Stockwell, Schachter, and Partee (1969) utilize a 'second lexical pass' for inserting many closed class items. Rizzi (1978:137) argues that the choice of perfect auxiliary in Italian depends on a prior syntactic operation termed restructuring. Otero (1976) is a broad extension of post-transformational lexical insertion. My own advocacy of extending and systematizing late insertion begins in Emonds (1985:chs. 4 and 5).

6. Within this framework the NP containing the noun is the locus of the Fregean 'sense' of the DP; in terms of Milner (1978:ch. 1) the N expresses the 'virtual reference' of the DP. The D is the locus of (co-)reference (Milner's 'actual reference'). According to Milner, the actual reference of a DP consists of the virtual reference of the NP being mapped into actual reference by the features of D; it then follows that a D lacking a sister NP will not have actual reference unless either deixis intervenes or some principle of coreference links D with some other actually referring D′; in other words a bare pronoun (D) lacks actual or independent reference.

7. Since XP by this definition of c-command is a nonhead, it is either a root (and the issue of c-command of material outside XP does not arise), or the node immediately dominating XP will necessarily branch. Hence, the definition in the text is equivalent for our purposes to the more commonly cited one of Reinhart's.

8. A pronoun may c-command a coreferential DP, but the pronoun's antecedent must be established independently of this latter DP: *Though the mayor$_i$ was rich, he$_i$ thought that the mayor$_i$ wouldn't be safe in a riot.*

9. A more detailed critique of Principle C can be found in Milner (1990). As he observes, Principle C is an interesting attempt to subsume probably different properties under a single principle. I claim that one of these properties, that a pronoun cannot c-command its antecedent, is more properly factored out and combined in (15) with Principle B.

A particular inadequacy of Principle C is presented by sets of examples like the following. I find no difference between (i) and (ii), although C allows (i) but not (ii).

(i) We had to introduce Mary's guest to Mary at the station.
(ii) We had to introduce Mary to Mary's guest at the station.

In contrast, the Antecedent Condition, subsuming B and part of C, correctly predicts (iii) through (vi), where *her* refers to *Mary:*

(iii) We had to introduce Mary's guest to her at the station.
(iv) We had to introduce her guest to Mary at the station.
(v) *We had to introduce her to Mary's guest at the station.
(vi) We had to introduce Mary to her guest at the station.

10. Researchers seduced by modern logic consistently 'discover' syntactic structures that reproduce logical formulations, such as quantifier-variable notation (i.e., where O is a quantifier, Ox $[_{Proposition} \ldots x \ldots]$). Since logic was invented by reflective speakers of natural language, but was never arrived at by investigation of linguistic properties, it seems more cogent to try to understand what properties of natural language logicians were unconsciously extrapolating from. If we take pronouns as natural language prototypes of 'variables,' antecedents and the material surrounding them as 'operators,' and Minimal Governing Categories as 'propositions,' we see that quantifier-variable notation is nothing but a simplified schematization of (15). From this point of view the essential characteristic of an 'operator position' is not in being adjoined to a proposition (i.e., an MGC) in some tree-based fashion, but simply in being exterior to the MGC in any syntactically sanctioned position whatsoever. This is natural enough, if we grant that early logicians had no notion of linguistic tree structure, but only the rougher intuition of 'exterior to a propositionlike unit.'

11. In my view subordinate adverbial clauses can be adjoined to trees at different heights, so that in some marginal readings they seem to act like sisters to V or (in the other direction) sisters to S rather than to a phrasal projection of V. Hence, the singular pronoun in (20b) is not sharply excluded.

12. See note 11. When an adverbial clause is separated by a comma, it is a sister to the modified S; consequently, the subject of such an adverbial clause is not bound by the main clause subject and can be a free pronoun or an epithet: *Many drivers$_i$ were tested, even though the fools$_i$ had been drinking.*

13. Lamiroy suggests that epithets and ordinary nouns differ with respect to Principle C in adverbial clauses. But if the c-commanding DPs are held constant, there is no difference. The following sentences are acceptable if the adverbial clause is a daughter of S·(for example, if set off by a comma and an emphatic such as *just*) and otherwise marginal.

(i) Jim will go (, just) if {Jim, the son of a gun} feels good.
(ii) John was hit by Mary (, just) before {John, the drunk} got a chance to get up.

The following sentences are not acceptable because they violate the Antecedent Condition (15).

(iii) *He$_i$ will go if Jim$_i$ feels good.
(iv) *He$_i$ was hit by Mary before John$_i$ got a chance to stand up.

14. Stevenson (1990:127) also suggests that the dichotomy imposed by c-command itself defines the linguistically significant class of free pronouns with pragmatic antecedents (those not c-commanded by their antecedent): "One possibility is that the processor is sensitive to the c-command relation. A pronoun that is c-commanded by an NP will trigger an initial search in the Discourse Representation Structure. A pronoun that is not c-commanded by an NP will trigger a search in the mental model."

15. Since at least some abstract case features are not assigned prior to transformations, the *phi-* features present prior to transformations may fail to include case. Such case features play no role in determining antecedents and hence are irrelevant to our concerns in this study.

16. Since semantic roles ('theta-roles') are assigned on the basis of deep structure information, this assumption implies that semantic roles can be assigned to DPs that are unspecified for their content at the deep or pretransformational level. While this presents no formal problems, it probably undermines an overly intuitive conceptualization of deep structure in terms of 'propositional content.'

17. If trees are considered to be constructed 'from the bottom up' as in Chomsky (1991), then (33) is a condition blocking any coreference during this process between two DPs, one of which is specified (only) for *phi*-features. In order to corefer a DP has to be specified either for no features (in which case it may qualify for bound pronoun status, as determined in section 4) or for more than *phi*-features, either by being a fully specified DP that can escape Principle C effects (cf. note 9) or by being in a context where the feature ANAPHOR is a possibility.

18. These successive reformulations are not meant to conceal the fact that they each impose a restriction on tree construction, namely, a personal pronoun whose features and coreference are specified in deep structure cannot come to stand in a c-command relation with its antecedent. Bound pronouns are then precisely those personal pronouns that escape this stricture.

19. In examples (36) and (37) we are not concerned with readings of the pronouns established outside the sentences at issue, which should be taken as isolated discourses.

20. Deep lexical pronouns are free, but the converse does not hold. Like other Romance clitics, French *en* and *y* license empty, that is nonlexicalized, pronominal DPs and NPs. As the discussion in the text has shown, these can under appropriate conditions, be free or bound.

21. This formulation draws on Reinhart's (1983:158–59) co-indexing rule (34b). However, the notion of an empty D representing bound pronouns, which is the key concept in this study, is absent in Reinhart's analysis.

As indicated in note 15, abstract case features are not a concern in this study. Since these features are generally assigned after transformations apply, we can assume they are assigned after (38) and so are not yet included in the *phi*-features of DP.

As is well known, antecedents are not uniquely determined; cf. the multiple ambiguity of *Pat said to Chris in front of Kim that she could describe him better than he could.* The formulation of Pronoun Binding affects this.

22. The analysis of pronouns here supports some aspects of the linear model of van Riemsdijk and Williams (1981), since a syntactic process with phonological effects (PB) follows a purely interpretive principle (VPI) in deriving a logical form from an underlying structure.

23. Recall that the stylistic convention for French pronominalization of all types, including the use of demonstratives, is that a +ANIMATE specification of an antecedent may be ignored in any position where +ANIMATE is not selected. Thus, as the examples of Lamiroy and Ruwet discussed in section 2.2 show, *en* and *y* may be bound by animate DPs as long as the animateness does not result from selection.

24. Possibly, English reflexive pronouns are simply a special case of (39), in which the idiomatic noun head *self* is allowed to appear freely in any VP-internal position.

25. The object nouns in these idioms are singular count nouns, and hence in English a determiner of some sort is required. The lexical entries of the idioms license the D as empty, definite, indefinite, of DP form, or in principle as any other element permitted in this position.

The empty DP in the idioms of (39) are additionally marked as requiring that antecedents be chosen within a strictly local domain, perhaps the same domain in which the anaphors subject to Principle A of Chomsky's binding theory are bound; how to represent the locality of antecedents for anaphors and other locally bound elements is not our concern here.

26. A pronoun with a 'split antecedent' as in *Mary told John that nobody would harm them* is a free pronoun, since c-command is not defined; there is no 'XP headed by the antecedent' that can c-command anything.

REFERENCES

Abney, S. 1987. *The English Noun Phrase in its Sentential Aspect.* Ph.D. Dissertation. MIT.

Blanche-Benveniste, C., J. Deulofeu, J. Stéfanini, and K. van den Eynde. 1984. *Pronom et syntaxe, l'approche pronominale et son application au français.* Paris: Selaf.

Borer, H. 1984. *Parametric Syntax: Case Studies in Semitic and Romance Languages.* Dordrecht: Foris.

Borer, H. To appear. *Parallel Morphology.* Cambridge: MIT Press.

Chomsky, N. 1957. *Syntactic Structures.* The Hague: Mouton.

Chomsky, N. 1965. *Aspects of the Theory of Syntax.* Cambridge: MIT Press.

Chomsky, N. 1981. *Lectures on Government and Binding.* Dordrecht: Foris.

Chomsky, N. 1986. *Knowledge of Language: Its Nature, Origins, and Use.* New York: Praeger.

Chomsky, N. 1991. Some Notes on Economy of Derivations and Representations. In *Principles and Parameters in Comparative Grammar.* R. Freidin, ed. Cambridge: MIT Press.

Chomsky, N. 1993. A Minimalist Program for Linguistic Theory. In *The View from Building 20: Papers in Linguistics in Honor of Sylvain Bromberger.* K. Hale and S. J. Keyser, eds. Cambridge: MIT Press.

Chomsky, N., and M. Halle. 1968. *The Sound Pattern of English.* New York: Harper and Row.

Dougherty, R. 1969. An Interpretive Theory of Pronominal Reference. *Foundations of Language* 5:488–519.

Emonds, J. 1985. *A Unified Theory of Syntactic Categories.* Dordrecht: Foris.

Emonds, J. 1987. The Invisible Category Principle. *Linguistic Inquiry* 18:613–632.

Emonds, J. 1991. The Autonomy of the (Syntactic) Lexicon and Syntax: Insertion Conditions for Inflectional and Derivational Morphemes. In *Interdisciplinary Approaches to Language. Essays in honor of S. Y. Kuroda.* C. Georgopoulos and R. Ishihara, eds. 1991. Dordrecht: Kluwer.

Emonds, J. In preparation. The Distance between Romance Clitics and their Phrasal Gaps.

Evans, G. 1980. Pronouns. *Linguistic Inquiry* 11:337–362.

Kubo, M. 1992. *Japanese Syntactic Structures and their Constructional Meanings.* Ph.D. Dissertation. MIT.

Lamiroy, B. 1985. Binding Properties of French *en.* In *Interdisciplinary Approaches to Language: Essays in honor of S. Y. Kuroda.* C. Georgopoulos and R. Ishihara, eds. 1991. Dordrecht: Kluwer.

Lamiroy, B. 1991. Coréférence et Référence Disjointe: Les Deux Pronoms *en. Travaux Linguistiques* 22:41–67.

Lamiroy, B. 1992. Le Pronom *en* et les Noms de Qualité. In *De la Musique à la Linguistique. Hommages à Nicolas Ruwet.* L. Tasmowski and A. Zribi-Hertz, eds. Ghent: Communication and Cognition.

Milner, J.-C. 1978. *De la Syntaxe à l'Interprétation.* Paris: Le Seuil.

Milner, J.-C. 1990. Some Remarks on Principle C. In *Binding in Romance: Essays in Honor of Judith McA'Nulty.* A.-M. diSciullo and A. Rochette, eds. Ottawa: Canadian Linguistic Association.

Otero, C. 1976. The Dictionary in a Generative Grammar. Paper presented at the Language Theory Session of the Modern Language Association in New York.

Postal, P. 1968. On So-Called "Pronouns" in English. In *Modern Studies in English: Readings in Transformational Grammar.* D. Reibel and S. Schane, eds. Englewood Cliffs: Prentice-Hall.

Reinhart, T. 1983. *Anaphora and Semantic Interpretation.* Chicago: University of Chicago Press.

Riemsdijk, H. van, and E. Williams. 1981. NP-Structure. *Linguistic Review* 117:1–217.

Rizzi, L. 1978. A Restructuring Rule in Italian Syntax. In *Recent Transformational Studies in European Languages.* S. J. Keyser, ed. Cambridge: MIT Press.

Ruwet, N. 1982. *La Grammaire des Insultes et autres Études.* Paris: Le Seuil.

Ruwet, N. 1990. *En* et *Y:* Deux clitiques pronominaux antilogophoriques. *Langages* 97:51–81.

Stevenson, R. 1990. Pronouns and their Antecedents. *Belfast Working Papers in Linguistics* 10:104–131.

Stockwell, R., P. Schachter, and B. Partee. 1969. *Integration of Transformational Theories of English Syntax.* Los Angeles: UCLA.

Wasow, T. 1979. *Anaphora in Generative Grammar.* Ghent: Story Scientia.

Superiority, Subjacency, and Economy*

Robert Freidin
Princeton University

In his introduction to volume four of *Noam Chomsky: Critical Assessments,* Carlos Otero writes:

> In true scientific inquiry (in fact, in any kind of rational inquiry, including the natural sciences), productive people try to identify and come to understand major factors and see what can be explained in terms of them. They anticipate that there will always be a periphery of unexplained phenomena (a range of nuances and minor effects that require auxiliary assumptions) which should be very sharply separated. (1994:17–18)

Generative grammar provides an ideal case study, as Otero has documented.[1] This inquiry has from the outset been a search for guiding principles, the dominant structures, and the major consequences.

In the history of generative grammar over the past four decades, among the major factors investigated have been rule systems and systems of grammatical principles and related parameters. One extremely successful line of research has been the elimination of language-particular and construction-specific transformations in favor of three optimally general and presumably universal transformational rules: Substitute α for β, Adjoin α to β, and Delete α (the former two referred to under the designation "Move α," or all three under the designation "Affect α"). This was brought about by the gradual development (1970 to 1979) of a set of general grammatical principles involving phrase structure, bounding, binding, Case, government, and predicate/argument structure,[2] many of which function as conditions on representations, rather than conditions on the application of rules (i.e., on derivations), raising a question about the role of derivations in grammar. If most grammatical principles function as conditions on representations, then perhaps all conditions on derivations could be replaced by conditions on representations so that derivations would become essentially epiphenomenal. One result in this direction was the demonstration in Freidin (1978) that the empirical effects of the Strict Cycle

Condition of Chomsky (1973) could be derived from independently motivated conditions on representations.[3] Such derivations highlighted the interconnection of the proposed conditions, beginning with Chomsky's demonstration of how many of Ross's island constraints (Ross 1967/1986[4])—and in particular the Complex NP Constraint—followed from the Subjacency Condition (Chomsky 1973, 1977—henceforth Subjacency). This led to the useful research strategy of trying to derive the empirical effects of one condition from another (or others) that appear to be more basic or have a broader empirical range. The guiding principle in this research is to eliminate redundancy (i.e., overlapping conditions) under the assumption that the language faculty is nonredundant. When a construction is prohibited by more than one condition, it is assumed that this construction is more strongly deviant than those that are prohibited by only one of the conditions. This is an empirical hypothesis, though not as yet particularly well motivated.

The Superiority Condition (Chomsky 1973) provides an interesting case study of the connections between grammatical principles and the effort to subsume certain ones under others. The original formulation of the Superiority Condition (henceforth Superiority) in Chomsky (1973) applies exclusively to leftward movement:[5]

(1) No rule can involve *X, Y* in the structure
$\ldots X \ldots [_{\alpha} \ldots Z \ldots - WYV \ldots] \ldots$
where the rule applies ambiguously to *Z* and *Y*, and *Z* is superior to *Y.*

A category Z is superior to Y when Z asymmetrically c-commands Y.[6] The standard examples involve *wh*-movement in a sentence containing multiple *wh*-phrases where one phrase is superior to the other, as in (2a–b):

(2) a. *What did who read?
b. Who read what?

Given a rule of *wh*-movement that can move either the subject *who* or the object *what* into [Spec,CP],[7] Superiority prohibits the movement of *what* because it is asymmetrically c-commanded by *who.* Under this formulation Superiority is a condition on the application of *wh*-movement and is thus a condition on derivations.

One widely discussed attempt to derive the empirical effects of Superiority involves the Empty Category Principle (ECP) of Chomsky (1981), under the crucial assumption that the ECP applies to LF representations.[8]

Under this proposal (2a) and (2b) would have the LF representations along the lines of (3a) and (3b) respectively:

(3) a. $[_{CP}\ [_{NP:2}$ who$_1$ $[_{NP:2}$ what]] $[_{IP}$ x$_1$ read y$_2$]]
b. $[_{CP}\ [_{NP:1}$ what$_2$ $[_{NP:1}$ who]] $[_{IP}$ x$_1$ read y$_2$]]

Note that this analysis assumes that unmoved *wh*-phrases in (2) are simply adjoined at LF to the *wh*-phrase in [Spec,CP]. It follows from the adjunction operation that the head of the phrase to which a *wh*-phrase is adjoined remains the head of the entire adjunction structure. Thus, in (3a) *who* fails to antecedent govern its trace because it does not c-command it—in contrast to (3b) where NP$_1$ c-commands and hence antecedent governs the trace in subject position. In both (3a–b) the trace in object position satisfies the ECP because it is lexically governed by the verb. On this analysis Superiority, a condition of derivations, is reduced to the ECP, a condition on LF representations. This analysis crucially depends on a disjunctive formulation of the ECP where either lexical head government or antecedent government suffices (as in Lasnik and Saito 1984, 1992).[9]

While this reduction may work for Superiority violations involving a superior subject in a finite clause, it fails for all other superior positions. Consider (4a–b) with the representations (5a–b):

(4) a. *What did John expect who(m) to read?
b. *What did John persuade who(m) to read?

(5) a. $[_{CP}$ what$_1$ did $[_{IP}$ John expect $[_{CP}$ t_1 $[_{IP}$ who(m) to read t_1]]]]
b. $[_{CP}$ what$_1$ did $[_{IP}$ John persuade who(m) $[_{CP}$ t_1 $[_{IP}$ PRO to read t_1]]]]

In (4a) the complement subject will undergo exceptional Case marking by the matrix verb. Under the standard GB analysis the infinitival subject position is lexically governed by the matrix verb. Thus antecedent government of the trace in complement subject position by the *wh*-phrase in [Spec,CP] is not required. Under the Spec/head agreement analysis of Case assignment (Chomsky and Lasnik 1993, Chomsky 1993), *who(m)* would move to [Spec,AgrO-P] in the matrix clause where it would antecedent govern its trace in complement subject position. (5a) therefore involves a Superiority, not an ECP, violation. In (5b) the superior *wh*-phrase is in object position where it is lexically governed. Thus (5b) is also a Superiority violation, but not an ECP violation.[11]

Another configurational analysis of superiority effects is given in

Pesetsky (1987) involving the relation between paths of moved *wh*-phrases (or in more contemporary terms, between *wh*-chains). Specifically, Pesetsky proposes a Nested Dependency Condition as formulated in (6):

(6) *Nested Dependency Condition* (NDC)
If two *wh*-trace dependencies overlap, one must contain the other.

(6) accounts for the following contrast (his (22a–b)):

(7) a. ?*What book*$_2$ don't you know *who*$_1$ to persuade t_1 to read t_2?
b. **Who*$_1$ don't you know *what book*$_2$ to persuade t_1 to read t_2?

In (7a) the chain (*who*$_1$, t_1) is nested inside the chain (*what book*$_2$, t_2), whereas in (7b), the chains intersect because *what book* lies inside the chain created by the movement of *who* while its trace is outside that chain.[12]

To handle Superiority violations within a single clause (e.g., (2a)), Pesetsky adopts the analysis of Jaeggli (1980/1981), where the *wh*-phrase that remains *in-situ* at S-structure is adjoined to the clause that dominates the moved *wh*-phrase—that is, adjunction to CP in our analysis or to S′ in Jaeggli's. This analysis corresponds to the standard raising analysis of quantifiers (May 1977) in which scope ambiguities are resolved in LF representations—specifically, the quantifier with wider scope will c-command the quantifier with narrower scope at LF. This seems inappropriate since multiple *wh*-phrase constructions do not manifest such scopal ambiguities. The answer to a question like (2b) is simply a paired list of people and objects. It involves a mapping from readers to things read. In contrast the LF representation allowed by the NDC (i.e., where *what* takes wide scope over *who*) corresponds to an interpretation where the mapping is from things read to readers. Yet a list of what was read by whom (e.g., "*Ulysses* was read by Bill and Mary, and *Middlemarch* was read by Jane, Fred, and Sally, . . . ") is a thoroughly unnatural response to a question like (2b).[13]

The NDC generalizes to certain Subjacency violations.[14] Thus (8) violates both the NDC and Subjacency:

(8) *[$_{CP}$ what$_1$ do [$_{IP}$ you wonder [$_{CP}$ who$_2$ [$_{IP}$ Bill gave t_1 to t_2]]]]

The chain (*who*$_2$, t_2) intersects the chain (*what*$_1$, t_1) and the link of the latter chain crosses two bounding categories (2 IPs). Nonetheless, (8) cannot be attributed to a crossed binding constraint like the NDC because of examples like (9), which are equally unacceptable but where there is no occurrence of crossed binding, as discussed in Freidin and Lasnik (1981).

(9) *[$_{CP}$ who$_2$ do [$_{IP}$ you wonder [$_{CP}$ what$_1$ [$_{IP}$ Bill gave t_1 to t_2]]]]

Presumably (9) is only a Subjacency violation (but see note 40 for a different analysis). It is not a Superiority violation because at the point in the derivation where *what* moves to the internal [Spec,CP], it asymmetrically c-commands *who* (on virtually every analysis of double object constructions that has been proposed in the literature). In contrast the movement of *who* to the internal [Spec,CP] in (8) violates Superiority because the *wh*-phrase *what* is superior.[15] Such paired examples suggest that a geometric approach to movement constraints like the NDC (or the Path Containment Condition of Pesetsky 1982) is not viable.

At this point we might raise the question of whether the movement in (9) of *who* to the external [Spec,CP] over *what* in the internal [Spec,CP] constitutes a Superiority violation. Undoubtedly, the internal [Spec,CP] c-commands the object of the PP in the embedded IP. Nonetheless, the *wh*-phrase in [Spec,CP] could not move to the external [Spec,CP] because then the selectional requirements of *wonder* would not be satisfied. If we change the matrix verb to *remember,* which does not require a [+WH] CP complement, then it is possible to derive (10):

(10) [$_{CP}$ what$_1$ do [$_{IP}$ you remember [$_{CP}$ t_1 [$_{IP}$ Bill gave t_1 to whom$_2$]]]]

The question is whether the movement of *what* to the matrix [Spec,CP] is driven by Superiority as well as Subjacency, which is violated in (9) by the movement of *who* to the external [Spec,CP]. In other words, is Superiority limited to *wh*-phrases in grammatical function positions? This seems like a reasonable way to sharpen the formulation of Superiority.[16] Note that those Romance languages in which a relative pronoun can be extracted out of a *wh*-island[17] provide some evidence that Superiority does not apply between a superior *wh*-phrase in [Spec,CP] and a *wh*-phrase in a grammatical function position. If it did, then those constructions should be blocked by Superiority.

Another connection between Superiority and Subjacency arises in constructions such as (11), which can be associated with two distinct S-structures (12a–b):

(11) *What did you forget who had borrowed?

(12) a. *[$_{CP}$ what$_1$ did [$_{IP}$ you forget [$_{CP}$ who$_2$ [$_{IP}$ t_2 had borrowed t_1]]]]

b. *[$_{CP}$ what$_1$ did [$_{IP}$ you forget [$_{CP}$ t_1 [$_{IP}$ who$_2$ had borrowed t_1]]]]

The chain (*what*$_1$, t_1) in (12a) violates Subjacency and Superiority (since *who,* which asymmetrically c-commands the complement object from the internal [Spec,CP], could also move to the external [Spec,CP]). In contrast, derivation of the chain link between the two traces in (12b) violates only Superiority. Suppose that the language faculty assigns examples like (11) a unique mental representation at each level of representation. Within the recent 'minimalist' framework (Chomsky 1993, 1994) in which the levels of representation are restricted to the interface levels PF and LF, the problem we have identified cannot be discussed in terms of assigning two distinct S-structure representations. Rather, the computation of (11) 'crashes'—that is, it fails to converge (meaning "yield a legitimate structural description") at one or both interface levels. Under a standard GB analysis (11) is computationally ambiguous. Computational ambiguity of this sort seems rather inefficient for language design, so perhaps it can be excluded. Let us conjecture that the only kind of computational ambiguity we will find in languages is that in which the two computations are convergent, as in the standard case of structural ambiguity (e.g. *a review of a book by two linguists*). Given this conjecture, the language faculty assigns a unique computation to (11) and therefore (11) crashes for a particular reason. If this is correct, then certain aspects of derivations are not epiphenomenal, as some earlier research was interpreted as suggesting.

From this perspective the problem with (11) is to determine why the computation crashes. Does the failure to converge involve PF or LF (or both)? The answer will depend on how and where Superiority and Subjacency apply to derivations or the representations they create, which in turn depends on other factors concerning the derivation of (11). Putting aside the issue of at what level or levels nonconvergence occurs, we have two distinct possibilities: the computation of (11) crashes because of Superiority or Subjacency. The choice between these two possibilities can be resolved if it follows from the theory of grammar that either the *wh*-phrase in subject position must move into [Spec,CP] prior to the movement of the *wh*-phrase in object position (in which case we get a Subjacency violation) or the *wh*-phrase in subject position does not move to a [Spec,CP] until after the *wh*-phase in object position moves to the external [Spec,CP]. Under the latter scenario Subjacency is not violated, but Superiority is.

Of course, in the absence of a theory that chooses one analysis over the other, we might try to identify some data whose analysis requires one option and excludes the other.

The standard versions of GB do not distinguish the two computations of (11) given in (12). Thus, (11) is excluded either because it violates two conditions or only one. Under the assumption that a construction that violates two general principles will be perceived as more deviant than one that violates only one of the two, this analysis of (11) cannot stand. One way of computing (11) must be wrong.

Fortunately, there is a way to tease apart the Superiority versus Subjacency analyses empirically. Consider the well-known fact that superiority effects disappear when bare interrogative pronouns are replaced by *which*-phrases, as illustrated in the contrast between (13a) and (13b):[18]

(13) a. *What did who borrow?
b. Which books did which students borrow?

This fact gives us a tool for testing the sort of violation that occurs in (11). If the corresponding construction with *which*-phrases instead of bare interrogative pronouns is less deviant, then we know that (11) involves a Superiority violation.

(14) Which books did you forget which students had borrowed?

Given that (14) is significantly better than (11)—some speakers (myself included) find it essentially normal, (11) appears to be a Superiority violation, not a Subjacency violation.

Having identified some empirical evidence for a unique analysis of (11), we now need to show how the analysis follows from the theory of grammar. I am assuming that examples like (13b) and (14) are not necessarily part of the primary language data of every child who acquires a grammar of English. Even if they were, the analysis of constructions like (11) does not follow automatically.

Within the current minimalist framework as sketched in Chomsky (1993) there are two economy of derivation principles that could be used to predict that a *wh*-phrase in subject position that is not moved out of its clause remains *in-situ* in the derivation to PF[19] (henceforth "overt syntax"[20]): Procrastinate and Greed. Procrastinate is based on the notion that LF movement is somehow preferable to overt movement (see Chomsky 1993:30). Thus, if nothing requires the movement of a subject *wh*-phrase in overt syntax, it will not move in the overt syntax. The derivation to LF does require the covert movement of a *wh*-phrase subject to [Spec,CP] in order to create a proper quantifier/variable structure. Otherwise, the derivation crashes at LF because the result violates Full Interpretation (FI)—a quantifier that does not bind a variable cannot be interpreted. Greed, a somewhat related principle, is characterized as self-serving Last Resort, where the Last Resort principle licenses a step in a derivation "only if it is necessary for convergence" (Chomsky 1993:32). "Derivations are driven by the narrow mechanical requirement of feature checking only, not by a 'search for intelligibility' or the like" (Chomsky 1993:33). Under Chomsky's version of Greed, an element moves only to check its own features. As will be discussed below, because this requirement appears to be too strong for *wh*-movement, a modified version of Greed will be proposed.

Given that quantifier/variable structures need not occur in overt syntax (as in the case of non-*wh*-quantifiers), it is reasonable to assume that the construction of these structures can be postponed to the derivation to LF. The application of Procrastinate to (11) therefore suggests that (12b) should be a viable PF representation. However, Greed pulls harder in the other direction.

Following the proposal for feature checking in Chomsky (1993), let us assume that languages have strong or weak features; that strong features are visible at PF whereas weak features are invisible; that features that are checked 'disappear'; and that strong features that remain unchecked at PF cause a derivation to crash. Let us further assume that [+WH] is a strong feature in English.[21] Therefore, it must be checked in overt syntax, or the derivation will crash at PF. For reasons that will become clear below, I am going to assume that this *wh*-feature is the one attached to C and that it is checked via Spec/head agreement when a *wh*-phrase moves into the relevant [Spec,CP]. Thus, if C contains [+WH], this feature must be checked in the overt syntax, or the derivation will crash at PF.

Consider a verb such as *expect* that does not allow indirect question complements. The sentence (15a) could be represented as either (15b) or (15c):

(15) a. *John expects the students read what.
  b. $[_{CP}$ $[_{C}$ +WH] $[_{IP}$ John expects $[_{CP}$ $[_{C}$ −WH] $[_{IP}$ the students read what]]]]
  c. $[_{CP}$ $[_{C}$ −WH] $[_{IP}$ John expects $[_{CP}$ $[_{C}$ −WH] $[_{IP}$ the students read what]]]]

In (15b) the *wh*-phrase has failed to move to the external [Spec,CP], hence the strong *wh*-feature in the external C is not checked, and the derivation crashes at PF because it is visible. At LF the *wh*-phrase can still move to the external [Spec,CP] to check the *wh*-feature (too late in this instance); however, this will create the requisite quantifier variable structure needed to interpret the *wh*-phrase at LF. So the derivation converges at LF. Greed applies both to LF, where it governs the movement of an object or infinitival complement subject NP to [Spec,AgrO-P], and to PF, where it determines the movement of the subject of a finite clause from [Spec,VP] to [Spec,AgrS-P] (= [Spec,IP]). In (15c) there is no strong feature to be checked, thus no reason for the *wh*-phrase to move at all in the overt syntax or the covert syntax, given Greed. Thus, the derivation of (15c) crashes at LF because the *wh*-phrase cannot be properly interpreted—a violation of FI.

If we substitute the verb *wonder,* which obligatorily selects a [+WH] C, for the matrix verb in (15a), the derivation crashes at PF because this strong feature is not checked. Greed would allow the *wh*-phrase to move to the internal [Spec,CP] at LF, hence the derivation would converge at LF. If that movement did not occur, then the derivation crashes at LF too for the familiar reason. If the matrix verb in (15a) is changed to *forget,* which optionally selects a [+WH] C, then either the matrix C or the complement C or both could contain [+WH]. If both do and there is only one *wh*-phrase, then one will not be checked, and the derivation crashes at PF. If there are two *wh*-phrases in the construction, then each *wh*-feature can be checked and the derivation converges at PF (as in (14)). If neither matrix nor complement C contains the *wh*-feature, then Greed causes the derivation to crash at LF as an FI violation.

Now consider the case in which there are multiple *wh*-phrases and only one [+WH] C—e.g., *who read what?* If feature checking applied to a feature of the *wh*-phrase, then such questions should crash at PF, contrary to the fact. For this reason we have been assuming that a *wh*-phrase checks the *wh*-feature in C and not conversely.[22] As for the LF representation of multiple *wh*-questions in which one *wh*-phrase remains *in-situ,* let us assume that the moved *wh*-phrase provides an adjunction site to which the *wh*-phrase *in-situ* can move at LF to create the appropriate quantifier/variable structure.

This analysis requires that we modify the analysis of Greed for *wh*-movement. The *wh*-phrase is not moving into [Spec,CP] to check its own [+WH] feature, but rather the one contained in C. Let us assume that the purpose of Greed is to maximize convergent derivations (i.e., profits). If a particular movement does not lead to a convergent derivation, then Greed blocks it.

Apparently the *wh*-feature in C is independent of whatever feature accounts for the formation of yes/no questions. Thus (16a) crashes either at PF because there is a [+WH] feature in the external C that is not checked or at LF because the *wh*-phrase cannot move to create a quantifier/variable structure.

(16) a. *Does John really expect [−WH] the students to read what?
b. What does John really expect [−WH] the students to read?
c. Does John really expect [−WH] the students to read *Barriers?*

In contrast the *wh*-phrase in (16b) converges at PF because the [+WH] feature in the matrix [Spec,CP] is checked by the *wh*-phrase and at LF for the familiar reason. (16c) does not involve a [+WH] C, as indicated by the contrast between (16a) and (16c).

With this analysis in mind we can return to the computation of (11) as a violation of Superiority rather than Subjacency. This concerns the way feature checking is carried out when a *wh*-phrase occurs in [Spec,IP]. To see what this involves, let us consider the verbs *expect, forget,* and *wonder,* which differ in their ability to take indirect question complements. As the paradigm in (17) illustrates, *expect* cannot take an indirect question complement, *forget* may (but does not have to), and *wonder* must.

(17) a. *John expects who to borrow the book.
b. Who does John expect to borrow the book?
c. John forgot who had borrowed the book.
d. Who did John forget had borrowed the book?
e. John wondered who had borrowed the book.
f. *Who did John wonder had borrowed the book?

(17a) crashes at LF for the same reasons that (15a) does, depending on which analysis of the external C we choose. In (17b) *who* winds up in the matrix [Spec,CP] to have its [+WH] feature checked by [+WH] C. The chain it forms involves the complement [Spec,CP]—in which case Subjacency is satisfied. (17c) and (17e) seem to be identical in the relevant respects. In both complements the *wh*-phrase subject raises to [Spec,CP] to check the [+WH] feature.[23] (17f) crashes at PF because the [+WH] feature of the complement C has not been checked. In contrast the feature of the complement C in (17d) is [−WH] and therefore does not require overt material in [Spec,CP].

Notice that we have been assuming that the *wh*-phrase in [Spec,IP] raises to [Spec,CP] so that checking of the *wh*-feature can occur. There is another possibility—namely, that checking occurs without movement to [Spec,CP]. If this is feasible, then Greed will rule out the string-vacuous movement of the *wh*-phrase in the overt syntax. The movement of the *wh*-phrase from [Spec,IP] to [Spec,CP] would occur in the covert syntax, the derivation to LF, as predicted by Procrastinate.

Such derivations would require that the [+WH] feature of complement C be checked by the *wh*-phrase in complement subject position. While this analysis might appear feasible for (17c) and (17e), it would create a problem for constructions such as (18) where the matrix verb selects a [−WH] C:

(18) a. Which books does John expect which students to borrow?

b. [$_{CP}$ which books$_1$ did [$_{IP}$ John expect [$_{CP}$$t_1$ [$_{IP}$ which students$_2$ to borrow t_1]]]]

If the selectional feature on C for *forget* and *wonder* can be transferred to I, then presumably the same thing should happen with *expect,* thereby creating a Spec/head agreement violation. Since (18) is perfectly acceptable, its computation should not violate any constraint on movement or selectional restriction. In this way constructions such as (18) argue against the possibility that the [+WH] feature on C can be checked by a *wh*-phrase in [Spec,IP]. (As we will see below, an even stronger empirical argument can be given against this analysis.)

Given Greed, the computation of (18a) cannot involve successive cyclic Move α through the internal [Spec,CP] because movement of the *wh*-phrase to this position is not motivated by feature checking. Also, a two-step derivation would violate the principle of Least Effort (Chomsky 1991), provided there is a way of accounting for this long-distance movement in a single step. Following Chomsky (1993), let us now assume that the basic movement operation is not Move α, but rather Form Chain. Form Chain constructs (18b) in one step by moving *which books* to the external [Spec,CP] and at the same time constructing the chain consisting of the trace in the internal [Spec,CP] and the trace in complement object position.[25] The chain is well formed since its links are minimal (i.e., satisfy Subjacency, etc.). Given this formulation, it follows that Subjacency, now a condition on chain links, must be construed as a condition on representations.[26] In this way (18) provides empirical evidence for Form Chain under a theory that includes Greed and a principle of Least Effort.

In (18) the *wh*-phrase in the complement subject position could not be raised to the internal [Spec,CP] position, thereby creating a putative Subjacency violation. However, a corresponding example with *forget* (e.g., (14) above) is susceptible to this analysis. Assuming the Form Chain analysis, the derivation of (14) with respect to *wh*-movement can be computed as two steps in (19) or one step in (20):

(19) $[_{CP}$ which books$_1$ did $[_{IP}$ John forget $[_{CP}$ which students$_2$ $[_{IP}$ t_2 had borrowed t_1]]]]

(20) $[_{CP}$ which books$_1$ did $[_{IP}$ John forget $[_{CP}$ t_1 $[_{IP}$ which students$_2$ had borrowed t_1]]]]

In (20) the one-step consists of moving the complement object to the external [Spec,CP] and forming a chain, which satisfies Subjacency. The two-step derivation in (19) can be given in two ways, depending on the order of the operations. If the complement subject *which students* is moved first to the complement [Spec,CP], then the application of Form Chain to the complement object *which books* will create a chain that violates Subjacency. The alternative derivation is countercyclic: *which books* moves long distance to the matrix [Spec,CP], forming a chain that satisfies Subjacency, and then *which students* moves into the complement [Spec,CP]. A principle of Least Effort selects (20) over (19) *ceteris paribus.* Given the status of (14), it seems clear that the proper computation for constructions such as (14) is (20) and not (19). As noted earlier, Subjacency violations do not exhibit varying effects depending on whether a *which*-phrase or a bare interrogative is involved. Furthermore, *forget* can, like *expect,* select a [−WH] C as discussed above.

If the complement C in (20) does not contain [+WH], Greed prevents the complement subject from moving to complement [Spec,CP] at LF to create a quantifier/variable structure. Instead, it must move to the external [Spec,CP], adjoining to the *wh*-phrase there to create a complex quantifier that is appropriate for the pair-list reading of such constructions.[27] However, when both *wh*-phrases in a multiple *wh*-question have moved to a [Spec,CP] in the overt syntax, the pair-list reading is blocked, as illustrated in (21):

(21) a. Which student did the professor tell which book to read?
b. Which book did the professor tell which student to read?

In (21b) the question asks for a pair-list answer, whereas in (21a) it does not—instead, it asks for the identity of student x such that the professor told x which book to read. The difference in interpretation is directly related to the difference in the syntactic structures of (21a) and (21b). In (21a) both *wh*-phrases have moved in the overt syntax to [Spec,CP] positions; therefore, at LF they form independent quantifier/variable structures. In contrast only one *wh*-phrase has moved to [Spec,CP] in (21b), the other remaining *in-situ.* However, at LF, the *in-situ wh*-phrase (*which student*) must move to [Spec,CP] in order to form a quantifier/variable structure. The only c-commanding [Spec,CP] position is already filled with a *wh*-phrase, therefore the *in-situ wh*-phrase adjoins to the *wh*-phrase in [Spec,CP], forming an absorption structure that gives the pair-list reading. Notice also that the nonpair-list reading of (14) may be computationally more complex than that of (21a) because it involves two intersecting quantifier/variable chains, while those in (21a) do not intersect.

Although this analysis accounts for *expect* and *forget* (e.g., (18) and (14)), the corresponding construction with *wonder,* which obligatorily selects [+WH] C, unlike *forget,* raises some further problems:[28]

(22) Which books did John wonder which students had borrowed?

The status of (22) is on a par with (14), though perhaps slightly degraded because of the computational complexity noted above. Significantly, (22) does not have a pair-list reading like (14), but only the one asking "for which books x did John wonder which students had borrowed x." The fact that (18) can only have a pair-list reading and (22) cannot would follow if the complement subject of (22) moves to [Spec,CP] in the overt syntax. In this way (22) provides evidence against the Vacuous Movement Hypothesis (cf. Chomsky 1986).

As with the corresponding example with *forget,* (22) has two potential analyses, given in (23):

(23) a. $[_{CP}$ which books$_1$ did $[_{IP}$ John wonder $[_{CP}$ which students$_2$ $[_{IP}$ t_2 had borrowed t_1]]]]
b. $[_{CP}$ which books$_1$ did $[_{IP}$ John wonder $[_{CP}$ t_1 $[_{IP}$ which students$_2$ had borrowed t_1]]]]

It would seem that (23b), the blocked Superiority violation derivation, and not (23a), the Subjacency violation, provides the appropriate computation. And yet the selectional feature of *wonder* requires (23a) at PF. If (23a) must feed the PF computation of (22), the countercyclic derivation seems the only way to avoid a Subjacency violation.

We have been assuming that feature checking of *wh*-features applies at PF for good reason. Consider what results if we adopt the alternative assumption—namely, that *wh*-features are checked at LF. (22) is no longer a problem because the *wh*-phrase in [Spec,IP] could raise to the complement [Spec,CP] at LF to check the *wh*-feature in C. However, this mechanism would also check the same feature in (24a), so that the explanation for the deviance of such constructions is lost.

(24) a. *John wondered Mary really admires who(m)
b. *John forgot Mary really admired who(m)

If *forget* in (24b) selects [+WH], checking features at LF will not account for such constructions—in contrast to feature checking at PF, where the *wh*-phrase remains *in-situ.* Thus, checking of *wh*-features occurs at PF, not LF.

It is worth noting that this account of (22) provides evidence for the derivational (as opposed to a representational) approach to grammar:

> Under a derivational approach, computation typically involves simple steps expressible in terms of natural relations and properties, with the context that makes them natural wiped out by later steps of the derivation and not visible in the representations to which it converges.[29] (Chomsky 1995)

The second step in the derivation of (23a) wipes out the context that allowed the first step.

Ironically, the proposed derivation for (22) violates the Strict Cycle Condition (SCC) as formulated in Chomsky (1973).[30] This would be a serious problem if the SCC were an axiom of the theory, but not if the empirical effects of the SCC followed from other considerations (see Freidin 1978, Kitahara 1995). Given the Form Chain analysis of *wh*-movement outlined above, it should be clear that Subjacency alone no longer accounts for any deviant *wh*-island construction.[31] Consider the derivation of (25):

(25) *Which students did John wonder which books had borrowed?

As in (22), the movement of each *wh*-phrase in (25) is motivated by Greed. If *which books* moves to the internal [Spec,CP] first, then the chain formed by a second movement of *which students* to the external [Spec,CP] will violate Subjacency. Presumably, this derivation converges at PF but crashes at LF. If, however, the two applications for Form Chain are reversed, then neither chain formed will violate Subjacency. The reason that (25) is deviant, but (22) is not, must follow from some other condition—in this case the ECP. The chain (*which students*$_1$, t_1) in (25) violates the ECP at LF because the trace is not properly governed. In contrast the trace in the LF chain (*which books*$_2$, t_2) in (22) must be properly governed. In the latter case it does not seem as if antecedent government will hold since both (22) and (25) appear to be relativized minimality violations of the same sort. This suggests that we may need to retain head government to explain the difference between (22) and (25), which involve another subject/object asymmetry.[32]

Chomsky (1993) proposes that the notion 'shortest link,' expressible in terms of the operation Form Chain, might be used to incorporate parts of Subjacency and the ECP under the intuitive formulation of a Shortest Movement Condition expressed in (26):

(26) 'Shortest Movement' Condition
Given two convergent derivations D_1 and D_2, both minimal and containing the same number of steps, D_1 blocks D_2 if its links are shorter. (Chomsky *op. cit.*:34)

Chomsky suggests that the phenomena of Superiority and Relativized Minimality (including superraising, the Head Movement Constraint, and [Spec,CP] islands (including *wh*-islands)) should fall out from such economy considerations, though an explicit account is not provided. (See Kitahara 1993 for a more detailed analysis of Superiority effects.)

To see how the Shortest Movement Condition (henceforth Shortest Movement) subsumes the effects of Superiority, consider how it would account for the simplest case, exemplified by (2). A question immediately arises about what part of the two derivations is relevant to the computation of this condition. Every derivation will involve an overt part, the derivation to PF, and a covert part, the derivation to LF. In the overt part, (2a–b) would involve (27a–b) respectively—pretending that the subject does not originate inside VP to keep the representations simple.

(27) a. $[_{CP}$ what$_2$ $[_{C^*}$ did$]$ $[_{IP}$ who$_1$ $[_{VP}$ read t_2 $]]]$
b. $[_{CP}$ who$_1$ $[_{C^*}$ $[_{IP}$ t_1 $[_{VP}$ read what$_2$ $]]]]$

The link between *what* and its trace in object position is obviously longer than the one between *who* and its trace. However, in the LF representations (3a–b) (repeated here for convenience), the links are the same for each derivation since both phrases have moved to the same two positions:[33]

(3) a. $[_{CP}$ $[_{NP:2}$ who$_1$ $[_{NP:2}$ what$]]$ $[_{IP}$ x_1 read y_2 $]]$
b. $[_{CP}$ $[_{NP:1}$ what$_2$ $[_{NP:1}$ who$]]$ $[_{IP}$ x_1 read y_2 $]]$

This shows that Shortest Movement applies in the overt syntax, not to LF.[34] It also shows that Shortest Movement will not account for the difference between (22) and (25) since each example involves the movement of both *wh*-phrases to the same two positions.

The same situation obtains in the more complicated case of (28) where the two *wh*-phrases start out in different clauses:[35]

(28) a. Who(m)$_1$ did John persuade t_1 [to visit who(m)$_2$]
b. *Who(m)$_2$ did John persuade who(m)$_1$ [to visit t_2]

Taking (28a–b) to represent a pair of two convergent derivations in the overt syntax (PF), the link between *who*$_1$ and its trace is, again obviously, shorter that the link between *who*$_2$ and its trace. Thus, the difference in acceptability between (28a) and (28b) follows from Shortest Movement. Given Greed, the *wh*-phrase in complement object position cannot move to the [Spec,CP] of the complement because *persuade* does not select a [+WH] C. (28b) is only a Superiority violation under the Form Chain analysis given that a trace of the moved *wh*-phrase will occur in the complement [Spec,CP], whereas under a Move α analysis (assuming Greed) it would be both a Superiority and a Subjacency violation.

As with the analysis of (11), these two analyses can be distinguished by replacing the bare interrogative pronouns in (28) with *which*-phrases:

(29) a. Which students$_1$ did John persuade t_1 [to visit which professors$_2$]
b. Which professors$_2$ did John persuade which students$_1$ [to visit t_2]

(29b) is perfectly normal.[36] However, the derivation of (29b) is identical to that of (28b), which is blocked by Shortest Movement. This contrast argues against Shortest Movement as formulated in (26). The condition is simply too general to make the fine distinctions apparently needed.[37]

Having dispensed with Shortest Movement, we can return to the two analyses of (28b) under Greed. With Form Chain (28b) is only a Superiority violation. Given this we would expect (29b) to be normal, as it is. Under the Move α analysis (29b) would still be a Subjacency violation since (28b) is both a Superiority and Subjacency violation. Thus (29b) shows that (28b) is only a Superiority violation, thereby providing further empirical evidence for the Form Chain analysis of movement. That is, Move α appears to be incompatible with Greed.

Notice that there are other constructions whose derivations involve no apparent difference between the Move α and Form Chain analyses and about which Shortest Movement also makes the wrong prediction. The derivation of (30a–b) involves one NP movement from complement subject to matrix subject and one *wh*-movement from matrix clause to [Spec,CP]:

(30) a. Which books$_1$ [t_1 seem to which students$_2$ [t_1 to be boring]]
b. To which students$_2$ do [which books$_1$ seem t_2 [t_1 to be boring]]

(30b) should be blocked by (30a) under Shortest Movement.[38] As might be expected, the same phenomena occur with passive constructions, which also involve one NP-movement:

(31) a. Which students$_2$ were [t_2 persuaded t_2 [to read which books$_1$]]
b. Which books$_1$ were [which students$_2$ persuaded t_2 [t_1 [to read t_1]]]

As illustrated, in (32) and (33), these constructions can be recast as indirect question complements of *forget* and *wonder:*

(32) a. I forgot which students were persuaded to read which books.
b. I forgot which books which students were persuaded to read.

(33) a. I wonder which students were persuaded to read which books.
b. I wonder which books which students were persuaded to read.

Moreover, all of these except (33a) can be turned into direct questions with only a slight degradation in acceptability, as in (34) and (35):[39]

(34) a. Which students did you forget were persuaded to read which books?
b. Which books did you forget which students were persuaded to read?

(35) a. *Which students do you wonder were persuaded to read which books?
b. Which books do you wonder which students were persuaded to read?

(35a) violates the selectional property of *wonder*, hence the derivation crashes at PF because the [+WH] feature in C of the CP complement of *wonder* is not checked. In (35b) that feature is checked by the movement of the complement subject *which students* into the complement [Spec,CP]. Notice that there are two possible derivations here using Form Chain. Given that there is a [+WH] feature in C of the CP complement of *wonder*, *which books* could move to the [Spec,CP] of that complement, forming a chain, and then move to the matrix [Spec,CP], forming a second chain. Alternatively, the *wh*-phrase could move directly to the matrix [Spec,CP], forming a single chain. Economy considerations along the lines of Least Effort (see Chomsky 1991) would preclude the first option. The *wh*-feature attached to the CP complement of *wonder* will be checked in PF by the overt movement of *which students* from [Spec,IP] to [Spec,CP]. Note that this derivation provides another more complicated example that necessarily violates the Strict Cycle Condition.

So far nothing precludes the possibility of a cyclic derivation of constructions like (22) and (35b), where the long-distance movement would invariably result in a chain that violates Subjacency. This is not a problem, however, as long as the countercyclic derivation is available. In general when the theory allows a convergent and a nonconvergent derivation for the same string, the convergent derivation usually masks the nonconvergent one. Thus, we can ignore the cyclic derivation that gives a bad result, though ideally the cyclic derivation would be blocked by some principle of grammar.

Under the countercyclic Form Chain analysis of *wh*-movement discussed above, no Subjacency violation could occur in a construction with a single embedded clausal complement. Thus the standard cases of *wh*-island violations involving the movement of two *wh*-phrase complements of V, as in (36), can no longer be explained as Subjacency violations.

(36) a. *Which books did you forget to which students Bill recommended?
b. *To which students did you forget which books Bill recommended?

On the cyclic derivation the examples in (36) violate Subjacency in the usual way, but not on the countercyclic derivation. Therefore, something aside from Subjacency must prohibit the countercyclic movement inside the complement CP. Just prior to this movement Form Chain creates the following structures:

(37) a. [$_{CP}$ which books$_1$ did [$_{IP}$ you forget [$_{CP}$ t_1 [$_{IP}$ Bill recommended t_1 to which students$_2$]]]]
b. [$_{CP}$ to which students$_2$ did [$_{IP}$ you forget [$_{CP}$ t_2 [$_{IP}$ Bill recommended which books$_1$ t_2]]]]

Since a trace is an empty category analogue of its antecedent, t_1 in (37a) is an NP, whereas t_2 in (37b) is a PP. The countercyclic movement of the *wh*-PP in (37a) or the *wh*-NP in (37b) should be ruled out by the nondistinctness on substitutions because the traces are categorially distinct from the phrases that replace them. In this way both possible derivations of (36) have a bad outcome.[40]

At this point we might wonder whether Subjacency plays any role at all regarding the movement of multiple *wh*-phrases in a sentence. That it does play a crucial role can be demonstrated with examples containing at least two successive sentential embeddings:

(38) *Which books couldn't Mary remember which students John expected to read?

With respect to *wh*-movement the derivation of (38) involves two steps: *which students* moves from the subject of *read* to [Spec,CP] of the complement of *remember*, and *which books* moves from the object of *read* to the [Spec,CP] of the root clause. This can be accomplished either cyclically or countercyclically. In the cyclic derivation the movement of *which books* is a straightforward Subjacency violation. The application of Form Chain in this instance creates a chain, one of whose links will cross two IPs because the intervening [Spec,CP] is occupied by *which students.* The countercyclic derivation is somewhat more interesting. Form Chain moves *which books* to the root CP and creates a chain with traces in all the intervening [Spec,CP] positions. This chain observes Subjacency. The next step in the derivation requires Form Chain to move *which students* to the [Spec,CP] of the complement of *remember.* If the resulting structure is as given in (39) (where t_2 is the trace of *which books*), then the chain formed by *which students* and its trace constitutes another Subjacency violation.

(39) . . . [$_{CP}$ which students$_1$ [$_{IP}$ John expected [$_{CP}$ t_2 [$_{IP}$ t_1 to read t_2]]]]

(39) results only if Form Chain cannot replace a trace with another trace. In contrast Form Chain can substitute a *wh*-phrase for a trace (for feature checking, as required by Greed). Note that even the cyclic derivation can be interpreted in this way. Thus Subjacency violations for such constructions follow as a consequence from the restriction on chain formation by the operation Form Chain.[41]

The analysis of *wh*-movement presented here has been motivated by principles of economy, primarily Greed with assistance from Least Effort. Taking Greed to be perhaps the major motivating force for substitution operations leads to the choice of Form Chain over Move α as the proper formulation for the movement transformation. As a result successive cyclic movement is revealed as an illusion, its effects subsumed under Subjacency (applied to the chain links created by Form Chain) and a rather natural prohibition against replacing one trace with another via Form Chain. The analysis of Superiority phenomena demonstrates that Form Chain is not subject to a Shortest Movement constraint (as proposed in Chomsky 1993) and therefore plays no role in motivating Form Chain over Move α. Furthermore, the analysis of *wh*-movement discussed in this paper suggests that some derivations may have to be countercyclic, not strictly cyclic. Therefore derivations may be countercyclic or cyclic, with improper consequences ruled out by other factors.

Much research in generative grammar over the past four decades has quite properly attempted to identify and explore large-scale generalizations about syntactic processes, including the A-over-A Principle, the *wh*-Island Condition, the Strict Cycle Condition, Subjacency, Koster's Locality Principle (Koster 1978), Connectedness (Kayne 1983), Global Harmony (Koster 1986), and currently the Shortest Movement Condition. It seems to me that the history of the field has shown that these large-scale syntactic generalizations tend to break down at various points and have to be restricted or replaced by more fine-grained principles (e.g., Greed, which essentially concerns morphological properties). It is therefore not surprising to find that a closer look at superiority phenomena and *wh*-movement under minimalist assumptions leads to the conclusion that successive cyclic movement is illusory, that derivations can be countercyclic and hence the empirical effects of the Strict Cycle Condition must be derivable from other principles of grammar, that the Shortest Movement Condition does not appear to be viable, and that the concept '*wh*-island' turns out to be completely spurious.

In the middle of Samuel Beckett's play *Endgame* a character exclaims ("With fervour"), "Ah the old questions, the old answers, there's nothing like them!" This is a profoundly irrational attitude, as anyone actively engaged in rational inquiry (including the natural sciences, as Carlos Otero pointedly notes in the quote at the beginning of this paper) knows. And as any generative grammarian who has been following the field over the past few decades knows all too well, it is demonstrably false. The great power of rational inquiry is that it can lead us to see the world in a new and hopefully clearer light. It liberates us from the tyranny of habit and the domination of concepts whose authority over us is without real justification. The more accurate our understanding of the world, the better our chances of finding real solutions to the problems we study. One hopes that this uniquely human ability can be applied to other aspects of human activity to improve the way we live as individuals and in society.

NOTES

* I am indebted to Len Babby, Sam Epstein, and Howard Lasnik for discussion of various portions of the material covered here and to audiences at USC and UC Irvine for comments on oral presentations of this material. I am further endebted to Epstein and Lasnik for extensive comments on a draft of this paper.

1. See also Otero (1984, 1991, and in preparation).

2. See Chomsky (1981) for the classic discussion and Freidin (1994a) for further discussion of the historical development.

3. For discussion of how strict cyclicity might be derived from the economy conditions of Chomsky (1993) see Kitahara (1995). See also Collins (1994), which attempts to derive the empirical effects of the Generalized Proper Binding Condition from conditions on the economy of derivations.

4. Henceforth, two dates separated by a slash indicate the date of an unpublished Ph.D. dissertation followed by the date of a subsequent published version.

5. It turns out, however, that Superiority, like Subjacency, applies to rightward movement as well. Consider the paradigm in (i):

(i) a. A report about the new power station that was written by three senators just appeared.
b. A report about the new power station just appeared that was written by three senators.
c. *A report that was written by three senators just appeared about the new power station.

Given that the PP *about the new power station* can extrapose when it is the sole adjunct in an NP, as shown in (ii), we now have to explain why it cannot extrapose when it occurs with another adjunct—in this case a reduced relative clause—in the NP:

(ii) A report just appeared about the new power station.

Under the natural assumption that the two adjuncts in the NP are in an asymmetric c-command relation, (i-c) is a straightforward Superiority violation now applied to rightward movement. This result is quite general across a range of NP constructions. For details and discussion see Freidin (1994b). It is worth mentioning that if Superiority generalizes to rightward movement, then it probably cannot be reduced to a condition on Operator Disjointness as proposed in Lasnik and Saito (1992) (see also Epstein 1993 for further discussion).

6. Recall that in 1973 the notion "c-command" had not been developed, and therefore Chomsky's original definition of the relation "superior" is not identical. Chomsky (1973) gives the following definition: "We say that the category A is 'superior' to the category B in the phrase marker if every major category dominating A dominates B as well but not conversely." The term "major category" designates N, V, and A and the categories that dominate them. However, if the rightward movement cases mentioned in the previous note fall under Superiority, then the formulation of the condition might be simplified to just asymmetric c-command.

The formulation of Superiority in (1) requires a further clarification under the Move α analysis. Since Move α does not distinguish between *wh*-movement and NP-movement (i.e., of non-*wh*-NPs), the condition should not be interpreted as applying to a construction where, for instance, a non-*wh*-NP is superior to a *wh*-phrase. Thus, (i) does not constitute a Superiority violation even though Move α applies to both the complement subject and object:

(i) Who does Mary seem to like?

It is not that Move α applies ambiguously to two constituents in an asymmetric c-command relation. What is crucial is that the application of Move α affects the same constituent X.

7. To avoid complicating the exposition, I will use current analyses rather than the historically accurate ones unless the difference is significant. In this case adopting the S′ → Comp S analysis rather than the CP/IP analysis of clauses does not affect the discussion.

8. This proposal appears in Jaeggli (1980/1981), who credits it to Chomsky (class lectures 1979). There is a somewhat different analysis involving the same idea in Aoun, Hornstein, and Sportiche (1980), which utilizes a special mechanism of Comp-indexing at S-structure. As we will see below, there is no need to posit such a mechanism under minimalist assumptions, hence the LF representations here are different from previous analyses (though most similar to May 1985), but the difference does not affect the ECP account.

It should be noted here that this was not the first attempt to derive Superiority. See Koster (1978), where a general c-command condition on locality (his Locality Principle) is proposed as an alternative to the Specified Subject Condition, parts of Subjacency, and Superiority among other phenomena. See also the Priority Filter of Fiengo (1980).

9. See the discussion of examples (22) and (25) below for some evidence that seems to support the disjunctive formulation.

This particular analysis also crucially depends on not adopting the May/Chomsky theory of adjunction structures (May 1985, Chomsky 1986, 1993), where an adjunction structure creates a two-segment category. Under this theory a category α Dominates (the capitalization indicates the special definition of the term) a category β if all the segments of α dominate β. (Notice that we still rely on the standard definition of domination to define "Dominates.") We then substitute "Dominate" for "dominate" in the definition of c-command. Thus, both *who* in (3a) and *what* in (3b) will c-command their respective traces because the first category that Dominates them is CP. We might try to save the ECP analysis by adjoining the *in-situ wh*-phrase to CP. For the examples in (2) this would have the effect that the phrase adjoined to CP would not c-command its trace because there would be no category that Dominates it. However, this strategy would immediately fail with embedded constructions as in (i), with the LF representation (ii):

(i) *I wonder what who read.
(ii) I wonder [$_{CP}$ who$_1$ [$_{CP}$ what$_2$ [$_{IP}$ x$_1$ read y$_2$]]]

In (ii) *who* would c-command its trace because the matrix VP is the first branching category that Dominates *who.*

10. See Pesetsky (1982) and Hendrick and Rochemont (1988) where such cases are discussed as 'pure' superiority effects.

11. Now we might try to save the ECP analysis of superiority effects by noting that at LF, *who(m)* in (4a) will be adjoined to *what* in the external [Spec,CP]. Although the trace of *who(m)* in complement subject position will be antecedent governed by the trace in [Spec,AgrO-P], the trace in [Spec,AgrO-P] would not be antecedent governed by *who,* if—crucially—we reject the May/Chomsky adjunction theory (see note 9). A similar analysis can be constructed for (4b). Nonetheless, this analysis creates a fatal problem. Given that an object must move to [Spec,AgrO-P] at LF for Case checking, the trace of *what* in [Spec,AgrO-P] for (2b) will also fail to be antecedent governed. Under the May/Chomsky adjunction theory and on the analysis that the LF movement of the *wh*-phrase involves adjunction to the *wh*-phrase in the matrix [Spec,CP], then the adjoined *wh*-phrase in [Spec,CP] will c-command and hence antecedent govern its trace in [Spec,AgrO-P]. Thus none of the Superiority violations in (2a) and (4) will violate the ECP. It is worth noting that the Pollock/Chomsky analysis of the functional category structure of clauses creates a problem for (2b) unless we abandon the LF analysis of the ECP or we adopt the May/Chomsky theory of adjunction.

See Cheng and Demirdash (1990) for an alternative ECP anlysis of the superiority effects in constructions like (4). Under this analysis the ECP applies at two distinct levels: antecedent (XP) government at S-structure and head (X^0) government at LF. Such anlyses are excluded under the minimalist framework of Chomsky (1993), given that S-structure is not a legitimate level of syntactic representation.

12. Pesetsky claims that the following pair of examples also demonstrates a difference that involves the Nested Dependency Condition:

(i) a. ?This is one book *which*$_2$ I do know *who*$_1$ to talk to t_1 about t_2
b. *John is one guy *who*$_1$ I do know *what book*$_2$ to talk to t_1 about t_2

These examples are unconvincing because they are essentially on a par with the corresponding examples where the *to*-phrase and *about*-phrase have been switched.

(ii) a. ?This is one book *which*$_2$ I do know *who*$_1$ to talk about t_2 to t_1.
b. *John is one guy *who*$_1$ I do know *what book*$_2$ to talk about t_2 to t_1.

(ii-a) is no more or less deviant than (i-a) even though the two *wh*-chains intersect in (ii-a) while they are nested in (i-a). The deviance of (ii-b) seems equal to that of (i-b), even though the former involves nested chains.

13. This problem does not arise for the analysis of (2b) if we assume that adjunction of *what* to *who* at LF creates an absorption structure along the lines of Higginbotham and May (1981), where the NP that dominates both *wh*-phrases bears the index of each. Alternatively, if we adopt the May/Chomsky analysis of adjunction, then both *wh*-phrases will c-command their respective traces. Further, it will not matter under either analysis whether adjunction occurs to the right or the left. For the NDC to hold for (2a) adjunction would have to occur to the right. Yet even if it did, it is not obvious that the resulting structure involves an instance of crossed binding—especially if the NP that dominates both *wh*-phrases bears the index of *who*.

14. Note that (7a) and (i-a) of note 12 also apparently violate Subjacency, though not the NDC.

15. Thus (i) (in contrast to (ii–iii) is a Superiority violation because the direct object asymmetrically c-commands the object of the PP:

(i) *Who(m) did John give what to?
(ii) To whom did John give what?
(iii) What did John give to whom?

Note that (ii) is problematic for some binary branching analyses of double object verbs (e.g., Larson 1988) where the NP *what* is superior to the PP *to whom*.

16. However, under the hypothesis that violations of multiple conditions increases the perceived deviance of a construction this formulation would not explain why (8) and (9) are perceived as equivalently deviant. If we abandon this hypothesis, nothing follows about the proper formulation of Superiority. Note that restricting Superiority to *wh*-phrases in A-positions eliminates a redundancy between Superiority and Subjacency that otherwise holds for *wh*-island violations in English-type languages.

17. See Rizzi (1980) and Sportiche (1981) for discussions of Italian and French respectively.

18. See Freidin (1974). The observation has also been credited to Richard Kayne and also to Michael Brame, and doubtless should be to many others who read Chomsky (1973) when it first appeared. Thus, whereas (2a) constitutes a Superiority violation, (13b) is absolutely normal. We will return to this and other related facts below.

19. Cf. the Vacuous Movement Hypothesis of Chomsky (1986:89–90)—namely, "vacuous movement is not obligatory at S-structure." See (Freidin and Lasnik 1981:n. 14) where the nonmovement of the *wh*-phrase complement subject in (ii) is proposed to explain the noticeable difference in acceptability between (i) and (ii), a problem raised in Chomsky (1980):

(i) Who did you wonder what saw?
(ii) What did you wonder who saw?

Thus only (i) would be a Subjacency violation, whereas (ii) would be a Superiority violation. Freidin and Lasnik suggest that the deviance of (ii) involves a relaxing of the requirement of *wonder* that its Comp (i.e., complement CP) contain a *wh*-phrase to the less stringent requirement of adjacency between the verb and the *wh*-phrase. See also George (1980) for further discussion of an analysis in which *wh*-phrase subjects do not move string vacuously. As we will see below, this particular analysis is not available under recent theory, nor is the Vacuous Movement Hypothesis more generally.

20. Note that we cannot say that the *wh*-phrase in subject position remains *in-situ* at PF, since at the level of PF the relevant structure is missing. See Chomsky (1991:n. 10). Since there is no level of S-structure in the framework, we can only talk about the differences between overt word order and LF representations in this more complicated way.

21. See Watanabe (1992) for an analysis in which the feature is also strong in *wh-in-situ* languages such as Chinese and Japanese.

22. Related to this is the analysis of echo questions in which the *wh*-phrase remains *in-situ*. Presumably the interpretation of such questions is not identical to the corresponding question in which the *wh*-phrase has been fronted. Let us assume provisionally that there is no *wh*-feature in C that requires checking in these constructions. Exactly how they are interpreted at LF remains to be determined.

23. There is a derivation of (17c) that would converge at PF and crash at LF—namely, the one in which the complement C was [−WH]. However, when we process a string to which the grammar can assign two distinct derivations, one legitimate and the other not, we generally ignore the illegitimate derivation. That is, we do not treat such cases as true structural ambiguity, where we can view the string one way and then another.

24. Note that this analysis does not need to refer to satisfaction of a selectional property, along the lines of Lexical Satisfaction as in Freidin and Babby (1984) and Freidin (1992), not to be confused with Satisfy of Chomsky (1993).

25. Form Chain is proposed in Chomsky (1993) to resolve a conflict between two natural notions of economy, shortest move and fewest steps. In what follows some empirical evidence will be discussed that supports Form Chain over Move α under certain assumptions about the economy of derivations. This evidence also concerns the choice between shortest move and fewest steps.

Form Chain bears a strong resemblance to the proposal for *wh*-movement in Bresnan (1971), which was offered to counter the argument against successive cyclic *wh*-movement in Postal (1970) concerning stranded prepositions by successive cyclic *wh*-movement. Translating Bresnan's proposal to the contemporary analysis, a *wh*-phrase moves directly to a [Spec,CP] governed by a [+WH] C. The rest of the Form Chain proposal is missing. However, Bresnan and Grimshaw (1978) proposes a single long-distance movement of a *wh*-phrase followed by coindexation of the Comp nodes intervening between the *wh*-phrase and its extraction site provided a Comp does not contain its own *wh*-phrase.

26. Notice that in this analysis Subjacency is not an interface condition. It applies immediately to the output of Form Chain, thus it has the flavor of a condition on rule application. Although it might be argued that Subjacency is a condition on the operation Form Chain, this interpretation seems weak. We do not know that any given application of Form Chain violates Subjacency until we have formed the chain and computed its links. If the argument that Subjacency applies to Form Chain as a condition of rule application were valid, then any condition on representations could be similarly construed as a condition on the application of rules. Thus, if filter F blocks the output of rule R, then we would be able to say that F blocks the application of R—which is true. However, F says nothing specifically about R, as is the case with true conditions on derivations.

27. This contradicts Pesetsky's D-linking analysis of *which*-phrases in which it is claimed that they do not move at LF, in contrast to bare interrogative pronouns—thus, they do not create crossed binding configurations that violate the NDC. However, without the NDC there is no explanation for the difference in behavior between D-linked versus non-D-linked *wh*-phrases. I am assuming that the previous discussion renders the NDC suspect at best. See Lasnik and Saito (1992) for further criticism of Pesetsky's analysis.

28. Chomsky (1986) refers to the corresponding example with bare interrogative pronouns (i) as "at worst a weak *wh*-Island Condition violation":

(i) What did you wonder who saw?

(See note 19 above for additional discussion and references.) Let us assume for the moment that (i) is also a Superiority violation under the Form Chain analysis. However, the derivation of (22) would not be, since a *which*-phrase may move over a superior *which*-phrase without inducing unacceptability. See note 18.

The selectional feature of *wonder* can also be checked by being morphologically instantiated as *if* or *whether.*

29. The examples Chomsky cites concern head movement and segmental phonology. (22), and perhaps (14) as well, provide an example involving XP movement.

30. It also violates the extension version of the strict cycle mentioned in Chomsky (1993). However, I will not pursue this issue here.

31. Under the Move α analysis, then Subjacency would have to be a condition on derivations because the intermediate trace in the internal [Spec,CP] would be destroyed by the movement of the complement subject *wh*-phrase to that [Spec,CP]. Thus, we arrive at a conclusion similar to that of Lasnik and Saito (1984), though for different reasons. In their analysis the *wh*-phrase does not have to leave a trace in [Spec,CP] and therefore does not. Hence Subjacency is violated if it is interpreted as a condition on representations, but not if it applies to derivations. What is correct about their analysis is the insight that Subjacency is directly tied to the operation of movement rules.

If the analysis proposed here is on the right track, it shows again how misleading our descriptive generalizations can be. *Wh*-islands come in varying strengths, depending on what grammatical principles their computations violate (i.e., ECP vs. Superiority).

32. This analysis requires a disjunctive formulation of the ECP as argued for most recently in Lasnik and Saito (1992). See also Chomsky (1981), Huang (1982), and Lasnik and Saito (1984) for discussion of the disjunctive formulation of the ECP.

33. It makes no difference whether we create absorption structures at LF or adjoin the *in-situ wh*-phrase to CP.

34. See Kitahara (1993) for a detailed discussion of how Shortest Movement accounts for a range of Superiority violations.

35. (28) is essentially the one cited in Chomsky (1993:14), except that the *who/whom* distinction is quite weak in my idiolect. Thus I prefer (28a) with *who* in both *wh*-phrase positions.

36. For me (29a) is slightly degraded compared to (29b), which is on a par with (28a).

37. (29b) not only provides empirical evidence against the notion of shortest move, but it also provides evidence for Form Chain as opposed to Move α, crucially assuming Greed. Thus, the motivation for Form Chain can no longer be credited to a conflict between two natural notions of economy, shortest movement and fewest steps, as mentioned in note 25.

38. The corresponding paradigm with bare interrogatives is interesting because both cases seem to be deviant.

(i) a. ?*What seems to whom to be boring?
    b. *To whom does what seem to be boring?

(i-b) is a straightforward Superiority violation. (i-a) seems only slightly less deviant than (i-b) for reasons that remain obscure.

39. There may be a reading where both (35a–b) are acceptable—namely, where the string *do you wonder* is parsed as a parenthetical. We are not considering that analysis, but rather the one in which *wonder* functions as the main verb of the sentence.

40. At best Subjacency provides only a partial explanation for the strong deviance of these constructions. Ideally, the cyclic derivation would be unavailable so that Subjacency would not be involved at all in explaining these examples.

Note that (8) and (9) still pose a problem under the assumption that only the movement of NPs is involved. However, given that such constructions are strongly deviant, on a par with those in (37) if not worse, a different analysis seems to be involved. Suppose that (8–9), like (37), involve the movement of two distinct categories (NP and PP) in spite of appearances. If so, then the stranding of the preposition must come about by some other process. This could be achieved under the copying+deletion analysis of movement discussed in Chomsky (1993). See Freidin (in preparation) for details.

41. It is worth noting that such examples cannot be subsumed under a nested dependency or path containment condition of the sort proposed in Pesetsky (1982, 1987).

REFERENCES

Anderson, S., and P. Kiparsky, eds. 1973. *A Festschrift for Morris Halle.* New York: Holt, Rinehart, and Winston.

Aoun, J., N. Hornstein and D. Sportiche. 1980. Some Aspects of Wide Scope Quantification. *Journal of Linguistic Research* 1:69–95.

Bresnan, J. 1971. Sentence Stress and Syntactic Transformations. *Language* 47:257–81.

Bresnan, J. and J. Grimshaw. 1978. The Syntax of Free Relatives in English. *Linguistic Inquiry* 9:331–91.

Cheng, L., and H. Demirdash. 1990. Superiority Violations. *MIT Working Papers in Linguistics* 13:27–46.

Chomsky, N. 1973. Conditions on Transformations. In Anderson and Kiparsky, eds., 1973.

Chomsky, N. 1977. On *Wh*-movement. In *Formal Syntax.* P. Culicover, T. Wasow and A. Akmajian, eds. New York: Academic Press.

Chomsky, N. 1980. On Binding. *Linguistic Inquiry* 11:1–46.

Chomsky, N. 1981. *Lectures on Government and Binding.* Dordrecht: Foris.

Chomsky, N. 1986. *Barriers.* Cambridge: MIT Press.

Chomsky, N. 1991. Some Notes on the Economy of Derivation and Representation. In R. Freidin, ed., 1991.

Chomsky, N. 1993. A Minimalist Program for Linguistic Theory. In *The View from Building 20: Essays in Linguistics in Honor of Sylvain Bromberger.* K. Hale and S. J. Keyser, eds. Cambridge: MIT Press.

Chomsky, N. 1995. Bare Phrase Structure. This volume.

Chomsky, N., and H. Lasnik. 1993. The Theory of Principles and Parameters. In *Syntax: Ein internationales Handbuch zeitgenössischer Forschung.* J. Jacobs, A. von Stechow, W. Sternefeld, and T. Vennemann, eds. Berlin: Walter de Gruyter.

Collins, C. 1994. Economy of Derivation and the Generalized Proper Binding Condition. *Linguistic Inquiry* 25:45–61.

Epstein, S. 1993. Superiority. Manuscript. Harvard University.

Fiengo, R. 1980. *Surface Structure: The Interface of Autonomous Components.* Cambridge: Harvard University Press.

Freidin, R. 1974. A Note on *Wh*-movement. *Purdue University Contributed Paper in Speech, Hearing, and Language* 3:55–60.

Freidin, R. 1978. Cyclicity and the Theory of Grammar. *Linguistic Inquiry* 9:519–49.

Freidin, R., ed. 1991. *Principles and Parameters in Comparative Grammar.* Cambridge: MIT Press.

Freidin, R. 1992. *Foundations of Generative Syntax.* Cambridge: MIT Press.

Freidin, R. 1994a. Conceptual Shifts in the Science of Grammar: 1951–92. In *Noam Chomsky: Critical Assessments.* 4 vols. C. Otero, ed. London: Routledge.

Freidin, R. 1994b. Superiority and Extraposition. Manuscript. Princeton University.

Freidin, R. In preparation. Superiority, Cyclicity, and Economy. Manuscript. Princeton University.

Freidin, R., and L. Babby. 1984. On the Interaction of Lexical and Syntactic Properties: Case Structure in Russian. *Cornell Working Papers in Linguistics* 6:71–103.

Freidin, R., and H. Lasnik. 1981. Disjoint Reference and *Wh*-trace. *Linguistic Inquiry* 12:39–53.

George, L. 1980. *Analogical Generalization in Natural Language Syntax.* Ph.D. Dissertation. MIT.

Hendrick, R., and M. Rochemont. 1988. Complementation, Multiple *Wh* and Echo Questions. *Toronto Working Papers in Linguistics* 9.

Higginbotham, J., and R. May. 1981. Questions, Quantifiers, and Crossing. *The Linguistic Review* 1:41–79.

Huang, C.-T. J. 1982. *Logical Relations in Chinese and the Theory of Grammar.* Ph.D. Dissertation. MIT.

Jaeggli, O. 1980/1981. *Topics in Romance Syntax.* Dordrecht: Foris.

Kayne, R. 1983. Connectedness. *Linguistic Inquiry* 14:223–50.

Kitahara, H. 1993. Deducing "Superiority" Effects from the Shortest Chain Requirement. *Harvard Working Papers in Linguistics.*

Kitahara, H. 1995. Target α: Deducing Strict Cyclicity from Principles of Economy. *Linguistic Inquiry* 26:47–77.

Koster, J. 1978. *Locality Principles in Syntax.* Dordrecht: Foris.

Koster, J. 1986. *Domains and Dynasties: The Radical Autonomy of Syntax.* Dordrecht: Foris.

Larson, R. 1988. On the Double Object Construction. *Linguistic Inquiry* 19:335–91.

Lasnik, H. and M. Saito. 1984. On the Nature of Proper Government. *Linguistic Inquiry* 15:235–90.

Lasnik, H. and M. Saito. 1992. *Move α: Conditions on its Application and Output.* Cambridge: MIT Press.

May, R. 1977. *The Grammar of Quantification.* Ph.D. Dissertation. MIT.

May, R. 1985. *Logical Form.* Cambridge MIT: Press.

Otero, C. 1984. *La revolución de Chomsky: Ciencia y sociedad.* Madrid: Tecnos.

Otero, C. 1991. The Cognitive Revolution and the Study of Language: Looking Back to See Ahead. In *Current Studies in Spanish Linguistics.* H. Campos and F. Martínez-Gil, eds. 1991. Washington, D.C.: Georgetown University Press.

Otero, C., ed. 1994. *Noam Chomsky: Critical Assessments.* 4 vols. London: Routledge.

Otero, C. In preparation. *Chomsky's Revolution: Cognitivism and Anarchism.* Oxford: Blackwell.

Pesetsky, D. 1982. *Paths and Categories.* Ph.D. Dissertation. MIT.

Pesetsky, D. 1987. *Wh-in-situ:* Movement and Unselective Binding. In *The Representation of (In)definiteness.* E. Reuland and A. ter Meulen, eds. Cambridge: MIT Press.

Postal, P. 1970. On Coreferential Complement Subject Deletion. *Linguistic Inquiry* 1:439–500.

Rizzi, L. 1980. Violations of the *Wh*-Island Constraint and the Subjacency Condition. *Journal of Italian Linguistics* 5:157–195.

Ross, J. R. 1967. *Constraints on Variables in Syntax.* Ph.D. Dissertation. MIT.

Ross, J. R. 1986. *Infinite Syntax!* Norwood, N.J.: Ablex.

Sportiche, D. 1981. On Bounding Nodes in French. *The Linguistic Review* 1:219–46.

Watanabe, A. 1992. Subjacency and S-structure Movement of *Wh-in-situ. Journal of East Asian Linguistics* 1:255–91

The Morphology of Spanish Clitics*

JAMES HARRIS
Massachusetts Institute of Technology

1 Introduction. The form and distribution of pronominal clitics in Spanish are determined by an intricate web of syntactic, morphological, and phonological factors. This paper explores the involvement of an autonomous morphological module of grammar that mediates between syntax and phonology and is the locus of insertion of vocabulary items into morphological terminal symbols. The formal operations of the morphological module include purging rules and operations of morphological adjunction and sequencing that manipulate an arboreal geometry of features along the lines of familiar phonological feature structures.

The obligatory starting point for any discussion of Spanish clitics is Perlmutter (1971) (P hereafter). One of P's most striking results was the substantiation of proposition (1):

(1) There are well-formed deep structures to which there corresponds no grammatical surface structure (P:19).

The centerpiece mechanism in the demonstration of (1) is the clitic template for Spanish shown in (2):

(2) Syntactic surface structure clitic template (P:45):[1]
se–2pers–1pers–3pers

This template performs a 'filtering function' at syntactic surface structure, "discarding any sentence generated by the transformational component that does not conform [. . .]" (P:86). In other words (2) dictates the selection and linear order of pronominal clitics in syntactic surface structure independently of their role and/or position in deep structure. In order for template (2) to work as intended the so-called 'spurious *se*' rule (3a) must first operate on third person DAT-ACC clusters as illustrated in (3b):

(3) a. Spurious *se* rule (P: 22):

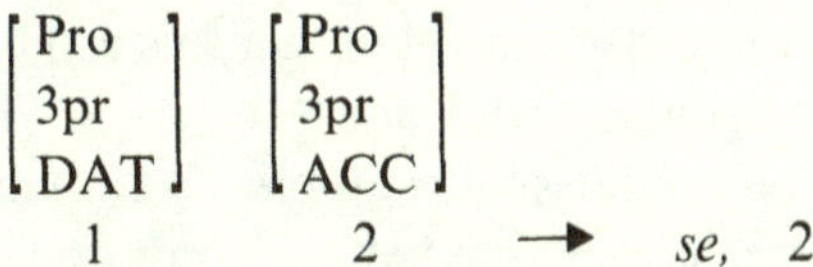

b. A José[1] LE leí cuento, pero a Héctor no SE no leí
'I read the story to José-DAT, but I didn't read it-ACC to Héctor-DAT'

As shown, the third person DAT clitic realized as *le* in isolation (and other contexts) is realized as *se* when clustered with a third person ACC clitic.[2]

Although the terms of syntactic discourse have changed radically since 1971 and numerous studies of Spanish clitics have appeared in the interim, the essential insight of (1) remains firmly established.[3] P's (2) and (3a) are less successful. I note first a property of Spanish clitic clusters that eludes (2). Consider the following examples (rashly shouted by a cruel king to his jester):

(4) a. Exijo que SE TE corte la cabeza . . . ¡que ?SE TE LA corte, digo!
'I demand that your head be cut off . . . Off with it, I say!'

b. Exijo que SE TE ME corte la cabeza . . . ¡que SE TE ME LA corte!
'I demand that your head be cut off for me-DAT . . . Off with it (for me)!'
'I demand that my head be cut off for you-DAT . . . Off with it (for you)!'

Two-clitic clusters (e.g., *se te*) are of course acceptable to all speakers. Many speakers flatly reject all longer clusters (e.g., *se te la, se te me, se te me la*) as ill-formed. Other speakers find them gradiently acceptable (and perhaps ambiguous as indicated). But very few speakers find any four-member cluster well formed. It is not understood what underlies this variation in grammaticality judgments.[4] In any event there are no alternative well-formed versions of sentences like (4a,b) not involving clitics; either the corresponding deep structures are realized as in (4) or they cannot be realized at all.

Strozer (1976:168) suggests that degraded acceptability of three- and four-member clusters "is probably due, at least in part, to the difficulty of interpreting them." It may well be true that some clitic clusters are hard to process in some contexts (or lack thereof), but this can hardly be relevant in cases like (4): even speakers who find (4b) grossly ill-formed find it easily interpretable. The trouble that examples like (4) make for P is that (2), the only relevant mechanism, predicts, contrary to fact, equal acceptability for all (conforming) clusters whatever their length.[5] This is an intriguing problem, but I leave it unresolved and turn to more tractable and substantive problems with (2) and (3a).

I note first that (2) contains a notational equivocation. The clitic *se* is no less third person than the items that occur in the rightmost position, which must exclude *se.* P simply takes this exclusion for granted and does not account for it. A deeper issue regarding (2) is its purely accidental character. The linear order *se*-2per-1per-3per is observationally correct (on the intended interpretation of (2), though not by its actual formalism), but nothing in P explains why it is not 3per-1per-2per-*se,* 1per-*se*-3per-2per, or any other.[6]

The spurious *se* rule (3a), too, has an unexpected and unexplained property: the fact that it yields precisely /se/ (homophonous with genuine *se,* cf. note 2) rather than some other arbitrary phonological string, for instance /ba/, /pu/, or /ran/, is purely accidental.

Clitic cluster well-formedness cannot be reduced to pure phonology, as can readily be seen in the spurious *se* phenomenon, all of whose inputs are impeccable *qua* phonological strings. For example, the clitic sequence **le lo* is disallowed in favor of *se lo* (cf. (3b)), but *lelo* 'dopey' is a well-formed word. Indeed, all inadmissible clitic sequences are perfectly well formed as strings of phonemes; for example, *lo te* and *la te* are impossible as clitic clusters although unexceptional words like *lotería* 'lottery' and *lateral,* 'lateral,' contain phonologically (even prosodically) identical sequences. Further, both syllables in the phonological string can be clitics, as illustrated in (5):

(5) Al hablarLE LO detesté.
'When I spoke to him I hated him.'

It is not controversial that some aspects of Spanish clitic structures are syntactico-semantic. I propose, however, that the specific effects of template (2), the absolute ill-formedness of **lo te* and **la te,* for example, are not syntactic at all, but are due instead to an autonomous morphological component not recognized as a formal element of generative grammar at the time of P and Strozer (1976). Moreover, clitic sequencing is not unitary as in (2). Rather, the overt effect is derived from several separate morphological and lexical factors.

2 The syntax-morphology connection. Let us distinguish between the placement/movement and the sequencing of clitics. The former refers to the relationship of clitics and clitic clusters to other syntactic constituents and is thus clearly a syntactic phenomenon; the latter refers to the distribution and order of clitics within clusters. Previous studies have established that syntax cannot completely determine clitic sequencing, and I claim that it is entirely morphological. This much is beyond controversy: sequencing is independent of placement in that the internal organization of clitic clusters is not affected by the location of the cluster in syntactic structure. Since clitic placement/movement is not the object of investigation here, I give short shrift to syntax. No detail of the cursory sketch I offer for background is crucial to our main enterprise.[7]

The syntactic literature leaves considerable room for speculation regarding the syntactic category of pronominal clitics and clitic clusters and their exact hierarchical relationships in deep and surface structure. Clitic clusters move as a unit, and they attach only to gerunds, infinitives, and person-marked verb forms. For example, various realizations of "He doesn't want to be able to continue giving IT to ME" are illustrated in (6):

(6)				
	not ME-IT	wants to be able to	continue	giving
a.	no ME-LO-	quiere poder	seguir	dando
	no	quiere poder-ME-LO	seguir	dando
	no	quiere poder	seguir-ME-LO	dando
	no	quiere poder	seguir	dándo-MELO
b.	*ME-LO-no	quiere poder	seguir	dando
	*no	quiere poder	seguir-ME	dándo-LO
	*no	quiere poder-ME	seguir-LO	dando

Clitic clusters are thus presumably a single constituent in surface structure, for which I use the theoretically neutral label CC. The position of this constituent in surface structure is something like (7):

(7)

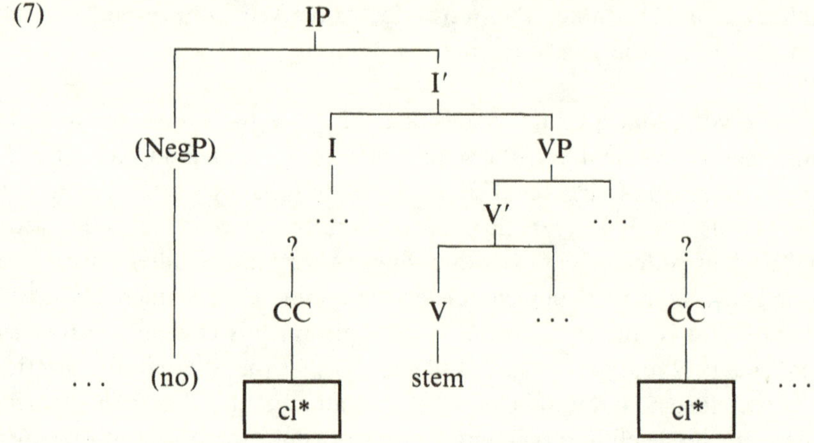

We need not be concerned with the factors that determine proclisis versus enclisis, since both are possible for all single clitics and all well-formed clusters, and (as already noted) the internal structure of the cluster is independent of position.

For concreteness I assume the basic organization of grammar schematized in (8), where a morphological structure component is included in the familiar Principles and Parameters layout:

(8) DS = D-structure, SS = S-structure, LF = Logical Form
MS = Morphological Structure, PF = Phonological Form

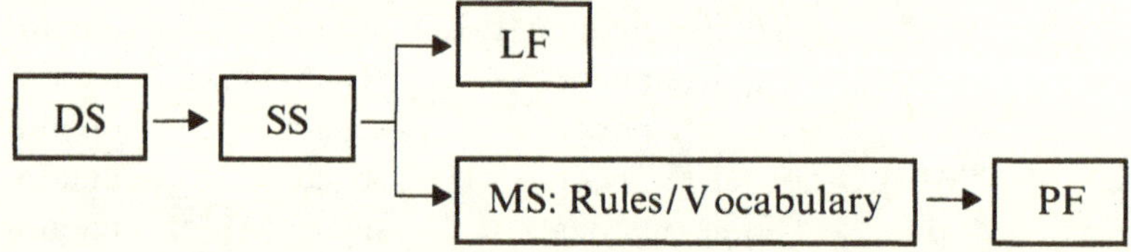

Following familiar arguments, I assume that SS representations are linearly unordered (mobile-like) and that the terminal elements of SS are fully specified for both all and only the features that play a role in syntax and/or depend on syntactic structure (e.g., syntactic category, case, etc.), but not for idiosyncratic declension-class membership, phonological properties, and so on.[8] In the specific case of Spanish pronominal clitics, SS representations look like these to a first approximation:[9]

(9) (^ = adjacent but linearly unordered)

a. $\begin{bmatrix} \text{dat} \\ \text{1p} \\ \text{plu} \end{bmatrix}$ (*nos*) b. $\begin{bmatrix} \text{acc} \\ \text{3p} \end{bmatrix} \wedge \begin{bmatrix} \text{acc} \\ \text{3p} \end{bmatrix}$ (*se lo*) c. $\begin{bmatrix} \text{acc} \\ \text{2p} \\ \text{plu} \end{bmatrix}$ (*sic*) (*los*)

Representations such as (9) are input to MS. Their features (no longer relevant to syntax) may be changed, removed, or augmented in MS. For example, [2per, plu] plays a role in syntax in every dialect of Spanish; but in Latin American dialects the overt realization of every syntactically second person plural item (clitics, stressable pronouns, long and short possessives, etc.) is identical to that of the corresponding (same gender and case) third person item. Thus, syntactic terminal (9c) undergoes restructuring in MS to a representation that refers only to the number and case features shown in (10):

(10) $\begin{bmatrix} \text{plu} \\ \text{acc} \end{bmatrix}$

There is no feature [3per] in (10). I claim that in Spanish 'third person' (the obviously 'unmarked' person) cannot in principle play any role in MS for the simple reason that there is no such entity in the MS of Spanish. Thus, (10), though derived from a [2per] terminal element of SS, is indistinguishable from the MS representation of a [3per acc plu] element of SS. We will see below other cases in which syntactically relevant features are purged from feature bundles in MS.

3 Internal structure of clitics; syncretism and form classes. The surface phonological form of all unclustered pronominal clitics is given in (11):[10]

(11)

<table>
<tr><th></th><th></th><th colspan="2">3pers
m f</th><th>2pers
m f</th><th>1pers
m f</th></tr>
<tr><td rowspan="2">ACC</td><td>SG</td><td>lo</td><td>la</td><td>te</td><td>me</td></tr>
<tr><td>PL</td><td>los</td><td>las</td><td>os</td><td>nos</td></tr>
<tr><td rowspan="2">DAT</td><td>SG</td><td colspan="2">le</td><td>te</td><td>me</td></tr>
<tr><td>PL</td><td colspan="2">les</td><td>os</td><td>nos</td></tr>
<tr><td rowspan="2">REF</td><td>SG</td><td colspan="2" rowspan="2">se</td><td>te</td><td>me</td></tr>
<tr><td>PL</td><td>os</td><td>nos</td></tr>
</table>

I now winnow out what is systematic in (11) from what is arbitrary and idiosyncratic.

Syntacticians and semanticists traditionally distinguish a variety of syntactic/semantic roles associated with Spanish clitics, for example, benefactive, malefactive, ethical, dative of interest, and so forth (Strozer 1976). All of these collapse into a single morphological realization, namely, DAT. We must evidently assume, then, some principle(s) of grammar whose effect is essentially that suggested in (12):

(12) {DAT, BEN, MAL, ETH, INT, . . . } ⇒ DAT

Similarly, as illustrated in note 2 with regard to genuine *se,* clitics are associated with a number of distinct syntactic/semantic roles that correspond to a single morphologically relevant category, for which I employ the traditional label REF(LEXIVE). Thus, we assume some principle(s), similar to (12), with the effect suggested in (13):

(13) {REFL, RECIP, MID, LEX, . . . } ⇒ REF

In short whatever distinctions are necessary in DS, SS, and LF, there are exactly three caselike categories in MS, namely, ACC, DAT, and REF. For these I will employ the neologism "kase" to serve as a reminder that (a) the labels ACC, DAT, and REF shed their syntactic connections in MS, and (b) all three are elements of the same type in MS.

Syncretism is rampant in (11); display (14) shows that 40 input matrices that already discount the distinctions eliminated by (12) and (13) converge on the 11 phonologically distinct clitics in (11):

<table>
<tr><td>(14) a.</td><td>1p
ACC
(f)</td><td>1p
DAT
(f)</td><td>1p
REF
(f)</td><td>1p
plu
ACC
(f)</td><td>1p
plu
DAT
(f)</td><td>1p
plu
REF
(f)</td></tr>
<tr><td>b.</td><td colspan="3">1p

(me)</td><td colspan="3">1p
plu
(nos)</td></tr>
<tr><td>c.</td><td>2p
ACC
(f)</td><td>2p
DAT
(f)</td><td>2p
REF
(f)</td><td>2p
plu
ACC
(f)</td><td>2p
plu
DAT
(f)</td><td>2p
plu
REF
(f)</td></tr>
<tr><td>d.</td><td colspan="3">2p

(te)</td><td colspan="3">2p
plu
(os)</td></tr>
<tr><td>e.</td><td>3p
ACC</td><td>3p
plu
ACC</td><td>2p
plu
ACC</td><td>3p
ACC
f</td><td>3p
plu
ACC
f</td><td>2p
plu
ACC
f</td></tr>
<tr><td>f.</td><td>ACC

(lo)</td><td colspan="2">plu
ACC

(los)</td><td>ACC
f

(la)</td><td colspan="2">ACC
plu
f
(las)</td></tr>
<tr><td>g.</td><td>3p
DAT
(f)</td><td>3p
plu
DAT
(f)</td><td>2p
plu
DAT
(f)</td><td>3p
REF
(f)</td><td>3p
plu
REF
(f)</td></tr>
<tr><td>h.</td><td>DAT

(le)</td><td colspan="2">plu
DAT

(les)</td><td colspan="2">[ ]

(se)</td></tr>
</table>

In this display (14a,c,e,g) contain the inputs to MS received from SS, while (14b,d,f,h) show the minimal specifications required to identify the 11 distinct outputs in MS tabulated in (11).[11] Phonological forms are given for easy identification of the morphological matrices.

The severe loss of overt distinctions shown in (14) is not random or accidental but is due instead, in large part, to operations that modify syntactic terminals by purging them of features that play no role in MS. One such operation was already mentioned in section 2, namely, the merger of second person plural forms with the corresponding third person forms in MS in Latin American dialects. I express this merger formally as in (15):

(15) [plu, 2per]
$\downarrow$
Ø

Application of (15) to feature terminals of the form [N, plu, 2per, KASE, (f)] correctly leaves in place the number, kase, and gender features necessary for phonological realization of all the contrasts in the six resulting third person forms *lo/los/la/las/le/les.* The decision to treat the merger in question precisely as deletion of a morphological feature is not taken casually; it is crucial at several points in the analysis developed below.

Let us now turn our attention to the internal morphological architecture of Spanish pronominal clitics. This structure is not arbitrary: clitics are (pro)nominals and have the same internal morphology of all Spanish 'nominals' (i.e., nonverb forms). This is illustrated in (16), where X is a variable over the appropriate category symbols:

(16)

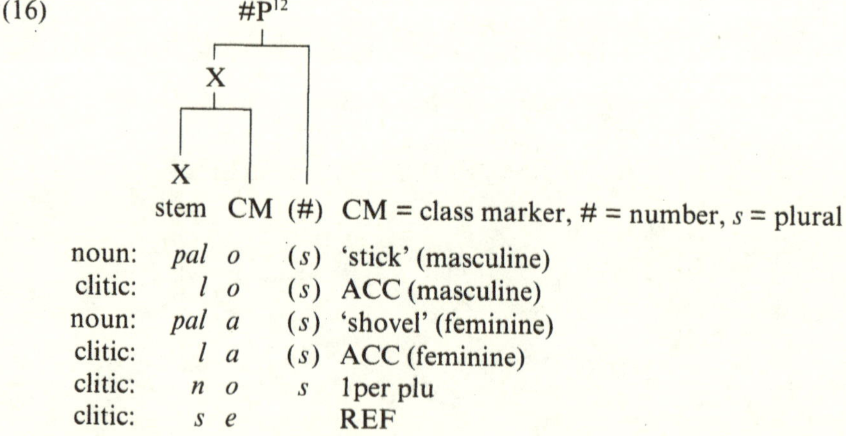

The isomorphism between ordinary nominals and clitics is obvious in *palo(s)/lo(s)* and *pala(s)/la(s),* though it is hardly transparent in *nos, se,* and other clitics.[13]

It is worth emphasizing that CM is not a gender inflection and that it plays no role in syntax; rather, the CM is adjoined to $[\text{stem}]_X$ in MS.[14]

CMs are the overt manifestation of five lexically arbitrary form classes; every nominal stem and nominal-forming affix belongs to one of these (Harris 1991a, b). As can be seen in (11), the form-class affiliation of clitics is as follows:

(17) III: me, te, le(s), se (CM-e)
II: la(s) (CM-a)
I: nos, os, lo(s) (CM-o)

For nonclitic nominals item-specific lexical assignment is necessary for classes III, IV, and V; lexically unspecified items are assigned to class II or class I by redundancy rule:

(18) a. feminine gender assigns class II
b. default class: I

Thus, for clitics as well, *me, te,* and *se* are assigned lexically to class III, while feminine *la(s)* and masculine *lo(s)* are assigned to II and I, respectively, by (18). Something more must be said about *nos* and *os,* which are class I even when syntactically feminine,[15] and dative *le(s),* which is gender invariant. For *nos/os* all that is required is a rule with the effect shown in (19):[16]

(19) [αpers, f]
↓
Ø

This rule applies in MS, removing the specification for feminine from any feature bundle that contains a person feature inherited from syntax. Thanks to (19), the stems of *nos* and *os,* like those of all nominal stems unspecified for gender or class, are assigned to default class I by redundancy rule (18b). Only first and second person clitics are affected by (19) since there is no formal mark for third person (section 2); the effect of (19) is detectable only in plural clitics since singular *me* and *te* are class III (which manifests no gender distinction) in any event.

We turn now to third person dative *le(s).* Note first that (11) shows total syncretism of kase in first and second person clitics. This systematic property of (11) can be captured by rule (20), which applies in MS to remove the irrelevant features:

(20) [per, KASE]
↓
Ø

Given the generalization expressed in (20), the class affiliation of *le(s)* is assigned by rule (21):

(21) [dat] → III

This maximally simple formulation is possible since (20) allows kase features to be present in MS only in the terminals of third person clitics, that is, those formally unmarked for person.

One syncretism not reflected in (11)/(14) is also formally a purging operation of a slightly different sort from (15), (19), and (20), different because the context is provided by an adjacent clitic. This is the spurious *se* rule, introduced as (3a), whereby syntactically dative *le* and *les* are realized as *se* when clustered with a third person accusative clitic. Given that (20) removes kase in MS from matrices that contain [per], only third person terminals (i.e., those unmarked for person) retain kase in MS. Therefore, the spurious *se* rule can be formalized as (22), which applies only to clusters of third person clitics:

(22) [acc]^[dat]
↓
Ø

After application of (22) erstwhile dative terminals have at most the feature(s) [X, (plu)]. This feature bundle has a single phonological realization, namely /s/, needed for the third person REF clitic in any event (see next section). Thus, (22), an irreducibly simple rule of the independently motivated class of purging operations in MS, directly yields the phonological instantiation of the existing clitic *se,* rather than an arbitrary string of phonemes (cf. P's (3a)).[17]

We have now identified most of the systematic properties of (11) relevant to the present discussion. The idiosyncratic information in (11) that remains to be accounted for relates primarily to the phonological realization of clitic stems. This information is provided by vocabulary entries of the type shown in (23), which also includes the phonological matrices for the class markers (CM) and number morpheme (#) of all nominals:

(23) Vocabulary:

a.	stem ↔	n	/1per,plu
		m	/1per
		[Ø	/2per,plu] (Spain only)
		t	/2per
		l	/acc/dat
		s	(default)
b.	plu ↔	Ø	/[[s-]__]$_N$[18]
			(default)
c.	CM ↔	e	/[III]__
		a	/[II]__
		o	(default)

Terminal nodes in SS do not contain information about idiosyncratic declension-class membership, phonological properties, and so on. Rather, lexical insertion takes place in MS after the purging operations described in the previous section. The phonological matrices (and identification of form-class membership, if unpredictable) of vocabulary items are inserted into but do not replace morphological matrices. Insertion obeys the condition that morphological matrices must be nondistinct from lexical contextual restrictions. The latter impose a partial ordering within sublists in accordance with the familiar universal Paninian principle of "more complex first." For example, the vocabulary item *n-* 'wins' over the item *m-* for insertion into the matrix [1per, plu] even though the contextual restriction on *m-* is compatible with (i.e., nondistinct from) this matrix. By the same token the item *s-*, which has no contextual requirement, can be inserted only into matrices that do not satisfy the more complex contextual restrictions of all other items in the same sublist of stems.

4 Morphological feature geometry. The previous section lays out a fairly detailed descriptive analysis of the morphological and phonological properties of Spanish pronominal clitics. We now explore ways in which the descriptive generalizations uncovered might be explained as specific consequences of certain general principles.

The traditional idea that morphological features are related hierarchically has reappeared in recent work (Bonet 1991, Halle and Marantz 1993, Harley 1993, and Noyer 1992, among others). For example, Noyer (1992) argues that the target and context features of morphological purging operations such as (15), (19) and (20) stand in the relationship CON-

TEXT FEATURE > TARGET FEATURE, where '>' means "dominates." Thus these purging rules imply (24a–c):[19]

(24) a. plu > 2per (15)
b. 1/2per > f (19)
c. 1/2per > dat/acc/ref (20)

Since the feature hierarchy is presumably universal, the prediction is that—if (24a–c) are empirically correct—no language can have a rule that deletes [plu] in the context of [2per], or [per] in the context of [f], and so on.[20]

Harley (1993) argues for a more elaborate hierarchy analogous to phonological feature geometry, *mutatis mutandis.*[21] For Harley this structure is not separate from feature bundles in MS as in Noyer; rather, the actual feature representation of morphemes is arboreal rather than consisting of unorganized sets. Like their phonological counterparts, feature trees in MS contain both terminal features and classificatory nodes that define natural classes for morphological rules and encode the possibilities of contrast. For Harley, (24a), for example, does not imply that [plu] directly dominates [2per]. Rather, [plu] is not more deeply embedded than [2pers], as in the following partial tree (where classificatory nodes and terminal features are written in uppercase and lowercase, respectively):[22]

(25)

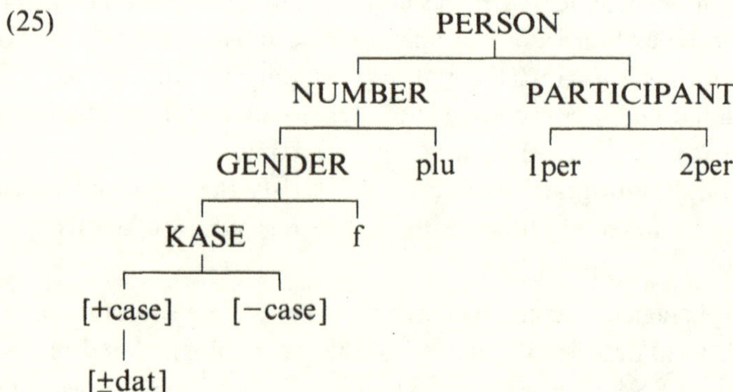

We immediately see one generalization that can be captured by (25): the two rules (19) and (20), both of which purge features in the environment of person features, can be expressed as the single rule (26):

(26) [PARTICIPANT, GENDER]
↓
Ø

Rule (26) correctly expresses the generalization that Spanish clitics marked for person cannot be marked for any feature in the natural class GENDER, that is, either 'gender' or 'case' in everyday terminology.

Harley proposes that 'degree of embedding' is proportional to the number of dominating nodes. By this measure [plu] and [2per] are equally embedded in (25), and either can be deleted in the context of the other.[23] In cases of unequal embedding the higher feature provides the context for the deletion of the lower feature. Thus, (25) encodes the context-target relationship in (26), for example, where PARTICIPANT triggers removal of GENDER and more generally predicts that gender and case features can never be directly responsible for purging person features.

Harley also proposes that morphological feature trees impose ordering on particular blocks of rules in cases of disjoint or overlapping structural descriptions, where the Paninian subset principle is inapplicable: the rule whose structural description contains the fewest nodes in the feature geometry takes precedence. Although the purging rules under discussion, to which the Paninian principle is irrelevant, are not obviously inconsistent with this proposal, it is not clear that they contain a meaningful test case: (15) applies beyond the clitic system, and the structural description of (22) encompasses two clitics; thus, our present limited understanding does not guarantee that the rules in question are all contained in a single rule block.

On the other hand the vocabulary insertion rules in (23) do present one case in which Harley's node-counting principle makes a valid prediction. Paninian complexity determines all of the empirically necessary orders in (23) except for that involving the item *l-* and those listed above it. Given that insertion is governed by nondistinctness rather than the stronger condition of identity between rule context and features of terminal nodes, why can't *l-* be inserted into terminals with person features? Harley's principle provides an answer: the insertion rule for *l-*, which mentions KASE features, involves a larger subtree than the rules higher on the list, none of which mentions anything in (25) lower than PERSON and NUMBER features. In sum, given Harley's proposal, no parochial ordering statement at all is required for (23).

5 More on plurality.

5.1 The plurality of *nos/os* and *se*. The obligatory *-s* of *nos/os* and the obligatory lack thereof in syntactically plural *se* are related. I outline here parts of the system that relates them.

Adjectives as well as nouns (and, I claim, clitics) have the overt morphology illustrated in (16) above (Harris 1991a, b). But there is a significant difference between nouns and adjectives with respect to gender and number. Nouns have gender and number; adjectives acquire gender and number through concord. Let us say that gender and number are 'proprietary' in nouns but 'vicarious' in adjectives. All plural nouns in Spanish manifest overt affixal plurality, with the suffix *-s.*[24]

In Spanish adjectives proprietary number occurs only in the special case of possessives. For example, *mi(s)* 'my' is proprietarily singular; it may or may not have a vicarious plural by virtue of concord. On the other hand the stem of *nuestr-* 'our' is proprietarily plural; it too may or may not have a concord-triggered vicarious plural. The stem *su(s)* 'your, his, her, its, their' is strikingly different: there is only one vocabulary item for both proprietarily singular and plural stems. In short there are thus two instantiations of plurality in first person *nuestro-s:* for example, one in the stem (vs. singular *mi-*) and another in the affix *-s.*

We now look at pronominal clitics in the same way.

(27)

		sing	plur	
a.	2 stems	*me*	*nos*	
		te	*os*	
b.		*le*	*les*	*-s*
		lo	*los*	
	1 stem	*la*	*las*	
c.		*se*	*seØ*	no *-s*

The forms in (27) cross-classify. The first and second person clitics (27a) have distinct stems, that is, separate vocabulary items, for singular and plurals opposed to the third person clitics (27b,c), which have a single stem for singular and plural. On the other hand, (27a) and (27b) group together, as opposed to *se,* in having a suffixal plural.

Compare (27) with the possessive adjectives. The first and second person clitics in (27a) and the adjective *nuestro-s/nuestra-s* uniquely share the characteristic of having two marks of plurality, one in the stem and another in the suffix *-s.* Since proprietarily plural nominals have suffixal *-s* without exception,[25] the clitics in (27a,b) are normal in this respect; *se* is uniquely exceptional among nominals in not manifesting *-s* when plural.

This exceptionality is a property of the root *s-*, not a peculiarity of the clitic *se.* Note first that both genuine and spurious *se* reject overt pluralization.[26] Second, other forms with the same root also reject suffixal manifestation of proprietary plurality; specifically, the possessive *su* 'your, his, her, its' and *nota bene* 'their' and the nonclitic (stressed) pronoun *sí* (**sís*) 'yourself, himself, herself, itself' and *nota bene* 'themselves.' Lack of suffixal plural -*s* is thus clearly an idiosyncracy of the single root *s*-.

It thus emerges clearly that some X^0s (first and second person plural clitics and the first person plural possessive adjective) contain two instances of [plu] corresponding to two sources of suffixal plurality, namely, proprietary plurality in nominals and concord in adjectives. The element # in (16) is thus a structural position in Spanish nouns, pronouns, and adjectives that houses the phonological realization of plurality, both proprietary and vicarious.[27] To account formally for the language-particular fact that suffixal plurality systematically accompanies proprietary plurality in Spanish nominals, I propose the following rule:

(28) $[[\text{plu}]_{N}\underline{\quad}]_{N^0}$
↓
plu

In the nominals with the root *s*-, that is, nonclitic and clitic pronouns *sí* and *se,* the suffixal [plu] inserted by (28) receives no phonological matrix because of the special first case of vocabulary insertion rule (23b). This rule pair captures the generalization that, of all the forms with root *s*-, only the two nominals *sí* and *se* reject suffixal -*s* (unlike all other nominals in the language), while the adjective *su* requires this suffix for concord.[28]

5.2 Parasitic plurals. Examples such as the following come from many dialects of Spanish, though not all:[29]

(29) The P(arasitic plural) effect:
La llegada de los federales SE LOS había impedido a las dos.
'The arrival of the soldiers had prevented the two women-DAT from doing it-ACC.'

In (29) the plurality of the DAT argument *las dos* is manifested not on the DAT clitic *se* but rather on the ACC clitic *los* 'doing it,' which is not only syntactically singular but also, *nota bene,* syntactically unpluralizable.[30] Examples like the following show that ACC clitics are never contaminated by the singularity of DAT arguments:

(30) Las codornices Tita SE *LA sirvió a Pedro.
'Tita served the quails-ACC to Pedro-DAT.'

This asymmetry is strongly explained if [plu] is monovalent (an independently motivated assumption taken for granted above). The following examples illustrate an additional interesting limit on the P effect for many, perhaps all, speakers:

(31) a. P effect:
El sombrero SE LOS quité a los hombres.
'I took the men's-DAT hat-ACC off (them).'

b. No P effect:
El sombrero SE LO/*LOS quitaron los hombres.
'The men took their-REF (own) hat-ACC off (themselves).'

The *se* in (31a) is spurious while the *se* in (31b) is genuine.[31] The former triggers the P effect, the latter does not. In other words the P effect appears in DAT^ACC but not in REF^ACC clusters.

Perhaps (32) provides a helpful visualization of the difference between third person DAT-ACC clusters in normative and P effect dialects:

(32) a. Normative dialects:

<table>
<tr><th></th><th></th><th>ACC SG
m/f</th><th>ACC PL
m/f</th></tr>
<tr><td rowspan="2">DAT</td><td>SG</td><td rowspan="2">se lo/la</td><td rowspan="2">se los/las</td></tr>
<tr><td>PL</td></tr>
</table>

b. P effect:

<table>
<tr><th></th><th></th><th>ACC SG
m/f</th><th>ACC PL
m/f</th></tr>
<tr><td rowspan="2">DAT</td><td>SG</td><td>se lo/la</td><td rowspan="2">se los/las</td></tr>
<tr><td>PL</td><td>se los/las</td></tr>
</table>

In normative dialects (32a) the DAT clitic has no effect on the ACC clitic: plurality is manifested on ACC *lo/la* iff that clitic itself is syntactically plural. Not so in P-effect dialects (32b): plurality is manifested affixally on the ACC clitic iff either DAT or ACC is syntactically plural.

There is a straightforward way to express these generalizations in our framework. The basic idea is shown in (33):[32]

(33) a. Normative:

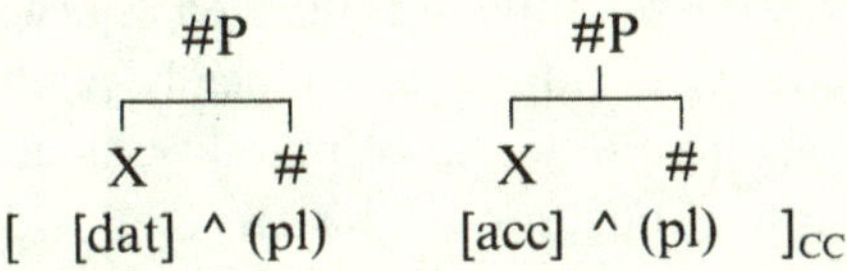

b. P effect:

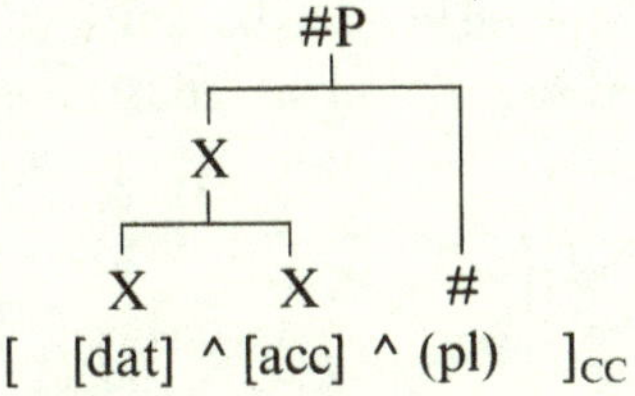

What is special about the P effect is the formation of structure (33b), which is not generated either in normative dialects or in P-effect dialects for REF^ACC clusters. Structure (33b) is the result of the familiar operation of adjunction, as shown in (34):

(34) X [dat (pl)] ^ X [acc (pl)] → X [X [dat (pl)] ^ X [acc (pl)]]

As expected, adjunction of the clustered DAT and ACC terminals in the input creates a new superordinate constituent of the same category. The normal constituent structure of (pro)nominals (see (16) in section 3) provides a node #P that dominates both the higher X and the node #, as shown in (35):

(35)

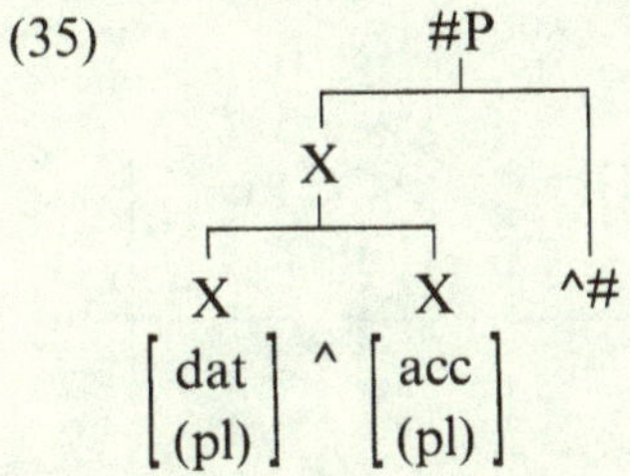

Since morphological terminals are linearly unordered prior to vocabulary insertion, # is equally adjacent to both subordinate X terminals; thus, rule (28) guarantees that [plu] is inserted into # if either X terminal contains that feature. Consequently, # is realized as *-s* according to (23) if either the DAT or the ACC clitic is syntactically plural, or if both are. There is only one overt manifestation of plurality, since there is only one # terminal. The rightmost position of this terminal is determined by the status of the vocabulary item (plural) *-s* as a suffix; the DAT and ACC clitic terminals are linearized by the principles of clitic sequencing (see next section). To summarize, the effects of the spurious *se* rule (22), rule (28), vocabulary insertion, and sequencing are illustrated in (36):

(36)

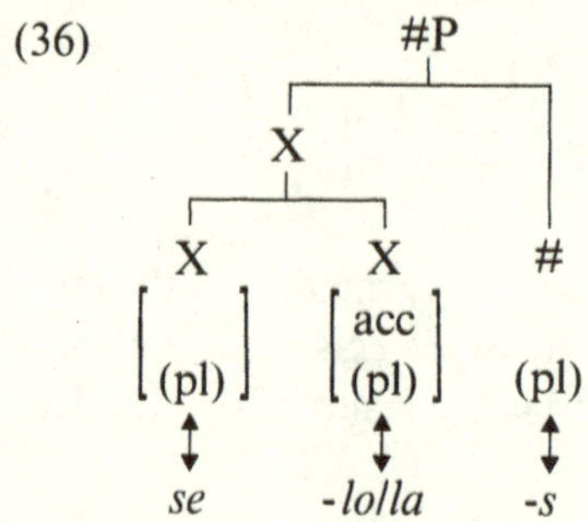

In an apparently small subset of P-effect dialects there is a phenomenon that I will call the P_{nos} effect:[33]

(37) P_{nos} effect:
¿Que si NOS leyó el cuento? Sí, NO LOS leyó.
'Did he read us-DAT the story-ACC? Yes, he read it-ACC to us-DAT.'

In *Sí, no los leyó* the plurality of the DAT argument is realized on the syntactically singular ACC clitic *los* (=*el cuento*) rather than on the DAT clitic, normally *nos.*[34] P_{nos} dialects, then, have the expanded version of (32b) shown in (38):

(38) P_{nos} dialects:

		ACC SG m/f	ACC PL m/f
DAT	SG	se lo/la	
	PL	se los/las	
	PL	no los/las	

As in all Latin American dialects, the only plural DAT clitics are *se* (optionally) and *nos* (inherently, proprietarily). When plural *se* and *nos* are clustered with a third person clitic in P_{nos} dialects, affixal plurality appears on the ACC clitic regardless of its syntactic plurality, but not on the DAT clitic. The output /no/ from *nos*-ACC inputs provides valuable confirmation of two details of our analysis above: (i) that the *-s* of *nos* really is the phonological instantiation of plurality rather than an arbitrary phonological piece of a monomorphemic terminal element and (ii) that inherent and suffixal plurality are empirically distinguishable and phonologically separable.

The P and P_{nos} effects are formally similar: both are instances of morphological adjunction, illustrated in (33) through (36). The essential difference is that the simple P effect restricts this adjunction to clusters with third person DAT clitics, while the P_{nos} effect generalizes it to all clusters with a plural DAT clitic. This descriptive difference might be the consequence of the following formal difference: In simple P-effect dialects adjunction follows purging rule (20), which removes KASE features from the terminal realized as *nos;* therefore adjunction targets only third person DAT^ACC clusters, as illustrated in (34). In P_{nos} dialects, on the other hand, adjunction precedes (20) and thus targets clusters with a first person clitic as well. This proposal would explain the (apparent) fact that P_{nos} dialects are a proper subset of simple P-effect dialects: given the proposed orderings, if adjunction targets *no(s)* then it necessarily targets *se,* but not conversely. Further investigation of P_{nos} dialects would be necessary to (dis)confirm this speculation.

6 Sequencing. I repeat P's template (2) as (39a) for the reader's convenience; the clitics that actually occur in each position are shown in (39b):

(39)					
	a.	se	2per	1per	3per
	b.	se	te/os	me/nos	lV(s)

For P, (39) is the sum of the following ordered pairs (in the examples on the right each clitic is identified by stem only):

(40)		Template pairs			Clitic pairs		
	a.	se-2	se-1	se-3	s-t	s-m/s-n	s-l
	b.	2-1	2-3			t-m/t-n	t-l
						o-m/o-n	o-l
	c.		1-3			m-l/n-l	

No other pairs of clitics surface in Spanish. The formulae in (40a–c) generalize to these three:

(41) a. se-X b. 2per-1per c. X-3per

I comment first on (41b). First and second person clitics together surface only in the order [2per]-[1per], regardless of case (CASE or kase). For example:

(42) a. TE-ME/TE-NOS presentaron.
'They introduced you to me/you to us.'
'They introduced me to you/us to you.'
b. *ME-TE/*NOS-TE presentaron.

The sequences *te-me* and *te-nos* are well formed in all standard dialects, but **me-te* and **nos-te* are not. For some speakers *te-me* and *te-nos* are ambiguous, either DAT-ACC or ACC- DAT; for others the ACC-DAT interpretation is preferred or obligatory. It is not obvious what to make of these differing interpretations. This much is clear, however: the sequence [2per]-[1per] must be imposed and *[1per]-[2per] disallowed in Spanish; if by stipulation as in (41b), so be it; if by some general principle yet to be discovered, so much the better.[35]

The content of (41a) and (41c) is that *s-* must precede and *l-* must follow all other clitics. This being the case, (41) is evidently empirically equivalent to the set of negative filters in (43):

(43) a. *X-s (41a)
b. *l-X (41c)
c. *[1per]-[2per] (41b)

The general conclusion is that templates in the sense of P are not empirically motivated by the data of Spanish clitics as a mechanism of Universal Grammar. The filters in (43) are sufficient to guarantee the correct sequencing of all syntactically and semantically well-formed clitic clusters—MS need not duplicate the work of the syntactic and semantic components. These filters also exclude sequences whose ill-formedness is purely morphological, including in particular the notorious case of multiple instances of *se* discussed in great detail in P in support of proposition (1).

It is possible that (43a,b) instantiate a deeper generalization that rests on the syncretism/purge phenomena discussed in section 3. Consider (44), where left-to-right order corresponds to increase in overt morphological contrasts:

(44) contrast:	Ø	<number	<number/gender/kase
	se=se=se	me=nos	lo=los
		te=nos	lo=la
			lo=le

The generalization that unites (43a) and (43b) can be expressed as the slogan in (45):

(45) Syncretism precedes contrast.

This is understood to mean that a clitic terminal that manifests an overt contrast with respect to a certain morphological property (number, gender, kase) can be preceded in a cluster only by a terminal that shows no overt contrast for that property. Slogan (45) has an arboreal interpretation as well. Given the conventional assumption that nodes without dependents are not present in geometrical representations such as (25), left-to-right order in clitic clusters corresponds to increasing tree size and leafiness: the tree for *se* contains no terminal features, that for *me/te/nos/os* contains participant features (and possibly [plu]), and the tree for the remaining clitics includes the features of the most distant kase branch.

In short, given morphological purging, the correct sequencing of Spanish clitics can be guaranteed by (41b)=(43c) and (45), whether the latter is interpreted arboreally or not. In either case the generalization embodied in (45) is obviously morphological rather than syntactic.

7 Conclusion. The present study adopts the basic tenets of the theoretical framework articulated in Halle and Marantz (1993), which they call distributed morphology (DM). DM is constrained in the first instance by the fact that in mediating between SS and PF, DM must meet the boundary conditions of both SS and PF: DM performs only the minimally necessary operations on structures independently motivated on syntactic and semantic grounds and required by independently determined phonological grounds.[36]

In the Spanish data studied here the perturbations in syntactic structure result mainly from the familiar operation of adjunction and (especially) purging in the MS component. Let us review certain consequences of the latter, more novel process.

Recall that syntactically [2per, plu] items surface in Latin American dialects as the corresponding third person forms. Purging rule (15), which removes [2per] in the context [plu], accounts for this fact. Latin American dialects obviously also have no need for a vocabulary entry for the clitic *os.* Interestingly, absence of this vocabulary entry alone does not account for the data; rule (15) is needed as well: without this purging operation there would be no principled reason not to expect that [2per, plu] clitics inherited from syntax would be realized as *te,* the sole vocabulary item for [2per]. Thanks to rule (15), however, *te* cannot replace *os,* because no plural clitic can have the feature [2pers] at vocabulary insertion. Rule (15) thus not only accounts for the fact that Latin American dialects lack *os,* it also explains why syntactic [2per, plu] clitics have realizations homophonous with the corresponding third person clitics *los/las/les* complete with the kase distinctions that *os* lacks rather than some other arbitrary phonological string: *l-* is the only vocabulary item that can be inserted into clitic terminals that have a kase feature but no person feature. Furthermore, it is easy to see that the same account also automatically predicts that spurious *se* is the only possible realization of a syntactically [2per, plu] clitic clustered with a third person ACC clitic. All of the correct results reviewed in this paragraph are generated without *ad hoc* machinery; indeed, *ad hoc* machinery would be required to prevent these results.

8 Postscript. To close, I would like to give additional illustration of the morphological adjunction operation in a tentative sketch of a phenomenon I will call inflectional cloning (IC) found in certain nonnormative dialects.[37]

(46)		IC occurs:	IC impossible:
	a.	vayaN-seN	no se/*seN vayaN
		go away (pl)	don't go away (pl)
	b.	va a ir-seN	se/*seN va a ir
		they're going to go away	they're going to go away

The morpheme *-n* is the unmarked form of the plural (subject) agreement suffix in verbs. Vocabulary list (23) should thus be expanded to include the following entry at the head of sublist (23b):

(47) plu $\leftrightarrow$ n $/ \_\_]_V$

As expected, *-n* appears in (46a) on the lexically reflexive affirmative imperative *vayan;* unexpectedly, *-n* is also cloned onto the reflexive clitic *se* (which does not normally show plural inflection, much less a verbal *-n*). As shown in the column on the right, IC does not occur with negative imperatives where clitics must be in preverbal position, that is, not adjacent to *-n.* In (46b) the appearance of *-n* on the clitic *se* following the infinitive *ir* is even more anomalous since Spanish infinitives themselves under no circumstance manifest person-number inflection. Nor can infinitives spawn *-n* in a proclitic *se,* as shown in the column on the right in (46b).

The plural imperative *vayan,* like all similar verb forms, has the morphological structure illustrated in (48) with minor irrelevant simplification:[38]

(48) I = (Tense/Mood/Aspect) Inflection
A = (Person/Number) Agreement, imp = imperative

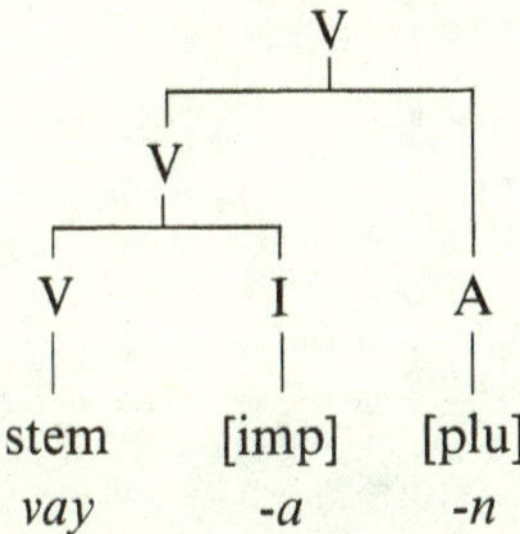

In normative dialects clitics are right sisters of affirmative imperatives in a syntactic constituent for which I will employ the theoretically neutral term Verb-plus-Clitic (VC). This is illustrated in (49):

(49)

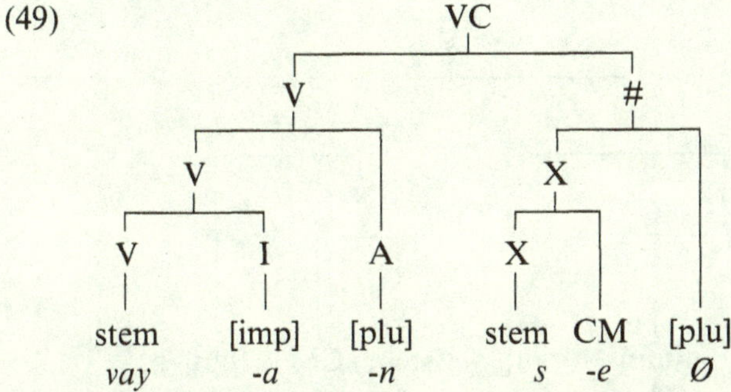

At the transition from SS to MS the derivational ancestor of (49) has the simpler form (50):

(50)

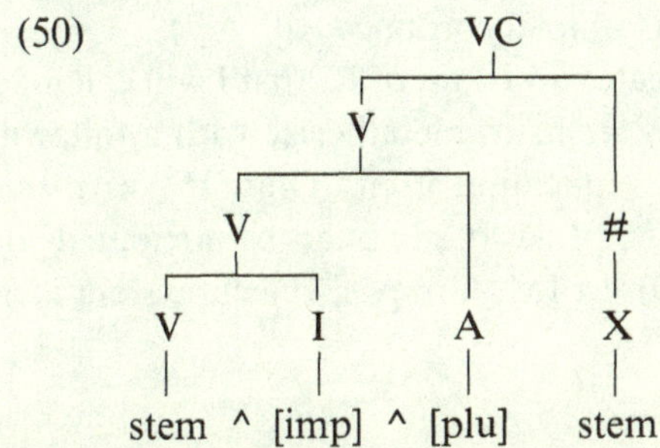

In normative dialects the hierarchical relationship between verb and clitic is not altered. In dialects with IC, on the other hand, the clitic is adjoined in the MS component to the verb. The resulting structure is shown in (51):

(51)

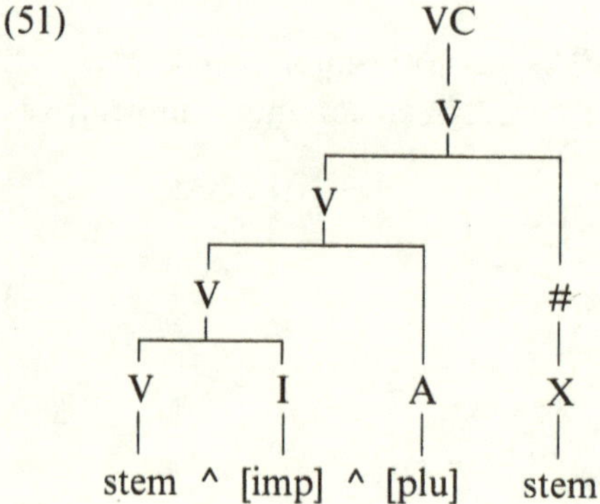

Application of all remaining MS rules and vocabulary insertion yield the structure shown in (52):[39]

(52)

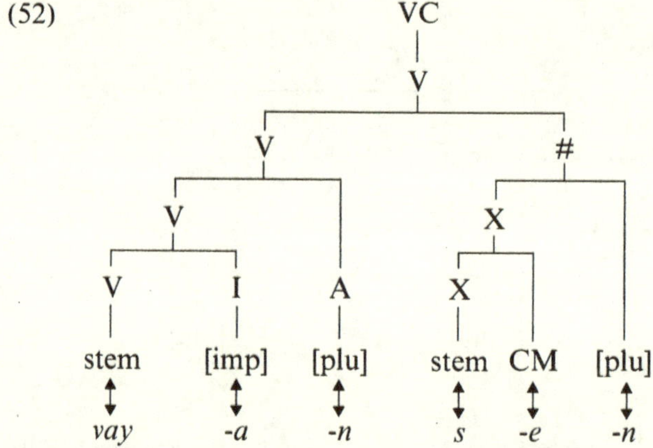

Thanks to adjunction, both instances of [plu] in (52) are dominated by V; therefore both are realized as *-n* in accordance with (47).

Minkoff (1993) investigates a variant of IC that I will call inflectional metathesis (IM), in which *-n* seems to metathesize with a following clitic or clitic cluster rather than replicating itself. Thus, IM *vaya-seN* is the counterpart of IC *vayaN-seN*.[40] Like IC, IM can be attributed to an MS adjunction operation on (50). In IM, however, the clitic stem is adjoined to A, as shown in (53):[41]

(53)

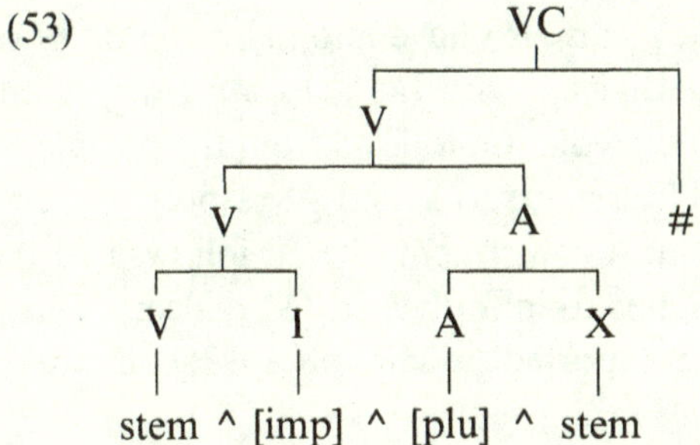

Subsequent MS operations, including vocabulary insertion, yield (54):

(54)

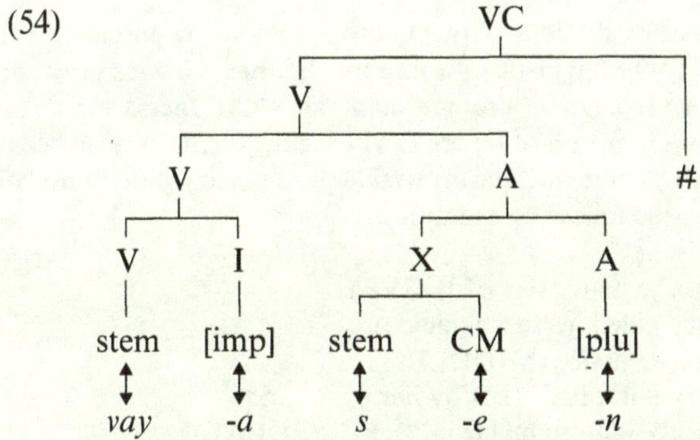

The empty # in (54) naturally receives no phonetic interpretation since there is no corresponding vocabulary item. More interestingly, the illusion that IM *vaya-seN* is related to normative *vayaN-se* by metathesis is an automatic result of the adjunction operation: once $[plu]_A$ and the clitic stem (with its adjoined CM) are sisters, their linear order is determined by the fact that the vocabulary item *-n* is inherently a suffix. No additional operations of movement or linearization are necessary.

It is clear why inflectional *-n* does not appear on clitics in preverbal position as illustrated in the right-hand column of (46a,b), in either IC or IM: there is no adjunction operation whereby $[plu]_A$ can become adjacent to the clitic stem while retaining its adjacency relation to $[imp]_I$, as the theory of morphological adjunction demands (Marantz 1989, Halle and Marantz 1993).

This account makes an interesting prediction on the natural assumption that the lack of person-number inflection on infinitives in Spanish is due to the fact that no A(greement) node is adjoined in structures otherwise like (48) in relevant respects. The prediction is that dialects with IC in imperatives, as in (46a), can also have anomalous *-n* on postinfinitival clitics, as in (46b), while dialects with IM (e.g., *vaya-sen*) will lack *-n* on postinfinitival clitics. This prediction follows from the postulation that IC and IM dialects adjoin clitic stems to V and A, respectively, as illustrated above: if infinitives lack an A constituent, then it follows that there can be no adjunction of clitic stems to infinitives in IM dialects. This prediction is true for the IM dialect reported in Minkoff 1993; it awaits wider confirmation or disconfirmation.

NOTES

* Dedico este estudio a Carlos Otero, quien me ha enseñado más de lo que él se da cuenta, sobre lingüística y sobre mucho más. Gracias por todo, Carlos.

1. I have replaced P's roman numerals with "1pers," etc.

2. This allomorph of [3pers DAT] is called 'spurious *se*' because it is homophonous with 'genuine *se*,' the invariable third person clitic, some of whose uses are illustrated in the following examples:

i. María se mató. (REFLEXIVE)
'Mary killed herself.' (suicide)

ii. María se mató. (MIDDLE)
'Mary got killed.' (not by her own hand)

iii. María y Juan se mataron. (RECIPROCAL)
'Mary and John killed each other.' (double murder)

iv. Se vive bien aquí. (UNSPECIFIED SUBJECT)
'People live well here/The living is good here.'

v. Juan se lavó las manos. (INALIENABLE)
'Juan washed his (own) hands.'

vi. Juan se queja. (LEXICAL)
'John complains.'

3. To the best of my knowledge Strozer (1976) remains unsurpassed as a source of both data and analysis, though the theoretical framework is out of date. Bonet (1991) provides dramatic support for a contemporary interpretation of (1).

4. One expects to find (among other statistical effects) that longer clusters occur less frequently in natural discourse than shorter ones. But the issue here is well-formedness, not statistics.

5. P states that for speakers who disallow greater-than-two-member clusters "some additional constraints appear to be operative" (P:52, note 28). The contrasting dialects do not seem to differ in any syntactically relevant way, and P makes no proposal as to what these constraints might be.

6. The same is true, *mutatis mutandis,* of Strozer's account, in which several aspects of clitic sequencing are stipulated in deep structure.

7. Readers interested in syntactic details should consult P, Strozer (1976), and the rich current syntactic literature such as Anderson (1993), Kayne (1991),

Marantz (1989), Otero (to appear), and Picallo (1991), with their extensive bibliographies.

8. For further discussion see Halle and Marantz (1993).

9. We can assume that all these matrices contain or are dominated by CL(ITIC), which will serve as a place holder for whatever category future research confirms to be the appropriate one.

10. Second person plural *os* is used only in Spain. In Latin America [2per plu] merges with [3per plu], as just noted.

11. In (14), "f(eminine)" is included in parentheses where possible in order to save space by reducing the number of input matrices. As we will see REF is superfluous in MS, but I will continue to use this designation for reflexive clitics where convenient.

12. I use this notation to distinguish the morphological 'number phrase' constituent from the NP of syntactic X′ structure.

13. The attribution of structure to clitics as in (16) is a radical departure from all the literature of which I am aware. Evidence is given in section 5.2 below that the *-s* of *nos*/*os* really is the plural marker rather than an arbitrary phonological segment.

14. On the other hand it is likely that 'number phrase' is a syntactic constituent, but the point is not crucial here.

15. As in examples like *Nosotras nos quejamos* 'We (fem) REF complained.'

16. The notation [αpers] in (19) and subsequently is a stand-in for the participant node introduced in section 4 below.

17. Whatever its source, the clitic *se* never shows overt pluralization (**ses*) even when clearly plural in DS/SS (cf. note 2, example iii). We will see below that this property of the lexical item *s-* is independent of the clitic system.

18. Cf. previous note. We return to this rule in section 5.

19. It is not clear how (22), where target and context features are in separate morphemes, relates to Noyer's proposal.

20. The decision to treat [plu] and [f] as monovalent rather than binary features, especially in (26) below, is not casual. An argument for [plu] is given in section 5.2 below in connection with example (29). Motivation for [f] appears at several points in Harris (1991a, b).

21. Morphological feature geometry has no natural relation to the anatomy of the human vocal tract, as does the phonological analogon.

22. This tree is not consistent with all subtrees proposed by Harley. The participant node obviates need for the notation [per], which subsumes [1per] and [2per]; absence of this node (and thus necessarily of its dependents) is equivalent to 'third person.' The KASE features [−case], [+dat], and [−dat] are equivalent to REF, DAT, and ACC, respectively. This treatment of KASE is merely an illustrative placeholder, needless to say.

23. I deliberately constructed (25) so as to illustrate this possibility, which Harley does not discuss. There is some empirical support for it: Noyer (1992) argues convincingly that person features induce number syncretism in Arabic and elsewhere; on the other hand we have seen above that number (specifically [plu]) obviously provides the context for reduction of person contrasts (specifically second and third) in Latin American Spanish.

24. A few Spanish nouns are inherently plural and thus have the plural suffix *-s,* e.g., *añicos,* 'smithereens.' I do not know of any native Spanish noun that is proprietarily plural but lacks *-s* like English *people* (for all speakers, I suppose), *cattle,* and *dice* (for some speakers).

25. See previous note.

26. See examples in note 2.

27. The # position also houses a form-class marker for numerous words, for example, nonplural *pancre-a-s* 'pancreas' (noun), *mochal-e-s* 'looney, nuts' (adjective), and the adverb *lej-o-s* 'far (away).' (The latter is especially instructive since adverbs are in no way connected with plurality.) Nouns and adjectives with the class marker *-s* in the singular never have a phonologically distinct form when syntactically plural (the plural of *pancreas* is *pancreas,* etc.). This follows from our analysis, since only one vocabulary item can be inserted into one terminal position.

28. The two most plausible descriptive alternatives to this proposal are empirically countermotivated: One, deletion of all instances of [plu] after the root *s-* is not viable: vicarious suffixal *-s* does appear in the possessive adjective *sus.* Two, deletion of [plu] in the stem constituent in the context [REF, ___] prior to the operation of (28) misses the generalization that **ses* is impossible for genuine and spurious *se* alike, that is, that impossibility of suffixal *-s* is a property of exactly the vocabulary item *s-*.

29. The P effect is considered a solecism by purists, but Kany (1951:109) states that in some areas "it is general even among the cultured and in literary style" and cites (unsolicited) written examples from virtually every Spanish-speaking country in the world. I ran across example (29) in Laura Esquivel's stylishly written 1990 novel *Como agua para chocolate* (p. 77).

30. The normative version of this sentence has *se lo.*

31. Without left dislocation of *el sombrero* the sentence in (31a) would be *les quité el sombrero a los hombres.* The sentence in (31b) without dislocation would be *se quitaron el sombrero los hombres.* As (29) shows the P effect is not dependent on dislocation; dislocation is merely a handy provider of transparent examples of third person DAT-ACC clitic clusters.

32. Recall the morphological structure shown in (16) in section 3.

33. I have found no mention of this effect in the standard literature. My sole source, whom I hereby gratefully acknowledge, is Minkoff (1993), who cites personal communication from Yolanda Rivera, a native P_{nos} speaker.

34. Normative and simple P-effect dialects have *nos lo.*

35. Strozer (1976) stipulates an *ad hoc* II-PERSON SHIFT transformation.

36. Indeed, the resolute agnosticism of the present study with regard to syntax is in fact a commitment to accept the consequences for the MS component of whatever structures independent syntactic and semantic argumentation eventually establish as necessary inputs.

37. IC is amply documented in Kany (1951:112–114) and can be heard on Spanish-language radio talk shows in the Boston area, for example. I have not, however, explored the phenomenon myself with a native speaker of an IC dialect.

38. This structure is minimally justified in that the allomorphy of [imp(erative)] and other I morphemes is governed by the idiosyncratic form class of the stem, and allomorphy of [pl] and other A morphemes is in turn governed by the Stem+Inflection constituent.

39. See discussion of the internal morphological structure of clitics in section 3.

40. IM is also amply documented in Kany (1951:112–114).

41. For clitic clusters, for example, *se lo(s),* the adjoined constituent is the superordinate X dominating both clitic stems: $[[\text{stem}]_X[\text{stem}]_X]_X$ (cf. (35), (36)). This yields (correct) IM outputs such as *dé-se-lo-N* 'give (pl) it/them to him/her/them' for normative *dé-N-se-lo(s).*

REFERENCES

Anderson, S. 1993. Wackernagel's Revenge: Clitics, Morphology, and the Syntax of Second Position. *Language* 69:68–98.

Bonet, E. 1991. *Morphology After Syntax.* Ph.D. Dissertation. MIT.

Esquivel, L. 1990. *Como agua para chocolate.* México, D.F.: Planeta.

Halle, M., and A. Marantz. 1993. Distributed Morphology and the Pieces of Inflection. In *The View from Building 20: Essays in Linguistics in Honor of Sylvain Bromberger.* K. Hale and S. J. Keyser, eds. Cambridge: MIT Press.

Harley, H. 1993. Hug a Tree. Manuscript. MIT.

Harris, J. 1991a. The Exponence of Gender in Spanish. *Linguistic Inquiry* 22:27–62.

Harris, J. 1991b. The Form Classes of Spanish Substantives. *Yearbook of Morphology* 1:65–88.

Kayne, R. 1991. Romance Clitics, Verb Movement, and PRO. *Linguistic Inquiry* 22:647–86.

Kany. C. 1951. *American-Spanish Syntax.* Chicago: University of Chicago Press.

Marantz, A. 1989. Clitics and Phrase Structure. In *Alternative Conceptions of Phrase Structure.* M. Baltin and A. Kroch, eds. Chicago: University of Chicago Press.

Minkoff, S. 1993. Plurality, Clitics, and Morphological Merger in Caribbean Spanish. In *Student Conference in Linguistics V.* V. M. Lindblad and M. Gamon, eds. Available from MITWPL.

Noyer, R. 1992. *Features, Positions, and Affixes in Autonomous Morphological Structure.* Ph.D. Dissertation. MIT.

Otero, C. P. To appear. Head Movement, Cliticization, Precompilation, and Word Insertion. In *Current Issues in Comparative Grammar.* R. Freidin, ed. Dordrecht: Kluwer.

Perlmutter, D. 1971. *Deep and Surface Structure Constraints in Syntax.* New York: Holt, Rinehart and Winston.

Picallo, M. C. 1991. Nominals and Nominalizations in Catalan. *Probus* 3:279–316.

Strozer, J. 1976. *Clitics in Spanish.* Ph.D. Dissertation. UCLA.

The Conceptual Structure of Intending and Volitional Action*

RAY JACKENDOFF
Brandeis University

1 Introduction. Much of the literature on the 'folk theory of mind' speaks of it in terms of 'propositional attitudes,' which are characterized simply as "beliefs, desires, etc." But in order to reason about the minds of others, it is necessary to have a more highly differentiated account of the attitudes. This paper investigates one particular case, intending, with attention to related and contrasting cases.

Why is it of interest to investigate intending in particular? I have chosen intending rather than believing because it has a somewhat more complex structure, which reveals more of the texture of the folk theory of mind. In particular the notion of volitional action—of performing an action intentionally—is crucial for the understanding of others' minds, and it has well-known grammatical repercussions as well. Some of these repercussions are dealt with in section 6. Moreover, an analysis of intending is fundamental for the treatment of all manner of social interaction. For instance, speech acts typically involve the speaker's intending the hearer to come to know something or intending to get the hearer to produce some response (see sections 6 and 7). Transactions involve each character doing something for the other with the intention of getting something in return. So an analysis of intending sets the stage for treating a wide range of important predicates.

Two important ground rules before I start: First, I will approach the question by asking what the word *intend* means, that is, how people conceptualize situations in which someone can be said to intend something. In doing so I take myself to be studying a human concept, not an aspect of ultimate reality: I am not concerned with what is really going on in people's brains when we attribute intentions to them. Put differently, unlike Fodor 1987, I do not assume that the folk theory of mind need bear any resemblance to a scientific theory of mind.

However, I also disagree with Churchland (1981) and Stich (1983), who regard the folk theory of mind as 'simply false' and therefore without scientific interest. Rather, my position is that a scientific theory of mind must describe the range of human concepts. It is therefore incumbent on it to describe concepts about other minds (Dennett's 1987 intentional stance), just as it is incumbent on it to describe concepts of space and force—regardless of how 'correct' or 'incorrect' such concepts are scientifically.

My second ground rule is that I will investigate the concept of intending within the general framework of conceptual semantics (Jackendoff 1983, 1990), adopting the general mode of formalization developed within that theory. This notation is not the only conceivable way to frame the investigation; any notation that makes similar distinctions is adequate for my purposes. However, it is important that the notation be construed as encoding regularities in the mind, not some general set-theoretical construct as in most varieties of formal semantics.

Much of my analysis here is based on discussion by Searle (1983) and Bratman (1987); Miller and Johnson-Laird (1976) has also been useful.

2 Predicates with actions as arguments. We begin with a general exploration of the syntax and semantics of propositional attitude verbs, then turn in section 5 to *intend* in particular.

A primary distinction among propositional attitude verbs is between *situational* attitudes and *actional* attitudes. A belief is an attitude adopted toward any situation (state or event), concrete or abstract, at any time, with any combination of characters in it. For example, the complement clauses in (1) express situations:

(1) John believed/claimed/imagined/doubted/assumed/presumed
{ that he was shorter than Bob.
that was born 10 years earlier than he really was.
that he was descended from royalty.
that the sky is green.
that Sue would bring a cake to the party. }

By contrast one can hold an intention only with respect to an event in which one is oneself the actor, a circumstance I will call an action (more precisely, a voluntary or self-initiated action). Thus, the standard syntactic expression uses a VP complement controlled by the subject, as in (2):

(2) John intended
{ to look at Sue.
to scratch his nose.
to prove Fermat's theorem. }

Intend contrasts with *want,* another subject-control verb, in that the complement must be self-controllable, as seen in (3)—that is, the subject of *intend* must be the actor of the complement. In other words, *want,* like *believe,* expresses a situational attitude, but *intend* expresses an actional attitude.

(3) { *John intended / John wanted }
{ to be shorter than Bob. / to have been born 10 years earlier than he really was. / to be descended from royalty. }

The same constraint on the complement occurs with two other predicates of actional attitude, *be willing* and *plan. Offer,* a speech act expressing willingness, follows suit. *Order* and *invite* are parallel except that the control goes with the postverbal NP.

(4) { John was willing/planned/offered / Bill ordered/invited John }
{ to look at Sue. / to scratch his nose. / to prove Fermat's theorem. / *to be shorter than Bob. / *to have been born 10 years earlier. / *to be descended from royalty. }

Intend also occurs with a *for-to* complement or a subjunctive *that*-clause. This option is not available with *offer* and *invite;* however, *order* permits a subjunctive clause, and *be willing* and *plan* permit a *for-to* clause.

(5) a. { John intended/*offered / *Bill invited John }
{ (for) Sue to bring a cake. / that Sue bring a cake. }

b. Bill ordered
{ ?for Sue to bring a cake / that Sue bring a cake. }

c. John was willing/planned
{ for Sue to bring a cake. / *that Sue bring a cake. }

At first glance these cases appear to violate the constraint just stated: the complements do not have subjects controlled by the matrix subject. However, closer examination reveals that their meanings do obey the constraint, even though their syntax does not: their interpretations are 'coerced'[1] into a meaning in which the subject of *intend* acts to bring about the situation described by the complement. For example, (5a) can be fairly well paraphrased by (6):

(6) John intended to bring about that Sue bring a cake.

Note that this *bring about* does not do so well when inserted in (2); evidently, coercion does not occur when the complement already expresses an action:

(7) ??John intended to bring about
{ that he look at Sue.
that he scratch his nose.
that he prove Fermat's theorem. }

Compare this situation with that of *wish,* a situational attitude. (8a) is not at all paraphrased by (8b): no coercion takes place. Furthermore, the *that*-complement of *wish* is not a subjunctive, but a conditional (or whatever one calls the verb form that produces *were* rather than *be* in (8c)); and this wish has no necessary connection with what John might do.

(8) a. John wished for Sue to be happy.
b. John wished to bring about that Sue be happy.
c. John wished that Sue were/*be happy.

In short the original semantic generalization stands. Actional attitudes require their complements to be interpreted as actions to be performed by the holder of the attitude. The apparent counterexamples are only so in the syntax: coercion inserts extra material that permits the offending complements to be interpreted in accordance with the constraint.

I will temporarily express the basic distinction as in (9); we will refine the story shortly.

(9) a. Situational (propositional) attitude (i.e., *X believes P*):
$[_{Sit}$ ATTITUDE ([X], $[_{Sit}$ P])]

b. Actional attitude (i.e., *X intends A*):
$[_{Sit}\ \text{ATTITUDE}\ ([X]^{\alpha}, [_{Act}\ \text{AFF}\ (\alpha,)])]$

In both cases X holds an attitude, here represented by the general predicate ATTITUDE. The first argument is the holder of the attitude; the second is the contemplated situation. In a situational attitude (9a) this second argument is an unconstrained situation. But an actional attitude (9b) requires as its second argument an action, a more specific element of the ontological universe than an ordinary situation. An Action must have an Actor role (encoded here as the first argument of the action tier function AFF—see Jackendoff 1990:ch. 7), and this role must be bound to the holder of the attitude as notated by the paired αs in (9b).

Because the Actor of the complement is bound, the standard syntactic realization of an Action is a controlled VP (either an infinitive or a gerund). If it so happens that the complement of *intend* expresses a more general situation, as in (5a), it cannot serve as a well-formed argument in (9b). Therefore an Action has to be constructed within which the situation in question is an argument, as in the paraphrases in (6). (10) shows formally the result; the part in boldface is the material introduced by coercion.

(10) Actional attitude toward an event

$$[_{Sit}\ \text{ATTITUDE}\ ([X]^{\alpha}, \begin{bmatrix} \text{CAUSE}\ ([\alpha], [_{Event}\ P]) \\ \text{AFF}\ (\alpha,) \end{bmatrix}_{Act})]$$

This is the proper interpretation for (5a). By contrast the complements in (2) are already Actions, so they do not require coercion and hence the putative paraphrases in (7) are inappropriate. Also by contrast, *wish,* being a situational attitude, allows any Situation as its second argument. Hence, it does not induce coercion on nonaction complements, so the putative paraphrase (8b) for (8a) is inappropriate.

3 Syntactic expression of situational and actional attitudes. We observed in (5) that *intend* and *offer* differ in their possibilities for syntactic complementation: *offer* permits only *to-VP,* but *intend* permits also *for-to-S* and *that*-subjunctive complements. Yet they both select semantically for Actions. How do we account for the syntactic difference? There are two possibilities: a difference in LCS argument structure or a difference in syntactic selection.

On the first possibility (which I will call the LCS hypothesis), *intend* but not *offer* includes the material indicated in bold in (10) as an optional part of its LCS. Just in case such material is present, complements other than VPs are semantically well-formed after all. In this view *John intended for Sue to come* involves not coercion, but simply the use of an expanded LCS.

In the second possibility (the subcategorization hypothesis), the LCS of both *intend* and *offer* is just the basic form in (8). The difference between them is only in what syntactic complement types they permit: *offer* syntactically permits only infinitival complements, while *intend* permits *for-to* and subjunctive complements as well. Such complements, although they cannot be strictly substituted into the argument position of *intend,* undergo a general process of coercion that inserts the boldface functions in the course of semantic composition in order to preserve well-formedness.

In short the LCS hypothesis puts more options in the semantics of *intend,* from which the syntactic differences follow, while the subcategorization hypothesis puts more options in the lexical syntactic structure (subcategorization), from which the differences in interpretation follow by general principles of coercion.

Before discussing the choice between these two hypotheses it is worth looking at some more data. Some verbs, for instance *persuade* and *convince,* express either situational or actional attitudes depending on their complement structure:

(11) a. Bill persuaded/convinced John [situational attitude]
{ that the sky was green.
that he has a big nose.
that Fermat's theorem was provable.
that Sue would bring a cake to the party. }

b. Bill persuaded/convinced John [actional attitude]
{ to look at Sue.
to scratch his nose.
to prove Fermat's theorem.
*to be shorter than Bob.
*to have been born 10 years earlier.
*to be descended from royalty. }

Persuade and *convince,* like *offer,* do not permit *for-to* and *that*-subjunctive complements:

(12) a. *Bill persuaded/convinced John
{ for Sue to bring a cake.
{ that Sue bring a cake.

Like these two verbs, *agree* expresses a situational attitude using an indicative *that*-complement (13a) or an actional attitude using a VP complement (13b). But like *intend* it also permits 'coerced' action complements (13c):

(13) a. John agreed that he has a big nose. (Situation)
b. John agreed
{ to look at Sue. (Action)
{ *to have been born 10 years earlier.
c. John agreed
{ for Sue to bring a cake.
{ that Sue bring a cake.
(= John agreed to bring it about that . . .)

A number of other verbs, including *swear, decide, forget,* and *occur to,* share this duality. The possibility of coerced action complements varies.

(14) a. John swore/decided/forgot that he was born 10 years before Bill.
b. John swore/decided/forgot to look at Sue/*to be born 10 years before Bill.
c. *John swore/decided/forgot for Sue to bring a cake/that Sue bring a cake.

(15) a. It never occurred to John that he was descended from royalty.
b. It never occurred to John to look at Sue/*to be descended from royalty.
c. It never occurred to John for Sue to bring a cake/*that Sue bring a cake.

In other cases it is more difficult to tease apart situational and actional attitudes. Verbs such as *want* and *prefer* allow their situational arguments to be expressed as infinitivals (16a,b). Hence, when they occur with plain VP complements, it is hard to tell whether these express an action (16c) or just a situation whose actor is bound to the holder of the attitude (16d).

(16) a. John wants (very much for) it to rain.
(≠John wants to bring it about that it rain.)
b. John would prefer for Bill to be descended from royalty.
(≠John would prefer to bring it about that . . .)
c. John wants to look at Sue. [action or situation?]
d. John would prefer to be descended from royalty.
[situation only]

Given this variety in syntactic behavior despite relative semantic homogeneity, I tend to favor the subcategorization hypothesis over the LCS hypothesis. For one thing there are other cases in which syntactic complement type must be syntactically selected. For instance, the relevant meanings of *believe* and *think* are approximately synonymous with a *that*-complement as seen in (17a). But only *believe* permits a synonymous NP+infinitive (ECM) complement as seen in (17b). Similarly, *want* and *desire* are semantically nearly indistinguishable in (17c,d), but they select different syntactic complements:

(17) a. John believes/thinks (that) Harry liked Susan.
b. John believes/*thinks Harry to have liked Susan.
c. John wants/?desires Sue to bring a cake.
d. John desires/*wants that Sue bring a cake.

The differences in (17) appear to be strictly syntactic (though this may be just my lack of imagination). If a difference in syntactic selection is necessary for such cases, there seems to be no reason not to invoke it in the difference between *intend* and *offer* as well.

This conclusion treats as rather superficial the fact that *order* permits a *that*-subjunctive but not a *for-to,* while *be willing* and *plan* are the other way around; it is just a matter of brute syntactic selection. This is similarly true for the varied syntactic behavior with the verbs in (11) through (15) that express either kind of attitude. In the subcategorization hypothesis these are simple (and eminently learnable) syntactic facts with no semantic significance.

This solution does have one potential drawback: it permits *intend* to syntactically select a complement that is, strictly speaking, semantically ill-formed and that must undergo a coercion in order for a well-formed interpretation to be constructed. I personally have no trouble with such an outcome on the grounds of general autonomy of syntax from semantics, but some readers may.

On the other hand it is incumbent on such readers to find an LCS difference between *order* and *plan* that reliably explains the difference between *that*-subjunctive and *for-to* complements, as well as the corresponding differences in (11) through (15)—not such an easy matter. Notice that it is not enough to say that verbs of ordering have such-and-such syntactic properties, while verbs of planning have such-and-such other syntactic properties: this is only a correlation. Such correlations may be of use in learning syntactic properties of verbs, à la Pinker (1989), but the syntactic properties are not automatic consequences of the semantics, as the LCS theory must predict.[2]

Summing up, this variety of verb types makes sense if we make three hypotheses:

1. The fundamental conceptual distinction is between situational attitudes such as (9a) and actional attitudes such as (9b). From this difference flows the difference in selectional restrictions on the complement clause: a situational attitude permits anything, but an actional attitude permits only an event whose Actor is the holder of the attitude.
2. The choice of syntactic complement type is governed in part by default principles: a Situation is most often expressed by an indicative *that*-clause, an Action by an infinitival or gerundive VP. But individual verbs can syntactically select additional complement types, which in the case of actional complements may have to undergo coercion in order to be semantically well-formed.
3. Verbs that semantically select either situational or actional attitudes express the same attitude in both cases; the cases differ only in whether the second argument is a Situation or an Action. Their LCS looks something like (18):

(18) $[_{Sit}$ ATTITUDE ([X], $[_{Sit/Act}$ P])]

4 Temporal dependency of intending. Intentions are also distinguished from beliefs by their time dependence. A belief and a claim can be directed toward a situation at any time, past, present, or future; but an intention cannot be directed toward an action in the past, as seen in (19):

(19) a. John believes himself to have talked to Sue yesterday.
b. John claims to have talked to Sue yesterday.
c. *John intends to talk/to have talked to Sue yesterday.

Like the necessity for a self-directed Actor, this is a well-formedness condition on intending.

Future-directedness (or better, nonpast-directedness) also occurs in other actional attitudes:

(20) * { John planned today
John decided today
Bill persuaded John today
John is willing today
Today it occurred to John
John is obliged
John swore today }
to talk/to have talked to Sue yesterday.

Future-directedness is not confined to actional attitudes. It also occurs with infinitival complements of the situational attitudes *wish, desire,* and *expect:*

(21) * { John wishes
John desires
John expects }
to talk/to have talked to Sue yesterday.

The *that*-complements of these verbs are all different, though. The conditional *that*-complement of *wish* can be past-directed, as seen in (22a).[3] On the other hand the subjunctive *that*-complement of *desire* cannot be past directed (22b). *Expect* preserves its future-directedness with an indicative *that*-complement: (22c), if acceptable, conceals a future-directed coerced interpretation something like (22d):[4]

(22) a. John wishes that he had talked to Sue yesterday.
b. *John desires that he talk/have talked to Sue yesterday.
c. ??John expects that Bill talked to Sue yesterday.
d. John expects to find out/John expects it to turn out that Bill talked to Sue yesterday.

To add future- (nonpast-) directedness to the formalism, it is necessary to introduce a Time constituent. Time is not normally considered part of the argument structure of the verb, but rather is signaled (if at all) by a combination of time adverbials and tense. Accordingly, I will notate the Time of a situation as a modifier beneath the function-argument structure of the situation, as in (23):

(23) $\left[_{\text{Sit}} \begin{matrix} F(X,Y) \\ [_{\text{Time}}\ T] \end{matrix}\right]$

In formalizing an intention (or any other attitude) two times are involved: the time at which the attitude is held and the time of the contemplated situation:

(24) at T_1, X 'attitudes' that P/to do P at T_2:

$$\left[_{\text{Sit}} \begin{matrix} \text{ATTITUDE}\left([X], \left[_{\text{Sit}} \begin{matrix} P \\ [T_2] \end{matrix}\right]\right) \\ [T_1] \end{matrix}\right]$$

The condition for future-directedness is that T_2 is not earlier than T_1. Any number of notations will do for this; the crucial part is that T_2 is somehow bound by T_1. This permits us to anchor the attitude itself at a known time, expressed by the tense of the main clause, but to leave open the time of the contemplated situation—all we know is that it is later:[5]

(25) Non-past directed attitude:

$$\left[_{\text{Sit}} \begin{matrix} \text{ATTITUDE}\left([X], \left[_{\text{Sit}} \begin{matrix} P \\ [_{\text{Time}}\ T \geq \beta] \end{matrix}\right]\right) \\ [_{\text{Time}}\ T_1]^{\beta} \end{matrix}\right]$$

5 The folk metaphysics of volitional actions. Having made all these observations, we now come to the meat of the discussion. Let us consider the formal difference between situational and actional attitudes. As shown by Searle (1983), Jackendoff (1985), and Bratman (1987), actional attitudes cannot in general be paraphrased as situational attitudes. For instance, the actional attitudes in (26) are subtly different from the putative paraphrases in (27):

(26) a. Bill persuaded John to look at Sue.
b. John agreed to bring a cake.
c. John forgot to open the door.
d. It never occurred to John to bring a cake.

(27) a. Bill persuaded John that he would/should look at Sue.
b. John agreed that he would/should bring a cake.
c. John forgot that he would/should open the door.
d. It never occurred to John that he would/should bring a cake.

To make the nonequivalence more vivid, notice that we can juxtapose each with the negation of the other without contradiction; for example (28):

(28) a. Bill persuaded John to look at Sue, but he didn't persuade him that he should look at Sue.
b. Bill persuaded John that he should look at Sue, but he didn't persuade him to (ACTUALLY) look at her.

Thus, there has to be some difference in the conceptual structure of parallel situational and actional attitudes. In (18) the difference is localized bluntly in the ontological category of the argument, the choice between *Sit* and *Act*. However, there is something suspect about making such a distinction. Actions appear to be—or to be derived from—a proper subset of events, rather than being a distinct ontological category. There are no actions that are not also events.

The usual sort of solution is to say that the two categories differ by a feature—say, that situations are [Sit, −A] and actions are [Sit, +A]. This allows us to account nicely for the facts of complement selection: verbs such as *intend* select for [Sit, +A]; verbs such as *believe* select for [Sit, −A], and verbs such as *persuade* select simply for [Sit]. But this is only part of the story. It does not explain why [Sit, +A] has the curious selectional restrictions it does, requiring a self-directed Actor bound to the holder of the attitude and a time not previous to the time of the attitude.

In order to address this question let us step back from formalism for a moment and think about the phenomenology of voluntary action. Searle's (1983) case of wiggling your finger will do as a simple example. It is as though you formulate an intention to wiggle your finger, say to yourself "Now!" and miraculously the finger moves. This step of execution, the translation of intention into action, seems miraculous because it is not open to introspection—it does not have a phenomenology.

Or so it is if someone is not holding your finger or if your finger is not broken or paralyzed. Under such circumstances you say "Now!" and the wrong thing happens—or nothing at all. In such a case we say you *tried* to move your finger but did not *succeed.*

Making this description sound a little more like cognitive science, we might say there has to be a way for the brain to convert conceptualized actions into motor instructions, that is, to actually act. But actions cannot just be executed the moment they are conceptualized: that would result in one's acting entirely on impulse. One could not, for instance, work up a sequence of actions before carrying it out—one would willy-nilly carry out whichever piece of the sequence one happened to think of first. Rather, in order for there to be any complexity in planning and behavior, it must be possible to conceptualize an action with a time attached to it that is different from the present and to just store this action plan in memory for later use.

If there has to be such a way to store and sequence conceptualized actions, the desired selectional restrictions on attitudes toward conceptualized actions follow immediately. Actional arguments require a self-directed Actor role because these are the only kinds of events that one could conceivably execute. Actional arguments must be nonpast-directed because the only times one could usefully attach to contemplated actions are future ones.

There is a further interesting consequence. How does the motor system know *which* conceptualized action in memory it should execute? It is reasonable to suppose it knows by the *time:* when the time attached to a conceptualized action corresponds to the present (Now!), this action suddenly becomes available to the motor system for execution. Under a modular conception of the mind we might say that no conceptualized actions are "visible" to the motor system except for those whose time is set to the present. Moreover, the motor system, being a fast and obligatory module, just executes such actions without any further instruction or intervention.

Such a story of how intention is converted into action is crude, vastly oversimplified, and perhaps completely wrong scientifically. But it does a rather nice job with the folk theory of voluntary action. A voluntary action is one that arises from a conceptualized action. The act of saying "Now!" to oneself and thereby setting an intention into action corresponds to setting the time of the contemplated action to the present—and then the motor system takes over without any awareness, until one receives the proprioceptive feedback that movement has taken place.

Moreover, suppose that because of an obstacle or injury the muscles fail to move the finger as intended. The instructions have still gone out to the motor system. It is just that the action perceived to have taken place fails to correspond to the action sent off to the motor system. That lack of correspondence is what we call "trying."

In order to give some formal shape to this 'folk metaphysics,' I want to propose a function in conceptual structure, called EXEC ('execute'). EXEC is a one-place function whose argument is a Situation. Intuitively, it converts the Situation into an Action—from something one can observe into something one can do. In order for it to have this characteristic a number of properties must be supposed.

1. [EXEC ($[_{Sit}$ X])] is well formed only if it is ascribed to a person's (animal's, computer's, etc.) mind. There are no contemplated actions in the physical world—only real physical actions.[6]
2. EXEC imposes two constraints on its argument X.
   a. X cannot be treated as a contemplated action unless it has an Actor and unless that Actor is identified with the person whose mind the contemplated action is in. You cannot do someone else's action.
   b. X has to have a time after the present. You cannot plan to do something yesterday.

These two constraints can be formalized as the further structure shown in (29) (EGO is an indexical to the person in whose mind EXEC resides; NOW is an indexical to the present):

(29) $$[\text{EXEC}\ (\begin{bmatrix} & \text{AFF (EGO,)} \\ {}_{\text{Sit}} & [_{\text{Time}}\ \text{T} \geq \text{NOW}] \end{bmatrix})]$$

Any Situation that is inserted as the argument of EXEC has this additional structure superimposed on it. This is why actional attitudes have the selectional restrictions they do.

3. A concept of the form (30) is automatically grabbed by the motor system for execution with no intervention from the conceptual system.

(30) $$[\text{EXEC}\ (\begin{bmatrix} & \text{AFF (EGO,)} \\ {}_{\text{Sit}} & [_{\text{Time}}\ \text{NOW}] \end{bmatrix})]$$

In addition, to account for the fact that many verbs select either Situations or Actions, we want to formally assign EXEC to an ontological category that is a featural variant of Situation as proposed at the beginning of this section. Accordingly, its final form is (31).

(31) $$[_{\text{Sit},+\text{A}}\ \text{EXEC}\ (\begin{bmatrix} & \text{AFF (EGO,)} \\ {}_{\text{Sit}} & [_{\text{Time}}\ \text{T} \geq \text{NOW}] \end{bmatrix})]$$

This can then be distinguished from a future Situation, which has the structure (32):

(32) $\left[_{\text{Sit.-A}} \begin{matrix} \ldots \\ [_{\text{Time}}\ T \geq \text{NOW}] \end{matrix} \right]$

For instance, the complement of *persuade Bill to VP* will have the conceptual structure (31) and that of *persuade Bill that he will VP* will have the structure (32)—close, but not identical.

I assume that, like all conceptual primitives, EXEC is innate: this conglomeration of special properties does not have to be learned. Rather, it is the specialized part of conceptual structure by which we conceptualize thought as translatable into action.

6 Intending, doing something intentionally, the volitionality of action, trying, and imperatives. The innovation of the function EXEC permits a whole range of notions centered around intentions to be formulated immediately.

6.1 The conceptual structure of *intend.* Jackendoff (1985) points out that *convince* and *persuade,* when used with *that*-complements, are causative inchoatives of *believe;* when used with infinitival complements, they are causative inchoatives of *intend:*

(33) a. Bill persuaded John that he was descended from royalty
= (By verbal argument,) Bill caused John to come to believe that . . . .

b. Bill persuaded John to scratch his nose
= (By verbal argument,) Bill caused John to come to intend to . . . .

This suggests that *believe* and *intend* are in fact the very same attitude, one of something like commitment, directed toward a situation and an action respectively.

Some of the other verbs mentioned above point toward the same parallelism. To *decide* that P is to come to believe that P in the face of other alternatives; to *decide* to do A is to come to intend to do A in the face of other alternatives. To *swear* that P is to publicly affirm one's belief that P (one's commitment to the truth of P), to *swear* to do A is to publicly affirm one's intention to do A (one's commitment to doing A).

Accordingly, I will formalize both *believe* and *intend* with a predicate COM (commitment), a taxonomic subcategory of ATTITUDE. Notice that (34a,b) are elaborated forms of (9a,b), respectively, just as they should be:

(34) a. X believes that P:

$[_{Sit}$ COM $([X], [_{Sit,-A}$ P$])]$

b. X intends to do Y:

$$[_{Sit}\ \text{COM}\ ([X]^{\alpha},\ [_{Sit,+A}\ \text{EXEC}\ \begin{bmatrix}\text{Y}\\ \text{AFF}\ (\begin{bmatrix}\alpha\\ \text{EGO}\end{bmatrix})\end{bmatrix}])]$$

Thus, we view believing and intending as parallel attitudes, differing only with respect to the category of their second argument. In accordance with the linguistic evidence, neither is derived (semantically) from the other; they are featural variants. *Decide* is then the inchoative of both, and *persuade* is the causative inchoative of both.

I leave it for further research to determine how COM fits into the general category of attitudes, that is, how the whole family of attitudes can be formally elaborated in such a way that COM fits in naturally. Presumably, COM will prove to have a feature decomposition that contrasts it with desiring, imagining, being willing, and so forth.

6.2 Doing something intentionally. Next let us consider what it means to do an action intentionally, a preoccupation of Searle (1983) and Bratman (1987).

Searle discusses a case in which he sets out in his car to kill his uncle, and on the way he is so agitated that in the fog he accidentally strikes and kills a pedestrian—who happens, unbeknownst to him, to be the very uncle he had set out to kill. Now it is clear that the act of striking and killing this pedestrian does *not* fulfill Searle's intention; he may well continue on his way to his uncle's house, knife firmly in hand, intention firmly in mind. (Why do people always use cases like this?)[8]

This case suggests that one can perform an action intentionally only by performing it with the intention that it fulfill an intention to perform that action. But how is this more complex intention fulfilled? It looks as though we are heading for an infinite regress. However, a possible way out involves a tricky use of the binding notation, shown in (35):

(35) X intentionally performs action Y at time T.

$$\begin{bmatrix}\text{Y}\\ \text{AFF}\ ([X]^{\alpha},)\\ [_{Time}\ \text{T}]\\ _{Sit,-A}\ [\text{FROM}\ [_{Sit,-A}\ \text{COM}\ (\alpha,\ [_{Sit,+A}\ \text{EXEC}\ (\beta)])]]\end{bmatrix}^{\beta}$$

What does this say? An English paraphrase that unpacks it pretty well is *X did Y out of an intention to do so.* The upper three lines encode the event Y, in which X is the Actor, taking place at time T. The bottom line is a modifier. Its main function, FROM, marks its argument as a Circumstantial Source (as in *They died **from** hunger*).[9] In (35) the argument of FROM is the situation of α's intending some Event β. In turn, because of the way β is bound, α's intention is toward the action itself, complete with intention. That is, the intention is in part self-referential (Searle uses the term "causally self-referential").

Notice in particular that T, the time of the Event Y, is automatically bound to the time of the intended Event. As a result, from the inside of X's head the time of the intended event is conceptualized as NOW. Hence, we can infer that X's motor system has taken over and executed the contemplated action.[10]

It is important as a formal part of Conceptual Semantics that we be able to extract an LCS for the adverb *intentionally* from (35), so that its meaning can be learned and stored in memory. I cannot go into the details, given that we have no general theory of adverb interpretation in which to evaluate it, but the desired LCS basically consists of the [FROM . . .] constituent plus the binding of α and β.

Let us now return to Searle's story. The hit-and-run death of his uncle does not count as an intentional killing, because the running down of the unknown pedestrian is not the act to which the intention is directed—that is, the commitment is not to *that very token act.* More generally, Bratman points out that, although one may perform a particular action intentionally, one does not necessarily intend the consequences. For example, if I intentionally run home in the rain, it does not mean I intentionally get my shoes wet. This follows from (35), because the action of getting my shoes wet is not bound to the intention to run home: only the action of running home is.

6.3 The intentional stance. Part of the folk theory of mind is a default assumption that actions are performed intentionally, that is, whenever possible, intentions are assumed to lie behind actions. That is how we manage to reason about other minds without being able to observe them. Of course, we often make mistakes, attributing intention to people for actions they do not (claim to) intend. But it works a lot of the time. In addition this assumption is the reason that we have a tendency to anthropomorphize inanimate objects that initiate action, such as wind, clouds, and especially computers, saying they 'want' to do whatever they do.

Formally, this assumption, part of Dennett's (1987) "intentional stance," can be stated as a default (or defeasible) inference rule of the form (36):

(36) $\begin{bmatrix} \text{Y} \\ \text{AFF }(\text{X},) \end{bmatrix}$ defeasibly entails

$$\begin{bmatrix} \text{Y} \\ \text{AFF }([\text{X}]^{\alpha},) \\ [\text{FROM [COM }(\alpha, [\text{EXEC }(\beta)])]] \end{bmatrix}^{\beta}$$

6.4 The volitional component of Agency. Jackendoff (1983, 1990), Dowty (1991), and others have argued that the traditional notion of Agency (the theta-role Agent) actually has a number of subcomponents that can appear independently. Dowty's list of components in what he calls "Proto-Agency" include the factors in (37a–e) (Dowty 1991:572):

(37)
  a. Volitional involvement in the event or state
  b. Sentience (and/or perception)
  c. Causing an event or change of state in another participant
  d. Movement (relative to the position of another participant)
  (e. Exists independently of the event named by the verb)

Of these (37e) probably has something to do with Topic, rather than Agent, as Dowty notes. (37d) has to do with the notion "Theme" in my work; because Theme precedes Location in the linking hierarchy (Jackendoff 1990:ch. 11); themehood creates a pressure toward subjecthood if there is no Agent. (37c) is the first argument of CAUSE (Instigator in Jackendoff (1990:ch. 7). Jackendoff (1990) has a further role, called Actor, which we have seen here as the first argument of the function AFF (Patient and Beneficiary are alternative realizations of the second role). Finally, the entailments of sentience appear when the character in question holds a situational or actional attitude; volitional involvement is a subcase of this.

Dowty does not say how these factors are encoded in semantic structure; we have seen that the relevant cases are all encoded in terms of structural positions as arguments of particular functions in conceptual structure. He also does not say how they are encoded in lexical entries. And rule (37) permits an interesting result. It has always been noticed that a verb such as *roll* is ambiguous as to whether its subject is volitional:

John's rolling down the hill may be a result of his having decided to do it or of his having been pushed. When the issue has been raised, the standard assumption (mine anyway) has been that all these verbs have an optional feature of volitionality in their LCS. But why is it true of all these verbs (including even psych verbs like *surprise*), rather than just some of them? An optional lexical feature leaves this unexplained.

Suppose, though, that the general principles of sentence interpretation contain the rule (37). Then any action verb with an animate subject will automatically present the possibility of a volitional interpretation. The feature of volitionality will not have to be included in the LCS at all, simplifying the lexicon considerably. (On the other hand verbs like *murder* that require a volitional subject will still include some volitional predicate in their LCS.)

6.5 Trying. We can now also formalize the intuitions of section 5 about trying. Trying to do Y is what happens when one sends an intention to do Y to the motor system for execution. Here it is:

(38) X tries to do Y:

$$\begin{bmatrix} \text{AFF } (X^{\alpha},) \\ [_{\text{Time}}\ T]^{\beta} \\ [\text{FROM } [\text{COM } (\alpha, [\text{EXEC } (\begin{bmatrix} Y \\ [_{\text{Time}}\ \beta] \end{bmatrix})])]] \end{bmatrix}$$

This says that X does something at time T—we do not know what—as a result of executing the intention to do Y at time T (X's subjective NOW). It may of course be the case that X is successful, but (38) does not say so; Gricean principles presumably account for the strong presumption that X has not succeeded.[11]

6.6 Imperatives. Finally, for what I find a rather surprising result, consider the relation between declarative and imperative sentences:

(39) a. Bill ate the pizza.
b. Eat the pizza.

The well-known selectional restrictions on imperatives are identical to those for actional attitudes. Imperatives require the thematic role of the understood subject "you" to be a volitional Actor, so statives (40a) and non-self-controllable events (40b) are unacceptable:

(40) a. *Be descended from royalty.
b. *Grow taller.

Where at all possible, such unacceptable cases are coerced into causative readings:

(41) a. Be quiet = Make yourself quiet.
b. Be examined by a doctor = Get yourself examined by a doctor.

And an imperative has to be nonpast-directed:

(42) Leave the room now/in 5 minutes/*5 minutes ago.

This parallelism should not be a coincidence. Accordingly, suppose the conceptual structure corresponding to imperative force is simply (43), from which the parallelism follows automatically.

(43) Do Y:
[EXEC ([Y])]

How will imperative force follow from this? Think about how a sentence acquires its illocutionary force. Just about every theory of illocutionary force supposes that conventional communication pastes some additional material around the content of the sentence; they differ in precisely what this additional material is. For instance, (44) gives an informal account of the extra information pasted around a declarative sentence (adapting for convenience the informal style of Wierzbicka 1987):

(44) For a declarative sentence S with conceptual structure
$[_{Sit}$ P], the illocutionary force is
I am saying S to you
out of the intention to cause you to come to believe $[_{Sit}$ P]

For present purposes the crucial part of this is *you believe,* which in our formalization comes out as (45):

(45) [COM ([YOU], $[_{Sit}$ P])]

Now suppose that we substitute for S in this formula an imperative sentence with the meaning (43). Then instead of (45) we get (46):

(46) [COM ([YOU], [EXEC [$_{Sit}$ Y]])]

But this is *you intend to do Y.* Putting this back into (44), we get (47):

(47) For an imperative sentence S with conceptual structure
[EXEC [$_{Sit}$ Y]], the illocutionary force is
I am saying S to you
out of the intention to cause you to come to intend [$_{Sit}$ Y]

This is just about right for the force of an imperative. In particular it abstracts away from whether the sentence is meant as a request or an order. In addition it predicts that the understood subject of an imperative is the addressee, since by the logic of EXEC, the Actor of [$_{Sit}$ Y] in (46) must be bound to the addressee.

In short, if we assume that the conceptual structure of an imperative is (42), we can unify the description of the illocutionary force of declarative and imperative sentences with no further ado. The more general description is (48):

(48) For a declarative or imperative sentence S with conceptual
structure [$_{Sit}$ X], the illocutionary force is
I am saying S to you
out of the intention to cause you$^{\alpha}$ to come to
[COM (α, [$_{Sit}$ X])].

More results along this line will follow in the next section.

7 Fulfilling versus voiding an intention. Fulfillment of an intention has the curious effect of wiping out the intention. Roughly speaking, if I intend to move my finger (or buy a new car) and actually do move my finger (or buy a new car), I no longer have the intention to do so.

What sort of entity is this that 'goes out of existence' through the occurrence of an event that it describes? Our beliefs do not go out of existence when we find out they are correct. On the other hand intentions are not unique in this respect. Wishes (some kinds, anyway) go away when they are satisfied. Going beyond attitudes, bodily sensations such as hunger, thirst, itches, and the need to urinate also go away when the relevant events for their satisfaction take place. Going beyond sentient beings, needs such as that of a house for a new roof cease to exist when a certain event takes place, namely, the house getting a new roof. So this odd metaphysical property of intentions is widely attested.

However, intentions can go out of existence for other reasons besides their fulfillment. Suppose Amy intends to feed the cats, but then discovers Beth has already done so. As a result of this discovery, Amy no longer has her intention—although she has not fulfilled it. I call this more general situation the *voiding* of an intention.

What are the conditions underlying the voiding of an intention? What is going on here is that we understand Amy's intention as really having more content than just feeding the cats. Rather, she intends to feed the cats in order to achieve some implicit purpose (or goal), presumably that the cats are not hungry. This is, of course, a pragmatic inference on our part: she may be determined to feed the cats come hell or high water, whether they want to be fed or not. But it is more charitable to attribute to her by default some reasonable purpose. And, intuitively, her intention is voided if she comes to believe that the purpose is satisfied. (Note that it is not enough that the purpose be satisfied pure and simple: Amy's intention does not go away when Beth feeds the cats, but only when Amy learns that Beth has fed the cats.)[12]

A purpose behind an intention can, of course, be overtly expressed, for example in (49):

(49) a. John intended to go home in order to see his mother.
b. John intended to buy a car in order to get to work more easily.

Again, if through some other means John gets to see his mother, or another way develops for him to get to work easily (say, he inherits a motorcycle or a new trolley line goes into operation), the intention may be voided.

Intuitively, I suggest, a purpose can be thought of as something one wants that causes a contemplated action.[13] I'll formalize this as (50):

(50) X intends Y in order to Z

$$[\text{COM } (\text{X}^{\alpha}, \begin{bmatrix} \text{EXEC } [\text{Y}] \\ [\text{FROM } [\text{WANT } (\alpha, \ [_{\text{Sit}} \ \text{Z}])] \end{bmatrix})]$$

In (50) the purpose is treated as a FROM modifier to conform to its subordinate role in the syntax. WANT is for present purposes treated as an unanalyzed situational attitude; this does not preclude further analysis. The crucial thing is that the desire for Z is the source of the contemplated action [EXEC [Y]].

Now notice that wanting has the same odd metaphysical property as intending, namely, that if a want is satisfied, it goes away. In (50) the want is what causes the intention. If it goes away, the intention does, too. In other words the voiding of an intention by the independent fulfillment of its purpose follows from the representation in (50) (plus some rough-and-ready rules of inference that cry out for formalization).

What about purposes with verbs other than *intend,* for instance (51)?

(51) a. John went home in order to see his mother.
b. John bought a car in order to get to work quicker.

The clue is that purposes can only go with volitional acts. One cannot *grow taller in order to . . .* or *be descended from royalty in order to . . . ,* and one cannot *buy a car today in order to get to work yesterday.* In other words, all purposes presuppose an intention. How does the intention get into the conceptual structure of (51)? The simplest possibility is that it is supplied by the rule of default entailment given in (36): if at all possible, assume an action is performed intentionally. By applying this rule we construct an intention to which the purpose can be attached. (52) gives the resulting structure for (51a):

(52)

$$\begin{bmatrix} \text{GO } (\alpha, \text{ TO HOME}) \\ \text{AFF } (\text{JOHN}^{\alpha},) \\ [\text{FROM } [\text{COM } (\alpha, \begin{bmatrix} \text{EXEC } [\beta] \\ [\text{FROM } [\text{WANT } (\alpha, [\text{SEE } (\alpha, [\text{MOTHER}])])]] \end{bmatrix})]] \end{bmatrix}^{\beta}$$

Notice that (51) has none of these strange properties of voiding: seeing his mother on some other occasion does not make John's going home to see her go away. This difference follows from the representation in (52). Here the intention is bound to the event of going home, which is asserted to have taken place. The intention is therefore asserted to have been executed and, hence, fulfilled.

Finally, let us return to imperative sentences. There is a form of imperative that is used not to make a request or an order, but to give instructions or advice:

(53) a. To make more money, work harder.
b. To bake a cake, take 3 cups flour, . . . , and put it in the oven for an hour.

Significantly, these sentences contain purpose clauses. Can we explain why these sentences have this force?

Let us elaborate a little further on our treatment of the illocutionary force of imperatives from the previous section. Suppose that adding a purpose clause to an imperative does the same thing as adding it to an intention. Then the conceptual structure of an imperative with a purpose clause comes out like (54):

(54) For Y to happen, do X

$$\begin{bmatrix} \text{EXEC} \begin{bmatrix} \text{Y} \\ \text{AFF} \quad (\alpha,) \end{bmatrix} \\ [\text{FROM} \ [\text{WANT} \ ([\alpha], \ \ [\text{Y}])]] \end{bmatrix}$$

If this is substituted into our formula for the illocutionary force of an imperative, the outcome is (55):

(55) For an imperative sentence S with conceptual structure (54), the illocutionary force is:
I am saying S to you out of the intention to cause you$^{\alpha}$ to come to

$$[\text{COM} \ (\alpha, \begin{bmatrix} \text{EXEC} \begin{bmatrix} \text{X} \\ \text{AFF} \quad (\alpha,) \end{bmatrix} \\ [\text{FROM} \ [\text{WANT} \ ([\alpha], \ \ [\text{Y}])]] \end{bmatrix})]$$

This is pretty close to the right force. For if the hearer does not want Y, and Y is what causes the contemplated action X to exist, then the intention disappears, too. On the other hand if the hearer does want Y, then the intention to do X appears. That is what instructions or advice are: if you want Y, then do X.

Now recall our initial example of Amy intending to feed the cats, with an implicit purpose whose satisfaction could void the intention. Similar cases occur with imperatives:

(56) Shake well.
Do not use near fire or flame.

These are not commands, but rather instructions: if you want this object to function properly, then do the following thing. So the more general use of imperatives for instructions follows from our analysis of the logic of implicit purposes.

This concludes the story. Summing up, we have analyzed *intend* as the composition of the two functions COM and EXEC. The former brings *intend* into parallelism with *believe,* as motivated by the fact that they have parallel causatives. The latter unifies *intend* with all the other actional attitudes and differentiates it from the situational attitudes. The special properties of EXEC account for the selectional restrictions on actional attitudes, for the coercion with *for-to* and *that*-subjunctive complements of *intend,* for the temporal properties of intentions, and for the peculiar relation of intentions to volitional actions. This treatment has led to a straightforward analysis of *doing Y intentionally* and of *try,* with its odd intermediate status between intending and successfully doing. The rule of defeasible inference in (36) has enabled us to eliminate the feature of optional volitionality from the LCS of a vast number of verbs. This account has enabled us also to give a more detailed analysis of purpose clauses and their relation to intention. Finally, it has led to a nice account of the illocutionary force of different sorts of imperatives. That ought to be enough consequences for one paper.

NOTES

* In 1969, fresh out of graduate school, I arrived in Los Angeles to teach at UCLA and do research for the RAND Corporation. There Carlos Otero befriended me and took enthusiastic interest in my work. At a time when I was deeply embroiled in what has now come to be called the "linguistic wars," Carlos's gentle support on matters substantive and political meant a tremendous amount to me. Thanks for all those lunches and walks on the beach, Carlos.

This paper is not a random offering of gratitude, either. A recent turn in my work has been toward the cognitive underpinnings of social behavior, the innate 'Universal Grammar' of the mental capacities that lie behind the ideals frequently expressed in Chomsky's political writings. Carlos has been an avid commentator on my preliminary attempts to lay out this domain. In studying the conceptual structure of intending and volitional action, I hope to set another small piece of this domain in place.

This research was supported in part by a fellowship from the John Simon Guggenheim Foundation and in part by NSF Grant IRI 92-13849 to Brandeis University.

1. The phenomenon of *coercion* (Pustejovsky 1991) is a situation in which the interpretation of a sentence contains extra semantic material that is not contributed by any of the lexical items in the sentence but that must be present in order for the sentence to be semantically well formed. A vivid example is from Talmy (1978):

(i) a. The light flashed.
 b. The light flashed repeatedly/over and over.
 c. The light flashed until dawn.
 d. The light flashed repeatedly/over and over until dawn.

Sentences (i-a) and (i-b) are not synonymous. Yet in the context of *until dawn,* they mean about the same. The reason is that *until dawn* semantically bounds a process, and *the light flashed* is not a process; hence, there is semantic incompatibility. The additional semantic function of repetition, not lexically expressed in (i-c) but part of its interpretation, 'coerces' *the light flashed* into an ongoing process, rendering it compatible with *until dawn.*

Four other rather well-known cases appear in (ii) through (v) in parallel format.

(ii) a. John was quiet.
b. John became quiet.
John stayed quiet.
c. Bill made John be quiet.
d. Bill made John become quiet.
Bill made John stay quiet. (Jackendoff 1983)

(iii) a. the book
b. read the book
write the book
c. John began the book.
d. John began to read the book.
John began to write the book. (Pustejovsky 1991)

(iv) a. his name
b. what his name is
c. Bill asked his name.
d. Bill asked what his name is (Grimshaw 1979)

(v) a. the ham sandwich
b. the man with (/who ordered) the ham sandwich
c. [One waitress to another:]
The ham sandwich wants more coffee.
d. The man with (/who ordered) the ham sandwich wants more coffee. (Nunberg 1979)

In (ii) a causative requires an event as its effect. Hence, a stative such as (ii-a) is coerced into either an inchoative or a durative event. In (iii) *begin* specifies the initial stages of an event; hence, an object such as (iii-a) is coerced into an activity one characteristically performs with it (alternatively, some other pragmatically prominent activity, as in *John was ripping lots of things up; after he finished ripping up the magazine, John began the book.*). In (iv) *ask* requires an interrogative as its complement, so (iv-a) is coerced into a related interrogative. In (v) *want* requires an animate subject, so *ham sandwich* is coerced into a person contextually associated with it.

An important point to notice in all these cases is that the nonlexical semantic material embeds within it the 'coerced' constituent. In (i) this material is "repetition of —"; in (iii), "read/write —"; in (iv) "what — is"; in (v) "the man with —." In (ii) this structure is less obvious, but it follows from the structure for inchoative and durative given in Jackendoff (1991).

Not enough is yet known about coercions to provide an exhaustive typology of them, nor to understand under what grammatical and pragmatic circumstances they are possible. But the phenomenon is robust enough to be unimpeachably a component of the syntax-semantics interface.

2. A rhetorical point here: In much of my work I have argued that what appeared to be syntactic properties of sentences are really semantic. The present case, in which I argue that they really are syntactic (in fact in opposition to syntacticians of the UTAH bent), should prove that I am not opposed to syntactic solutions all the time. It is an empirical issue. In this respect I differentiate myself from Cognitive Grammar, especially Langacker (1987), one of whose basic claims is that all syntactic behavior is completely predictable on semantic grounds. I claim only that lots more syntactic behavior is predictable on semantic grounds than we are used to thinking.

3. There is another difference between the two kinds of complements of *wish.* The infinitival complement carries a strong sense that it is contrary to fact. But it is not necessarily contrary to fact, as shown in (i). On the other hand the conditional *that*-complement is necessarily contrary to fact, as seen in (ii).

(i) I wish to be exactly as I am.
(ii) *I wish that I were exactly as I am.

4. My impression is that future-directedness has some influence on complement selection for situational attitudes, in particular creating a pressure toward *for-to* complements; but as can be seen from these examples it certainly is not determinative.

5. The notation $[T \geq \beta]$ can be formalized further in the notation of Jackendoff (1991) as (i), which says intuitively that T_2 is an element of the time interval bounded at its earlier end (BDBY-) by T_1.

(i) $[_{Time}\ \text{ELT}\ ([\text{BDBY}^{-}\ ([\beta])])]$

6. The social world is another matter. An obligation, for example, involves the performance of an action at some point in the future, and I have accordingly treated it as an actional attitude here. But this is not strictly accurate. Although we can (sort of) say *Where is John's intention?—in his mind,* we cannot say *Where is John's obligation?—in his mind.* Rather, the folk metaphysics of obligation puts it in a social space; an obligation is not a personal attitude, but a publicly available interpersonal entity. In folk metaphysics, though, social space is doubtless supervenient on minds: one cannot imagine a 'society' of rocks or clouds without imagining them as somehow sentient. So the claim that EXEC may be located only in minds requires a bit of extension, though not implausible extension, to deal with social concepts.

7. Actually not the motor system, since even thinking can be a voluntary action. But the phenomenology is substantially the same, so I will assume that the conceptualization of voluntary action applies to thinking as well as wiggling one's finger. As I said in the introduction, it is not the responsibility of a folk theory to account for how the mind really works — only for how it seems to work if you do not examine it too closely.

8. It is worth mentioning that the description of intentions, like that of other attitudes, raises the notorious problem of referential opacity. Searle's hit-and-run situation provides a good illustration. Under his scenario both the sentences in (i) have true readings.

(i) a. Searle did not intend to kill the unknown pedestrian.
b. Searle intended to kill the unknown pedestrian.

How can this be, given that the two sentences are apparently contradictory?

The reason is that there is a systematic ambiguity in all the terms within the description of an attitude. These terms may record the way the holder of the attitude describes the contemplated event to himself (the opaque description, also known as a description of the narrow content of the attitude). Alternatively, they may record the speaker's description of the individuals, situations, or properties to which the attitude pertains, independently of the way the holder of the attitude may happen to describe them to himself (the transparent description, also known as a description of the broad content of the attitude). Assuming the narrow content of Searle's intention is expressed by "I intend to kill my uncle," (i-a) is true on the opaque reading of *the unknown pedestrian.* But because, unbeknownst to Searle, the person *he* describes as "my uncle" happens also to be describable as "the unknown pedestrian," (i-b) is true on the transparent reading of *the unknown pedestrian.* (Of course, (i-a) is false on the transparent reading and (i-b) is false on the opaque reading.) This distinction has received copious discussion in the literature, starting with Russell (1905) and Quine (1956) and moving through an unmentionably large number of subsequent references (see Linsky 1971, Heny 1981, Searle 1983, Jackendoff 1983:ch. 11 for representative references).

I will not go into the millions of subtleties and complexities of this distinction, nor the millions of different accounts of it. The crucial point for our purpose here is that attitudes are individuated by their narrow content. For instance, Searle may at once hold beliefs that his uncle is alive and that the unknown pedestrian is dead, even though in terms of broad content the two turn out be contradictory. Similarly, he has an intention to kill his uncle but also (in the moment prior to the accident when he is swerving wildly) an intention not to kill the unknown pedestrian. So, when we are asking what intention he is satisfying by performing some action, we have to know how he himself individuates his intentions.

The upshot is that the argument of EXEC in X's mind has to be evaluated in X's terms, and we cannot tell from a transparent description exactly what X has in mind. Inferences based on people's intentions require opaque descriptions. Unfortunately, there is nothing in the normal linguistic description of attitudes that distinguishes the transparent and opaque readings. Choose whatever formalization you like to distinguish them.

9. FROM is proposed in Jackendoff (1990:section 5.4). Intuitively, its argument is a Situation that brings about the Event that it modifies (e.g., *hunger caused him to die*). Any equivalent formalization will do the trick.

10. Let me be a bit more careful about how this works in light of the discussion in note 8. Recall that (28), the formal structure of EXEC, includes the two indexical elements EGO and NOW. In embedding EXEC under actional attitudes I have said that EGO is bound to the holder of the attitude. This is to say that EGO describes this character opaquely (in the character's terms), while the bound variable describes the same character transparently (in the speaker's terms). Similarly, I say that "from the point of view of the character holding the attitude the time is NOW"; i.e., NOW is an opaque description. Meanwhile, the variable is bound to the speaker's description of the time, i.e., a transparent description.

11. This is quite a different analysis of *try* than in Jackendoff (1990:section 7.2), where *try* is treated as CS^{u}, an application of force with indeterminate outcome. What the present analysis has going for it is that *try* requires a sentient subject: one cannot talk of the wind or the waves trying to knock down a building except by anthropomorphizing them and ascribing intentions to them. (By contrast, *The wind managed/failed to knock down the building* carry no such sense of sentience.)

Alternatively, both analyses could be correct: the CS^u function could be what happens in the physical world, with a concomitant intention:

$$\begin{bmatrix} CS^u\ (X^\alpha,\ [_{Sit}\ ] \\ [_{Time}\ T]^\beta \\ [FROM\ [COM\ (\alpha,\ [EXEC\ (\begin{bmatrix} Y \\ [_{Time}\ \ ] \end{bmatrix})])]] \end{bmatrix}$$

(Though this does feel a bit baroque.)

12. A slightly trickier case of voiding an intention occurs if we continue Searle's story from section 6.2. At the point at which he has killed the unknown pedestrian, his intention is intact. But somewhat later he gets arrested for a hit-and-run accident and learns the identity of his victim. At this point his intention is presumably voided. This case falls under the present one if we attribute to Searle a reasonable although somewhat redundant purpose behind his intention: that his uncle be dead. Since he now knows that the purpose is satisfied, the intention vanishes.

13. This applies only to purposes attributed to beings that can have intentions. Purposes can also be attributed to artifacts *(a phone rings to let us know someone is calling)* and to nonsentient living things *(a tree has leaves to collect sunlight).* These have somewhat different structure; an ideal analysis would unify them all as variations on a common theme. I will not do it here.

REFERENCES

Bratman, M. E. 1987. *Intentions, Plans, and Practical Reason.* Cambridge: Harvard University Press.

Churchland, P. M. 1981. Eliminative Materialism and the Propositional Attitudes. *Journal of Philosophy* 78:67–90.

Dennett, D. C. 1987. *The Intentional Stance.* Cambridge: MIT Press.

Dowty, D. 1991. Thematic Proto-Roles and Argument Selection. *Language* 67:547–619.

Fodor, J. A. 1987. *Psychosemantics.* Cambridge: MIT Press.

Grimshaw, J. 1979. Complement Selection and the Lexicon. *Linguistic Inquiry* 10:279–325.

Heny, F., ed. 1981. *Ambiguities in Intensional Contexts.* Dordrecht: Reidel.

Jackendoff, R. 1983. *Semantics and Cognition.* Cambridge: MIT Press.

Jackendoff, R. 1985. Believing and Intending Two Sides of the Same Coin. *Linguistic Inquiry* 16:445–459.

Jackendoff, R. 1990. *Semantic Structures.* Cambridge: MIT Press.

Jackendoff, R. 1991. Parts and Boundaries. *Cognition* 41:9–45.

Langacker, R. 1987. *Foundations of Cognitive Grammar,* Vol. 1. Stanford: Stanford University Press.

Linsky, L., ed. 1971. *Reference and Modality.* London: Oxford University Press.

Miller, G., and P. Johnson-Laird. 1976. *Language and Perception.* Cambridge: Harvard University Press.

Nunberg, G. 1979. The Nonuniqueness of Semantic Solutions Polysemy. *Linguistics and Philosophy* 3:143–84.

Pinker, S. 1989. *Learnability and Cognition: The Acquisition of Argument Structure.* Cambridge: MIT Press.

Pustejovsky, J. 1991. The Generative Lexicon. *Computational Linguistics* 17:409–41.

Quine, W. V. O. 1956. Quantifiers and Propositional Attitudes. *Journal of Philosophy* 53:177–87.

Russell, B. 1905. On Denoting. *Mind* 14:479–93.

Searle, J. R. 1983. *Intentionality.* Cambridge: Cambridge University Press.

Stich, S. C. 1983. *From Folk Psychology to Cognitive Science: The Case Against Belief.* Cambridge: MIT Press.

Talmy, L. 1978. The Relation of Grammar to Cognition: A Synopsis. In *Proceedings of TINLAP—2: Theoretical Issues in Natural Language Processing.* D. Waltz, ed. New York: Association for Computing Machinery.

Wierzbicka, A. 1987. *English Speech Act Verbs: A Semantic Dictionary.* Sydney: Academic Press.

From the Lexicon to the Syntax: The Problem of Subjunctive Clauses

PAULA KEMPCHINSKY
University of Iowa

1 Introduction. The shift in linguistic theory from the language-specific and construction-specific rules of early generative grammar to the 'particularly simple design' of minimal conceptual necessity of Chomsky (1993) has transferred, in great part, the burden of explanation for overt syntactic differences between languages from the computational component of the language faculty to the lexicon. In fact, the point of departure for a major line of research within the principles and parameters framework has been the idea that the syntactic properties of a head should be inducible from the interaction of its semantic properties with general principles of syntactic representations and lexicon to syntax mapping. Concomitantly, our view of the lexicon has changed; what once was perceived as a list of individual lexical items, each with its own syntactic, phonological, and semantic particularities, is now seen as a structured set of entities, perhaps bilevel (cf. Hale and Keyser 1986, Rappaport and Levin 1988, and work in that vein). The semantic content of each lexical item is represented in terms of conceptual structures that are composed of certain semantic primitives such as 'cause,' 'event,' 'path,' and so on; similarities across lexical items are at least partially derivable from their shared semantic primitives.

The idea that lexical items are structured representations built up from certain conceptual primitives has two possible consequences, which I want to explore here. First of all, on the assumption that conceptual structures are located in a separate component, parallel to the language component and linked to it via systematic correspondence rules, we have some explanation for how language acquisition gets started, the 'semantic bootstrapping' hypothesis of Pinker (1984, 1989). The simplest version of this hypothesis suggests that children, equipped with innate principles for linking syntax and semantics, derive the semantic representation of a particular sentence via nongrammatical means (i.e., via general strategies of perception and cognition) and then proceed to do some preliminary syntactic analyses. Once the child has acquired in this way some syntactic coding of semantic relations, s/he can then apply these syntactic cues to sentences where the syntax to semantics link is not as obvious. Second, if in fact we do have as part of our mental equipment a conceptual component that supplies us with 'meaning,' the question arises as to whether we need anything else for semantic interpretation. Jackendoff (1983:95) explicitly takes the position that conceptual structures are sufficient: "... semantic structure and conceptual structure denote the same level of representation," but this viewpoint has not been unchallenged.

In what follows I will explore these issues with respect to clausal complementation, specifically, subjunctive complements to the class of verbs that can be termed 'volitional' and 'directive.' I will argue that patterns of language acquisition and language loss indicate that there has to be a systematic relationship between the meaning of volitional verbs such as *querer,* 'to want' and the fact that they take subjunctive clausal complements. I will then review the work on argument structure of lexical items and will show that missing from this line of research has been any systematic examination of clausal complementation. I will argue that the conceptual structure of verbs such as *querer,* when combined with the theory of extended projections proposed by Grimshaw (1991), can account for the existence of clausal complements but cannot account for types of clausal complements, particularly with respect to the mood distinction of subjunctive versus indicative. I will then discuss the analysis of subjunctive clauses within model-theoretic semantics and will suggest that conceptual structures must be augmented with another level of semantic representation to fully account for the interpretation of propositions. Finally, I will suggest some consequences of this line of thinking for both the 'semantic bootstrapping' hypothesis and the implications of the minimalist program for language acquisition theory.

2 Subjunctive clauses in Spanish Patterns of acquisition and loss. As is well known, in Spanish subjunctive clauses appear as complements to three main classes of verbs: (i) volitional predicates such as *querer,* 'to want,' *desear,* 'to desire' and directive predicates such as *ordenar,* 'to order,' *aconsejar,* 'to advise,' *animar,* 'to encourage,' *obligar,* 'to require' and so on; (ii) negated epistemic predicates such as *no creer,* 'to not believe,' *dudar,* 'to doubt,' *no ser seguro,* 'to not be certain'; and (iii) factive-emotive predicates such as *lamentar,* 'to regret,' *alegrarse de,* 'to be glad about,' *ser natural,* 'to be expected' and the like. With respect to the acquisition of subordinate subjunctive clauses, the salient fact to be captured is this: in the course of first language acquisition, children acquiring languages such as Spanish acquire subordinate subjunctive clauses first as complements to volitional verbs and only (much) later as complements to either negated epistemic predicates or factive emotive predicates. The appearance of subjunctive complements to volitional verbs, primarily *querer,* may be as early as four years, while subjunctive complements to negated epistemics characteristically appear between five and a half and six years, and subjunctives with factive emotives as late as ten, although more commonly around seven to eight years (for some discussion see Padilla-Rivera (1985) and references cited therein).

Conversely, studies on Spanish language attrition show that the use of subjunctive, particularly in the present tense, tends to be conserved. A particularly illustrative study is the research on Los Angeles Spanish carried out by Silva-Corvalán (1991). Her focus was the restructuring of the Spanish verbal system as a result of contact with a superordinate language, in this case English, where in principle such restructuring can be traced to various processes: simplification resulting in the loss of forms, and transfer from and subsequent convergence with English. With respect to the subjunctive the initial hypothesis was that simplification and loss would affect first the conditional and the subjunctive forms, both because these are used in "contexts of higher hypotheticality or weaker assertiveness" and because the lack or at the very least low occurrence in spoken speech of subjunctive forms in English would be predicted to influence the relative frequency of subjunctive forms in the Spanish of bilinguals. Nevertheless, the results of the study showed that although there is simplification of the tense system of the subjunctive mood, resulting in the loss of the imperfect subjunctive, the present subjunctive is retained until very late stages of Spanish language loss.

Although Silva-Corvalán's study does not examine the retention of the subjunctive by syntactic context, research by Ocampo (1991) on Spanish-English bilinguals has shown that use of the subjunctive is most highly retained in complement clauses to volitional and directive predicates. Note that this pattern is somewhat surprising from the point of view of semantic transparency; since volitional predicates such as *querer* allow only subjunctive complements when tensed, there is no semantic or pragmatic information carried by a contrast in mood. The alternation between subjunctive and indicative complements to negated epistemic predicates and factive emotive predicates, on the other hand, does convey semantic/pragmatic information such as the speaker's degree of commitment to the truth of the complement clause or the speaker's assumption of previous knowledge on the part of the hearer (cf. Farkas 1993 and Guitart 1978, 1980). Thus the pattern of retention of the subjunctive mood also calls for an explanation.

Silva-Corvalán (1990) notes that the pattern of language attrition in situations of language contact is in many cases the mirror image of first and second language acquisition, which of course is true in this case. This is not surprising if we consider language loss as simply a manifestation of incomplete acquisition on the part of subsequent generations. So we are back again to the acquisition problem. Intuitively, it seems clear that the appearance of subjunctive complements in volitional and directive contexts is directly related to the lexical meaning of the superordinate predicate.[1] Therefore, it should be the case that the lexical structure of a verb such as *querer* must project into the syntax not only the number of arguments it takes and their relative hierarchy, but also the categorial identity of the internal argument—not merely that it is a CP, but that it is a subjunctive CP. The particular problem posed by subjunctive complementation is thus the following: what aspect of the (matrix) verb's semantic representation entails syntactic projection of a subjunctive clause? This brings us to the general question of lexicon to syntax mapping, to which I now turn.

3 Approaches to lexicon-to-syntax mapping.

3.1 Semantic representations and semantic conceptual structures. If the syntax of a given head-complement structure is to be derivable from the semantic properties of the head, there are at least three salient syntactic properties that need to be accounted for. These are (i) the number of arguments that appear with that head, (ii) their relative position in the initial syntactic representation (including possible alternations, as in the case of the class of *spray/load* verbs studied by Rappaport and Levin (1988)), and (iii) the categorial identity of those arguments. Much of the research on argument structure of the past decade has focused on the first two properties, as illustrated by Baker's (1988) Universal Theta Assignment Hypothesis or by Perlmutter and Postal's (1984) Universal Alignment Principle (although clearly this is a line of research that can be traced back to Fillmore's (1968) work on Case grammar). A common although not universal conclusion of this work has been to consider that theta roles are not primitives of linguistic theory, but are rather a function of the location of a given argument in a highly articulated lexical conceptual structure (LCS). The original syntactic position of this argument is, in turn, mediated by a second level of lexical representation, predicate-argument structure (PAS), which is merely an annotation for variables that are projected into positions in the syntax according to the position that they occupy in LCS. An example of such a bilevel lexical representation is given in (1):

(1) *dar* 'to give'
LCS: x cause [y come to be at (possession)z]
PAS: < 1 2 3 >
(Ana le dio una manzana al niño)
'Ana gave the boy an apple'

The LCS in (1) is meant to capture the fact that the argument represented by the variable 'x' is interpreted as an agent by virtue of occupying the slot '____ cause,' the 'y' argument is interpreted as theme because it is in the position '____ come to be,' and 'z' is goal. The LCS links to the PAS in left-to-right fashion, so that in the syntax the argument corresponding to 'x' should be in the highest position (the 'external argument') and so on.

The LCS in (1) is only a 'bare bones' representation, and we will turn directly to research in this area. What is important to note here is that neither the LCS nor the PAS of (1) gives any information as to categorial identity of the three arguments. *Dar,* of course, takes three NP arguments (assuming, for sake of discussion, that the indirect object in Spanish is an obliquely marked NP rather than a PP headed by the preposition *a,* 'to'). But neither the LCS nor the PAS of *dar* is significantly different from the respective representations for *explicar,* a verb whose second argument may be either a CP or an NP:

(2) *explicar* 'to explain'
LCS: x cause [y come to be at (perception)z]
PAS: < 1 2 3 >
(Ana le explicó al niño que un asteroide es un planeta pequeño)
'Ana explained to the boy that an asteroid is a small planet'

Now, obviously, the difference in categorial selection here is a well-known fact, and the approach taken in most studies utilizing some notion of bilevel lexical representation is to assume that categorial selection obeys something like the Canonical Structural Realization principle first proposed by Grimshaw (1979, 1981), assuming sufficiently 'robust' LCS representations.[2] We must then explore what is meant by 'sufficently robust' Lexical Conceptual Structures, particularly in regards to the question of selection for clausal complements.

The most rigorous proposal—or more accurately, set of proposals—to date regarding the nature of conceptual structures is Jackendoff's work on conceptual representations (cf. Jackendoff 1983, 1985, 1990). It should be noted that here already we are on somewhat shaky terminological ground. Work on lexical conceptual structures such as the various analyses that have emerged from the MIT Lexicon Project assume, as we have already seen, a level of conceptual structure that is within the lexicon. In his work, however, Jackendoff explicitly proposes semantic conceptual representations that are within a conceptual component linked to the linguistic component via the lexicon, which is conceived of as a set of correspondence relations among conceptual, syntactic, and phonological representations. This difference is significant, and we will return to this issue in section 4.3 below. For now I would like to give a brief overview of how conceptual structures work, to see what they can tell us about syntactic complementation.

In Jackendoff's system the building blocks of conceptual representations are conceptual types, such as 'event,' 'path,' 'thing,' 'property,' and so on, which he terms the 'semantic parts of speech.' These are located in semantic fields (e.g., 'possessive,' 'spatial,' 'identificational') via functions such as STAY, BE, CAUSE, ORIENT, and others. Examples of (partial) conceptual representations are given in (3) and (4) (from Jackendoff 1983)

(3) $$\left[_{\text{Event}}\ \text{GO}_{\text{Poss}}\left([_{\text{Thing}}\ ],\ \left[_{\text{Path}}\ \begin{matrix}\text{FROM } [_{\text{Thing}}\ ] \\ \text{TO } [_{\text{Thing}}\ ]\end{matrix}\right]\right)\right]$$

(cf. John gave a book to Bill)

(4) $$\left[_{\text{State}}\ \text{GO}_{\text{Ident}}\left([_{\text{Thing}}\ ],\ \left[_{\text{Path}}\ \begin{matrix}\text{FROM } [_{\text{Property}}\ ] \\ \text{TO } [_{\text{Property}}\ ]\end{matrix}\right]\right)\right]$$

(cf. This theory ranges from the sublime to the ridiculous)

As can be seen by comparing (3) and (4), *give* and *range* both contain the GO function in their semantic representations, with the former being located in the possessive field and the latter in the identificational field. Hence, both these verbs will 'assign' the same theta roles, since theta roles are defined relationally in terms of positions within the semantic conceptual structure. (For ease of comparison I have omitted the CAUSE function in the representation of *give.*)

3.2 Mapping to clausal complements. Our primary interest here is to determine to what extent categorial identity of syntactic complements is derivable from the semantic properties of the selecting head. Jackendoff (1993b) assumes something along the lines of Grimshaw's Canonical Structural Realization Principle, linking conceptual types to syntactic categories, with a 'residue' of syntactic selection that must be specified. He suggests the following pairs of conceptual types to syntactic categories, with the canonical structural realization italicized:

(5) a. Thing *NP*
b. Path *PP,* NP
c. Property *AP,* NP, PP
d. Event *CP,* NP
e. Proposition *CP,* IP, NP

The immediate question raised by the above list is the nature of the proposed conceptual type 'proposition.' In particular it is not clear how within conceptual structures 'proposition' is to be distinguished from 'event' or 'state.' Consider (6):

(6) a. Ana es inteligente.
'Ana is intelligent.'
b. Pedro cree que Ana es inteligente.
'Pedro believes that Ana is intelligent.'

(6a) would have a conceptual structure something like (7), with the relevant lexical items inserted into the appropriate argument positions:

(7) $[_{\text{State}}\ \text{BE}_{\text{Ident}}\ ([_{\text{Thing}}\ \text{ANA}], [\text{AT}_{\text{Ident}}\ ([_{\text{Property}}\ \text{INTELLIGENT}])])]$

In (6b), of course, the proposition embodied in (7) is embedded in a belief context, which Jackendoff (1983, 1985) represents with the semantic function REPRESENTATION, so that a possible conceptual structure representation would be as in (8):

(8) $[_{\text{State}}\ \text{BE}\ ([\ \text{REP}\ [_{\text{State}}\ \text{BE}_{\text{Ident}}\ ([_{\text{Thing}}\ \text{ANA}],$
$[\text{AT}_{\text{Ident}}\ ([_{\text{Property}}\ \text{INTELLIGENT}])])]\ \text{IN}\ ([_{\text{Thing}}\ \text{PEDRO'S}$
$\text{MIND}])])]$

Note that in (8) REPRESENTATION is a semantic function, not a conceptual category. As such, it does not seem a likely candidate for the semantic correlate of the syntactic category CP. That this is so can be seen clearly from the conceptual representation proposed by Kornfilt and Correa (1993) for the verb *tell.* These researchers follow Jackendoff's framework in its essentials, adding the semantic field of 'mental' to include abstract movement of information between or within cognitive agents. For *tell,* therefore, they propose the structure in (9), in which the argument positions are unspecified for conceptual type:

(9) tell: CAUSE (x, GO_{mental} (REP (y), $PATH_{mental}$ [FROM (x) to (z)]))
(x tell z that y)

Now, of the research that has been carried out using Jackendoff's proposed conceptual structures, the study by Kornfilt and Correa is the one that deals most directly with the problem of determining syntactic categories. At the same time it illustrates some of the problems in dealing with clausal complementation. The basic set of conceptual types that they assume is presented in (10):

(10)

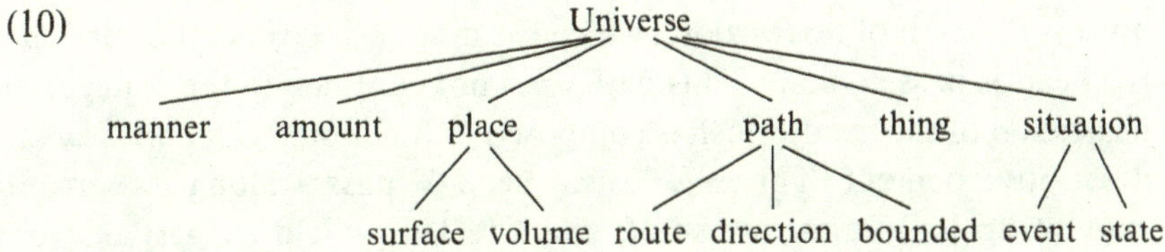

Kornfilt and Correa note that the subontology of 'places,' 'paths,' and 'situations' is more elaborate than the other conceptual types because lexical semantics has been traditionally concerned with the syntax and semantics of verbs and prepositions, where the latter correspond to places and paths and "Situations correspond loosely to the kind of entities referred to by verbs" (*op. cit.*:85). However, only two sentences later they claim that there are correspondence principles that express the relationship between conceptual types and syntactic categories, with one of these principles being that "clauses correspond to situations."

In fact their proposal regarding the categorial realization of arguments is much more refined than simply a list of conceptual types with their corresponding syntactic categories. They argue that a general lexical redundancy rule essentially 'assigns' the syntactic category as a function of the semantic primitive, the position of the argument in the conceptual expression, and the conceptual type.

A partial 'map' of these relations is given in (11):[3]

(11)	Primitive	Position	Type	Category
	BE	1	thing	NP
			situation	CP
	GO	1	thing	NP
		2	path	PP
	LET	1	thing	NP
		2	situation	CP
	AT	1	thing	NP
			property	AP

Since for them the conceptual type 'situation' includes the conceptual types 'event' and 'state,' we seem to have made little progress with respect to where the putative conceptual type 'proposition' fits in. Now, looking at the map in (11) or the list in (5) with the eyes of a syntactician, what becomes immediately noticeable is that the proposed syntactic correlates to conceptual types are a heterogeneous set: alongside NP and AP, clearly lexical projections, we have CP, a functional projection. And here, I would like to suggest, is one source of difficulty. It will be recalled that as part of his proposal that NPs are included in a functional projection of type DP, Abney (1987) suggested that the s(emantic)-projection path of a node is the path of nodes along which the descriptive, semantic content of the head is passed along. This path does not continue to the c(ategorial)-projection of the head, which is composed of functional categories lacking descriptive content. Thus the lexical head V passes along its semantic content up to VP, but not to IP and CP. This would suggest that only lexical categories correspond to conceptual categories, while functional categories are purely syntactic. Here, I think, is one way out of the dilemma.[4]

3.3 The lexical/functional distinction and extended projection. What I want to explore is the following idea: there is indeed a set of correspondences or mappings between conceptual types and syntactic categories along the lines developed by Kornfilt and Correa. However, this mapping is, on the syntactic end of things, strictly to lexical categories such as NP, VP, and AP.[5] The functional categories do not derive from conceptual structure, but rather are projected from the appropriate lexical categories within a system of extended projection as proposed by Grimshaw (1991). She proposes that functional elements such as Det and Infl are not, strictly speaking, members of a category distinct from N and V, respectively, but rather have the same categorial status, being distinguished from the lexical heads only by the feature [+F(unctional)]. Thus Det is [+N, −V, +F] while N is [+N, −V, −F]. Crucially for us, she analyzes Comp (and hence CP) as the highest functional projection of the verbal system.

As Grimshaw notes, this proposal has straightforward consequences for long-standing problems of clausal selection. Since Bresnan (1972) it has been assumed that selection for types of clausal complements reduces to selection for elements in Comp, as exemplified by the English *that* versus *for* versus *wh* distinction. But in many languages the subjunctive/indicative distinction is not morphologically encoded in Comp, as illustrated below for Spanish and English:

(12) a. Han recomendado que los estudiantes lleguen/*llegan preparados.
'They have recommended that the students arrive (SUBJ/*IND) prepared.'
b. Han afirmado que los estudiantes llegan/*lleguen preparados.
'They have affirmed that the students arrive (IND/ *SUBJ) prepared.'

(13) a. I demanded that the students arrive/*arrived prepared.
b. I thought that the students arrived prepared.

Selection for subjunctive versus indicative, then, appears to be a case of non-local selection, regardless of whether subjunctive is seen as a feature of a 'nondecomposed' Infl or as the head of a modal projection MP (cf. Laka 1990 and Rivero 1992, among others). In Kempchinsky (1986, 1990) I argued that selection for subjunctive clauses had to involve selection for an element in Comp because of the mutual exclusion of subjunctive and *wh*-operators. The subjunctive operator in Comp, in turn, selects the subjunctive feature in Infl. Such an approach works technically but raises the question of learnability: if there is no morphological difference in Comp for the language in question (leaving aside the good fortune of children acquiring a language such as Romanian), then how does the child acquire these selectional facts? Grimshaw, having noted the facts in English, shows that the notion of extended projection provides a solution. Assuming that the mood distinction is encoded on the verb, then that particular feature will project all the way through the complete extended projection to CP, where it is then (locally) selected by the superordinate verb.[6]

This then gives us the following picture: A verb in its semantic representation may contain the conceptual type 'situation,' which includes the subtypes 'event' and 'state.' By a general map relating conceptual types to syntactic categories, as proposed by Kornfilt and Correa, this conceptual type will map to the lexical category VP. By the theory of extended projection this VP will then project all the relevant functional categories, that is, those containing the feature [+V]—hence, CP. Conversely, the conceptual type "thing" will map to the lexical category NP, which will then form its extended projection set DP (and possibly PP). As an example, consider the verb *querer,* which syntactically may appear with either a CP or a DP complement. Following Jackendoff (1990), we will take the semantic representation of *querer* to be as in (14):[7]

(14) $[_{Event}$ WANT $([_{Thing}\ x], [_{Thing/Situation}\ y])]$

a. Ana quiere una bebida bien fría. y = Thing
'Ana wants a very cold drink.'

b. Ana quiere que le sirvas una bebida bien fría. y = Situation
'Ana wants that you serve her a very cold drink.' (event)

c. Ana quiere que haga mucho sol. y = Situation
'Ana wants that it be sunny.' (state)

With this set of assumptions then, we need make no appeal to the semantic function of REPRESENTATION. However, the primary motivation for proposing this function was not to account for the projection of clauses as a syntactic category, but rather to provide a means for accounting for the semantic interpretation of clauses within the scope of propositional attitude verbs. This in turn is made necessary by the explicit assumption that there is no additional level of semantic representation beyond the set of semantic conceptual structures. Further, at this point we still have made little progress on the specific problem of selecting for types of complement clauses. This is the focus of the following section.

4 Selection for subjunctive CPs.

4.1 Semantic function as an arbiter of mood. As I observed in section 2, the class of verbs that invariably take subjunctive complements when tensed are the volitional and directive predicatives, where the latter term is being used somewhat broadly to also include permissive predicates such as *permitir,* 'to permit' and *dejar,* 'to allow' and interdictive predicates such as *prohibir,* 'to forbid' and *impedir,* 'to prevent.' Now, one way to account for the projection of subjunctive versus indicative mood would be to complicate the mapping algorithm from conceptual types to syntactic categories by specifying that 'situations' in the scope of certain functions, say WANT, CAUSE, or LET, map to subjunctive VPs. That at least these three functions, if not more, would entail subjunctive complements is illustrated by the following examples:

(15) a. Ana desea que tú la acompañes.
'Ana desires that you accompany (SUBJ) her.' (WANT)

b. Ana forzó a Pedro a que saliera sin ella.
'Ana forced Pedro (to) that he leave (SUBJ) without her.' (CAUSE)

c. Ana permitió que los niños vieran la película.
'Ana permitted that the children see (SUBJ) the movie.' (LET)

Recall that by extended projection selection for mood, although 'syntactically' represented by both a M(odal)P and a CP with the appropriate complementizer, is initially selection for the verb on which the mood distinction is encoded. This approach, furthermore, is also compatible with the minimalist framework, according to which the verb is inserted into the syntactic structure 'full strength'[8] and then checked against the (strong or weak) morphological features in the various functional heads through which it moves, either before or after Spell-out.

However, this approach, although I think it can be made to work technically, seems to me to miss an important generalization. The class of verbs with which we are dealing appears on this account to be a rather heterogeneous set, and the list of semantic functions seems to be arbitrary—why these and not others? One would expect that the 'cut' could vary from language to language, so that, say, Spanish required subjunctive complements to verbs whose semantic representation contained the functions WANT and LET but not CAUSE, while French evidenced subjunctive complements to verbs with LET and CAUSE but not WANT. But within the Romance languages such differences do not emerge, whereas there are differences in the mood of clausal complements to epistemic verbs and factive-emotive verbs. I would therefore like to turn away for a moment from semantic conceptual semantics and explore a different avenue of approach.

4.2 Subjunctive clauses in model-theoretic semantics. A unified account of this class of verbs is provided by Farkas (1993) within the framework of model-theoretic semantics. Farkas starts with the assumption that since selection for the subjunctive is invariant (in the Romance languages) only for the general class of volitional and directive predicatives, mood selection must be derivable from the meaning of these predicates—exactly our assumption here. Now it would seem that a straightforward way for accounting for this selection would be to appeal in some way to the traditional notion of 'irrealis.' The proposition embodied by the clausal complement to volitional and directive predicates is necessarily not true at the moment of wishing or ordering, and so the complement appears in the subjunctive mood. Clearly, this is too simplistic given the complexities of propositional attitude verbs. Minimally, some appeal must be made to the beliefs of the matrix subject: if this subject believes that the proposition embodied in the subordinate clause is true, the clause is in the indicative mood; otherwise, the clause appears in the subjunctive. However, the truly problematic cases, as Farkas points out, are fiction verbs such as *dream* and, in a class by itself, the verb *promise.* Both these classes introduce complements that are necessarily not true from the point of view of the matrix subject but that in the Romance languages almost invariably appear with indicative complements.

What Farkas proposes, therefore, is that an analysis of the semantics of subjunctive complements must be based on the idea that the truth of the proposition is evaluated with respect to times and (possible) worlds, with these possible worlds being anchored in turn to individuals. Mood choice is then dependent on two factors: (i) the truth of the complement proposition as far as that individual anchor is concerned and (ii) whether the matrix verb introduces one particular world, that is, is an extensional predicate, or introduces a set of worlds, that is, is an intensional predicate. Extensional predicates govern the indicative and intensional predicates govern the subjunctive.

Consider on this account verbs of reporting, which govern the indicative. These verbs introduce one world, the world taken to be the real world at the time of the reported conversation. The primary anchor is the matrix subject, who reports what she or he understands to be this real world. Fiction verbs such as *dream* introduce a new world that the matrix subject (and the speaker) understand as not equaling the real world, while *promise* introduces a particular world that is identical to the future real world as understood by the subject. Since in all of these cases there is only one world, the complement appears in the indicative mood.

In contrast volitionals and directives introduce a set of worlds, the set of possible futures. These two subclasses differ in that a subset of the worlds introduced by directive predicates is the set in which the directive is fulfilled, while desiderative predicates have no such subset. Nonetheless, their crucial shared property is that the set of worlds introduced by the predicate does not contain the world at the time referred to by the matrix. This captures the traditional intuition of 'irrealis,' while still providing a means of distinguishing between, say, *want* and *promise.*[9]

The semantic basis of the subjunctive/indicative mood distinction, therefore, rests on the difference between extensionality versus intentionality. Further, the property of being an intensional predicate is imputed to be a part of the lexical meaning of a verb such as *querer.* The obvious question now is whether an account based on model-theoretic semantics can be compatible with a highly mentalistic approach such as Jackendoff's semantic conceptual structures.

4.3 Model-theoretic semantics and mentalist approaches. Jackendoff's basic complaint with model-theoretic semantics is that the basic entities of the model are assumed to have an existence or reality independent of the mind of the language user; truth is therefore defined as a predetermined relationship between a sentence and the real world. (He accordingly terms model-theoretic semantics, as usually practiced, as 'E-semantics' versus a more psychologically based 'I-semantics.'). Whether model-theoretic semantics can in fact be made to harmonize in some way with a psychologically based view of grammar has been a preoccupation for some time for Partee (cf. Partee 1979, 1982, and 1993). On the one hand she is not convinced that semantic representations should necessarily look something like syntactic representations as in a Jackendovian-type framework; on the other she recognizes the clash between the notion of theoretically nondenumerable possible worlds and the limitations of the finite brain. In Partee (1979, 1982) she proposes that this problem can be overcome if we assume that it is not necessary to represent all of the possible worlds distinctly in order to know a function that has them as a domain, while in Partee (1993) she observes that recent work in model-theoretic semantics (she mentions explicitly work by Heim and Kratzer) has made the compatibility of this type of semantics with mentalist conceptions of grammar more feasible. Further, in this latter work she discusses analyses in model-theoretic semantics that appear to capture important linguistic generalizations but that are not transferable to syntactic-type formal semantic representations, which in spirit I have tried to do here as well.

I would like to suggest that both of these approaches to semantics, each of which captures important linguistic generalizations, do play a role in a psychological model of grammar. I noted earlier that there is a crucial terminological distintion between lexical conceptual structures and semantic conceptual structures. Recall that Jackendoff makes the explicit claim that semantic conceptual structures are identical to semantic representation; that is, they form the basis not only of lexical knowledge (what words mean) but also of the semantic interpretation of sentences. It seems to me that this view of things limits the task of the computational component—that is, syntax—to 'filling in,' as it were, the slots (the argument variables). What I propose here is that lexical meaning, as represented in conceptual structures, must be separated from propositional meaning, as represented ultimately at the level of LF.

I assume, as stated explicitly in Chomsky (1993), that language ('I-language') is a separate component of the mind alongside an independent conceptual component. The interface level between language and the conceptual system is assumed to be LF. But of course the lexicon, from which items enter into the computational system, is also an interface level with the conceptual system, since the meanings of individual lexical items, as thoroughly demonstrated by Jackendoff, are functions of basic conceptual types and semantic fields. However, propositional meaning seems to need an additional layer of semantic interpretation; more precisely, a proposition, in the linguistic sense, is a predicate-argument structure (the contribution of the conceptual component) with a time index and a world index. These latter are the contribution of the syntax, specifically, the contribution of the functional categories. Thus, the functor Infl (or Tense) relates the event or state embodied in the predicate-argument structure to a temporal index or point. The functor Comp marks the propositional value (the truth conditions, informally), of the IP/TP. Similarly, for noun phrases the functor Det determines the referent or token of the head N, which represents the type. The essence of this idea, then, is that s-selection phenomena are derived from the conceptual component via the individual lexical items, while c-selection phenomena are derived from the syntax, the computational component.

At this point the logical question is the following: If c-selection derives from the syntax, in what sense can we say that selection for subjunctive complements to volitional and directive predicates is to be derivable from the meaning of these predicates? I turn to this question in the next section.

5 Extended projections, acquisition, and minimalism. The picture we now have is the following: The child approaching the task of language acquisition has two sets of tools: the conceptual component and the computational component. The conceptual component gives her or him a network or grid that allows her to impose some organization on direct sensory input. Assuming the existence of some set of correspondence principles, the conceptual component also feeds into the lexicon, which in turn projects structure into the syntax. In effect, therefore, the lexicon is a set of correspondence relations between syntactic structures and conceptual structures, as Jackendoff proposes.

The correspondence principles take the form of a map, along the lines proposed by Kornfilt and Correa (1993), relating conceptual types to lexical categories. Thus, the argument in position 1 of the semantic primitive GO of conceptual type *thing* is an NP, the argument in position 2 of the semantic primitive GO of conceptual type *situation* is a VP, and so on. These lexical categories in turn form part of an extended projection set with their related functional categories.

Now the heads of functional categories (C, D, T, etc.) are morphemes, often bound, sometimes free, that have by Grimshaw's theory of extended projection both a lexical category value [+N, +V] and the functional value [+F]. Of course, morphology is exactly that aspect of language that is 'visible' to the child and that has to be learned; indeed, in the minimalist program morphology plays a paramount role in determining the line between overt and covert syntax.

Recall the assumption mentioned above that a verb enters the syntactic representation with all of its morphology (rather than acquiring this morphology via head-to-head movement as in Baker (1988)). Now this assumption, taken together with the VP-internal subject hypothesis, means that at an early stage of acquisition it is possible for the child to have 'acquired' full clauses when in fact the grammar at that point only projects lexical categories. In a language such as Spanish, *querer* followed by a 'clause' whose verb is inflected for the subjunctive could first be acquired as a chunk. Acquisition proceeds as the child begins to induce the projection of functional categories from the existence of morphological markers. Thus, working 'backwards,' as it were, the child learns as part of the lexical entry of *querer* that this verb selects a verb inflected for the subjunctive mood. By the theory of extended projections this feature is then carried up through the entire projection, ending at CP. Now for the volitional and directive predicates the subjunctive mood of the complement clause, as we have seen, is directly relatable to the propositional value in terms of possible worlds of that clause, as interpreted in LF. The lexical entry of verbs such as *querer* therefore comes to include the relevant c-selection facts—what we used to call subcategorization—as part of the child's acquiring syntax.[10]

The idea therefore is that input into the acquisition process comes from both the conceptual component and the computational component. What does this mean for semantic bootstrapping? Pinker (1989) observes that in its initial form (Pinker 1984) the semantic bootstrapping hypothesis essentially equated semantic structures with conceptual structures, as in the diagram shown in (16):

(16)

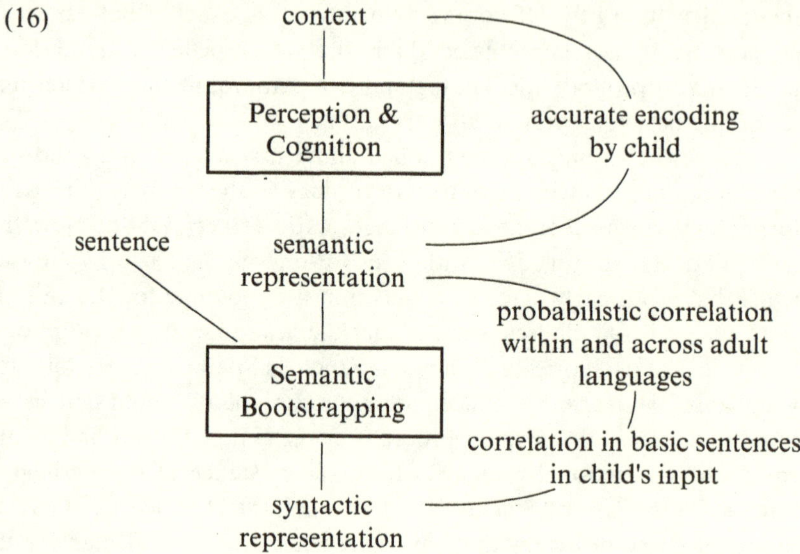

However, he comes to reject this view, arguing (on the basis of the argument alternations studied in his 1989 work) that semantic representations are linguistic representations that are partially specific to a given language. Therefore, semantic representations "must be a separate component created from context" (1989: p. 361). In the new picture there is an additional link, as shown in (17):

(17)

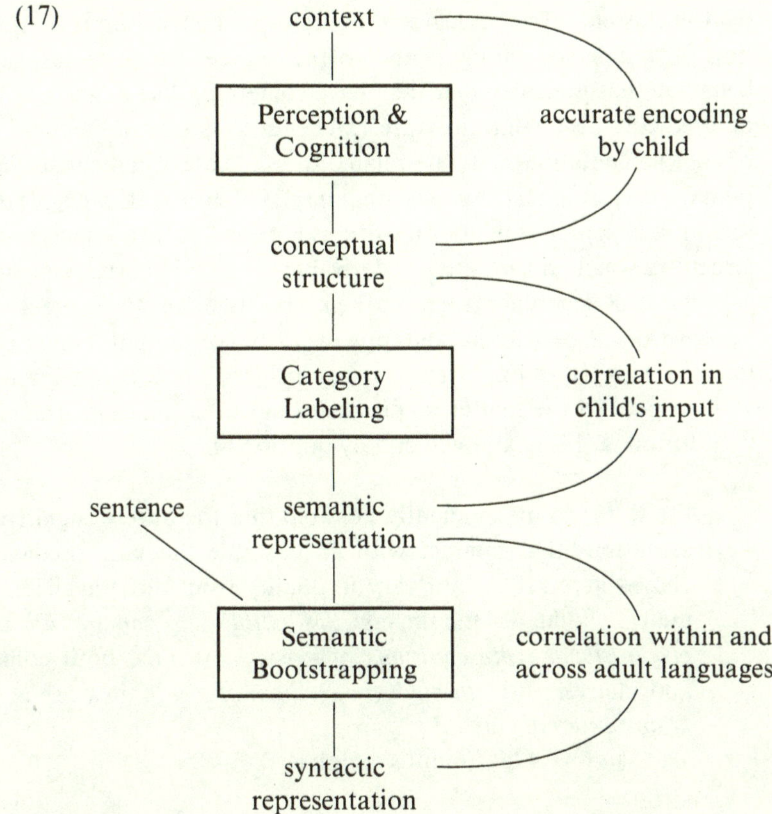

The crucial linking now is between syntax and semantics, not between syntax and conceptual structures. As Pinker notes (1989:363), this is preferable on conceptual grounds: "Heuristic correlations between perceptually derivable conceptual/semantic categories and syntax are both undesirable formally and difficult to defend empirically, compared to linking regularities between syntax and abstract semantics." Essentially, what is argued here is that there is a level of semantic representation independent from conceptual structures that also plays a role in acquisition, which is precisely what I have suggested must be the case with the acquisition of subcategorized subjunctive clauses. This may appear to some to be too complex a picture. However, the facts of human language may not be as simple as we might like, and I think that it is not insignificant that the acquisition of subjunctive clauses, even with verbs like *querer,* is relatively late in the acquisition process, as might be expected from the schema proposed here.

6 Conclusion. To the degree that conceptual structure is a representation of 'connected thought' and to the degree that primates, say, show behavior that indicates that they have something like connected thought or predicate argument structure (Jackendoff 1993a), then those aspects of complementation structure related to predicate argument structure are perhaps not uniquely 'human' or 'linguistic.' But to the degree that the semantic interpretation of propositions is derivable from aspects of clausal structure, which in turn are not derivable from or in correspondence with aspects of conceptual structure, then what is linguistic is precisely that: propositions. I believe that the framework of conceptual semantics elaborated by Jackendoff has given us many insights into lexical semantics. But with respect to the matter of propositional interpretation, I agree more with Emonds (1991) and will end by quoting him:

> "It seems to me eminently possible that the purely cognitive representations that interact with at least the thematic predicates discussed here . . . do not vary in quality from those available to primates. What is human is *the ability to conjure up complex propositional representations* of possible worlds, both consciously and inadvertently, *through the medium of syntax and in the absence of any external stimuli.*
>
> (*op. cit.*:425; Emonds' emphasis)

NOTES

1. This pattern of acquisition and loss is repeated in terms of cross-linguistic distribution. As Farkas (1993) notes, in a language with an 'active' subjunctive/indicative distinction, subjunctive clauses will appear minimally as complements to volitional and directive predicates. In Romanian, if we abstract away from the replacement of the infinitive with the subjunctive mood, it is only with volitionals and directives that subjunctive complements appear. In English the so-called *that*-subjunctives appear almost exclusively with directive predicates (*ask, demand, recommend,* and so on), while the use of *for-to* infinitives is limited primarily to volitional verbs (*prefer, desire*) and factive-emotives in modal contexts (cf. Kempchinsky 1986, following Emonds 1976).

2. It is worth noting that the appeal to Grimshaw's CSR is in fact incompatible with the explicit assumption taken in much of the work on lexical structures that syntactic structure is mapped directly from PAS. Concretely, the problem is that a principle such as Canonical Structural Realization makes reference to conceptual categories located in the LCS, but this information is not represented at the level of argument structure. There are two possible solutions to this loss of information: either the PAS must contain more than simply 'contentless' variables, or the PAS as an intermediate level between the lexicon and the syntax should be dispensed with altogether, in which case lexicon-to-syntax mapping will need to be expressed as correspondence rules between 'conceptual' nodes in an LCS-type representation and syntactic nodes, as proposed by Bouchard (1991). I am not unaware of this problem but will not deal with it here.

3. The formal rule that they propose is the following

(i) Grammatical function assignment rule
Abstraction variable x in LCS L has syntactic relation [V′,XP] if
  (i) P is the conceptual primitive immediately containing x,
  (ii) the argument position of x in P is I,
  (iii) T is the required conceptual type of x in L, and
  (iv) XP = S(P,I,T) where S is a map [such as (11) in the text]

4. Beyond the particular theoretical difficulties posed by clausal complementation, I believe there is another source of confusion with respect to the relation held by CP vs. VP to conceptual structure, namely, our incomplete assimilation of recent and not so recent advances in linguistic theory into our 'everyday' linguistic discourse. Clausal categories, whether they be labelled 'S,' 'S′,' 'CP,' or whatever, have formed part of our theoretical inventory since the earliest days of generative grammar, along with such familiar categories as 'NP,' 'VP,' and the like. The DP hypothesis has allowed us to perceive much more clearly the parallelism between the NP-DP relationship and the VP-IP-CP relationship, while we still persist in the use of a language of discourse that refers to NPs and CPs as maximal projections in argument position vs. VPs and PPs (as, for example, in *Barriers*).

5. As always, PPs have a somewhat problematic status. See Grimshaw (1991), who proposes, following Emonds (1985), that PPs are the maximal functional category of NPs, i.e., they are the nominal counterparts of CPs. On the other hand PPs behave more like a lexical category in lexicon-to-syntax mapping, since they seem to straightforwardly correspond to given conceptual types, as discussed by Jackendoff in his work and by Kornfilt and Correa.

6. An interesting question here is whether selection for IP vs. CP should be possible, given that they are members of the same categorial set. Grimshaw suggests that this is possible on the assumption that IPs and CPs are different semantic types, the former being of the type 'event' and the latter of the type 'proposition.' This distinction is exploited in recent work by Ormazabal (1994), who proposes that the propositional vs. eventive interpretation of a complement corresponds syntactically to the presence vs. absence of a CP projection. Concretely, he analyzes control infinitives, which semantically correspond to unrealized or prospective events, as IPs rather than CPs. This proposal, while attractive, runs into an immediate problem with subjunctive complements to volitional and directional predicates, which regularly alternate with control infinitives. It also, as may become clear below, somewhat contradicts the spirit of my proposal here.

7. Jackendoff (1990) suggests that WANT may be a basic semantic function, on a par with CAUSE and LET, as evidenced by the fact that it may appear in several semantic fields. The representation I give in (14) is therefore my interpretation of this suggestion.

Jackendoff (this volume) offers an extensive proposal for the semantic conceptual structure underlying volitional and directive predicates in English (the c-selection properties of which are not as straightforward as those of their Romance counterparts). I had not seen this proposal when I was writing this article.

8. This particular turn of phrase is due to Frank Drijkoningen (cf. Drijkoningen 1994).

9. The fact that negated epistemics may also take subjunctive complements is explained by appealing to the idea that these predicates introduce a set of epistemically possible worlds that are ordered with respect to what the individual anchor—the matrix subject—takes to be the actual world. Thus, the indicative may appear when these worlds are closely overlapping with the actual world. This account therefore captures the pragmatic considerations that are observable with negated epistemics, illustrated below:

(i) a. No creo que él tenga la culpa (pero tendremos que esperar los resultados de la investigación).
'I don't believe that he is (SUBJ) guilty (but we'll have to wait for the results of the investigation).'

b. No creo que él tiene la culpa (porque he visto evidencia de que el otro lo hizo).
'I don't believe that he is (IND) guilty (because I have seen evidence that the other one did it).'

10. The germ of this idea was planted by Rob Chametzky in the form of a question he asked at a presentation of this material in a colloquium at the University of Iowa. He is not, of course, responsible for my elaboration of it.

REFERENCES

Abney, S. 1987. *The English Noun Phrase in its Sentential Aspect.* Ph.D. Dissertation. MIT.

Baker, M. 1988. *Incorporation: A Theory of Grammatical Function Changing.* Chicago: University of Chicago Press.

Bouchard, D. 1991. From Conceptual Structure to Syntactic Structure. In *Views on Phrase Structure.* K. Leffel and D. Bouchard, eds. Dordrecht: Kluwer.

Bresnan, J. 1972. *Theory of Complementation in English Syntax.* Ph.D. Dissertation. MIT.

Chomsky, N. 1993. A Minimalist Program for Linguistic Theory. In *The View from Building 20: Essays in Linguistics in Honor of Sylvain Bromberger.* K. Hale and S. J. Keyser, eds. Cambridge: MIT Press.

Drijkoningen, F. 1994. Morphological Strength and Word Order Variation in French. Paper presented at the Fourth Colloquium on Generative Grammar. Tarragona, Spain.

Emonds, J. 1976. *A Transformational Approach to English Syntax.* New York: Academic Press.

Emonds, J. 1985. *A Unified Theory of Syntactic Categories.* Dordrecht: Foris.

Emonds, J. 1991. Subcategorization and Syntax-based Theta-role Assignment. *Natural Language and Linguistic Theory* 9:369–429.

Farkas, D. 1993. On the Semantics of Subjunctive Complements. In *Romance Languages and Modern Linguistic Theory.* P. Hirschbühler and K. Koerner, eds. Amsterdam/Philadelphia: John Benjamins.

Fillmore, C. 1968. The Case for Case. In *Universals in Linguistic Theory.* E. Bach and R. J. Harms, eds. New York: Holt, Rinehart and Winston.

Grimshaw, J. 1979. Complement Selection and the Lexicon. *Linguistic Inquiry* 10:279–326.

Grimshaw, J. 1981. Form, Function, and the Language Acquisition Device. In *The Logical Problem of Language Acquisition.* C. L. Baker and J. J. McCarthy, eds. Cambridge: MIT Press.

Grimshaw, J. 1991. *Extended Projection.* Manuscript. Brandeis University.

Guitart, J. 1978. Sobre el subjuntivo en hablas del Caribe hispánico: Teoría y datos. Paper presented at the 5th International Congress of ALFAL. Caracas, Venezuela.

Guitart, J. 1980. On the Pragmatics of Spanish Mood in So-called Semi-factive Predicates. In *Contemporary Studies in Romance Languages.* F. Nuessel, ed. Bloomington: Indiana University Linguistics Club.

Hale, K., and S. Keyser. 1986. Some Transitivity Alternations in English. *Lexicon Project Working Papers* 7. Cambridge: MIT Center for Cognitive Science.

Jackendoff, R. 1983. *Semantics and Cognition.* Cambridge: MIT Press.

Jackendoff, R. 1985. Believing and Intending: Two Sides of the Same Coin. *Linguistic Inquiry* 16:445–59.

Jackendoff, R. 1990. *Semantic Structures.* Cambridge: MIT Press.

Jackendoff, R. 1993a. On the Role of Conceptual Structure in Argument Selection. *Natural Language and Linguistic Theory* 11:279–312.

Jackendoff, R. 1993b. The Combinatorial Structure of Thought: The Family of Causative Concepts. In *Knowledge and Language,* vol. 2. E. Reuland and W. Abraham, eds. Dordrecht/Boston: Kluwer.

Kempchinsky, P. 1986. *Romance Subjunctive Clauses and Logical Form.* Ph.D. Dissertation. UCLA.

Kempchinsky, P. 1990. Más sobre el efecto de referencia disjunta del subjuntivo. In *Indicativo y subjuntivo.* I. Bosque, ed. Madrid: Taurus.

Kornfilt, J., and N. Correa. 1993. Conceptual Structure and its Relation to the Structure of Lexical Entries. In *Knowledge and Language,* vol. 2. E. Reuland and W. Abraham, eds. Dordrecht/Boston: Kluwer.

Laka, I. 1990. *Negation in Syntax.* Ph.D. Dissertation. MIT.

Ocampo, F. 1991. El subjuntivo en tres generaciones de hablantes bilingües. In *Spanish in the United States: Sociolinguistic Issues.* J. Bergen, ed. Washington, D.C.: Georgetown University Press.

Ormazabal, J. 1994. Deriving Factivity from the Syntax. Paper presented at the Fourth Colloquium on Generative Grammar. Tarragona, Spain.

Padilla-Rivera, J. 1985. *On the Definition of Binding Domains in Spanish.* Ph.D. Dissertation. Cornell University.

Partee, B. 1979. Semantics—Mathematics or Psychology? In *Semantics from Different Points of View.* R. Bauerle, et al., eds. Berlin: Springer-Verlag.

Partee, B. 1982. Belief-sentences and the Limits of Semantics. In *Processes, Beliefs and Questions.* S. Peters and E. Saarinen, eds. Dordrecht: Reidel.

Partee, B. 1993. Semantic Structures and Semantic Properties. In *Knowledge and Language,* vol. 2. E. Reuland and W. Abraham, eds. Dordrecht/Boston: Kluwer.

Perlmutter, D., and P. Postal. 1984. The 1-Advancement Exclusiveness Law. In *Studies in Relational Grammar.* D. Perlmutter and C. Rosen, eds. Chicago: University of Chicago Press.

Pinker, S. 1984. *Language Learnability and Language Development.* Cambridge: Harvard University Press.

Pinker, S. 1989. *Learnability and Cognition: The Acquisition of Argument Structure.* Cambridge: MIT Press.

Rappaport, M., and B. Levin. 1988. What to Do with Theta-roles. In *Thematic Relations.* W. Wilkins, ed. New York: Academic Press.

Rivero, M. L. 1992. Clitic and NP Climbing in Old Spanish. In *Current Studies in Spanish Linguistics.* H. Campos and F. Martinez-Gil, eds. Washington, D. C.: Georgetown University Press.

Silva-Corvalán, C. 1990. Current Issues in Studies of Language Contact. *Hispania* 73:162–76.

Silva-Corvalán, C. 1991. Spanish Language Attrition in a Contact Situation with English. In *First Language Attrition.* H. Selinger and R. Vago, eds. Cambridge: Cambridge University Press.

Verbal Morphology: *Syntactic Structures* Meets the Minimalist Program*

Howard Lasnik
University of Connecticut

One of the major breakthroughs in the history of generative transformational grammar was the discovery by Chomsky (1955, 1957) of the regularities underlying English verbal morphology. Much of the apparent chaos of this central portion of English morpho-syntax was rendered systematic by the fundamental insight that the tense-agreement inflectional morpheme ('C') is syntactically independent, even though always a bound morpheme superficially. The analysis was brilliantly successful and paved the way for numerous refinements and extensions over the past forty years, the large majority of them sharing the same fundamental insight. The refinements can be viewed as attempts to maintain the leading ideas of the analysis but to reconcile them with the growing concern for explanatory adequacy.

For example, Lasnik (1981) was particularly concerned with the stipulated rule ordering and the arbitrary marking of particular transformations as obligatory or optional in Chomsky's early system and proposed that these problematic language-particular formal mechanisms can be eliminated in favor of the general filter in (1):

(1) The 'stranded affix' filter: A morphologically realized affix must be a syntactic dependent of a morphologically realized category, at surface structure. (Lasnik 1981)

Notice that this filter crucially assumes, along with Chomsky (1955, 1957) and many succeeding analyses, that the inflectional material on a verb is a morphological affix, even though it begins its syntactic existence as an autonomous entity. Given this assumption and given (1) and the restrictive theory of transformations it presupposes, a typical analysis of the English verb system of the early 1980s looks something like (2):

(2) a. S is the maximal projection of the inflectional morpheme Infl (= C of Chomsky 1957).
b. Infl takes VP as its complement.

c. When the head of VP is *have* or *be* it raises to Infl, the next head up.
d. Otherwise Infl lowers to V: Affix Hopping.
(e. Otherwise *do* adjoins to Infl.)

Such a system is descriptively comparable to that of Chomsky (1955, 1957) in the way it handles the familiar paradigms below, and is superior in terms of explanatory adequacy,[1] for the reasons already alluded to.

(3)	John left.	*John leftn't.
	John has left.	John hasn't left.
	John is leaving.	John isn't leaving.
(4)	John left.	*Left John.
	John has left.	Has John left.
	John is leaving	Is John leaving.

Emonds (1978), based on a similar model, insightfully explored certain differences between English and French. Taking *pas* to be the analogue of *not*, he was concerned with the fact that while only auxiliary (finite) verbs precede negation in English, any (finite) verb does so in French:

(5) a. *John likes not Mary.
b. Jean (n')aime pas Marie.

Emonds proposed that the basic difference between English and French is that in the latter language verb raising is not limited to auxiliaries. Then, given the priorities in (2), Affix Hopping will never be necessary in French.

Pollock (1989) developed Emonds's idea further, offering an explanation of the verb raising difference between English and French. First, he argued that Infl should be split:

(6) 'Infl' is not one head; it consists of (at least) Tense and Agr(eement), each heading its own projection. Raising to Tense proceeds via Agr.

Given (6), the difference between English and French is accounted for by (7):

(7) a. English Agr, because it is not morphologically rich, is opaque to Θ-role transmission. Thus, if a verb with Θ-roles to assign were to raise, it would be unable to assign them, resulting in a violation of the Θ-criterion.

b. French Agr, because it is morphologically rich, is transparent to Θ-role transmission, so any sort of verb can raise.

Chomsky (1991), building on Pollock's analysis, offers the following economy explanation of why raising takes place whenever it can:

(8) Raising is preferred to lowering, because lowering will leave an unbound trace that will have to be remedied by re-raising in LF.

Notice that (8) assumes re-raising is, in general, possible when not blocked by a more economical derivation. If this were not so, even (9) would not be possible:

(9) John likes Mary.

The next question, then, is why (10), with overt lowering and LF re-raising, is not the English version of (5)b:[2]

(10) *John not likes Mary.

Chomsky's answer to this question is stated in terms of his more articulated version of Pollock's split Infl hypothesis. Note that Chomsky follows Pollock in taking negation to be a head:[3]

(11) 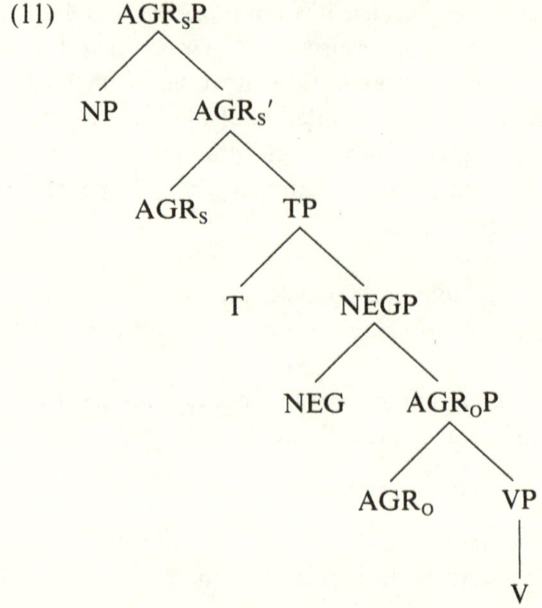

According to Chomsky, the Head Movement Constraint (reduced to an ECP antecedent government requirement) prevents the LF re-raising needed in the derivation of (10).[4] The intervening head Neg cannot be crossed. On the face of it the overt raising across negation in French, and that in English with *have* and *be,* would seem to run afoul of the same requirement. Chomsky accounts for the difference in the following way, where (12) lists the relevant principles and (13) and (14) sketch the French and English derivations, respectively:

(12) a. If Agr moves, its trace can be deleted, since it plays no role in LF.
b. If V moves, its trace cannot be deleted.
c. Deletion of an element leaves a category lacking features, [*e*].
d. Adjunction to [*e*] is not permitted.

(13) a. When V overtly raises (French) (5b), it first adjoins to AgrO, creating [$_{AgrO}$ V AgrO].
b. Next, AgrO raises to T, crossing Neg, thus leaving a trace that is marked [-γ], indicating a violation of the ECP. That trace is an Agr,

c. Eventually, in accord with (12a) the [-γ] trace is deleted, so there is no ECP violation (where ECP is, as in Lasnik and Saito 1984 and 1992, an LF filter: *[-γ]).

(14) a. When V vainly attempts to covertly (re-)raise in LF (English) (10), AgrS has already lowered overtly to T, leaving an Agr trace (which deletes, leaving [*e*]), and creating a complex T,

b. which has already lowered overtly to AgrO, leaving a T trace and creating a still more complex Agr,

c. which has already lowered overtly to V, leaving an Agr trace (which deletes, leaving [*e*]), and creating a complex V.

d. This complex V raises to the [*e*] left by the deletion of the AgrO trace, a movement that is by (12d) necessarily substitution, thus turning [*e*] into V.

e. This element now raises across Neg to (the trace of) T, leaving behind a [−γ] trace that is crucially a V trace, hence nondeletable. The resulting LF is in violation of the ECP.

There is a potential technical problem with this account of French, in that (12a) and (13c) seem to be inconsistent with a central economy condition of Chomsky (1991): Deletion is only permitted to turn an ill-formed LF object into a well-formed LF object, where the relevant well-formed objects are Operator-variable pairs and uniform chains (chains all the members of which are X^0s, are in A-positions, or are in A′-positions). This is precisely to prevent making a short licit head-, A-, or adjunct-movement, followed by a long illicit movement, with subsequent deletion of the offending trace of the latter movement.[5]

A related problem is that generally a long movement (i.e., one in violation of relativized minimality) results in some degradation (e.g., Subjacency effects, as discussed by Chomsky and Lasnik 1993), even if the offending trace is eventually eliminated. But the long overt V-movement at issue here is fully grammatical. I will not pursue these technical problems further, since the minimalist framework of Chomsky (1993), which I turn to now, rejects the account for other reasons and provides another perspective on verbal morphology.

Chomsky (1993) departs in an important respect from his earlier treatments of verbal morphology by adopting a strictly lexicalist view under which verbs are taken from the lexicon already fully inflected. They still must associate syntactically with the appropriate functional heads, but only in order for their inflectional properties to be checked against abstract features of the functional heads (rather than acquired as affixes). This checking approach mirrors Chomsky's checking view of Case, which holds that Case features are already associated with (the heads of) DPs as they are first inserted into syntactic structures. These DPs must wind up in positions where the Case they already have can be suitably licensed.[6] Note that in this view there is no obvious need for Affix Hopping. The fact that verbs overtly appear with their inflectional morphology even in English is no longer a relevant consideration in determining exactly how the derivation proceeded.

Intrinsic to this checking theory is that the features of verbs and functional heads must be checked against each other, but that this checking can in principle take place anywhere in a derivation on the path to LF. Chomsky also proposes, as a matter of execution, that once a feature of Agr has done its checking work it disappears.

From this point of view the difference between French and English is not verb raising versus affix lowering. Rather, it is whether verb raising takes place in overt syntax (French) or in the LF component (English). Further, since Chomsky argues that LF and PF are the only levels of linguistic representation, this difference cannot be attributed, as it might have been in previous theories, to any S-structure property. Chomsky thus proposes (15) as the core difference between French and English. The relevant notions are explicated in (16):

(15) a. In French the V-features of Agr (i.e., those that check features of a V) are strong.
b. In English the V-features of Agr are weak.

(16) a. V-features are not legitimate PF objects.
b. Strong features are visible at PF; weak features are not. Surviving strong features cause the derivation to crash at PF.

In French, since the V-features of Agr are strong, if V raises to Agr overtly, the V-features of Agr check the features of the V in overt syntax and disappear. Both LF and PF are thus well formed. If on the other hand V were to delay raising until LF, the V-features of Agr would survive into PF, causing the derivation to crash at that level, even though LF requirements would be satisfied. This correctly forces overt V-raising in French.

In English delaying V-raising until LF does not result in an ill-formed PF object, so such a derivation is possible. What makes it necessary is

(17) PROCRASTINATE: Delay an operation until LF whenever possible, that is, whenever delaying would not cause the derivation to crash.

(17) thus plays a central role in excluding (5a), repeated as (18):

(18) *John likes not Mary.

But, as already discussed, *have* and *be* do raise overtly. Chomsky proposes that this happens because *have* and *be* are semantically vacuous, hence not visible to LF operations. Thus, if they have not raised overtly, they will not be able to raise at all. Their unchecked features will cause the LF to crash.

This proposal raises certain questions. First, it is not clear that *be* is always semantically vacuous, yet the syntactic behavior of *be* in finite clauses is always the same. For example, it is reasonable to assume that in (19), *is* has the meaning of *exists.* Yet, as seen in (20), it raises overtly nonetheless:

(19) There is a solution.

(20) a. There is not a solution.
b. Is there a solution?

Second, even apart from the empirical considerations just mentioned, there is the conceptual question of whether syntactic operations, even those in the LF component, should be sensitive to purely semantic properties. LF is after all a syntactic rather than a semantic component. Finally, there is reason to believe that even instances of *have* and *be* that are vacuous in Chomsky's sense can undergo LF raising. For example, if the functional head in an English subjunctive clause has a V feature to be checked,[7] *have* and *be* evidently can raise in LF (and, along with main verbs, do so across negation):

(21) a. I desire that John not leave.
b. I desire that John not be here.

As noted by Wexler (1994), the potential problem in (21) does arise in other languages, such as Swedish, where auxiliary verbs pattern exactly with main verbs in remaining *in-situ* in embedded clauses, even though they are undoubtedly inflected:[8]

(22) a. . . . , om hon inte ofte har sett honom.
whether she not often has seen him.
b. *om hon har inte ofte sett honom.
c. *om hon inte har ofte sett honom.

Note incidentally that Chomsky (1993) does not provide an account of (10), repeated as (23):

(23) *John not likes Mary.

The analysis of Chomsky (1991), summarized in (14) above, does not carry over to this framework, since it relies crucially on properties of the traces left by affix lowering, an operation that has now been eliminated.[9] This much is clear: it must be ruled out, but its derivation must not crash. If it crashed, it could not block (24), since Procrastinate only chooses among convergent derivations.

(24) *John likes not Mary.

The analytic options are severely limited, particularly under the proposal of Chomsky (1995), apparently contra Chomsky (1991), that a [$-\gamma$] trace causes a derivation to crash. Below, I will suggest a new (actually very old) perspective on these facts that avoids this particular problem.

We have seen that Chomsky's lexicalist-minimalist account of verbal morphology demands that Agr and T are just abstract features that check against features of fully inflected verbs that raise to them. The earlier accounts treated such Infl items exclusively as bound morphemes that had to become affixes on otherwise bare verbs. We have seen that each approach has substantial problems. I will argue that the most important of these problems can be overcome under a hybrid approach that allows both mechanisms to coexist. (25) sketches such a possibility, where the fundamental difference between French and English (and between English auxiliary and main verbs) is with respect to choice of mechanism, that is, with respect to lexical representation.

(25) a. French verbs are fully inflected in the lexicon (possibly correlating with the fact that there are no bare forms; even the infinitive has an ending).
b. *Have* and *be* are fully inflected in the lexicon (possibly correlating with the fact that they are highly suppletive, but see below).
c. All other English verbs are bare in the lexicon.

With the lexical properties of verbs outlined in (25) no further stipulations are needed for Infl, at least for the core phenomena. As I will show momentarily, (26), the null hypothesis under the theory I advocate, suffices for French and English finite clauses:

(26) Infl is freely an affix or a set of abstract features.

Given that English *have* and *be* behave just like French verbs and given that English main verbs are not lexically represented with inflectional features ((25c)), the Infl feature strength difference posited by Chomsky ((15), (16) above) becomes superfluous. Instead, we have (27):

(27) Finite featural Infl is strong in both French and English.

The final necessary mechanism is for all intents and purposes the original one: Affix Hopping. Further, as conjectured by Lasnik (1981) and developed further by Halle and Marantz (1993) and Bobaljik (1993), the rule is a morphophonemic one rather than a syntactic one:

(28) Affixal Infl must merge with a V, a PF process (distinct from head movement) demanding adjacency.

Consider now the various combinations made available by this theory. First, suppose that we select a verb with inflectional features (notated here as +F) and a featural (as opposed to affixal) Infl:

(29) . . . Infl . . . V . . .
+F +F

This configuration is, of course, well formed. V raises (overtly) to Infl, and all relevant features are checked. This is the situation with all French verbs, as well as with English *have* and *be.*

Next, consider the case of a bare verb and an affixal (as opposed to featural) Infl:

(30) . . . Infl . . . V . . .
Af bare

This is the situation with English main verbs. In this configuration PF merger takes place as long as adjacency obtains, and the PF affixal requirement of Infl is satisfied.

Given (26), two other configurations could potentially arise, but, since both of them will ultimately crash, there is no need to replace (26) with a stipulation. The first such mismatched configuration is shown in (31):

(31) . . . Infl . . . V . . .
+F bare

Here, the features of Infl will not be checked, so the derivation crashes at LF. And under the assumption that the features are strong, there is a PF crash as well.

Finally, consider (32), the reverse of (31):

(32) . . . Infl . . . V . . .
Af +F

This time the features of V will fail to be checked, causing an LF crash. Additionally, if in principle affixal Infl cannot attach to an already inflected verb, this failure leads to a PF crash.

(33) summarizes the immediately preceding discussion:

(33)			
	a.	. . . Infl . . .V . . . +F +F	OK. V will overtly raise.
	b.	. . . Infl . . .V . . . Af bare	OK. PF merger.
	c.	. . . Infl . . .V . . . +F bare	*at LF. +F of Infl will not be checked; *at PF as well, since +F is strong.
	d.	. . . Infl . . .V. . . Af F+	*at LF. +F of V will not be checked. *at PF also, if merger fails.

Thus, it follows automatically from the lexical properties of French verbs that French Infl will always have to be featural, just as it follows from the lexical properties of *be* and auxiliary *have* that English Infl will always have to be featural when the verb is *have* or *be.* The parallelism in behavior between French verbs and English auxiliaries has a unified account in this theory, following from a parallelism in morphological properties. With a main verb in English, on the other hand, English Infl will always have to be affixal, and this too follows automatically.

Consider now the ill-formed negative sentences in English. (34) involves an apparently inflected verb *in-situ* in overt syntax:

(34) *John not walked.

Recall that Chomsky had assumed that such a configuration is universally ungrammatical, invariably leading to an ECP violation. However, we have seen that the theory leading to that conclusion for Chomsky, in which LF verb raising is preceded by overt affix lowering, has been rejected in favor of a lexicalist approach. And in the latter it is not clear that the result obtains. Further, there is empirical reason for doubting the conclusion in the first place, as seen, for example, in the Swedish example (22) above.

My account of (34) is that of Chomsky (1957).[10] *Walked* is not in the lexicon of English: all main verbs are 'bare.' Hence, (34) must arise from the merger of affixal Infl with *walk*. But *not* intervenes between Infl and *walk* so the former cannot merge with the latter.[11] Crucially, then, the Swedish example (22) must not involve merger. Rather, it must involve the covert analogue of the overt raising seen in French or with English *have* and *be*. That is, the verb is pulled from the lexicon fully inflected. Infl, then, is necessarily featural, so the verb must raise to Infl for the matching features to be checked. The different property of Swedish is that the V-features of Infl are weak, while those in French and English are strong. Procrastinate dictates that the Swedish verb will remain *in-situ* in overt syntax. (35) is fundamentally similar:

(35) *John walked not.

Walked is not in the lexicon, so even though featural Infl exists in English and even though its V-features are strong, *walked* could never be created by raising.[12]

We have seen that raising across negation overtly, as in (36) and (37), and covertly, as in (38), is available:

(36) Jean (n')aime pas Marie.
(37) John has not left.
(38) . . . , om hon inte ofte har sett honom.

We now must ask why this is possible. One possibility is the analysis of Chomsky (1991) sketched above in (13). That analysis was actually part of an account of a difference between overt and covert verb-raising that I have argued is spurious. Further, the most problematic aspect of Chomsky's analysis was (14), exactly the portion of it designed to block covert raising. Under the assumption that overt and covert verb-raising are equally allowed, (14) is eliminable, leaving (13) for *both* overt and covert movement. However, I pointed out that even (13) is not entirely without difficulties. I will therefore briefly consider two further possibilities for why verb-raising across negation is possible, somehow evading a relativized minimality ECP violation.

The first further possibility, along the lines of Roberts (1993, 1994), is that Neg and V are heads of different sorts (A vs. A′) and that relativized minimality is even more relativized than in the original proposal of Rizzi (1990). If a head only blocks movement of a head of the same type, Neg would then not block movement of V. The second possibility is that Neg is not a head, but a modifier. Note that, at least for Chomsky, its central role as a head had been to block (34), via the ECP. But under the present approach the ECP is irrelevant to the issue. There is still, though, the unanswered question of why *not,* but not adverbs, blocks the adjacency needed for merger. Conceivably, head status of *not* is relevant to this difference.[13]

I have argued that there is a fundamental morphological difference between French verbs and English main verbs and that this difference is mirrored internal to English by one between English auxiliary and main verbs. Certain surprising facts about VP ellipsis first discussed by Warner (1986) provide interesting evidence bearing on the English internal claim.

It has long been known that VP ellipsis can ignore certain inflectional differences between antecedent verb and elided verb. For example, Quirk et al. (1972), reported by Sag (1976), observe that a finite form of a verb can antecede the deletion[14] of the bare form that follows a modal, as in the following example:

(39) John slept, and Mary will too.

(40) a. *John *slept,* and Mary will *slept* too.

b. John *slept,* and Mary will *sleep* too.

In (39) the past tense form *slept* serves as antecedent for the deletion of the bare form *sleep.*

As expected, given (39) and (40), the present tense form can also antecede the bare form:

(41) John sleeps (every afternoon), and Mary should too.

(42) a. *John *sleeps,* and Mary should *sleeps* too.

b. John *sleeps,* and Mary should *sleep* too.

Similarly, the progressive and perfect forms can antecede the bare form:

(43) ?John was sleeping, and Mary will too.

(44) a. *John was *sleeping,* and Mary will *sleeping* too.

b. John was *sleeping,* and Mary will *sleep* too.

(45) John has slept, and Mary will too.
(46) a. *John has *slept,* and Mary will *slept* too.
b. John has *slept,* and Mary will *sleep* too.

It appears that a sort of sloppy identity is at work here, permitting tense and aspectual differences to be ignored in the same way that *phi*-feature differences typically can be. But, as Warner notes, there are certain exceptions to this general pattern. (47) is seemingly parallel to (39), but, surprisingly, it is unacceptable:

(47) *John was here, and Mary will too.
(48) a. *John was here and Mary will was here too.
b. John was here and Mary will be here too.

Evidently *was* cannot antecede *be;* nor can *is* antecede *be:*

(49) *John is here, and Mary will too.

There is no general prohibition on VP ellipsis of a VP headed by *be* following a modal. (50) is virtually perfect and far better than (47) and (49):

(50) John will be here, and Mary will too.

Note that the failed antecedent in (47) and (49) has undergone raising out of the VP while the target V has not, unlike the situation in the successful examples among (39) through (45) and (50), where neither target nor antecedent V has undergone raising. One might therefore conjecture that a trace cannot serve as (part of) an antecedent for VP deletion. There is reason to doubt that conjecture, however. In (51) the antecedent of the elided VP in the second conjunct contains the trace of topicalization:

(51) Linguistics_1, I like t_1, and you should too.

Further, the trace of raising to subject position can, to a reasonably acceptable extent, antecede an NP *in-situ:*

(52) a. Someone_1 is t_1 in the garden, isn't there.
b. Someone_1 will be t_1 in the garden, won't there.

Finally, even a form of *be* that presumably has not raised has difficulty anteceding a distinct form of *be,* as in (53), from Warner (1986), or (55):

(53) ?*The children have been very good here. I wish they would at home.

Compare (54), with *behave* instead of *be:*

(54) ?The children have behaved very well here. I wish they would at home.

(55) *John was being obnoxious, and Mary will too.

Similar effects obtain with auxiliary *have.* Ellipsis is markedly better in (56) with identical forms of *have* than in (57) with distinct ones:

(56) a. John should have left, but Mary shouldn't ~~have left~~.
b. ?John should have left, but Mary shouldn't.

(57) a. John has left, but Mary shouldn't have left.
b. *John has left, but Mary shouldn't ~~have left~~.

Note that, as might be expected, the ellipsis site in (57b) is fine when interpreted as *leave.* That is roughly the situation we have seen before, with one form of a main verb anteceding a distinct form of that verb (in this case perfect *left* anteceding bare *leave*[15]). Note too that the identity of form demanded for ellipsis of auxiliary *have* is somewhat abstract, making reference to morphological features and not just phonetic ones. (58) is no better than (57b):

(58) *The men have left, but the women shouldn't ~~have left~~.

The present plural of auxiliary *have* cannot antecede the bare form, even though they are both superficially *have.* Note too that main verb *have* patterns with other main verbs and not with auxiliary *have:*

(59) John has a driver's license, but Mary shouldn't.

The descriptive generalization covering the data considered so far is stated in (60):

(60) The bare form of a verb V other than *be* or auxiliary *have* can be deleted under identity with any other form of V. *Be* or auxiliary *have* can only be deleted under identity with the very same form.

As Warner observes, this difference does not follow directly from (degree of) suppletion. The paradigm of *go* is highly suppletive, yet that verb patterns with all the other main verbs considered above:

(61) John went, and now Mary will ~~go~~.

The progressive form of all verbs (even including *be*) is also completely regular, yet such deletion under partial identity is disallowed:

(62) a. *John slept, and Mary was too.
 b. John slept, and Mary was sleeping too.

(63) a. *John will sleep. Mary is now.
 b. John will sleep. Mary is sleeping now.

Thus, the relevant difference seems to be between main verbs and auxiliaries[16]. where the latter category includes *be* and certain instances of *have.* Interestingly, as Chomsky (1957) observed, main verb *have* sometimes marginally behaves like an auxiliary:

(64) ?John hasn't a driver's license.
 (cf. John doesn't have a driver's license)

It is significant that when it does behave like an auxiliary it patterns with auxiliary *have* with respect to ellipsis:

(65) ?*John hasn't a driver's license, but Mary should.
 (cf. John doesn't have a driver's license, but Mary should.)

The inflectional features that cause it to raise make it distinct from the bare form for the purposes of deletion under identity.

Sag (1976) briefly discusses the main verb phenomena, taking them to be representative. He observes that these cases could be accounted for by ordering verb phrase deletion before affix hopping. Note that on the strictly lexicalist view discussed above there is no such point in a derivation. However, on the analysis of Chomsky (1957), adopted in its essentials here, there is indeed such a point. I have departed from Chomsky (1957) in just one major respect: for him ALL verbs are introduced into syntactic structures bare and achieve their inflectional form via affix hopping, while I have argued that auxiliaries are pulled from the lexicon fully inflected.[17] This difference between English main and auxiliary verbs was part of my explanation of the verb-raising asymmetries. Strikingly, the very same difference can explain the ellipsis asymmetries along essentially the lines suggested by Sag:

(66) A form of a verb V can only be deleted under identity with the very same form.
Forms of *be* and auxiliary *have* are introduced into syntactic structures already fully inflected. Forms of 'main' verbs are created out of lexically introduced bare forms and independent affixes.

Given (66), deletion under apparent incomplete identity is actually deletion under full identity but at a point in the derivation before the bare stem has associated with the inflectional affix. This is schematically illustrated in (67), a structure for *John slept, and Mary will too:*

(67) John Infl sleep, and Mary will ~~sleep~~ too.

We have seen numerous instances in which the finite form of a main verb antecedes a bare form. Quirk et al. (1972), cited by Sag (1976), give several examples where the progressive and perfect forms likewise antecede the bare form. This possibility indicates on the present account that the Chomsky (1957) affix hopping analysis is in order for these forms as well. Schematically, we have the following:

(68) a. John was sleeping, and now Mary will.
b. John was ing sleep, and now Mary will ~~sleep~~.
(69) a. John has slept, and now Mary will.
b. John has en sleep, and now Mary will ~~sleep~~.

Quirk et al. (1972) indicate that the reverse situation from (68), with bare form anteceding progressive, is not possible. They give (70), which is parallel in structure and behavior to (71):

(70) ?*John won't enter the competition, but Peter is.
(71) ?*John slept, and Mary was too.

A consideration of the structure of (71) suggests an immediate solution to this puzzle:

(72) John Infl sleep, and Mary was *ing* ~~sleep~~ too.

The progressive affix *ing* is stranded. Hence, (71) and (72) run afoul of the stranded affix filter. These examples thus provide additional evidence for the Chomsky (1957) type analysis of main verbs that I advocate. For reasons that I do not understand, though, the perfect affix diverges in behavior from the progressive, the perfect form of a main verb being deletable in just the same circumstances that the bare form is. Quirk et al. give (73) and (74), which are far better than the progressive examples just considered:

(73) John may be questioning our motives, but Peter hasn't.
(74) Peter saw your parents last week, but he hasn't since.

These ought to involve a stranded *en.* I will have to leave their acceptability as an open problem.[18]

The conclusions about the negation and ellipsis phenomena reviewed thus far potentially provide a microscope for the examination of additional inflectional forms of verbs. Consider simple imperatives in English:

(75) Leave.

What is the morphological analysis of such a sentence? Lasnik (1981) argues that there is an imperative affix (occupying the position normally occupied by Tense) that must associate with the bare stem, based on the ungrammaticality of (76):

(76) *Not leave.

The ungrammaticality is due to the stranded affix filter, since lack of adjacency blocks the merger of Imp and *leave.* The analysis fits completely into the framework I have outlined above. Two alternatives are excluded. It cannot be that there is no Imp morpheme at all, since that would leave (76) unexplained. Nor could there be a featural Imp to which already inflected *leave* would raise, since, if the hypothesized feature were weak, (76) would be good, and if it were strong, (77) would:[19]

(77) *Leave not.

Thus far, Imp is behaving just like finite Infl. The parallelism extends still further: (76) is salvaged (however that is to be captured in the theory) by *do* support:

(78) Do not leave.

The parallelism breaks down with respect to auxiliary verbs, however. Not even *be* can raise:

(79) *Be not foolish.

This indicates on the present account that either (80a) or (b) must be correct as a lexical property of English:

(80) a. The Imperative morpheme is strictly affixal, hence there will never be raising to it (just merger with it).
b. OR Imp is freely affixal or featural, and *be* and auxiliary *have* lack imperative forms in the lexicon.

On either account, in this particular construction *be* is pulled from the lexicon bare, just as main verbs are. This predicts that imperative of *be* should parallel imperative of main verbs in ellipsis behavior. (81) shows that prediction is confirmed:[20]

(81) a. Leave. I don't want to.
I won't.
b. Be quiet. I don't want to.
I won't.

(81) is in direct contrast with (82), the properties of the latter following from the fact that *is* never arises via affixation:

(82) a. Mary left. I don't want to.
b. Mary is quiet. *I don't want to.

Finally, earlier I considered the possibility that English subjunctives involve covert raising. Ellipsis facts indicate that this is incorrect:

(83) I require that John leave, but Bill doesn't have to.
(84) I require that John be here, but Bill doesn't have to.

The subjunctive form of a main verb or *be* can antecede the bare form. This indicates that the subjunctive is not a lexically inflected form at all in English. In this regard subjunctives are like imperatives. But the negative subjunctive sentences diverge from the negative imperatives, as in (85), repeated from (21):

(85) a. I desire that John not leave.
b. I desire that John not be here.

Thus, subjunctives cannot involve affixation either. They must be what they superficially appear: bare forms.[21] Under the standard assumption that nominative Case on a subject must be licensed by an appropriate functional head that combines with AgrS, subjunctive clauses must have a subjunctive functional head. The above argument indicates that that head is not an affix and, further, does not have V-features.

In conclusion, I have presented an analysis that, not surprisingly, differs from that of Chomsky (1957) in significant respects. For Chomsky, all of the descriptive machinery was syntactic, while I have argued, from the perspective of more recent theorizing, that affix hopping is a PF process rather than a syntactic one and that the differential behavior of verbs of the two sorts is stated in the lexicon and not in particular transformations. Perhaps more striking than the differences, though, are the similarities. In many respects we arrive at the end of this journey almost where we began: with an analysis of core facts of English verbal morphology highly reminiscent of the classic one in its reliance on a form of affix hopping and in its formal distinction between main verbs and auxiliaries. Sometimes old ideas are not merely interesting—they can even be right.

Appendix

For ease of exposition I have reduced the system of verbal inflection to simply 'Infl,' but this obscures a number of potential questions. Given standard assumptions about clause structure, as in Chomsky (1991), AgrS is higher than Tense, which is in turn higher than AgrO. In a simple sentence with no auxiliary verbs all of these associate with the verb. Now there is ample evidence that the association with AgrO must be syntactic: in many respects an object or an ECM subject behaves as if it were outside the VP.[22] The task is to reconcile this with my proposal about merger, which presumably involves Tense and possibly AgrS. Here are three possibilities

A. V has Agr features lexically, and these can be ignored for ellipsis (just as such features of DPs can, as in standard sloppy identity constructions *I read my book and they did too*). V raises to Agr in LF to check these features but merges with tense in PF. This demands that AgrO be invisible in determining the adjacency needed for merger. This follows from Bobaljik's (1993) definition of adjacency.

B. V raises to AgrO overtly along the lines of Koizumi (1993) and Ura (1993). In PF, AgrS merges with Tense, which merges with the V-AgrO complex.

C. Like 2, except that raising to AgrO is in LF.

Both (B) and (C) posit a formal difference between AgrS and AgrO. If we are to follow Chomsky (1993) in taking 'AgrS' and 'AgrO' to be merely mnemonics for distinguishing two different functional roles of Agr, these two possibilities must presumably be excluded. See Borer (1994), though, for arguments that AgrO is better regarded as an aspectual head than as purely an agreement head.

NOTES

* Portions of this material were presented in a course at the University of Connecticut, at the Washington Area Generative Society Second Minimalist Fest, in a colloquium at the Keio University Institute of Cultural and Linguistic studies, and at the First Numazu Linguistic Seminar. I am grateful to all of those audiences for their stimulating suggestions and devastating counterexamples, which led to substantial improvements in the analysis. I am especially indebted to Željko Bošković and Roger Martin for many hours of discussion and for an extraordinarily careful reading of the manuscript under panic conditions.

1. I return to the question of why verb raising takes precedence over Affix Hopping. As for the apparent 'last-resort' nature of *do*-support, see Watanabe (1993) and Baker (1991) for proposals (and see the latter for important critical discussion of the kind of economy analyses I will examine below). See also Bobaljik (1993) for discussion in terms of a Chomsky (1957) style analysis of English verbal inflection similar to one I will argue for below.

2. Chomsky (1991) takes Affix Hopping to be a standard instantiation of syntactic Move α. Hence, no simple adjacency requirement of the sort in earlier analyses could be relevant.

3. AgrS is the subject agreement projection, and AgrO is the object agreement projection.

4. As Roger Martin observes, the mechanism by which re-raising remedies the violation is not entirely clear. Chomsky (1991:426) states that "[s]ubsequent LF raising . . . to the position of *t* is required to create a proper chain." Note though that, if the raising is adjunction, and if the chain is originally improper because the *t* is marked [$-\gamma$] in the ECP notation of Lasnik and Saito (1984, 1992), then the violation is not obviously eliminated. One possible approach to this problem is to allow γ-marking to freely apply anywhere in the derivation, rather than insisting that it apply immediately as the trace is created. Once all raising is completed, every trace is arguably in a configuration of antecedent government.

5. The illicit A′-movement in question is long adjunct movement, for example, of the sort discussed by Lasnik and Saito (1984):

(i) *Why$_1$ do you believe the claim that John said [Bill left t_1]?

The derivation to be excluded involves a short movement to the lowest [Spec,CP] followed by a long move out of the complex NP to the matrix [Spec,CP]. Similarly, the relevant illicit A-movement would be such 'super raising' as (ii):

(ii) *John seems that it is likely to be arrested *t*

with a short movement to the lowest [Spec,IP] followed by a long move to the matrix. For head movement Želko Bošković suggests (iii), where *have* has moved through AgrO on its way to the matrix Infl:

(iii) *You have not believed Peter to *t t* gone there.

6. Interestingly, this checking view more precisely captures the insight of the earliest modern version of Case theory, that of Vergnaud (1977), than does the Case assignment approach of Chomsky (1980 and 1981).

7. Later, though, we will see reason to doubt this.

8. These examples are taken from Wilder and Ćavar (1993). See also Bošković (1994) for discussion of a Serbo-Croatian construction that allows fully inflected finite auxiliary verbs to remain *in-situ.*

9. See Epstein (to appear) for discussion, and a possible analysis.

10. See also Halle and Marantz (1993) and Bobaljik (1993).

11. One remaining question concerns the obvious grammaticality of (i):

(i) John never left.

While *not* evidently blocks the adjacency needed for merger, adverbs in general do not. Bobaljik (1993) suggest that adverbs (or, more generally, adjuncts) are not relevant to PF adjacency, while heads and specifiers are. In fact, he assumes that *not* in English is actually a specifier.

12. I continue to assume that movement is driven solely by features of the appropriate sort. In particular, I assume that the property of being an affix is not a feature relevant to syntactic head-raising. Thus, as Roger Martin notes, under either Chomsky's (1993) Greed constraint or the weaker Enlightened Self Interest of Lasnik (1994), movement of bare V will be blocked by general economy considerations.

13. If *not* is a head, a radical alternative to Roberts's idea would be to eliminate the head movement constraint entirely. Obviously, it is far beyond the scope of this paper to explore that possibility. I will merely note in passing that one standard argument for the constraint, from Chomsky (1986), is not clearly relevant. Chomsky observes that in (i) *will* must move to Comp; an alternative in which *be* moves to *Comp* across *will* is barred:

(i) a. How tall will John be?
b. *How tall be John will?

As Chomsky notes, the Head Movement Constraint (HMC)/ECP will rule (i-a) out. However, in any theory where movement is driven solely by the need for features to be satisfied, the HMC is superfluous here. In V-to-C constructions in English there is no morphological need of either V or C that is satisfied by the raising of V *per se.* Rather, the requirement involves Tense: it is only a finite verb that ever raises to C. Thus, general economy considerations block (i-b) because no feature will drive the movement of *be* to Comp. See Roberts (1994) for related discussion.

14. I use the term 'deletion' merely for ease of exposition. As far as I can tell, all of the arguments I present are neutral between a PF deletion approach to ellipsis and an LF copying one.

15. I return to such constructions below.

16. Kayne (1989) conjectures that universal grammar makes available a categorial distinction between the class of lexical verbs and the class of auxiliary verbs. Such a distinction is at the core of Akmajian, Steele, and Wasow (1979) and Steele (1981). Wexler (1994) shows that a consistent pattern of inflectional errors in child language reflects a fundamental main verb vs. auxiliary verb dichotomy. For children acquiring English his findings are reminiscent of my proposals: for main verbs, but not for auxiliaries, children would freely substitute the infinitival form for the appropriate finite form.

17. This is essentially the formal analogue of the insightful semantic proposal of Warner (1986), though he argued that such a treatment is appropriate for *be* but not for *have* (based on subtle acceptability differences that I am putting aside).

18. Descriptively, it is as if stranded *en* is spelled out as zero, much as stranded Infl is spelled out as a form of *do.* We have seen that stranded *ing* lacks the first possibility. (i) shows that it lacks the second as well:

(i) *John slept and Mary was doing too.

19. Željko Bošković points out that this conclusion does not quite follow. Suppose that negation is an A′-head in the sense of Roberts (1993) and that verb movement in imperative constructions also involves movement to an A′-head across negation. Then a simple positive imperative could involve raising, while a negative imperative could not. A special form would be needed for the negatives (*do*-support in English). Rivero (1994) shows just such a pattern for several Balkan languages. Ellipsis provides some evidence against such an approach to the English facts, however, as we will see directly.

20. (i) indicates that even in a positive imperative *be* behaves strictly like a bare verb and does not undergo raising:

(i) a. Should I be quiet? Please do.
b. *Please be.

If imperative *be* could raise, (i-b) could arise from raising and deletion of the residual VP, just as in (ii):

(ii) John is.

If such phenomena establish that auxiliary verbs in English have bare forms that are capable in principle of undergoing merger, the central ellipsis phenomena I have presented must be reconsidered. I showed how (49), repeated as (iii), is ruled out if *is* is necessarily taken fully inflected from the lexicon:

(iii) *John is here, and Mary will too.

But with *be* in principle able to merge with a particular inflectional affix (Imp) the question is why there cannot be an alternative merger derivation of *is,* alongside the lexicalist one. I suspect that the answer lies in the domain of what is often termed morphological blocking. If *is* exists as a word, the merger derivation will be blocked, on the assumption that inflectional slots are uniquely filled, at least in the unmarked case. See Aronoff (1976), Kiparsky (1982), and Pinker (1984) for discussion.

21. An alternative, suggested by Željko Bošković, is that the relative height of negation and subjunctive head differs from that of negation and tense. I put that possibility aside for future research.

22. See Lasnik and Saito (1991) and Lasnik (1993) for discussion.

REFERENCES

Akmajian, A., S. Steele, and T. Wasow. 1979. The Category AUX in Universal Grammar. *Linguistic Inquiry* 10:1–64.

Aronoff, M. 1976. *Word Formation in Generative Grammar.* Cambridge: MIT Press.

Baker, C. L. 1991. The Syntax of English *not:* The Limits of Core Grammar. *Linguistic Inquiry* 22:387–429.

Bobaljik, J. D. 1993. What does Adjacency do? Manuscript. MIT.

Borer, H. 1994. On the Projection of Arguments. In *Functional Projections. University of Massachusetts Occasional Papers* 17. E. E. Benedicto and J. T. Runner, eds. Amherst: GLSA.

Bošković, Ž. 1994. Participle Movement in Serbo-Croatian and Related Issues. Manuscript. University of Connecticut.

Chomsky, N. 1955. The Logical Structure of Linguistic Theory. Manuscript. Harvard University. [1975. New York: Plenum].

Chomsky, N. 1957. *Syntactic Structures.* The Hague: Mouton.

Chomsky, N. 1980. On Binding. *Linguistic Inquiry* 11:1–46.

Chomsky, N. 1981. *Lectures on Government and Binding.* Dordrecht: Foris.

Chomsky, N. 1986. *Barriers.* Cambridge: MIT Press.

Chomsky, N. 1991. Some Notes on Economy of Derivation and Representation. In *Principles and Parameters in Comparative Grammar.* R. Freidin, ed. Cambridge: MIT Press.

Chomsky, N. 1993. A Minimalist Program for Linguistic Theory. In *The View from Building 20: Essays in Linguistics in Honor of Sylvain Bromberger.* K. Hale and S. J. Keyser, eds. Cambridge: MIT Press.

Chomsky, N. 1995. Bare Phrase Structure. This volume.

Chomsky, N., and H. Lasnik. 1993. The Theory of Principles and Parameters. In *Syntax: An International Handbook of Contemporary Research.* J. Jacobs, A. von Stechow, W. Sternefeld, and T. Vennemann, eds. Berlin: Walter de Gruyter.

Emonds, J. 1978. The Verbal Complex V′-V in French. *Linguistic Inquiry* 9:151–75.

Epstein, S. D. To appear. Scope Marking and LF V2. *Linguistic Inquiry.*

Halle, M., and A. Marantz. 1993. Distributed Morphology and the Pieces of Inflection. In *The View from Building 20: Essays in Linguistics in Honor of Sylvain Bromberger.* K. Hale and S. J. Keyser, eds. Cambridge: MIT Press.

Kayne, R. S. 1989. Notes on English Agreement. Manuscript. CUNY Graduate Center.

Kiparsky, P. 1982. From Cyclic Phonology to Lexical Phonology. In *The Structure of Phonological Representations (Part I).* H. van der Hulst and N. Smith, eds. Dordrecht: Foris.

Koizumi, M. 1993. Object Agreement Phrases and the Split VP hypothesis. In *Papers on Case and Agreement I.* J. D. Bobaljik and C. Phillips, eds. Cambridge: MIT.

Lasnik, H. 1981. Restricting the Theory of Transformations. In *Explanation in Linguistics.* N. Hornstein and D. Lightfoot, eds. London: Longmans. [Reprinted in H. Lasnik, 1990.]

Lasnik, H. 1990. *Essays on Restrictiveness and Learnability.* Dordrecht: Kluwer.

Lasnik, H. 1993. Lectures on Minimalist Syntax. In *University of Connecticut Occasional Papers in Linguistics* 1.

Lasnik, H. 1994. Case and Expletives Revisited: On Greed and Other Human Failings. Manuscript. University of Connecticut.

Lasnik, H., and M. Saito. 1984. On the Nature of Proper Government. *Linguistic Inquiry* 15:235–89.

Lasnik, H., and M. Saito. 1991. On the Subject of Infinitives. In *Papers from the 27th Regional Meeting of the Chicago Linguistic Society, Part One: The General Session.* L. M. Dobrin, L. Nichols, and R. M. Rodriguez, eds. Chicago: CLS.

Lasnik, H. and M. Saito. 1992. *Move α.* Cambridge: MIT Press.

Pinker, S. 1984. *Language Learnability and Language Development.* Cambridge: Harvard University Press.

Pollock, J.-Y. 1989. Verb Movement, Universal Grammar, and the Structure of IP. *Linguistic Inquiry* 20:365–424.

Quirk, R., S. Greenbaum, G. Leech, and J. Svartik. 1972. *A Grammar of Contemporary English.* London: Seminar Press.

Rivero, M. L. 1994. Clause Structure and V-movement in the Languages of the Balkans. *Natural Language and Linguistic Theory* 12:63–120.

Rizzi, L. 1990. *Relativized Minimality.* Cambridge: MIT Press.

Roberts, I. G. 1993. *Verbs and Diachronic Syntax.* Dordrecht: Kluwer.

Roberts, I. G. 1994. Two Types of Head Movement in Romance. In *Verb Movement.* D. Lightfoot and N. Hornstein, eds. Cambridge: Cambridge University Press.

Sag, I. 1976. *Deletion and Logical Form.* Ph.D. Dissertation. MIT.

Steele, S. 1981. *An Encyclopedia of Aux.* Cambridge: MIT Press.

Ura, H. 1993. On Feature-Checking for Wh-traces. In *Papers on Case and Agreement I.* J. D. Bobaljik and C. Phillips, eds. Cambridge: MIT Press.

Vergnaud, J.-R. 1977. Personal Letter to H. Lasnik and N. Chomsky. Paris.

Warner, A. R. 1986. Ellipsis Conditions and the Status of the English Copula. *York Papers in Linguistics* 12:153–72.

Watanabe, A. 1993. *Agr-based Case Theory and its Interaction with the A'-System.* Ph.D. Dissertation. MIT.

Wexler, K. 1994. Optional Infinitives, Head Movement, and the Economy of Derivations. In *Verb Movement.* D. Lightfoot and N. Hornstein, eds. Cambridge: Cambridge University Press.

Wilder, C., and D. Ćavar. 1993. Word Order Variation, Verb Movement, and Economy Principles. *Sprachwissenschaft in Frankfurt Arbeitspapier* 10. Frankfurt.

Participle Agreement and Object Shift in Old Spanish: A Minimalist Theory Approach*

Claudia Parodi
UCLA

1 Introduction. Considerable effort within the theoretical framework proposed by Chomsky in the *Minimalist Program for Linguistic Theory* (MPLT) has been devoted to agreement phenomena in order to explain the Case Filter (see Chomsky 1993, Branigan 1992, Jonas and Bobaljik 1993, and Zwart 1993). This inquiry has focused mainly on overt and covert structural Case-checking of subjects and objects. Evidence for overt Case-checking of objects has been provided by languages such as Icelandic, Swedish, French, and Italian,[1] in which the verb may agree overtly with the object. Modern Spanish has been excluded from these studies, since it has overt participle agreement in passive constructions only. However, Old Spanish, from the Middle Ages up to the first half of the Sixteenth Century had participial agreement in a wide range of contexts. In this paper I will concentrate on Old Spanish Object Shift Constructions (OSCs) and constructions with cliticized, relativized, or scrambled objects to show how overt and covert accusative Case-checking was implemented.[2]

In the *MPLT* framework OSC such as **Mary the door opened* are ruled out by the Shortest Movement and the Strict Cycle Condition principles. These principles also exclude grammatical examples of shifted objects in Old Spanish such as (1):

(1) Dixol cuemo avia su obra acabad-a.
(He) told him how (he) had his work-FEM finished-FEM
'He told him that he had finished his work.' (*Cron.* 12.28a)

Adapting part of Jonas and Bobaljik's proposal (1993), I argue that it is possible to have cases of Object Shift in overt syntax without violating the Shortest Movement and the Strict Cycle Condition principles. Moreover, I show that OSCs are possible in clauses with compound tenses, contrary to what has been claimed (Branigan 1992:28, Jonas and Bobaljik

1993:89 fns. 37, 93). I propose that the same mechanisms required to generate shifted objects in clauses with simple verb tenses are at work in clauses with compound verb tenses. I show that OSCs are different from other constructions in which cliticized, relativized, or scrambled and quantified objects optionally agree with the participle such as in the examples in (2). (The feminine forms are taken from the source mentioned on the right after each example; the neutral forms are reconstructed based on parallel examples found in these sources.)

(2) a. Cosas que yo he dich-as/-o.
Things-FEM that I have said-FEM-PL/0 (*Corbacho* 165)
b. Desque la a ganad-a/-o.
Since (he) her has won-FEM/0 (*Buen Amor:*46/97a)
'Since he has won her.'
c. Pues que (todas) estas cosas ovo dicha-as/-o.
Since that all these things-FEM (he) had said-FEM-PL/0
'Since he told all these things.' (*Crónica:*38 29a)

Object Shift Constructions have disappeared from most modern Romance languages and dialects because their generation has many requirements that burden the acquisition process.

In the first part of this paper I present the theoretical assumptions that I adopt, which are outlined in Chomsky (1993) and related works. I concentrate on feature checking and the movements required to generate structures with shifted objects, such as the example in (1). In the second part I analyze the position occupied by shifted objects, and I compare OSCs with the other constructions included in (2), in which the participle optionally agrees with the object. In the third part I discuss the loss of Object Shift Constructions in Old Spanish.

2 Theoretical background. Within the *MPLT* framework lexical elements are drawn from the lexicon with all their morphological features, including Case and *phi*-features. They are projected in a structure such as (3), in which the subject and the object are VP internal:

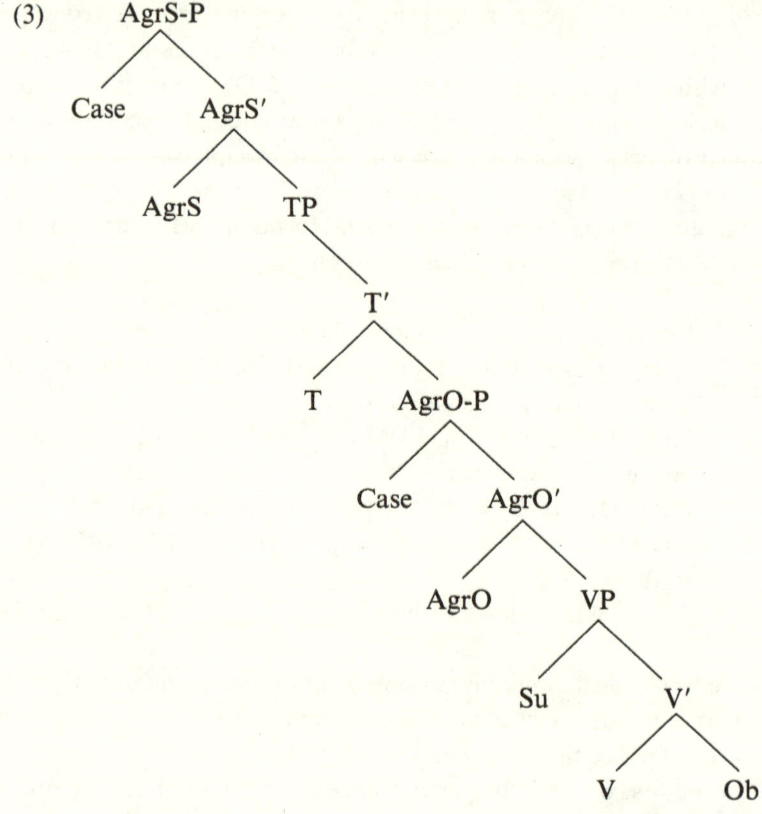

In this structure subjects and objects must raise to the agreement phrases to check their Case and agreement features with the appropriate functional head in a Spec/head relationship. The inflectional heads, T and the two Agrs, each have two features, one verbal and one nominal. The verbal features check the inflectional features of the verb (V), and the nominal features (N) check the morphological features of the DPs, such as Case and agreement. The N and the V features can be either weak or strong and vary arbitrarily across languages. However, rich overt morphology does not necessarily mean strength, but it may. Weak features need to be checked at LF (Logical Form). Strong features are visible in the PF (Phonetic Form) component and must be checked prior to Spell-Out. Feature checking takes place by movement, which may be overt (at S-structure) or covert (at LF). The role of functional heads is exclusively formal. Agr has no substantive component at LF. Chomsky (1993:30) claims that Agr plays a mediating role and that it disappears as soon as it has checked all the features in its inventory. Thus, Agr deletes as soon as it has checked the features of V. If any inflectional feature remains at LF, the derivation crashes at that level.

As shown in (3), the subject and the object raise to their respective agreement phrases by crossing paths instead of by nesting. In order to prevent the arguments from raising to the Spec of the inappropriate agreement projections, overt and covert movements must always be constrained by principles of Economy. One such principle, that of the Shortest Movement, subsumes the ECP, as interpreted by Rizzi (1990). Thus, the target of head movement, A movement, and A′ movement should not be farther than the next proper landing site:

(4) (i) A Head position for Head movement.
(ii) Spec of AgrP, TP, VP for A movement.
(iii) Spec of CP and adjoined positions for A′ movement. (see Jonas and Bobaljik 1993:63)

As a consequence of the operation Generalized Transformation, a Spec position is generated only if it is filled or targeted for movement. For instance, in (3) the subject raises to [Spec,AgrS-P] without violating the Shortest Movement Condition, since [Spec,AgrO-P] is not filled. The subject, however, could also raise to [Spec,AgrO-P], because it is the next available A-position. However, this movement blocks Case checking of the object, since it remains 'frozen in place,' and is unable to raise to [Spec,AgrO-P]. Thus, the construction is not convergent (see Chomsky 1993:19). The object must raise to [Spec,AgrO-P] for Case checking, crossing the subject or its trace, in violation of the Shortest Movement Condition. However, this violation can be avoided if the verb head adjoins to AgrO before the object raises to [Spec,AgrO-P]. The movement of V to AgrO creates the chain (V, t_{verb}) whose minimal domain[3] is {[Spec,AgrO-P], [Spec,VP] and Ob} in (3). V-raising forms an enlarged minimal domain for the chain. Within the enlarged minimal domain the object may raise to [Spec,AgrO-P], skipping over the subject or its trace in [Spec,VP]. After the verb has raised to AgrO the Specs of AgrO and VP stand in the same minimal relationship to this chain. If two targets of movement are in the same minimal domain, they are equidistant. Thus, in (3) the two Spec positions of AgrO and VP are equidistant from the complement of V. This correlation is defined by Chomsky (1993:17) as follows:

(5) If α, β are in the same minimal domain, they are equidistant from γ (where α, β could be the Specs and γ the object).

The other principle, the Strict Cycle Condition, imposes an order on syntactic derivations and requires that every structure-building transformation enlarge the phrase. Movement into a Spec of a phrase adds structure to the phrase. Adjunction to a phrase does not. Thus, if a countercyclic movement raises an object into the middle of a phrase, the phrase is not made larger and the Strict Cycle is violated. If a head is moved, forming a chain, the intermediate positions do not enlarge the structure. The landing site of the head, however, does enlarge the structure. Thus, the head of the chain is relevant to the Strict Cycle Condition. Adjunction of a category to another category does not enlarge the number of categories, since additional segments do not count as more structure (see Branigan 1992:18–19).

In summary, raising the object to [Spec,AgrO-P] is possible in a structure such the one depicted in (3) only if V has previously head-adjoined to AgrO. The movement of the verb head to AgrO renders the Specs of AgrO and VP equidistant from the object position. Thus, the object phrase may skip [Spec,VP]—where the subject or its trace is located—without violating the Shortest Movement and the Strict Cycle conditions.

If V raising only occurs at LF, as in English, the object must raise to [Spec,AgrO-P] also at LF.

3 The structure of Object Shift Constructions. The term Object Shift, like scrambling, has been used in different ways in the bibliography of Generative Grammar. Here I follow Jonas and Bobaljik (1993:68) who separate Object Shift from cliticization and scrambling. Direct object cliticization and scrambling, like relativization, entail an A′-(or non-L-related) movement of a pronoun or a DP. Object Shift, instead, is an overt A- (or L-related) movement of a full definite DP inside a clause. It is triggered by Case and Agreement checking.

In a language with overt object raising, the movement of the verb, the object, and the subject must follow a specific order to generate a convergent construction, because of the Shortest Movement and the Strict Cycle conditions. The object must raise overtly to [Spec,AgrO-P] after the verb has moved to AgrO and before the subject raises to a higher position. Then the subject must move to [Spec,TP] after the verb has raised to T. Jonas and Bobaljik have shown that this sequence of movements is required by the Shortest Movement Condition, according to which no more than one filled Specifier can be skipped within a minimal domain. Thus, the chain ([V+Agr]. . .*t*) must be formed for the object in VP to skip over the internal subject. Likewise, the [Verb+Agr] complex must adjoin to T, forming a second chain ([[V+Agr]+T]. . .*t*′) for the subject to be able to move. Within the minimal domain of the second chain {[Spec,TP], [Spec,AgrO-P] and [Spec,VP]}, the internal subject may exit VP, since [Spec,TP] and [Spec,AgrO-P] are equidistant from [Spec,VP]. The formation of the second chain is required, since the shifted object has already filled [Spec,AgrO-P]. The Shortest Movement Condition again forces the subject to raise to [Spec,TP]. Thus, [Spec,TP] must be an available position for the subject in languages that have Object Shift. Otherwise, the derivation would crash, because the subject would not be able to raise. Jonas and Bobaljik claim that this set of movements must be overt. However, I will show below that it is possible to have OSCs in which the second chain is formed covertly and the first chain overtly. The movements to generate OSCs are depicted in (6):

(6)

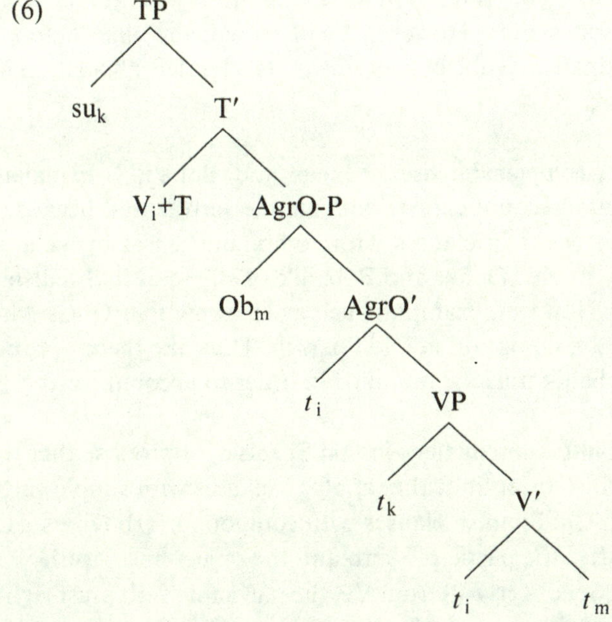

In OSCs the subject cannot raise to [Spec,AgrS-P] directly, across a potential [Spec,TP], because the Shortest Movement Condition would be violated. Jonas and Bobaljik point out that there is an apparent paradox in the fact that, on the one hand, potential (i.e., unfilled) specifiers do not count for purposes of the Shortest Movement Condition, as in the case of the subject raising in English, but, on the other hand, once a filled Specifier is skipped, the next potential Specifier must be targeted. In fact this is only an apparent paradox, since intervening nonfilled specifiers are not relevant for determining the first appropriate landing site for the Shortest Movement Condition, as in English. However, the first intervening filled Specifier will always count as the first appropriate landing site, and the Shortest Movement Condition will preclude movement to any position farther than this. But when a verb head is moved, as was shown before, the Specifier of the next phrase above the starting point of the chain will be equidistant from the Specifier of the phrase whose verbal head starts the chain. For example, the movement of the verb from AgrO to T will render only [Spec,TP] equidistant from [Spec,AgrO-P]. Hence, if a language does not license [Spec,TP], OSCs are prohibited. [Spec,TP] is in principle unattainable in English and Modern French. Thus, these languages do not have OSCs. Conversely, if a language has OSCs, it must license [Spec,TP] as an available, final, or intermediate position for the subject. An important implication of Jonas and Bobaljik's proposal is that there is no convergent sentence in which the subject stays in its VP internal position in overt syntax. However, I will show below that there are cases in which the small *pro* subject may stay in its VP internal position in OSCs in overt syntax.

4 OSC with compound tenses. Jonas and Bobaljik's explanation of OSCs takes into account clauses with simple verb tenses, because Object Shift does not occur in clauses with compound tenses in Icelandic, the language they studied (Jonas and Bobaljik 1993:93), or in Swedish (Branigan 1992:28). However, examples such as (1) show that OSCs with compound tenses are an option in Old Spanish. Thus, the theory proposed by Jonas and Bobaljik must be modified in order to account for these cases.

4.1 Object Shift Constructions in Old Spanish. I propose that the same mechanisms for Object Shift that apply to clauses with simple verb tenses are at work in Old Spanish clauses with compound verb tenses. However, I claim that after the participle verb and the object have overtly raised to AgrO and to [Spec,AgrO-P] from VP, the participle verb must right or left adjoin to the auxiliary, immediately above AgrO-P. The movement of the participle into the auxiliary is required by the Shortest Movement Condition. This movement will allow the subject to exit its VP internal position and land in [Spec,TP] in its way to AgrS, skipping the object in [Spec, AgrO-P].

4.2. OSCs with overt subject. Consider the following examples in (7):

(7) a.	El ovo dich-as	estas cos-as.	
	He has said-FEM-PL	these things-FEM-PL	(*Estoria* 99.19)

b. Hercules ouo conquist-a toda Esperia.
Hercules had conquered-FEM all Spain. (*Hercules* 52.29)

In (7), after the participle and the object have raised to AgrO the participle right-adjoins to the auxiliary verb, forming a second chain, as shown below in (10). This movement allows the subject to exit its VP internal position and land in [Spec,TP] on its way to AgrS, skipping the object in [Spec,AgrO-P]. We have seen that the Shortest Movement and the Strict Cycle Conditions force the subject to raise to [Spec,TP] on its way to [Spec,AgrS-P]. In (7) the auxiliary verb must raise to T before the subject can exit its VP internal position in order to enlarge the minimal domain of the auxiliary verb and comply with the Shortest Movement Condition. The auxiliary verb could raise to T and to AgrS either alone by excorporating from the participle[4] or together with the participle as a compound head. Evidence from Modern Italian dialects gathered in the examples in (13) points toward the possibility that the auxiliary and the participle move together to T and to AgrS in OSCs. Right or left adjunction of the participle to the auxiliary and movement of the verb to C depend on different factors, such as focalization of the verb or the Wackernagel or Tobler-Mussafia laws.[5]

4.3 OSCs with small *pro* subject. Now consider the examples in (8):

(8) a. Cogid-a han la tiend-a.
Taken-FEM have (they) the tent-FEM
'They have taken the tent.' (*Cid* 988.2706)
b. Dixol cuemo avie su obra acabad-a.[6]
He) told-him how (he) had his work finished-FEM
'He told him that he had finished his work.' (*Cron.* 12.28a)

The subject in both sentences is a small *pro.* When the subject is a small *pro,* the adjunction of the participle to the auxiliary may be overt, as in (8a), or covert, as in (8b). We have seen that the movement of the participle to the Auxiliary verb is required by the Shortest Movement Condition. If the participle does not adjoin to the auxiliary verb, the subject will not be able to exit its VP internal position and the sentence would be nonconvergent. In (8a), after the participle and the object have raised overtly to AgrO the participle left-adjoins overtly to the auxiliary verb, and the compound verbal head then raises to C, passing through T and AgrS. The small *pro* subject may raise to [Spec,Agr S] overtly or covertly, since the domain of the auxiliary verb and T have already been enlarged.

In (8b) the first chain has been formed overtly. I will argue, however, that the second chain is formed covertly. The word order of this sentence shows that the first chain has been formed overtly, since the participle verb is in AgrO and the object is in [Spec,AgrO-P]. We have seen that the Shortest Movement Condition requires that the participle adjoin to the Auxiliary verb, before the subject exits from its VP internal position, after the first chain has been formed. In (8b) the small *pro* subject is in [Spec,VP], since the participle is in AgrO. Therefore, the adjunction of the participle to the auxiliary verb and to T must be completed covertly before the subject can exit its VP internal position. The small *pro* subject must then also raise covertly to [Spec,TP] and [Spec,AgrS-P] to be properly identified. Thus, the second chain is formed covertly.[7]

My proposal that the participle must adjoin to the auxiliary verb before the subject exits its VP internal position in OSC with compound tenses also explains the examples of Old French, such as the reconstructed example in (9) and the examples of Modern Italian reproduced in (13) below, which are parallel to Old Spanish OSCs:

(9)	Jean a repeintes	les tables.
	Jean has repainted-FEM-PL	the tables-FEM-PL

These examples were left unexplained by Branigan (1992:42) and others (see references cited in Branigan).

4.4 The structure of OSCs with compound tenses and overt subjects. (10) depicts the relevant structure and movements I suggest for Object Shift with compound tenses and overt subjects:

(10)

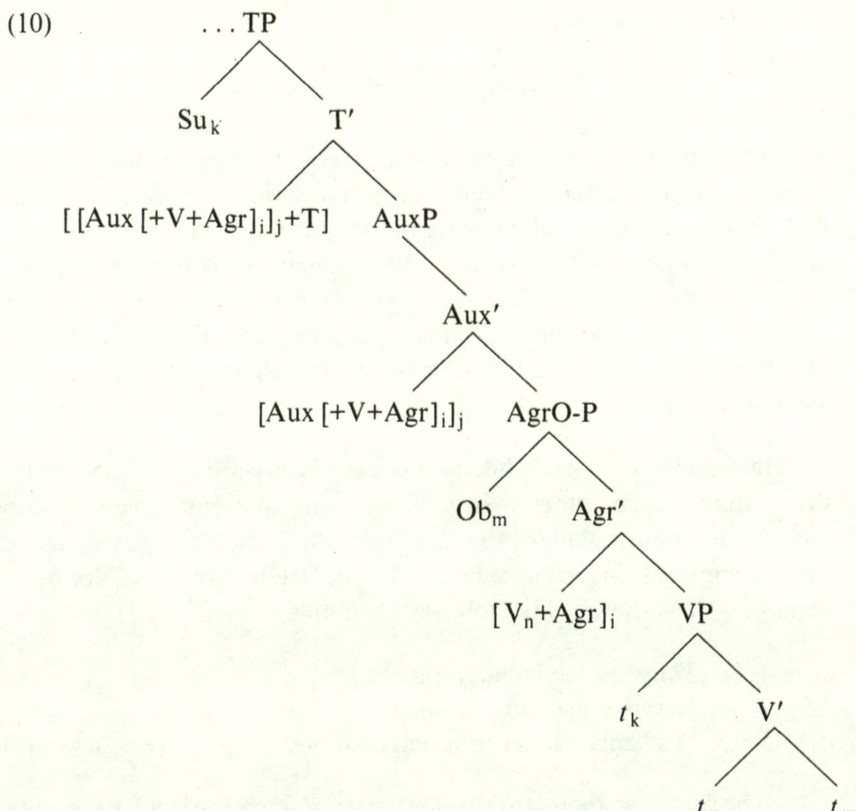

Object Shift in compound tense sentences is allowed in limited contexts since it has many requirements, which burden the acquisition process. One of these requirements is that for the subject to exit VP, the object and the participle verb must move overtly to AgrO-P. Then, prior to Spell-Out or at LF, the participle must adjoin to the Auxiliary verb, and the subject must raise to [Spec,TP] in a certain sequence to comply with the Shortest Movement and the Strict Cycle Conditions. The fact that the verb and the object must be in AgrO-P in overt syntax implies that they check their agreement features at S-structure. Therefore, there are no possible cases of shifted objects without agreement. In fact, I did not find examples of Object Shift without participle agreement such as the ungrammatical example (11) in the texts that I analyzed (Spanish literary and legal texts from the twelfth century through the sixteenth century):

(11) *Avia sus obras acabado.
had his works-FEM-PL finished-NEUTR
'He had his works finished.'

In summary I have shown that in OSCs it is crucial that the participle adjoins to the auxiliary verb, forming a chain that expands the minimal domain of AgrO and allowing the subject to exit VP. [Spec,AgrO-P] and [Spec,TP] become equidistant. The auxiliary verb alone or the compound [auxiliary+participle] then raise to T before the subject moves to the next available specifier, which is [Spec,TP]. Next, the subject and the auxiliary verb—compound or alone—move to AgrS to check Case and agreement features.

5 More evidence on participle to auxiliary incorporation. There is evidence from sources other than OSCs proving that participles could be incorporated into auxiliaries in Old Spanish. If the verb was focalized, the participle was incorporated from the AgrO-P into the auxiliary before raising to C, as shown in the following example:

(12) Vengado-me-habia Ysmenia.
Revenge-me-had Ysmenia
'Ysmenia has taken revenge for me.' (*Keniston:* 453)

The fact that there are no interposed elements, except for a clitic, between the auxiliary and the participle in these contexts proves that the participle is adjoined to the auxiliary (see Parodi in press for discussion and section 8 below).

Modern Italian dialects that have OSCs also adjoin the participle to the auxiliary verb. However, unlike Old Spanish, the auxiliary verb cannot be excorporated from the participle, and the participle must right adjoin to the auxiliary verb. Consider the following examples:

(13) a. Gianni ha mangiat-i gli spaghetti.
Gianni has eaten-MASC-Pl the spaghetti
b. *Gianni ha gli spaghetti mangiat-i.
Gianni has the spaghetti eaten-MASC-PL
c. *Gianni non ha mai mangiat-i gli spaghetti.
Gianni not has never eaten-MASC-PL the spaghetti
'Gianni has never eaten the spaghetti.'
d. Gianni non ha mai mangiato gli spaghetti.
Gianni not has never eaten the spaghetti
'Gianni has never eaten the spaghetti.'

Example (13a) shows that the object was moved to [Spec,AgrO-P] and that the participle has adjoined to the auxiliary verb. This example is parallel to the Old Spanish examples in (7). Example (13b) demonstrates that if the object is shifted and the agreeing participle is not raised to the auxiliary, the construction is not convergent. Example (13c) shows that nothing may be interposed between the participle and the auxiliary in OSCs. Example (13d) is not an OSC, since the object does not agree with the participle. Thus, the participle verb does not need to be adjoined to the auxiliary verb. In this sentence the subject has raised overtly to the Specifier of AgrS. The participle and the direct object stay in their VP internal position due to Procrastination. The object will check its Case covertly, after the participle has also raised covertly to AgrO. This example and the example in (14) reflect the Case-checking pattern of Modern Spanish and most languages.

Now consider the example in (14), which is parallel to (13d):

(14) Auia fecho muchos enojos.
(He) had done many offenses
'He had committed many crimes.' (*Juan Manuel* 57.30)

In (14) the object is not shifted either, since it does not agree with the participle. Due to Procrastination it may be assumed that the small *pro* subject, the participle verb, and the object raise to their checking positions covertly. The only element that raises overtly to AgrS passing through T is the auxiliary verb. I propose that (13d) and (14) are generated by building a structure similar to (3).

Within the framework of the *MPLT*, covert movement operations are preferred because of Procrastination, a principle of Economy by which a "system tries to reach PF as fast as possible minimizing overt syntax" (Chomsky (1993:30–31)). Overt movement is allowed only if an element must be checked before Spell-Out in order to eliminate its strong features (morphological features), which disappear at LF. Thus, if the [N] features of a subject are strong at S-structure, [Spec,TP] must be generated to check them overtly, but it will disappear after checking the features of the subject. Bobaljik and Jonas (1993:73) claim that [Spec,TP] is not available as an intermediate position at LF. They argue that [Spec,TP] will not be generated at LF if the phonetic noun has strong features, because they must be checked overtly. They add that [Spec,TP] will not be generated at LF if the phonetic subject has weak [N] features, since these features do not have to be checked. However, I have already shown that [Spec,TP] is required at LF to account for structures such as (8b), in which the subject is a small *pro* and the object and the participle have been moved overtly to AgrO.[8]

6 The position of shifted objects. Holmberg (1986) has demonstrated that in Swedish and Icelandic shifted objects are in an A-position, since they do not induce weak crossover effects. Further evidence from parasitic gaps in Italian dialects that contain shifted objects proves that these objects are in an A-position, as shown in (15):

(15) a. Gli spaghetti che ho mangiat-I senza riscaldare.
The spaghetti that (I) have eaten-MASC-PL without heating.
b. *Ho mangiat-I gli spaghetti senza riscaldare.
(I) have eaten-MASC-PL the spaghetti without heating

Parasitic gaps are allowed in examples such as (15a) since the null operator in the parasitic gap construction is c-commanded by a *wh*-element or an empty operator in an A′-position in the relative clause. However, in (15b) the gap is ungrammatical, since the shifted object in A-position does not c-command the null operator. Thus, we may conclude that [Spec,AgrO-P] is an A-position and Object Shift is an instance of A-movement (see Tellier 1991 for a detailed discussion on the properties of parasitic gaps.)

7 Other constructions with participal agreement. In addition to shifted objects, there are other constructions with participle agreement. In these constructions, in which the object is extracted by *wh*-movement, clitic placement, or scrambling, the agreement of the participle with the direct object is optional, as shown in (2), repeated as (16):

(16) a. Cosas que yo he dich-as/-o.
Things that I have said-FEM-PL/0 (*Corbacho:*165)
b. Desque la a ganad-a/-o.
Since (he) her has won-FEM-PL/0 (*Buen Amor:*46/97a)
'Since he has won her.'
c. Pues que (todas) estas cosas ovo dich-as/-o.[9]
Since that (all) these things (he) had said-FEM-PL/0
'Since he told (all) these things.' (*Cronica:*38 29a)

The sentences in which the participle agrees with the relative pronoun, a scrambled DP, or the clitic have been treated as belonging to the same class as OSCs (see Kayne 1989, Branigan 1992, Déprez 1989, etc.). However, here I will depart from this assumption. I will argue that the movement of the object to [Spec,AgrO-P] is part of an A′-chain in the examples in (16). This chain is different from the A-chains that I have shown are formed when a lexical DP lands in [Spec,AgrO-P] in OSC.

Despite the fact that in all the examples in (16) the movement of the object to [Spec,AgrO-P] is part of an A′-chain, there are some differences in the sequence in which the subject raises to [Spec,AgrO-P] to check Case and agreement in each type of sentence due to the Strict Cycle Condition. Recall that this Condition requires that every transformation make the phrases larger. Therefore, I will account for each type of sentence separately.

7.1 Relative clauses. In relative clauses when the participle agrees with the relativized object, the main verb raises overtly to the head of AgrO, as in example (16a), which is repeated as (17):

(17) a. Cosas que yo he dich-as.
Things-FEM-PL that I have said-FEM-PL. (*Corbacho:*165)

To comply with the Strict Cycle Condition, the subject may raise to [Spec, AgrS-P] to check its Case and agreement features before or after the participle has moved to AgrO but before the object raises to [Spec,AgrO-P]. The movement of the subject satisfies the Shortest Movement Condition, since there is no intervening A-position and the phrase is made larger. Raising of the subject to [Spec,AgrO-P] would give the wrong results, as I have shown above in the explanation of example (1). The relative pronoun—or the null operator—*wh*-moves overtly to [Spec,CP] to check the strong features of C. Within the *MPLT* framework, raising the operator to [Spec,CP] is driven by morphological necessity. Chomsky (1993:32) assumes that C has an operator feature, which is a morphological property [+WH/Q]. Moreover, by raising to [Spec,CP], the operator satisfies its scopal properties. The Shortest Movement Condition is met because there are no A′ or non-L-related positions between the direct object and [Spec,CP]. The Strict Cycle Condition is fulfilled since the phrase is made larger with this movement. In (17) the agreement of the object with the participle can be explained by assuming along with Branigan (1992:38–39) that the Form Chain operation, which places the relative pronoun or the null operator in [Spec,CP], creates a number of intermediate traces. One of these intermediate traces is in [Spec,AgrO-P], an A-position. The movement through [Spec,AgrO-P] does not violate the Shortest Movement

Condition, since the previous movement of the participle to AgrO enlarges the domain of the verb and the object is not forced to land in [Spec,VP]. The trace in [Spec,AgrO-P] checks its strong features with the head before Spell-Out applies. This derivation, as Branigan points out, allows A′-chain formation operations to form A-chains as subparts of larger chains. Improper movement, which can be derived as a violation of principle C, results when a trace in an A-position binds a trace in A′-position. However, if A′-movement leaves one or more traces in A-positions, principle C will not be violated, since only the highest trace will be subject to this principle. Hence, a chain will be properly formed if its head is in an A′-position and its tail and one or more intermediate traces are in an A-position, as in (17). The relevant movements are shown in (18):

(18) Estas cosas $[_{CP}$Op$_i$ que $[_{AgrS\text{-}P}$ yo$_k$ he $[_{AgrO\text{-}P}$ t_i $[_{AgrO}$ dichas$_j$ $[_{VP}$ t_k $[_{V'}$ t_j $t_i]]]]]]$

(19) is the same as (12), except that (19) does not have agreement:

(19) Estas cosas que yo he dich-o.
'These things that I have said.'

I propose that the movements to generate this sentence are the same as the movements of (18). However there is one difference because of the lack of agreement. In (19) the relative pronoun[10]—or the null operator—adjoins to [Spec,AgrO-P] to check structural Case on its way to [Spec,CP]. Case-checking for *wh*-traces is needed because of the Chain Condition, which requires an A-chain to have one structural Case position. We have seen above that an A-chain may be part of a whole *wh*-chain. Thus, Case checking is required. Case-checking in a broadly L-related position is possible for *wh*-traces in overt syntax, as Ura (1993) has shown. Ura (1993:257) has demonstrated that a broadly L-related position may or may not count as an A-position. He assumes that all Case- (or feature) checking positions are A-positions, and he formulates the following definitions concerning the A/A′ distinctions:

(20) i. A narrowly L-related position is always an A-position. A broadly L-related position counts as an A-position only if it is actually L-related to an L-head; otherwise, it is an A′-position.

ii. A position is actually L-related if feature checking actually takes place between that position and some L-head.[11]

The Economy principle on Chain length allows *wh*-chains only to check their Case in the adjunction position of AgrO-P. This principle precludes Case-checking of DP movement in an adjoined position of AgrO-P, such as the object in OSC, since this movement would generate a longer chain than the chain whose head ends in [Spec,AgrO-P].[12] This principle explains why OSCs without participle agreement do not check their Case in an adjoined position to AgrO, but covertly, in [Spec,AgrO-P].

In (19) the position adjoined to AgrO-P, a broadly L-related position, is occupied by a trace. The participle verb, previously adjoined to AgrO, checks the Case features of the chain with the trace in that position. Thus, the position adjoined to AgrO-P counts as an A-position. Overt agreement, however, is not possible because the feature checking of the *wh*-chain takes place at the position adjoined to AgrO-P. In contrast, in (18) overt agreement appears because the agreement features of the chain are checked in [Spec,AgrO-P]. Independent evidence for this analysis comes from French ECM verbs (see Ura 1993).

Since in relative clauses the subject must move before the object to comply with the Strict Cycle Condition, the participle is not forced to adjoin to the auxiliary verb, and the subject is not required to pass through [Spec,TP] on its way to [Spec,AgrS-P]. Thus, the derivation of relative clauses is more economical than the derivation of OSCs.

7.2 Clitic constructions. When the object is cliticized it may agree with the participle as in (17b), repeated here as (21):

(21) Desque la a ganad-a.
Since (he) her has won-FEM-PL
'Since he has won her.' (*Buen Amor:*46/97a)

Following Sportiche (1992), I will assume that object clitics are generated as heads of a functional phrase, which he calls clitic voice. For the sake of simplicity I will use the term Accusative Phrase to refer specifically to the phrase of direct object clitics. The Spec position of the Accusative Phrase is an A′-position that selects an Accusative XP* argument as shown in (22).[13] The XP* argument, whose head is a small *pro*,[14] originates in a VP internal object position and must raise overtly or covertly to the Spec of the Accusative Phrase. It raises overtly to [Spec,AccP] if the participle agrees with the direct object clitic. The XP* Phrase must raise to [Spec,AccP] to be properly identified. On its way to [Spec,AccP] the XP* Phrase moves to [Spec,AgrO-P] to check Case and agreement. After the XP* phrase has reached [Spec,AccP] it is properly identified by the clitic head in a Spec/head relationship. Then the clitic head left-adjoins to the auxiliary verb in the clause, as an instance of head movement. Considering certain movements of the participle, which will become clear below, I propose that the Accusative Phrase is located below the Auxiliary Phrase in sentences with compound tenses in Old Spanish, as shown in (22).

(22)

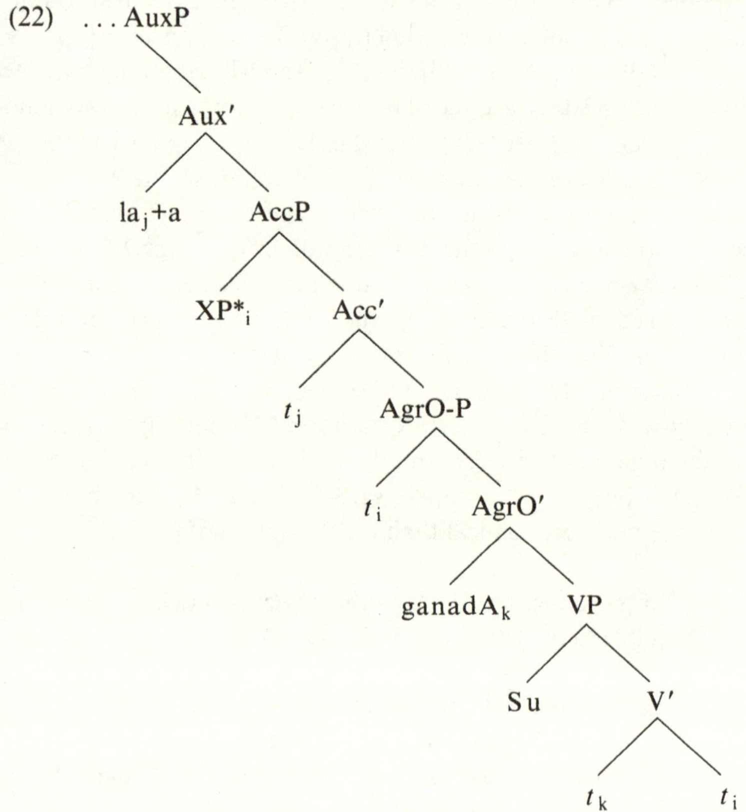

The clitic head of AccP has operatorlike properties since it licenses specificity to the raised argument in [Spec,AccP]. The raised argument in [Spec,AccP] complies with the Clitic Criterion (Sportiche 1992:25), which is equivalent to the *wh* or Q-criterion. The Clitic Criterion states that at LF:

(23) i. A clitic must be in a Spec/head relationship with a [+F] XP.
ii. A [+F] XP must be in a Spec/head relationship with a clitic.

The fact that the clitic and the XP* in [Spec,AccP] agree in Case and *phi*-features is a consequence of the Clitic Criterion. Accusative Case is not checked in [Spec,AccP], since it would be a violation of the Chain Condition.

In sentences with clitics the participle must first raise to the head of AgrO. Because the Strict Cycle Condition requires the phrase to be made larger, the object XP* must move to [Spec,AccP] before the subject raises to [Spec,AgrS-P]. The agreement of the object with the participle can be explained by assuming that the XP* on its way to [Spec,AccP] forms a chain with intermediate traces, equivalent to the chain formed in relative clauses. As in the case of relative clauses, one of the intermediate traces is in [Spec,AgrO-P]. The movement through [Spec,AgrO-P] does not violate the Shortest Movement Condition, since the previous movement of the participle to AgrO enlarges the domain of the verb and the object is not forced to land in [Spec,VP]. The trace in [Spec,AgrO-P] checks its strong features with the head before Spell-Out applies. As in the case of *wh*-movement, this derivation requires that A′-chain formation operations form A-chains as subparts of larger chains.

The subject may then move out of its VP internal position. The trace of the object in [Spec,AgrO-P] will not force the subject to move to [Spec,TP], as in OSCs, since this trace is part of an A′-chain. The trace in [Spec,AgrO-P], as part of an A′-chain, does not preclude the movement of the subject to [Spec,AgrS-P], the movement of which is an instance of A-movement. Thus, the adjunction of the participle to the auxiliary verb is not required for the subject to exit its VP internal position. This is shown in (24), where the locative adverb is interposed between the auxiliary and the participle verb (see also below, paragraph 7.3).

(24) Desque la ovo alli poblad-a.
Since (he) her had there populated-FEM
'Since he had it populated there.' (*Crónica:*9/30a)

When the participle does not agree with the direct object, clitic sentences such as (25) are generated:

(25) Desque la a ganado.
Since (he) her has won
'Since he has won her.' (*Buen Amor:*46/97a)

The movements to generate sentences with direct object clitics with or without participle agreement are the same (see movements in (22) above). In constructions without participle agreement, such as (25), the movements of the argument XP* to [Spec,AgrO-P] and to AccP must be covert (see also Sportiche 1992:31). We have seen above that covert movement operations are preferred because of Procrastination. Overt movements are allowed only if an element must be checked before Spell-Out in order to eliminate its strong features, which disappear at LF.

7.3 Scrambled and quantified objects. Scrambling, which is a case of focus movement, and Quantifier Raising are other instances of A′-movement. Consider the following examples:

(26) a. Habia toda la tierra en su amor tornad-a.
Had all the land (he) to his love turned-FEM
'He had turned all the people to love him.' (*Apol* 51/95b)
b. Pues que todas estas cosas les ovo dich-as.
Since that all these things (he) to them had said-FEM-PL . . .
'Since he had told them all these things. . . .' (*Cronica* 38:29a)

In these examples the object is quantified, but the subject is a small *pro*. The shifted object raises overtly to [Spec,AgrO-P]. Then it adjoins, as an instance of Quantifier raising, to some non-L-related position (A′) in the sentence, such as AgrS-P. Thus, Q-raising, as in the examples of *wh*-movement and Accusative clitics, is preceded by object shift, forming a chain. This chain has its head in an A′-position and its tail and one intermediate trace in A-positions. In these constructions the object and the participle agree, which forces the object to raise overtly to [Spec,AgrO-P] after the participle verb has adjoined to AgrO. This movement enlarges the minimal domain of the verbal chain. The form chain operation will create a number of intermediate traces. The trace in [Spec,AgrO-P] checks its strong features with the head before Spell-Out applies. Again, I will assume that a small *pro* subject may move covertly at LF. I assume that *pro* subject is generated in VP internal position, where it is licensed, and that it raises to AgrS to be properly identified by the head AgrS in a Spec/head relationship. Since the object has been A′-moved by adjunction overtly, the null subject is not forced to move to [Spec,TP] in its way to AgrS in order to exit VP and comply with the Shortest Movement Condition. Moreover, adjunction operations, such as Q-raising, are not subject to the Strict Cycle Condition. The relevant movements of (26a) are depicted in (27):

(27) $[_{CP}$Habia$_l$ $[_{AgrSP}$ toda la tierra$_i$ $[_{AgrS}$ *pro*$_k$ t_l en su amor $[_{AgrOP}$ t_i $[_{AgrO}$ tornada$_j$ $[_{VP}$ t_k $[_{V'}$ t_j t_i]]]]]][15]

When the subject is lexical, as in (28), it must move overtly out of VP.

(28) Habie la buena dueña tan gran haber ganado.
Had the good lady such great property won
'The good lady had won such great property.' (*Apol:* 152/420b)

In this derivation, after the object has been scrambled or Q-raised, the subject may move to [Spec,AgrS-P] directly from its internal VP position. Since the object has been removed from [Spec,AgrO-P] by A′-movement, the participle does not need to adjoin to the Auxiliary, and the Subject does not need to pass through [Spec,TP] in its way to [Spec, AgrS-P]. We have seen that A-movement and A′-movement do not interfere with each other and that movements by adjunction do not fall under the Strict Cycle Condition. The participle does not need to adjoin to the auxiliary verb, but it may, as it does in (28). In (28) the auxiliary verb is in C, since it precedes the phonetic subject. The auxiliary verb, which excorporates from the participle, moves to C, passing through T and AgrS. The movement of the auxiliary to C is triggered by independent reasons other than the movement of the subject or the scrambling of the object.[16]

In the cases of object scrambling and Q-raising the agreement of the participle and object is not required, since there are examples such as (29):

(29) Desque (todas) estas rrazones ouo dicho.
Since all these reasons (he) had said.
(*J. Manuel:* 57/38)

We may assume that the mechanics that generate examples such as this are the same as those that generate the examples of *wh*-movement without agreement. The scrambled object A′-adjoins to [Spec,AgrO-P] on its way to adjoining to [Spec,AgrS-P]. We have seen in section 6.1 that a trace may check its Case features when it is adjoined to [Spec,AgrO-P].

8 Movement of the participle. I have shown above that in OSCs the participle verb must raise to AgrO to allow the movement of the object to [Spec,AgrO-P] because of the Shortest Movement Condition and the Strict Cycle Condition. Moreover, the participle must right- or left-adjoin to the auxiliary verb in order to allow for the subject to exit its VP internal position and land in [Spec,TP]. The auxiliary verb must raise to T and to AgrS to check its tense and the Case and agreement of the subject. The auxiliary may raise overtly to T and AgrS by itself, as in (8b), or together with the participle, as in (7). The auxiliary by itself or the compound auxiliary+participle may then optionally move to C (as in 8a) through independent reasons.

Because of the Shortest Movement Condition and the Strict Cycle Condition in the cases of *wh*-movement, XP* movement, and Q-raising and scrambling, the participle verb must also raise overtly or covertly to AgrO to allow the movement of the object. However, in these constructions the participle is not forced to adjoin to the Auxiliary verb, since the object is raised to an A′-position. The subject may then raise directly from its internal VP position to [Spec,AgrS-P], since the domain of AgrO does not need to be made larger for the subject to exit VP. A′-movement does not interfere with A-movement. The Strict Cycle Condition, which requires each substitution movement to make the phrases larger, forces a sequence of movements in the cases of *wh*-movement and XP*-movement. The Strict Cycle Condition does not apply to scrambling, since adjunction operations are not subject to this principle. Neither *wh*-movement, XP* movement nor scrambling or Q-raising require the subject to land in [Spec,TP], since in all these constructions the object is removed from [Spec,AgrO-P] by A′-movement. Thus, these constructions are more economical than OSC, which must raise their subject to [Spec,TP].

The participle verb in the cases of *wh*-movement, XP* movement, or scrambling may stay in AgrO, as shown in (26a) and (27a). When the subject is a small *pro,* the participle may also stay in AgrO in OSCs, as in (8b).

In the cases of XP* movement the participle may left-adjoin to the clitic. Then the compound participle+clitic must left-adjoin again to the auxiliary verb, as an instance of clitic head movement, and raise to T and to AgrS to check tense and agreement. From there the compound participle+clitic+auxiliary may optionally raise to C due to independent reasons, as shown in (12), repeated as (31):

(31) Vengado-me-habia Ysmenia.
Revenged-me-has Ysmenia
'Ysmenia has taken revenge for me.' (*Keniston:*453)

In compound tenses the clitic must raise to the auxiliary verb, since there are no examples such as (32):

(32) a. *Ysmenia habia vengado-me.
Ysmenia had revenged-me.
b. *Habia Ysmenia vengado-me.
Had Ysmenia revenged-me.

However, the clitic may left- or right-adjoin to the auxiliary verb, as shown in (21), repeated as (33):

(33) a.

Desque	la	a	ganad-a.
Since (he)	her	has	won-FEM

'Since he has won her.' (*Buen Amor*:46/97a)

b.

Habian-lo	en su	casa de	pequeno criado.
Had-him (they)	in their	house from	childhood raised

'They had raised him from childhood in their house.' (*Apol.* 33/37c)

In the case of relative clauses the whole compound verb may raise to C, as shown in (33):

(33)

Como dicho-ha,	vido la tierra	paçifica.
How said-has (he) (he)	saw the land	peaceful

'Like he has said, he saw the land peaceful.' (Garay:1523)

9 The loss of Object Shift Constructions. Object Shift Constructions have disappeared in Modern Spanish and in the majority of Romance languages. I have claimed above that Object Shift is a costly derivation, since it has many requirements. One of the requirements is the projection of [Spec,TP] and adjunction of the participle verb to the auxiliary, as shown in (3). Speakers of Old Spanish had the option of expressing the same content that can be expressed with Object Shift constructions using simpler, covert mechanisms. By the end of the first half of the sixteenth century, shifted objects were replaced with a simpler and less costly construction. The structure of clauses with shifted objects, depicted in (3), was replaced by the structure in (2). The loss of Object Shift Constructions is diachronic proof that speakers minimize overt syntax because of Procrastination.

XP* and *wh*-movement have had a longer life than OSCs in the Romance languages, since their derivation is more economical than the derivation of OSCs. Speakers of languages such as Spanish that have lost participle agreement with direct objects seem to have avoided reduplication, which can be considered another aspect of the principle of Economy of language.

NOTES

*I would like to thank Louis Greenwald for his help in preparing this article and Carlos Quicoli for his careful reading of the text. At the time I wrote this article I was unable to consider Kayne (1993).

1. Previous relevant accounts on participle agreement with the object and its correlation with Case in French and Italian is the article of Kayne (1989). Additional studies on this topic are Burzio (1986), Déprez (1989), and Sportiche (1990), among others. Recently Kayne (1993) has proposed a new theory on auxiliary selection in which *have* and *be* are identical. The difference between the two auxiliaries is that *have* is the result of the incorporation of an abstract preposition to *be* before Spell Out.

2. In addition, Old Spanish had participle agreement in passive sentences, small clauses and constructions with unaccusative verbs. In Old Spanish, as in modern French and Italian, the auxiliary was *ser*, 'to be' with unaccusative and passive verbs. The following cases exemplify these constructions

(i) a. A otro [fin] so venid-a.
To another [matter] (I) am come-FEM
'I have come for another matter.' (*Celest:*98/9)

b. Si los moros fuesen vencid-os. . .
If the Moors were defeated-MASC-PL. . . (*J. Manuel:*57)

c. Hela viv-a hallad-a.
(I) have-her alive-FEM found-FEM
'I have found her alive.' (*Apol:*217)

3. Chomsky (1993:11–12) defines the domain of a head α as the set of nodes contained in Max(α) that are distinct from and do not contain α. However, since the operative relations are local, only the minimal subsets are relevant. Thus, the minimal domain of a head excludes the elements dominated by the nodes that conform a domain. For example, consider (i)

(i)

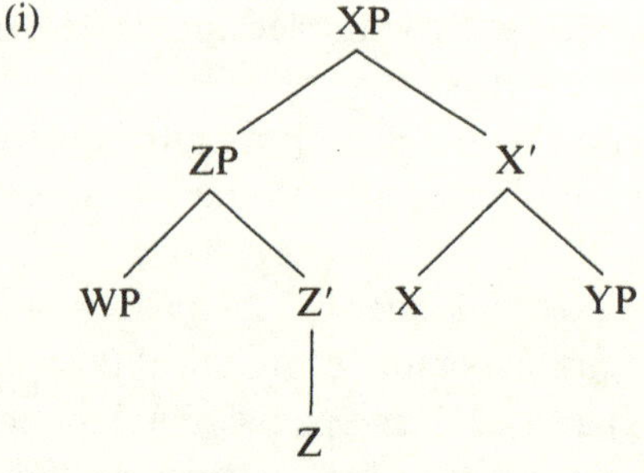

In (i), the domain of the head X is {YP, ZP, WP}, but the minimal domain of X is {ZP, YP}.

4. In this type of excorporation either the host or the incorporee are free to move on. See Roberts (1991:216) for details.

5. See Wanner (1992) for discussion and an alternative point of view of these laws in Old Spanish.

6. The example in (8) could be interpreted as a small clause. However, this example is an OSC since the participle is part of the predicate of the subject. In

Object Small Clauses the participle or the adjective is the predicate of the object, as in example (i-c) in note 2.

7. For the impossibility of VP internal subjects in Icelandic see Jonas and Bobaljik (1993).

8. [Spec,TP] is a required position to avoid a Shortest Movement Condition violation in examples such as (8) and other OSCs. However, there is no empirical evidence showing differences between OSC subjects and the subjects of other sentences. I leave the question open for further research.

9. In addition to these examples there are cases of topicalization or *wh*-focus, and clitic left dislocation with optional participle agreement such as the following

(i) a. La carrera, has errad-a/-o.
'The course, (you) have mistaken-FEM/0' (*Buen Amor:*46)

b. La missa, acabad-A/-O-la-han.
The mass, finished-it-have-FEM/0 (they)
'The mass, they have finished it.' (*Cid:*920/366)

Since the cases of topicalization are like the examples in (16a) and the cases of clitic left dislocation are like the examples in (16b), I omit them for the sake of conciseness.

10. When the Operator is null and there is no participle agreement, the movement of the operator could be covert. However, Chomsky (1993:32) suggests that the *wh*-operator feature may be universally strong. Thus, its movement will be always overt.

11. For the concepts narrowly L-related and broadly L-related, see Chomsky (1993:28); for details on Case checking for *wh*-traces, see Ura (1993:255).

12. *wh*-chains have the same length when the object trace is adjoined to [Spec,AgrO-P] or if it is in [Spec,AgrO-P]. Thus, they fulfill the Economy Principle on chain length in the same fashion. Consider the following chains:

(i) a. wh_i/XP^*_i ... $[_{AgrO\text{-}P}\ t'_i\ [_{AgrO\text{-}P}\ Agr\ [_{VP}\ V\ t_i]]]$
b. wh_i/XP^*_i ... $[_{AgrO\text{-}P}\ t'_i\ Agr\ [_{VP}\ V\ t_i]]]$
c. ... $[_{AgrO\text{-}P}\ DP_i\ [_{AgrO\text{-}P}\ Agr\ [_{VP}\ V\ t_i]]]$
d. ... $[_{AgrO\text{-}P}\ DP_i\ Agr\ [_{VP}\ V\ t_i]]]$

The chains (a) and (b) have the same length. The chain link between the trace in V and the intermediate trace in AgrO-P in (a) is geometrically longer than the chain link in (b). But the chain link between the intermediate trace in AgrO and the head of the chain in (a) is shorter than that in (b). However, (c) and (d) are not equivalent with respect to chain length. The chain in (c) is longer than that in (d). The Economy principle prefers (c) over (d), but it has nothing to say about the choice between (a) and (b).

13. Sportiche argues that the Spec position of the Accusative Phrase is an A′-position because it licenses parasitic gaps and relieves weak crossover effects throughout.

14. In certain languages it may be a lexical DP; see Sportiche (1992:26).

15. Notice that in (27) the second internal argument of the verb is also scrambled. I leave for further research the mechanics of this movement and the motivation for raising of the auxiliary verb to C. In the example in (26a) the auxiliary verb raises to C, but in (26b) it stays in AgrS. Notice that the example in (26a) is a main clause and the example in (26b) is a subordinate clause.

16. However, in languages such as Albanian, scrambling of the object to [Spec,CP]—which is equivalent to Cinque's (1991) Clitic Left Dislocation—triggers the movement of the verb to C, but scrambling to a position adjoined to AgrS does not; see Massey (1992) for details.

17. Old Spanish is similar to Albanian, which also allows a complex verb to be raised to C, see Massey (1992:151).

REFERENCES

Auto de los Reyes Magos. 1300 [1966]. D. J. Gifford and F. W. Hodcroft, eds., 1966.

Branigan, P. 1992. *Subjects and Complementizers.* Ph.D. Dissertation. MIT.

Burzio, L. 1986. *Italian Syntax: A Government-Binding Approach.* Dordrecht: Kluwer.

Cantar de Mio Cid. 1140 [1969]. R. Menéndez Pidal, ed. Madrid: Espasa-Calpe.

Chomsky, N. 1993. A Minimalist Program for Linguistic Theory. In *The View from Building 20: Essays in Linguistics in Honor of Sylvain Bromberger.* K. Hale and S. J. Keyser, eds. Cambridge: MIT Press.

Cinque, G. 1991. *Types of A' Dependencies.* Cambridge: MIT Press.

Déprez, V. 1989. *On the Typology of Syntactic Positions and the Nature of Chains.* Ph.D. Dissertation. MIT.

Garay, F. 1523. *La llegada de Francisco de Garay al Panuco.* C. Parodi, ed. Manuscript. UCLA.

Gifford, D. J., and F. W. Hodcroft. 1966. *Textos Lingüísticos del Medioevo Español.* Oxford: The Dophin Book.

Holmberg, A. 1986. *Word Order and Syntactic Features.* Ph.D. Dissertation. University of Stockholm.

Jonas, D., and J. Bobaljik. 1993. Spaces for Subjects: The Role of TP in Icelandic. In *Papers on Case and Agreement* I. J. Bobaljik and C. Phillips, eds. Cambridge: MIT Press.

Kayne, R. 1989. Facets of Past Participle Agreement. In *Dialect Variation and the Theory of Grammar.* P. Benincà, ed. Dordrecht: Foris.

Kayne, R. 1993. Toward a Modular Theory of Auxiliary Selection. *Studia Linguistica* 47:3–31.

Libro de Apolonio. 1300 [1976]. Manuel Alvar, ed. Madrid: Castalia.

Massey, V. W. 1992. Compositionality and Constituency in Albanian. *MIT Occasional Papers in Linguistics* 3.

Manuel, J. 1238–1348 [1966]. *El Libro de Patronio o El Conde Lucanor.* D. J. Gifford and F. W. Hodcroft, eds., 1966.

Parodi, C. In press. Verb Incorporation and the HMC in XVIth-century Spanish. In *Contemporary Research in Romance Linguistics.* J. Amastae, G. Goodall,

M. Montalbetti, and M. Phinney, eds. Amsterdam and Philadelphia: John Benjamins.

Primera crónica general de España. 1400 [1955]. R. Menéndez Pidal, ed. Gredos: Madrid.

Rizzi, L. 1990. *Relativized Minimality.* Cambridge: MIT Press.

Roberts, I. 1991. Excorporation and Minimality. *Linguistic Inquiry* 22:209–18.

Rojas, F. de. 1499 [1968]. *La Celestina.* J. Cejador, ed. Madrid: Clásicos Castellanos.

Sportiche, D. 1990. *Movement, Agreement and Case.* Manuscript. UCLA.

Sportiche, D. 1992. *Clitic Constructions.* Manuscript. UCLA.

Talavera, A. de. 1423 [1970]. *El Corbacho.* J. González Muela, ed. Madrid: Castalia.

Tellier, C. 1991. *Licensing Theory and French Parasitic Gaps.* Dordrecht: Kluwer.

Ura, H. 1993. On Feature Checking for *wh*-Traces. In *Papers on Case and Agreement I.* J. Bobaljik and C. Phillips, eds. Cambridge: MIT Press.

Wanner, D. 1992. The Tobbler-Mussafia Law in Old Spanish. In *Current Studies in Spanish Linguistics.* H. Campos and F. Martínez-Gil, eds. Washington, D. C.: Georgetown University Press.

Zwart, J.-W. 1993. Verb Movement and Complementizer Agreement. In *Papers on Case and Agreement I.* J. Bobaljik and C. Phillips, eds. Cambridge: MIT Press.

On Compounding in English and Spanish*

Carlos Piera
Universidad Autónoma de Madrid

1 Introduction. The standard accounts of nominal compounding in a language such as English view this process as, in itself, fairly unproblematic. This raises the issue of why other languages, such as Spanish, cannot make use of compounding as freely and productively as English does.

My goal here is to outline a treatment of some aspects of compounding from which both the freedom of English and the limitations of Spanish may follow. I will then suggest that a parallel account can be given of the resistance to Noun Incorporation exhibited by these two languages, among many others. Throughout the paper I will concentrate on English and Spanish. I will also concentrate on maximally productive N-N compounding.[1]

2 Compounding without lexical insertion. The structure most linguists would attribute to a simple English root compound like *apple pie* is as given in (1):

(1) $[_N [_N X] [_N Y]]$

(1) appears since at least Chomsky and Halle (1968:16 and *passim*) within otherwise very different morphological frameworks, for example, recently in Anderson (1992:297) and Lieber (1992:54–56). These authors also coincide in attributing to compounds, in Anderson's words, a 'quasi-syntactic' structure: composition is exceptional for Anderson and regular for Lieber, in that it makes use of essentially the same devices that syntax provides for the organization of phrases. As Anderson puts it, "it involves the combining of lexical stems in a syntactic structure" (1992:293). An analogous approach is revealed in the Romance domain by the use of terms like "compostos sintagmàtics" (Mascaró 1986:71–73).

Let us assume now that productive compounding is indeed literally the output of a syntactic process. The question then arises as to what sort of syntactic process results outside of compounding in a structure like (1). My claim is that no such process exists and therefore that (1) cannot be the correct structure for compounds unless the hypothesis of their syntactic origin is abandoned.

The representation in (1) owes its syntactic legitimacy to the notion of 'lexical insertion.' In the framework of Chomsky (1965) and elsewhere phrase-markers are objects with intrinsic properties, as specified by phrase structure rules and, in later work, by X′ theory. These objects can be constructed independently of their terminal nodes—typically lexical items—and terminal nodes can be seen as inserted under their preterminal mother. Thus, for example, *pie* is inserted under the nonbranching $[_N\ ]$ node, perhaps by means of a substitution transformation affecting a terminal Δ. This creates the standard representation (2):

(2) $[_N$ pie]

Note that (2) is not the output of the lexicon. A lexical item has—actually, consists of—several sets of features. One such set is the set of syntactically relevant features—call them grammatical features—and it is fair to assume that N, or rather +N, is one of these. If we use the spelling *pie* to represent the phonological part of the corresponding lexical entry, what the lexicon provides is not (2) but something closer to (3):

(3) {pie, {grammatical features}, {semantic features}},
where {grammatical features} = {+N, +Count, etc.}

The point to be considered here is whether (3) can be the source of (1) once the specific tenets of the Chomsky (1965) model are given up.

Along the lines of Chomsky (1993) I will assume here that there are no DS and SS levels, hence no structures into which lexical insertion may be said to occur in a theoretically meaningful way. I will also assume that the expansion of a lexical item such as (3) into a larger constituent, be it X^0 or higher, can take place only in one of two ways, namely, through either substitution or adjunction. Some version of the latter assumption is standard in current syntactic work (e.g., Kayne 1994); for our present purposes it will be sufficient to extend it to the 'quasi-syntactic' domain of compounding without making any claims about other morphological processes. One of its consequences is that pure concatenation is excluded from that domain, as it has been from syntax for quite a long time.

Given the first of these assumptions, (2) can only arise through projection, specifically through projection of at least the set of grammatical features in (3). But projection—an aspect of the algorithm whereby grammatical structures are put together—should not in principle be allowed to take place *per se* and in isolation. I am not aware of any motivation for allowing such a possibility, whereas its exclusion appears to be next to inevitable within the framework adopted here, apart from being a consequence of fairly basic economy requirements. We can then adopt a constraint allowing projection only under branching, with obvious consequences for syntactic representation. If we wished to preserve X′ theory in its standard form (but see Muysken 1982, among others), we might let projection take place whenever (a) the projected node branches, and/or (b) the projected node is nonmaximal and is dominated by a maximal projection of the same node. Condition (b) is only relevant to (phrasal) syntax proper; as far as compounding is concerned, therefore, we may assume that only branching can trigger any sort of projection.

Consider, then, a compound such as *apple pie.* Which of its two components should project? What is at stake is the nature of the node resulting from compounding, a nature that is of course determined by the head of the compound. This is most visible in compounds involving two different grammatical categories: *blackbird* is a noun, not an adjective. Hence the structure so far motivated for simple root compounds should be as in (5):

(5) a. $[_{+N,+F1,\ldots}$ {black, $\{+A, +F_a, +F_b, \ldots\}$} {bird, $\{+N, +F_1, +F_2, \ldots\}$}]
b. $[_{+N,+F3,\ldots}$ {apple, $\{+N, +F_c, +F_d, \ldots\}$} {pie, $\{+N, +F_3, +F_4, \ldots\}$}]

In simplified tree form we would have:

(6) $\{+N, +F_3, \ldots\}$
/ \
apple $\{+N, +F_c, \ldots\}$ pie $\{+N, +F_3, \ldots\}$

To repeat, the features on the lefthand constituent of these forms do not need to be projected: they can be recovered from the constituent itself. The features on the righthand constituent are projected—given that there is branching—because they are the head's features: they must be available as features of the entire compound.

(5) and (6) should correspond to what in syntax is a standard adjunction structure. Compounding is, to put it in X′ terms, same-level recursive, while so-called substitutions are the operations whereby phrasal constituents are expanded—that is, again in X′ terms, it is through substitution that X^0 becomes X′ and so on. Also, as adjunction structures, (5) and (6) allow the head of the compound to be determined essentially as it

is determined in syntax, through the converse of feature projection. The structure in (1) on the other hand could only be created (a) if projection were allowed to take place without restriction and (b) either through substitution or through sister adjunction. Sister adjunction is not contemplated in current syntactic work. It is then legitimate to propose (5) and (6) as the structure of English compounds. Let us now consider the empirical consequences of this proposal.

3 A proposed restriction. The most salient formal differences between English and Spanish compounding (on the latter see Bustos Gisbert 1986, Varela 1992, Rainer 1993a, and the bibliography in Rainer 1993b) are stated descriptively under (7):

(7) a. English compounds are right headed (*police dog*), whereas Spanish compounds are left headed (*perro policía*), and

b. English compounding is recursive (*DEA police dog*), whereas Spanish is not (**perro policía Departamento de Narcóticos*).

We must now show that, given (5) and (6) above, these properties can be made to follow from independently motivated differences in the morphological makeup of English and Spanish substantives, for there is nothing else that can cause them.

Now, the first difficulty we face is that (5)–(6) do not make any predictions about ordering: their linear organization is an artifact of our written representation. Note that the usual convention whereby the head of an adjunction structure projects twice (so-called Chomsky-adjunction) does not solve this problem by itself, unless further assumptions about X′ structure are also made. Since we would like to keep our assumptions to a minimum, we will explore the possibility of reducing all our ordering requirements to morphology proper. To put it another way, we are considering an aspect of the following topic: How much structure should morphology provide, and in what shape, in order for syntax to behave as it does? In this connection we must keep in mind that in our particular domain we cannot resort directly to general syntactic well-formedness restrictions, such as have been proposed by Kayne (1994): we have nothing to gain from a straightforward exclusion of left-headed compounds like *perro policía* 'police dog'.

The crucial construct here will be the notion 'word marker'—henceforth WM. As Harris (1991a, b) has shown convincingly and in great detail, Spanish nouns and adjectives—as well as adverbs, which will not concern us here—minimally have the shape given in (8), where *d* marks a derivational constituent and *i* an inflectional constituent:

(8) $[\,[X]_d\ Y]_i$

I refer the reader to Harris's work for the motivation and the specifics of this proposal, which has parallels in other languages (see Halle 1991 among others). It will be sufficient to note that even Harris's class 3 nominals, which do not exhibit a WM, conform to the bracketing structure in (8).

Our first task is to account for the absence of regular right-headed structures such as *apple pie* in Spanish; let our example be a hypothetical translation **manzana tarta* (or *torta*). I would like to suggest that the relevant restriction can be stated—in a provisional and informal way—as follows:

(9) A double bracket at the edge of a word blocks adjunction of a word

The operation of (9) is straightforward. We may represent Spanish *tarta* in isolation as (10)—a simplified representation whose full form should be closer to (3) above:

(10) [[tart] WM]

The corresponding compound would be (11)—where the eventual shape of the WM is given in parentheses strictly for readability:

(11) $[_{+N....}$ [[manzan(a)] WM] [[tart(a)] WM]]

In (11) the double bracket to the left of *tart(a)* violates (9), which I will refer to as the Double Bracket Restriction—henceforth, DBR. Thus, if this restriction is correct, (11) is not a possible Spanish compound. Since (10) has the minimal shape of all Spanish substantives, (11) is the minimally complex right-headed structure any Spanish compound may have. Therefore, all right-headed compounds are ruled ungrammatical in Spanish by the DBR. Note how the parallel English compound does not include any internal double bracket, thus being allowed by the DBR whether we adhere to the minimal representation in (5b) or carry out a two-segment projection as in (12):

(12) $[_{+N\ldots}$ apple $[_{+N\ldots}$ pie]]

Consider now the fact that Spanish does have left-headed compounds. Let our example be *perro policía,* literally, 'dog police,' that is, 'police dog.' Assume that the direction of compounding is entirely free, specifically that it need not take place to the left of the head. What this implies in the present context is that the structure of English and Spanish compounds is formally identical, except for the fact that they are mirror images of each other (and of course for the presence in Spanish of WMs). Compare (11) to (13):

(13) $[_{+N\ldots}$ [[perr(o)] WM] [[policí(a)] WM]]

Clearly, (13), since its head noun has no double bracket to its right, is compatible with the DBR.

This concludes our account of the properties under (7a). As for recursiveness, note that the form *perro policía* in (13) has a double bracket at its leftmost edge. In accordance with the DBR, adjunction to it should be ruled out, which is the desired result. Spanish compounds are thus predicted to be maximally binary. A translation of (14) as its mirror image is correctly ruled out as ungrammatical: (15).

(14) pet police dog
(15) *perro policía mascota

On the other hand it is equally clear that (14) and all similar English forms are compatible with the DBR. What the DBR restricts is the context for adjunction—the adjunction site—not the character of the adjoined element. Hence, any element, no matter how complex its edges, can be adjoined in English (*Early Middle English scholar, man-in-the-moon marigold*), as long as the leftmost edge of its would-be head is single bracketed. The addition of any number of simple items in English will only increase the depth of embedding of the compound head, not the number of brackets at the leftmost edge of the compound, that is, the depth of embedding of its leftmost adjunct. English compounding is thus correctly characterized as recursive, which completes our account of the properties under (7) above. Observe that synthetic compounds (*paperback writer*) pose no additional problems within the standard analysis in which their deverbal head is in turn headed by an affix: the leftmost edge of the resulting word is still single bracketed, as shown in (16) (cf. (5)and (6)):

(16) $[_{+N,\ldots}$ {write, {+V, . . . }} {er, {+N, . . . }}]

We may note that traditional grammarians have often tried to derive the properties of compounding from those of the internal inflectional elements, typically by invoking the limitations existing on internal inflection in compounds (Geert Booij clarifies the extent of such limitations in unpublished work). If I am correct, these attempts do invoke the right constructs but look for them in the wrong place: it is not the inflectional properties of the adjoined element, hence the internal ones, that are relevant here, but those of the head.

4 Some related issues. Although many issues related to our topic will have to be left out entirely, a few comments on some potential implications of the preceding proposals are in order.

In the first place we may have advanced toward the solution of a classic problem in Spanish grammar. As shown below, a Spanish noun can be preceded by one adjective, and only one ((17a,b)), and this adjective cannot be a compound ((17c)), whereas no such restriction applies to postnominal adjectives ((17d,e)):

(17) a. el azul océano
the blue Ocean
b. *el agitado azul océano
the agitated blue Ocean
c. *el azul Prusia océano
the Prussia blue Ocean
d. el océano azul agitado
e. el océano azul Prusia

Suppose that through syntactic substitution-expansion only one position is available for an adjectival modifier to the left of a head noun (which could follow from Kayne 1994, if I interpret it correctly). If prenominal adjective recursion is the result of an adjunction process, then no more adjectives can be added to the left by the DBR, since Spanish adjectives, as noted, have the same structure as nouns; this gives (17b). Furthermore, if all prenominal adjectives were taken to be adjoined to the head noun, the exclusion of compound adjectives would also follow, giving (17c). This latter move is problematic, however, insofar as the DBR should exclude even a first adjunction in Spanish. There are a number of ways to circumvent this difficulty, but they all involve other aspects of the grammar and must be left unexplored here.

Turning to a more general issue, I have made no attempt to clarify the exact nature of the label on the upper node of compounds (see Lieber 1992, for an especially thorough treatment of feature projection). If indeed they are a subclass of adjunction structures, this problem must be dealt with in connection with the entire class. Note at any rate that the analysis above would not be affected by the adoption of the usual two-head node, two-segment representation of adjuncts: whatever the effects of one more pair of brackets around the leftmost element in Spanish or the rightmost element in English, as in (12) above, these brackets would be there only after adjunction and hence affect only later operations. Since these operations are already excluded in Spanish on the one hand and take place in English at the righthand end of the compound on the other, no new predictions are made.

As Lieber has stressed, English compounds may have the structure of any well-formed syntactic phrase in the language (*while-you-wait, over-the-counter, hard-to-get, hand-me-down, salt-and-pepper,* etc.). Many of these forms, if represented according to the standard syntactic conventions, will include multiple internal bracketings, which might be taken to violate the DBR. I believe that such an objection would be unwarranted. The exact correspondence between these and standard syntactic structures must be captured by generating them through substitution, not adjunction, and this exempts them from the DBR. On the other hand it can be argued that the outside label on these forms does not derive in the usual way from the head of the internal construction, since they do not behave as VPs, CPs, PPs, and so on, but as [+N] elements. They appear in other words to be exocentric—an unsurprising property among compounds even of the more regular type, as in the semantics of *girlfriend* (Marchand 1969) in English or in the well-known Romance pattern of *pickpocket* and *sacacorchos* (lit., 'drawcorks,' 'corkscrew') (for different views see, among others, Di Sciullo and Williams 1987:79ff., Varela 1992:108ff., and Anderson 1992:316–319).

In any case, judging from their behavior with respect to the DBR, these forms seem to behave as complex elements. Let us review briefly what the DBR can tell us about the complexity of individual compound constituents. We have seen that it does not restrict the complexity of English adjuncts. As for heads, some authors (Marchand 1960:199–200) would like to exclude from English all compound-headed compounds, whereas others (Chomsky and Halle 1968:92–93) point out that "such constructions are rare," but mention as possible examples *chemistry research-laboratory, kitchen towel-rack,* and *evening mathematics-class.* With only the minimalist assumptions adopted so far no distinction can be made between triple compounds and double-headed ones, and these forms are all compatible with the DBR, as can be seen in (18a); compare to the equally acceptable *chemistry-research laboratory* in (18b):

(18) a. [{chemistry{ . . . }} [{research { . . . }} {laboratory { . . . }}]]
b. [[{chemistry { . . . }} {research{ . . . }}] {laboratory { . . . }}]

The rarity of these forms will need to be accounted for, then, through other means—perhaps related to their structural ambiguity—unless some justification can be found for excluding them through further bracketing of the two rightmost items.

In its present form, however, the DBR does rule out definite cases of compound-internal compounds, since any adjunction of a compound will create a double bracket. Although the facts are not altogether clear, compounds having a phrasal structure seem to be excluded from compound-internal position; this suggests, as pointed out above, that, even though not formed through adjunction, they are treated as having double, or multiple, brackets around them. Thus, in spite of the fact that all of (19a,b,c) are well formed, (20a,b) are not:

(19) a. across-the-board faculty pay cut
b. across-the-board pay cut
c. across-the-board cut

(20) a. *faculty across-the-board pay cut
b. *faculty pay across-the-board cut

The complexity that (20) appears to reflect could be because phrasal bracketings are recognized at the point when actual (adjunction-type) compounding takes place. Alternatively, it may be caused by their exocentric character; whether we take it to be represented by the addition of a null head (see, e.g., Lieber 1992:67) or by one further step of rebracketing and relabeling, it will entail the presence of one more bracket to the left. Notice that, as opposed to other instances of category changing, the categorial anomaly of these items cannot be attributed to relisting in the lexicon (Lieber 1992:157ff.), since—at least when they are semantically compositional—they do not appear in the lexicon in the first place.

To conclude these remarks on complexity, notice that the DBR tolerates Spanish compounds that have a compound as their second term. This seems to be correct, as shown in (21):

(21) a. un primo guardia civil
a cousin Guard Civil
'a Civil Guard cousin'
b. una cama estilo Luis XV
'a Louis XV style bed'
c. un traje príncipe de Gales
'a Prince of Wales (a kind of pattern) suit'

5 A remark on Noun Incorporation. The basic constructs used in this paper are of course open to different interpretations, from which different refinements, reformulations, and applications will follow. Of crucial importance is the actual implementation of the notions 'inflectional' and 'derivational,' as reflected in the subscripts in (8). Notice that, as things now stand, the notions 'subject to inflection' and 'having an obligatory word marker' are disjoint, although the notion 'pertaining to a (morphological) word class' may be dependent on the latter. The DBR is undoubtedly too crude in its present form and will need to be revised in the light of the interpretation given to these and other notions. Eschewing this major issue here, I will merely point out how the line of inquiry exemplified above may be used to clarify other aspects of universal grammar by reducing syntactic variation and much of linear ordering to the consequences of morphological diversity (Chomsky 1993; cf. Emonds 1986).

Consider Noun (to Verb) Incorporation—NI. Since Baker (1988:ch. 3 and *passim*), NI has been viewed as the output of a syntactic adjunction that is perfectly simple and entirely independent of language. Now, it was precisely the simplicity of English compounding that suggested to us that Spanish, and other languages like it, must have properties amounting to limitations on compounding, properties that ideally should be of a morphological nature. By the same token we may expect other languages like English and Spanish, which cannot resort productively to NI, to have morphological properties that cause this limitation. If treated as strictly syntactic, as in Baker's work, the verbal forms created by the incorporation of a noun onto a verb are normal adjunction structures; their standard two-segment representation would be as in (22), which is entirely parallel to (12) above:

(22) $[_V$ N $[_V$ V]]

Other authors (Di Sciullo and Williams 1987:63–69; and Anderson 1992:267–270) argue for the morphological nature of the N+V units present in NI constructions. Thus, Anderson—who mentions Sapir (1911) as a precedent—suggests that a form such as (23) below, the result of "a kind of compounding . . . is formed directly in the lexicon, and not by adjunction in the syntax" (Anderson 1992:268):

(23) $[_V [_N$ meat$] [_V$ eat$]]$

Notice that, except for the category on the head, (23) is identical to (1)—understandably so, since it is meant to show how NI verbal forms can be taken to be just like standard compounds. Therefore, (23) is subject to the same criticisms and open to the same alternatives as (1). I conclude that the conflict between syntactic and lexical hypotheses on the generation of NI configurations has no bearing on the issue of their exact constituent structure, which is all that we are concerned with here.[2]

Suppose, then, that the morphological shape of Spanish and English verbs had at least the complexity of Spanish substantives, as reflected above in (8). That is, suppose that—using a terminology that is as neutral as possible—their derivational core is accompanied by an external inflectional slot to be filled or filtered out according to the requirements of its head and of the surrounding phrasal constituents. This assumption is nearly uncontroversial with regard to the rich verbal paradigms of Spanish. Although no compelling morphological motivation can be offered for it in the case of English, it is also quite well founded on syntactic grounds in this language, given what we know of its grammar. English and Spanish verbs must raise to successive inflectional positions (Chomsky 1993:27–28) on the basis of the principle of Greed, which allows movement of an element α "only if morphological properties of α itself are not otherwise satisfied" (Chomsky 1993:33). Thus, for example, an English verb amounting to a single or purely derivational unit—a structure such as {*eat*, +V, . . .} or $[_V$ *eat*$]$—would not move to the T(ense) and Agr(eement) nodes. This all but forces us to adopt for English verbs a structure having, as was assumed above, at least the complexity of (8); a variant of this structure is discussed by Chomsky (1993:28).[3]

Given this assumption, all the verbal forms of English and Spanish that are capable of inflection would be at least double bracketed to the left; hence, by the DBR, they could not host an adjoined element. This would exclude from these languages all forms like (22) and (23) and all the forms they are meant to represent, that is, all the forms in which a noun is adjoined to an inflectable verb head. It is surely no accident that in all the languages considered by Baker that exhibit verbal agreement, with a single exception, the person-gender-number morphemes precede the incorporated noun, whereas in Spanish and English, as in other nonincorporating languages, this marker would follow the V head of the compound.[4] Be that as it may, the resistance to Noun Incorporation in languages like Spanish and English—a topic on which there has not been any research so far, to my knowledge, but one that has important implications—seems to be the consequence of a strictly local, strictly morphological property of a class of words in these languages. If this is indeed correct, it indicates that the research program in which syntactic variation is attributed to morphological idiosyncracies is very much on the right track.

NOTES

* This paper is the written version of a talk I gave in May 1992 at Tilburg University and later at the Universidad de Castilla-La Mancha and the Madrid Autónoma. A longer and more detailed version, initially prepared for this volume, ventured into and drew on theoretical subtleties that may turn out to be more profitably examined in the light of Chomsky's contribution to this volume. Nothing surprising there, neither in general nor in this particular case, since the initial stimulus for my paper came from Chomsky (1993, circulated in 1992) and from some of his Fall 1991 lectures. This remark is, then, prompted by that most personal feeling: guilt. For the extent of my debt to Carlos Otero is such that only a work of Paninian proportions would seem to me remotely indicative of it.

I was not able to include discussion of an important contribution by Cinque (1993), and I took only the most superficial notice of Kayne (1994) and Halle and Marantz (1993). I am grateful to Joe Emonds, Bart Hollebrandse, Riny Huybreghts, Amaya Mendikoetxea, and Roberta Quance for kindness, comments, and corrections, and, very specially, to Henk van Riemsdijk, for all the above plus wonderful hospitality. All are exonerated. My stay at Tilburg was made possible by a grant from the Programa de movilidad del personal investigador of the Dirección General de Ciencia y Tecnología, of the Spanish Ministry of Education and Science, while I was included in Research Project PB90-0181. Both the institution and its very helpful personnel deserve gratitude.

Y a Carlos ¿qué le voy a decir?

1. This means, in particular, trying not to rely on the semantically noncompositional cases that constitute the bulk of the examples in Spanish grammars, while allowing for examples like *libro lavadora* ('washing machine book'), which refer in a perfectly clear way to nonexisting and perhaps impossible objects. Needless to say, care must also be taken to exclude apparent counterexamples that can be built through coordination.

2. In unpublished work Joseph Emonds formulates and justifies a principle of Generalized Incorporation, which would reduce the syntactic relevance of this debate as well.

3. Halle and Marantz (1993, especially 166–170) propose a detailed alternative to Chomsky's treatment, which deserves careful examination. All I can say at this point is that unfortunately it does not seem to be compatible with the minimalist assumptions about phrase structure adopted here.

4. The languages in question are Onondaga, Southern Tiwa, Mohawk, Nahuatl, Oneida, and Tuscarora. A similar order appears to be obeyed by the antipassive morpheme in Mam and Chamorro. The exception is Greenlandic, on which, for this and many related issues, see Sadock (1991).

REFERENCES

Anderson, S. R. 1992. *A-morphous Morphology.* Cambridge: Cambridge University Press.

Baker, M. C. 1988. *Incorporation: A Theory of Grammatical Function Changing.* Chicago: University of Chicago Press.

Bustos Gisbert, E. de. 1986. *La composición nominal en español.* Salamanca: Ediciones de la Universidad de Salamanca.

Cinque, G. 1993. A Null Theory of Phrase and Compound Stress. *Linguistic Inquiry* 24: 239–97.

Chomsky, N. 1965. *Aspects of the Theory of Syntax.* Cambridge: MIT Press.

Chomsky, N. 1993. A Minimalist Program for Linguistic Theory. In *The View from Building 20: Essays in Linguistics in Honor of Sylvain Bromberger.* K. Hale and S. J. Keyser, eds. Cambridge: MIT Press.

Chomsky, N., and M. Halle. 1968. *The Sound Pattern of English.* New York: Harper and Row.

Di Sciullo, A. M., and E. Williams. 1988. *On the Definition of Word.* Cambridge: MIT Press.

Emonds, J. E. 1986. *A Unified Theory of Syntactic Categories.* Dordrecht: Foris.

Halle, M. 1991. The Latvian Declension. In *Yearbook of Morphology* 4. G. Booij and J. van Marle, eds. Dordrecht: Kluwer.

Halle, M., and A. Marantz. 1993. Distributed Morphology and the Pieces of Inflection. In *The View from Building 20: Essays in Linguistics in Honor of Sylvain Bromberger.* K. Hale and S. J. Keyser, eds. Cambridge: MIT Press.

Harris, J. W. 1991a. The Exponence of Gender in Spanish. *Linguistic Inquiry* 22:27–62.

Harris, J. W. 1991b. The Form Classes of Spanish Substantives. In *Yearbook of Morphology* 4. G. Booij and J. van Marle, eds. Dordrecht: Kluwer.

Kayne, R. 1994. *The Antisymmetry of Syntax.* Cambridge: MIT Press.

Lieber, R. 1992. *Deconstructing Morphology.* Chicago: University of Chicago Press.

Marchand, H. 1960. Die Länge englischer Komposita und die entsprechenden Verhältnisse im Deutschen. *Anglia* 78:411–16. Reprinted in *Studies in Syntax and Word-formation: Selected Articles by Hans Marchand.* 1974. D. Kastovsky, ed. Munich: Wilhelm Fink.

Marchand, H. 1969. *The Categories and Types of Present-day English Word-formation.* Munich: C. H. Beck.

Mascaró, J. 1986. *Morfologia.* Barcelona: Edicions de l'Enciclopèdia Catalana.

Muysken, P. 1982. Parametrizing the Notion 'Head.' *Journal of Linguistic Research* 2:57–75.

Rainer, F. 1993a. *Spanische Wortbildungslehre.* Tübingen: Max Niemeyer.

Rainer, F. 1993b. Sesenta años (1921–1990) de investigación en la formación de palabras del español moderno: bibliografía crítica selectiva. In *La formación de palabras.* S. Varela, ed. Madrid: Taurus.

Sapir, E. 1911. The Problem of Noun Incorporation in American languages. *American Anthropologist* (n.s.) 13:250–82.

Sadock, J. 1991. *Autolexical Syntax: A Theory of Parallel Grammatical Representations.* Chicago: University of Chicago Press.

Varela, S. 1992. *Fundamentos de morfología.* Madrid: Síntesis.

NP Traces and the ECP/Binding Overlap*

CARLOS QUICOLI
UCLA

1 The ECP/Binding overlap. Current theories formulated under the Principles and Parameters framework (Chomsky 1981, 1982, 1986a, and related work) permit two possible explanations for the distribution of NP-traces. According to one hypothesis, NP-traces are anaphors, and their distribution is regulated by Principle A of Binding Theory. According to the other hypothesis, all traces (including NP-traces) must conform to the Empty Category Principle (ECP), which requires that traces be 'properly governed.'

Thus, given the literature, there are in principle two ways of accounting for the distribution of NP-traces in Portuguese and English raising structures such as the following:

(1) a. Nos parecemos ignorar as regras.
We seem-1pl. to ignore the rules.
b. Nos_1 parecemos [t_1 ignorar as regras]
(2) a. We seem to ignore the rules.
b. We_1 seem [t_1 to ignore the rules]
(3) a. *Nos parecemos que ignoramos as regras.
We seem-1pl that ignored-1pl. the rules.
b. Nos_1 parecemos [que [t_1 ignoramos as regras]
(4) a. *We seem that ignored the rules.
b. We_1 seem [that [t_1 ignored the rules]

According to the ECP hypothesis, such facts follow from the ECP, a specific condition on traces (cf. Lasnik and Saito 1992; Chomsky 1986a and 1986b, among others). Under this view the Portuguese structure P(1) and its English counterpart E(2) would be well formed because the NP-trace in them is 'properly governed'—either 'lexically governed' under the familiar assumption that the embedded clause is an IP (= S) rather than CP (= S′), or 'antecedent governed' (cf. Lasnik and Saito 1984), or both—so that the ECP is satisfied. However, Portuguese P(3) and English E(4) would be excluded by the ECP since the trace would not be 'properly governed'. The embedded clause is a CP, a 'barrier' to government, so that the trace is neither lexically governed nor antecedent, violating the ECP.

Alternatively, according to the Binding hypothesis, the facts above would follow from Principle A of Binding Theory. Structures such as P(1) and E(2) are well formed because the NP-trace (an anaphor) in such structures is bound in a Binding Domain (the domain c-commanded by the matrix subject). However, structures such as P(3) and E(4) would be excluded as violations of Principle A of Binding Theory: the embedded verb in such structures contains the agreement element (Agr), which makes the embedded clause a Binding Domain (cf. Chomsky 1981:section 3.2.3, and related work). Since in both P(3) and E(4) the traces are not bound within the Agr domain (a binding domain), the structure is ruled out by Principle A of Binding Theory.

The above exemplify what I shall refer to here as the ECP/Binding overlap. There are essentially two possible outcomes concerning such an issue. One possibility is that this is simply a harmless overlap of two general theories that are independently required to explain other phenomena but that converge on a particular domain of data. The other possibility is that the overlap reveals an unwelcome redundancy that needs to be resolved. In this article I discuss evidence based on a number of contrasts involving the distribution of NP traces in Portuguese and English in hope of contributing to the resolution of this issue.

In the discussion I present evidence favoring the Binding approach over the ECP approach to NP-traces. I argue that the requirements to satisfy the ECP—both 'lexical government' (or 'theta-government') and 'antecedent government'—present a number of empirical problems, which can be overcome by Binding Theory.

2 Brief review: Binding principles and the ECP. Studies within the Principles and Parameters framework (cf. Chomsky 1981, 1982 and 1986a) have led to the formulation of two major subtheories: Binding Theory and Government Theory.

Binding Theory is relied on to explain referential possibilities of NPs occurring in sentences. Based on Chomsky (1981), its three basic principles can be stated as follows (cf. Chomsky 1981:221; Chomsky 1986a:166):

(5) Binding Theory:
   A. An anaphor must be bound within a binding domain.
   B. A pronominal must be free within a binding domain.
   C. An R-expression must be free.

There has been considerable work aimed at sharpening the notion of 'Binding Domain' (or 'binding category').[1] For present purposes I shall assume (following Chomsky 1981) that there are essentially two Binding Domains: α) the domain c-commanded by the closest subject (incorporating the earlier SSC) and b) the domain c-commanded by the agreement morphology identifying the subject (Agr) (incorporating the earlier TSC/NIC). These two notions can be brought together, constituting the domain of an 'accessible SUBJECT' (Chomsky 1981). Accordingly, based on Chomsky (1981:220), we shall adopt the following formulation of Binding Domain:

(6) Binding Domain:[2]
β is a binding domain for α if and only if
β is the minimal category containing α and a SUBJECT accessible to α.
(SUBJECT = [NP, S] or Agr)

As for the notion 'bound' I will assume the following definition:3

(7) α is bound by β if and only if
a. α is coindexed with β and
b. α is c-commanded by β.

The theory of binding summarized above is essentially as formulated in Chomsky (1981:220) and differs from some versions in the literature. Some previous and later versions of binding make reference to the notion of 'government' in the definition of binding domains (cf. the notion of 'governing category' discussed in Chomsky 1981, and the notion 'minimal governing category' identified as "a maximal projection containing both a subject and a lexical category governing [A]" as in Chomsky 1986a:169). The version that I am assuming here is a 'strict' binding theory based exclusively on the concept of 'accessible SUBJECT,' making no reference to 'government' (see note 2). If terminological distinctions are necessary, we may refer to the theory adopted here as Strict Binding Theory.

Binding Theory refers to two basic properties of NPs—'anaphor' and 'pronominal.' By combining these two properties a typology of seven elements can be derived: three phonetically realized, or overt, NPs (lexical anaphors, lexical pronominals, and R-expressions) and four phonetically null NPs (null anaphors such as NP-traces, the null pronominal *pro,* null names or variables such as *wh*-traces, and the pronominal-anaphor *PRO* (Chomsky 1982).

Binding Theory regulates the distribution of both overt NPs (e.g., lexical anaphors and pronominals), as well as null NPs (e.g., NP-traces, *pro,* and so on). Of particular relevance here is the assumption that overt and null anaphors are regulated by Principle A, overt and null pronominals are governed by Principle B, while R-expressions and null-variables (e.g., *wh*-trace) are regulated by Principle C. More recently, Aoun (1986) has argued that all traces, including NP-traces and *wh*-traces, fall under Principle A—a version of Binding Theory referred to as Generalized Binding Theory.

On the other hand Government Theory regulates the assignment of Case to NPs (principles of Case Assignment) and enforces Case requirements of lexical NPs (Case Filter). It is also widely assumed since Chomsky's LGB (Chomsky 1981) that government is involved in the licensing of traces left by movement, which is accomplished by the ECP:

(8) Empty Category Principle (ECP)
Traces must be properly governed.

In some versions (cf. Chomsky 1981 for discussion) the ECP was thought to apply to all empty categories. In more recent studies, however, the ECP has been regarded exclusively as a condition on traces (cf. Lasnik and Saito 1984, 1992 and Chomsky 1986a, b), which is reflected in the formulation given in (8).

Following standard assumptions, the definitions of 'proper government' and 'government' are reproduced below:

(9) Proper government
a properly governs β iff α governs β and
a) α is a lexical category X^0, or (lexical government)
b) α is coindexed with β (antecedent government)
(cf. Chomsky 1981; Aoun and Sportiche 1982)

(10) Government
α governs β iff every maximal projection dominating α also dominates β and conversely.
(Aoun and Sportiche 1982)

The standard formulation of the ECP is disjunctive. It requires either 'antecedent government' or 'lexical government' as in (11):

(11) Standard ECP
Traces must either be lexically governed or antecedent governed.

The standard ECP, or disjunctive ECP, was initially formulated by Chomsky (1981) and utilized in much of the later work. Subsequently, there were a number of attempts at redefining the ECP. Thus, it has been argued that the ECP must be formulated 'conjunctively' (conjunctive ECP). According to the conjunctive ECP, both lexical and antecedent government must be met in order to satisfy the principle. The conjunctive ECP appears in various forms in works such as Jaeggli (1982), Stowell (1985), and Johnson (1988), among others. One might also pursue the idea of a restricted ECP, according to which only antecedent-government is relevant to the ECP, a suggestion made by Chomsky (1986b) in the context of *Barriers.* In the discussion of the standard ECP approach we shall focus on (11), making reference to the other versions as relevant.

A different and very stimulating approach to ECP phenomena has been outlined in Chomsky's *Barriers* (Chomsky 1986b). Chomsky suggests a theory of movement in which the relation between a trace and a moved category ('antecedent-government') is restricted by the presence of 'barriers,' defined in terms of concepts such as blocking category, L-marking, and related notions. Under the *Barriers* model the ECP reduces to antecedent-government. The presence of 'barriers' blocks antecedent government, yielding the phenomena covered under the standard ECP. Subsequently, in an important study Lasnik and Saito (1992), elaborating on their earlier work (Lasnik and Saito 1984) and on Chomsky's *Barriers,* introduce several important modifications in the *Barriers* model and present a different version of the ECP, which they extend to an impressive range of phenomena.

In the discussion to follow we shall examine some consequences of the Binding approach, the standard ECP approach, and the *Barriers* approach with respect to structures containing NP-traces, primarily in Portuguese and English.

3 NP-Traces: Binding and the standard ECP. In this section we compare the theoretical consequences of the Binding approach and the standard ECP approach to NP-traces in a range of data from Portuguese and English. As a preliminary, let us sharpen the main differences between these two approaches.

The standard ECP is based on the concept of 'government.' Both the core notion of 'lexical government' (i.e., government of a category by a lexical head) and the extended notion of 'antecedent government' (government by coindexation with a c-commanding category) are subcases of the notion 'government.' Lexical government is straightforward, but antecedent government requires comment.

As can be seen from their definitions above, the concept of 'antecedent government' utilized by the standard ECP is formally similar to the concept of 'binding' of an anaphor by an antecedent (or 'antecedent binding') utilized by Principle A of Binding Theory, in that both require coindexation with a c-commanding category, though there are essential differences between them. So let us attempt to make the distinctions sharper.

A central assumption of the theory of government is that certain categories (i.e., CP, NP) prevent 'lexical government' from outside. Thus, consider the structures below:

(12) a. John [$_{VP}$ saw NP*]
 b. John believes [$_{IP}$ NP* to be innocent]
 c. John tried [$_{CP}$ [$_{IP}$ NP* to leave]]

In (12a) the verb *see* governs NP* in object position, since there is no category intervening between them, so that the verb can assign Case and theta role to its object. In (12b) *believe,* an ECM verb, has an IP complement. IP does not block government, so the main verb is able to govern NP* in the embedded subject position. In (12c), however, the main verb cannot govern NP* in the embedded subject position since, under the standard ECP approach, CP is considered an absolute barrier to government.[5]

Now, in many cases the same categories that block lexical government (e.g., CP and NP) appear to block also the association between a moved category and its trace, making it plausible to suppose that 'government' is implicated in such cases as well. Consider for instance the structures below:

(13) a. John seems [$_{IP}$ *t* to like Mary]
 b. John seems [$_{CP}$ [$_{IP}$ *t* to be intelligent]]

Under the standard ECP approach a verb such as *seem* allows 'CP-deletion' (= S′ deletion) or, rather, may occur either with a CP or IP complement. Analyses under the standard ECP approach assume that *seem* lexically governs the trace in (13a) because IP is not a barrier, so that the ECP is satisfied.[6] But if CP is present, as in structure (13b), the trace would not be antecedent governed since CP is an absolute barrier to government.

On the other hand the concept of 'binding' by an antecedent (or 'antecedent binding') under the strict version of Binding Theory adopted here (i.e., 'Strict Binding Theory') is based on the concept of 'accessible SUBJECT,' which creates binding domains. Thus, under the Strict Binding

Theory the trace is bound in both structures in (13), regardless of the IP/CP distinction. In both cases the binding domain for the NP-trace is the domain c-commanded by the matrix subject, and the traces are correctly 'bound' within their respective binding domains. Throughout this presentation Binding Theory refers to the strict version of this theory.[7]

In sum the essential distinction between 'antecedent government' of the ECP versus 'antecedent binding' of Strict Binding Theory is that they scan the structure for different properties. 'Antecedent government' searches for 'barriers to government,' while 'antecedent binding' searches for an 'accessible SUBJECT.' So it should be possible to determine the empirical differences between these two approaches. Let us now turn to the relevant data bearing on this issue.

3.1 NIC Effects. In many languages, including English and Portuguese, lexical anaphors cannot occur in Nominative position (cf. Chomsky 1980)—the so-called NIC effect illustrated in (14):

(14) a. John believes [himself to be competent]
b. *John believes [himself Agr-is competent]

Such NIC effects with lexical anaphors are currently explained by Principle A of Binding Theory. In the well-formed (14a) the lexical anaphor is bound (by the matrix subject) within its binding domain (the domain c-commanded by the matrix subject), satisfying Principle A. However, (14b) is a violation of Principle A, since the lexical anaphor is free within its binding domain (the domain c-commanded by the Agr in the subordinate clause).

On a par with lexical anaphors the behavior of some traces, particularly NP-traces, appears to display similar NIC effects:

(15) a. John seems [*t* to be intelligent]
b. *John seems [*t* Agr-is intelligent]

(16) a. John is believed [*t* to be guilty]
b. *John is believed [*t* Agr-is guilty]

In Portuguese similar effects obtain, with the interesting nuance that such apparent NIC effects are found also with inflected infinitives (Quicoli 1976a, 1982, 1992; Rouveret 1980):

(17) a. Os senadores parecem [*t* ser inteligentes]
b. *Os senadores parecem [*t* Agr-serem inteligentes]
'The senators seem to be intelligent.'

(18) a. ?Os marginais foram vistos [*t* entrar pela janela]
b. *Os marginais foram vistos [*t* Agr-entrarem pela janela]
'The outlaws were seen enter by the window.'

As can be seen from (17) and (18), NP-movement is possible in structures with noninflected infinitives but not with inflected infinitives, which shows that NIC effects are related to the presence of Agr (George and Kornfilt 1981; Chomsky 1981). Under the Binding approach the facts of NP-traces in such structures are explained in a straightforward manner. In the grammatical sentences the traces are bound, while the ungrammatical sentences violate Principle A, since the NP-traces are free in the domain of Agr (a binding domain) (cf. Chomsky (1982) for such an approach).[8]

On the other hand there are suggestions in the literature to the effect that Binding Theory should be restricted to lexical anaphors, so that Principle A would not apply to NP-traces (or traces in general), which are assumed to be regulated by the ECP. Thus, Chomsky (1986a) argues that Principle A is redundant with the ECP in NIC structures containing NP-traces and proposes to dispense with Principle A in the account of NIC phenomena (though he maintains that Principle A is still required to account for SSC effects with NP traces; cf. Chomsky 1986a:175ff).

But let us examine more closely the assumptions underlying the ECP approach with respect to such data. As noted in the previous section in connection with (15), standard ECP analyses of NP-movement in raising constructions hinge on the IP/CP nature of the embedded complement. Raising verbs are assumed to occur with either IP or CP complements. A well-motivated approach would be to allow IP or CP to occur freely, letting general principles rule out the unwanted cases. Thus, in principle, raising structures containing infinitives might occur with either IP or CP complement as in (19):

(19) a. John seems [$_{IP}$ *t* to like Mary] (= 3a)
b. John seems [$_{CP}$ [$_{IP}$ *t* to be intelligent]]

Assuming that IP and CP are freely selected, we see that the standard ECP would have no problems with such structures. Structure (19a) would be allowed to surface. The complement is IP so that the embedded trace subject can be properly governed (i.e., 'lexically governed,' as in Chomsky 1981; 'antecedent governed' as in Lasnik and Saito 1984, or perhaps both). Structure (19b) would be excluded by the ECP, since the presence of CP, an absolute barrier, prevents proper government of the embedded trace. No stipulation concerning IP or CP would be necessary for these facts, as desired.

By parity we should also expect IP or CP complements when the embedded verb is finite. Thus, an ungrammatical structure such as (20), in principle, might arise from either an IP or CP complement as in (20):

(20) *John seems is intelligent (= 15b)
(21) a. $John_1$ seems $[_{IP}$ t_1 Agr-is intelligent]
b. $John_1$ seems $[_{CP}$ $[_{IP}$ t_1 Agr-is intelligent]]

Standard ECP analyses usually assume that (20) is traceable to (21b) with a CP complement. Since the presence of CP would prevent proper government of the embedded trace, the structure would be correctly excluded by the ECP. But suppose the structure were (21a) with an IP complement. Then the trace would be properly governed, and the ECP would incorrectly allow the ungrammatical (20) to surface.[9]

Short of stipulating that finite complements must be CP, ECP analyses must rely on additional assumptions (see below). But then NIC effects in such raising structures would follow from such additional assumptions, not from the ECP, which seems ineffective in dealing with NIC phenomena. The same problem arises in connection with English passive structures in (16) above, where identical considerations apply.

The same would be true of Portuguese raising structures. Under the standard ECP approach *parecer* would also have to be analyzed as taking an IP or CP complement. If we assume IP or CP to be freely selected, noninflected and inflected infinitives would each have two possibilities:

(22) a. Os senadores parecem ser inteligentes. (=17a)
'The senators seem to be inteligent.'
b. Os senadores parecem $[_{IP}$ t ser inteligentes]
c. Os senadores parecem $[_{CP}$ $[_{IP}$ t ser inteligentes]
(23) a. *Os senadores parecem serem inteligentes. (=17b)
The senators seem-3pl to-be-3pl inteligent.
b. Os senadores parecem $[_{IP}$ t Agr-serem inteligentes]
c. Os senadores parecem $[_{CP}$ $[_{IP}$ t Agr-serem inteligentes]

The ECP would be able to account for the facts in (22) with noninflected infinitives. S-structure (22c) with a CP complement would be excluded as an ECP violation, since the presence of CP blocks government of the trace. However, S-structure (22b) with an IP complement is permitted by the ECP since the trace is properly governed across IP, so that (22a) is correctly allowed by the ECP.

But consider now the problem posed by (23) with an inflected infinitive complement. Here, sentence (23a) is ungrammatical, and both S-structures (23b) and (23c) must be excluded. The ECP is able to exclude (23c) since the presence of CP prevents proper government of the trace. But in the case of structure (23b) with an IP complement, the trace would be able to be properly governed, leading the ECP approach to an incorrect prediction.

Again, the ECP approach would require additional assumptions depending on whether the complement is an inflected or a noninflected infinitive, just like in the case of English finite versus infinitival complements. Notice that the same problem would arise in the case of Portuguese passive structures in (18), where identical considerations apply.

By contrast, as noted, none of these facts pose problems for the Binding approach. NP-extraction out of finite clauses in Portuguese and English, as well as NP extraction out of inflected infinitives in Portuguese, constitutes NIC effects and would be correctly ruled out by Principle A of Binding Theory.

Before moving to another topic let us consider a third possibility to account for NIC effects, which has been suggested by Chomsky (1986a). Notice that one might propose that NIC effects such as the above are actually excluded neither by the ECP nor by Principle A, but rather by an independent principle, the Chain Condition (Chomsky 1986a:136), which excludes structures in which an NP chain receives more than one Case. Since in the examples above this clearly happens, it could be argued that such facts are ruled out by the Chain Condition.

Of course, it would be more desirable if the effects of the Chain Condition could be subsumed under more general principles. In fact, there seems to be some evidence to show that such a condition against double Case assignment fails in NIC effects, while Principle A holds, which suggests that the Chain Condition may be reduced to Principle A. Consider for example the facts in (24), given with its D-structure and S-structure in (25):

(24) *It seems John to be likely is concerned.

(25) a. It seems [$_{NP}$ to be likely [John Agr-is concerned]]

b. It seems [John-Nom to be likely [*t* Agr-is concerned]]

In D-structure (25a) the NP subject of 'be likely' is empty, forcing movement of the embedded subject 'John' to that position,[10] so as to produce S-structure (25b). Notice that in S-structure (25b), 'John' has a unique Case (Nominative), assigned by the Agr of the embedded predicate 'is concerned.' Further, since 'John' has Case, there is no need to raise it to the matrix subject position of 'seem' (the standard assumption being that raising is obligatory with 'seem' in order for the subject to receive Case; cf. Chomsky 1982, Quicoli 1992). Notice further that other familiar principles are not violated. The Case Filter is satisfied, and the movement is permitted by Subjacency. More importantly, notice that the Chain Condition is not violated since 'John' has only one Case: the predicate 'be likely' is a regular infinitive, and 'seem' is not an ECM verb. Yet (24) is clearly ungrammatical—an incorrect prediction of the Chain Condition.

By contrast, facts above can be explained straightforwardly if we assume that Principle A applies to NP-traces. As can be seen from S-structure (25b), the NP-trace is free in its binding domain (the domain created by the embedded Agr), so that the structure is correctly excluded as a violation of Principle A. Such facts therefore provide evidence in favor of Principle A and against both the standard ECP and the Chain Condition.

A similar phenomenon bearing on the issue concerning Principle A and the Chain Condition has to do with the behavior of Portuguese clitics, which display NIC effects similar to those observed in NP-movement structures (cf. Quicoli 1976a and 1992). Thus, clitic movement is possible with noninflected infinitives but not with inflected infinitives:

(26) a. José nos viu sair.
José us saw leave
'José saw us leave.'
b. José nos_1 viu [t_1 sair]

(27) a. *José nos viu sairmos.
José us saw leave-1pl.
b. José nos_1 viu [t_1 Agr-sairmos]

The clitic facts above would pose a problem for the standard ECP approach. If IP or CP complements are freely selected, the trace in (26b) would be properly governed when the complement is IP, so that the ECP would not be able to exclude the ungrammatical (27b). Further, notice that familiar principles such as Subjacency and the Case Filter are not violated and hence cannot rescue the ECP. More importantly for the issue at hand, notice that the Chain Condition cannot exclude (27b) either, since in S-structure (27b) the clitics would have only one Case. Thus, we see that under either the standard ECP or the Chain Condition NIC effects such as (27) appear to be quite problematic.

However, as before, a plausible explanation can be given if we assume that Principle A applies also to clitic traces (as argued in Quicoli 1976a, 1980, 1992; Kayne 1975, 1981; Rouveret and Vergnaud 1980; and Varela 1988, among others), though there are differing views on the matter.[11] The clitic facts in (26) and (27) here are parallel to the paradigm of NP-traces in (22) and(23) and under the Binding approach they would be explained by Principle A exactly in the same way. The well-formed (26) is permitted since the clitic trace is correctly bound in its binding domain. But in the ill-formed (27) the presence of the Agr of the inflected infinitive creates a binding domain and the trace is not bound within this domain, so that the structure is correctly excluded as a violation of Principle A.

3.2 Complement structure and NP/wh combinations. As noted in the above section in connection with (3), the standard ECP approach to NP movement in raising structures hinges greatly on the nature of the IP/CP nature of the embedded complement. Under the Binding approach (assuming the Strict Binding Theory), this is not crucial since 'binding' looks for 'accessible subjects' instead of 'barriers to government.'

Consider in this regard the problem posed by NP/*wh* combinations such as the following:

(28) a. Quem os senadores parecem ter visitado?
Who the senators seem-3pl to have visited.
b. Quem$_2$ eles Agr-parecem [$_{CP}$ t_2 [$_{IP}$ t_1 ter visitado t_2]]
(29) a. Who did they seem to have visited?
b. Who$_2$ did they$_1$ seem [t_2 [t_1 to have visited t_2]]

Such examples pose problems for the ECP approach. Because of subjacency considerations, *wh*-movement must first move to the lower CP, hence the complement must be CP. This would ensure that the *wh*-trace in object position is properly governed (in this case it is both lexically governed and antecedent governed). However, since the complement is CP, the NP-trace in subject position is neither antecedent governed nor lexically governed, so that the ECP would exclude such sentences—an incorrect prediction of the ECP.

One might invoke a rule of CP-deletion for such cases, so as to allow the embedded NP trace to be lexically governed by the matrix verb. However, this seems tó be a rather dubious move in light of current results. Thus, in more articulated ECP analyses such as Lasnik and Saito (1984), it is argued that 'proper government' of arguments, as in the present case, must be done at S-structure. Assuming this, their 'gamma-marking' mechanism would apply to (28b) and (29b), marking the object trace [$+\gamma$], and the subject trace [$-\gamma$] indicating that the latter is not properly governed, yielding an ECP violation. Since deletion of the trace under CP can only occur at LF (cf. Lasnik and Saito 1992:95), it is not possible to invoke CP-deletion at S-structure in order to allow *seem* to lexically govern the trace.[12]

On the other hand the behavior of NP traces in NP/*wh* combinations such as P(28) and E(29) above presents no problem for the Binding approach. The NP-trace in such structures is bound, satisfying Principle A. As for *wh*-traces, as noted before, there are a number of possibilities available at the moment. One hypothesis (cf. Freidin and Lasnik 1981, Chomsky 1981), is that *wh*-traces are 'variables' and are thus subject to Principle C rather than Principle A of Binding Theory. According to another hypothesis, Aoun's Generalized Binding Theory (Aoun 1986), the relation between *wh*-traces and their antecedents (in fact all traces) is also regulated by Principle A of Binding Theory. Choosing among these hypotheses is a difficult matter. Here I will tentatively assume that *wh*-traces also require Principle A, as in Generalized Binding Theory, although this is not crucial to this discussion.

3.3 *That*-trace and NIC effects. As is well-known, in finite '*that*-clauses' *wh*-extraction of objects and subjects appears to yield systematic cross-linguistic differences. Thus, *wh*-extraction of objects in such structures is possible in a null subject language such as Portuguese and in an overt subject language like English:

(30) a. Quem parece que os embaixadores admiram?
b. Quem [$_{IP}$ NP parece [$_{CP}$ que [$_{IP}$ os embaixadores admiram *t*]
(31) a. Who does it seem that the ambassadors admire?
b. Who does [$_{IP}$ it seem [$_{CP}$ that [$_{IP}$ the ambassadors admire *t*]

However, *wh*-extraction of a subject in such structures in general is permitted in null subject languages but not in overt subject languages:

(32) Que embaixadores parece que chegaram?
(33) *Which ambassadors does it seem that arrived?

Such effects ('subject-object asymmetries') have been attributed to differences in lexical government and are taken to constitute evidence in favor of the ECP. An appealing explanation, due to Rizzi (1982), is that *wh*-movement from object position, as in P(30) and E(31), would systematically leave a lexically governed trace, satisfying the ECP. However, *wh*-extraction of a subject is related to parametric differences. It is permitted in null subject languages because such languages allow 'free subject-verb inversion (i.e., 'free inversion'), while overt subject languages do not. Thus, according to Rizzi's analysis, the possibility of subject extraction here correlates with the following difference in structure between Portuguese and English:

(34) Que embaixadores [*pro* parece [*t* que [(*t*) chegaram *t′*]

(35) Which ambassadors [does it seem [*t* that [*t* arrived]

In a language that allows null subjects such as Portuguese,[13] 'free inversion' would provide a lexical governor for the trace of the postposed subject (*t′*), so that P(32) would be allowed by the ECP. On the other hand overt subject languages such as English do not allow free inversion, and hence extraction of the subject would leave a lexically ungoverned trace in subject position, so that E(33) would be excluded as a violation of the ECP. Notice that the explanation above hinges exclusively on lexical government, while antecedent government plays no explanatory role, since the traces would be antecedent governed by the trace in CP in both languages.

However, we see that such an ECP account would make incorrect predictions in the case of NP-traces. Thus, consider the effect of NP movement in the same structures:

(36) P. *Os embaixadores parecem que chegaram.

(37) E. *The ambassadors seem that arrived.

If we assume that Portuguese allows 'free inversion,' we should expect free inversion to provide a lexical governor for the NP-trace in such structures, while the absence of free inversion in English would leave an ungoverned trace in subject position in this language, as before. Thus, given the ECP analysis above, we should expect P(36) to be well formed and E(37) to be ill formed. However, such structures are ill formed in both languages, contradicting the ECP hypothesis. As we see, contrary to Rizzi's hypothesis, the facts pertaining to *that*-trace effects in null subject versus overt subject languages do not, in fact, provide evidence for the ECP since the assumptions needed to account for *wh*-traces are contradicted by the facts of NP-traces and vice versa. There is thus no support for the ECP approach derived from such data.

In light of the above one might propose that instead of lexical government, what is involved in such cases is actually antecedent government. That would account for the NP structures in P(36) and E(37), but the ECP explanation given for the differences involving the *that*-trace effect in P(32) and E(33) would be voided. In fact, the ECP analysis of these facts becomes equivalent to a Generalized Binding analysis.

The approach I would like to suggest is as follows. Let us assume the Portuguese situation to be the general case, with *that*-trace effects in English representing a special case—a rather problematic phenomenon at the moment.[14] In Portuguese *that*-clauses extraction of a subject can be accomplished by *wh*-movement but not by NP-movement. Under the Binding approach NP-movement out of such structures as in P(36) (and E(37)) would be correctly excluded by Principle A, while *wh*-movement in P(32) would be permitted by assuming either that *wh*-traces are subject to Principle A (as in Aoun's Generalized Binding approach) or that they are exempt from Principle A but subject to Principle C. Either way the facts would be unproblematic for the Binding approach.

Before leaving this topic let us briefly examine an interesting paradigm involving the inflected versus noninflected infinitive observed in Portuguese examples such as the ones below (cf. Quicoli 1982, 1992; Rouveret 1980):

(38) a. As notícias parece que tem asas.
b. *As notícias parecem que tem asas
The news-3 pl seem-3 sg that have-3pl wings
'It seems that the news has wings.'

(39) a. As notícias parece terem asas.
b. *As notícias parecem terem asas
The news-3pl seem-3sg to have-3pl wings
'It seems that the news have wings.'

In the well-formed (a) sentences the moved NP *as notícias* must agree only with the subordinate verb—the finite verb in (38a) and the inflected infinitive in (39a). If the moved NP agrees also with *parecer*, as in (38b) and (39b), the resulting sentences are ungrammatical. As argued in Quicoli (1976, 1982, 1992) such contrasts are because (38a) and (39a) involve topicalization (e.g. *wh*-type of movement), while the ungrammatical (38b) and (39b) involve NP-movement, resulting in a NIC effect. According to our analysis, the structures corresponding to such sentences are as follows:

(40) a. $[_{CP}$ as notícias $[_{IP}$ *pro* parece $[_{CP}$ *t'* que [*t* Agr-tem asas]]]]
b. $[_{IP}$ as notícias parecem $[_{CP}$ que [*t* Agr-tem asas]]]

(41) a. $[_{CP}$ as notícias $[_{IP}$ *pro* parece $[_{CP}$ *t'* $[_{IP}$ *t* Agr-terem asas]]]]
b. $[_{IP}$ as notícias parecem $[_{CP}$ $[_{IP}$ *t* Agr-terem asas]]]

As we can see, the patterns here correspond to the examples involving *wh*-movement and NP-movement discussed above, so that identical considerations apply. Under the standard ECP approach, if we assume that the traces are 'lexically governed' via 'free inversion' to allow topicalized structures such as (40a) and (41a), we would not be able to account for the facts of NP-movement in (40b) and (41b), which are problematic under the standard ECP approach.

Under the Binding approach structures with NP-traces such as (40b) and (41b) would be NIC effects and would be correctly ruled out by Principle A. Structures involving topicalization (which behaves like *wh*-movement) would be allowed under either the assumption that such traces involve Principle A (Aoun's Generalized Binding), or the assumption that *wh*-traces are regulated by Principle C, so that the facts are unproblematic, raising the question of whether the ECP is needed to account for such facts.

3.4 SSC and super-raising effects. As is well known, lexical anaphors display typical SSC effects, as illustrated below:

(42) John believes [Mary to like only herself]
(43) *John believes [Mary to like only himself]

Such SSC effects with lexical anaphors are widely believed to be explained by Principle A of Binding Theory. As pointed out since the early days of current Binding Theory (Chomsky 1973, 1975), SSC appears to occur also with NP-traces. A standard example is (44):

(44) E. *The Zapatistas seem [José to admire *t*]
P. *Os Zapatistas parecem [José admirar *t*]

Under the Binding approach such structures would violate Principle A in an obvious way and would be excluded. Under the standard ECP approach the traces would be lexically governed, so that such structures are problematic, requiring other assumptions. In this case these structures must be excluded by the Case Filter, which rescues the ECP analysis.

Consider now familiar examples involving SSC/NIC effects, such as the following:

(45) E. *The Zapatistas seem [that [José admires *t*]
P. *Os Zapatistas parecem [que [José admira *t*]

Here the Case Filter is inapplicable. Under the Binding approach these are unproblematic; the structures would be ruled out by Principle A, as before.

However, under the standard ECP approach, the trace in such structures would be lexically governed by the embedded verb and constitute a problem for the ECP, requiring recourse to other conditions. Thus, it is sometimes argued that such structures would actually be permitted by the standard ECP but would be ruled out by Chomsky's (1986a) Chain Condition, which prevents double Case assignment to an NP chain. Of course this diminishes the empirical content of the standard ECP and raises the further question of whether the Chain Condition is sufficient to rule out SSC effects that escape the ECP.

Recall that we have already argued that the Chain Condition is not sufficient to rule out NIC effects with NP-traces that escape the ECP, so that Principle A is required. So the question here is whether the Chain Condition can be relied on to rule out SSC effects, supplementing the ECP.

Consider in this regard the problem posed by structures involving the passive and raising subcases of NP-movement such as the following:

(46) P. José parece ser admirado.
E. José seems to be admired.

In principle such sentences might be associated with long or short NP movement, as indicated below:

(47) a. José$_1$ seems [t_1 to be admired t_1]
b. José$_1$ seems [NP* to admired t_1]

However, under reasonable theoretical assumptions only (47a) with successive short NP movement is a desirable theoretical result. Structure (47b), where the object is 'misraised' in a single long NP movement from the embedded object position to the matrix subject position without going first into the embedded subject position NP*, must be excluded on theoretical grounds. The question then is which of the principles considered here would allow (47a) and rule out 'misraised object' structures such as (47b).

Under the Binding approach structure (47a) would be permitted since the trace is correctly bound in its binding domain, while the theoretically bizarre structure (47b), an (invisible) SSC effect, would be correctly excluded as a violation of Principle A, as desired.

Consider now the standard ECP approach. The ECP would allow (47a), which is fine. But it would also allow the bizarre (47b) since the object trace is properly governed—a negative result of the ECP. Notice now that the Chain Condition cannot exclude the theoretically undesirable (47b) either. The embedded verb is passive and does not assign Case to its object, so that the misraised object receives Case once, in the matrix clause. Thus, neither the standard ECP nor the Chain Condition can exclude the theoretically bizarre (47b)—a negative theoretical result for both these principles.

Notice further that other principles such as Subjacency, the Theta Criterion, and the Case Filter would also not be able to block the unwanted (47b). Subjacency is respected. The Case Filter is also satisfied, since the subject receives Case under the matrix subject position. Finally, the Theta Criterion is also satisfied, since the misraised object receives only one theta-role from the embedded verb.

It thus appears from the above facts that the desirable theoretical results can only be obtained here if we assume that Principle A applies to NP-traces. The facts in question thus provide evidence showing that Principle A is indeed required in the explanation of NP-trace phenomena.

A similar argument can be constructed on the basis of the behavior of Portuguese clitics, which also display SSC effects (cf. Quicoli 1976a) comparable to those found in cases of NP-movement discussed above:

(48) a. José nos viu insultar Pedro.
'José saw us insult Pedro.'
b. José nos_1 viu [t_1 insultar Pedro]

(49) a. *José nos viu Pedro insultar.
José saw Pedro insult us.
b. José nos_1 viu [Pedro insultar t_1]

The standard ECP would be able to account for (48). However, (49) is problematic. Since the clitic is lexically marked by the embedded verb, the ECP is satisfied. Further, since the clitic in (49) has only one Case, the Chain Condition is again not applicable, which shows once again that such a condition is not sufficient to account for SSC effects that escape the ECP. It is thus difficult to see how such facts can be accounted for under the standard ECP approach.

Under the Binding approach, however, such facts are unproblematic. Assuming that Principle A applies also to clitic traces, the principle would allow the well-formed (48), since the clitic trace is bound within its binding domain. At the same time, the ill-formed (49) would be correctly excluded as a Principle A violation since the clitic trace is not bound in its binding domain.

As an additional test case, consider the problem posed by 'super-raising' structures such as (50):

(50) a. *John seems that it is likely to win.
b. John_1 seems $[_{CP}$ that $[_{IP}$ it is likely $[_{IP}$ t_1 to win]]]

Under the standard ECP approach the embedded trace would be lexically governed by the matrix adjective, satisfying the standard ECP. The only principle blocking such structures is Subjacency. However, subjacency violations yield relatively mild effects in acceptability, while (50) is severely deviant, suggesting that other principles are also violated. But since the ECP is satisfied, the ECP cannot be used to explain the severity of deviation. Nor can the Chain Condition, since the misraised subject in such examples has only one Case.

On the other hand, assuming the Binding approach, (50) violates both Subjacency and Principle A, since the embedded subject trace is free in its binding domain. The double violation would explain why (50) is more severely deviant than cases where only Subjacency is violated. Thus, the Binding approach provides a better account of the facts of super-raising than the standard ECP approach.

As a final problem, consider 'object misraising' structures such as (51) discussed by Lasnik and Saito (1992:129), who attribute it to Mark Baker:

(51) a. *John seems that it was told that Mary is a genius.
b. John_1 seems [that it was told t_1 [that Mary is a genius]]

Here the object 'John' was raised from the object position of *told* to the matrix subject position, and the sentence is clearly ill-formed. The NP trace is 'lexically governed' (hence properly governed), since it is the theta-marked object of *told.* So the standard ECP would not exclude such sentences. Moreover, since the embedded verb is passive, it cannot assign Case; consequently, the misraised object would be assigned Case only once in the matrix clause, so that the Chain Condition against double Case assignment cannot exclude such structures either. Under the standard ECP such facts are thus quite problematic.

By contrast such ungrammatical examples can be correctly excluded if we assume that Principle A applies to NP-traces. The embedded clause is a double binding domain for the trace (a combined SSC/NIC effect), created by the presence of both the embedded subject and the Agr of the finite verb, constituting a 'strong binding domain.' Since the trace is free in its binding domain, the sentence is excluded as a violation of Principle A—a strong violation in this case because of the presence of the 'strong binding domain'—which would explain the higher degree of deviance of such examples.[15]

3.5 Conclusion. Let us now conclude this part of the discussion. In the various sections above we have examined a number of specific situations in which the standard ECP—even when supplemented by additional assumptions, particularly the Chain Condition barring double Case assignment—seems to be deficient in the account of NP-trace and related phenomena. At the same time we have seen that such problems can be resolved if we assume that Principle A of Binding theory applies to NP-traces. Although the evidence discussed here is quite limited and hence not sufficient to invalidate the standard ECP, it suggests that the effects of Principle A as it applies to NP-traces cannot be subsumed under the standard ECP. We thus conclude that Principle A provides an explanation for a significant range of NP-trace phenomena that is not explained by other principles and is thus necessary for the explanation of NP-traces, regardless of the status of the standard ECP.

4 *Barriers* and Binding Domains. Thus far we have compared the Binding approach to the standard ECP approach. As noted, Binding Theory relies on the concept of 'accessible SUBJECT,' while the standard ECP relies on the concept of 'government' (lexical government and antecedent government) and categories that block government relations. In *Barriers,* Chomsky (1986b) outlines a far-reaching theory attempting to integrate the theory of movement (i.e., principles such as Subjacency and the CED) and the theory of government (ECP). The central idea is to develop a theory of 'barriers' to the effect that the same categories in the same structural configurations constitute barriers precluding both movement and government. The theory of movement proposed in *Barriers* will not be of concern here. Instead, we shall focus on the *Barriers* approach to ECP phenomena and compare this approach to the Binding approach in light of some relevant data involving NP-traces.

4.1 The *Barriers* model and binding. According to the *Barriers* model (henceforth 'B-model'), the relation between a moved category and its trace in general reduces to 'antecedent government' (the ECP). Certain categories in certain structural configurations act as 'barriers' preventing the association of a moved category and its trace across them, with the result that such structures would violate the requirement of 'antecedent government,' thus violating the ECP.

To define 'barrier,' Chomsky first introduces the notion of 'blocking category' (BC) and then defines 'barriers' in terms of 'blocking categories.' Blocking categories are in turn defined in terms of L-marking (which is accomplished by 'theta-marking' or 'theta government'). Essentially, a blocking category that is L-marked does not constitute a barrier, so that 'antecedent government' can go through it, while a category that is not L-marked constitutes a barrier to such a relation. As Chomsky correctly notes, the concept of 'government' (including 'lexical government') cannot play any role in the definition of 'barriers,' to avoid circularity. Hence, the concept of 'lexical government,' the core notion of the standard ECP, no longer plays a role in the explanation of trace phenomena under the model, so that the ECP reduces to 'antecedent government' (coindexation).

To illustrate the B-model, consider the analysis of *wh*-sentences such as (52), given with their respective D-structures in (53):

(52) P. Quem você viu?
Who you saw?
E. Who did you see?

(53) P. $[_{CP}$ $[_{IP}$ você $[_{VP}$ viu quem]]]]
E. $[_{CP}$ $[_{IP}$ you $[_{VP}$ saw who]]]]

Under the B-model movement of the *wh*-phrase (*who*/*quem*) directly from object position to the CP would yield an ill-formed structure. VP would be a barrier preventing antecedent government of the object trace by the *wh*-phrase under CP, so that the structure would be in violation of the ECP. To permit sentences such as (52), Chomsky proposes that *wh*-movement first adjoins the *wh*-phrase to VP, then moves it to [Spec,CP]. Thus, according to Chomsky's analysis, the S-structure for sentences such as (52) would be as in (54):

(54) P. $[_{CP}$ quem$_1$ $[_{IP}$ você $[_{VP'}$ t_1 $[_{VP}$ viu t_1]]]]
E. $[_{CP}$ who$_1$ did $[_{IP}$ you $[_{VP'}$ t_1 $[_{VP}$ see t_1]]]]

The first movement, adjunction to CP creating the subprojection VP′, is assumed not to 'cross' VP, but is rather a 'segment' of VP, so no barrier intervenes, and the trace in object position is antecedent governed by the trace under VP′. Similarly, the trace under VP′ is antecedent governed by the *wh*-word in CP. IP (a 'defective category') is a barrier only when it dominates a blocking category. Since VP′ (unlike VP) is not a blocking category, IP is not a barrier, so that antecedent government obtains, and the ECP is satisfied.

Let us now turn to the treatment of NP-movement under this model. Consider first simple passive sentences such as (55), given with their more conventional S-structure typified by (56):

(55) P. José foi promovido.
E. José was promoted.

(56) $[_{IP}$ José$_1$ $[_{VP}$ was promoted $t_1]]$

VP is a barrier here (the head of IP does not L-mark VP), so that antecedent government between 'José' and its trace (t_1) does not obtain. Such structures would then be excluded as ECP violations. But, of course, sentences such as (55) must be allowed.

Notice that, unlike *wh*-movement, NP-movement cannot adjoin the object to VP and then move it to the subject position, as this would constitute 'improper movement' of an A'- to an A-position, yielding a Principle C violation (cf. Chomsky 1981, 1986b, based on earlier work by May 1981). In view of this Chomsky argues that the S-structure for sentences such as (55) is not (56) but rather (57):

(57) John$_1$ $[_{\alpha}$ be-I$_1]$ $[_{VP'}$ t_j $[_{VP}$ arrested $t_1]]$

In (57) first the auxiliary 'be' moves to I leaving a trace (t_j). This movement is permitted, since it is across a segment of VP. Now, the inflection element I contains Agr and is coindexed with *John,* so that the category hosting 'be' (i.e., α) has the same index as the subject (i.e., j=1). Chomsky argues that the verbal trace (t_j) then receives the trace of its hosting category (i.e., j=1). He then proposes to extend the notion of 'antecedent government' to the effect that the verbal trace ($t_j = t_1$) becomes the antecedent governor of the trace under VP.

Consider now the treatment of raising structures. According to the B-model, sentences such as (58) would have an S-structure as in (59):

(58) E. José seems to be intelligent.
P. José parece ser inteligente.

(59) $[_{IP}$ John$_1$ $[_{\alpha}$ seems-I$_1]$ $[_{VP}$ t_j $[_{IP}$ t_1 $[_{VP}$ to be intelligent$]]]$

NP movement raises *José* from the embedded subject position (t_1) to the matrix subject position. IP is not a barrier. But the matrix VP is, so that *John* cannot antecedent govern the embedded trace. However, Chomsky argues, *seem* moves to the head of I (V to I movement). The inflection element I is coindexed with the subject position, so that the hosting category α has same index as the subject (α = 1). As before, the verbal trace

t_j receives the index of α (i.e., j = 1). Under the extension of the concept of antecedent government the verbal trace antecedent governs the embedded trace, satisfying the ECP.

The strategy I will pursue here, following the Binding approach, is to interpret the *Barriers* model as a theory of movement—encompassing the effects of Subjacency and the CED[16]—leaving NP-trace phenomena to be accounted for by Principle A. In that case movement would look for 'barriers,' while antecedent-trace phenomena, at least in the case of NP-traces, would look for 'accessible subjects.' Under this alternative the traces in (56) and (59) would be bound, as required by Principle A, without the need of extending the notion of antecedent to verbs.

Let us now compare the *Barriers* approach with the Binding approach in light of the facts discussed earlier in connection with the standard ECP. As a first test, consider NIC effects in examples such as the following:

(60) *John seems is intelligent. (=15b)

Since *seem* may occur with IP and CP, there are in principle two S-structures that can be associated with such ill-formed sentences. Adopting the analytical assumptions of the *Barriers* model, these would be as in (61):

(61) a. John$_1$ seems-I$_1$ [$_{VP}$ t_j [$_{CP}$ [$_{IP}$ t_1 Agr-is intelligent]]]
b. John$_1$ seems-I$_1$ [$_{VP}$ t_j [$_{IP}$ t_1 Agr-is intelligent]]

The problem, as before, is how to exclude both such structures. Consider the role of ECP under the B-model. Structure (61a) with a CP complement would be correctly excluded by the ECP. Since CP dominates IP, which is not L-marked by *seem,* CP becomes a barrier 'by inheritance,' thus preventing the embedded NP-trace from being antecedent governed by the verbal trace (t_j), and the structure is excluded as an ECP violation. Suppose, however, the structure were (61b) with IP. Since IP is L-marked by the main verb, IP is not a barrier, and the trace in subject position would be antecedent governed by the verbal trace, so that the ECP would give an incorrect result here, just as in the standard ECP approach.[17]

By contrast, under a Binding approach, as noted earlier, both structures would be excluded by Principle A since in both cases the NP-trace is not bound in its binding domain.

A second problem for the ECP in the context of the B-model arises also in connection with NIC effect with NP traces in Portuguese sentences containing inflected infinitives. Thus, assuming IP and CP to be freely selected, ungrammatical sentences such as (62) might arise from either one of the structures in (63):

(62) *Os senadores parecem serem inteligentes. (=17b)
The senators seem to-be-3pl intelligent.

(63) a. Os senadores$_1$ [parecem-I$_1$] [$_{VP}$ t_j [$_{CP}$ [$_{IP}$ t_1 Agr-serem inteligentes]]]
b. Os senadores$_1$ [parecem-I$_1$] [$_{VP}$ t_j [$_{IP}$ t_1 Agr-serem inteligentes]]

As in the case of English finite structures above, the ECP would give the right results in (63b) with a CP complement, which would be ruled out as an ECP violation. However, in (63b) the subject trace under IP would be antecedent governed, so that the ECP would not be able to exclude such cases, a negative result.

As a third test, let us turn now to NP/*wh* combinations such as (64):

(64) E. Who does José seem to admire? (cf. (28))
P. Quem José parece admirar? (cf. (29))

Following the analytical assumptions of the *Barriers* model, such sentences would have an S-structure of type (65):

(65) Who$_2$ [$_{IP}$ José$_1$ seems-I$_1$ [$_{VP'}$ t_2 [$_{VP}$ t_j [$_{CP}$ t_2 [$_{IP}$ t_1 [$_{VP'}$ t_2 [$_{VP}$ to admire t_2]]]]]]]

Here, because of VP adjunction, the traces left by *wh*-movement would all be antecedent governed, satisfying the ECP. However, the NP trace (t_1) is not antecedent governed. The trace of *seem* (i.e., t_j) L-marks CP. But IP is not L-marked and hence it is a BC, and, since CP dominates IP, which is a BC, CP becomes a barrier by inheritance, so that the verbal trace (t_j, with j=1) cannot antecedent govern the NP trace (t_1). Hence, the ECP would predict that such sentences are ill formed, an incorrect prediction of the ECP.[18]

Under the Binding approach (assuming 'strict binding') such facts would pose no problem. The NP-trace is bound within its binding domain. At the same time, assuming Generalized Binding, the *wh*-traces would also be bound, so that such examples are unproblematic.

However, the argument just given is not conclusive, since under the *Barriers* approach there is yet another possibility. Assuming that IP or CP may be freely selected and that *wh*-movement adjoins to VP, the following S-structure with an IP complement would also be available:

(66) Who$_2$ [$_{IP}$ José$_1$ seems-I$_1$ [$_{VP'}$ t_2 [$_{VP}$ t_j [$_{IP}$ t_1 [$_{VP'}$ t_2 [$_{VP}$ to admire t_2]]]]]]

Under these assumptions the facts in question can also be accounted for under the B-model in terms of the ECP. In (66) the NP-trace would be antecedent governed by the verbal trace (t_j, j=1), as before. At the same time successive VP adjunction of *wh*-movement allows antecedent government of *wh*-traces. In particular, movement from the embedded VP to the matrix VP dispenses with the need of an embedded CP to host the *wh*-phrase. Thus, while such NP/*wh* combinations pose problems for the standard ECP approach, they do not appear to constitute a problem for the *Barriers* approach. We thus again have a Binding/ECP overlap.

However, as we will now show, VP adjunction poses problems that seem to go beyond the power of the ECP. The behavior of Romance clitics is in many respects similar to that of NP-traces (Quicoli 1976a, 1980; Kayne 1975, 1981; Varela 1986, among others), though some problems remain. Consider the facts of cliticization in Spanish examples such as (67):

(67) a. Juan quería comprarlo.
Juan wanted to-buy it.
b. Juan lo quería comprar.
Juan it wanted to-buy
'Juan wanted to buy it.'

Under the B-model, VP is a barrier, so that movement of the clitic from the embedded VP to the matrix VP as in (67) would require VP-adjunction. This would give the correct results here.

However, we see that movement of the clitic from the object position of *romper* to the matrix VP via VP-adjunction would also produce ungrammatical sentences such as (68), associated with S-structure (69):

(68) *Juan lo vio la pelota romper.
Juan it saw the ball break
'Juan saw the ball break it.'
(69) Juan [$_{VP}$ lo$_1$ vio [$_{IP}$ la pelota [$_{VP'}$ t'_2 [$_{VP}$ romper t_2]

Following the B-model, clitic movement via successive VP adjunction as in (67b) would be permitted (cf. the analysis of *wh*-movement in (52)).

Notice that in (69) all traces are properly governed, satisfying the ECP. The object trace (t_2) is antecedent governed by the trace (t'_2) under the VP-adjoined structure, so VP is not a barrier. Likewise, movement from the segment VP′ to the matrix VP does not cross any barriers. VP′ is not a BC, hence not a barrier, while IP is L-marked by the matrix verb and is not a barrier either. Hence, under the B-model there seems to be no way of excluding the ill-formed (68) by the ECP.

The problem here seems rather clear and highlights a basic difference between the ECP and the effects of Principle A. Structure (69) is plainly an SSC effect. The problem here, as seems obvious, has to do with the presence of a *subject* in the embedded clause, which creates a binding domain for the clitic trace. Since the clitic trace is not bound within this binding domain, the structure is correctly excluded as a Principle A violation.

The ECP, on the other hand, is based on a different concept, the concept of antecedent government that is constrained by 'barriers'—a concept very different from that of 'accessible subject' required by Binding Theory. Because of this, the ECP and Principle A make entirely different predictions for such facts. Principle A gives the correct results here, while the ECP does not. So, to exclude such sentences, it appears that the B-model must also incorporate Principle A to exclude such SSC effects with clitic traces, regardless of the status of the ECP.

Notice that the same would be true for NIC effects involving Portuguese clitics in inflected versus noninflected infinitival clauses. Thus, consider the examples in (70):

(70) a. José nos viu sair. (=26)
'José saw us leave.'
b. *José nos viu sairmos. (=27)
José us saw leave-1pl

Assuming free selection of IP and CP complements, one of the options that allows both inflected and noninflected infinitives may occur with IP, as shown in (71):

(71) a. José nos_1 viu $[_{IP}\ t_1$ sair]
b. José nos_1 viu $[_{IP}\ t_1$ Agr-sairmos]

Movement of the clitic to the matrix VP crosses only IP, which is not a barrier, since IP is L-marked by the matrix verb. So antecedent government of the embedded subject should be possible in both cases. Since the ECP is satisfied we would expect both sentences in (70) to be grammatical.

However, (70a) is well formed, while (70b) is not, contrary to what is predicted by the ECP.

Again the facts seem to be clear. The problem seems to be related to the presence versus absence of subject-verb agreement, which implies the existence of a subject. Principle A is sensitive to subject agreement (Agr) and can account for such NIC effects. The ECP on the other hand is not sensitive to subject Agr, but to 'government' and 'barriers' and hence cannot account for the facts. It thus appears that the theory of movement provided by the B-model must also incorporate Principle A in order to exclude such NIC effects with clitics.

A parallel situation arises in connection with the phenomenon of leftward movement of quantifier in French (L-*tous*), whose behavior is in many ways similar to that of anaphoric NP-traces (cf. Quicoli 1976b, Pollock 1978), though the matter is not uncontroversial (cf. note 19). Thus, consider the L-*tous* paradigm below (cf. Quicoli 1976b:588, Kayne 1975:11):

(72) a. Jean a voulu manger tout.
b. Jean a voulu tout manger.
c. Jean a tout voulu manger.
'John wanted to eat everything.'

As (72c) shows, *tout* is able to move from the embedded VP to the matrix VP. Under the B-model a plausible assumption is that L-*tous* also involves successive VP adjunction. This would allow the facts in (72) to be accounted for by the ECP since the quantifier traces in such structures would all be antecedent governed.

Now, parallel to NP-traces, the Q-trace left by L-*tous,* like NP-traces, also seems to display SSC effects (Quicoli 1976b), though the matter is not uncontroversial.[19] Thus, consider the ungrammatical (73), which, according to the B-model, would be assigned an S-structure such as (74):

(73) *Jean a tout laissé Pierre manger.
Jean has everything let Pierre eat
'Jean let Pierre eat everything.'

(74) Jean a tout$_1$ laissé [$_{IP}$ Pierre [$_{VP'}$ t'_1 [$_{VP}$ manger t_1]

As in the case of clitics, if L-*tous* movement involves VP-adjunction, as indicated in (74), all the quantifier traces would be antecedent governed, satisfying the ECP. Yet, the resulting sentence (73) is ungrammatical, contradicting the ECP.

But again the facts seem to be clear: these are SSC effects. What makes the difference here is the presence of the embedded subject, which creates a binding domain. Since Principle A is sensitive to subjects, it will correctly exclude such structures; the trace under VP′ is not bound in its binding domain, a Principle A violation. By contrast the ECP, which is sensitive to other properties, does not appear to able to account for such facts.

To conclude this portion of the discussion, we have examined a number of facts involving NP-traces, and related clitic and quantifier movement phenomena, that pose problems for the ECP—now in the context of the theory of Barriers. At the same time we have shown that in the same theoretical context the facts do not pose problems for the Binding approach to NP-traces and anaphoric-like traces such as clitic and quantifier traces. In particular we have shown that movement requiring VP-adjunction often creates SSC effects and NIC effects that are beyond the scope of the ECP but that can be correctly excluded by Principle A. Moreover, the application of Principle A to NP-trace phenomena and other anaphoric-like traces seems entirely consistent with the mechanisms of movement utilized by the *Barriers* model, which can be enhanced by incorporating Principle A to regulate the behavior of such traces.

4.2 The Revised *Barriers* model. In an important study Lasnik and Saito (1992) introduce various modifications in Chomsky's B-model, redefining the ECP and extending what they refer to as the Revised *Barriers* model to an impressive range of phenomena. Here we will briefly discuss aspects of Lasnik and Saito's Revised *Barriers* model (henceforth, RB-model) as it applies to data involving NP-traces.

According to the RB-model, VP is usually not a barrier since it is L-marked by I, thus avoiding some complications having to do with the need for VP-adjunction in the B-model. Second, IP is not a defective category and, like other categories, becomes a barrier when not L-marked. As for the ECP, Lasnik and Saito define the notion of antecedent government in terms of Fiengo's (1974, 1980) concepts of proper binding and subjacency (Cf. Lasnik and Saito (1992:24, 106)). Their definition is as follows:

(75) α antecedent governs β if and only if
  a. α binds β, and
  b. α is subjacent to β.
  (α is subjacent to β if for every γ, γ a barrier for α, the maximal projection immediately dominating τ dominates β. Cf. p. 106)

According to the RB-model, binding of proper binding (the requirement that traces be coindexed with a c-commanding antecedent) applies to all traces at both S-structure and LF (Lasnik and Saito *op. cit.*:106, 141).[20] The effect of the (b) clause is to make S′ (=CP) and NP 'absolute barriers' to antecedent government "in the sense that only the head is accessible to such government from outside" (*op. cit.*:24). Furthermore, as they point out, 'antecedent government,' unlike the standard ECP, is not a subcase of 'government,' and is more similar to 'subjacency' than to 'government.' As for 'lexical government,' Lasnik and Saito argue (contra the standard ECP) that for this relation to hold the governor must theta-mark or Case-mark the governed category; simple 'government' by a lexical head is not sufficient to satisfy the ECP. Further, they argue that Case-marking and theta-marking also involve coindexation, so that 'lexical government' can be collapsed with 'antecedent government' since the latter also involves 'binding' and 'subjacency'; thus, the definition of 'proper government' is interchangeable with that of 'antecedent government' in (75).

There is, however, an important difference between the B-model and the RB-model with regard to the formulation of the ECP. The B-model employs a restricted version, according to which only antecedent government is relevant to the ECP (call it 'restricted ECP'), while the RB-model homogenizes 'antecedent government' and 'lexical government' (call it 'unified ECP'), thus retaining properties of the earlier disjunctive formulation of the principle. This has consequences. For example, theta-marking may be sufficient to satisfy the 'unified ECP' of the RB-model but not the 'restricted ECP' of the B-model, a consequence that we explore below.

To illustrate the RB-model, passive sentences such as (77a) are assumed to have an S-structure like (77b):

(77) a. John was arrested.
b. John_1 Infl_1 $[_{VP}$ be arrested $t_1]$

Here Infl is coindexed with the subject, just as in the B-model. Infl also c-commands the trace (satisfying (75a)), and it is a head (satisfying (75b)). Further, no barriers separate Infl from the trace; VP is not a barrier under the RB-model, since it is L-marked by Infl so that antecedent government holds, satisfying the ECP.

The approach to raising structures is also quite similar to that of the B-model. Thus, simple raising sentences would be analyzed as follows:

(78) a. John seems to be smart.
b. John_1 Infl_1 $[_{VP}$ seems $[_{IP}$ t_1 to be smart$]$

According to the RB-model, 'lexical government' of the NP-trace by the main verb is precluded in such structures since *seem* neither theta-marks nor Case-marks the embedded subject position. In their previous work (Lasnik and Saito 1984), Lasnik and Saito had assumed that the embedded subject in such structures was 'antecedent governed' since IP is not a barrier. However, under the RB-model this is no longer possible. Since *John* is not a 'head,' it is not accessible for antecedent government (an effect of (75b)). In view of this Lasnik and Saito propose that the NP trace in the structure in (78) is antecedent governed, not by *John,* but by the Infl coindexed with *John* (as we see, an approach similar to that adopted under the *Barriers* approach.)

Let us now examine the RB-model with respect to the NP-trace phenomena that we have been considering. As a first test, let us consider the issue pertaining to the choice of complements. Here it seems that the RB approach has the same problems with respect to the selection of IP/CP complements in the raising construction as the standard ECP approach. Thus, if IP and CP are freely selected, ungrammatical sentences such as (78) might arise from either one of the structures in (79):

(78) *John seems is smart. (cf. (15b))

(79) a. John_1 Infl_1 seems $[_{CP}$ $[_{IP}$ t_1 Agr-is smart]]

b. John_1 Infl_1 seems $[_{IP}$ t_1 Agr-is smart]

In (79a), with a CP complement, the unified ECP of the RB-model would give the right results, since CP is a barrier. But, in (79b), with an IP complement, the subject trace would be antecedent governed by Infl, a problem for the ECP. By contrast, as pointed out earlier, these are not problematic under the Binding approach, since both would be excluded as Principle A violations.

As a second test, consider the analysis of NP/*wh* combinations under the RB-model:

(80) a. Who does John seem to admire? (cf. (29))

b. who_2 does $[_{IP}$ John_1 Infl_1 seem $[_{CP}$ t_2 $[_{IP}$ t_1 admire t_2]]]

Since t_1 and t_2 are argument traces, the 'gamma-marking' mechanism of the RB-model requires that they be properly governed at S-structure. Under this assumption the *wh*-trace t_2 would be properly governed since it is antecedent governed by the t_2 under CP and lexically governed since it is the theta-marked complement of admire. But the trace of the NP subject is neither lexically governed nor antecedent governed from above, since CP is a barrier. Recall that the trace t_2 under the RB-model can delete only at LF, so that CP deletion cannot be invoked to rescue the ECP. Thus, these facts seem problematic under the RB approach.

Under the Binding approach such structures present no problem. The NP trace is correctly bound, as required by Principle A. The *wh*-trace would also be bound, if we assume Generalized Binding, so that such facts are correctly accounted for.

As a third test, let us consider SSC effects. Consider initially the problem posed by object misraising structures such as (81) analyzed in terms of the RB-model in (82):

(81) José seems to be admired. (=46b)

(82) a. José$_1$ Infl$_1$ seems [$_{IP}$ t_1 to be admired t_1]

b. José$_1$ Infl$_1$ seems [$_{IP}$ NP* to be admired t_1]

As we recall, structure (82a) with NP movement in a stepwise fashion, with the object going first to the embedded subject position, is theoretically desirable, while (82b) with misraising of the embedded object directly to the matrix subject position is a theoretically bizarre result that must be prevented.

The RB-model has no problem with (82a). However, exclusion of (82b) is problematic. Since the object trace is theta-marked by *admire,* it is properly governed, satisfying the ECP. Also, since the verb is passive and does not assign Case, the misraised object receives only one Case, so recourse to Chomsky's Chain Condition barring double case to rescue the ECP has no effect here. The Theta Criterion is also satisfied, as is Subjacency, since IP is not a barrier. It is thus difficult to see how (82b) would be ruled out under the RB approach.

Under the Binding approach (82b), as noted, these would not be a problem. Such structures (invisible SSC effects) would be correctly excluded by Principle A, since the object NP trace is free in the domain created by the empty subject NP*, a violation of Principle A.

As a fourth test, straight SSC effects with Portuguese clitics such as (83) also seem to be problematic under the RB approach:

(83) a. *José nos viu Pedro insultar. (=48)

b. José nos$_1$ viu [$_{IP}$ Pedro insultar t_1]

The clitic trace in object position would be properly governed, since it is Case-marked and theta-marked by *insultar.* In addition, if clitic movement involves head-movement, the object trace would also be antecedent governed: IP is L-marked by a matrix verb and is not a barrier, while VP is not a barrier under the RB approach. Similar problems seem to arise in connection with SSC effects with French quantifiers such as (73) above, which are also problematic under this analysis.

Likewise, NIC effects with clitics in inflected infinitive structures such as the ill-formed (70) above would also be problematic, since the clitic traces would be antecedent governed in such structures, so that it is difficult to see how the approach can be extended to Romance.

By contrast none of the facts in question pose problems for the Binding approach, where they are correctly explained in terms of Principle A of Binding theory.

On the plus side we see that the RB proposal is able to account quite naturally for superraising structures such as (84) (cf. Lasnik and Saito 1992:128):

(84) *Bill$_1$ Infl$_1$ is believed [$_{CP}$ that [$_{IP}$ it$_2$ Infl$_2$ seems [t_1 to be smart]]] (cf. (50))

Under the RB approach *seem* 'governs' the NP trace t_1. However, it does not 'lexically govern' this trace, since it neither Case-marks nor theta-marks t_1. Antecedent government also fails. The adjacent Infl$_2$ is not coindexed with the subject trace, while the matrix Infl$_1$ coindexed with it is 'too far' to antecedent govern it since the intermediate IP constitutes a barrier for the trace in question and Infl$_1$ is outside that barrier.

However, as pointed out before, such facts can also be accounted for under the Binding approach. The trace t_1 is free in the domain created by the subject of *seem* (i.e., *it*$_2$), a violation of Principle A. So the two proposals would simply overlap here.

As a final set, consider the object misraising structures such as (85) discussed by Lasnik and Saito (Lasnik and Saito 1992:129):

(85) a. *John seems that it was told that Mary is a genius. (=51)
b. John$_1$ seems [$_{CP}$ that it was told t_1 [that Mary is a genius]]

As Lasnik and Saito observe, the example involves movement of the object of *told* to the matrix subject position and is clearly ungrammatical. As they note, this is a problem for the RB approach. Since the object trace is a theta-marked complement of *told,* it would be 'properly governed,' so that the 'unified ECP' of the RB-model would not be able to rule out such structures, which are thus problematic under the RB-model.[21]

By contrast, under the Binding approach adopted here object misraising structures such as (85) would be correctly excluded as a violation of Principle A. The trace of *told* is free in the 'strong binding domain' created by the presence of both the subject of the clause (*it*) and of Agr, yielding a strong Principle A violation.

To conclude this portion, the discussion above is quite limited in scope and is restricted primarily to NP-traces, and even here many facts were not considered. However, the facts pertaining to NP-traces that we have considered seem to constitute an important diagnostic, since they raise complex problems for the analysis of NP-trace phenomena. From the above discussion we have seen that, at least in the cases considered, the Binding approach gives a better account of the facts than the ECP approach in the context both of the *Barriers* model and the revised *Barriers* model, suggesting that Principle A is required to account for NP-trace phenomena within *Barriers*-type approaches.

5 Conclusion. During the discussion we compared the empirical effects of Principle A applying to NP-traces (the Binding approach) to the various versions of the ECP in the context of the standard ECP approach, the *Barriers* approach, and the Revised *Barriers* approach. In each case it was shown that, at least for the limited range of facts under consideration, the application of Principle A to NP-traces provides a better account for the facts of NP-traces than the various versions of the ECP. In particular it was shown that the concept of 'SUBJECT' (i.e., [NP, IP] and Agr), as required by the Binding approach, in many cases seems to be the only relevant factor determining grammaticality versus ungrammaticality in structures containing NP-traces.

On the other hand the concept of 'lexical government' (the core notion of the standard ECP) appears not to play a role in the explanation of NP-trace phenomena, where it encounters a number of serious problems (confirming Chomsky's (1986b) claim that lexical government may not be relevant for trace phenomena). At the same time it was shown that a certain range of NP-trace phenomena (along with clitic traces and quantifier traces) seems to go beyond the scope of the ECP formulated in terms of 'antecedent government' regulated by 'barriers' (a conclusion shared by Lasnik and Saito (1992), though they suggest a different alternative).

In connection with the *Barriers* model it was shown that movement requiring VP to VP movement (such as clitic movement and L-*tous* phenomena) often systematically creates SSC effects and NIC effects that seem to go beyond the scope of the ECP but that can be correctly excluded by Principle A. Since the application of Principle A to NP-trace phenomena and other anaphoric-type traces seem entirely consistent with the mechanisms of movement utilized by the *Barriers* model and the Revised *Barriers* model, the latter can be enhanced by incorporating Principle A to regulate the behavior of anaphoric trace phenomena instead of the ECP.

NOTES

* Research leading to this article was supported in part by a grant from the UCLA Academic Senate, which I gratefully acknowledge. I am indebted to Claudia Parodi for comments and to the students in my Portuguese Linguistics seminar (Fall 1993) for discussion.

1. For an illuminating discussion of this topic see Freidin (1986). See also Chomsky (1981; 1986a), Harbert (1991), Huang (1983), Yang (1983), and Progovac (1993), among others, for relevant discussion.

2. Notice that, contrary to the more familiar formulations given in the literature (cf. Chomsky 1986a; Huang 1983), no reference is made to 'governor' or 'governing category' in the definition of 'binding domain, since I assume 'government' plays no role in the determination of 'binding domains.' Under the strict version of Binding Theory that I adopt here, 'binding domains' are determined strictly on the basis of the concept of 'accessible SUBJECT,' perhaps with some parametrization due to factors such as the difference between subjunctive vs. indicative mood, as suggested by the facts of long-distance binding in Icelandic (Yang 1983; Johnson 1985) and other languages (cf. articles in Koster and Reuland 1991).

There are many reasons for this. First, there is a certain naturalness in formulating 'binding domains' in terms of 'accessible SUBJECT.' Anaphors, for example, must get their reference from an antecedent in the sentence containing them and are often subject-oriented, so that it is plausible to define their 'binding domain' in terms of a potential antecedent—that is, a syntactic subject or the Agreement element that implies the presence of a subject (see Freidin 1986 for discussion). Second, reference to 'government' and 'governing category' has the effect of excluding NIC effects with NP-traces from the scope of Binding Theory (cf. Chomsky 1986a), which, as argued above, seems incorrect (cf. also Harbert 1991).

Of course, this move has some problematic consequences as well. The most obvious one is that Chomsky's (1981) 'PRO theorem' (i.e., the generalization that PRO must always be ungoverned) can no longer follow from Binding Theory in the familiar way. However, recent studies suggest that PRO may in fact occur in governed positions (cf. Kayne 1991), and have Case (Freidin and Sprouse 1991), so that this may not be a loss of generalization.

3. Some studies include an additional condition requiring that the NP be also 'A-bound.' In my view this is a residue of an earlier assumption (now abandoned). This was necessary for instance under the hypothesis of 'functional determinations of empty categories,' according to which a single empty category is defined 'functionally' (cf. Chomsky 1982:section 5), depending on whether the EC is A-bound or A′-bound—a theory now believed to be untenable (cf. Bouchard 1984). Another instance where such distinction seemed necessary is the requirement that theta-marking is restricted to sisterhood in multiple branching structures, which is also believed to be untenable, rendering the A-position vs. A′-position distinction unnecessary, as Chomsky (1993) noted. Thus, at the moment the concepts A-bound/A′-bound, though largely employed, do not seem to have any theoretical reality and must be reinterpreted as informal descriptive terms used in exposition on a par with terms such as 'raising' and '*wh*-island,' among others.

4. As noted in the text, there are at the moment some questions involving the status of *wh*-traces. According to many analyses (cf. Chomsky 1981, Freidin and Lasnik 1981, among others) *wh*-traces behave like null variables. Hence, under present assumptions their behavior would be regulated by Principle C. On the other hand Aoun (1986) argues that *wh*-traces (in fact all traces) enter into an anaphoric relation with their antecedents and, hence, are regulated by Principle A. It is unclear to me at this point which hypothesis is to be preferred. I will tentatively assume Aoun's Generalized Binding version, according to which *wh*-traces also involve Principle A, though this is not crucial here, since we shall focus on NP-traces.

5. This is unlike the treatment in Chomsky's (1986b) *Barriers* model, where the concept of 'barrier' is relativized. Essentially a category is a barrier unless it is L-marked. The *Barriers* model is discussed in section 4.

6. Not all ECP analyses assume this, however. Thus, Lasnik and Saito (1984) have argued that lexical government does not obtain in such structures since *seem* neither 'theta-marks' nor 'Case-marks' the trace (cf. Chomsky 1986b for a similar view), so that the ECP is satisfied via 'antecedent government' of the trace by the matrix subject, which is possible since IP (unlike CP) does not block government. In more recent work Lasnik and Saito (1992) give a different analysis to these facts, which we discuss in detail later in section 4.

7. Recall that some versions of the Binding Theory utilize either the concept of 'government' in the definition of binding domains, as represented by the concept of 'governing category' (Chomsky 1981), or both 'government' and the concept of 'accessible SUBJECT' as represented by the concept of 'minimal governing category,' a functional complex containing the governor and an accessible subject as in Chomsky (1986a). Under the Strict Binding Theory that I am assuming here 'government' plays no role in the definition of binding domains, which are based solely on the concept of 'accessible SUBJECT,' for the reasons given in note 2.

8. For relevant discussion of the issues involving the application of Principle A in NIC effects, see Chomsky (1986a), Harbert (1991), and Progovac (1993), among others.

9. Obviously, if an ECP analysis of traces is to be maintained, at least antecedent government must be able to govern the subject of a finite verb; otherwise, the ECP would be violated in sentences such as (i):

(i) a. Who do you think won the race?
    b. Who do you think [*t*′ [*t* Agr-won the race]]

For analysis of such facts in terms of the ECP see Lasnik and Saito (1992:95).

10. This would be necessary if we assume that principles of economy of the type proposed in Chomsky (1991) require movement to always be induced ("move only when you have to"). Under a theory where movement applies freely ('move alpha' anywhere), raising of the subject to the empty NP position would be an option. Induced or otherwise, it would be possible to derive such S-structures. Notice also that there is no reason to suppose that the problem has to do with the placement of 'it,' which allegedly must be placed in the subject position of 'be likely' and then raised to *seem.* Obviously, 'it' can appear as the subject of *seem* independently of raising, as evidenced by sentences such as *It appears that Bill is concerned.* I am indebted to Claudia Parodi for comments on this section.

11. For relevant discussion see Strozer (1976), Jaeggli (1982), Kayne (1989, 1991), Borer (1986), and Burzio (1986), among others. For a recent approach to clitics under the Minimalist approach see Sportiche (1992).

12. Notice that even if CP deletion is allowed in such structures under more elaborated ECP analyses, the trace subject would not be lexically governed. Thus, as argued by Lasnik and Saito (1984, 1992) and Chomsky (1986b) 'lexical government' requires a relation of Case-marking or theta-marking, not simply government by a lexical head, as here. If these claims are correct, then CP deletion to allow lexical government here would be pointless.

13. There are some questions about Brazilian Portuguese, which appears to be moving toward a non-null subject language (Zubizarreta 1982, Kempchinsky 1984). This would not be relevant to the issue at hand, since the same argument can be given for other languages such as Italian and Spanish, which are the prototypes of null subject languages.

14. Chomsky (1986b:47–48) suggests that *that*-trace effects in English follow from the ECP by assuming the Minimality Condition. He considers the following examples:

(i) Who did you believe $[_{CP} t\ [_{C}$ e] $[_{IP} t$ would win]]
(ii) *Who did you believe $[_{CP} t\ /_{C}$ that] $[_{IP} t$ would win]]

Chomsky suggests that in (i) antecedent government between the trace in [Spec,CP] and the trace in IP is possible since the head of CP is empty. In (ii), on the other hand, since the head of CP is present, the Minimality Condition would make the trace in [Spec,CP] unavailable for antecedent government, so that (ii) would be ruled out as an ECP violation. Unfortunately, however, this does not appear to be consistent with the facts of Portuguese and Romance, which do allow the counterpart of English (ii). Lasnik and Saito (1992:section 5.5) attempt to make their analysis consistent with Chomsky's (1986b) account above in terms of a revised [±WH] feature system. However, since their analysis of *that*-trace facts seems equivalent to Chomsky's, the Romance facts seem to pose much the same problems. For an argument against the ECP account of *that*-trace effects, see Culicover (1993).

15. This hypothesis seems plausible under the assumption that cumulative violations correlate with a higher degree of unacceptability. If this view is in the right direction, Principle A violations should yield gradually worse effects in examples (i) through (iv), as the distance between antecedent and anaphor increases:

(i) ?The boys think that [pictures of each other] are on sale.
(ii) *The boys think that [John's pictures of each other) are on sale.
(iii) *The boys think that Judy will put [pictures of each other] on the wall.
(iv) **The boys think that Judy will put [John's pictures of each other] on the wall.

It is difficult to make precise judgements in such cases. But it seems, according to my informal query of informants, that (iv) is much worse than (ii) and (iii), while (ii) and (iii) are worse than (i), which seems acceptable. However, I will not pursue these matters here.

16. But see Browning (1989) for an argument that the CED cannot be reduced to the ECP.

17. Notice that recourse to the Minimality Condition here does not seem to give the right effects. Minimality cannot preclude antecedent government of the subject of a finite clause; otherwise it would exclude examples such as (i):

(i) Who do you think $[_{CP} t\ [_{IP} t$ Agr-likes Mary]].

So Minimality would not be able to block antecedent government of the NP trace in subject position under IP.

18. Again notice that CP deletion would have no effect here. Since the traces in question are arguments, the 'gamma-marking' mechanism assumed by the *Barriers* model would apply at S-structure and mark the NP-trace $[-\gamma]$ as a violation of the ECP. Later CP deletion would not be able to rescue the structure.

19. For a differing view on the matter see Kayne (1981) and Sportiche (1988). Kayne argues (contra Quicoli 1976b) that traces of quantifier movement are 'variables,' not 'anaphors,' and hence are exempt from SSC and NIC (i.e., Principle A of Binding Theory). Kayne gives essentially two arguments.

The first is that L-*tous* does not yield SSC effects in sentences with PRO subjects such as (i):

(i) Marie a tout voulu faire.
'Marie wanted to do everything.'

However, this argument does not seem to hold. First, as is well known, such structures in Romance often involve restructuring (Rizzi 1982), so that the behavior of L-*tous* in (i) is unproblematic (what seems exceptional is the behavior of clitics in such constructions in contemporary French, which escapes the general Romance paradigm). Second, as shown in the text, SSC effects do occur with lexical subjects. Third, as noted by Pollock (1978:67), SSC effects in general hold in PRO structures of obligatory control; compare

(ii) *Jean a tous certifié les avoir lus.
'Jean has certified to have read them all.'

Kayne's second argument is the acceptance by many speakers (though not all; cf. his note 7) of sentences such as (iii):

(iii) ?Je veux tout que tu leur enleves.
'I want you to take everything from them.'

Such examples suggest that Q-traces are not subject to SSC and NIC. However, this argument is not compelling. As Pollock (1978:section 3.2) has shown, such effects occur only when the embedded verb is subjunctive. When the embedded verb is indicative, NIC and SSC effects clearly obtain; compare

(iv) *Je dis tous qu'ils sont partis.
'I say that they have all left.'

Thus Kayne's argument does not hold. Speculating on the acceptability of (iii), as we know from Icelandic, subjunctive makes binding domains transparent (for discussion of subjunctive in Romance see Kempchinsky 1986). This, plus the fact that *tous* is also a quantifier at LF and, hence, must bind a variable at LF, may explain the marginal acceptability of (iii), though I will not pursue the matter here.

20. This formulation of 'antecedent government' brings the ECP close to the theory of generalized binding. Because of such similarities Hornstein and Lightfoot (1991) have argued that 'antecedent government' is redundant with respect to generalized binding and can be dispensed with in favor of the latter, though it seems to me that more investigation is needed to settle this issue.

21. In view of facts such as these Lasnik and Saito conclude that while their formulation of the ECP accounts for a wide range of NP-trace phenomena, certain cases such as (85) are found to be outside the domain of the ECP. For the latter they argue for an alternative approach based on an extension of Chomsky's (1986a) Uniformity Condition (cf. Lasnik and Saito 1992:section 4.3.3; cf. also p. 107 for discussion). However, I will not examine this possibility here.

REFERENCES

Aoun, J. 1986. *Generalized Binding.* Dordrecht: Foris.

Aoun, J., and D. Sportiche. 1982. On the Formal Theory of Government. *The Linguistic Review* 2:211–36.

Aoun, J., N. Hornstein and D. Sportiche. 1981. Some Aspects of Wide Scope Quantification. *Journal of Linguistic Research* 1:69–95.

Borer, H. 1986. *The Syntax of Pronominal Clitics.* New York: Academic Press.

Bouchard, D. 1984. *On the Content of Empty Categories.* Dordrecht: Foris.

Browning, M. A. 1989. ECP = CED. *Linguistic Inquiry* 20:481–91.

Burzio, L. 1986. *Italian Syntax.* Dordrecht: Foris.

Chomsky, N. 1973. Conditions on Transformations. In *A Festschrift for Morris Halle.* S. R. Anderson and P. Kiparsky, eds. New York: Holt, Rinehart, and Winston.

Chomsky, N. 1975. Conditions on Rules of Grammar. *Linguistic Analysis* 2:303–51.

Chomsky, N. 1980. On Binding. *Linguistic Inquiry.* 11:1–46.

Chomsky, N. 1981. *Lectures on Government and Binding.* Dordrecht: Foris.

Chomsky, N. 1982. *Some Concepts and Consequences of the Theory of Government and Binding.* Cambridge: MIT Press.

Chomsky, N. 1986a. *Knowledge of Language.* New York: Praeger.

Chomsky, N. 1986b. *Barriers.* Cambridge: MIT Press.

Chomsky, N. 1991. Some Notes on Economy of Derivation and Representation. In *Principles and Parameters in Comparative Grammar.* R. Freidin, ed. Cambridge: MIT Press.

Chomsky, N. 1993. A Minimalist Program for Linguistic Theory. In *The View from Building 20: Essays in Linguistics in Honor of Sylvain Bromberger.* K. Hale and S. J. Keyser, eds. Cambridge: MIT Press.

Culicover, P. W. 1993. Evidence Against ECP Accounts of *That-t* Effect. *Linguistic Inquiry* 24:372–81.

Fiengo, R. 1974. *Semantic Conditions on Surface Structure.* Ph. D. Dissertation. MIT.

Fiengo, R. 1980. *Surface Structure,* Cambridge: Harvard University Press.

Freidin, R. 1986. Fundamental Issues in the Theory of Binding. In *Studies in the Acquisition of Anaphora.* B. Lust, ed. Dordrecht: Reidel.

Freidin, R., and H. Lasnik. 1981. Disjoint Reference and *Wh*-Trace. *Linguistic Inquiry* 12:39–53.

Freidin, R., and R. Sprouse. 1991. Lexical Case Phenomena. In *Principles and Parameters in Comparative Grammar.* R. Freidin, ed. Cambridge: MIT Press.

George, L., and J. Kornfilt. 1981. Finiteness and Boundedness in Turkish. In *Binding and Filtering.* F. Heny, ed. Cambridge: MIT Press.

Harbert, W. 1991. Binding, Subject, and Accessability. In *Principles and Parameters in Comparative Grammar.* R. Freidin, ed. Cambridge: MIT Press.

Hornstein, N., and D. Lightfoot. 1991. On the Nature of Lexical Government. In *Principles and Parameters in Comparative Grammar.* R. Freidin, ed. Cambridge: MIT Press.

Huang, J. 1983. A Note on the Binding Theory. *Linguistic Inquiry* 14:554–61.

Huang, J. 1982. Logical Relations in Chinese and the Theory of Grammar. Pd.D. Dissertation. MIT.

Jaeggli, O. 1982. *Topics in Romance Syntax.* Dordrecht: Foris.

Johnson, K. 1985. Some Notes on Subjunctive Clauses and Binding in Icelandic. In *MIT Working Papers in Linguistics* 6. Cambridge: Department of Linguistics and Philosophy, MIT.

Johnson, K. 1988. Clausal Gerunds, the ECP, and Government. *Linguistic Inquiry* 19:583–610.

Kayne, R. 1975. *French Syntax.* Cambridge: MIT Press.

Kayne, R. 1981. Binding, Quantifiers, Clitics, and Control. In *Binding and Filtering.* F. Heny, ed. Cambridge: MIT Press.

Kayne, R. 1989. Null Subjects and Clitic Climbing. In *The Null Subject Parameter.* O. Jaeggli and K. Safir, eds. Dordrecht: Kluwer.

Kayne, R. 1991. Romance Clitics, Verb Movement, and PRO. *Linguistic Inquiry* 22:647–86.

Kempchinsky, P. 1984. Brazilian Portuguese and the Null Subject Parameters. *Mester* 13:3–16.

Kempchinsky, P. 1986. *Romance Subjunctive Clauses and Logical Form.* Ph.D. Dissertation. UCLA.

Koster, J., and E. Reuland, eds. 1991. *Long-Distance Anaphora.* Cambridge: Cambridge University Press.

Lasnik., H., and M. Saito. 1984. On the Nature of Proper Government. *Linguistic Inquiry* 15:235–89.

Lasnik, H., and M. Saito. 1992. *Move Alpha: Conditions on Its Applications and Output.* Cambridge: MIT Press.

May, R. 1981. Movement and Binding. *Linguistic Inquiry* 12:215–43.

Pollock, J. Y. 1978. Trace Theory and French Syntax. In *Recent Transformational Studies in European Languages.* S. J. Keyser, ed. Cambridge: MIT Press.

Progovac, L. 1993. Long-Distance Reflexives: Movement-to-Infl versus Relativized SUBJECT. *Linguistic Inquiry* 24:755–72.

Quicoli, A. C. 1976a. Conditions on Clitic Movement in Portuguese. *Linguistic Analysis* 2:199–223.

Quicoli, A. C. 1976b. Conditions on Quantifier Movement in French. *Linguistic Inquiry* 7:583–607.

Quicoli, A. C. 1980. Clitic Movement in French Causatives. *Linguistic Analysis* 6:131–86.

Quicoli, A. C. 1982. *The Structure of Complementation.* Ghent: Story-Scientia.

Quicoli, A. C. 1992. Agreement and Parametric Variation: Spanish versus Portuguese. To appear in *Current Issues in Comparative Syntax.* R. Freidin, ed. Dordrecht: Kluwer.

Rizzi, L. 1982. *Issues in Italian Syntax.* Dordrecht: Foris.

Rouveret, A. 1980. Sur la Notion de Proposition Finie: Gouvernment et Inversion. *Recherches Linguistiques* 9:76–140.

Rouveret, A., and J.-R. Vergnaud. 1980. Specifying Reference to the Subject: French Causatives and Conditions on Representations. *Linguistic Inquiry* 11:97–202.

Sportiche, D. 1988. A Theory of Floating Quantifiers and Its Corollaries for Constituent Structure. *Linguistic Inquiry* 19:425–49.

Sportiche, D. 1992. Clitic Constructions. Manuscript. UCLA.

Stowell, T. 1985. Null Operators and the Theory of Proper Government. Manuscript. Department of Linguistics, UCLA.

Strozer, J. 1976. *Clitics in Spanish.* Ph.D. Dissertation. UCLA.

Varela, A. 1988. *Binding in Spanish: A Theoretical and Experimental Study.* Ph.D. Dissertation. University of Connecticut.

Yang, D. 1983. The Extended Binding Theory of Anaphors. *Language Research* 19:169–92.

Zubizarreta, M. L. 1982. Theoretical Implications of Subject Extraction in Portuguese. *The Linguistic Review* 2:79–96.

Sketch of a Reductionist Approach to Syntactic Variation and Dependencies*

DOMINIQUE SPORTICHE
UCLA

1 Some restrictive boundary conditions. I want to explore a strongly universalist and reductionist view of syntactic theory that seeks to radically restrict the inventory of (a) variations between different languages and (b) variations among different processes. The general proposal is that (surface) syntactic structure is cross-linguistically invariant, principles are not parametrized, and variation is essentially confined to the pairing between morphophonological properties and semantico-syntactic properties of morphemes.

Syntactic theory has so developed in recent years that some fairly radical hypotheses can be entertained concerning cross-linguistic variation. In the principle and parameters approach (see Chomsky (1981)), languages are seen as sharing a common core grammar of available principles. With some of these are associated parameters whose value may vary along finite discrete scales from language to language. What aspects of grammatical systems can be parametrized in this way? Borer (1984) suggests that parametric differences between languages are found only in the lexicon. Given that a certain amount of lexical variation among languages is incontrovertibly found, the idea of limiting linguistic variation to the lexicon appears to be the strongest initial hypothesis. I will therefore adopt it. Lexical variation itself is not unlimited. Thus, Borer (1984) suggests that variation might be restricted to the inflectional properties of different formatives and the inventory of inflectional rules. In modernized terms we might take this to mean that variation is limited to the inventory and properties of functional projections. This proposal does not state exactly how inflectional properties may vary. If indeed syntactic representations are projected to a substantial extent from lexical properties (as the Projection Principle, in whatever guise, entails), lexical differences could entail the existence of important differences in the structure of syntactic representations as well. For example, if inflectional heads may vary in their selectional or subcategorizing properties, possible structural variation that ensues could be quite substantial. I would like to suggest a stronger possibility, namely, that neither the inventory of inflectional processes nor the functioning of inflectional processes may vary. In terms of functional categories this means that languages differ neither in the functional categories they use in a given syntactic context nor in the inflectional properties correlated with the presence of a particular functional category. More generally, I would like to suggest that syntactic structures are cross-linguistically invariant.

Functional heads either instantiate grammatical properties (e.g., Case, agreement, subordinating functions (complementizers), etc.) or realize interpretive properties (tense, clause typing, clause polarity, focus, definiteness). Clearly, languages differ in the way they exhibit Case, agreement, or tense, if at all. Restricting variation to functional projections is thus quite natural. However, although their audible correlates vary, the properties expressed by functional heads that have a grammatical function are not obviously absent in any language for either formal or semantic reasons. For example, if (structural) Case is a necessary property of certain DPs, and if structural Case is assigned in [Spec,AgrP] (Chomsky (1991), Mahajan (1990), Sportiche (1990)), all languages will have to have Case and Agr even if they are not overtly realized. Postulating variations for functional heads expressing interpretive properties is dubious, if, as appears plausible (are there languages without yes/no questions or *wh*-questions, without definiteness, or without negation?), the set of interpretive functions that have to be expressed and the conditions under which they are expressed are universal. Furthermore, every serious grammatical theory reasonably assumes the existence of phonologically or phonetically unrealized syntactic or interpretive properties, e.g., a non-past tense morpheme in English. This simple observation raises a very general problem concerning the availability of silent morphemes and in particular of silent functional heads (that may be equivalently viewed as features of particular heads) and more generally of silent categories. Because we know that they are not necessarily phonologically realized, their observed absence is not an indication of their structural absence.

To begin to accommodate the cross-linguistic or cross-constructional observed variations in this area, I will resort to a type of lexical difference that is incontrovertibly available, namely, the pairing between a *signifié* and a *signifiant* (*l'arbitraire du signe*), that is, the pairing between morphophonological properties of a given item and its syntactic and semantic properties. Clearly, languages differ as to how the same head is pronounced. As an initial assumption, I want to suggest that this is, apart from lexical vocabulary differences (e.g., lack of a French word for *shallow* or the systematic absence of, say, adjectives in a given language),[1] the only type of difference found in the lexicon. Thus, the sound associated to a particular referent or property varies. This is, of course, a substantial window of variation. However, if it is plausible that there are no syntactically relevant variations with respect to lexical categories, the only type of parameter will concern morphophonological properties of functional heads and in particular how functional heads may be realized.

There are two fundamental types of effects arising from the morphophonological space of variation, which I will address in turn.

1.1 Affixation and conflation.

1.1.1 Affixation. Let us begin with the idea that the mapping from words or morphemes to syntactic heads can be one-to-many. Consider first surface structure words. A surface word or morpheme does not necessarily correspond to an atomic property. For example, neither of the words *derives* or *derivation* is atomic. However, they are usually treated differently depending on the version of the Lexicalist Hypothesis adopted. *Derivation* is usually considered to enter syntax as one nominal unit without further internal structure, as it is assumed that its internal structure has no bearing on and is not dependent on syntax. The internal structure of the third person singular verb derives is syntax dependent (on what the subject of its clause is and whether its distance to Tense is short enough). This means that, fundamentally, it is not atomic from the point of view of syntax. There are a variety of ways to handle this observation. One that has been dominant in recent years is to suppose that *derives* is syntactically two morphemes *derive+s,* each heading a different projection (V and AgrS) and concatenated by a syntactic rule (of head movement relating V and AgrS). In this account some stipulation has to be introduced to the effect that the head of AgrS is both overt and affixal in English. This description of the realization of Agr, or more generally of functional heads, is not cross-linguistically stable. Thus English AgrO is always silent, whereas French AgrO may be overt. In English the future of the present morpheme may be an independent word (*will*), while in French it is a bound morpheme (*-er-*). The French future of the present is a morphologically affixed bound morpheme, while in English it may be a clitic (*'ll*). Finally, the French preverbal definite third person clitic pronoun is a phonological clitic, while in Trentino Italian it is a syntactic clitic (see Sportiche (1993a)). More generally, we find the following kind of variation:

(1) Functional Heads may be realized as silent (covert) or as overt
if overt as independent words
or as bound morphemes
if as bound morphemes
as morphological affixes (with or without segmental content)
or as clitics
if as clitics
as phonological clitics only
or as syntactic clitics (hence phonological clitics)

To take a clear case, the correspondence between the French word *mangeront (will eat-3rdPL)* and correlated syntactic heads is one to many (in fact, here, one to three: AgrS, Tense, and V). However, there is a sense in which it is not a one-to-three mapping, as there are three clearly identifiable morphemes *mang+er+ont,* each corresponding to, and very possibly syntactically generated as, one head. Notice that the English case *eats, eat (eat+Present+3rdSG, eat+present+non3rdSG)* can be treated in similar way if, as is standard, appeal is made to silent morphemes, here Non-past.

1.1.2 Conflation. Some cases of one-to-many correspondences cannot be handled in this fashion. Consider the English form *ate.* Here the word *ate* contains two morphemes in a sense (morphosyntactically: V+past) but is atomic in another (phonologically), and presumably this irregular spellout of the concatenation of two morphemes is stored in the lexicon. Suppose, thinking in derivational terms,[2] that morphosyntactically complex inflectional forms of this sort are always formed by head movement. This forces the existence of lowering rules in syntax: In English, there is good evidence that a main verb inflected for Tense, say Past, does not raise to T in the syntax (since it follows all VP initial material). Allomorphy checking will require concatenation of Past and V, that is, lowering or affix hopping of T to V. This raises problems because (a) lowering is extremely restricted (it seems to occur only with affixes): unlike raising, it does not occur with phrasal movement; and (b) lowering of an affix A to a head H is possible iff raising of H to A is possible in principle. One solution adopted in Chomsky (1991) to explain the second property is to require that, in case A overtly lowers to H, LF raising of H+A to A takes place in order to erase the effects of A to H lowering. Besides the unnaturalness of this proposal (why lower to raise later?), this says nothing of the first problem (why can DPs not lower overtly and raise back at LF?).

Chomsky (1993) proposes a simpler and more principled approach to this problem that explains both (a) and (b). He suggests dissociating the concatenation process itself from the process of checking the form and ordering of morphemes composing a complex word. According to this view—call it the checking approach[3]—a verb is drawn from the lexicon fully inflected, say [[V+T]+AgrS]. This verbal complex must raise by LF to T and AgrS in order to check (or cancel out) the properties of the inflectional affixes, tense, and agreement features of the verb. One immediate advantage of this approach is that it does away with lowering entirely but keeps the idea that head movement is involved. Second, the treatment of suppletion, that is, of forms such as *eat+past=ate,* becomes identical from the point of view of the syntax to that of nonsuppletive forms *like+ed=liked.* Finally, it explains why lowering occurs only with affixes, that is, heads: it will occur only when a word made of several morphemes is involved.

This proposal does not eliminate incorporation as a syntactic process of concatenation. Incorporation could be the result of either syntactic movement or the morpholexical process subject to syntactic checking just discussed. In the first case incorporation takes place in the syntax proper as a result of overt movement, as is the case of, say, preverbal pronominal cliticization in Romance. Call it "syntactic incorporation" (SI). Because the concatenation of morphemes is the result of the application of head movement, we expect (a) that it will always involve upward movement, never lowering, and (b) that the properties of the compound will be strictly compositionally computed (since input from the lexicon is unavailable). When concatenation is not syntactic, call it "morpholexical incorporation" (MI).[4] Because the concatenation of morphemes is a lexical operation, we expect to find (a) apparent cases of lowering (since a word may be generated with an affix whose licensing position is higher in the tree) and (b) noncompositionality of the concatenation (lexical exception, suppletion, etc., or meaning idiosyncrasies, as in the case of derived nominals discussed in Chomsky (1970)). Both phonological and semantico-syntactic information about lexical items is stored in the lexicon. If the lexicon interfaces with the rest of the grammar at only one point, phonological features would be inserted at the same time as others: in this case phonological allomorphy and suppletion are indicative of MI. Alternatively, phonological properties of lexical items are not present at all in syntax and are accessed by morphophonological rules that map syntactic representations onto phonological representations (that is, the 'phonological lexicon' interfaces with postsyntactic representations input to morphophonology only, unlike the 'syntactic/semantic lexicon'). This has some conceptual and other advantages, which I will not discuss here, and the drawback that access to the lexicon occurs twice. If this view is correct, morphophonological suppletion has no bearing on whether MI or SI is involved in concatenation (unlike what is assumed in Sportiche (1993a)).

Cases of morpholexical incorporation or "conflation" are cases of one-to-many mapping from words to syntactic heads. I believe recent work shows this phenomenon to be extremely pervasive, both when functional categories are involved and when lexical categories are involved (thus considerably reducing the actual syntactic variation observed for lexical categories).

Extremely general instances of morpholexical incorporation for lexical categories are illustrated by (an interpretation of) the recent work of Hale and Keyser (1991) on lexical decomposition of verbs and other predicators. They demonstrate that an illuminating account of the existence of systematic gaps in the set of available verbs can be given by assuming that verbs have a sort of internal syntactic structure subject to syntactic well-formedness conditions (e.g., the ECP). For example, they postulate incorporation of the head of internal arguments in a great variety of cases (very roughly: the verb *dance* has the VP internal structure of *do a dance,* with the noun *dance* incorporating into the verb *do;* similarly, *put the book on shelf* → *shelve the book.*). I read them as assuming that these processes take place in the lexicon (their L-syntax level). However, because they are subject to constraints defining syntactic processes, operative in syntax, they should be viewed as belonging to syntax proper (thus explaining why syntactic constraints are relevant). In the perspective of Chomsky's checking approach we can analyze a V+N category such as [*dance*] as generated syntactically in the V slot licensing its V part with its N part incorporated (whether by MI or SI) in it.[5]

We can slightly modify Larson's (1988) VP shell proposal so that it can be looked at from the same point of view. It is because *kill* is the 'lexical' concatenation of CAUSE and DIE that *kill* projects two VPs, one with the agent as specifier and the other with the patient as specifier. Under this modification the lower VP has the same internal structure as that projected by DIE and the higher one as that projected by CAUSE.[6] In effect, this is a contemporary version of Lexical Decomposition analyses.[7] However, because there is a lexical component to it—the verb *kill=cause-to-die* is formed in the lexicon and is listed as such in the lexicon—it is immune to the arguments leveled against lexical decomposition, as nothing prevents these conflated words from displaying idiosyncratic properties beyond their basic 'decomposed' meaning (indicating in the present instance that MI is involved).[8]

Other examples are found in the work of Kayne (1993), which justifies the derivation of the verb *have* from *be+F,* that is, from the verb *be* incorporating a category F (which Kayne takes to be a P or a D—another illustration involving functional categories), or in the work of Bhatt and Yoon (1991), which we discuss below.

Since conflation exists and is available in principle, we must inquire, any time we find linguistic variation, whether the observed variation is not reducible to conflation being used in one case but not in another. This is especially significant where variation is most obvious, the cross-linguistic distribution of functional properties, which involve closed classes.

1.2 Universal constituent structure and recoverability. Perhaps only because of the way in which functional properties differ cross-linguistically in their realization (or lack thereof), one central question concerns variability in the way functional heads are syntactically mapped. Essentially because of the way we construe affixation and conflation and the possibility of invoking the existence of silent morphemes (as English present tense), it seems to me plausible to assume the most restrictive position from the point of view of syntax, namely, that languages simply differ neither in the stock of functional heads that they have, nor in the principles that govern their appearance in structure. Functional heads being associated with lexical categories,[9] I will assume that every lexical category is uniquely and invariantly associated with a set of functional projections, all of which which are always projected with the same hierarchical organization.[10] In effect this is saying that from the point of view of syntactic structure, there is only one language, that is, that syntactic structure is invariant. The price to pay for syntactic invariance is analytic abstractness. Some of it is inevitable but I would like to limit it to a certain extent by requiring a degree of overtness.

The choice among the various modes of realization listed in (1) seems arbitrary from the point of view of synchronic grammars except for the overt/covert distinction. It seems reasonable to require that the presence of a given property be somehow "recoverable." Let us distinguish between "necessary" and "contingent" properties of clauses and other constituents and between predictable and arbitrary properties of heads. Necessary properties need not be overt: their existence is required. Such are AgrO, AgrS, Nominative, T, and so on. Among contingent properties of clauses, predictable properties of heads may be left covert. Thus, knowing what the verb of a clause is, we may infer how many arguments there are and their categories. These arguments may thus stay covert if there is some universal convention allowing the recovery of their content. There seem to be such principles: the content of a covert category may be recovered through some antecedent; or antecedentless covert DPs must be pronouns—*pro.* There seems to be no such general predictability for other lexical categories. As they by definition have idiosyncratic, hence nonrecoverable, properties, they must be overt except, of course, when they have antecedents (e.g., VP deletion, gapping).

Among contingent properties of clauses we also find properties expressed by functional heads. Take clause type (the statement/question distinction) or polarity (the affirmation/negation distinction), for example. The clause type information must be recoverable. A clause is not necessarily a question or necessarily a nonquestion, but it is necessarily one or the other. This suggests that it is not the presence of the functional category that is contingent, but rather the value that its head assumes. A plausible construal of this recoverability requirement is that these values must in a given paradigm, say, of clause type, all be overt save one[11] (thus, nonquestion clause typing may be left covert but question must be overt; affirmation may be covert but negation must be overt; and so on). Whether this is tenable is unclear. I assume for the moment that it is. Making explicit this discussion, assume (2):

(2) *Recoverability Principle:* Optional properties of heads must be recoverable.

Let us understand it as follows: if a head (or some property of this head) is present in a particular location in which its occurrence is paradigmatically optional, there must be a way to recover its presence. We will try to specify how this is possible as we go along, introducing modifications as we proceed with particular case studies.

It is possible that we also find truly contingent properties expressed by functional heads (although it is not completely obvious that they exist). Thus, we may argue that Focus is not necessarily present (some sentences may lack a focused constituent). If so, Focus (and other such properties), when present, must be overtly indicated.

1.3 Movement. Superficially, languages do look different in ways other than the type of realization heads may have, that is, abstracting away from the affixal or the conflated nature of heads. Ordering is the most visible such case. We need to provide other plausible sources for the observed differences. A partial answer compatible with what was said so far is inherent in (1). The relative ordering of a functional or a lexical head with respect to other material in a clause will be affected by whether it is overt, and in the former case whether the head is a syntactically bound morpheme. If it is, it might precede material that an independent head would follow. For example, the respective order of a head and one of its arguments could change as a result of the head appearing before its arguments, instead of after, because as a syntactically bound morpheme it must appear incorporated in another—possibly covert—head to the left of the argument (see, for example, the alternation *an interesting one/someone interesting*).

Ordering differences are not limited to alternation between a head and some other material. We also find such alternations between phrases. Combining ideas of Chomsky (1993) and Kayne (1994), we can reduce this type of variation to the first one, that is, to properties of heads.

Examining the properties of head-initial/head-final languages, Kayne (1994) notes that the expected mirror image distribution of properties in head-initial and head-final languages is not found. Instead, bias toward initial headedness is found. He proposes to account for this asymmetry by postulating that all languages are essentially head-initial and that the appearance of final headedness is given by post-head arguments of a head moving around this head (that is, to its left) overtly. This position is more restrictive than the more usual head initial/head final parameter, and I will adopt it.

Dependencies between two positions exhibiting movement properties are not always realized as overt movement, as the literature on LF *wh*-movement illustrates. A reasonable account of this observation postulates that nonovert movement dependencies between two positions showing movement properties are cases of covert movement as suggested, for example, in the case of *wh*-movement in Aoun, Hornstein and Sportiche (1981), or Huang (1982). We may assume then that different constructions in the same language or the same construction in different languages can differ in whether they involve covert movement instead of overt movement. Kayne's proposal concerning the head-initial/head-final alternations can be straightforwardly integrated with Chomsky's (1993) proposals by construing head-final languages, namely, languages moving (some) arguments around to the left of their heads, as languages doing overt rather than covert movement.

There is an alternative approach to the question of covert movement that simply denies its existence while maintaining that movement is involved by postulating that 'covert movement' constructions actually involve overt movement of a covert element, as the work of Aoun and Li (1993), Watanabe (1992), and Cheng (1992) points out in the case of *wh*-movement. This approach looks quite plausible in such cases. If it could be extended quite generally, cross-linguistic variation based on overt versus covert movement could be entirely eliminated, obviously a desirable move if the overt movement/covert movement distinction was reduced to some independently necessary property.[12] Although I believe there is some advantage to an approach eliminating covert movement, I will keep to the familiar overt/covert assumption, making occasional remarks on the alternative.

The remaining question asks what exactly differentiates overt movement constructions from covert movement constructions. In the cases he looks at, Chomsky, pursuing his minimalist ideas, suggests that overt movement constructions involve overt movement because some phonological property of some head must be licensed. He calls this diacritic property of heads 'strong' and the lack thereof 'weak.' If indeed this could be maintained (and it is surely conceptually desirable—movement must feed the phonology because some phonological property is involved—even though it is most unclear how to do it precisely), it would reduce the overt movement/covert movement distinction to the phonological property of some head, that is, it would fall within the range of parametric properties listed in (1).

1.4 Summary. In sum the general picture that emerges is in effect a generalized version of the Universal Base Hypothesis in which there are no cross-linguistic differences in the syntactic structures of the various levels of syntactic representations: a given ordered set of properties exhaustively instantiated as a string of (possibly covert, possibly affixlike, possibly conflated) heads in any language is associated with a unique syntactic structure. Observed variations arise either (a) because of morphophonological properties of the string of heads involved as in (1), conflation, or (b) because some movement dependency involved is instantiated overtly instead of covertly—quite possibly a subcase of (a). This set of constraints may appear too restrictive to handle the observed cross-constructional or cross-linguistic variations. The opposite is probably closer to the truth. It is easy to realize that an extremely large number of (but not every possible) cases of ordering and concatenation can be generated, given a universal (and possibly invariant) clausal structure augmented with the possibility of leftward movement of phrases and of heads.

Movement plays a prominent role in such a view. I will argue that this role extends to more cases than is customarily acknowledged but at the same time that possible types of movement are radically restricted. More specifically, I will propose that (almost) all syntactic dependencies should be analyzed the same way, say, as movement dependencies:[13]

(3) a. There is only one type of nonlocal syntactic dependency.
  b. There is only one type of local syntactic dependency.

In the rest of this article I will explore ways to substantiate these proposals. Essentially, I will explore the possibility that the only nonlocal syntactic dependency is movement to specifier of some designated projection and that the only local dependency is incorporation.

2 Types of syntactic dependencies.

2.1 A preliminary inventory of syntactic dependencies. The following list illustrates the variety of syntactic dependencies.

1. Movement (landing site, trace): the moved item may be a head or a phrase and must command its trace.
2. C-selection or subcategorization: a lexical category imposes categorial identity on some phrase that it commands.
3. S-selection: a word-level category imposes a particular property on some head that it commands.[13]
4. Anaphor/pronominal binding (antecedent, anaphor/pronoun): the antecedent must command the anaphor/pronoun.
5. Scope (scope 'position,' quantifier): the scope position of a quantifier must command the quantifier.
6. Clitics (clitic, argument position): the clitic must command the argument position it stands for.
7. Polarity items (polarity licenser, polarity item): the licenser must command the polarity item.
8. Quantifier split constructions (English *only, even* or French *beaucoup*): the quantifier modifies another constituent in its command domain.

Recent work extends this inventory to include:

9. Case for DPs (Case position, theta position): the Case position commands the theta position.[14]
10. Agreement processes in general (Koopman (1992), Kayne (1989)) are construed as relations between a head and its phrasal specifier.
11. Number for DP (number determination, NP): the locus of number commands the NP position that has this number (see Ritter (1991), Valois (1991), Koopman (1993b)

How many primitives are needed to describe these relations? If this sample is significant, it suggests that this set is quite narrowly constrained. Putting agreement processes aside, which I analyze as instances of specifier/head relationships, any of these dependencies D obeys two properties:[16]

(4) a. D is a binary relation D(x,y)
    b. One of {x,y} must command the other

where (4b) is stated in terms of some unique appropriate primitive of 'command,' which we will take to be i-command, roughly defined in (5):

(5) *I-command*
I-command (x,y) iff the first constituent containing x contains y, x ≠ y.

These two properties are neither syntactically nor semantically necessary. It is easy to manufacture a language, syntax and semantics, that would use different structural requirements for each of these dependencies. If this uniform characterization is correct, this uniformity needs to be explained. One way of explaining it, and the one that I will pursue, is that there is a central uniformity to the way in which the syntax of these dependencies ought to be construed. I want to pursue a line of explanation that at the most abstract level of analysis simply reduces all these relations to the same one. This approach is inspired by that adopted by Chomsky (1977). There he suggested that, if some constructions had a sufficient number of common properties, they should be analyzed as involving the same process (*wh*-movement in this instance). Carrying this further, I propose that if constructions have any property in common, they should, at the proper level of analysis, be analyzed as identical. Given that movement is essentially a binary relation and that movement is always to a (i-)commanding position, I will suggest that all these relations are cases of movement.

Naturally, these movement relations are not identical. The varying locality conditions constraining these relations illustrate one prominent difference. But this does not affect their being movement processes, as the difference between A-movement and A′-movement demonstrate. Some differences, however, do seem to bear on the question of how to treat these dependencies. Consider again the examples of dependencies listed above, still leaving agreement aside. Each is of the type D(*x,y*), where *x* (i-) commands *y*. This set can be subdivided into three subsets according to the categorial nature of *x* and *y*. *X* can be a phrase, as in phrasal movement, scope (*wh*-movement), antecedent anaphor, or polarity licensing (*None of them gives a damn*). Or it can be a head, as with clitics (see Sportiche (1992, 1993a) and references therein for extensive justification), polarity licensing

(*He denies giving a damn*), or scope (*il ne regardera personne.*). Similarly, *y* can be a phrase (XP movement relation, subcategorization) or a head (head movement).

Thus we find homogeneous relations (head/head) or (phrase/phrase) and heterogeneous relations (head/phrase). We consider each type in turn.

2.2 On the domains of syntactic dependencies. Postulating that all these syntactic dependencies are cases of movement derives both that they are binary relations and that they involve a command requirement. Some finer distinctions appear necessary, as we discuss now, since different dependencies take different sets as domains and exhibit systematically different properties.

2.2.1 Homogeneous head/head relations. Head/head relations are primarily exemplified by head movement constructions such as V to I (in French), I to C (in Germanic), P to V (in English reanalysis, Dutch, or Bantu), and V to V (in Romance restructuring or more generally 'clause union' constructions). These relations are extremely local, a locality reducible to antecedent government imposed by the ECP[18] (see Koopman (1984)) and usually described in terms of Travis's (1984) *Head Movement Constraint* (HMC), which requires that the trace of a head be (i-)commanded by an antecedent without any barrier intervening, that is, that the trace of a head be governed by an antecedent:

(6) *Head Movement Constraint*
The trace of a head must be governed by an antecedent of this head.

Head/head relations are also exemplified by s-selection (linked to theta assignment). Thus, a verb may require of the lexical head of one of its arguments that it be [+animate] or [+concrete]. S-selection as well is an extremely local relation (see Chomsky's (1965) strict locality). Apart from s-selection of its external argument by some predicate—to which we will return later—this locality condition requires that an s-selector (i-)command a head that it selects without any barrier intervening between them, that is, the s-selector must head-govern its selectee:

(7) *S-selection*
S-selection requires head government.

2.2.2 Homogeneous phrase/phrase relations. XP/XP relations comprise a variety of different relations allowing apparently less local dependencies. NP-raising as in *John$_i$ seems to be likely to have been seen t$_i$*, *wh*-movement as in *who$_i$ do you think Mary saw t$_i$* or polarity item licensing as in *Nobody demands that you do anything,* illustrate the apparent unboundedness of these relations. Even though the movement dependencies are analyzed as a succession of small local steps, it is a kind of derivation that is not allowed for head movement. A head cannot move successive cyclically; at each step it incorporates into the next head up (which may be silent) and the combination may move. In another words, a particular head may only move once:[19]

(8) U $[_{WP}$ $[_W$ W+X $]$ $[_{XP}$ $[_X$e$]]]$

Once X has incorporated into W, only W itself (excorporation) or W+X can move to the higher head U.

2.2.3 Heterogeneous X/XP relations. Heterogeneous relations split into two subsets: The first subset comprises the head complement relation such as is exemplified by c-selection. These relations, just like the head/head relations, are extremely local and the locality restriction appears to be the same, namely, head-government: a head may c-select a phrase iff it (i-)commands it and no barrier intervenes.

The second subset comprises exactly the same relations as are found in XP/XP relations—LF *wh*-movement (dependency between a [+Q] particle and a *wh*-phrase, polarity item licensing (e.g., *deny . . . anything*), expression of scope (e.g., *ne . . . personne*—compare with expression of scope in terms of movement, that is, in terms of an XP/XP relation)—and exhibit fundamentally the same properties (for example, the locality of polarity item licensing is independent of whether the licenser is a head or a phrase).

This raises several questions. First, is it accidental that binary relations are both heterogeneous in terms of their domain (a pair head/phrase) and heterogeneous as a set in terms of their properties? Second, why should some head/phrase relations exhibit a behavior similar to that of head/head relations, and other head/phrase relations exhibit a behavior similar to that of phrase/phrase relations? Finally, why do phrase/phrase relations systematically appear to be expressible in terms of head/phrase relations (descriptively, these relations are the same: *wh*-structures, polarity licensing, scope assignment)? This immediately suggests that some head/phrase relations are covert head/head relations, and the other head/phrase relations are covert phrase/phrase relations. This is the line I am going to pursue.

3 Unifying head/head relations.

3.1 Generalized incorporation. Let us begin with head/head relations. It is easy to reduce strictly local head/phrase relations to cases of head/head relations. Take c-selection, for example. It suffices to construe c-selection not as a relation between a head X and a phrasal category P, but rather as a relation between X and the head of P. More generally, it suffices to construe the head complement relation not as a relation between a head H and a phrase P, but between a head H and the head. Given the assumption that every category strictly conforms to the X′ schema, there are exactly as many heads as there are phrases.

But this still leaves one question unanswered. Why is strict locality expressed in terms of either the Head Movement Constraint or head government? If indeed we are dealing with some unitary phenomena involving both locality (no intervening barrier) and also a hierarchical requirement (i-command), there should be a unitary account underlying head government and the HMC.

Expanding on Koopman's (1993a) proposal, which considerably extends the scope of incorporation rules and discusses it in much more detail, we may derive a unitary account by eliminating head government altogether and replacing it by the Head Movement Constraint.[20] This raises no direct problem as the configurations of head government are identical to the configurations of antecedent government by a head, apart from the involvement of movement. In order to achieve this result I suggest that all cases of head/head dependencies are in fact cases of movement.

Consider first cases of s-selection or c-selection by some head H. Let us adopt Stowell's (1981) idea of theta grid, augmenting it to include a notion of categorial grid in the following way:

> A head H will c-select an XP by imposing the categorial feature [+x] and s-select its head by imposing some property [+p] iff the lexical representation of H contains a slot marked [+x,+p] that must literally be filled by movement of some [+p] head X into it by LF.

For example, the verb *witness* takes as internal argument an NP (c-selection), whose denotation can be construed as an 'event' (s-selection); call this property [+event].[21] These requirements will be instantiated as follows:

(9) $[_{V}$ witness $[_{[+N,-V,+event]}]\,]$ $[_{DP}$ D $[_{NP}$N$]\,]$

Lexical encoding of this sort can be further elaborated. For example, the Theta Criterion can be reformulated as stating that (a) unincorporated (argument) heads at LF are deviant; this would replace 'every argument must have a theta role,' and (b) a head with unfilled slots at LF will be interpreted as an unsaturated predicate (and default rules might apply to fill this slot); this would replace 'every theta role is assigned to one argument.' Note that we do not need a uniqueness requirement—replacing 'one' by 'one and only one'—because of the impossibility of moving two items into the same position or that of heads moving twice.

Elaborating still further the internal structure of the lexical representation of the verb, we may encode the hierarchy of arguments that predicates take (external, $internal_1$, $internal_2$. . .) and enforce a particular hierarchy of syntactic realization of these arguments (we need to specify further principles by which these lexical slots can be filled). To give a concrete example, consider the transitive verb *pour.* Assume it imposes the complex of s- and c-selection [+p] on its external argument and the complex [+q] on its internal argument. Then it will have the following lexical representation:[22]

(10) pour (_, _) = P (_ , Q (_))
with [+p] linked to the first slot of P and [+q] linked to the slot of Q

and enter in the following syntactic representation (modified from Larson's 1988 proposal):[23]

(11)
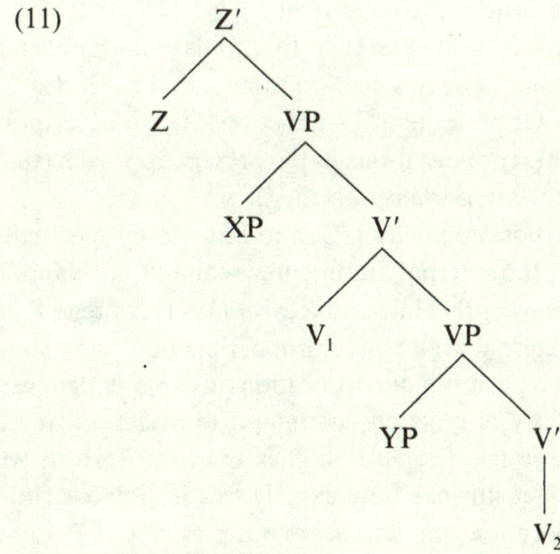

This representation will be well formed if P contains a [+q] head that can (and then must) incorporate into the [+q] slot of the V and XP contains a [+p] head that can (and then must) incorporate into the [+p] slot of the V. Given that incorporation is movement, hence upward only, it means that the verb must move from V_2 to V_1 to allow the first incorporation and then from V_2 to some higher head Z to allow for the second incorporation, namely, that of the external argument.[24]

One important result emerging from Baker's (1988) work on incorporation was that agglutinative languages could be reduced to underlying analytic languages by invoking analytic underlying structures and attributing the observed compounding to a syntactic process of incorporation. The difference between agglutinative languages and analytic languages can be reevaluated given the central role processes of incorporation are postulated to play in general, in particular, to license selection, for it makes all languages uniformly agglutinative at LF.

3.2 Some cases and some problems.

3.2.1 C-selection/incorporation/s-selection asymmetries. If c-selection and s-selection are cases of incorporation, we expect all three to behave in the same way. In some areas they apparently do not. Although all arguments of a predicate are by definition s-selected by it, the external argument is neither c-selected by its predicate (see Chomsky (1965), Carter (1976)), nor can it incorporate into it (Baker (1988)). I have no explanation to offer for these facts (if indeed they are facts), nor do I know of any, however these various notions are construed.

In the case of c-selection it is easy to stipulate the answer in any number of ways. The usual way has been to require that c-selection is only of i-commanded or sister material at D-structure. Such a description can also be stated on lexical representations in the present approach (the external argument slot is not categorially specified).

The case of incorporation is trickier, and I have only speculations to offer. Incorporation of the external argument is required, we claim, by LF. Baker (1988) and more recently Hale and Keyser (1991) contend that overt incorporation of an external argument is impossible (although some care is needed, viz. subject pronoun incorporation in VSO languages). Although this impossibility is typically attributed to a lack of antecedent government because the incorporee is higher than the verb in which it incorporates, it is in fact unclear how exactly this is supposed to work. This is because the relevant asymmetries are not present at LF, sometimes not even at S-structure as, for example, in cases in which the verb raises higher than the subject. Possibly, if indeed the generalization is correct, external argument*s* are not lexical arguments of the predicate at all, that is, they would be neither c- nor s-selected. Their licensing then would have to be done differently (e.g., Spec/head).

I leave this as unresolved, simply making the following programmatic remarks. First, there is no evidence that external arguments do not incorporate at LF. I am led to postulate that they do, although I need to explain why they do not do it overtly. Notice that, given the decompositional analysis of nonmonadic predicates (e.g., *kill*) implicit in Larson's (1988) proposal and reanalyzed here as involving a conflation of several monadic predicates (*cause to die*)—in fact several clauses—the notion that external arguments cannot incorporate appears highly dubious since the direct object of *kill* is indeed the external argument of *die* and may, as direct object of *kill,* in principle incorporate *to kill.* The problem then becomes why the highest argument of a V (whether conflated or not) cannot incorporate to V overtly. An obvious difference is the following: for incorporation of some argument into this V to take place, the verb must raise to a position higher than this argument (to guarantee i-command). Consider the structure in (11): the nominal head of YP may incorporate into V if V_1 raises to V_2 and this is done without category change (V to V raising). In fact, with conflated verbs it is arguable that it is the same V. To incorporate the nominal head of XP, however, this raising must be by definition to a non-V category F (presumably a functional category). We may argue that the target slot within V is no longer available given the derived internal structure $[_F$ F + V].[24] At LF, however, categorial distinction may be irrelevant and $[_F$ F + V] is indistinguishable from $[_v$ V + V], allowing the required incorporation.

3.2.2 Postposed or preposed arguments. If internal arguments must incorporate to their selector at LF, what happens when these arguments appear moved leftward or rightward? Some head part of this argument (the head noun for DPs) must incorporate, we claim, into its selector. How can this be reconciled with the overt movement that arguments may undergo to positions not governed by the relevant selector? The usual reconstruction option is plausible but not general enough. It would work for movement to an A′-position (left or right) but not for cases of A-movement, such as raising to subject, as A-movement does not display the typical binding effects associated with reconstruction. Chomsky (1993) offers a construal of movement rules as a copying process (plus PF deletion)—in effect an enriched version of Burzio's (1986) 'layered trace' proposal—that provides a way to reconcile movement of a phrase with incorporation of a subpart of it into its selecting predicate. Traces are full copies of the moved phrases. Incorporation of the relevant subpart into its selector can take place exactly as if movement had not taken place.

3.2.3 Silent complementizers. The previous proposal suggests an approach to a couple of puzzles concerning the distribution of silent complementizers in English. Complementizer 'deletion' is allowed only in complement contexts:

(12) a. *(That) Mary left bothered Lewis.
b. Mary said (that) Lewis was too fat.

The central generalization concerning their distribution can be phrased as follows (Kayne (1984) or Stowell (1981)):

(13) Silent Cs can occur only in head-governed contexts.

Stowell (1981) naturally attributed this restriction to Chomsky 's (1981) ECP, requiring that silent categories be head governed by an appropriate head (a proper governor, here a head). Such an approach is especially desirable since a silent *that* seems to be allowed precisely in the C projections that allow an intermediate trace of *wh*-movement: *that* may be omitted only in complement position of bridge verbs. The problem with this approach, apparent throughout in Chomsky (1986), is that the ECP applies only to traces (i.e., actually involves antecedent government), not to silent categories in general, e.g., *pro.* But an omitted *that* appears to be the C equivalent of *pro* rather than trace.

This problem can be circumvented within the present approach. Consider a *that*-headed argument clause. Its complementizer *that,* expressing the tensed and declarative status of the embedded clause, is selected by some higher predicate. It will have to incorporate into this predicate by LF. Suppose we look at a missing complementizer not as a silent allomorph of *that,* but as the *trace* of a silent allomorph of *that* that has incorporated in the overt syntax into its selector.[26] Silent *that* will occur precisely in contexts in which it can overtly incorporate into its selector in the syntax. It follows that this can happen only in contexts in which they are head governed by their selector or, to put it equivalently, in contexts in which this incorporation leads to a proper configuration of antecedent government of the trace of silent *that* by its incorporated antecedent. In terms of the list in (1) the difference between *that* and silent *that* is that the latter would have to be lexically designated as a bound morpheme requiring overt incorporation. This extends to cases of clauses that are complements of prepositions, such as *before* $[_C\ t]$ *John left,* which select the silent option of the complementizer.[27]

As H. Koopman (p.c.) suggests, this approach can provide the beginning of a reason as to why only certain classes of verbs allow silent Cs. Manner-of-speaking verbs such as *whisper* do not allow silent Cs but verbs such as *say* do. Capitalizing on the idea of conflation (lexical decomposition), suppose that a verb such as *whisper* is in fact a conflated verb+manner adverbial combination, that is, it is syntactically projected as two projections—say, for concreteness here, an adverb heading an AdvP taking as complement a V heading a VP:[28] To license its internal structure, the verb *whisper=softly speak* will have to appear in the Adv slot binding a silent V in the V slot: $[_{AdvP}$ [$[_{Adv}$ softly-speak$_i$ $[_{VP}$ $[t_i]$]]]]. This makes overt incorporation of the complementizer impossible, as the verb *whisper* is separated from C by an intervening head (the silent V).[29] Verbs such as *say,* which lack this internal structure, allow overt C incorporation.[30]

4 Unifying phrase/phrase relations.

4.1 Generalized Spec/head licensing. Let us turn now to XP/XP relations and nonstrictly local relations of the form X/XP (e.g., polarity licensing). As discussed earlier, it is desirable to reduce them all to the same type of relation in order to explain why they are both binary relations and require the command requirement. There is no a priori bias in favor of unifying all these relations under the movement banner, except that which comes from the discussion of the previous sections: regarding head distribution, movement does seem to be a primitive. Why then introduce any other if we can avoid it? Many of the relations here might be argued to resemble each other because some sort of scope taking is involved (e.g., *wh*-movement, negative quantifier licensing, polarity item licensing). However, a generalized scope approach does not seem to extend to cases of A-movement (subject or object raising) in any plausible way. It is precisely because movement is a formal relationship that we have the (dangerous) freedom to make it encompass everything. This freedom would not exist if all the dependencies were reduced to some general process with interpretive correlates (e.g., scope assignment). The existence of A-movement or head movement shows that we need the additional leeway.

Assuming then that they should be reduced to movement, an immediate difficulty is that it is not immediately obvious how to make head/phrase relations into phrase/phrase relations or vice versa. The structural relations involved, although they all involve command, do not do it in quite the same way. Thus, in a head/phrase relation H/P, the phrasal projection of H contains P. In a phrase/phrase relation XP/P neither contains the other. In order to achieve this unification I would like to suggest that all of these relations actually involve three terms: two phrasal positions and a head. To instantiate this general idea in a way that also captures the i-command requirement, let us postulate the following approach: in each case the relevant property (*wh,* quantificational, polarity, specificity for clitics, anaphoricity, Case, Number, being quantified over by *only,* etc.) must be licensed in the same way: the XP bearing the property P in question can only be licensed in an appropriate subject predicate relationship with the proper predicate. To put it in contemporary terms, the element carrying the syntactic property P (i.e., a lexical property with syntactic reflexes)[31] in question must, in order for P to be properly licensed, be in a specifier/head relationship with a head of the P type, that is, one whose only content is the property P. In other words, for each relevant property P, a configuration of the following sort must obtain:

(14)

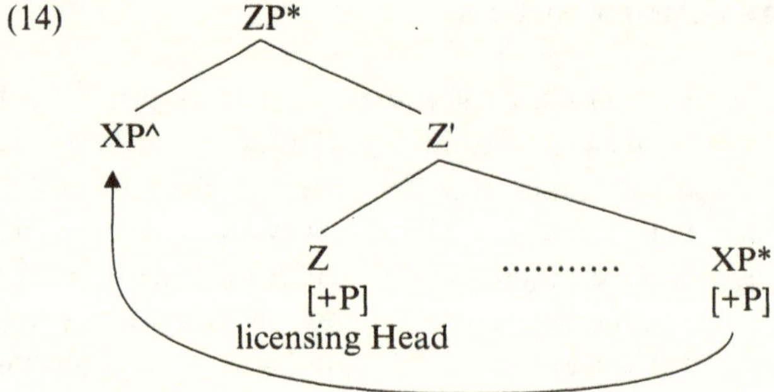

In order to ensure this state of affairs we postulate (15):

(15) *Generalized Licensing Criterion (GLC)*
Syntactic properties must be licensed in Spec/Head configurations.

Movement is the means by which the licensing Spec/head relationship is realized in case the phrase to license is not generated in the appropriate position. This in general will be the case. The existence of movement is a reflection of another (unexplained) linguistic property, namely, that a word or a phrase does not express an atomic (syntactically relevant) property, but rather a concatenation of atomic properties, each of which has to be satisfied under the GLC. Note that under this view movement cannot be optional. It is a driven process. If it can apply—because some property needs licensing—it must (whether covertly or overtly).

A uniform analysis of these dependencies must still leave room to explain their difference of appearance (that is, what we see) and their difference of properties. Concerning the first one, it is easy to see that the variation is a function of which of the three heads involved in this ternary relation[32] is phonologically realized (this is congruent with our earlier discussion of parametric variation):

(16) In the ternary relation (XP^, H^{0}. XP*)
each of them may be overt or covert.

The two types we have been discussing (phrase/phrase versus head/phrase) correspond to which of XP^ in [Spec,HP] and H^0 is overt, respectively. But the typology is actually richer, as we may have cases where all three are overt: if both XP^ and XP* are overt, it does not look like a movement relation (e.g., as in *who saw what*), but we would argue that it is. Furthermore, if H^0 is also overt,[33] we will have an overt ternary relation. With XP^ in [Spec,HP] overt and XP* covert we have a usual movement relation. With XP^ covert and XP* overt we will have a covert movement relation.

Other properties differentiating these dependencies will have to capitalize on particulars of each dependency as is standardly assumed:

(17) a. Overt versus covert movement
b. The properties of XP^ and XP* (A/A′-position, Case/Caseless, etc.)
c. Lexical properties of the moving item itself

The contribution of the first two factors is clear. The third might play a crucial role in determining the appropriate locality domains. Thus, the binding domain for English anaphors (e.g., *himself*) is narrower than the binding domain of long-distance anaphors (e.g., Chinese *ziji* or Japanese *zibun*). Neither of these domains is identical to the domain over which a relation between the French negative quantifier *personne* and its scope position marked by *ne* is allowed. Still, none of these is identical to the domain over which *wh*-movement is allowed. Rather than attributing these differences to anaphoric binding relations not being movement relations, we have to attribute them to differences in the internal structures and properties of the moving items. For example, the internal structure and properties of lexical anaphors are different from those of *wh*-phrases; anaphors differ from each other—for example, "self" in Chinese vs. "X-self" in English. The anaphorizing item may also differ—for example, "self" in Chinese or English versus "same" in French). Consequently the kind of 'interveners' to which these movement relations will be sensitive will differ as well.

4.2 Elimination of adjunction. In this section I briefly outline, without arguments, some assumptions that I defend elsewhere but that I will use later on. I propose in Sportiche (1993b) that syntactic adjunction is not an available option. Neither is adjunction under movement (all movements are substitution in the Spec position of some projection along the lines of the GLC) and there are no (base-generated) adjuncts either, such as adverbs, adjectives, PPs, and extraposed clauses. The aspect of this proposal relevant to what follows is the latter, namely, the treatment of adverbs and adjectives. Informally speaking, I will assume that adverbs and adjectives are all dominated by a projection whose head takes the modifiee of the adverb or the adjective as an argument, that is, as complement (or sometimes as specifier). The general intuition is that adjectives and adverbs bear the same kind of relation to their modifiee that determiners bear to their noun phrases or predicates to their arguments.

A constituent such as *the book* is, since Abney (1987), analyzed as having a head/complement structure:

(18) a. $[_{DP}$ $[_{D'}$ $[_{D}$ the] $[_{NP}$ book]]]
     b. $[_{DP}$ $[_{DP}$ the] $[_{D'}$ $[_{D}$ e] $[_{NP}$ book]]]

Although the structural skeleton of determiner phrases that this assumes is well motivated, the particular distribution of the lexical material within it indicated in (18a), as proposed by Abney (1987), is not obviously correct and might have to be modified to (18b).[34] Adverbs and adjectives, I propose, should be treated exactly the same way. This is illustrated in the following structures (where for each case it must be decided which of the two options is the correct one and what the identity of the complement is):

(19) a. John will stupidly answer:
     . . . $[_{AdvP}$ $[_{Adv'}$ $[_{Adv}$ stupidly] $[_{VP}$ answer]]]
   b. John will answer stupidly:
     . . . $[_{AdvP}$$[_{VP}$ answer]$[_{Adv'}$$[_{Adv}$ stupidly]]]
   c. A proud mother:
     . . . $[_{AP}$ $[_{A'}$ $[_{A}$ proud]$[_{NP}$ mother]]][35]
   d. A mother proud of her son:
     . . . $[_{AP}$$[_{NP}$ mother]$[_{A'}$$[_{A}$ proud] $[_{DP}$ of her son]]]

e. John always buy books:
. . . $[_{AdvP}[_{Adv'}[_{Adv}$ always] $[_{XP}$ buy books]]]

f. John always buys books:
. . . $[_{AdvP}$ $[_{AdvP}$ always] $[_{Adv'}$ $[_{Adv}$ $[_{Adv}$ e $][_{XP}$ buy books]]]

As a final remark on this topic, I also assume that the adjunct status of adjuncts is directly encoded by stipulating that these adjunct projections are totally transparent to government. In other words government (hence, head movement) may behave exactly as if the entire projection were absent.

4.3 The program. In the next section we will turn to what motivates this approach in one individual case. In the case of the typical A-movement dependencies this approach just recapitulates the currently adopted positions. Thus, NP-movement, as in the case of VP-internal subject raising, object raising, or Passive, is motivated by Case licensing; that is, it is a tripartite relation between the moving phrase, the Case licensing head—the appropriate Agr projection—and the landing site—the specifier of that AgrP. It straightforwardly extends to theta assignment if we adopt a slightly modified version of Larson's (1988) VP shell proposal by requiring that all arguments of a verb, and more generally of a predicate P, be generated as specifiers and only specifiers of layered phrasal projections of this predicate P, as illustrated in (11). In this case the ternary relation reduces to a binary relation as XP* and XP^ are identical.

We will therefore primarily concentrate on A′ movement. I will illustrate this approach here with the well-known example—and we will conclude arechetypal case—of *wh*-questions, discuss its syntax, modify some existing proposals concerning it (mostly Rizzi (1991)), and draw some consequences about characteristic properties of such dependencies.

5 Questions. The GLC is inspired by Rizzi's (1991) update of May's (1985) WH-Criterion; the former takes into account Chomsky's (1986) generalized X′ proposal extending the X′ schema to all projections:[36]

(20) *WH- Criterion or Q-criterion:*
At LF
A [+wh] head must be in a Spec/head relationship with a [+wh] XP
A [+wh] XP must be in a Spec/head relationship with a [+wh] head.

The underlying motivation for this proposal is the syntactic attribution of scope to *wh*-quantifiers: the scope of a *wh*-question phrase is syntactically marked by the presence of a [+Q] head. It is directly motivated by the syntax of *wh*-questions in English-like languages. In the present approach it is simply motivated by the need for the *wh*-property to be properly licensed by an appropriate head. Since there is no principled motivation for why the scope of *wh*-question words should be what it is observed to be, a primitive motivation in terms of scope is no better *a priori* than a syntactic licensing motivation, although *a posteriori* the two should obviously interact (moving *wh*-phrases has consequences for their scope properties). This proposal encodes in a simple manner a number of assumptions concerning the functioning of *wh*-question quantification and the nature of LF representations. It 'derives' the existence of *wh*-movement. It makes all languages essentially identical at LF, regardless of whether *wh*-movement is overt or not. Furthermore, modulo minimal assumptions concerning the difference between selected clauses and unselected clauses, it derives the existence of V or I to C movement in *wh*-questions. Departing from Rizzi's proposal, I will suppose that the [+wh] feature is always a property of certain Cs indicating the question property. Remember, however, that the locus of a property and the locus of its realization in overt syntax are not necessarily the same (Past may be generated on a V in the V slot head of VP even though it is a property of the head T of TP).

5.1 English questions. I will suppose without discussion a particular organization of the English auxiliary system. First, I will suppose that every verb (including modals, see Sportiche (1993b), for justifications) is generated in a V slot. Second, I will suppose that main verbs may not overtly raise to T, unlike auxiliary verbs, which may (possibly because, as we interpret Pollock (1989) in terms of a clause structure containing AgrO below T, they cannot even reach AgrO) and must when tensed. Following Chomsky (1993) I assume that in English and more generally (given the existence of suppletion) Tense features are generated on V in the V slot of VP.

5.1.1 *Wh*-questions. Let us begin with embedded *wh*-questions:

(21) Mary asks [+Q you should see who]

By LF both the WH-Criterion and Recoverability must be satisfied: first, *who* must raise to [Spec,CP]; second, [+Q] must be recoverable. In English the first requirement must in fact be met at S-structure, that is, the *wh*-element moves overtly (when there is only one; if there are several *wh*-elements, only one must and may move). I know of no proposed explanation as to why this is so.[37] English does not have an overt [+Q] complementizer. What happens to the [+Q] C property? Suppose that the English [+Q] is a covert bound morpheme and, more precisely, a morphological affix or a syntactic clitic; that is, it requires morpholexical or syntactic incorporation. As such, it must incorporate into some other category. This incorporation must be into the verb *ask* itself, which in its lexical representation contains an open clausal slot specified [+Q]; as I have earlier suggested following Koopman (1993a), this movement is the way selection is always satisfied. This is then similar to what happens with silent instances of the complementizer *that.* Note that the presence of this silent [+Q] C is recoverable, since the Q feature is realized on [Spec,CP]. Since the verb *ask* or the verb *know* allow both declarative and interrogative complements, the presence of +Q is contingent. One of +Q/−Q may be recoverable as the unmarked option. Since silent *that* can be covert without any visible reflex, it must be construed as the unmarked option. Hence +Q must be visible. Complement clauses of certain verbs such as *wonder* require a +Q setting. But they behave exactly like complement clauses of verbs such as *know* and *ask.* We must therefore take contingent (or optional) as meaning 'paradigmatically contingent' (or optional), that is, contingent in general, even though it may be necessary for particular choices of lexical items.

The main clause case is more complicated. Here I will rely extensively on some of Chomsky's (1991) Economy ideas. The first part of the account of (21) would apply unchanged: the *wh*-word must raise in the syntax. The bound morpheme status of the [+Q] C cannot be handled the same way. The option available in embedded clauses is excluded, since there is nothing to incorporate the [+Q] C upward to (I am going to ignore intermediate heads such as AgrS and AgrO, limiting the discussion to C, T, and V):

(22) a. [+Q Mary should teach what] → What should Mary teach?
b. [+Q Mary taught what] → What did Mary teach?

Consider first (22a). The tense morphology is generated on the verb *should,* which raises to T overtly to license its T features (say, +T). How is the bound morpheme status of +Q licensed? One way would be to generate +Q on T. I would like to exclude this possibility by invoking a principle of "Paradigmatic Uniformity" (PA). If +Q could in general be generated on T, causing overt T to C in main clauses, we would expect overt T to C in embedded clauses as well (at least with non-subject *wh*-phrases, given the lack of overt T to C in subject questions, viz. *who left*). Because of paradigmatic uniformity, I will assume—for the moment—that it never can. So, +Q is generated in C in main clauses, and its bound morpheme status requires that T raise to C overtly. This derivation violates Chomsky's (1993) principle of Greed, which requires movement to be motivated solely by properties of the moving item, that is, for the purpose of licensing one of its own properties. Here, T to C is triggered by C, not by T. I suggest that we interpret Greed as an Economy principle: it can be violated as a last resort.[38]

Consider next (22b). By Paradigmatic Uniformity, the tense features +T must be generated on V (as simple declaratives show). If they are, +Q could not be licensed at all, since for whatever reason non-auxiliary verbs cannot overtly raise to T, a fortiori not higher. No well-formed output is predicted possible. However, English has a dummy verb *do,* on which it can generate +T. So +T is generated on *do. Do* as an auxiliary verb may raise to C, and raising to C is required to license the bound morpheme +Q in C.

A further complication arises in the case of subject *wh*-movement:

(23) a. [+Q [who taught calculus]]
b. [who +Q [should teach calculus]]

In either of the forms PA forces +T to be generated on V. The bound morpheme nature of the [+Q] C should force some head to raise to C, but this is the structure of neither example in (23).[39] Why is this raising to C prevented? Koopman (1983) suggests a reason; she makes an analogy between the lack of raising to C in the present case with the obligatory absence of *that* in *Who do you think (*that) t left.* Her idea is that the trace is illicit (due to the ECP) if the C position is filled. Whichever implementation of this idea is the right one, this generalization applies to the present situation:

(24) * [who$_i$ should$_j$ [t_i t_j teach calculus]]

If +Q was in C, forcing T to C in the syntax as in (23a), a violating configuration would be created (at S-structure). This means we must relax Paradigmatic Uniformity. I suggest we weaken it by allowing violations of it as a Last Resort Strategy: in the absence of any alternative toward a well-formed output, minimal departures from Paradigmatic Uniformity are allowed. In the present case PA can be relaxed with respect to either the T features or the Q features, yielding the two following minimal options: +Q may be generated on T+V in V instead of C, or +T may be generated in the T slot instead of the V slot, both violating PA. The second option is ruled out, however, because it still leaves +Q unbound (and raising to it is impossible as it would violate Koopman's generalization). The only option is to violate PA by generating +Q on whichever verb bears +T:

(25) a. [who [*t* taught_{V+T+Q} calculus]]
b. [who [*t* should_{V+T+Q} teach calculus]]

At LF, V+T+Q will raise successively first to T and then to C to license the +T and +Q morphemes it bears.

Let us recapitulate the ingredients we need. We postulated that the English +Q morpheme is a bound morpheme, we introduced a principle of Paradigmatic Uniformity, and we also mentioned Chomsky's principle of Greed. Greed may be violated when PA is not. PA can be violated as a last resort if no well-formed output is derivable. This gives a ranking of strength among these principles:

Lexical properties (+Q is a bound morpheme) cannot be violated.
ECP (or whatever is responsible for *that*-trace effects) cannot be violated.
PA can be violated to avoid violations of the previous two.
Greed may be violated to avoid violations of the previous three.

5.1.2 Yes/no questions. Let us turn now to yes/no questions. Given Larson's (1985) arguments that the disjunction(s) introduced by a yes/no question marker in some clause can affect any clause from within which operator movement could have taken place to the yes/no marker, we postulate, adopting his conclusions, that yes/no questions involve the movement of a (mostly covert) disjunctive or yes/no *wh*-operator to [Spec,CP]. Postulating such an operator explains why *wh*-question and yes/no or disjunctive questions are incompatible. There is only one position: the yes/no operator and a *wh*-phrase cannot both overtly move to it.[40] Thus, consider the sentences below:

(26) a. Who did you see?
b. What did Gloria write to Mary or Lewis?
c. Did Gloria write to Mary or Lewis?

Even though (26a) exhibits both a preposed *wh*-word and subject/aux inversion, it cannot mean "who did you see or who did you not see." Similarly, (26c) is ambiguous (and disambiguated by intonation). It may call for a yes/no answer or for a term of the alternative answer (it may then be paraphrased as "Did Gloria write to Mary or did Gloria write to Lewis"). (26b), however, cannot be a request for both what was written and which of Mary and Lewis it was written to (although, pragmatically, it may be answered this way).

Consider an indirect question. Assume that *whether* is the *wh* disjunction operator as suggested by its resemblance with *wh*-either (see Kayne (1991a) for recent arguments). Then the derivation of (27) below is not significantly different from the previous cases:

(27) Mary asks [Q you should leave whether]

At LF, *whether* must have raised to the embedded [Spec,CP] and the [+Q] C must have incorporated into the verb *ask*. Note that *whether* has the option of being silent in certain dialects.[41] Incorporation of the Q morpheme into *ask* would leave the [+Q] value of the head C opaque. The [+Q] head must not incorporate into its selecting verb. The derivation invoked in (25) is not available either: if +Q was generated on V with LF raising to C, the question nature of the embedded clause would be opaque as well. The last option, since the Q morpheme is a syntactically bound morpheme, is for raising to C to take place overtly in a way similar to main clause subject/aux inversion, yielding:

(28) Mary asks [[$_{wh\text{-operator}}$ e]$_k$ should$_j$ [you t_j leave t_k]]

In main clauses *whether* must be silent for unknown reasons (but cf. below). If it did not have to, we would presumably derive (29a). Otherwise, we must have raising to C exactly as in the previous case of non-subject *wh*-movement, yielding (29b):

(29) a. [whether$_k$ should$_j$ you t_j leave t_k]
b. [[$_{wh\text{-operator}}$ e]$_k$ should$_j$ [you t_j leave t_k]]

Finally, consider a simple declarative such as *They (should) sleep.* Such a clause must contain a highest projection, headed by [−Q], indicating the declarative status of the clause. This we may assume is the default value and, since it triggers no word order changes at all, is analyzed as a silent independent morpheme. Its recoverable character follows from its being the default setting.

5.2 French questions.

5.2.1 Questions with word order changes. French *wh*-questions and yes/no questions fundamentally function like English questions:

(30) a. Quand Marie est partie/Quand (Marie) est-elle partie/ Quand est partie Marie?
When Mary has left/When (Mary) has-she left/When has left Mary?
b. Lequel d'entre eux a mangé /Lequel d'entre eux a-t-il mangé?
Which one of them has eaten /which one of them has-he eaten?
c. Il demande quand Marie est partie/*quand (Marie) est-elle partie/quand est partie Marie.
He asks when Mary has left/*when (Mary) has-she left/ when has left Mary.
d. (Marie) est-elle partie?/ Je demande si Marie est partie.
Has Mary left?/ I ask whether Mary left.

As (30a) illustrates, matrix *wh*-questions all have a preposed *wh*-phrase.[42] The rest of the sentence may stay unaffected, and may display Complex Inversion, Subject Clitic Inversion, or Stylistic Inversion. Stylistic Inversion appears to be a French-specific (and poorly understood) construction, properties of which are discussed in Kayne and Pollock (1978) and Kayne (1972) and which I will basically ignore here. Complex Inversion and Subject Clitic Inversion are excluded in embedded questions. They have been traditionally analyzed as involving overt raising to C (cf. Kayne (1984), Rizzi and Roberts (1989). I analyze them in Sportiche (1993a) as involving covert T to C only in main clauses. This is also true of yes/no questions. The yes/no operator in French is always silent. In embedded yes/no questions, the [+Q] property is spelled out on C as *si.* In main clauses this +Q C is silent. Sportiche (1993a) argues that French lacks overt raising to C altogether. In effect, then, French main clause yes/no questions behave like English subject *wh*-questions in which overt raising to C is prohibited. As in the case of (25b), [+Q] must be generated on T (which is generated on the verb itself), and T to C applies covertly.

Now recall the pattern of Standard English

(i) In standard English [+Q], a bound morpheme, is always generated in C, except when doing so yields violations of some principle.

(ii) In embedded *wh*-questions we have both a preposed *wh*-phrase and [+Q] C incorporation into a higher head. In main clauses we have both a preposed *wh*- phrase and T to C movement to license the morphological requirement of the [+Q] C, except when the *wh*-phrase is the subject. In that case overt T to C is disallowed. Instead, we must resort to generating [+Q] on T and raise T to C covertly. Yes/no questions work exactly like *wh*-questions except for the fact that the main clause yes/no operator is silent.

French then appears identical to English except for the fact that French *whether* is always silent, and French lacks overt T to C altogether.

5.2.2 Why main clause *whether, si* are silent. Why do we find main clause/embedded clause distinctions in the way yes/no is marked (viz. the French alternation Ø/*si*)? A possible reason is the following: suppose, following Bhatt and Yoon (1991), that we distinguish the subordinating property of C from its clause-typing property. They argue that in certain languages these two properties are represented by different morphemes. The only way to make this idea compatible with the general assumptions we make is to split CP in two, replacing it by a subordinating projection SP taking a clause-typing projection TypeP as complement, and so universally. What they analyze as cases of conflation, for example, a unique English CP headed by C, we must reanalyze as a case of two morphemes, Type and S, morpholexically incorporated to each other.[43] Hence, the complementizer *that* is really morphologically complex (tensed declarative + subordination), is generated in TypeP, and must raise to SP to check its subordinating feature. Suppose that French *si* is such a conflated head (subordination+Q). What would we expect to see in main clauses? Clauses seem to be unique in that they are the only constituents that may lawfully appear unembedded (in nonelliptic contexts). It is not unreasonable then to expect that the subordination/nonsubordination of clauses be marked in some way, for example, by the presence of SP.[44] A correlate of this is that main clauses should lack SP. If French *si* indeed is S+Q, it cannot appear in main clauses. We could then state that the unincorporated form of the +Q head of Type P is a silent bound morpheme, like English '*s*.[45]

In what follows I will continue using CP and C as shorthand.

5.2.3 Questions with no word order change. Some (non-echo) questions have the same word order as statements, such as intonation yes/no questions:

(31) Louis a mangé un oeuf?
'Did Lewis eat an egg?'

Compared to statements, the only change is intonational. For example, in (31a) intonation rises at the end of the sentence, unlike what happens in statements. Intonation plays a disambiguating or interpretive role in many constructions and in particular in other kinds of questions that I will not discuss.[46]

How should these kinds of questions be treated? I want to outline a proposal consistent with the kind of restrictive assumptions made in the first section and with the overall organization of the various components of grammar.

First of all, since intonation plays a role both in PF (obviously) and at LF (it provides the question property), it should be represented at S-structure (spell-out), namely, syntactically.

How should it be represented? The null hypothesis, it would seem, is that it should be represented exactly as it always is, that is, as [+Q] in C. This is also the only one consistent with the restrictive assumptions we made in the first section: if the question/statement distinction is sometimes represented on the head of a designated functional category, then it universally always is. This would mean that one of the realizations of the French [+Q] head in main clauses has no segmental value but only a suprasegmental value (equivalent to a tonal melody in tone languages), which manifests itself on the intonational melody. Two properties need to be explained. First this question intonation is in complementary distribution with all the syntactic operations, such as Subject Clitic Inversion, diagnostic of a main clause question. Second, and quite surprisingly, the intonational effect is a rising intonation at the end of the sentence, whereas typically (care is needed here to avoid any parasitic contrastive focus), the [+Q] property triggers a High effect on the element bearing the [+Q] property or immediately preceding its syntactic position (thus *Marie a t-ELLE mangé/Has Marie eaten?* and *Avez-VOUS mangé/Have you eaten?;* similarly, *QUI a vu ce film/Who saw this movie?* and *QUAND êtes-vous parti/When did you leave?*).

Consider then the syntactic structure of an intonation yes/no question such as (32):

(32) $[_{CP}$ [+Q] $[_{IP}$ Louis a mangé un oeuf]]

Rules of phonological interpretation of syntactic information will have to readjust the effects of the presence of the question morpheme by interpreting its effects sentence-finally; that is, away from its syntactic position. This raises the question of how exactly the syntax/phonology interface works. One of the present practices, consisting of postulating rules of phonological interpretation that sometimes rearrange syntactic structures, seems *a priori* unacceptable.[47] Its unacceptable character is illustrated by imagining what it would mean if it were applied at other interfaces, for example, the lexicon/syntax interface or the syntax/interpretation interface. Keeping again to minimal assumptions, the strongest approach concerning syntax-to-phonology readjustments rules is that they do not exist at all: phonological rules simply interpret the syntactic and lexical information present in their input congruent with the structure of the phonological vocabulary. If the phonological rules in general are faithful to syntactic information, but in some cases credibly appear to rearrange it, then taking phonological evidence seriously entails that the postulated syntactic structure is wrong. In the case at hand we would have to postulate either that an intonational Q suprasegmental morpheme is generated sentence-finally or that it is generated in C but its phonological effects are shifted to the end of the sentence. Neither option is acceptable. I would like to suggest instead that the structure (32) is incorrect and that it should be replaced by (33):

(33) $[_{CP}$ $[_{IP}$ Louis a mangé un oeuf$]_i$ [+Q] [t_i]]

in which the entire IP has preposed to [Spec,CP], that is, to a position preceding the [+Q] morpheme. The obligatoriness of this preposing can be made to follow from the lexical stipulation that the suprasegmental version of the [+Q] morpheme is a leftward phonological clitic; that is, it needs material to its left. Since the question/statement distinction is a property of the entire IP following it, the silent question operator usually moving to [Spec,CP] (and sometimes lexicalized as *whether* in English) is an IP level modifier. Since the Q morpheme needs phonological material to its left, the only way to produce a well-formed output is to pied-pipe the entire IP as in (33).

This structure explains some odd features of this intonation yes/no question. In simple clauses it derives the complementarity noted above between other phenomena involving T to C (such as Subject Clitic Inversion) and this intonational pattern, since the material that would potentially raise from T to C (recall that T to C occurs only at LF in French) is already higher than the C. It also explains why these intonation yes/no questions, although they have the interpretive properties of questions, lack their syntactic properties. For example, polarity items are not licensed in intonation yes/no questions. Thus, the polarity item *qui ce soit* 'whoever' can occur as a bare object only in polarity environments, for example, those commanded by some negative item or by [+Q]. It cannot appear in an intonation question for lack of appropriate command:

(34) a. *Il a vu qui que ce soit (statement).
'He saw anybody.'
b. A-t-il vu qui que ce soit/Il n'a pas vu qui que ce soit.
'Has he seen anybody/He has not seen anybody.'
c. *Il a vu qui que ce soit (question)?
'Has he seen anybody?'

Licensing by a commanding yes/no operator in [Spec,CP] at S-structure is required and this configuration is not met in (34c), since the operator is embedded inside the preposed IP.[48]

5.2.4 Multiple questions. Consider multiple questions:

(35) Who saw what?

Given the requirements imposed by the WH-Criterion, both *wh*-operators must be in a Spec/head relationship with the same [+Q] head (since there is only one such head). Since the *wh* property of both *wh*-operator properties must be licensed by a unique head, we must postulate the existence of a process reducing these two phrases to one. One way this rule may be functioning would be by reducing these two operators to one, namely, by creating a binary *wh*-quantifier out of two unary quantifiers so that there would be one relevant *wh*-property to Spec/head license. Call this "Absorption." Semantically, this might seem gratuitous because the *wh*-question operators are idempotent (i.e., have the property $x^2=x$), although it could explain why we get the pair-list reading (i.e., we cannot answer *who* and *what* independently as in *who saw something and what was seen*). The same phenomenon is observed in negative constructions (negative concord) with a clear case of nonidempotent operators (negation).

Although the treatment we have sketched above is the standard treatment for multiple questions, some of its properties are unclear. First of all, Chomsky (1993) has advanced some arguments for wanting to conclude that *wh*-movement should universally be overt. But many languages, including English and French, that tolerate multiple questions clearly exhibit both moved *wh*-phrases and *wh-in-situ* at the same time. How is this to be reconciled with the requirement that *wh*-movement be obligatorily overt? One possibility could be to claim that the +Q property of C is strong in Chomsky's (1993) sense and thus requires a *wh*-operator in [Spec,CP] in overt syntax. Second, the precise mechanism by which absorption takes place is most unclear: it is a definitional property of syntactic positions that they can contain only one item at a time. Yet, in the case of the standard account of multiple questions we want several *wh*-phrases to occupy exactly the same [Spec,CP] at LF at the same time. This suggests an alternative treatment along the following lines that takes advantage of the approach to *wh*-movement to Japanese or Chinese *wh*-questions advocated by Aoun and Li (1993), Watanabe (1992), or Cheng (1992). Current analyses of DPs headed by English *who, what* or French *qui* assume that the *wh*-word is itself the question operator. A word like *who* seems to stand both for the question operator and for its range (here [+human]). We may claim instead that the *wh*-operator in French or English is always covert and that the *wh*-words are *wh*-polarity items ([+human] nouns such as *who,* [−human] nouns such as *what,* determiners such as *which,* and so on) that must occur in the scope of these *wh*-operators. The structure of a *wh*-phrase would then be [*wh*-operator [who]]. In a sentence with a unique *wh*-phrase, this *wh*-phrase must move to [Spec,CP]. When there are two, only one of them can contain a *wh*-operator (otherwise there is no possibility to satisfy the GLC) and it must move to [Spec,CP]. The other one must then be parasitic on the first one (i.e., exactly like a parasitic gap). The structure of a sentence such as (35) would then be as in (36):

(36) $[_{DP}$ *Wh*-op$_j$ [who] $]_i$ [t_i saw $[_{DP}$ $[_{pg}$ *e*] [what]]]

Here, movement of the *wh*-operator must pied-pipe (in English but not with, say, French *combien*) the entire DP. Languages in which *wh*-words always are *wh*-operators themselves (possibly conflated with the head noun or some other category) would then simply not allow multiple questions (Italian might be such a case; see Rizzi (1982)).

5.3 Diagnostic properties. This analysis of *wh*-constructions evidences a number of properties that we expect to see recur elsewhere and that we can use as diagnostic for the idea that something like the configuration mandated by the GLC is indeed met:

1. *Wh*-question words (now including the yes/no operators) are related to a particular, designated, and fixed position in the syntactic structure of a sentence.

2. It is a relation between a head ([+Q] C) and a ([+wh]) XP that must be Spec/head at LF. Because this relationship is established by movement, the specifier of the [+Q] C, hence apparently the [+Q] C itself, is in a possible movement relationship (i.e., subject to islandhood, etc.) with the *wh*-XP.
3. Doubly filled Comp effects may be found (which we can now analyze as a prohibition against filling both the specifier and the head position of any projection at the same time; call this the Doubly Filled Projection Prohibition).
4. Absorption effects are observed.
5. The specifier of this [+Q] head is an A′-position (as exemplified by its licensing parasitic gaps).

5.4 Further and future extensions. I discuss elsewhere how this general approach extends to clitic constructions (Sportiche (1992, 1993a)) and to negative constructions (Sportiche (1993c)). I hope to extend it in future work to a number of other syntactic constructions: anaphoric binding dependencies (binding of anaphors and hopefully pronominal binding), scopal and other properties of non-*wh* non-negative quantifiers (see Stowell and Beghelli (1994)), Focus, etc. The general proposal we put forth allows very little analytical leeway, but I try to push it as far as I can. In each instance it forces us to postulate a designated projection to fulfill the role of ZP* in (14). In the case of non-*wh* non-negative quantifiers, the way to take the analogy with *wh*-questions is straightforward and leads us to postulate designated 'Q' projections for each type of these quantifiers with concomitant movement. In the case of anaphor binding it leads us to postulate designated positions—for example, [Spec,ReflexiveP]—that anaphors have to move to be properly licensed. The general idea is clear. It will lead to fairly abstract analyses of individual lexical items of the kind postulated by Klima (1964) in the case of negative polarity items. It will also lead to the view that the same property expressed in different sites of a single clause cannot be a property licensed *in-situ.* Take, for example, the case of Focus. In a simple French clause it may be marked prosodically *in-situ* but felicitously only on one constituent at a time. This uniqueness suggests immediately that the Focus property is associated with a particular unique position. We are then led to postulate both the existence of a Focus Phrase with a Focus head, the morphemic content of which is responsible for the prosodic effect, and movement of the focused constituent to the specifier position of this phrase.

The abstractness price we pay for this kind of unification is reduced in some cases by the overt similarity found in some languages between constructions that are treated differently in English or French. Extremely significant in this respect is the work of Li (1992), showing that Chinese *wh*-words (*wh*-one), polarity items (*any*-one), and existential quantifiers (*some*-one) are one and the same word, the interpretive import of which is contextually determined by the kind of elements in the scope of which they are found. It should come as no surprise that they should have closely related syntactic functioning, as we propose.

NOTES

*Various parts of this work have been presented at the 1992 GLOW Colloquium in Lisbon, the University of Indiana at Bloomington, Cornell University, and the European Science foundation in Strasbourg and in graduate seminars at UCLA in 1990, 1991, 1992, and 1993. Thanks to their audiences for their input. A grant from the UCLA Academic Senate partially supporting this research is gratefully acknowledged.

1. The discussion of conflation later on might be taken to suggest that even this kind of variation is even more superficial than it appears. For example, *shallow* might be analyzed in English as the conflated *not-deep.*

2. As we will see, the conclusion of this section and all others in this article are consistent with a model of syntax comprising a unique level of representation conflating D-structure and S-structure as in Sportiche (1983). In fact, it is consistent with a model comprising a unique level of representation conflating D-structure, S-structure, and LF, i.e., one lacking syntactic derivations altogether. I will continue talking in derivational terms to keep exposition on familiar terms.

3. This is a generalization to head movement of an approach that has been suggested for phrasal movement in Jaeggli (1980), who suggested replacing Case assignment by Case checking.

4. This distinction is reminiscent of Marantz's (1992) distinction between D-structure incorporation and S-structure incorporation. Differences between the two incorporation processes are recently discussed in Sportiche (1993a) in connection with pre- and post-verbal subject clitics in French. For a more general approach to these questions see Koopman (1993a) and references therein.

5. This would depend mostly on whether strict compositionality is respected. In general with these cases, it is not.

6. Larson's proposal differs in that it would allow *kill* to project the agent as the specifier and the patient as the complement within the same unique VP.

7. In ongoing work (Sportiche (1993b)), building on Collins and Thráinson (1993), I argue that we can and should go one step closer to lexical decomposition analyses in postulating that there is full clausal structure per verb and even per VP: (a) each verb has its own full clausal structure and (b) each VP (of a VP shell) projection has its own full clausal structure; there is no VP shell literally. Thus, *kill=cause to die* corresponds to two full clauses (see Collins and Thrainson's (1993) work arguing that Icelandic double object constructions are biclausal).

8. For example, the verb *die* is not present in the syntax at all as such and so cannot be modified by adverbs, as in cause-to-die. Note also that, correlatively, it is also possible to have a syntactic aspect to derivational morphology exactly as in the case of inflectional morphology, a conclusion with some merits (see Valois 1991).

9. Lexical categories are V, N, A, and perhaps P, i.e., predicative categories. I use "lexical" also in the sense of idiosyncratic, as in lexical properties of some functional head, e.g., how future Tense is pronounced in French.

10. This means, for example, that every verb is always associated with a full clausal structure, as I discuss in Sportiche (1993b). Alternatively, there may be general principles predicting which, if any, of these functional projections is not present in given contexts.

11. It appears that which one is covert (statement, affirmation) is constant cross-linguistically, a generalization that has no explanation but demands one.

12. For example, following Cheng's (1992) suggestion, we could analyze a Chinese *wh*-phrase as [OP *wh*-word], with overt movement of the silent operator OP, much as *combien* movement in French *combien as-tu vu d'enfants.* We could then treat English *wh*-words the same way but with OP movement of this null operator requiring pied-piping of the entire phrase in English; in the case of Chinese *wh*-movement this pied-piping would be prohibited.

13. Note that, strictly speaking, it makes no sense, if we reduce all movement and binding relations to one type, to say that we have reduced them to movement (or binding). They now are all and the same and, if the text is correct, of the type antecedent/trace relation. Saying that they reduce to movement is saying that the driving property is a formal one (properties are licensed in spec/head relations) rather than an interpretive requirement (anaphors must be provided with reference, variables with a range, and so on.).

14. I am for the moment ignoring selection for the external argument, to which I will return.

15. Although this is the usual account for NP-movement in passive or raising structures, it has been considerably extended recently by Chomsky (1991), Koopman (1992), Mahajan (1990), and Sportiche (1990).

16. It is quite possible that the following extends to all syntactic dependencies. For example, although there are superficial cases of, say, n-ary relations, essential cases are possibly nonexistent. N-ary relations can always be factored as a conjunction of (n-1) binary relations, each involving a distinguished element among the n. Thus, although *who saw what when* could be seen as a relation between a scope position, *who, what,* and *when,* it can be construed as three relations, each between a scope position and a *wh*-phrase. One possible irreducible case is the case of a plural pronoun bound by two independent quantifiers as in *Every girl told some boy that they* (i.e., *he* and *she*) *should leave.*

17. This is instead of the usual c-command or m-command (as discussed in Sportiche (1990)). Roughly for $x \neq y$, c-command (x,y) iff the first branching constituent (or its immediate projection) containing x contains y, m-command (x,y) iff the first phrasal consistent containing x contains y (see Aoun and Sportiche (1981) and references therein).

18. Throughout, I will assume a version of ECP stated in terms of antecedent government and barrierhood. Part of this could be translated in an Economy approach in terms of shortest steps, as Chomsky (1993) has recently suggested.

19. See Koopman (1993a) for a discussion of these questions (long-distance head movement, excorporation). See also Sportiche (1990, 1992, 1993a) for the particular case of pronominal clitics.

20. A similar suggestion was made by R. Kayne at the 1992 GLOW in Lisbon and a more restricted version of it by N. Chomsky at the Irvine Lectures, Winter 1993.

21. Some important quesions are left unaddressed here. The complement is really a DP, but I would claim that this is a derived property. C-selection is of an argumental category (it gets a theta role) whose lexical content is nominal, i.e., NP (nouns are predicative categories). Ds make NPs into arguments. Thus, the conjunctive requirement nominal and argument will force the projection of a DP (see Stowell (1989, 1991) for discussion of these questions). On why the N of a DP may incorporate into its selecting V, see Koopman (1993b), who suggests that the NP raises to [Spec,DP] first, whence incorporation takes place.

22. This internal structure completely follows from the internal structure of the verb *pour*: Because it may be very roughly analyzed as the conflated verbal cateogry *cause-to-flow (like a liquid),* it is actually a sequence of two verbs, each with its own subject.

23. Actually, a biclausal structure if the proposals referred to in footnote 6 are taken into account.

24. If an external argument must incorporate (but cf. discussion below), the necessary existence of the higher head Z entails that every predicative category (i.e., the lexical categories A, V, N, and perhaps P) must be complements of some functional category.

25. Recall that I in fact take conflated verbs to literally comprise two (or more) verbs and that each must project a full clausal structure. This means that in *kill=cause to die,* a full clause, i.e., functional projections such as T, C, and so on, should intervene between the two verbs. However, because incorporation of *die* to *cause* is obviously selected and overt, these functional projections must count as nonintervening, i.e., as defective. If for some reason the F of the text was defective, we would for the same reason expect external argument incorporation to be possible. I would argue that this is exactly what happens in agentive nominalizations, e.g., *killer=one who kills,* which I would take to be exactly a relative clause with a defective clausal structure and an incorporated agent (see Potter (1994) for relevant discussion of related Navajo and Cherokee facts).

26. Note that recoverability of this silent complementizer is obviously satisfied.

27. Below we will see another case of silent C with similar properties. Unfortunately, the distribution of the silent infinitive complementizer that is not subject to restriction (13) (viz. *I tried [$_{C}$e] to win/[$_{C}$e] to win is easy*) prevents generalizing the bound morpheme status of silent heads.

28. This approach to adverbial adjuncts is discussed and justified in Sportiche (1993b). See section 4.3 below for a quick summary.

29. If covert incorporation is blocked as well, the *that*-clause complement of *whisper* will have to be treated as extraposed.

30. See Koopman (1993a) for discussion of other such cases. As for the other generalization explored by Kayne (*op. cit.*) and Stowell (*op. cit.*), i.e., that verbs allow silent complementizers in tense complements if they are bridge verbs, it is tempting to relate it also to C incorporation: CPs would be opaque for extraction unless the C can incorporate to its selecting verb.

31. For example, being a Q is a syntactic property: it is coded lexically but has syntactic, i.e., structural, relational consequences, namely, scope.

32. I use this term descriptively here. There are actually two binary relations: a Spec/head relation and a movement dependency.

33. We return later to apparent restrictions concerning co-occurence of H and its specifier as, for example, in cases of *wh*-movement and doubly filled Comps.

34. The first one is probably correct for French *le livre,* while the second one has some plausibilty for the English case of *the book.*

35. Abney (1987) suggests this structure for certain adjective-noun combinations.

36. Throughout I will suppose that [+wh] or [+Q] is an optional property of certain complementizers, but nothing essential turns on this. As Bhatt and Yoon (1991) discuss, the subordinating function must be distinguished from the clause type function. English or French conflates the two in C. It is thus likely that +Q is a property of an independent declarative/interrogative head.

37. Chomsky (1993) suggesets that *wh*-movement is always overt.

38. The alternative, closer to Rizzi's (1991) proposal, would generate the +Q feature on T—much as Tense may be generated on the verb in VP in English, as Chomsky (1993) suggests. Raising of T+Q to C would then not violate Greed. But this violates PA.

39. In the first case this conclusion is supported since the tensed main verbs follow VP adverbs. In the second it is, for example, by *have* contraction:

(i) John should have taught
(ii) John should've taught.
(iii) Should John have taught.
(iv) *Should've John taught.
(v) Should John've taught.
(vi) Who should have taught.
(vii) Who should've taught.

If the modal had raised to C in (vii), we would expect contradiction to be impossible as in (iv) or (v).

40. We return below to the question of why multiple questions with one of them moved and the other *in-situ* are also excluded.

41. This is because in the paradigm of *wh*-question operators it is the only one that can be silent without an antecedent and is thus recoverable. Again, the question arises: why it is this particular operator that can be silent?

42. With a complication concerning *que/what.* See Obenauer (1976,1977) for discussion.

43. They propose that in languages with two morphemes, SP is adjoined to TypeP, although they leave open the possiblity we suggest. For English-type languages they assume because of the conflated head—and it is essential for their analysis of V2—that there is one projection only: CP. If necessary, some of their results could be duplicated here by distinguishing languages incorporating Type to S (because of recoverability or morphological boundedness) from languages raising V (or more precisely V+T) to Type (for the same reasons).

44. This is why we would want SP to be higher than TypeP: TypePs would then be internally identical in main and embedded clauses, SP added on main clauses only. The alternative order is compatible with the test, even if conceptually less desirable. The data on the question is contradictory. The bimorphemic languages Bhatt and Yoon discuss show the hierarchy S>Type. So does, for example, Spanish (viz. *pregunto que a quién hablaste (I ask that who you spoke to = I ask who you spoke to),* now analyzed with *que* in S and *a quien* in [Spec, TypeP]). The Germanic languages seem to suggest otherwise. For example, Dutch embedded questions allow the co-occurence of three morphemes. Thus, corresponding to the underlined CP material *I wonder who John saw,* it is possible to have *wie of dat (who if that),* i.e., a *wh*-phrase, a [+Q] complementizer, and a "that" complementizer co-occurring. The presence of the *wh*-word leaves no room but to analyze *of* as the clause-typing particle marking the question, which thus seems higher than the subordinating particle *that.*

45. The same analysis could be applied to English *ø/whether* alteration if, unlike what we have supposed, *whether* also is the conflation of S+Q, an assumption otherwise consistent with our analysis.

46. For example, *in-situ* normal *wh*-questions vs. echo *wh*-questions (*Marie a vu qui/Marie a vu QUI*) and *wh*-questions from *wh*-exclamatives (*Quel tableau il a peint/Quel tableau il a peint*).

47. This is not to say that all of syntactic structure is relevant. For example, some syntactic information might simply be irrelevant, but then, systematically so; e.g., syntax provides for infinite embedding possibility.

48. Left unexplained so far is why pied-piping must be of the largest IP viz. **[[(que) Il a mangé)$_i$ [il a dit (que) t$_i$].* We might take advantage of Bhatt and Yoon's conflation idea: complementizers such as *que* conflate Type and S. Pied piping a lower IP, in fact a lower TypeP, would carry the trace of *que* (raised to S) higher than its antecedent. This kind of situation is not allowed (it would be the equivalent of passivizing a DP whose N head has incorporated to V).

REFERENCES

Abney, S. 1987. *The Noun Phrase in its Sentential Aspect.* Ph.D. Dissertation. MIT.

Aoun, J., N. Hornstein and D. Sportiche. 1981. Aspects of Wide Scope Quantification. *The Journal of Linguistic Research 1:*69–95.

Aoun, J., and Y. A. Li. 1993. *Wh*-elements *in-situ:* Syntax or LF. *Linguistic Inquiry* 24:199–238.

Aoun, J., and D. Sportiche. 1983. On the Formal Theory of Government. *The Linguistic Review* 2:211–36.

Baker, M. 1988. *Incorporation.* Chicago: University of Chicago Press.

Bhatt, R., and J. Yoon. 1991. On the Composition of COMP and Parameters of V2. In *Proceedings of the Tenth West Coast Conference on Formal Linguistics.* D. Bates, ed. Stanford: Center for the Study of Language and Information.

Borer, H. 1984. *Parametric Syntax.* Dordrecht: Foris.

Burzio, L. 1986. *Italian Syntax.* Dordrecht: Reidel.

Carter, R. 1976. *On Linking: Papers by Richard Carter.* Cambridge: MIT Center for Cognitive Science Lexicon Project.

Cheng, L. 1992. On *Wh*-movement and *wh-in-situ.* Colloquium presented at UCLA.

Chomsky, N. 1965. *Aspects of the Theory of Syntax.* The Hague: Mouton.

Chomsky, N. 1970. Remarks on Nominalizations. *Studies in Semantics in Generative Grammar.* The Hague: Mouton.

Chomsky, N. 1977. On *Wh*-movement. In *Formal Syntax.* P. Culicover, T. Wasow, and A. Akmajian, eds. New York: Academic Press.

Chomsky, N. 1981. *Lectures on Government and Binding,* Dordrecht: Foris.

Chomsky, N. 1986a. *Barriers.* Cambridge: MIT Press.

Chomsky, N. 1991. Some Notes on Economy of Derivation and Representation. In *Principles and Parameters in Comparative Grammar.* R. Freidin, ed. Cambridge: MIT Press.

Chomsky, N. 1993. A Minimalist Program for Linguistic Theory. In *The View from Building 20: Essays in Linguistics in Honor of Sylvain Bromberger.* K. Hale and S. J. Keyser, eds. Cambridge: MIT Press.

Collins, C., and H. Thráinsson. 1993. *Object Shift in Double Object Constructions and the Theory of Case.* Manuscript. Harvard University.

Hale, K. and J. Keyser 1991. *On Argument Structure and the Lexical Expression of Syntactic Relations.* Manuscript. MIT.

Huang, C.-T. J. 1982. *Logical Relations in Chinese and the Theory of Grammar.* Ph.D. Dissertation. MIT.

Jaeggli, O. 1980. Remarks on *to* Contraction. *Linguistic Inquiry* 11:239–45.

Kayne, R. 1972. Subject Inversion in French Interrogatives. In *Generative Studies in Romance Languages.* J. Casagrande and B. Saciuk, eds. Rowley: Newbury House.

Kayne, R. 1984. *Connectedness and Binary Branching.* Dordrecht: Foris.

Kayne, R. 1989. Facets of Romance Past Participle Agreement. In *Dialect Variation and the Theory of Grammar.* P. Benincà, ed. Dordrecht: Foris.

Kayne, R. 1991a. Romance Clitics, Verb Movement and PRO. *Linguistic Inquiry* 22:647–86.

Kayne, R. 1991b. *Italian Negative Infinitival Imperatives and Clitic Climbing.* Manuscript. CUNY.

Kayne, R. 1993. Toward a Modular Theory of Auxiliary Selection. *Studia Linguistica* 47:3–31.

Kayne, R. 1994. *The Antisymmetry of Syntax.* Manuscript. CUNY.

Kayne, R., and J.-Y. Pollock. 1978. Stylistic Inversion, Successive Cyclicity and Move NP in French. *Linguistic Inquiry* 9:595–621.

Klima, E. S. 1964. Negation in English. In *The Structure of Language Readings in the Philosophy of Language.* J. A. Fodor and J. J. Katz, eds. Englewood Cliffs, NJ: Prentice-Hall.

Koopman, H. 1983. ECP Effects in Main Clauses. *Linguistic Inquiry* 14:346–51.

Koopman, H. 1984. *The Syntax of Verbs: From Verb Movement Rules in the Kru Languages to Universal Grammar.* Dordrecht: Foris.

Koopman, H. 1992. On the Absence of Case Chains in Bambara. *Natural Language and Linguistic Theory* 10:555–94.

Koopman, H. 1993a. Licensing Heads. In *Verb Movement.* N. Hornstein and D. Lightfoot, eds. Cambridge: Cambridge University Press.

Koopman, H. 1993b. *The Internal and External Distribution of Pronominal DPs.* Manuscript. UCLA.

Larson, R. 1985. On the Syntax of Disjunction Scope. *Natural Language and Linguistic Theory* 3:217–64.

Larson, R. 1988. On the Double Object Construction. *Linguistic Inquiry* 19:335–92.

Li, Y. A. 1992. Indefinite *Wh* in Mandarin Chinese. *Journal of East Asian Linguistics* 1:125–56.

Mahajan, A. 1990. *The A/A' Distinction and Movement Theory.* Ph.D. Dissertation. MIT.

May, R. 1985. *Logical Form.* Cambridge: MIT Press.

Obenauer, H-G. 1976. *Etudes de Syntaxe Interrogative du Français.* Tübingen: Niemeyer.

Obenauer, H-G. 1977. Syntaxe et Interprétation: *que* Interrogatif. *Le Français Moderne* 45:305–41.

Pollock, J.-Y. 1989. Verb Movement, Universal Grammar, and the Structure of IP. *Linguistic Inquiry* 20:365–424.

Potter, B. 1994. *Navajo and Cherokee Nominalizations.* Manuscript. UCLA.

Ritter, E. 1991. *Two Functional Categories in Noun Phrases: Evidence from Modern Hebrew.* Manuscript. UQAM, Montreal.

Rizzi, L. 1982. *Issues in Italian Syntax.* Dordrecht: Foris.

Rizzi, L. 1991. Residual Verb Second and the WH-Criterion. *Technical Report in Formal and Computational Linguistics* 2. Faculty of Letters, University of Geneva.

Rizzi, L., and I. Roberts. 1989. Complex Inversion in French. *Probus* 1:1–30

Sportiche, D. 1983. *Structural Invariance and Symmetry in Syntax.* Ph. D. Dissertation. MIT.

Sportiche, D. 1990. *Movement, Agreement and Case.* Manuscript. UCLA.

Sportiche, D. 1992. *Clitic Constructions.* Manuscript. UCLA.

Sportiche, D. 1993a. *Subject Clitics in French and Romance, Complex Inversion and Clitic Doubling.* Manuscript. UCLA.

Sportiche, D. 1993b. *Adjuncts and Adjunctions.* Manuscript. UCLA.

Sportiche, D. 1993c. *Remarks on the Structural Representation of Negation.* Manuscript. UCLA.

Stowell, T. 1981. *The Origins of Phrase Structure.* Ph.D. Dissertation. MIT.

Stowell, T. 1989. Subjects, Specifiers, and X′ Theory. In *Alternative Conceptions of Phrase Structure.* M. Baltin and A. Kroch, eds. Chicago: University of Chicago Press.

Stowell, T. 1991. Determiners in NP and DP. In *Views on Phrase Structure.* K. Leffel and D. Bouchard, eds. Dordrecht: Kluwer.

Stowell, T., and F. Beghelli. 1994. Direction of Quantifier Movement. GLOW 94.

Travis, L. 1984. *Parameters and Effects of Word Order Variations,* Ph.D. Dissertation. MIT.

Valois, D. 1991. *The Internal Syntax of DP.* Ph.D. Dissertation. UCLA.

Watanabe, A. 1992. *Wh-in-situ,* Subjacency, and Chain Formation. Manuscript. MIT.

On the Nature of Clitic Doubling*

ESTHER TORREGO
University of Massachusetts, Boston

1 **Introduction.** In this article I present a view of clitic doubling rooted in the selection of a functional head by a light verb. Following Hale and Keyser (1991), I assume that the arguments of certain verbs (or perhaps all) are organized within a Larsonian type of VP shell in a binary branching X′ theory, along the lines of Kayne (1984).[1] The leading idea is that light verbs may select not just for a V, as it is commonly assumed, but for a functional head, a kind of Infl, which I represent as a D below:

(1)
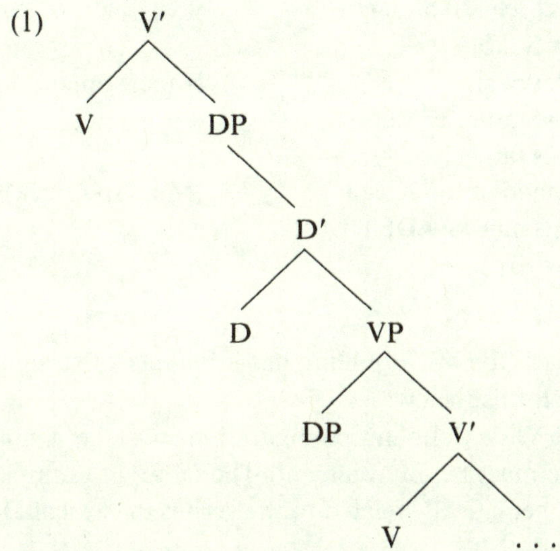

Intervening between the higher and the lower verb there is a DP whose head I assume is the accusative clitic of the Spanish example below:

(2) Lo empujaron a Juan.
him-pushed to John
'They pushed John.'

The accusative clitic corresponds to the functional head D. The lexical DP, which appears with the dative preposition *a,* 'to,' is the argumental object. Morphologically, the accusative clitic and its double are in the same gender, person, and number. Semantically, they are interpreted as a single argument. For the time being I assume that the object is in the Specifier of the lower VP (see note 9).

In the 1970s and 1980s, the clitic-doubling phenomenon received a great amount of attention. The following are examples involving clitic doubling of a direct object in (a) Lebanese Arabic, (b) Romanian, (c) Albanian, (d) Macedonian, and (e) Modern Greek:[2]

(3) a. sefit-o la karim. (Lebanese Arabic)
saw-she-him (to Karin)
'She saw Karin.'
b. l-am vazut pe Popescu. (Romanian)
him-have-I seen to Popescu
'I have seen Popescu.'
c. Agini e pa Sokolin. (Albanian)
Agin-def cl see Sokol-def
'Agim saw Sokol.'
d. Go vide tatka si. (Macedonian)
him he-saw father to-self
'He saw his father.'
e. o Yanis ton idhe ton Kosta. (Modern Greek)
DET Yanis him-saw DET Kosta
'Yanis saw Kosta.'

The sketched approach to clitic doubling has a number of straightforward implications which I list below:

First, the clitic of a clitic-doubling configuration must be a non-argument, and the double must be an argument. Therefore, in examples such as (3) the XP that is thematically related to the verb is the lexical DP, not the clitic.[3]

Second, in syntactic contexts such as in (4) below in which the functional category D (the clitic) is selected but it does not appear overtly, an argumental null pronominal must be postulated:

(4) Lo empujaron *pro.*
him-pushed *pro*
'They pushed him.'

Third, the functional head selected by the light verb (the clitic) does not have to appear overtly. For clitic-doubling contexts such as (5) below, a null clitic must be part of the structure:

(5) Empujaron a Juan.
pushed to Juan
'They pushed Juan.'

Factually, there is cross-linguistic variation concerning the overt expression of an accusative clitic in non-dislocated contexts with non-pronominal and non-anaphoric objects. To my knowledge the main variables controlling the phenomenon in all clitic-doubling languages are the definiteness of the object and its pronominal versus its non-pronominal nature. Here I will ignore these variables, unless they become relevant in the course of the discussion.[4]

Next I will discuss what verbs, and in what contexts, select for the functional category that I argue surfaces as the clitic of clitic-doubling structures and in what contexts they do so.

2 Transitive verbs that select D. The type of transitive verbs that select D can be found by looking at the Case-marking of the object. Descriptively speaking, D appears only with 'specific' animate objects.

To facilitate the presentation, I provide below a summary of the data in my work in progress that lead to this conclusion:[5]

(6)

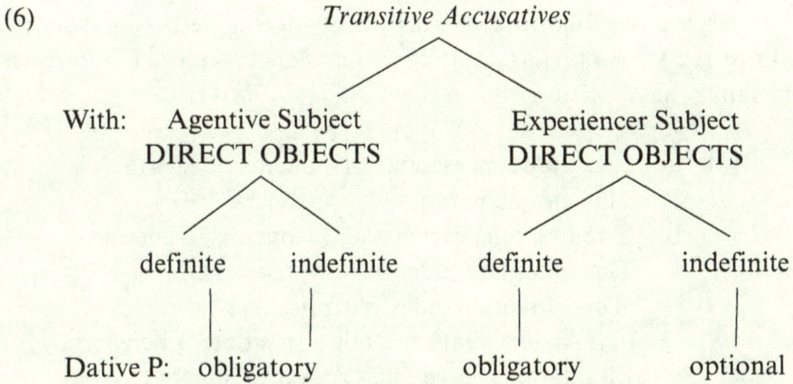

2.1 The Agent/Theme (or Patient) class. Within the eventive class of transitive accusative verbs two main subclasses can be distinguished:

(a) the *see*-class and (b) the *push*-class. Here I will discuss only the empirical evidence that separates the two: non-specific indefinites. An indefinite object can appear with the dative preposition (a) optionally with the *see*-class of verbs and (b) obligatorily with the *push*-class of verbs. We should point out, however, that this distinction holds only for 'animates,' as we will see in section 3.1.1:

(7) a. Empujaron *(a) una niña.
pushed to a girl
'They pushed a girl.'
b. Vieron/besaron (a) una niña.
her-saw/kissed (to) a girl
'They saw/kissed a girl.'

In (7a) the dative preposition occurs obligatorily with the object, whereas in (7b) the preposition is optional. Since the presence of the preposition signals a hidden D, we can infer from these data that verbs such as *push* (or *hit*) have an underlying light verb that in some languages selects D obligatorily. Verbs of the *see*-class, however, have a choice.

Once this premise is established, let us look more closely at the apparent optionality of the dative preposition with verbs of the *see*-class. Upon closer inspection we realize that there is a difference in meaning whenever the object of these verbs comes accompanied by the preposition. More concretely, the subject receives a different interpretation depending on whether D is selected. If the dative P appears on the object, the subject of the clause has a more agentive meaning than otherwise.

Observe the following contrast involving the verb *hide,* which belongs to the same class as *see* (Cf. *La familia escondió (a) un prisionero* 'The family hid a prisioner'):

(8) a. Esta montaña esconde prisioneros de guerra.
This mountain hides war prisoners.
b. *Esta montaña esconde a prisioneros de guerra.
This mountain hides to war prisoners.
'This mountain hides war prisoners.'
(Cf. Alguna gente esconde a prisioneros de guerra
Lit., 'Some people hides to war prisoners')

As we see in these examples from Spanish, a non-agentive subject with *esconder* ('hide') is precluded when the object is preceded by the dative preposition (8b). In other words the presence of the dative P on the object makes the sentence an action. An action needs an agentive subject. Since the subject of (8b) cannot be agentive for lexical reasons, (8b) is excluded.

The existence of two types of readings with *hide* and similar verbs is argued for by Jackendoff (1990) for English. According to Jackendoff, *hide* alternates between a state and an event reading. As illustrated in (8), this holds true in Spanish also. In Spanish the presence of the dative preposition on the object forces the event reading of this verb. Since the event reading of the verb correlates with an agentive subject, (8b) is impossible.

Jackendoff suggests that the difference in the two readings of *hide* must be encoded in the lexical entry. I take the position that each reading of *hide* correlates with a different light verb. What gives rise to the event reading is the presence of the light verb, which selects for a special Infl—the clitic—and not 'the flexibility' of the particular verb (in this case, *hide*).

The sketched approach makes one prediction with respect to the selection properties of verbs such as *hide* and *see.* Both of these verbs select for stage-level small clauses. Since the event reading of these verbs describes a change that culminates in the state reading, the small clause will force the event reading of the verb. In this case, in clitic-doubling languages the light verb corresponding to the event reading will select for the clitic. As shown below, this prediction is borne out:

(9) a. Allí vieron una mujer muerta.
there (they) saw a woman dead
'There they saw a dead woman.'
b. Allí vieron a una mujer muerta.
there (they) saw to a woman dead
'There they saw a woman dead.'

The examples in (9) differ in interpretation. As suggested by the glosses, the object of *ver* ('see'), which has the dative preposition, can be clausal only in (9b).

We see then that the event reading emerges depending on whether verbs like *hide* or *see* have one or the other light verb. Light verbs that are eventive (presumably, verbs close to *get, give,* etc.) select for a special Infl in some languages–the clitic. From this point of view direct objects associated to accusative clitics are event participants in a subordinate VP shell with a special form of Case.[6] This result recalls the morphological Case-marking of subjects and objects interpreted as 'specific' in a variety of languages.[7] In sum the selection of light verbs is not the same across languages; it is parametrizable.

2.1.1 The Experiencer/Theme class. There is another class of transitive accusative verbs that, like eventive verbs, take a special Infl, but these verbs are stative. Verbs such as *know* and *love* are in this class:

(10) a. Juan conoce *(a) una bailarina.
John knows (to) a dancer.
b. Juan la conoce a ella.
Juan her-knows to her
(11) a. Juan ama *(a) una bailarina.
John loves (to) a dancer.
b. Juan la ama a ella.
Juan her-loves to her.

The clitic-doubling facts in (10) and (11) do not differ from those of eventive verbs.

A similar situation arises with both *considerar* 'consider' and *tener* ('have' with possessive meaning). These two verbs select for a special Infl (the clitic) with small clauses:

(12) Pedro considera un genio *(a) un violinista.
Pedro considers a genius (to) a violinist.

The subject of the predicate embedded under *considerar* receives the Case associated to a hidden D. This verb, like *judge,* might be considered eventive, but it is less clear than in the previous cases.

Stative *tener* ('have') can take a small clause with its subject marked by the dative preposition:[8]

(13) a. Tienen (*a) un hijo.
pro have (to) my son
'They have a son.'
b. Tienen (a) un hijo en el hospital.
pro have (to) a son in the hospital
'They have a son in the hospital.'

What the verbs in this subsection have in common is that they all take an Experiencer as subject and a Theme (or a Patient) as object.[9]

It appears then that there are two classes of accusative verbs that, in terms of the proposals of this article, have an underlying light verb that selects for a special Infl in Spanish: (a) verbs that take an Agent and a

Theme (or a Patient); and (b) verbs that take an Experiencer and a Theme (or a Patient).[10] I will leave this generalization in this descriptive stage.

2.1.2 On the animacy variable. One of the possible variables restricting clitic doubling cross-linguistically is animacy. Spanish and Macedonian contrast along this dimension. In Spanish only nouns that can be 'actors' by virtue of their inherent lexical content can co-occur with the clitic:

(14) a. *(La) empujaron la mesa.
(it)-pushed the table
'They pushed the table.'
b. (La) empujaron a la niña.
(it) pushed to the girl
'They pushed the girl.'

Although the verb is the same in (14a) and (14b), only the animate clitic of (14b) can be appear doubled. This does not hold in Macedonian, where non-animates also appear with a clitic (cf. *skrsi ja casa-ta* (break it the glass, 'Break the glass').[11]

Animacy also restricts the overt case marking of objects in Hindi. It appears, then, that the special form of Case that singles out objects in Spanish correlates with the Infl selected by light verbs and may surface as a clitic. In Hindi, on the other hand, the special Case of animates seems to correlate with object Agr (see Mahajan (1990a, b)).

It may seem that animacy and specificity are entirely unrelated. However, why then do only direct objects that are semantically 'specific' get this special inflection? I would like to propose that animacy is to be encoded as a morphological feature in the definite determiner. The basic idea is to make 'animacy' dependent on D:

(15) D
|
P(articipant)
|
Oblique

The parametric variation with respect to animacy can be seen as reflecting different choices in the features of D.

The animacy restriction that holds of clitic doubling in Spanish and similar languages creates a split in the status of clitics with respect to theta and movement theory. Everything else being equal, the argument status of clitics in Spanish will differ according to whether they are the expression of the functional category selected by the light verb or they are the actual complement of V. Thus, in the minimal pair in (14) below the clitic is an argument in (16a) and a nonargument in (16b):

(16) a. La empujaron (= la mesa).
it-pushed (the table)
'They pushed the table.'
b. La empujaron (= a la niña).
her-pushed (to the girl)
'They pushed her.'

Similarly, we expect that non-argumental clitics will move as heads from the beginning, whereas clitics that are arguments could in principle move as XPs, in whatever manner clitics move in non clitic-doubling languages.

2.2 On ditransitive verbs. So far only single transitive verbs have been discussed. This section will look at the state of affairs presented by ditransitive verbs.

Despite the cross-linguistic similarities that can be observed in the examples of (3), languages differ with respect to the complements that enter into clitic doubling. Both direct and indirect objects can appear doubled by a clitic in present-day Spanish. This is shown in (17) below:

(17) Se la presentaron (a ella) (al profesor).
him-her-introduced (to her) (to the professor)
'They introduced her to the professor.'

The view of clitic doubling put forward here requires us to posit two light verbs underlying the representation of verbs such as *presentar* ('introduce').

But ditransitive verbs do not behave uniformly with respect to clitic doubling. Strozer (1976) shows that the particular verb involved and the realization of each of its objects crucially matters.

2.2.1 How many Ds per verb? With a slight marginality some ditransitives allow two *a*-objects with no overt clitic; however, others do not:

(18) a. Presentamos a Juan al professor.
introduced to Juan to the teacher
We introduced Juan to the teacher.
b. Describimos a Juan (*al profesor).
described to Juan (to the teacher)
We described Juan (to the teacher).

As shown, the verb *presentar,* 'introduce,' can take two *a*-objects whereas *describir,* "describe," cannot.[12]

Similarly, with a slight marginality the verb *presentar,* 'introduce,' allows the direct object to be realized as a clitic and the indirect object to have no overt clitic; however, this combination yields ill-formedness with *describir,* 'describe':

(19) a. Lọ presenté al editor.
him-introduced to the editor
I introduced him to the editor.
b. *Lo describí al editor.
him-described to the editor.
I described him to the editor.

The contrast shown in (19) suggests a difference in the underlying representation of each of these verbs.

Let us suppose that the underlying representation of *presentar* ('introduce'), contrary to that of *describir* ('describe'), allows for two (rather than one) light verbs, each of which may select D. This is illustrated in (20) for *Presentó a Juan a su professor* 'S/he introduced Juan to the professor':

(20)

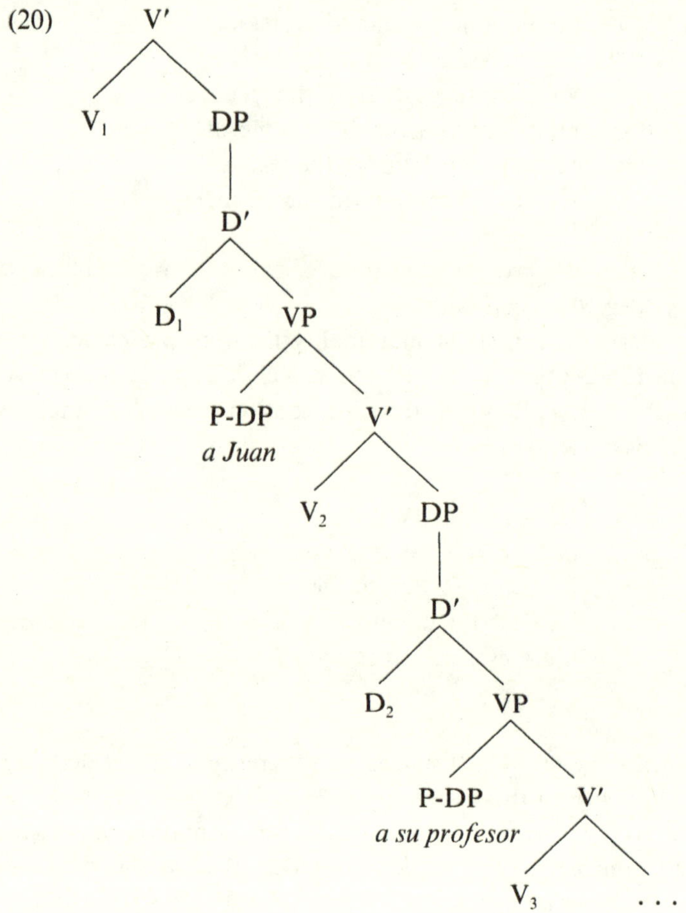

This assumption makes the prediction that *presentar* ('introduce') should permit doubling of both objects in the same sentence and *describir,* ('describe') only one. This prediction is borne out. As pointed out to me by I. Laka (p.c.), the following contrasts holds:

(21) a. Se los presenté (a ellos) (al editor).
to him-them-introduced (to them) (to the editor)
'I introduced them to the editor.'

b. Se los describí (*a ellos) (al editor).
to him-them (to them) (to the editor)
'I described them to the editor.'

As shown here, both of the objects of *presentar* can be doubled by a clitic, whereas with *describir* only the indirect object can.

I have not yet provided syntactic evidence in favor of the postulated functional head associated to dative objects. I will do so in the next section.

3 On the syntactic effects of D. In Chomsky's (1993) theory both the subject and the object move from within the VP to a Spec of an AgrP projection for Case and agreement feature checking. Feature checking must occur in the checking domain of the relevant head. Strong features are visible at PF. Visible unchecked features are not interpretable at the interface levels of PF and LF. Therefore, strong features must be checked by Spell-Out, whereas weak features need not be checked until LF.

In the spirit of current work by Chomsky and others on Agr I will assume that once D checks its features, its trace deletes and its D-projection is no longer visible. As a result, the D selected by light verbs will play no direct role at LF.

Let me first make explicit my basic assumptions about overtly case-marked objects.

3.1 Case checking of dative objects. A natural assumption is that the strength of the agreement features of the selected D vary depending on whether D appears overtly in the accusative. If D is realized as *lo* (accusative), I assume that D has strong agreement features. If D is nonovert, I assume that it has weak agreement features. In either case D has agreement features (Ferguson 1993). It is important to note that definite objects come with an overt accusative clitic in some dialects and that indefinites do not (cf. **(los) escondieron a los prisioneros* 'They hid the prisoners' versus *(*los) escondieron a unos prisioneros* 'They hid some prisoners'). The strength of the morphological features of the DP argument determines the kind of agreement in each instance: strong agreement features require an overt D (*lo(s)/la(s)*) and weak agreement features involve a null D.

The selection of D entails one specific form of Case realization: the dative. If D is selected, the direct object appears in the dative. If D is not selected, the object appears in the regular accusative.

Here it becomes important to view the dative preposition as a Case-feature on the object. I assume that the dative preposition in Romance is not a true preposition, but the spelling out of a Case feature.[13] Note that if direct objects in the dative are DPs in the appropriate configuration, we expect to find a past participle agreeing overtly with an *a*-DP; this case is attested in small clauses such as *tienen a los soldados castigad*(**os*) (Lit. 'they have to the soldiers punished'). I assume that this instance of agreement is mediated by an AgrP, along the lines of Kayne (1985).[14]

I make the assumption that the dative Case feature manifested by the preposition of direct objects is checked against V, since V, and not D, ultimately supplies the accusative Case. This amounts to claiming that accusative in Spanish can be strong or weak. Strong accusative is manifested by the dative preposition.[15]

There are different ways of achieving feature checking of objects with the dative preposition. In principle the dative object could raise to AgrO via the Spec position of the DP projection. Here it will check the nominal features of the head D in a Spec/head agreement relation.[16] Then it will proceed to the Spec position of AgrO to check its Case:

(22)

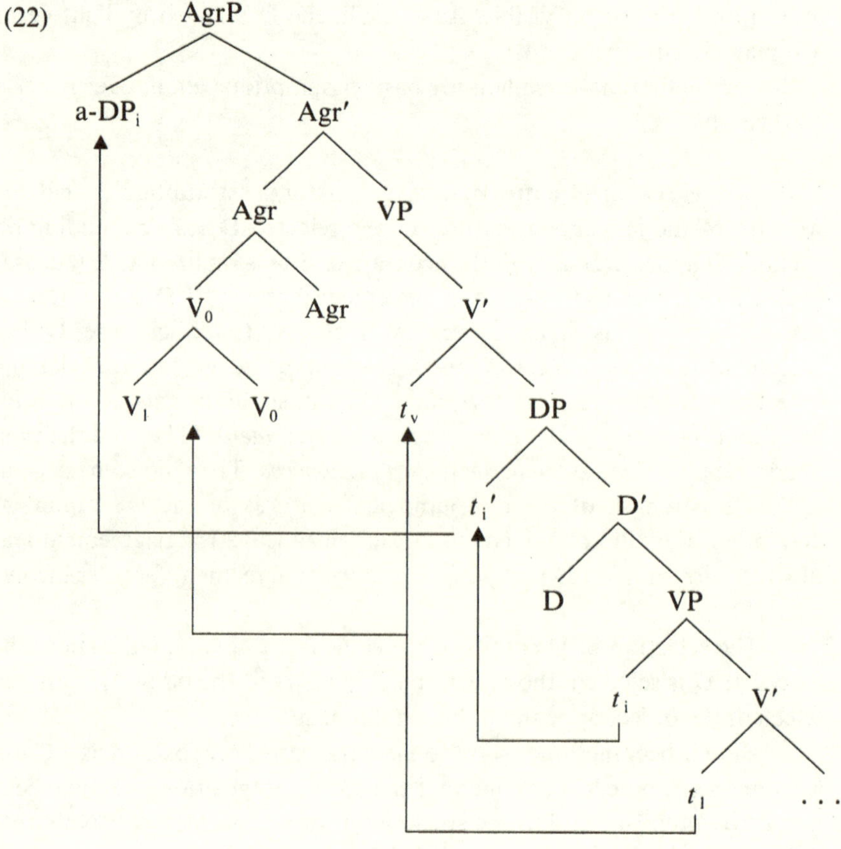

The second option is that the null D moves and adjoins to V (Baker (1988)) (adjunction is a standard form of formal licensing for null elements); then the dative object will raise to [Spec,AgrO-P] directly:

(23)

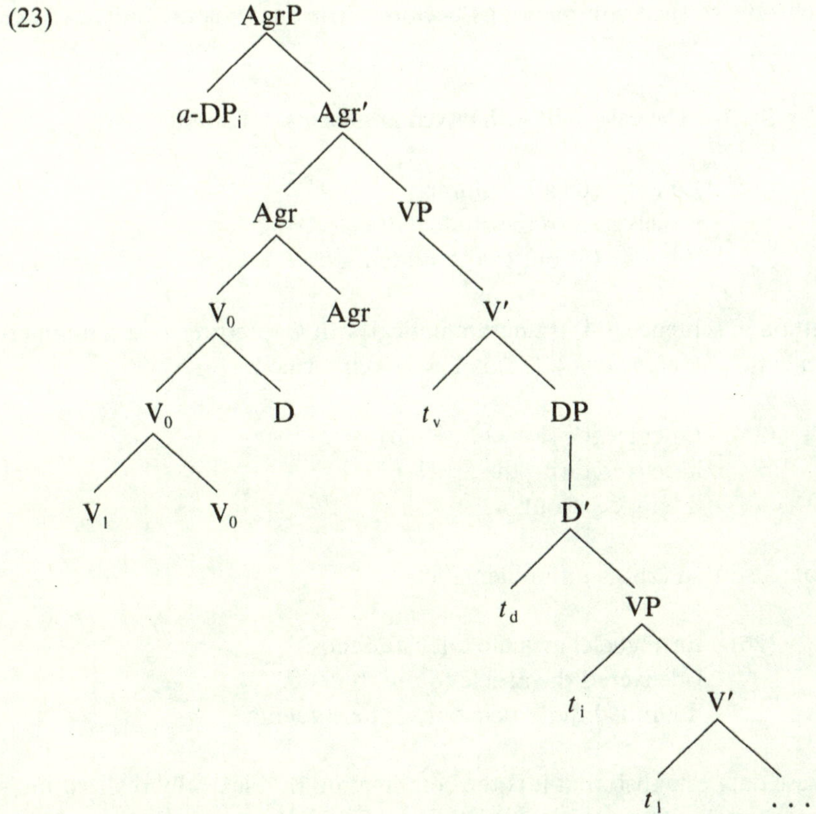

I believe each of these derivations is instantiated in the grammar in different contexts: the former when D surfaces in the accusative, the latter when D is null. There is a great amount of dialectal variation in this area. Such variation will reflect different choices of the grammar concerning the strengh of morphological features, as well as subsequent differences in their checking. What is important for my purposes here is that (a) accusative clitics bear strong agreement features, and (b) the dative Case of accusatives is checked by the verb.

The syntactic system gives us the Case-properties of one dative object with no problem. However, we have seen that when a verb takes more than one dative object, the data can get fairly complex.

I want to outline the main tenets of my approach vis-à-vis one particular case that does not require much data. It deals with combinations of a non-animate accusative clitic and a lexically realized indirect object. Such a combination yields ill-formedness with all verbs in Spanish and was noted by Strozer (1976). Morphology cannot be responsible for the exclusion of such combinations because their analogue in Italian is well formed.

3.1.1 The case split with mixed arguments. Examine (24):

(24) *Lo entregué a los alumnos.
it-delivered to the students
'I handed it out to the students.'

Although sentence (24) is ungrammatical with *lo* interpreted as a non person clitic (*lo=el artículo*), (25) below is well formed:

(25) Lo entregué (lo=el artículo).
it-delivered (it=the article)
'I handed it out.'

Note also that (26) is unproblematic:

(26) Entregué el artículo a los alumnos.
I-delivered the article to the students
'I handed the article out to the students.'

These data establish that it is the combination of a lexically realized indirect object (with no clitic) and the accusative third person clitic that is potentially in conflict.

There is a key fact that must be borne in mind. Clitic doubling in Spanish is attested with ALL objects in the dative. In the syntax this translates as there being a D, null or overt, for each dative object. Everything hinges on the postulated D.

Suppose that the argumental clitic crosses to AgrO over DP. This is possible when D moves and adjoins to V. In this derivation the Spec position of the intervening functional projection DP and the Spec position of AgrO-P are equidistant once V raises to AgrO:[17]

(27)

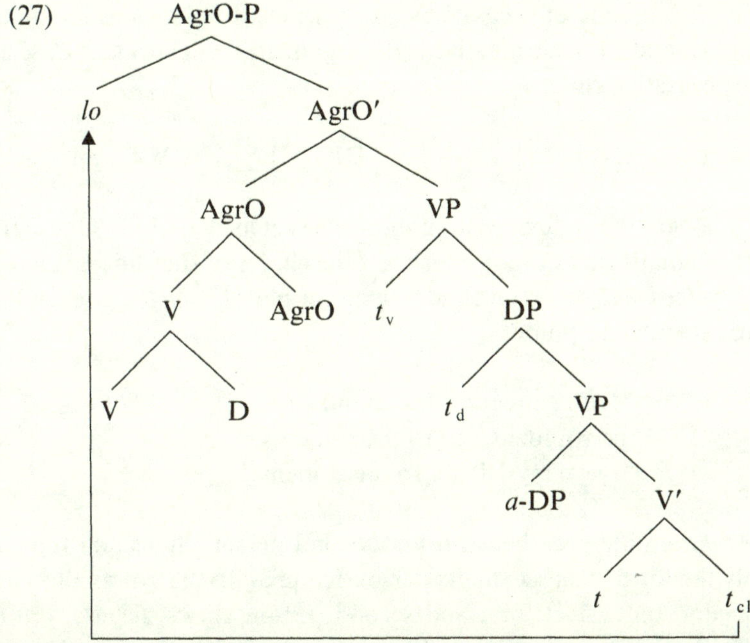

Since V carries along the agreement features of the incorporated D, it is reasonable to suppose that they are checked by Agr. If so, the clitic will be able to check accusative Case, but not its agreement features. If left unchecked, the agreement features of the accusative clitic will be visible at the interface levels of PF and LF, causing the derivation to crash.

It is crucial that the accusative clitic have strong agreement features. This, I assume, is responsible for the grammaticality contrast between (24) and (26):

(24) *Lo entregué a los alumnos.
it-delivered to the students
'I handed it out to the students.'

(26) Entregué el artículo a los alumnos.
I-delivered the article to the students
'I handed the article out to the students.'

Unlike the accusative clitic D, there is no reason to assume that the direct object in (26) has strong agreement features.

It is quite telling that the accusative non-animate clitic and the lexical dative in (24) are wrongly understood as if they were one and the same argument. This interpretation corresponds to the derivation of an instance of clitic doubling of accusatives.[18] In essence, the clitic *lo* is the functional head D, and the lexical dative is the argument that checks its Case against the accusative clitic:

(28) INFL. . . $[_{VP}$ . . .V $[_{DP}$ *a*-DP $[_{D'}$ [lo] $[_{VP}$ *t* [V . . .]]]]]

Two kinds of evidence support the sketched analysis. One is that the ungrammaticality of (24) vanishes if the choice of the clitic is not a D *(lo)* but *me/nos,* a first person clitic singular or plural, or *te/os,* a second person clitic singular or plural:

(29) Me/te entregué a los alumnos.
me/you-delivered to the students
'I gave myself/you to the students.'

One difference between first/second person clitics and third is that only the former class exhibits person-features. In the syntax this can have an important effect: first and second person clitics 'license' *pro* (Borer (1984)). However, *lo* (Ds) will not license *pro.* We can now hypothesize that *pro* has weak agreement features. Under these assumptions the only pronominal element that is compatible with the functional head D in derivation (28) will be *pro.* In this account (30) and (24) share the fact that their objects have weak agreement features; hence, they do not have to be checked before LF.

Further evidence in support of this approach comes from dative clitics. To put the matter in simple terms: a dative clitic causes any combination of accusative clitic and lexical dative to be well formed:[19]

(30) (*Se) lo presenté (a los alumnos).
(to them)-it-introduced (to the students)

The dative clitic, which in (30) is realized as *se,* appears, doubling the indirect object *a los alumnos.* Note that here the accusative clitic *lo,* a D with strong features, causes no problem. The saving role of the dative clitic is valid for all verbs, regardless of their lexical class.

There is a crucial morphological difference between the dative clitic *le(s)* and the accusative clitic *lo(s)/la(s)* (masculine and feminine in the singular and plural, respectively): the dative clitic has weak agreement features.[20] If, instead of a null D, D is realized overtly in the dative, the cause of ungrammaticality of derivation (28) ceases to exist. There is no functional head D that interferes with the checking of the agreement features of the accusative clitic *lo.*

I neglect to discuss a number of other effects having to do with dative clitics. The arguments that led me to conclude the assumptions presented here form a body of independent research. Let me just anticipate that there is a default D that supplies dative case to a dative object, namely the clitic *le,* and that this clitic plays a crucial role throughout the grammar.

NOTES

*This is a study that articulates ideas presented in a graduate course on Syntactic Theory at the Universidad del País Vasco in Vitoria (Spain) in 1991. The issues dealt with here are developed more extensively in a manuscript in progress. I am especially indebted to C. P. Otero for his seminars on clitic doubling in the seventies, which triggered my initial interest for the topics of this article. For discussion and observations, I am grateful to N. Chomsky, K. Hale, S. Iatridou, R. Kayne, J. Lacarra, I. Laka, D. Pesetsky, C. Piera, K. Sainz, and J. Uriagereka.

1. Unlike in Larson's (1988) proposal, I assume that the verb that heads the higher VP shell has morphological features, rather than being empty. An attempt to relate some aspects of Pesetsky's (1995) theory of layered structures to the claims of this article is made in work in progress.

2. On Romanian and Spanish, see Jaeggli (1982), Borer (1984), and Hurtado (1981) among many others. For Lebanese Arabic, see Aoun, Borer, and Halle (1981), Aoun and Sportiche (1981). The Albanian example is taken from Massey (1991). Thanks to A. Marantz for alerting me to Massey's (1991) dissertation and making it available early enough. I am in debt to K. Chvany for acquainting me with Macedonian; see Berent (1980).

3. This result is in agreement with the behavior of clitic-doubling structures with respect to Binding Theory. It has been argued by Aoun (1985) and, far more extensively, by Varela (1988) that the element subject to Binding Theory is the double instead of the clitic.

4. I examine the least central issues of doubling in my manuscript in progress.

5. I omit the animacy variable from the graph, as well as proper names. There is one other case missing from (6) that is too complex to explain here and irrelevant for the purposes of this article.

6. Massey (1991) notes that verbs of the class that I am arguing obligatorily select D are expressed in Japanese by the light verb *suru.* She classifies them as the DO-TO class. It is quite common for these verbs to have paraphrases with light verbs in Spanish: *empujar/dar un empujón; golpear/dar un golpe; asustar* (in its agentive meaning)/*dar un susto,* and so on. The same happens with *echar*: *echar la culpa.* A detailed discussion of the syntactic and semantic issues involving classes of transitive verbs is provided in my work in progress.

7. It is a well-known fact that there are semantic distinctions such as

Carlson's (1977) classification of stage-level predicates and individual-level predicates, which have syntactic effects in some languages. See Kuroda (1972, 1992), Higginbotham (1985), Diesing (1992), Kratzer (1989), and Raposo and Uriagereka (1993), among others. Other semantic distinctions (whatever the label is) can be marked syntactically by the grammar. We seem to be dealing here with one of them.

8. Independently of any other consideration, D could not surface as a pronominal clitic with the object of *tener* if this verb were to be the lexicalization of *be* and a selected D, as proposed by Kayne (1993) for possessive *have* in English. Kayne assigns the following structure to possessive *have*: *be* [[D/P] [possesive]], where the possessive DP raises to the matrix Infl for case reasons. Incorporation of the D/P to *be* will preclude the surface realization of D. The behavior of *tener* with small clauses is compatible with this alternative, since *tener* selects one more predicate.

9. With this class of verbs it ceases to be an advantage of the system to have the overtly Case-marked object in the Specifier of the lower VP shell. In the case of eventive verbs this makes more sense, particularly in the case of the object of the *push*-class of verbs, which is affected (see Tenny (1987)). Marantz (1990) generates affected objects exactly in this position. This issue needs further investigation, especially in light of Pesetsky's (1993) Cascade theory.

10. This comes close to the description that traditional grammarians of Spanish gave for the marker *a.* They took a functional approach and observed that the marker is used when either of the two arguments of the verb could be taken as holding the grammatical relation of subject and object. The ambiguity is possible when both arguments appear postverbally, as in

(i) Persigue el gato el ratón
chases the cat the mouse
'The cat chases the mouse' or 'The mouse chases the cat'

Agents and Experiencers share with Patients the fact that they are potential actors.

11. For the purposes of this presentation I refer to animates and inanimates. But animacy is not the correct notion to characterize the nominals that can be clitic-doubled in Spanish. Either participant or Jackendoff's (1983) notion of [actor] seems to be more adequate. I discuss this issue in more depth in my work in progress.

12. I thank I. Bosque and C. Piera (p.c.) for pointing out this contrast to me.

13. Thanks to R. Kayne (p.c.) for helping me clarify this point. Despite the fact that animate indefinites can appear as objects in the configuration in (1), their interpretation is constrained by specificity in Spanish (Enç (1991) and Diesing (1992)).

14. This statement does not imply that there is no difference in the syntactic behavior of dative complements in Romance direct and indirect objects. Although indirect objects in Romance behave like DPs rather than like PPs for Binding (see Rizzi (1988) and Branchadell (1992)), they act differently in many other respects. See Kayne (1984) and Emonds (1985).

15. For relevant discussion about the nature of the dative P in Romance see Emonds (1985).

16. The idea that D mediates in the Case relation between V and its direct object finds support in the fact that the clitic and the argument have to match in animacy, gender, number, and person: Hurtado's (1981) and Suñer's (1988) Matching Hypothesis.

17. I have placed the accusative clitic lower than the lexical dative, but this is not crucial for the analysis. What is important is that the accusative clitic be lower than the functional projection DP.

18. In dialects that allow clitics to double accusatives (as in River Plate Spanish) these examples are good under this reading.

19. The Spanish clitic *se* is the form that corresponds to the dative clitic *le* in combination with a third person accusative clitic. See Bonet (1991).

20. Whereas accusative clitics manifest gender overtly, the dative clitic does not. In addition there are dialects in which a singular form of the dative clitic can co-occur with a lexical object in the plural.

REFERENCES

Aoun, J. 1985. *A Grammar of Anaphora.* Cambridge: MIT Press.

Aoun, J., H. Borer, and M. Halle. 1981. Introduction, Theoretical Issues in the Grammar of Semitic languages. *MIT Working Papers in Linguistics* 3:1–20.

Aoun, J., and D. Sportiche. 1981. The Domain of Weak Cross-Over Restrictions. *MIT Working Papers in Linguistics* 3:43–52.

Baker, M. C. 1988. *Incorporation.* Chicago: University of Chicago Press.

Berent, G. P. 1980. On the Realization of Trace: Macedonian Clitic Pronouns. In *Morphosyntax in Slavic.* C. Chvany and R. D. Brecht, eds. Columbus: Slavica.

Bonet, E. 1991. *Morphology after Syntax: Pronominal Clitics in Romance.* Ph.D. Dissertation. MIT.

Borer, H. 1984. *Parametric Syntax.* Dordrecht: Foris.

Branchadell, A. 1992. *A Study of Lexical and Nonlexical Datives.* Ph.D. Dissertation. Universitat Autónoma, Barcelona.

Carlson, G. 1977. *Reference to Kinds in English,* Ph.D. Dissertation. University of Massachusetts, Amherst.

Chomsky, N. 1993. A Minimalist Program for Linguistic Theory. In *The View from Building 20: Essays in Linguistics in Honor of Sylvain Bromberger.* K. Hale and S. J. Keyser, eds. Cambridge: MIT Press.

Diesing, M. 1992. *Indefinites.* Cambridge: MIT Press.

Emonds, J. 1985. *A Unified Theory of Syntactic Categories.* Dordrecht: Foris.

Enç, M. 1991. The Semantics of Specificity. *Linguistic Inquiry* 22:1–26.

Ferguson, S. K. 1993. Notes on the Shortest Move Metric and Object Checking. *Harvard Working Papers in Linguistics* 3:65–80.

Hale, K., and J. Keyser. 1991. *On the Syntax of Argument Structure.* Manuscript. Center for Cognitive Science. MIT.

Higginbotham. J. 1985. On Semantics. *Linguistic Inquiry* 16:547–93.

Hurtado, A. 1981. *Clitic Chains.* Manuscript. Simon Fraser University.
Jackendoff, R. 1983. *Semantics and Cognition.* Cambridge: MIT Press.
Jackendoff, R. 1990. *Semantic Structures.* Cambridge: MIT Press.
Jaeggli, O. 1982. *Topics in Romance Syntax.* Dordrecht: Foris.
Kayne, R. 1984. *Connectedness and Binary Branching.* Dordrecht: Foris.
Kayne, R. 1985. L'accord du participe passe en français et en italian. *Modeles Linguistiques* 7:73–89.
Kayne, R. 1993. Toward a Modular Theory of Auxiliary Selection. *Studia Linguistica* 47:3–31
Kratzer, A. 1989. Stage and Individual Level Predicates. *Papers on Quantification.* NSF Grant Report, Department of Linguistics, University of Massachusetts, Amherst.
Kuroda, S.-Y. 1972. The Categorial and the Thetic Judgment: Evidence from Japanese. *Foundations of Language* 9:153–85.
Kuroda, S.-Y. 1992. *Japanese Syntax and Semantics: Collected Papers.* Dordrecht: Kluwer.
Larson, R. 1988. On the Double Object Construction. *Linguistic Inquiry* 19:335–392.
Mahajan, A. 1990a. Clitic Doubling, Object Agreement and Specificity. *Proceedings of NELS 19.*
Mahajan, A. 1990b. *The A/A-Bar Distinction and Movement Theory.* Ph.D. Dissertation. MIT.
Marantz, A. 1990. Implications of Asymmetries in Double Object Constructions. MIT Lecture. March.
Massey, V. 1991. *Compositionality and Constituency in Albanian,* Ph.D. Dissertation. University of North Carolina, Chapel Hill.
Pesetsky, D. 1995. *Zero Syntax.* Cambridge: MIT Press.
Raposo, E., and J. Uriagereka. 1993. Two Types of Small Clauses. GLOW talk and manuscript. UCSB and UMCP.
Rizzi, L. 1988. Il sintagma preposizionale. In *Grande Grammatical Italiana di Consultazione* 11. L. Renzi, ed. Bologna: Mulino.
Strozer, J. R. 1976. *Clitics in Spanish.* Ph.D. Dissertation. UCLA.
Suñer, M. 1988. The Role of Agreement in Clitic-Doubled Constructions. *Natural Language and Linguistic Theory* 6:391–434.
Tenny, C. 1987. *Grammaticalizing Aspect and Affectedness.* Ph.D. Dissertation. MIT.
Varela, A. 1988. *Binding in Spanish: A Theoretical and Experimental Study.* Ph.D. Dissertation. University of Connecticut.

www.ingramcontent.com/pod-product-compliance
Lightning Source LLC
LaVergne TN
LVHW050300080826
844660LV00012B/663

* 9 7 8 0 8 7 8 4 0 2 4 8 9 *